Fuzzy Methods for Customer Relationship Management and Marketing:

Applications and Classifications

Andreas Meier
University of Fribourg, Switzerland

Laurent Donzé
University of Fribourg, Switzerland

T0350105

Managing Director: Lindsay Johnston
Senior Editorial Director: Heather Probst
Book Production Manager: Sean Woznicki
Development Manager: Joel Gamon
Acquisitions Editor: Erika Gallagher
Typesetters: Adrienne Freeland
Print Coordinator: Jamie Snavely
Cover Design: Nick Newcomer, Greg Snader

Published in the United States of America by
        Business Science Reference (an imprint of IGI Global)
        701 E. Chocolate Avenue
        Hershey PA 17033
        Tel: 717-533-8845
        Fax: 717-533-8661
        E-mail: cust@igi-global.com
        Web site: http://www.igi-global.com

Library of Congress Cataloging-in-Publication Data

Fuzzy methods for customer relationship management and marketing: applications and classifications / Andreas Meier and Laurent Donze, editors.
    p. cm.
  Summary: "This book explores the possibilities and advantages created by fuzzy methods through the presentation of thorough research and case studies"-
-Provided by publisher.
  Includes bibliographical references and index.
  ISBN 978-1-4666-0095-9 (hardcover) -- ISBN 978-1-4666-0096-6 (ebook) -- ISBN 978-1-4666-0097-3 (print & perpetual access) 1. Customer relations--Management. 2. Marketing. 3. Fuzzy logic. I. Meier, Andreas, 1951- II. Donzi, Laurent.
  HF5415.5.F89 2012
  658.8'12--dc23
                            2011042182

British Cataloguing in Publication Data
A Cataloguing in Publication record for this book is available from the British Library.

All work contributed to this book is new, previously-unpublished material. The views expressed in this book are those of the authors, but not necessarily of the publisher.

List of Reviewers

Spyridon Arvanitis, *KOF ETHZ Zurich, Switzerland*
Patrick Bosc, *ENSSAT Lannion Cedex, France*
Philippe Cudré-Mauroux, *University of Fribourg, Switzerland*
Rodolphe Dewarrat, *tecData AG, Switzerland*
Bruno Jeitziner, *Swiss Federal Tax Administration, Switzerland*
Michael Kaufmann, *Swiss Mobiliar Insurance, Switzerland*
Martial Pasquier, *University of Lausanne, Switzerland*
George Smith, *University of East Anglia, UK*
Bruno Trstenjak, *Medimurje University of Applied Sciences, Croatia*
Maurizio Vanetti, *University of Fribourg, Switzerland*
Marino Widmer, *University of Fribourg, Switzerland*

Table of Contents

Chapter 1
Applying Fuzzy Logic and Fuzzy Methods to Marketing..1
> Laurent Donzé, *University of Fribourg, Switzerland*
> Andreas Meier, *University of Fribourg, Switzerland*

Section 1
Fuzzy Modeling

Chapter 2
Fuzzy Soft Social Network Modeling and Marketing...16
> Ronald R. Yager, *Iona College, USA*
> Rachel L. Yager, *Metropolitan College of New York, USA*

Chapter 3
Fuzzy Dynamic Groups: Measures and Implications for Television Audiences.................................41
> José-Domingo Mora, *University of Massachusetts-Dartmouth, USA*

Chapter 4
Using Case Data to Ensure 'Real World' Input Validation within Fuzzy Set Theory Models..............61
> Sara Denize, *University of Western Sydney, Australia*
> Sharon Purchase, *University of Western Australia, Australia*
> Doina Olaru, *University of Western Australia, Australia*

Section 4
Market Analysis

Detailed Table of Contents

Chapter 1

Laurent Donzé, University of Fribourg, Switzerland
Andreas Meier, University of Fribourg, Switzerland

The chapter introduces fundamental concepts such as fuzzy sets, fuzzy logic, and computing with linguistic variables and terms. This set of fuzzy methods can be applied in marketing and customer relationship management. In the conclusion, future research directions are given for applying fuzzy logic to marketing and customer relationship management.

Section 1
Fuzzy Modeling

The first section is principally theoretical in orientation. Chapter 2 introduces a fuzzy set of operators designed to retrieve human-focused network information. Chapter 3 next examines the conceptualization of dynamic groups and their fuzzification. Finally, in Chapter 4 a process for the validation of fuzzy models is presented.

Chapter 2

Ronald R. Yager, Iona College, USA
Rachel L. Yager, Metropolitan College of New York, USA

The chapter focuses on the modeling of social networks. The authors provide a language that can be used to query a social network. Using fuzzy set theory and granular computing, the authors have constructed a bridge between the human analyst and the formal model of the network.

Chapter 3

José-Domingo Mora, University of Massachusetts-Dartmouth, USA

The characteristics of the individuals in a group and / or the individual memberships in the group may change. These effects, which are due to time, introduce fuzziness into the definition of the group. The authors attempt to model dynamic groups of this kind. Analysis of members of a family watching television is offered as one application of such modeling.

Chapter 4

Sara Denize, University of Western Sydney, Australia
Sharon Purchase, University of Western Australia, Australia
Doina Olaru, University of Western Australia, Australia

As fuzzy set theories open up new ways of investigating business networks, it becomes necessary to validate these fuzzy models with real-world data. The chapter illustrates a fuzzy model validation process and concludes with recommendations to assist researchers in validating their fuzzy models.

Section 2
Customer Relationship Management and Web Analytics

There are five chapters in the second section, which is the cornerstone of the book. These chapters address the main focus of the book: Customer Relationship Management. In Chapter 5, fuzzy clustering is applied to Web user profiles. In Chapter 6, a second application of fuzzy clusters is given, for e-Elections. A framework for a fuzzy online reputation analysis is demonstrated in Chapter 7. In Chapter 8, the concept of fuzzy target groups is used, and finally, in Chapter 9, an inductive fuzzy classification method is proposed.

Chapter 5

Stanislav Kreuzer, Goethe University, Germany
Natascha Hoebel, Goethe University, Germany

This chapter addresses the problem of how to define, calculate, and visually represent fuzzy clusters of Web visitors with respect to their behavior and supposed interests. The authors introduce a fuzzy clustering approach named CORD (Clustering of Ordinal Data). A fuzzy k-modes algorithm extension for categorical data is the basis of this method. The results can be presented in two ways: in a table or with an animation.

Chapter 6

Luis Terán, University of Fribourg, Switzerland
Andreas Ladner, Institut de Hautes Études en Administration Publique, Switzerland
Jan Fivaz, University of Bern, Switzerland
Stefani Gerber, University of Bern, Switzerland

The authors propose a fuzzy recommender system for e-Elections. A user-friendly interface has been developed to help the voters to find the most similar candidates according to the preferences of the voters. A fuzzy c-mean algorithm is applied to constitute these clusters of similar candidates.

Chapter 7

Edy Portmann, University of Fribourg, Switzerland
Tam Nguyen, National University of Singapore, Singapore
Jose Sepulveda, National University of Singapore, Singapore
Adrian David Cheok, National University of Singapore, Singapore

The authors have set up a fuzzy online reputation analysis framework (foRa) in order to permit communications operatives to search the Social Web to find meaningful information in a straightforward manner. An interactive user interface known as the dashboard allows the browsing of related topics.

Chapter 8

Michael Kaufmann, Swiss Mobiliar Insurance & Pensions, Switzerland
Cédric Graf, ITpearls AG, Switzerland

An inductive fuzzy classification based on normalized likelihood ratios permits the authors to generate customer profiles based on a target class and relevant customer attributes. The method is particularly well suited for selection, visualization, and prediction in the field of analytics. A case study is described, together with an implementation of the method proposed.

Chapter 9

Darius Zumstein, University of Fribourg, Switzerland

As Web metrics are not adequately classified in a sharp manner, the author proposes an inductive fuzzy classification. This method seems particularly adapted to Web mining. It makes it possible to rank Web pages using a gradual degree of membership in classes. As a consequence, the results are easier to interpret.

Section 3
Performance Analysis

The third section focuses on the economic activity or the performance of a firm. Chapter 10 examines a data warehouse and shows how to integrate fuzzy concepts as meta-tables. The assessment of online customers can be realized with a fuzzy logic approach, as described in Chapter 11. A hybrid fuzzy multiple objectives approach can also help to develop a model for lotsizing, pricing, marketing, and planning. This is presented in Chapter 12.

Chapter 10

Daniel Fasel, University of Fribourg, Switzerland
Khurram Shahzad, Royal Institute of Technology (KTH), Sweden

In constructing a fuzzy data warehouse, the authors integrate fuzzy concepts as meta-tables without affecting the core of a classical data warehouse. Despite the integration of the fuzziness, the time-invariability of the data is preserved. This approach allows analyses of data in both sharp and fuzzy modes. A case study demonstrates the validity of the approach.

Chapter 11

Nicolas Werro, Swisscom AG, Switzerland
Henrik Stormer, Edorex Informatik AG, Switzerland

This chapter is devoted to the hierarchical fuzzy classification of online customers. A combination of relational databases and fuzzy logic allows the classification of a customer into several classes at the same time. As a result, customer equity is greatly improved, which can help to refine marketing campaigns.

Chapter 12

R. Ghasemy Yaghin, Amirkabir University of Technology, Iran
S.M.T. Fatemi Ghomi, Amirkabir University of Technology, Iran

The imprecise and fuzzy nature of parameters, such as unit costs and marketing functions, has led the authors to develop a fuzzy multiple objectives model. The objective functions considered are profit, return on inventory investment, and a qualitative objective related to customer satisfaction. The model is able to determine the joint pricing, lotsizing, and marketing plan of the manufacturer.

Section 4
Market Analysis

The concluding section is addressed to marketers. The question of segmentation is revisited in chapter 13 with the introduction of fuzzy concepts. And finally, in Chapter 14, a fuzzy set qualitative comparative analysis, particularly well adapted to the analysis of complex configurations of causal conditions, is applied to the identification of market mavens.

Chapter 13

Mònica Casabayó, ESADE-URL, Spain
Núria Agell, ESADE-URL, Spain

This chapter presents a fuzzy segmentation model, which combines statistical and artificial intelligence techniques to identify and quantify multifaceted consumers. This LAMDA technique is proposed as an alternative to non-overlapping segmentation techniques. The fuzzy method appears to have a number of advantages, as is demonstrated in a genuine Spanish business case study.

Chapter 14

Miri Chung, University of Rhode Island, USA
Arch G. Woodside, Boston College, USA

The authors apply a fuzzy set qualitative comparative analysis to distinguish between Market Mavens and Market Gurus using multi-year data from a national U.S. omnibus survey. This technique makes possible the analysis of complex configurations of causal conditions as explanations of an outcome condition. Truth tables are constructed to display all possible combinations of causal conditions and case distributions, and this allows the discovery of multiple pathways to an outcome.

Foreword

When I was asked to write a foreword to this book "*Fuzzy Methods for Customer Relationship Management and Marketing*," I was glad to see one more important application of fuzzy models. Nowadays, fuzzy models are applied in many fields of science and its applications, ranging from mathematics to engineering, from medical diagnosis to quality control, and from metrology to marketing, just to mention some of them. The bases for fuzzy methods are fuzzy sets which are founded on a generalization of the abstract concept *set*. A classical set A is characterized by its indicator function $I_A(\cdot)$ which is based on dual logic, i.e. indicator functions are allowed to assume only the two values 0 or 1. For an element x in A the indicator function takes the value $I_A(x) = 1$, and for an element x which doesn't belong to A we have $I_A(x) = 0$.

In reality, it turns out that not all sets can be characterized in this way. An example is the set of good books. As far as I know the first mathematical publication on a generalization of indicator functions is from the year 1951 by Karl Menger. He allowed the generalized indicator functions $\mu(\cdot)$ to assume any value in the unit interval $[0; 1]$. This is a generalized logic with a continuity of truth values, where $\mu(x)$ is the degree of membership of the element x to this generalized set. These generalized indicator functions $\mu(\cdot)$ were called *membership functions* by Lotfi Zadeh more than one decade later, and the so defined generalized sets he called *fuzzy sets*. This was the starting point of so-called fuzzy logic and fuzzy methods.

Fuzzy models were flourishing during the last decades of the 20th century and in the first decade of the 21st century. Presently even statistics is taking care of fuzziness of data and a-priori information. Especially for decision making and other executive work, fuzzy logic models are important methods to support managers. Moreover, for marketing and related data mining, fuzzy concepts are essential.

Fortunately this book is continuing quantitative modeling based on fuzzy methods and constitutes a valuable contribution to management science.

Reinhard Viertl
TU Wien
June 2011

Reinhard Viertl *was born in 1946 in Hall in Tyrol, Austria. He studied in civil engineering, philosophy, and engineering mathematics, earning Dipl.-Ing. degree 1972, and Doctor of engineering sciences 1974. He was Assistant at the Technische Hochschule Wien, University docent 1979, Research fellow and visiting Lecturer, University of California, Berkeley, 1980-1981, and Visiting docent, University of Klagenfurt, 1981-1982. Since 1982, he has been full Professor of Applied Statistics with special emphasis on Regional and Information Sciences, Vienna University of Technology. He has also been Visiting* *professor, University of Innsbruck, 1991-1993, Seasonal instructor, University of Calgary, 2003, Visiting professor, University of Salatiga, Indonesia, 2010, Visiting professor, University of Brno, Czech Republic, 2011. He is a Member of the International Statistical Institute, Fellow of the Royal Statistical Society, London, President of the Austrian Statistical Society 1987-1995, and received invitation to membership in the New York Academy of Sciences, 1999. He gained election as honorary member of the Austrian Statistical Society, 2008. Scientific publications include: Statistical Methods in Accelerated Life Testing (1988), Introduction to Stochastics (in German, 2003), Statistical Methods for Non-Precise Data (1996), Description and Analysis of Fuzzy Information (in German, 2006), Statistical Methods for Fuzzy Data (2011). He has been Editor and co-Editor of several other books, and the author of over 100 scientific papers in mathematics and statistics.*

Preface

With today's information overload, it has become increasingly difficult to analyze the huge amounts of data and to generate appropriate management decisions. Furthermore, the data are often imprecise and will include both quantitative and qualitative elements. For these reasons it is important to extend traditional decision making processes by adding intuitive reasoning, human subjectivity, and imprecision.

To deal with uncertainty, vagueness, and imprecision, Lotfi A. Zadeh introduced fuzzy sets and fuzzy logic. In the present volume, fuzzy classification is applied to extend portfolio analysis, scoring methods, customer segmentation, and performance measurement, and thus, to improve managerial decisions. As an integral part of the book, case studies show how fuzzy classification with its query facilities can extend customer equity, enable mass customization, and refine marketing campaigns.

Most publications in management and marketing do not address the problem, which can arise when using traditional, non-fuzzy or 'sharp' methods. With fuzzy classification, a customer can belong to more than one class with differing degrees of membership. This approach to membership not only provides a better description of the elements, it also helps to reveal both the potential strengths and the possible weakness of the class elements under consideration. As a result, marketing managers can treat their customers according to their true value. This book explores the possibilities and advantages created by fuzzy methods, through the presentation of thorough research and case studies.

The book covers a great variety of possible fuzzy logic approaches to customer relationship management and marketing. Examples are:

- Segmentation with Fuzzy Customer Classes
- Fuzzy Scoring Methods for Marketing
- Fuzzy Data Warehousing
- Inductive Fuzzy Classification for Marketing Programs
- Fuzzy-based Recommender Systems
- Fuzzy Portfolio Techniques in Marketing
- Community Marketing based on Fuzzy Logic
- Fuzzy Clustering of Web User Profiles
- Online Reputation and Fuzziness
- Building Fuzzy-based Ontologies
- Web Analytics and Web Controlling with Fuzziness
- Fuzzy-based Performance Measurement
- Improving Social Networks through Fuzzy Control

This book is not only intended for students and researchers but will also be valuable for executives, managers, marketing experts, and project leaders who would like to apply fuzzy classification to managerial decisions. The book presents a set of fuzzy methods, case studies, and Web-based tools, which together, make it possible to test the efficiency and effectiveness of fuzzy classification.

OVERVIEW OF BOOK CHAPTERS

The book has been divided into four sections. The first section, *Fuzzy Modeling*, is characterized by its rather theoretical orientation. The second section, *Customer Relationship Management and Web Analytics*, addresses the main focus of the book and is its cornerstone. In the third section, *Performance Analysis*, the object of attention is the economic activity or the performance of a firm. The concluding section, *Market Analysis*, is particularly aimed at marketers.

Fuzzy Modeling

Three chapters form the first section. Chapter 1, by the book's editors, introduces the topic area and begins the book. Yager and Yager in Chapter 2, *Fuzzy Soft Social Network Modeling and Marketing*, set out to model social networks. Their aim is to provide a language or a framework, which can be used to intelligently query a social network. A fuzzy set of operators is presented which can be used to retrieve human-focused network information. Perhaps the main difficulty the authors have to face is in translating linguistic descriptions into mathematical concepts. Fuzzy set theories or granular computing may help to construct the bridge between the human analyst and the formal model of the network.

First, the authors present a short introduction to graph theory. The notions of path, connected graph, and bridge are introduced. The composition operator, which is essential in relationships, is also explained. Then, the concept of *precisiation* is borrowed from Zadeh, which attempts to make the world understandable to the machine. Fuzzy set theory helps to bridge the gap between man and machine. In fact, man's common vocabulary is expressed in terms of fuzzy sets that are in a form the machine can manipulate. The authors use the linguistic modeling capability of fuzzy sets to provide more realistic formulations of concepts available in social networks analysis.

The notions of node importance, cluster, congested nodes, duration, directed graphs, and authority figures are each introduced and described. A section devoted to vector valued nodes and social network databases concludes the chapter. All these concepts can be formalized using fuzzy sets and permit the evaluation of any given social network.

Chapter 3, *Fuzzy Dynamic Groups: Measures and Implications for Television Audiences*, is by Mora. The author first notes that time affects groups of consumers in two fundamental ways: the characteristics of the individuals in the group change and the individual memberships in the group may change too. These two aspects introduce fuzziness into the definition of the group, which becomes dynamic. A dynamic group presented by the author is made up of the members of a family watching television.

The main question for the author is how to define and measure a group of viewers. In the context of television audiences, the author describes two important group characteristics: size and composition. The author proceeds first to the fuzzification of dynamic groups. Then he defines the degree of membership of individuals in the group. Group composition is a multidimensional construct reflecting the proportion of specific types of individuals in the group. Finally a generalized linear model is presented with individual viewership as the dependent variable and as independent variables a set of individual characteristics and the proposed measures of cardinality and fuzziness. The estimation of the model confirms the hypotheses made about the characteristics of the group.

The contribution of Denize et al. forms Chapter 4, *Using Case Data to Ensure 'Real World' Input Validation within Fuzzy Set Theory Models*. As fuzzy set theories open up new ways of investigating business networks, the authors contend, it becomes necessary to validate the fuzzy models used within real-world contexts. They also note that these theories have not been used extensively within marketing and management disciplines. Furthermore, model validation and verification are not yet the rule. According to the authors, the process of validation has a number of advantages. First, it allows model builders to develop a fuzzy rule based system without working from a full factorial set of rules. Second, it checks for consistency and coverage of the fuzzy rule based system. Finally, it validates the simulation models within real world data sets. Thus this process improves both the efficiency of the validation and the sufficiency of the model.

First of all, the authors clarify the concept of validation. They argue that modelers make comparisons at critical points and that these comparisons constitute verification or validation. The authors are particularly interested "in the emergent processes in innovation networks and what combinations of network characteristics contribute to innovation success." As they say, innovation processes occur within business networks.

The case study selected by the authors considers the solar cell industry in Australia during the period 1985-2008. Particularly illustrative is the flow chart given by the authors describing the validation process. The fuzzy modeling process is shown in three main steps. The first step is the identification of the variables' domains and their description (deriving fuzzy inputs). In the second step, the extraction of the initial set of rules is presented (deriving rules). The third step is devoted to the review and refinement of the fuzzy-rule based system. After this third step, it is possible to demonstrate the extent to which the fuzzy model results correspond to real-world case data. Finally, the authors conclude the chapter with six valuable lessons. Fuzzy models are not well understood and accepted by the research community. According to the authors, further improvements in the validation process will be achieved once the fuzzy set theory model becomes a more prominent tool within marketing research.

Customer Relationship Management and Web Analytics

Five chapters make up this second section. In Chapter 5, *Fuzzy Clustering of Web User Profiles for Analyzing their Behavior and Interests*, Kreuzer and Hoebel address the problem of how to define, calculate, and visually present fuzzy clusters of Web visitors with respect to their behavior and supposed interests. The authors introduce a fuzzy clustering approach named CORD (Clustering of Ordinal Data) to analyse website contents, users' interests, and behavior. The CORD approach combines three modern clustering techniques and is able to process very large sets of ordinal data. The concept of "non-obvious user profiles" (NOPs) is introduced in order to measure the Web users' supposed interests. This profile is inferred from the user's behavior in one or more sessions on the website and represents the interests of one user in different topics.

A fuzzy k-modes algorithm extension for categorical data constitutes the basis of the CORD method. This algorithm uses the degree to which a record belongs to a certain centroid. This fuzziness, saved during the iteration process, makes it possible to choose the centroids and produce the cluster with greater accuracy. A valuable contribution of the authors is the presentation of a modified fuzzy centroid algorithm. In fact, implementing the algorithm in a naïve way will greatly slow the computations. The authors have developed the idea of parallelizing the computations. In this way they can improve the speed considerably and are able to cluster very large datasets efficiently.

A case study based on a website gives the authors the opportunity to test the fuzzy CORD approach. The non-obvious profiles and feedback profiles of the Web users are stored. Then one can apply the algorithm and present the results visually, together with the fuzzy centroids. Two presentations are provided: a table view and an animation view. These representations appear very helpful in analyzing the data. The animation view permits the analysis of the behavior of the Web users and the study of the cluster changes over time.

Terán et al., in Chapter 6, *Using a Fuzzy-Based Cluster Algorithm for Recommending Candidates in E-Elections*, propose a fuzzy recommender system for e-Elections. The authors have developed a user-friendly interface – a Web application called smartvote – to help voters to find the most similar candidates according to the preferences of the individual voters. Their recommender system needs inputs from voters and candidates and is then able to make recommendations based on similarities that exist between voters and candidates. A fuzzy c-mean algorithm is applied to constitute these clusters of similar candidates. The recommender system is supported by an attractive graphic interface, which is able to display the cluster – N-closest candidates – together with the location of the voter.

Portmann et al., in Chapter 7, *Fuzzy Online Reputation Analysis Framework*, have set up a fuzzy online reputation analysis framework (foRa) in order to allow communications operatives to search the Social Web to find meaningful information in a straightforward manner. The foRa framework has three main parts. A fuzzy grassroots ontology collects data and converts them into an ontology. The ontology is managed and stored on a storage system. A reputation analysis engine carries out the analysis, and an interactive user interface called the dashboard allows the browsing of related topics.

The tagspace is a representation of a consistent picture and serves as the input for the ontology adaptor, which is intended to separate the tagspace into hierarchies of classes. A fuzzy c-means algorithm is used to do this. A prototype (youReputation) of a reputation analysis tool demonstrates the features of the foRa framework. The prototype gives reputation results based on search inputs.

According to Kaufmann and Graf in Chapter 8, *Fuzzy Target Groups in Analytic Customer Relationship Management*, three analytic techniques can be very helpful in supporting Customer Relationship Management activities: the selection of relevant attributes, the visual presentation of relevant associations, and the prediction of relevant class membership. The authors emphasize that inductive fuzzy logic techniques support these three types of analysis.

Based on a likelihood inductive approach, fuzzy membership degrees in the desired target classes are computed. This inductive fuzzy classification, which is based on normalized likelihood ratios, allows the authors to generate customer profiles based on a target class and the relevant customer attributes. The chapter concludes with the presentation of an implementation of the software.

For their case study, the authors consider the financial services provider *Swiss Post,* which wishes to contact customers with personal advertisement messages. Based on relevant customer attributes, a predictive inductive fuzzy model is constructed that assigns a numerical value to every customer record. A fuzzy target group can thus be identified.

Chapter 9, *Web Analytics with Fuzziness*, is by Zumstein. In its restrictive definition, Web analytics is essentially the measurement and analysis of Web data. As noted by the author, one significant problem in this context is that Web data often consist of metrics values and raw numbers, and are therefore difficult to interpret. The aim of the chapter is to propose a fuzzy logic concept making this analysis possible.

A first remark made by the author is that traditionally, Web metrics values are classified in a sharp way, which is not a very good solution. The need for a fuzzy classification is argued and an inductive fuzzy classification method proposed for the analysis of Web usage patterns. This fuzzification has a number of advantages in this context. Fuzzy classification in Web mining makes it possible to rank Web pages by a gradual degree of membership in classes. Furthermore, it appears that the results of methods based on fuzzy logic are easier to interpret. As an illustration, the author provides a case study concerning the use of fuzzy classification with real Web data.

Performance Analysis

The third section has three chapters and begins with a contribution from Fasel and Shahzad. In Chapter 10, *Fuzzy Data Warehouse for Performance Analysis*, these authors consider classification with linguistic terms in the context of data warehousing. They argue that if a crisp strategy is applied, true values cannot be measured, and it is not possible to have a smooth transition between classes. Their approach, based on a fuzzy data warehouse model, attempts to integrate fuzzy concepts as meta-tables without affecting the core of a traditional data warehouse. One can immediately see the potential of such an approach. Both sharp and fuzzy analyses of data are made possible.

A fuzzy OLAP cube makes it possible to implement fuzziness within the data warehouse. Yet, by allowing the querying of both crisp and fuzzy data, thanks to their meta-table structure, they combine fuzzy association rules mining and other data mining techniques which require less effort than the proposed cube. The cube contains the membership degrees of the fuzzy sets as measures. The application of fuzzy association rules is thus made possible. This approach appears greatly to simplify the integration and aggregation of fuzzy concepts and can be integrated into existing traditional data warehouses rather simply.

An original part of the chapter is the presentation of a method for modeling a fuzzy data warehouse. In two specific steps, "Defining classification elements" and "Building a fuzzy data warehouse model," the modeler is guided in the development of a fuzzy data warehouse without requiring a deep knowledge of fuzzy logic.

The case study presented by the authors is very helpful, not only to illustrate the implementation of a fuzzy data warehouse, but also to demonstrate the performance of this form of data warehouse. The case concerns a movie rental company. Particularly interesting is the integration of fuzzy concepts in the data warehouse. At the end of the process, the company benefits from a new set of performance measures. As the authors show, these measures can be very useful, for example for the analysis of customer revenue.

Werro and Stormer in Chapter 11 propose *A Fuzzy Logic Approach for the Assessment of Online Customers*. The authors adopt the customer equity principle to analyze and manage customer relationships. They argue that the fuzzy classification approach can improve the customer equity, launch loyalty programs, automate mass customization, and refine marketing campaigns. The toolkit supplied by the authors, which is an extension of the fuzzy classification query language, aims to reduce the complexity of customer data and through fuzzy classification makes possible the extraction of valuable hidden information. This is done by extending the relational database schema with meta-tables added to the system catalogue.

Furthermore, the authors show that it is possible to decompose a complex fuzzy classification into a hierarchy of fuzzy classifications. As a result, the complexity of the initial problem will be reduced, allowing a better definition and optimization of the different fuzzy sub-classifications. According to the authors, a hierarchical fuzzy classification allows marketers to carry out better analyses. As an illustration, a practical example is given.

Ghasemy Yaghin and Fatemi Ghomi, in Chapter 12, *A Hybrid Fuzzy Multiple Objectives Approach to Lotsizing, Pricing and Marketing Planning Model*, note that few studies have simultaneously considered profit maximization and Return on Inventory Investment (ROII) maximization as performance criteria for the shortage constrained inventory model. The imprecise and fuzzy nature of parameters such as unit costs and marketing functions has led the authors to develop a fuzzy multiple objectives model. The profit, return on inventory investment, and a qualitative objective related to customer satisfaction are the objective functions considered. The model is able to determine the joint pricing, lotsizing, and marketing plan of the manufacturer. A real-world industrial case study illustrates the method.

Market Analysis

The fourth and final section includes two chapters. Casabayó and Agell, in Chapter 13, propose *A Fuzzy Segmentation Approach to Guide Marketing Decisions*. As the authors note, the market segmentation concept has been widely used in market analysis and has had great success since its introduction. Yet there are numerous limitations in this approach. The consumer is a plural person, which cannot be reduced to a single category. The fuzzy segmentation approach proposed by the authors is an attempt to overcome this problem. Using a multi-behavioral model, they have been able to interpret non-exclusive segments and obtain a clearer image of market realities. In this way, the decision-making process is considerably improved.

The LAMDA technique is advocated as an alternative to non-overlapping segmentation techniques. LAMDA (Logical Association in Multivariate Data Analysis) is a fuzzy clustering method, which uses a fuzzy membership function as the measure of adequacy of a unit for a cluster. The authors reveal numerous advantages of the LAMDA method over traditional classification techniques. First, in comparison to classic data mining or the artificial intelligence methods, there is its simplicity, both in the understanding and the interpretation of the results. Beyond this, the method works with both quantitative and qualitative data, is fast, very intuitive, and requires less memory than other classifying techniques.

The case study is based on data from a leading company in the Spanish energy sector. Two segmentation techniques were applied: a non-hierarchical cluster analysis and the LAMDA method. A compatibility analysis of the two methods was undertaken. It appears that the fuzzy segmentation reveals more pertinent information than the other segmentation method and permits the firm to identify more accurately the multiple segments customers belong to and why.

Chapter 14, *Causal Recipes Sufficient for Identifying Market Gurus versus Mavens*, is by Chung and Woodside. The identification of Market Mavens, i.e. information diffusers, plays a central role in the study of consumer behavior. However, a second category of information diffuser has to be considered: Market Gurus. These are consumers others frequently seek out for advice but who do not seek advice from others. The authors' aim is to develop a theory of the characteristics of Market Gurus, to search for them, and thus to confirm the existence of Market Gurus among consumers.

The authors apply a fuzzy set qualitative comparative analysis to distinguish between Market Mavens and Market Gurus using multi-year data from a national U.S. omnibus survey. This method makes it possible to analyze complex configurations of causal conditions as explanations of an outcome condition. Configurations of behavior may be demographics, attitudes, interests, and opinions. The authors proceed first by calibrating fuzzy-set scores. This procedure allows them to describe the degree of membership for a given case. Next "truth tables" are constructed to display all possible combinations of causal conditions and case distributions. Theses tables allow the authors to find multiple pathways to an outcome. The results obtained corroborate and extend previous research.

If you want to gain knowledge about recent research in fuzzy marketing methods or to build your company's customer assets for optimal performance, then this book is for you.

Andreas Meier
University of Fribourg, Switzerland

Laurent Donzé
University of Fribourg, Switzerland

Acknowledgment

We thank all the authors for their excellent contributions to this book. In addition, we acknowledge the help of the reviewers who made many suggestions to improve the quality. Finally, special thanks go to the publishing team at IGI Global. In particular, we thank Joel Gamon for giving us much valuable advice and supervising our book project.

Andreas Meier
University of Fribourg, Switzerland

Laurent Donzé
University of Fribourg, Switzerland

Chapter 1
Applying Fuzzy Logic and Fuzzy Methods to Marketing

Laurent Donzé
University of Fribourg, Switzerland

Andreas Meier
University of Fribourg, Switzerland

ABSTRACT

Marketing deals with identifying and meeting the needs of customers. It is therefore both an art and a science. To bridge the gap between art and science, soft computing, or computing with words, could be an option. This chapter introduces fundamental concepts such as fuzzy sets, fuzzy logic, and computing with linguistic variables and terms. This set of fuzzy methods can be applied in marketing and customer relationship management. In the conclusion, future research directions are given for applying fuzzy logic to marketing and customer relationship management.

BRIDGING ART AND SCIENCE

Marketing is "the activity, set of institutions, and processes for creating, communicating, delivering, and exchanging offerings that have value for customers, clients, partners, and society at large" (see American Marketing Association, 2011). Kotler and Keller (2006, p. 6) define marketing as "a social process by which individuals and groups obtain what they need and want through creating, offering, and freely exchanging products

and services of value with others". Marketing therefore deals with identifying and meeting human and social needs.

Marketing is both an art and a science. It is the art and the knowledge to manage customer relationships, extend customer life cycles, tailor the marketing mix (product, price, place, promotion), and optimize customer equity (Blattberg et al., 2001). Robert Lauterborn (1990, p. 26) suggested connecting the company's four P's with the customers' four C's, product with customer

DOI: 10.4018/978-1-4666-0095-9.ch001

solution, price with customer cost, place with convenience, and promotion with communication. In electronic business and commerce especially, winning companies will be those that meet customers' needs economically and with effective communication (Meier & Stormer, 2009)

Today, with Social Web and Semantic Web opportunities (Hitzler et al., 2010), companies and marketers are searching for a holistic marketing concept. This must be based on the design and implementation of marketing programs, processes, and activities that recognize the needs of online customers. The dictum that "everything matters" means that marketing and customer relationship management have to cope with complexities. Fuzzy Logic or fuzzy thinking, first established by Lotfi Zadeh's work on fuzzy sets (Zadeh, 1965), suggests that binary thought is a way of simplifying a complex world and is in most cases not adequate. Simplification distorts reality. In Zadeh's words: "As the complexity of a system increases, our ability to make precise and significant statements about its behaviour diminishes until a threshold is reached beyond which precision and significance become mutually exclusive characteristics" (Kosko, 1994, p. 148).

Fuzzy logic is an extension of classical logic with only two truth values, 'true' and 'false'. It can be considered as an infinite value logic covering the whole interval from true (1) to false (0). Fuzzy logic focuses on linguistic variables in natural languages and provides a foundation for approximate reasoning with imprecise propositions. It reflects both the rightness and vagueness of human thinking.

A holistic marketing or customer relationship management concept has to take into account approximate reasoning (Bojadziev & Bojadziev, 1997; Grint, 1997). The behavior of customers, customer communication, and customer relationships are neither 'black' nor 'white' but there are a variety of grey scales with which to differentiate marketing programs and, hopefully, to improve customer equity.

This chapter is organized as follows. First, an introduction to fuzzy and crisp sets is given followed by a discussion of fuzzy logic and linguistic variables. An overview of possible applications in marketing and customer relationship management will then be provided. Finally, future trends and research issues are outlined.

CRISP SETS VS. FUZZY SETS

The concept of a set or a collection of objects is common in marketing and relationship management. For instance, all customers with their properties, such as name, age, address, and customer value are stored in the customer database or data warehouse. The objects in the set are called the elements of the set. Traditional data sets are also called ordinary or crisp sets in order to distinguish them from fuzzy sets.

An important notion in set theory is that of membership. If an element x belongs to a set A then $x \in A$, otherwise $x \notin A$. For each element x of a set A there are only two possibilities: either x belongs to A or it does not. The membership rule that characterizes the elements of a set A can be described by the characteristic function. The characteristic function χ takes only two values 1 and 0 or 'true' and 'false'. More precisely: if X is the universal set (universe of discourse) and A is a subset $A \subset X$ then the characteristic function χ of a set A indicates whether or not x belongs to A, i.e., $\chi_A : X \rightarrow \{0,1\}$. In other words every crisp set is uniquely defined by its characteristic function.

In Figure 1, the classical set *Teenager* is described by its characteristic function. A teenager is defined by her age: if x has an age between 13 (thirteen) and 19 (nineteen) then x belongs to the class of teenagers, otherwise it does not. The characteristic function of the set *Teenager* is:

Figure 1. The crisp set Teenager defined by its characteristic function

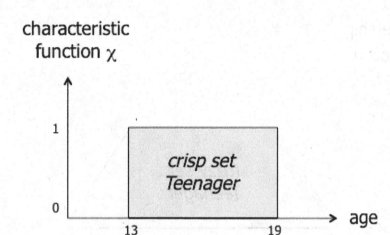

$$\chi_{\text{Teenager}}(x) = \begin{cases} 1 & for \ \ 13 \leq x \leq 19 \\ 0 & for \ \ x < 13 \ \ and \ \ x > 19 \end{cases}$$

For marketers the description of teenagers as a crisp set is not satisfactory. For instance, a young person waiting for his or her thirteenth birthday a few seconds before midnight is not yet a teenager, though a few seconds later she moves abruptly into the teenager group. Crisp sets do not allow gradation: parents or relatives of a teenager see the teenager gradually growing into a teenager before the thirteenth birthday celebration. And the reverse is also true: a teenager slowly says goodbye to the teenager group after the age of nineteen. When dealing with linguistic concepts or gradual transitions, crisp sets in which the characteristic function can only take two values, 1 or 0, are simply inadequate (Figure 1).

Instead of describing teenagers as a crisp set, an alternative would be to use a fuzzy set. Zadeh (1965) assigns a number to every element in the universe set, which indicates the degree or grade to which the element belongs to the set. For instance, young people with different ages may have different degrees of belonging to the teenager group. To formulate this fuzziness mathematically, Zadeh proposes the following definition:

If X is the set of universe and $A \subset X$, then the set A={(x, $\mu_A(x)$)| x ∈ X} is called a fuzzy set with the membership function μ_A: X –> [0,1].

A fuzzy set A is a set of pairs (x, $\mu_A(x)$) where each element x also has a grade $\mu_A(x)$. The grade is a number between 0 and 1 and measures the property of belonging to the set. The grade $\mu_A(x)=1$ means full membership (x belongs 100% to the fuzzy set A). The value 0 means non-membership while intermediate values between 0 and 1 describe partial membership.

An example of a fuzzy teenager set is given in Figure 2. A young person of age 10 is not yet a teenager, i.e., $\mu_{\text{Teenager}}(10)=0$. However that person gradually becomes a teenager. At the age of 11 for instance, she is already a teenager to the extent of one third if $\mu_{\text{Teenager}}(11)=1/3$. At the age of 12 she is two-thirds a teenager and at thirteen a full teenager. A similar graduation can be adopted for persons leaving the teenager group.

The membership functions for modeling marketing issues should be chosen according to the perception and experience of the marketers. Different functions are possible to define the concept of teenagers. In the proposed example in Figure 2, the membership function for teenagers is the following:

Figure 2. The fuzzy set Teenager defined by its membership function

Figure 2. The fuzzy set Teenager defined by its membership function

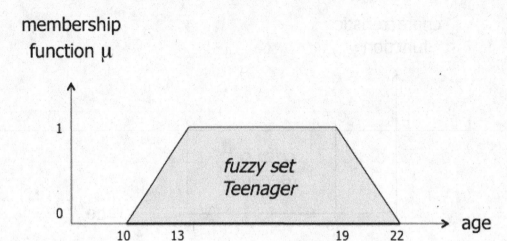

$$\mu_{\text{Teenager}}(x)=\begin{cases} 1 & for \quad 13 \leq x \leq 19 \\ \dfrac{x-10}{3} & for \quad 10 \leq x \leq 13 \\ \dfrac{22-x}{3} & for \quad 19 \leq x \leq 22 \\ 0 & for \quad x \leq 10 \quad and \quad x \geq 22 \end{cases}$$

Classical sets can be considered as a special case of fuzzy sets where all elements of the set have a membership degree of 1. Comparing the crisp set Teenager with the fuzzy set Teenager shows that sets with gradation describe reality better. In Figure 3 for instance, the customer segment Teenager overlaps the customer segment Youngster. As in real life, a young person gradually passes from the teenager class into the youngster class.

If marketers decide to use fuzzy segmentation according to figure 3, then neighboring segments may overlap. In other words, a person can belong to more than one customer segment. In Figure 3 for instance, a young person aged 20.5 belongs 50% to the segment of teenagers and 50% to the segment of youngsters. Being a member of a fuzzy segment implies a degree of membership. This

Figure 3. Introducing fuzzy customer segments

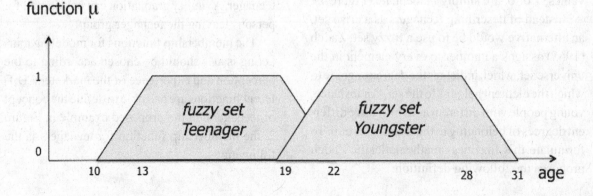

notion of membership results in the disappearance of sharp borders between customer segments (Hruschka, 1986). It can be shown that fuzzy customer segments reflect reality better and allow marketers to treat their customers according to their real value (Meier et al., 2008; Meier & Werro, 2007).

Fuzzy set theory generalizes the classical set theory. The functions used for the intersection of fuzzy sets are called t-norms and those used for union are called t-conorms (Buckley & Eslami, 2002; Wang et al., 2009). Other fuzzy set oriented operators, such as complement, implication, comparison, and equivalence can also be studied.

FUZZY LOGIC AND LINGUISTIC VARIABLES

Classical or two-valued logic deals with propositions, which are either true or false. Fuzzy logic is an extension of many-valued logic where propositions have more than two truth values. It incorporates fuzzy sets and relations, deals with linguistic variables and defines modifiers such as *very*, *mostly*, *not*, and so on. In other words, fuzzy logic facilitates common sense reasoning with imprecise and vague propositions.

A proposition (often called a statement) is a declarative sentence, which is logically either true (truth value 1) or false (truth value 0). Mathematicians and philosophers have always had doubts about describing the world with only two truth values. For instance, it is difficult to estimate a truth value for propositions, which express future events (e.g., "tomorrow it will be sunny"). A number of different three-value logics have been introduced, differing according to how the third truth value is defined. In addition, many-valued logics have been derived and in cases where the truth values are represented by all real numbers in the interval [0,1], infinite-valued logics (see Bergmann, 2008). In addition, there is an isomorphism between the fuzzy set theory and the infinite-valued logic: complement, intersection and union in fuzzy sets correspond to negation, conjunction, and disjunction in the infinite-valued logic, if propositions are replaced by the truth values.

Variables whose values are words in a natural or artificial language are called linguistic variables. For instance, when defining customer segments based on age, Age can be defined as a linguistic variable (see Figure 4). Defining fuzzy sets via the basic domain measured in years (the base variable), a number of different linguistic terms can be derived such as *Child, Teenager, Youngster,*

Figure 4. Linguistic variables and terms defined over fuzzy sets

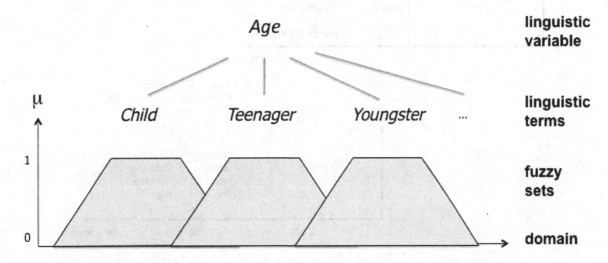

Middle Aged, Senior and *others*. Each customer segment is then defined approximately by these different linguistic terms. The linguistic terms or labels are chosen by marketers; they also have to define adequate membership functions, perhaps in cooperation with data analysts or data mining experts. Well-known membership functions are triangular, trapezoidal, s-shaped, or a combination of these.

Linguistic variables and terms can play an important role in marketing and customer relationship management. Besides Age, for instance, other linguistic variables with appropriate terms for Turnover, Gain, Investment, Customer Value, Risk, Loyalty, Customer Satisfaction etc. can be defined. These pre-defined linguistic variables and terms can then be used in query languages to control marketing and business issues. Applying fuzzy logic to different business sectors such as finance, marketing, human resources, logistics and other managerial application domains can

help to develop a successful performance measurement tool (see next section).

Databases are used intensively in database marketing as well as in customer relationship management. The query language SQL (Structured Query Language, Chamberlin, 1976) is the standard for defining and querying relational databases where data is stored in two-dimensional tables. The structure of SQL is the following:

select attributes
from tables
where selection condition

In Figure 5, a query example evaluates all customers with a turnover between 500 and 1000 Euros. Since the classical relational database model is defined with sharp sets, a sharp judgment of customers take place at the border of the class.

In order to query databases with fuzzy classes, the classification language fCQL (fuzzy Classification Query Language, Meier et al., 2005;

Figure 5. Extending query languages with linguistic variables and terms

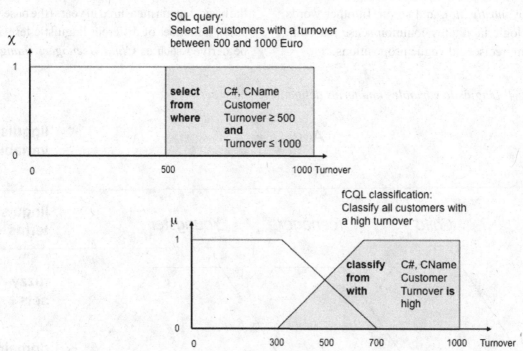

Meier et al., 2008) has been defined and implemented. The structure of this classification query language is:

classify attributes
from tables
with classification condition

It is in the **with** clause of fCQL that the user can take advantage of the predefined linguistic variables and their associated linguistic terms. In the classification example of Figure 5 all customers with the classification condition 'Turnover is high' are retrieved.

The classification language fCQL is a data analysis tool that allows marketers and users to query a predefined fuzzy classification of existing databases. Classification queries improve the quality of necessary decisions, for example, for marketing campaigns or when analyzing a product portfolio (Werro, 2008). Marketers and database experts determine the linguistic variables and define appropriate membership functions for the linguistic terms. Consequently, the fCQL approach hides the complexity of the domain from the users and allows them to focus on the querying process.

From the user's point of view, fCQL and similar fuzzy language extensions (Bosc & Kacprzyk 1995; Pons et al., 2000; Zadozny et al., 2008) can be seen as human-oriented query languages as they function at the linguistic level. Managers or marketers can easily formulate classification queries, as they are intuitive, that is, the meaning of the queries is linguistically expressed.

APPLYING FUZZY LOGIC TO MARKETING

Marketing deals with identifying and meeting the needs of customers. The customer-oriented strategy for building customer equity is called customer relationship management. With the systematic analysis, planning, organization and control of customer relationships the company can improve its financial performance. Fuzzy logic can be applied to a range of managerial tasks in marketing as well as to customer relationship management. In what follows, five possible application areas are outlined in order to show the advantages of fuzzy logic.

Planning and Optimizing Marketing Campaigns

Launching a marketing campaign can be very expensive. It is therefore crucial to select a customer group with potential. Fuzzy classification offers considerable advantages when planning and selecting customer subgroups (Meier & Werro, 2007; Werro, 2008). An example of a fuzzy-controlled marketing campaign is given in Figure 6. Here, the strategy is to select customers with attractive behaviour but low turnover. Using membership functions, a subset of customers in class C_3 can be chosen. The application of membership functions allows marketers to evaluate attractive customers in relation to the available campaign budget. Once the marketing campaign or testing process has been started, the fuzzy customer classes can be analyzed again. It is important to find out if the money invested is moving the customers in the planned direction, i.e., improving their customer value.

With fuzzy classification, marketers can monitor the development of customers or customer groups. By comparing the value of a customer over time, it is possible to determine whether a customer has increased, maintained, or decreased in customer value. The most valuable application of this monitoring of customers could be the detection of churning customers: automated triggers can respond to trends in customer values; if a good customer begins to show churning behavior, an alert to the marketing department may help to retain the customer.

Figure 6. Controlling the development of a target group after a marketing campaign

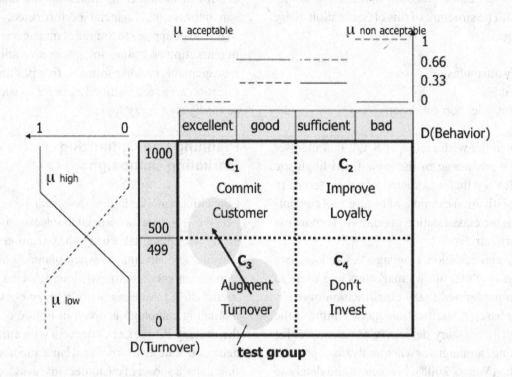

Mass Customization and Personalization

Customization and low cost are often mutually exclusive. Mass production provides low cost but at the expense of uniformity. Mass customization is defined as customization and personalization of products and services for individual customers at a mass production price. Digital goods and services are costly to produce but cheap to reproduce (Meier & Stormer, 2009). Versioning of products and services can easily be achieved.

Another advantage of fuzzy classification is its potential for personalized privileges. For instance, the membership degree of customers can determine the privileges they receive, such as a personalized discount. Discount rates can be associated with each fuzzy class; the individual discount of an online customer could then be calculated as the aggregation of the discounts of all the classes she belongs to in proportion to

her various degrees of membership (Werro et al., 2005). Using fuzzy classification for mass customization and personalization results in transparent and fair judgments.

Applying the fuzzy classification model with personalized discounts has additional advantages: first, all customers are motivated to improve their buying attitude and/or behavior. Second, only a small group within the premium class gets the maximum discount; the same is true for other classes provided with a discount. In other words, the total budget for personalized discounts will be smaller compared with conventional discount methods. The savings can then be used for acquisition or retention programs.

The automated calculation of a personalized discount is an obvious and pertinent example but the mass customization principle is not limited to this. Depending on the company's activity, many other applications can be found such as establishing the risk level in terms of the interest rate and own funds for credit worthiness; or a customer priority rating which can be used, for instance, to manage the queue at a call center; or, more generally, monitoring the performance of the company.

Web Analytics and Customer Performance Measurement

Customer relationship management has become an important issue in recent years. A first strategic objective is to acquire new customers and win back lost customers with attractive market and resource potential. The second strategic objective is to maintain and improve customer equity by cross- and up-selling together with retention programs during the customer lifetime (Blattberg et al., 2001; Rust et al., 2000). It is therefore important to treat customer relationships as an asset. This means managing customer relationships, measuring them, and maximizing them.

One example of a hierarchical fuzzy classification space is the calculation and monitoring of customer equity. Customer equity has to consider monetary assets (turnover, margins, service costs etc.) and also hidden assets such as loyalty and attachment. Harrison (2000) proposes an expression of customer loyalty based on two dimensions, attachment and buying behavior. On the basis of these two aspects of customer equity, a hierarchy of fuzzy classes for the calculation of customer values can be derived (Figure 7).

In our example, customer value depends on the two linguistic variables profitability and loyalty; loyalty is linked to buying frequency and attachment; attachment to visiting frequency and involvement frequency; and so on. It is important to note that marketers can evaluate the fuzzy classification space in a more structured way and with clearly defined semantics at every level of the hierarchy. For instance, if loyalty problems appear for a given customer, then the buying, visiting and involvement behavior can be studied in more depth in order to identify a suitable retention program.

Based on the above-mentioned attributes and a decomposition mechanism (see Werro et al., 2006), it is possible to calculate the customer value for each customer; the customer equity is then the total sum of the customer values of all customers. The fuzzy classification calculation schema allows marketers to extract the customer value of each customer and to analyze the potential and the weaknesses of these customers at different levels of the hierarchy. Indeed, each level of the hierarchy expresses a concept defined by a fuzzy classification; it is therefore possible to derive appropriate marketing actions to be taken for every customer in order to augment the customer value.

Recommendations of Products and Services

Using company data and market information in a customer database or data warehouse, analysis can be generated, such as prognoses for relationship maintenance and the optimization of marketing activities (Meier & Stormer, 2009). For the analysis of the customer, his/her sales behavior, and the involvement in the customer relationship, the following fuzzy marketing methods are attractive:

- **Fuzzy Clustering and deviation analysis:** The goal of fuzzy clustering is to group together customers with similar customer profiles and customer behavior. Using fuzzy customer classes allows the classes to overlap in a multi-dimensional classification space. Deviation analysis aims to recognize changes in developmental and behavioral patterns. Using fuzzy clustering and deviation analysis together allows the customer base to be evaluated with respect to a range of criteria and provides a differentiated understanding of the behavior of customer groups and sub-groups.
- **Recommender Systems:** Dependencies between the characteristics of individual customers can be captured in fuzzy associ-

Figure 7. Hierarchical decomposition of fuzzy customer classes

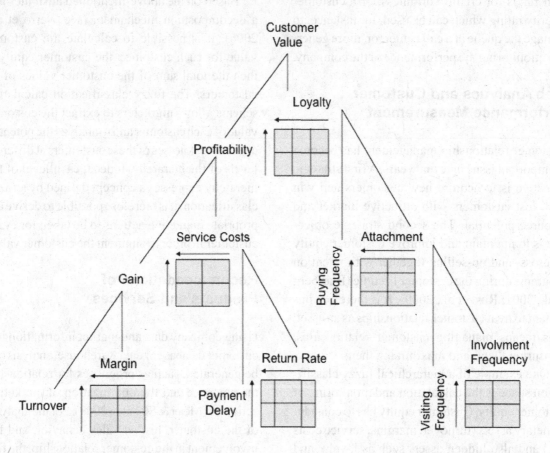

ation rules. Also included are shopping cart analyses based on click streams and web analytics. Recommender systems based on content-based or collaborative-based fuzzy filtering allow recommendations for products and services to be made (Yager, 2003).

- **Inductive Fuzzy Classification:** Characteristic individual trends of customers can be estimated using a prognosis analysis. A data mining methodology for an inductive fuzzy classification has been proposed (Kaufmann & Meier, 2009). The induction step is based on deriving fuzzy restrictions from data whose membership functions are inferred from normalized likelihood ratios of target class membership. An individual marketing campaign using this approach showed that fuzzy

classification led to a higher product selling ratio than crisp classification or random selection.

These and other research issues illustrate the need to combine marketing research with fuzzy logic. A fuzzy classification approach with appropriate software tools and query languages remains a fruitful toolkit for different application domains in marketing and relationship management.

Controlling Loop for Customer Relationship Management

In recent years, managers in a range of industries have been rethinking how to measure the performance of their businesses. They have recognized that a shift is needed towards treating financial statistics in the context of a broader set of measures. Edvinsson and Malone, for instance, propose the introduction of an intellectual capital report, which brings together indicators from finance, customer base, process management, renewal, and development as well as from human resources (Edvinsson & Malone, 1997). The customer focus requires indicators such as market share, number of customers, customer equity, customers lost, average duration of customer relationship, ratio of sales contacts to sales responses, satisfied customer index and service expenses per customer.

Figure 8 illustrates the closed loop for performance measurement and controlling customer relationships. This loop has been implemented in the webshop eSarine with the help of a fuzzy-based performance measurement system (Werro et al.. 2004). At the strategic level, objectives for customer acquisition, retention, and add-on selling must be defined, as must also the process and service quality goals of the webshop. The traditional

tasks in marketing, sales and after-sales activities will be carried out. Applications for collaborative services such as customized push, personalized offers and care of online communities will also be developed. In addition, all customer contacts information, i.e., click streams, has to be analyzed and stored in a contacts database.

The glue between the strategic and operational layer is the customer profile database with fuzzy classes, extended by the contacts database. The webshop administrator or a specialized team is responsible for a consistent customer database, and for the analysis of the contacts and the behavior of online customers. The fuzzy classification model with a corresponding query facility allows the webshop owner to improve customer equity, launch loyalty programs, automate mass customization, and refine online marketing campaigns.

Figure 8. Closed loop for controlling online customers and their behavior

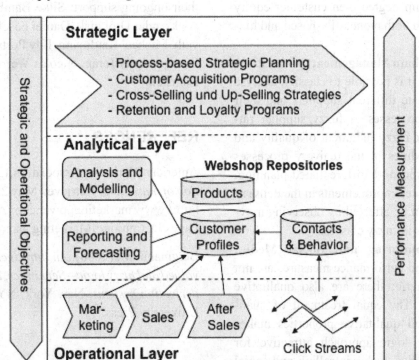

CONCLUSION

This chapter has presented an introduction to fuzzy sets, fuzzy logic, fuzzy methods for marketing and customer relationship management.

The research issues raised in this book illustrate the need to combine fuzzy logic with managerial application areas. In summary, fuzzy logic helps to analyze and control both quantitative and qualitative performance indicators in the following fields:

- **Strategic Management and Marketing:** For the analysis of markets, fuzzy logic allows demographic, geographic, behavioral and psychographic market segmentations. It is more successful and realistic to target markets fuzzily and to fuzzily position brands or companies in their markets.
- **Customer Relationship Management:** For customer analysis and segmentation, fuzzy customer classes give the marketers a differentiated judgment of customers and customer groups. In addition, if customer value is calculated as an aggregated membership degree then customer equity is based on both monetarily-based and hidden assets.
- **Supply Chain Management:** With a fuzzy approach, it is possible to classify, analyse and evaluate different suppliers and their delivery processes. A fuzzy supplier rating and/or fuzzy judgment of quality and time schedules of the delivery processes provides for more differentiated planning. For instance, improvements in the delivery system can be effected by observing moving targets in fuzzy classes.
- **Web Monitoring and Social Media:** Quality and performance measures are not only numeric; there are also qualitative measures. The equal treatment of quantitative and qualitative properties makes the fuzzy logic approach attractive for web analytics, web controlling and social media monitoring. It is possible to fuzzily categorise, analyse and control smart objects, customers, products, services and processes.
- **Risk Management:** It is not only in banking or insurance that individuals or companies have to be divided into risk classes. Very often, pricing components directly depend on risk levels. With a fuzzy logic approach, the calculation of risk degrees, creditworthiness or other indicators can be carried out with finer granularity.

Fuzzy logic can be seen as a management method, and appropriate software tools and languages are a powerful instrument for analysis and control of a business.

ACKNOWLEDGMENT

The authors would like to thank their current and former colleagues of the research center for Fuzzy Marketing Methods (www.FMsquare.org) for their ongoing support: Silke Bambauer-Sachse, Aleksandar Drobnjak, Daniel Fasel, Zoltan Horvath, Michael Kaufmann, Edy Portmann, Henrik Stormer, Luis Terán, Nicolas Werro, and Darius Zumstein.

REFERENCES

American Marketing Association. (2011). *Definition of marketing*. Retrieved May 25, 2011, from http://www.marketingpower.com/AboutAMA/Pages/DefinitionofMarketing.aspx

Bergmann, M. (2008). *An introduction to many-valued and fuzzy logic – Semantics, algebras, and derivation systems*. New York, NY: Cambridge University Press.

Blattberg, R. C., Getz, G., & Thomas, J. S. (2001). *Customer equity – Building and managing relationships as valuable assets*. Boston, MA: Harvard Business School Press.

Bojadziev, G., & Bojadziev, M. (1997). *Fuzzy logic for business, finance, and management*. Singapore: World Scientific Publishing Co.

Bosc, P., & Kacprzyk, J. (Eds.). (1995). *Fuzzines in database management systems*. Heidelberg, Germany: Physica Publisher.

Buckley, J. J., & Eslami, E. (2002). *An introduction to fuzzy logic and fuzzy sets*. Heidelberg, Germany: Physica Publisher.

Chamberlin, D. D., Astrahan, M. M., Eswaran, K. P., Griffiths, P. P., Lorie, R. A., & Mehl, J. W. (1976). A unified approach to data definition, manipulation, and control. *IBM Journal of Research and Development, 20*(6), 560–575. doi:10.1147/rd.206.0560

Edvinsson, L., & Malone, M. S. (1997). *Intellectual capital – Realizing your company's true value by finding its hidden brainpower*. New York, NY: Harper Collins Publisher.

Grint, K. (1997). *Fuzzy management – Contemporary ideas and practices at work*. New York, NY: Oxford University Press.

Harrison, T. (2000). *Financial services marketing*. Essex, UK: Pearson Education Press.

Hitzler, P., Krötzsch, M., & Rudolph, S. (2010). *Foundations of Semantic Web technologies*. Boca Raton, FL: Taylor and Francis Group.

Hruschka, H. (1986). Market definition and segmentation using fuzzy clustering methods. *International Journal of Research in Marketing, 3*, 117–134. doi:10.1016/0167-8116(86)90015-7

Kaufmann, M., & Meier, A. (2009). An inductive fuzzy classification approach applied to individual marketing. In *Proceedings of the 28th North American Fuzzy Information Processing Society Annual Conference*. Cincinnati, Ohio, Kosko, B. (1994). *Fuzzy thinking*. London, UK: Flamingo.

Kotler, P., & Keller, K. L. (2006). *Marketing management*. Upper Saddle River, NJ: Pearson Prentice Hall.

Lauterborn, R. (1990). New marketing litany – 4P's Passe, C-words take over. *Advertising Age, 1*, 26.

Meier, A., Schindler, G., & Werro, N. (2008). Fuzzy classification on relational databases. In Galindo, G. J. (Ed.), *Handbook on research on fuzzy information processing in databases* (*Vol. 2*, pp. 586–614). Hershey, PA: IGI Global. doi:10.4018/978-1-59904-853-6.ch023

Meier, A., & Stormer, H. (2009). *eBusiness and eCommerce – Managing the digital value chain*. Heidelberg, Germany: Springer Publisher.

Meier, A., & Werro, N. (2007). A fuzzy classification model for online customers. *Informatica, 31*, 175–182.

Meier, A., Werro, N., Albrecht, M., & Sarakinos, M. (2005). Using a fuzzy classification query language for customer relationship management. In *Proceedings of the 31st Very Large Data Bases Conference: VLDB 2005* (pp. 10889-1096). Trondheim, Norway.

Pons, O., Vila, M. A., & Kacprzyk, J. (Eds.). (2000). *Knowledge management in fuzzy databases*. Heidelberg, Germany: Physica Publisher.

Rust, R. T., Zeithaml, V. A., & Lemon, K. N. (2000). *Driving customer equity*. New York, NY: Free Press.

Wang, X. Ruan, D., & Kerre, E. E. (2009). *Mathematics of fuzziness – Basic issues*. Berlin, Germany: Springer Publisher.

Werro, N. (2008). *Fuzzy classification of online customers*. PhD Thesis, University of Fribourg, Switzerland, also available as eThesis. Retrieved May 25, 2001, from http://diuf.unifr.ch/main/is/research/fuzzy-classification-query-language-fcql

Werro, N., Stormer, H., Frauchiger, D., & Meier, A. (2004). eSarine – A Struts-based webshop for small and medium-sized enterprises. In *Lecture Notes in Informatics EMISA2004 – Information Systems in E-Business and E-Government* (pp. 13-24). Luxembourg, Belgium.

Werro, N., Stormer, H., & Meier, A. (2005). Personalized discount – A fuzzy logic approach. In *Proceedings of the 5th IFIP International Conference on eBusiness, eCommerce and eGovernment* (pp. 375-387). Poznan, Poland.

Werro, N., Stormer, H., & Meier, A. (2006). A hierarchical fuzzy classification of online customers. In *Proceedings of the IEEE International Conference on e-Business Engineering – ICEBE2006* (pp. 256-263). Shanghai, China.

Yager, R. R. (2003). Fuzzy logic methods in recommender systems. *Fuzzy Sets and Systems, 136*, 133–149. doi:10.1016/S0165-0114(02)00223-3

Zadeh, L. A. (1965). Fuzzy sets. *Information and Control, 8*, 338–353. doi:10.1016/S0019-9958(65)90241-X

Zadrozny, S., de Tre, G., de Caluwe, R., & Kacprzyk, J. (Eds.). (2008). An overview of fuzzy approaches to flexible database querying. In J. Galindo (Ed.), *Handbook on research on fuzzy information processing in databases* (pp. 34-54, vol. 1). Hershey, PA: IGI Global.

KEY TERMS AND DEFINITIONS

Customer Equity: The customer equity of an individual customer or of a customer group is the sum of the acquisition equity, the retention equity, and the add-on selling equity which results from up- and cross-selling activities.

Customer Relationship Management: A strategy to develop and improve customer equity by managing the relationships of customers and potential customers.

Fuzzy Clustering: The process of dividing data elements into classes by means of a similarity measure. In fuzzy clustering the similarity measure is based on membership functions where the elements of the classes can belong to more than one class.

Fuzzy Logic: Classical or two-valued logic deals with propositions or sentences, which are either true (truth value 1) or false (truth value 0). Fuzzy logic is an extension of many-valued logic, i.e., it is an infinite-valued logic where the truth values can be represented by all real numbers of the interval $[0,1]$.

Fuzzy Set: A classical or crisp set is uniquely defined by its characteristic function χ. For each element of the set this function indicates whether it belongs to the set (truth value 1) or not (truth value 0). In a fuzzy set, the membership function μ assigns to each element of the set a number or truth value from the interval $[0,1]$ (called the membership degree), which indicates the degree to which the element belongs to the set.

Linguistic Variable: Variables whose values are words in a natural or artificial language are called linguistic variables. Terms or labels for the linguistic variable are expressed by fuzzy sets on a universal set called the domain. As an example, age can be considered as a linguistic variable whose values are words like young, middle aged, old and so on.

Marketing: Identifying and meeting the needs of customers. It organizes all the processes required in creating, communicating, offering, and delivering products and services of value to customers or partners.

Section 1
Fuzzy Modeling

Chapter 2
Fuzzy Soft Social Network Modeling and Marketing

Ronald R. Yager
Iona College, USA

Rachel L. Yager
Metropolitan College of New York, USA

ABSTRACT

Facebook, Linkedin, Myspace, and other social networks have become a very important environment in which people interact, exchange information about products, services, movies and music, and so forth. New trends and hot items rapidly move through these networks. Clearly, modern marketing has to focus on the possibilities of taking advantage of these networks. The determination of people who are leaders and trendsetters within a social network would be a great benefit for marketing. In recent papers, the authors have developed a model of social networks based on the use of fuzzy set theory and other soft granular computing technologies. This is called the Framework for Intelligent Social Network Analysis (FISNA). Using granular computing, the authors express concepts associated with social networks in a human-focused manner. Since human beings predominantly use linguistic terms in order to communicate, reason, and understand, they are able to build bridges between human conceptualization and the formal mathematical representation of the social networks. Consider, for example, a concept such as "leader." An analyst may be able to express, in linguistic terms, using a network relevant vocabulary, the properties of a leader. The authors' framework enables translation of this linguistic description into a mathematical formalism that allows for determination of how true it is that a particular person, a node in the network, is a leader. The authors use fuzzy set methodologies, and more generally granular computing, to provide the necessary bridge between the human analyst and the formal model of the network. In this chapter, the authors investigate and describe the use of the FISNA technology to help in the modeling of market related concepts in social networks.

DOI: 10.4018/978-1-4666-0095-9.ch002

INTRODUCTION

A social network provides a vast amount of information in the form of a social graph of human relationships, interactions and behaviors. The usefulness of this information to advertisers and marketers is readily apparent. For example, identifying people who are high influencer of their social circle, known as opinion leaders and trendsetters, can be useful in the preliminary steps of preparing a marketing plan and strategy (Doyle, 2007). In the pharmaceutical industry, key opinion leaders are medical professionals whose opinions are frequently consulted for decisions in products and treatments (Nair, Manchanda & Bhatia, 2010). Marketers are also interested in setting apart followers and trendsetters for music, fashion, and media; the buying patterns of trendsetters provide insights for future trends, directly and indirectly promotes the sale of products (Maldonado, 2010). The complex inter-relational structure of these networks greatly complicates the task of extracting the kinds of information desired by marketers. Our goal here is to provide a language which can be used to intelligently query a social network. Here we shall describe fuzzy set operators developed by Yager (2008, 2010a, 2010b) which can be used to develop human focused network information retrieval techniques.

Considerable recent interest has been focused on social relational network analysis (Carrington, Scott & Wasserman, 2007). A notable example of this has been in the analysis of terrorist and criminal organizations (Popp & Yen, 2006). Another area of applicability is in the domain of social networks such as Facebook, Myspace and LinkedIn that are rapidly gaining importance on the Internet.

In trying to extend our capabilities to analyze social relational networks, an important objective is to associate human concepts and ideas with these networks. Since human beings predominantly use linguistic terms, in which to communicate, reason and understand, we become faced with the task of trying to build bridges between human conceptualization and the formal mathematical representation of the social network.

Consider for example a concept, such as "leader". An analyst may be able to express, in linguistic terms, using a network relevant vocabulary, properties of a leader. Our task then becomes a translation of this linguistic description into a mathematical formalism that allows us to determine how true it is that a particular node is a leader.

In this work we began looking at the possibility of using fuzzy set methodologies and more generally granular computing (Zadeh, 1998; Lin, Yao & Zadeh 2002; Bargiela & Pedrycz 2003; Yager, 2006) to provide the necessary bridge between the human analyst and the formal model of the network.

Our interest in focusing on this technology is based on the confluence of two important factors. One of these is that fuzzy set theory and particularly Zadeh's paradigm of computer with words (Zadeh, 1996, 1999) which was especially developed for the task of representing human linguistic concepts in terms of a mathematical object, a fuzzy subset. Fuzzy logic has large repertoire of operations that allows for the combination of these sets in ways that mimic the logic of human reasoning and deduction. The second important factor is the nature of the formal mathematical model of social networks. The standard formal model used to represent a social network is a mathematical structure called a relationship. Using this structure, the members of the network constitute a set of elements, the connections in a network are represented as pairs of elements, and the network is viewed as the set of all these pairs. The key observation here is that the standard form of network representatives is in terms of set theory. The fact that the underlying representation of the social network is in set theoretic terms makes it well-suited to a marriage with the fuzzy set approach. In Figure 1 we show the FISNA, Framework for Intelligent Social Network Analysis.

Figure 1. Framework for Intelligent Social Network Analysis (FISNA)

An introduction to basic ideas of graph (relational network) theory is first provided in the following sections. We then discuss concepts from granular computing, in particular the fuzzy set paradigm of computing with words. The natural connection between graph theory and granular computing, particularly fuzzy set theory, is pointed out. This connection is grounded in the fact that these are both set based technologies. Our objective here is to take a step toward the development of intelligent social network analysis using granular computing. In particular one can start by expressing in a human focused manner, concepts associated with social networks; we can then formalize these concepts using fuzzy sets and evaluate these concepts with respect to social networks, which have been represented using set based relational network theory. We capture this approach in what we call the framework for intelligent social network analysis, FISNA. Using this paradigm we provide definitions of a number of concepts related to social networks.

BACKGROUND: BASIC RELATIONAL NETWORK THEORY

The technology underlying modern social networks can be viewed as coming from four directions. The oldest of these is mathematics which dates back to Euler in 1736 and his interest in solving the Konigsberg bridge problem (Chartrand, 1977; Bollobas, 2000; Berge, 2001).

Mathematicians refer to this field as of graph theory[1]. The second direction is social network theory (Wasserman & Faust, 1994; Scott, 2000). This work dates back to the 1930's when social scientist notable anthropologist started using networks to model social organizations and relationships. The third direction has focused on the growth and evolution of networks (Newman, Barabási & Watts, 2006). This direction has made considerable use of probabilistic techniques, while it has roots in the early work on random graphs by Solomonoff and Rapoport (1951) and Erodos and Renyi (1960), it has recently flourished with its focus on small world models (Watts & Strogatz, 1998) and scale free models (Barabási & Albert, 1999). These have been particularly useful in modeling the Internet. A fourth direction has been from the area of computational intelligence which has been interested in using network methods to model human reasoning (Cook & Holder, 2007). The concept of network used in this area is much more heterogeneous than the one used by the others.

Mathematical Graph Theory

In this section, we introduce some of the basic ideas from mathematical graph theory. Our purpose here is to focus on the view of a graph as a mathematical relationship. The view will be useful when we apply fuzzy set theory to model human concepts. Since we are drawing heavily from the ideas of classic mathematics, here we shall most often use the mathematicians preferred term of *graph*;

however for our ultimate purposes, a more intuitive designation would be a *relational network*.

Two major classes of graphs are undirected and directed. Since for the most part we shall concentrate on undirected graphs, we use the unmodified term *graph* to mean undirected, and we specifically use the modifier *directed* when we refer to directed graph.

A typical graph is shown in Figure 2. It consists of a set of vertices (nodes) with some of them connected with undirected lines. We denote this graph as $G = <V, E>$ here $V = \{a,b,c,d,e\}$ is the set of vertices and $E = \{ab, ad, ae, bc, cd\}$ is the collection of undirected lines called edges. The number of vertices in V is called the **order** of G. The number of edges in E is called the **size** of G. We shall find it convenient to let U indicate the collection of all distinct unordered pairs[2].

Using this we see that $E \subseteq U$. We see that if V has n elements then the cardinality of U is $\frac{n(n-1)}{2}$. We shall also find it useful to designate U_x for any $x \in V$ as the subset of U consisting of the terms involving x. Here we see that $|U_x| = n-1$.

If xy is an edge of G we say that x and y are adjacent. The word incident can be used synonymously with adjacent. We say that a graph G is complete if all vertices are adjacent, and there is an edge between all vertices. We note a complete graph with n vertices has $\frac{n(n-1)}{2}$ edges.

For our purposes we will find it useful to associate with G a relationship $R: V \times V \rightarrow \{0,1\}$ such that $R(x,y) = R(y,x) = 1$ if xy is an edge of G, and $R(x,y) = R(y,x) = 0$ if xy is not an edge of G. Thus we see that for an undirected graph R is a symmetric relation, $R(x,y) = R(y,x)$. For some purposes, it will be useful to assume that R is reflexive, $R(x, x) = 1$. Alternatively, starting with a reflexive symmetric relationship on a set V, we can generate an undirected graph.

An additional mathematical construct that can be associated with a graph G is a symmetric matrix M. Here the component $m_{ij} = 1$ if $v_i v_j$ is an edge of the graph and is zero if the vertices v_i and v_j are not adjacent. Here again we let $m_{ii} = 1$.

When we are dealing with multiple graphs, we shall refer to the vertices and edges of a graph G as $V(G)$ and $E(G)$. We shall also use the notation E_G and V_G. Assume $G = <V, E>$ is a graph its complement is a graph $\overline{G}$ having the same vertex set as G, but two vertexes are adjacent in $\overline{G}$ if they a not adjacent in G. Thus $V(\overline{G}) = V(G)$ and $E(\overline{G}) = U - E(G)$. We note that if R and $\overline{R}$ are the associated relations then $\overline{R}(x, y) = 1 - R(x, y)$ for $x \neq y$ and $R(x, x) = \overline{R}(x, x) = 1$.

The concept of *isomorphism* allows us to consider different graphs as equivalent. Assume $G_1 = <V_1, E_1>$ and $G_2 = <V_2, E_2>$. An isomorphism from G_1 to G_2 is a bijective, one to one and onto, mapping $f: V_1 \rightarrow V_2$ such that two vertices $a, b \in V_1$ are adjacent in G_1 if $f(a)$ and $f(b)$ are adjacent in G_2. In this case we say that G_1 and G_2 are isomorphic. We note if R_1 and R_2 are the associated relationship, then G_1 and G_2 are isomorphic if there exist an f such that $R_1(a,b) = R_2(f(a), f(b))$. If f is an isomorphic from G_1 to G_2 then f^{-1} is an isomorphism from G_2 to G_1. We shall denote an isomorphism G between G_1 and G_2 as $G_1 \sim G_2$. It is clear that if G_1 and G_2 are isomorphic, then $|V_1| = |V_2|$ and $|E_1| = |E_2|$. Isomorphism is an equivalence relation. Thus if $G_1 \sim G_2$ and $G_2 \sim G_3$ then $G_1 \sim G_3$.

Let $G = <V_G, V_E>$ be a graph. A graph $H = <V_H, E_H>$ is called a subgraph of G if $E_H \subseteq E_G$ and $V_H \subseteq V_G$. We note that a subgraph H of G does not need to contain all the edges in E_G between

Figure 2. Typical undirected graph

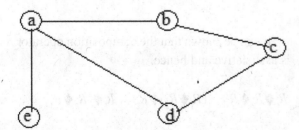

the vertices in V_H. A stronger requirement would be that V_H contains all the edges in V_G between the elements in E_H. We call such a subgraph, an induced subgraph from using V_H.

An important operation in graphs is moving between vertices, graph transversal. Here we define some important ideas in this regard.

If x and y are two distinct vertices, and an x-y path in G is a sequence of distinct vertices beginning with x and ending with y so that there is an edge between any two adjacent vertices in the sequence. Consider the sequence of distinct nodes $a_1 a_2 a_3 \ldots a_q$ this can be said to provide a path for a_1 to a_q if $\underset{i=1 \text{ to } q-1}{\text{Min}}[R(a_i, a_{i+1})] = 1$.

We note in an undirected graph if $a_1 a_2 a_3 \ldots a_q$ is a path from a_1 to a_q then its reverse $a_q\, a_{q-1}\, a_{q-2} \ldots a_1$ is a path from a_q to a_1.

Two vertices x and y are said to be connected if x = y or there is an x-y path. A graph G is said to be connected if every two vertices in G are connected. A connected subgraph H of G is called a component of G if H is not contained in any connected subgraph of G having more vertices or edges than H. H is a maximal connected subgraph. If a graph has only one component, the graph is a connected graph.

A cycle is an x-y path in which x = y and contains at least three edges. It must contain at least three distant vertices. A graph is called Hamiltonian if there exist a cycle containing every vertex.

Assume $G = <V, E>$ is a graph in which $x \in V$ and $e \in E$. By G - e we mean the subgraph $<V, E - e>$, it contains all edges except e and has the same vertices as G. By G - x we mean the subgraph $<V$ - $x, E - U_x>$. It contains all the vertices of G except x and all the edges of G except those that are incident on x. We note $E - U_x = E \cap \overline{U_x}$.

If G is a connected graph, then an edge e is called a bridge if G - e is disconnected. If G is a connected graph, then a vertex x is called a cut-vertex if G - x is disconnected.

A connected graph that has no cycles is called a tree. We note that every edge of a tree is a bridge.

A graph $G = <V, E>$ is called bipartite if it is possible to partition the vertex set into two subsets, V_1 and V_2 so that every edge of G joins a vertex of V_1 with a vertex of V_2 and no vertices in the same subset are adjacent.

A number of measures have been associated with a graph. Among the most useful of these is the degree of a vertex, denoted deg(v). It is the number of edges incident to the vertex. For example in the graph of Figure 1 we have deg(a) = 3. The sum of the degrees over all vertices is equal to twice the number of edges.

Another important idea is the length of a path, defined as the number of edges the path contains. The distance between two vertices is the length of the shortest path between them. We refer to a shortest path as a geodesic and denote the shortest path between x and y as Geo(x, y). If we use Len(p) to indicate the length of a path then the distance(x, y) = Len(Geo(x, y)). If no path exists between two vertices we say that the distance is infinite.

We shall find a graph's description in terms of its relationship R to be extremely useful in many applications. This will be particularly useful for the case when we try to associate human cognitive concepts with a graph.

A useful mathematical operation associated with relationships is composition. Assume R_1 and R_2 are relationships over the same vertex set V. The composition of R_1 and R_2 denoted $R_1 \blacklozenge R_2$ is also a relationship on V defined so that,

$$R_1 \blacklozenge R_2 (x, z) = Max_{y \in V}\left[Min\left(R_1(x, y), R_2(y, z)\right)\right].$$

It can be shown that the composition operator is associative and hence,

$$R_1 \blacklozenge R_2 \blacklozenge R_3 = (R_1 \blacklozenge R_2) \blacklozenge R_2 = R_1 \blacklozenge (R_2 \blacklozenge R_3).$$

A special case of composition is $R \blacklozenge R$, , the composition of a graph with itself, we shall denote this R_2. More generally we shall denote the composition of R with its self k times as R^k,

$$R^k = R \blacklozenge R \blacklozenge \ldots \blacklozenge R.$$

We observe that since $R(x, x) = 1$ then,

$$R^2\left(x,\, z\right) = Max_y\left[\left(R\left(x,\, y\right) \wedge R\left(y,\, z\right)\right]$$
$$\geq R\left(x,\, x\right) \wedge R\left(x,\, z\right) \geq R\left(x,\, z\right).$$

More generally it can be shown that $R^k (x,y) \leq R^{k+1} (x,y)$ and $R^k (x,x) = 1$. From this we see $R^k \subseteq R^{k+1}$ for all $k \geq 1$.

It is most important to observe that if $R^k (x,y) = 1$, then there exists a path of at least length k from x to y. Thus distance (x, y) can be seen as the smallest k for which $R^k (x,y) = 1$. Thus we see composition operation provides a useful tool for working with paths.

In the preceding, we have introduced some of the basic ideas of mathematical graph theory. As we now turn to some applications in the following sections, we shall find it more intuitively appealing to refer to graphs as relational or social networks.

MODELLING SOCIAL NETWORK NOTIONS WITH FUZZY CONCEPTS

As we have indicated, our goal here is to extend our capabilities of analyzing relational networks by associating with these networks, various concepts with which humans understand the world. As already noted, human beings predominantly use linguistic terms in which to communicate, comprehend and reason. Machines, on the other hand, require much more formal symbols in which to "comprehend and reason." Considerable interest has focused on the use of ontologies and other semantic technologies to bring human like reasoning and comprehension to our computational system. One of the most successful approaches to providing a bridge between man and machine comprehension has been Zadeh fuzzy set based paradigm of computing with worlds (Zadeh, 1996) and the more general idea of granular computing (Bargiela & Pedrycz, 2003).

These technologies allow for a high level of man-machine cooperation by providing a framework in which concepts, ideas and knowledge can be modeled in a manner amenable to both man and machine.

Here we are interested in using this framework for mutual understanding in the domain of social network analysis. As previously noted, the potential here is particularly promising given that computer's understanding of these networks is in terms of a mathematical relationship, which is a type of set object.

In the following, we shall introduce some ideas from these fuzzy set based approaches to computing with words.

Let U be some attribute that takes its value in a space Y. An example of this is age. For humans, this takes its value in the set $Y = \{1 \text{ to } 100\}$. A linguistic value is some word that can be used to describe the value of U. In the case of age some examples of linguistic values are "old", "young" and "about 30". A linguistic value can be seen as a granule, it is a collection of values from X. In providing information about U in addition to using precise values people also use linguistic values as well as other granular objects such as ranges. By a vocabulary associated with an attribute we mean a collection of linguistic values that are used to discuss the attribute and are commonly understood. It is part of the social environment.

Fuzzy sets have provided a useful tool for formalizing the idea of vocabulary in a way that allows for the type of formal computation needed by machines. Here if W is a linguistic value about the attribute U then we can express it as a fuzzy subset W over the domain Y of U. In particular for any element $y \in Y$ its membership grade in W,

$W(y) \in [0,1]$, indicates the compatibility of the value y with the linguistic concept W.

With the aid of fuzzy sets, we are able to bridge the gap between man and machine, by allowing the man to define the common vocabulary in terms of fuzzy sets. Man can now communicate his ideas using words, and the machine can understand these words as fuzzy sets; the fuzzy sets are in a form that the machine can manipulate. This is what Zadeh (2006) has referred to as machine precisiation. We are making the world understandable to the machine.

In studying social networks, there are a number of attributes about which it will be useful to have vocabularies. One such attribute is the strength of connection between vertices. This is an attribute whose domain is the unit interval, $I = [0, 1]$. Terms like strong, weak, none would be linguistic values that would be part of a vocabulary associated with this attribute. In this case we would define the word "strong" as a fuzzy subset S of $[0, 1]$ such that for any $y \in [0,1]$ the value $S(y)$ would indicate the degree to which y satisfies the communal definition of the concept strong.

Another attribute for which it would be useful to have a communal vocabulary is the number of links in a path, link-length. Here we can express this in terms of fuzzy subsets defined over the domain $Y = \{0,..., N\}$.

Linguistic values in addition to being associated with attributes corresponding to physical objects can be associated with variables corresponding to universal type concepts. One such example we shall find useful is proportion. Here U is an attribute that takes its value in the set $I = [0. 1]$ where $r \in [0,1]$ is a proportion. Examples of linguistic values that would be part of a vocabulary associated with this attribute are "many", "most", "about half" and "few". As noted by Zadeh (1983), these terms provide a generalization of the quantifiers "all" and "none" often used in logic. We can refer to this as linguistic quantifiers.

In the following, we shall use the linguistic modeling capability of fuzzy sets to provide more realistic formulation of some concepts available in social networks analysis as well as some new some concepts. Since our goal is to focus on the procedures and operations involved in providing this type of capability, we shall not dwell upon the construction of the vocabulary, but assume that all necessary linguistic terms are available as appropriate fuzzy sets. In addition with an understanding of the mechanism provided, we are certain that future researchers can provide alternative formulations of the concepts other than those provided here.

On the Concept of Node Importance

A useful concept introduced in the social network literature involves the idea of importance of a vertex in a network. This is related to the centrality of a node (Scott, 2000). The basic measure of centrality, sometimes called local centrality, is the number of vertices adjacent to a node. Thus,

$$C(x_i) = \sum_{\substack{j=1 \\ j \neq i}}^{n} R(x_i, x_j).$$

Here we are measuring the centrality of a vertex by the number of other vertices to which it directly connected. Here n is the number of nodes in the network.

A somewhat more general definition is to measure the number of nodes it is connected to by at most k steps. In this we get,

$$C^k(x_i) = \sum_{\substack{j=1 \\ j \neq i}}^{n} R^k(x_i, x_j).$$

Since $R^k(x_i, x_j) \geq R^p(x_i, x_j)$ for $k > p$ then we see that $C^k(x_i)$ $C^p(x_i)$ for $k > p$.

A softening of this concept can be achieved by considering the "number of close connections". In order to do this, we take advantage of the OWA aggregation operator (Yager, 1988) and the ability of fuzzy subsets to express linguistic terms. Here we assume the linguistic term *close* is in our common vocabulary. In particular, we have definition of the concept *close* as a fuzzy subset Q on the space $N = \{1, 2,..., n, n + 1\}$. Here for each $j \in N$ we have $Q(j) \in [0,1]$ as the degree to which being connected at most by j links is considered as *close*. We note that such a definition for close must satisfy the following properties:

1. $Q(j) \geq Q(k)$ if $j < k$,
2. $Q(1) = 1$ and
3. $Q(n+1) = 0$.

Using this definition, we obtain a set of n weights to be used as the parameters for the OWA aggregation operator, $w_k = Q(k) - Q(k+1)$. We note that the w_k's satisfy the following two conditions $w_k \geq 0$ and $\sum_{k=1}^{n} w_k = 1$.

Using these weights we calculate the number of close connections that x_i has as,

$$C^{Close}\left(x_i\right) = \sum_{k=1}^{n} w_k C^k\left(x_i\right).$$

In the above, $C^k\left(x_i\right) = \sum_{j=1, j\neq i}^{n} R^k(x_i, x_j)$ as defined in the preceding.

A special case of *close* is where $Q(j) = 1$ for $j \leq q$ and $Q(j) = 0$ for $j > q$. This corresponds to a definition of *close* as "at most q links." Using this definition, we obtain that $w_k = 1$ for k = q and $w_k = 0$ for $k \neq q$. In this case we get $C^{Close}(xi) = C^q(xi)$.

Another special case is where $Q(j) = 1$ for $j \leq q_1$, $Q(j) = \alpha$ for $q_1 < j \leq q_2$ and $Q(j) = 0$ for $j > q_2$. In this case we get,

$w_k = \alpha$ for $k = q_1$

$w_k = 1 - \alpha$ for $k = q_2$

$w_k = 0$ for all other k

Using this we get $C^{Close}(x_i) = \alpha C^{q1}(x_i) C^{q1}(x_1) + (1-\alpha) C^{q2}(x_1)$.

Another notable definition of *Close* is the following quasi-linear type. Here we define *Close* as follows,

$$Q\left(j\right) = \frac{q-j}{q-1} \text{ for } j < q$$

$Q(j) = 0$ for $j \geq q$.

In this case, $w_k = 0$ for $k \geq q$ and $w_k = Q\left(k\right) - Q\left(k-1\right)\frac{1}{(q-1)}$ for $k < q$.

Using this definition we get,

$$C^{Close}\left(x_i\right) = \frac{1}{(q-1)} \sum_{k=1}^{q-1} C^k\left(x_i\right).$$

Recalling that that $C^k(x_i)$ is the number of nodes connected to x_i by at most k steps let us define $T^k(x_i) = C^k(x_i) C^{k-1}(x_i)$. Here $T^k(x_i)$ is the number of nodes whose shortest path to x_i is equal to k steps. We note here that $C^0(x_i) = 0$. From this we see that $C^k\left(x_i\right) = \sum_{j=1}^{k} T^j(x_i)$. Using this with the quasi-linear definition of *Close* we get,

$$C^{Close}\left(x_i\right) = \frac{1}{(q-1)} \sum_{k=1}^{q-1}\left[\sum_{j=1}^{k} T^j\left(x_i\right)\right] = \sum_{k=1}^{q-1} \frac{q-k}{(q-1)} T^k\left(x_i\right).$$

Here $C^{Close}(x_i)$ is a weighted sum of the number of nodes that have shortest path to x_i of length k. We further observe that the weights are a linearly decreasing function of k.

An alternative and perhaps more universal expression for $C^{Close}(x_i)$ can be obtained if we define a path as *Close* in terms of the proportion of internal vertices it contains rather than the absolute number of links. In order to accomplish this introduce term *Close*$_p$ standing for close in proportional terms, which we define using a membership function $f: [0,1] \rightarrow [0,1]$. We illustrate this in Figure 3. Here with $p \in [0,1]$ indicating a proportion of the vertices term $f(p)$ indicates the degree to which two vertices being connected through at most p proportion of the other vertices in network are considered as being close. Here we observe that $f(p_1) \geq f(p_2)$ if $p_1 < p_2$, $f(0) = 1$ and $f(1) = 1$.

We can use this to generate a value for number of close connections to x_i. Here again,

$$C^{Close}(x_i) = \sum_{k=1}^{n-1} w_k C^k(x_i).$$

But in this case, we have $w_k = f((k-1)/(n-2))$.

Once we have calculated the number of close connections to x_i, $C^{Close}(x_i)$, we can answer a question such as "Does x_i have at least five close connections?". More generally using the ability of fuzzy subsets to represent linguistic numeric concepts, we can answer questions as to whether x_i has *many* or *few* close connectors. In particular if L is a linguistic quantity such as *many*, *few* or *about twenty* we can define it as a fuzzy subset L of the real line R. Here for any number $y \in R$, $L(y)$ indicates the degree to which y satisfies the concept L. Using this we can express the answer to the question how true is it that x_i has L close connections by obtaining $L(C^{Close}(x_i))$, the membership grade of $C^{Close}(x_i)$ in L. We note that if we define L as a proportional fuzzy subset L_p on [0, 1], then we obtain the answer to the question as $L_p(C^{Close}(x_i) / n)$.

Generalizing the Concept of a Cluster

The concept of a cluster of nodes and the related idea of clique are important and useful ideas in studying social networks. Again let $G = <V, E>$ be an undirected graph representing a social network. Assume R is the associated relationship. A subset $S \subseteq V$ is called a cluster of order k if,

Figure 3. Close in proportional terms

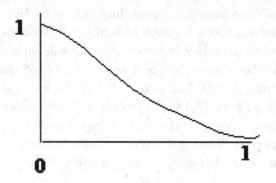

1. For all $x,y \in S$ we have $Geo(x,y) \leq k$
2. For all $z \notin S$ we have $Geo(x,z) > k$ for some $x \in S$.

In terms of R we see that for all $x,y \in S$ we must have $R^k(x,y) = 1$ and for $z \notin S$ then $R^k(x,z) = 0$ for at least one $x \in S$. In the special case where $k=1$ we call the set S a clique and for $k=n$ then S is called a connected component.

Here we suggest a softer definition of the idea of clique, more in the spirit of human perception of the concept of a clique. With the aid of fuzzy sets we are able to precisiate this concept to provide a machine understandable interpretation of the definition.

Following is our proposed definition of the concept of a clique. A subset S is a clique if most of elements in S are closely connected, none of the elements are too far from each other, and no element not in the clique is better connected to the members of the clique than any element in the clique. We can see that the concept of clique requires the satisfaction of three criteria. Let us look at these criteria and then see how to evaluate their satisfaction

- C_1: Most of the elements in S are closely connected
- C_2: None of the elements in S are too far from any of the others

- C_3: No element not in the clique is better connected to the members of clique than any element in the clique

Our procedure for the determining whether a subset S is a clique will be the following. For the subset S we shall find for each of the criteria C_j the value $C_j(S) \in [0,1]$, indicating the degree to which the subset S satisfies the criteria C_j. Once having these values, we obtain the degree to which S is a clique, $Clique\,(S) = Min_j\,[C_j(S)]$.

We now focus on how to evaluate each of these criteria, and we must provide a machine understanding of each of these criteria. We start with the first criterion. Here we must use two linguistic concepts from our communal vocabulary, *Closely connected* and *Most*. *Closely connected* can be defined using a function Q: Positive Integers $\rightarrow$ [0,1] such that $Q(k)$ is the degree to which a shortest path between two nodes of at most k edges is considered as *close*. A prototypical example of such a function is shown in Figure 4 in which,

$Q(k) = 1$ for $k \leq a$

$$Q(k) = \frac{b-k}{b-a}\ \text{for}\ a \leq k < b$$

$Q(k) = 0$ for $k \geq b$

Here a shortest distance of a or less is considered as close. A shortest distance of equal or greater than b is not *close*. Distances between these extremes partially satisfy the concept *close*.

Note: While the function Q will only be evaluated at integer values from users perspective it will be easier for users to express it as a continuous function rather than only on the integers.

Now for any two nodes x and y we can calculate the degree to which they are close as,

$$\text{Close}(x,\,y)\ =\ \underset{k=1\,to\,b}{\text{Max}}\Big[Q(k) \wedge R^k(x,\,y)\Big].$$

We note that if the shortest distance between x and y is q, then $R_k(x,y) = 0$ for $k < q$ and $R^k(x,y) = 1$ for $k \geq q$ and since $Q(k)$ is monotonically decreasing, then $\text{Close}(x,\,y) = Q(q)$.

The next concept we need is *Most*. Formally most can be expressed as a fuzzy subset M: [0,1] $\rightarrow$ [0,1] where for any $p \in [0,1]$ the value $M(p)$ indicates the degree to which the proportion p satisfies the concept of *Most* We see the fuzzy subset set M should have the following properties: $M(0) = 0$, $M(1) = 1$ and $M(p_2) \geq M(p_1)$ if $p_2 > p_1$. A basic form for the fuzzy subset M corresponding to the concept Most is shown in Figure 5.

A special case of this is where $\alpha = 0.5$ and $\beta = 0.75$. Using this we get,

$M(p) = 0$ for $p \leq 0.5$

$$M(p) = \frac{0.75 - p}{0.25} = 3 - 4p\ \text{for}\ 0.5 < p \leq 0.75$$

$M(p) = 1$ for $p > 0.75$

Using these linguistic concepts, we can now describe a procedure to obtain $C_1(S)$. Assume $S = \{x_1,\,...,\,x_{n_s}\}$ is some subset of nodes where n_s indicates the number of elements in S. For each pair x_i and x_j in S, we can calculate $Close\,(x_i,x_j) = Q(q_{ij})$ where q_{ij} is the shortest distance between x_i and x_j. For each x_i we can calculate the degree to which it is close to *Most* of the other elements in S as $W(x_i) = M(p_i)$ where,

$$p_i\ =\ \frac{\displaystyle\sum_{\substack{j=1\ to\ n_s \\ j \neq i}} Close(x_i,x_j)}{n_s - 1}.$$

Figure 4. Prototypical definition of close

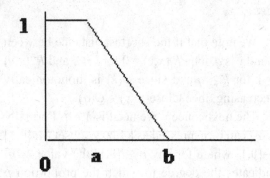

Figure 5. Concept: Most as a fuzzy set

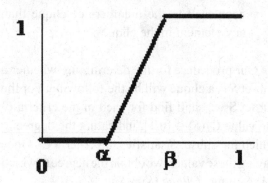

Using this we can calculate $C_1(S) = \underset{x_i \in S}{\text{Min}}[W(x_i)]$.

We now consider the second criterion, "none of the elements in S are far from any other element in S." We first need the concept *Far*. To obtain this we start with a fuzzy subset from the non-negative real numbers, $F: R \rightarrow [0,1]$ so that $F(k)$ is the degree to which a shortest distance of k links is *Far*. We see that F should be a monotonically increasing function, prototypically illustrated in Figure 6. A crisp definition of *Far* can be had if we make $c = d$.

We now obtain from this the concept not far. We denote this as a fuzzy set $\overline{F}$ and express it as the negation of F thus $\overline{F}(k) = 1 - F(k)$.

Using this we can obtain the degree to which any two nodes are not far,

$$\text{Not.Far}(x, y) = \underset{k=1 \text{ to } n}{\text{Max}}\left[R_k(x, y) \wedge \overline{F}(k)\right].$$

Let U_s indicate the collection of distinct unordered pairs of elements in S. Once having obtained for every pair $u \in U_s$ a measure of the degree to which they are not far as calculated above we then can obtain,

$$C_2(s) = \underset{u \in U_s}{\text{Min}}\left[\text{Not.Far}(x, y)\right].$$

Thus here we simply need to find the furthest pair of vertices in S and calculate the degree to which they are not far.

The third condition requires that no element not in S be better connected to the elements in S then any of the elements in S. We shall suggest a method for precisiation of this condition. We note that the method is not unique and other ways can surely be envisioned for capturing this condition, our goal here is more to be illustrative than definitive.

Our definition will be based on the requirement that all the elements in S should be closer to most of the other elements in S than any element not in S.

Thus if $y \notin S$, we can calculate degree to which it is close to most of the elements in S as,

Figure 6. Fuzzy set: Far

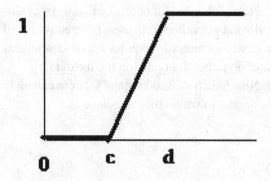

$$W\left(y \,/\, S\right) = \text{Most}\left(\frac{\sum_{j=1}^{n_s} Close(y, x_j)}{n_s}\right).$$

In addition for any $x_i \in S$ we can calculate as we have already shown,

$$W\left(x_i \,/\, S\right) = \text{Most}\left(\frac{\sum_{\substack{j=1 \text{ to } n_s \\ j \neq i}} Close(x_i, x_j)}{n_s - 1}\right).$$

We now order the $W\,(y/S)$ and $W\,(x_i/S)$ for $x_i \in S$ and $y \in S$ in descending order. If one of the y is ahead of any of the x_i on this list, then $C_3(S) = 0$, otherwise $C_3(S) = 1$.

Congested Nodes

The concept of path in an undirected graph $G = <X, R>$ is clearly defined. A sequence of nodes $\rho = x_1 x_2 \ldots x_q$ is a path between x_1 and x_q if $\text{Min}_{i=1 \text{ to } q}\left[R(x_i, x_{i+1})\right] = 1$. Here we want to consider an idea of congestion and try to formulate an idea of an *uncongested path*. Our interest here is motivated by the observation that in some applications, the number of arcs incident upon a node can interfere with the performance of the node in a path.

Consider a social networking system such as LinkedIn. This is a system in which people, generally for the purpose of business, try to make connection with another person using connections through other people. Here for example, let us assume **A** wants to contact **B** who is a person he doesn't know. **A** however sees that **M**, a person he knows, has a connection with **B**. **A** therefore has a path to **B** thru **M**. In this LinkedIn social network, **A** would contact **M** and ask him to make

an introduction to **B**. However, if **M** has a lot of connections, incident nodes, he may be very congested and not be very efficient in making the connection. If **A** has an alternative connection to **B** through **D** a node with not many incident nodes he may prefer to go through **D**. Even if the path through **D** requires him also to go through an additional node **E**, he may prefer this to the path thru **M** if **E** also has not many incident nodes. Typically binary social networks don't have the capability to make these kinds of distinctions. Here we begin to look into the inclusion of these types of considerations by introducing the idea of "uncongested" path and the related idea of path duration.

We first introduce a predicate "congested node" which we can express as a fuzzy set C over the set X of nodes in the network. Here for each node $x_i \in X$ the value $C(x_i) \in [0,1]$ indicates the degree to which x_i is a congested node. This membership grade is the truth of the statement xi is a congested node. We must now define what we mean by a congested node. We shall start here with a simple definition, although one that is cointensive with our idea of congestion. We shall say that a node is a congested node if it has many incident nodes. It has a high density. In order to take advantage of this definition, we must make machine understandable the term *many*. The approach we shall use is to express *many* as a fuzzy subset. Let N = {0, 1, 2,..., n} where n is the number of nodes in the network. We now define *many* as a fuzzy subset **MANY** over the space N such that for any $y \in N$, the value **MANY**$(y) \in [0,1]$ indicates the degree to which the quantity y satisfies the concept many. We can see that **MANY** must be a monotonically increasing function of y, this if $y_2 > y_1$ the **MANY**$(y_2) \geq$ **MANY**(y_1). A prototypical example of the concept of many is shown in Figure 7.

Using our definition of a congested node as one with many incident nodes and our precisiation of the concept many by the fuzzy subset **MANY**,

Figure 7. Many incident nodes

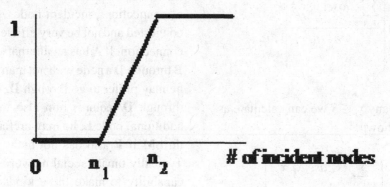

we can obtain the degree to which a node x_i is congested node,

$$C\left(x_i\right) = \text{MANY}(\sum_{\substack{j=1 \\ j \neq i}}^{n} R(x_i, x_j)).$$

It is the degree to which the number of incident nodes on x_i satisfies **MANY**.

Using the concept of a congested node, we can consider the formulation of the meaning of the idea of an uncongested path in a social network $<X, R>$. Here we shall initially use a very basic understanding of the concept, uncongested path, as a sequence of nodes that is a path in which all intermediary nodes are uncongested. Let us now see to what degree the sequence $\rho = x_1 x_2 \ldots x_q$ provides an uncongested path from x_1 to x_q.

For any node x_i in the sequence, we can obtain the degree to which it is uncongested node as $\overline{C}\left(x_i\right) = 1 - C\left(x_i\right)$, where $C(x_i)$ is the degree to which it is a congested node.

We can now calculate the degree to which "all the intermediary nodes are not congested" as $\text{Min}_{i=2 \text{ to } q-1}[\overline{C}(x_i)]$. In addition we can calculate the degree to it is true that the sequence ρ is a path from x_1 to x_q as $\text{Path}\left(\rho\right) = \text{Min}_{i=1 \text{ to } q-1}[R(x_i, x_{i+1})]$. Using these we can now express the concept, uncongested path, as a predicate UNCONG that

we can associate with any sequence of nodes $\rho = x_1 x_2 \ldots x_q$ and evaluated as,

$$\text{UNCONG}\left(\rho\right) = \text{Path}\left(\rho\right) \text{Min}_{i=2 \text{ to } q-1}[\overline{C}(x_i)].$$

Here then for the sequence $\rho = x_1 x_2 \ldots x_q$ we have that UNCONG(ρ) is;

$$R\left(x_1, x_2\right) \wedge \overline{C}\left(x_2\right) \wedge R\left(x_2, x_3\right) \wedge \overline{C}\left(x_3\right)$$
$$\wedge \ldots \wedge R\left(x_{q-2}, x_{q-1}\right) \wedge \overline{C}\left(x_{q-1}\right) \wedge R\left(x_{q-1}, x_q\right)$$

It is intuitively interesting that we rewrite this as,

$$\text{UNCONG}\left(\rho\right) = R\left(x_1, x_2\right) \wedge \text{Min}_{i=2 \text{ to } q-1}[\overline{C}(x_i) \wedge R\left(x_i, x_{i+1}\right)].$$

Here the term $D\left(x_i\right) = \overline{C}(x_i) \wedge R\left(x_i, x_{i+1}\right)$ can be viewed the degree to which the node x_i can effectively perform its leg of path.

Actually for this case where $R(x_i, x_j) \in \{0,1\}$ we will get that either UNCONG(ρ) = 0 if the sequence is not a path or

$$\text{UNCONG}\left(\rho\right) = \text{Min}_{i=2 \text{ to } q-1}[\overline{C}(x_i)].$$

While the approach just suggested is a basic approach, the framework that it provides is rich enough to allow for the inclusion of more sophisticated considerations with respect to the idea of congestion and more generally, the ease of attainment of connection. We shall now investigate some of the available extensions.

We first begin with the definition of the concept of congested node which we described in terms of how many incident arcs a node has. We suggested that the degree of congestion of node xi is equal to the truth-value of the predicate the node x_i has many incident nodes,

$$C\left(x_i\right) = \text{MANY}(\sum_{j=1, j \neq i}^{N} R(x_i, x_j))$$

where **MANY** is defined as a fuzzy subset of the space $N = \{0, 1,..., n\}$, it is fuzzy subset over the set of integers. We first note that we can define *Many* in terms of a proportion rather than an absolute value. That is we can define *Many* as **MANY**$_p$: $[0,1] \rightarrow [0,1]$, here for any proportion y of nodes in the network **MANY**$_p$ (y) indicates the degree to what y satisfies the concept *many*. In this case,

$$C\left(x_i\right) = \text{MANY}_p\left(\frac{\sum_{j \neq i}^{N} R\left(x_i, x_j\right)}{N}\right).$$

This allows for a more universal definition of *Many*.

More generally, we can define a predicate *congested node* using a Takagi-Sugeno type fuzzy systems model (Pedrycz & Gomide, 2007). Let V be a variable denoting the number of incident arcs on a node. Let C indicate the degree to which it is true that a node is a congested node. Let A_i, $i = 1$ *to r*, be a collection of linguistic terms describing the number of arcs incident on a node. Here then the A_i will be terms like *few, many, about 10*, etc. Using these terms, we can formulate a fuzzy systems model definition of the concept congested node using r rules of the form

If V is A_i then C is α_i.

Here $\alpha_i \in [0,1]$ is the degree to which it is true the node is considered as congested. In order to calculate the degree of congestion of an arbitrary node x_j, we first calculate the number of incident arcs it has: $q_j = \sum_{k=1, k \neq j}^{n} R(x_j, x_k)$. Using this we obtain,

$$C\left(x_j\right) = \frac{\sum_{i=1}^{r} A_i(q_j) \cdot \alpha_i}{\sum_{i=1}^{r} A_i(q_j)}.$$

Even more generally, we can use additional features of the node external to its network parameters to calculate degree to which it is a congested node. These features are of course dependent on the type of object the node is representing. Let U be some additional feature associated with nodes. Let B_i, $i = 1$ to be some predicates describing values of the feature U. In addition assume for any node x_j we can obtain $B_i(x_j) \in [0,1]$ the degree to which feature value B_i is satisfied by node x_j. A typical example of a feature value is a fuzzy subset, however other descriptions are possible.

Using these ideas we can now formulate our definition of the degree of congestion of a node using a collection of r rules of the form

If V is A_i and U is B_i then C is α_i.

With q_j as calculated above being the number of arcs incident on x_j we can obtain,

$$C\left(x_j\right) = \frac{\sum_{i=1}^{r} A_i(q_j) B_i(x_j) \alpha_i}{\sum_{i=1}^{r} A_i(q_j) B_i(x_j)}.$$

The main point is that we can use, in addition to information of the network structure, sophisticated knowledge about a node to determine whether it will smoothly perform its task or introduce congestion into a path. In social networks such as LinkedIn, providing such knowledge of the personality and objectives of individual node would be useful.

Let us now look at another aspect of our framework for calculating the degree to which a path constitutes an uncongested path. Our definition was that all the nodes on the path must be uncongested. A softer definition of this concept can be obtained if we use in our definition that most of the nodes on the path are uncongested, that is we replace all with most. More generally use can use any quantifier such as *all*, *almost all*, or *some*, to specify what we mean by an uncongested path. We further recall that these types of linguistic quantifiers can be expressed as a fuzzy subset $Q: [0,1] \rightarrow [0,1]$ so that for any proportion $p \in [0,1]$, the value $Q(p)$ indicates the degree to which the proportion p satisfies the concept of the quantifier (Zadeh, 1983). Furthermore these types of quantifiers display the properties that $Q(0) = 0$, $Q(1) = 1$ and $Q(p_1) \geq Q(p_2)$ if $p_1 > p_2$.

Yager (1996) showed how one could use the OWA operator to evaluate the truth of the predicates such as Q of the nodes on the path are uncongested.

In particular, we assume having a path with m intermediary nodes. Let $\overline{C}(x_i) = 1 - C(x_i)$ be the degree to which the ith intermediate node on the path is uncongested. Using these values and the fuzzy set Q we are able to determine UNCONG(ρ), the degree to which path ρ satisfies our definition of being an uncongested path. We describe the procedure as follows. We first calculate a set of m weights associated with the quantifier Q as $w_j = Q(j/m) - Q((j-1)/m)$ for $j = 1$ to m. These are a set of weights lying in the unit interval and summing to one.

Next we let b_j be the jth largest of $\overline{C}(x_j)$. Using these we then calculate,

$$\text{UNCONG}(\rho) = \sum_{j=1}^{m} w_j b_j.$$

We point out that in the special case where $w_n = 1$ and $w_j = 0$ for $j \neq n$ we get,

$$\text{UNCONG}(\rho) = b_m,$$

where b_m is the smallest of the $\overline{C}(x_i)$, that is $\text{UNCONG}(\rho) = \text{Min}_i\left[\overline{C}(x_i)\right]$, which was our original formulation.

Duration

In describing paths in networks, a useful concept is the number of links or length of the path. Here we shall provide a generalization of this idea by introducing the concept of duration, which will allow us to consider the impact of congestion on the length of a sequence of nodes.

Consider the sequence of nodes: $\rho = x_1 x_2 \ldots x_q$. We shall define the duration of ρ as,

$$\text{Dura}(\rho) = \sum_{j=1}^{q-1} \frac{1}{R(x_j, x_{j+1})} + \sum_{j=2}^{q-1} \left(\frac{1}{\overline{C}(x_j)} - 1 \right).$$

Let us first consider this for the standard case where we don't consider congestion, which is obtained by letting $\overline{C}(x_i) = 1$. In this case,

$$\text{Dura}(\rho) = \sum_{j=1}^{q-1} \frac{1}{R(x_j, x_{j+1})}.$$

If ρ is a true path, then $R(x_j, x_{j+1}) = 1$ for all j, we get to Dura(ρ) = $q-1$, the number of links in the path. If any of $R(x_j, x_{j+1}) = 0$, then the sequence ρ is not a path. In this case Dura(ρ) = ∞ since $\frac{1}{0} = \infty$. Thus a sequence that is not a path has Dura(ρ) = ∞.

Now let us look at situations where we can have some congestion. First consider the term $1/\overline{C}(x_i) - 1$. We see:

$$\frac{1}{\overline{C}(x_i)} - 1 = \frac{1 - \overline{C}(x_i)}{\overline{C}(x_i)} = \frac{1 - (1 - C(x_i))}{\overline{C}(x_i)} = \frac{C(x_i)}{\overline{C}(x_i)} = \frac{C(x_i)}{1 - C(x_i)}.$$

Thus it is the ratio of the degree of congestion divided by the degree of non-congestion. If the congestion is zero, then $C(x) / (1 - C(x)) = 0$ on the other hand if $C(x) = 1$, then this becomes infinite. Most generally in the case, where ρ is a true path, then $\text{Dura}(\rho) = \#$ of links $+ \sum_{j=2}^{q-1} C(x_j) / 1 - C(x_j)$. Here we can refer to $C(x_j) / (1 - C(x_j))$ as the delay associated with node x_i.

Directed Graphs

Another class of graphs is those shown in Figure 8. These are called directed graphs or digraphs. A digraph consists of a number of vertices or nodes with directed lines between. These lines are referred to as directed edges or arcs. We can denote this directed graph as $D = <V, A>$ where V is the set of nodes and A the collection of arcs. The arc denoted (a, b) is used to indicate a directed edge from a to b.

We can associate with D a reflexive relationship R on V. Thus $R: V \times V \rightarrow \{0, 1\}$. In this relationship, $R(x, y) = 1$ if there is a directed edge from x to y. In point of fact, an undirected graph can be seen as a special case of a directed graph

Figure 8. Typical directed graph

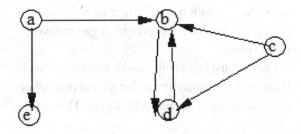

in which R is symmetric, $R(x, y) = R(y, x)$. Thus at the formal level, we can view both undirected and directed graphs as the same type of objects, both are relationships $R: V \times V \{0,1\}$, the only difference between them is that an undirected graph is symmetric. As a result of this unification, many of the concepts that we have introduced for (undirected) graphs are valid for digraphs. Actually from a formal mathematical point of view, it is more natural to start with the idea of a directed graph and express an undirected graph is a special case.

The operation of composition, $R \blacklozenge R = R^2$ is the same for these digraphs,

$$R^2(x,z) = Max_y[R(x,y) \wedge R(y,z)].$$

The concept of path naturally extends. If x and y are two distinct vertices, an $x - y$ path is a sequence of distinct vertices beginning with x and ending with y so that there is a directed edge between any two adjacent vertices. More formally if x and y are two distinct vertices an $x - y$ path is a sequencing of distinct vertices beginning with x and ending with y so that $R(a, b) = 1$ for any two adjacent vertices in the sequence. Formally we say that the sequencing $a_1 a_2 a_3 \dots a_q$ is a path from to a_1 to a_q if $R(a_1, a_2) \wedge R_2(a_2, a_3) \wedge \dots \wedge R(a_{q-1}, a_q) = 1$; this is thus the degree to which it is a path.

Closely related to this is the idea of a semi-path. Formally we say that the sequence $a_1 a_2 a_3 \dots a_q$ is a semi-path from a_1 to a_q if,

$$(R(a_1, a_2) \vee R(a_2, a_1) \wedge R(a_2, a_3) \vee R(a_3, a_2)) \wedge \dots \wedge C(R(a_{q-1}, a_q) \vee R(a_q, a_{q-1}) = 1.$$

Thus here all we must need is a directed edge either way between any of the adjacent vertices. More generally, we can associate with a directed graph R on a new graph $\hat{R}$ defined so,

$$\hat{R}(x, y) = Max\left(R(x, y), R(y, x)\right).$$

One can see that $\widehat{R}(x, y)$ is always symmetric $\widehat{R}(x, y) = \widehat{R}(y, x)$. Furthermore if R is symmetric then $\widehat{R} = R$. Thus $a_1 a_2 a_3 ... a_q$ is a semi-path from a_1 to a_q if,

$$\widehat{R}(a_1, a_2) \wedge \widehat{R}(a_2, a_2) \wedge ... \wedge \widehat{R}(a_{q-1}, a_q) = 1.$$

The concepts of connected and connectivity can be extended to the more general idea of a directed graph (Chartrand, 1977). Let a and b be two nodes in D. We say a and b are:

1. Weakly connected if there exists a semi-path between a and b.
2. Unilaterally connected if there are joined by a path from a to b or b to a.
3. Strongly connected if there are joined by both a path from a to b and b to a.
4. Recursively connected if they are strongly connected, and the paths from a to b and from b to a use the same nodes but in reverse order.

We note that recursive implies *strong*, and unilaterally implies *weak*. For any of the four terms Z – *weak, unilaterally, strong*, and *recursive* – we say the D is Z connected if all nodes are Z connected.

The concept of degree of a node can be generalized to the case of digraph, however here we need two concepts in-degree, Deg_i and out-degree, Deg_0. In particular,

$$\text{Deg}_i(x) = \sum_{y \in V - \{x\}} R(y, x),$$

it is the number of edges coming into x. The out-degree is,

$$\text{Deg}_o(x) = \sum_{y \in V - \{x\}} R(x, y).$$

We say a digraph is *strongly directed* if for all vertices x and y we have $R(x,y) \wedge R(y,x) = 0$. This means we never can have an arc going both ways between vertices.

Authority Figures

A prototypical directed graph is hierarchical structure or rooted tree shown in Figure 9. Here we are interested in providing a generalization of the node #1 for any directed relational network by introducing a node type concept called an *authority figure*. Our objective is to define some procedure via some network features, so that for any node x_j in a directed graph, we can determine the degree of truth of the statement: x_j is an authority-figure. We shall formulate this as a fuzzy subset AFig over the set of nodes, X. Thus for any node x_j its membership grade $\text{AFig}(x_j)$ will be the degree to which it is an authority figure.

Our procedure will be to define what properties constitute our concept of authority figure, and we provide a mechanism that allows us to calculate whether a node satisfies these conditions in terms of using the network structure. Here we shall consider a network $<X, R>$ in which R: $X \times X \to [0,1]$ such $R(x,y) = 1$ if there is an edge from x to y and $R(x,y) = 0$ if no edge exists. The fact that it is a directed network means that $R(x, y)$ and $R(y, x)$ are not necessarily equal. We assume R is a reflexive relationship, $R(x,x) = 1$.

We now consider our generalization of the concept of an authority figure. We first see that the basic feature of node x_1 in Figure 9 is that all nodes have a path from x_1 while no nodes have a path to x_1. We shall now provide a generalization in this idea.

What must be kept in mind is that our generalization will be subjective in that it is our perception of the concept of an authority figure. Thus while

Figure 9. Typical hierarchical network

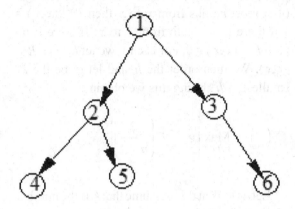

we feel that our definition basically captures the idea of authority figure, other people may have somewhat different variations of our formulation. However what is of importance here is that the procedure that will be described to implement our definition is general enough to be used to implement other specific formulations of this concept.

We shall define authority figure type node as one that satisfies the following conditions:

- C_1: The node has a path to all other nodes in the network.
- C_2: For most nodes the path from the authority node to it is short.
- C_3: Few nodes have a path to the authority node.

Here then we need to satisfy three criteria. We now suggest how to determine the satisfaction of each of these criteria using the network structure $<X, R>$. We shall assume the cardinality of the network is $|X| = n$. We recall that for any network $R^k(x_i, x_j) = 1$ if there exists a path from x_i to x_j with at most k edges. If no such path exists it is zero. Using this we can easily formulate the first criteria. For any node x_i we can define,

$$C_1(x_i) = Min_j(R^{m-1}(x_i, x_j)).$$

The second condition requires us to use fuzzy sets to introduce two concepts "*most*" and "*short*". We first define the concept *most* using a fuzzy subset Q on the unit interval, Q: $[0,1] \rightarrow [0,1]$, where for any proportion p the value $Q(p)$ indicates the degree to it satisfies the concept *most*. Such a fuzzy subset should satisfy the conditions: $Q(0) = 0$, $Q(1) = 1$ and if $p_2 > p_1$ then $Q(p_2) > Q(p_1)$. A prototypical example of this using a piecewise linear definition for most such as,

$$Q(0) = 0 \text{ if } p \leq a$$

$$Q(p) = \frac{p-a}{b-a} \text{ if } a < p \leq b$$

$$Q(p) = 1 \text{ if } p > b$$

Alternatively we can use a power type function such as $Q(p) = p^r$ with $r > 2$.

The concept of short path can also be expressed as a fuzzy subset S defined on the set of positive integers. Here S must be such that $S(1) = 1$ and $S(l_1) \geq S(l_2)$ if $l_1 < l_2$. Again a prototypical definition of this concept can be had using a piece-wise linear fuzzy subset as shown in Figure 10.

Our interest now is to determine $C_2(x_i)$, the degree to which the node x_i has a short path to most nodes. First we determine for any x_j the truth of the proposition that there is a short path from x_i to x_j. Here we shall let the $SP_i(x_j)$ denote this value and express it as,

$$SP_i(x_j) = \underset{k=1 \text{ to } n-1}{\text{Max}} \left[S(k) \wedge R^k(x_i, x_j) \right].$$

Since $S(k)$ is decreasing with respect to k we see $SP_i(x_j)$ will be equal to $S(k)$ for the first k for which there is a path from x_i to x_j. If we denote this k_j then $SP_i(x_j) = S(k_j)$.

Using the preceding we can obtain for each $x_j \neq x_i$ the value $SP_i(x_j)$ the degree to which there is a short path for x_i to x_j.

We now use a version of the OWA aggregation operator (Yager, 1992) to determine $C_2(x_i)$, the degree to which x_i has a short path to most of the other nodes. We proceed as follows. We first order the $SP_i(x_j)$ and let d_k be the value of the kth largest of the $SP_i(x_j)$. Using this and the fuzzy subset Q representing our concept of *most* we calculate,

$$C_2(x_i) = \max_{k=1 \text{ to } n-1} \left[Q\left(\frac{k}{n-1}\right) \wedge d_k \right].$$

An alternative way of obtaining $C_2(x_i)$ is to use the regular OWA operator. Here we first obtain,

$$w_k = Q\left(\frac{k}{n-1}\right) - Q\left(\frac{k-1}{n-1}\right),$$

for $k = l$ to $n - 1$ and then we obtain,

$$C_2(x_i) = \sum_{k=1}^{n-1} w_k d_k.$$

We now consider the third requirement, *few* nodes have a path to the authority, xi. Here we can define *few* in similar way to how we defined *most*. Let it be a fuzzy set $F: [0,1] \rightarrow [0,1]$ such that for any proportion p, $F(p)$ indicates its satisfaction to the concept *few*. Here F must be such that: $F(0) = 1$, $F(1) = 0$ and if $p_2 > p_1$ then $F(p_2) F(p_1)$.

Since $R^r(x_j, x_i) = 1$ if there is a path of length of at most r links from x_j to x_j then $R^{n-1}(x_j, x_i) = 1$ if there is any path from x_j to x_i. If there is no path $R^{n-1}(x_j, x_i) = 0$. For each x_j we let $h_j = 1 - R^{n-1}(x_j, x_i)$. We then order the h_j and let g_k be the kth smallest of h_j. Using this we obtain,

$$C_3(x_i) = \max_{k=1 \text{ to } n} \left[g_k \wedge F\left(\frac{k}{n-1}\right) \right].$$

Let us look at this. Assume that k_i is the number of nodes for which $R(x_i, x_j) = 1$. In this case, $h_j = 0$ for k_i values, and $h_j = 1$ for $(n-1) - k_i = n - (k_i+1)$ values. In this case $g_k = 1$ for $k \geq k_1 + 1$ and hence,

$$C_3(x_i) = F\left(\frac{k_i}{n-1}\right).$$

It is degree to which $\left(\frac{k_i}{n-1}\right)$ satisfies the concept *few*.

We are now in a position to determine the truth of the statement that x_i is an authority figure. We first calculate the value of $C_1(x_i)$, $C_2(x_i)$ and $C_3(x_i)$ and then,

$$\text{AFig}(x_i) = \min [C_1(x_i), C_2(x_i), C_3(x_i)].$$

Figure 10. Fuzzy subset corresponding to concept short path

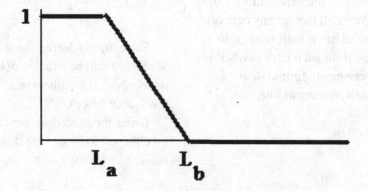

VECTOR VALUED NODES AND SOCIAL NETWORK DATABASES

In the following, we shall consider a weighted network $<X, R>$ where each of the nodes has an associated vector of attribute (feature) values. This type of situation is of particular relevance to Web based social networks such as LinkedIn and Facebook as well terror networks and criminal networks. In these types of networks, each of the node objects have various attributes properties and features. This structure can be viewed as combination of relational network and database.

In these networks, we have a collection of q attributes $U_1,...,U_q$. In the case where the nodes are people examples of attributes could be nationality, age or income. Each of the attributes takes a value from a domain Y_i. In this situation each node has an associated q vector whose i^{th} component is the value of the ith attribute for that node.

We shall use the notation $U_i(x_j)$ to indicate the variable corresponding to the attribute U_i in the case of node x_j. For example with U_i being the attribute age, then $U_i(x_j)$ would indicate the variable age of x_j. If U_i is the attribute country of birth, then Y_i would be a list of countries, and $U_i(x_j)$ would be the variable corresponding the country of birth of x_j. We shall let v_{ij} indicate the value of the variable $U_i(x_j)$, thus $U_i(x_j) = v_{ij}$. Thus in this case, any node in our network has an associated vector V_j whose i component v_{ij} corresponds to the value of attribute U_i for node x_j. We should observe that the above network could in some ways be viewed as a kind of database.

In the following, we shall begin to describe techniques that can be used to analyze, investigate and question networks with vector-valued notes. Here we shall be using flexible/fuzzy-querying techniques (Zadrozny, de Tré, de Caluwe, & Kacprzyk, 2008).

In the following we shall assume that country of residence is one of the attributes, we shall denote this as U_1. Thus $U_1(x_j)$ is the variable denoting the country of residence of x_j. In this case, the domain Y_1 associated with U_1 is the set of countries. In addition, a communal vocabulary associated with this attribute would consist of terms such as "Middle East", "North America", "South America" and "Southeast Asia". Other terms such as "mountainous country", ""Spanish speaking", and "Oil producing" can also be part of the vocabulary. Each of the terms in the vocabulary would be defined in terms of subsets of Y_1. Some of these terms can be defined using crisp subsets while others will require fuzzy subsets.

In addition we shall assume that age is another of the attributes associated with the network nodes. We shall denote this as U_2 with its domain Y_2 being the set of non-negative integers. Here we shall also assume the availability of mutually understandable vocabulary of commonly used linguistic term to describe a person's age. These terms will be defined in terms of subsets of Y_2.

Assume x_j is some node in our network. We can ask "What is the strength of x_j's strongest connection to a person residing in South America?" Here strong is a user defined predicate. In the following we shall let **SA** indicate the subset of Y_1 corresponding to South America. Using this we can obtain as the answer to our question,

$$\underset{i,i\neq j}{\text{Max}}\left[\text{SA}\left(U_1\left(x_i\right)\right)\wedge R^n\left(x_i,x_j\right)\right].$$

More specifically we can ask "What is the strength of x_j's strongest connection to a young person residing in South America?" In this case, with U_2 being the attribute age and **Young** being the subset corresponding concept of young person, we get as the answer:

$$\underset{i,i\neq j}{\text{Max}}\left[\text{SA}\left(U_1\left(x_i\right)\right)\wedge \text{Young}\left(U_2\left(x_i\right)\right)\wedge R^n\left(x_i,x_j\right)\right].$$

We note this value is also the truth of the question "Does x_j have a connection to a Young South American".

We note that if we want to find out "Does x_j have a strong connection to a Young South American" then we obtain the truth of this as,

$$\underset{i,i \neq j}{\text{Max}} \left[\text{SA}\left(U_1\left(x_i\right)\right) \wedge \text{Young}\left(U_2\left(x_i\right)\right) \wedge \text{Strong}\left(R^n\left(x_i, x_j\right)\right) \right].$$

Here we have replaced the predicate $R^n(x_i, x_j)$ with Strong $(R^n(x_i, x_j))$.

A related question is the following. Let B be some crisp subset of X. We now ask what is strongest connection between an element in B and a Young South American not in B. The answer is the obtained from the following,

$$\underset{x_i \in B}{\text{Max}} \left[\underset{x_j}{\text{Max}} \left[\text{SA}\left(U_1\left(x_i\right)\right) \wedge \text{Young}\left(U_2\left(x_j\right)\right) \wedge R^n\left(x_i, x_j\right) \wedge \overline{B}\left(x_j\right) \right] \right].$$

If in the above, we are interested in only direct connections rather than any connection we replace R^n by R.

We now consider the question: Do all people residing in South America have a strong connection with each other? We shall denote the truth of this question $\text{Tr}(Q)$. We calculate this truth-value as,

$$\text{Tr}(Q) = \underset{x_i, x_j \in X}{\text{Min}} \left[\left(1 - \text{SA}\left(U_1\left(x_i\right)\right)\right) \vee \left(1 - \text{SA}\left(U_1\left(x_j\right)\right)\right) \vee \text{Strong}\left(R^n\left(x_i, x_j\right)\right) \right].$$

Let us look at this for the special case where SA is a crisp set. We first see that in the case of a pair (x_i, x_j) in which at least one of the elements do not reside in South America, then either $\text{SA}(U_1(x_i)) = 0$ or $\text{SA}(U_1(x_j)) = 0$, and therefore,

$$(1 - \text{SA}(U_1(x_i))) \vee (1 - \text{SA}(U_1(x_j))) \vee \text{Strong}(R^n(x_i, x_j)) = 1.$$

This case will not be the min. For the case in which both x_i and x_j reside in South America, then $\text{SA}(U_1(x_i)) = \text{SA}(U_1(x_j)) = 1$, and hence,

$$(1 - \text{SA}(U_1(x_i))) \vee (1 - \text{SA}(U_1(x_j))) \vee \text{Strong}(R^n(x_i, x_j)) = \text{Strong}(R^n(x_i, x_j)).$$

From this we get as expected,

$$\text{Tr}(Q) = \underset{x_i, x_j \in SA}{\text{Min}} \left[\text{Strong}\left(R^n\left(x_i, x_j\right)\right) \right].$$

Now we shall consider the slightly more complicated question of whether "*most* of the people residing in *western* countries have *strong* connections". We shall here assume the term *most* is available in our common vocabulary, where it is defined as a fuzzy subset over the unit interval. In addition, we shall assume that the concept, *western country*, is a concept that is defined by the fuzzy subset W over the domain Y_1. In this case for each $x_i \in X$ we have $W(U_1(x_i))$ indicates the degree to which it is true that x_i is from a western country. In the following we shall set P be the set of all unordered pairs of distinct elements from X. P is the set of all the subsets of X consisting of two elements. We see that the number of elements in P, $n_P = \dfrac{n(n-1)}{2}$ where n is the number of elements in X. We shall denote an element $\{x_i, x_j\}$ in P as p_k. Here then k goes from 1 to n_P.

For each pair $p_k = \{x_i, x_j\}$ we obtain two values. The first $V_k = \text{Min}(W(U_1(x_i)), W(U_1(x_j)))$ indicates the degree to which p_k consists of pair of elements both from a western country. The second value is $S_k = \text{Strong}(R^n(x_i, x_j))$, indicates the degree to which there is a strong connection between the pair $\{x_i, x_j\}$. We shall use the technology of OWA operators to answer our question (Yager, 1996). We proceed to obtain the answer as follows:

1. Order the S_k and let $\text{ind}(j)$ be the index of the jth largest of the S_k. Thus here $S_{\text{ind}(j)}$ is the jth largest of the S_k, and $V_{\text{ind}(j)}$ is its associated V value.

2. We next calculate $R = \sum_{j=1}^{n_p} V_{ind(j)}$

3. We next obtain a set of weight w_j for $j = 1$ to n_p, where

$$w_j = \text{Most}\left(\frac{R_j}{R}\right) - \text{Most}\left(\frac{R_j - 1}{R}\right).$$

Here $R_j = \sum_{i=1}^{j} V_{ind(i)}$.

4. We finally calculate the truth of the question

as $\text{Tr}(q) = \sum_{j=1}^{n_p} w_j S_{ind(j)}$.

An interesting special case of the preceding occurs if the subset W, Western Country, is a crisp set. In this case $V_k = \text{Min}(W(U_1(x_i)), W(U_1(x_j)))$ is a binary value, either one or zero. It is one if both x_i and x_j are from western countries and zero if either is not from a western country.

Another question we can ask is whether the young people form a clique. Since the young people provide a fuzzy subset over the space X, and we have previously indicated a process for determining whether a fuzzy set is a clique, we can answer this question.

FUTURE RESEARCH DIRECTIONS: SOLUTION FOR DETECTING TRENDSETTERS AND OPINION LEADERS

One objective of our future research is to focus on the problem of detecting trendsetters and opinion leaders. Here we briefly describe some of ideas related to this task. One approach is to first identify cliques in which most number of members purchase the same product (say a smart phone). Then assuming that we have a database that records the time of purchase, we can define the concept

of a trendsetter: the individuals who, most of the time, made the earliest purchase in the clique.

Similar to the idea of identifying trendsetters is the research on identifying key players (Ortiz-Arroyo, & Akbar, 2008), where the method of detection is to measure the centrality entropy of each node, and how this changes when the node is removed from the network. An obstacle for such approach is the size of the network, and the centrality entropy can be computationally intensive when we measure for every node in the entire social network. One way to resolve this problem is by applying the concept of cliques, as described earlier in this chapter, to reduce the number of paths. This allows marketers to identify the concept of key trendsetters, people who are critical in influencing massive adoption and purchase of products.

The use of directed graph and the resulting concepts such as Authority Figure, may not be useful for Facebook, as everyone has the same role as friend. However, in Linkedin, the roles can be boss, subordinate, coworkers, partners etc. The behavior of the people in forums (e.g. the start and end of the discussions of new business topics) allows us to trace the set of Authority Figures, and the cliques that they can influence.

In addition to focusing on concepts involving people in social networks, another research direction is to focus on the organizations that are associated with these people, thus allowing us to explore the concepts related to organization effectiveness. For example, we can associate concepts of "collaboration", "partnership", "dominance" and "autonomous" with inter-organisational cooperation (Fearon, Ballantine & Philip, 2010) that can help companies and business decisions in supply chain management. Political links and the concepts of politicians, affiliations, and connections are important to understand the influence and power of states and governments (Dulio, Skinner, & Masket, 2009; Mizoguchi, 2009). We can also examine the concept of network effectiveness in terms of the use of knowledge for R&D (Mote, Jordan, Hage, & Whitestone, 2007).

CONCLUSION

We provided an introduction to the basic ideas of graph (relational network) theory. We discussed some concepts from the fuzzy set paradigm of computing with words. The natural connection between these two technologies was pointed out. Our main objective here was to introduce a framework to help in development of intelligent social network theory using granular computing.

Using this framework, one starts by expressing, in a human focused manner, concepts associated with social networks. We then formalize these concepts using fuzzy sets. Having this set based formulation we can evaluate these concepts with respect to a given social network which have been represented using set based relational network theory. This approach forms the basis of what we call the framework for intelligent social network analysis, FISNA. Using this framework, we provided definitions of a number of concepts related to social networks. Finally we introduced the idea of vector–valued nodes and began developing a technology of social network database theory. Clearly this newly introduced idea of social network database theory will provide many applications and will need a more formal mathematical, a task for future research.

REFERENCES

Barabási, A. L., & Albert, R. (1999). Emergence of scaling in random networks. *Science, 286*, 509–512. doi:10.1126/science.286.5439.509

Bargiela, A., & Pedrycz, W. (2003). *Granular computing: An introduction*. Amsterdam, The Netherlands: Kluwer Academic Publishers.

Berge, C. (2001). *The theory of graphs*. New York, NY: Dover.

Bollobas, B. (2000). *Modern graph theory*. New York, NY: Springer.

Carrington, P. J., Scott, J., & Wasserman, S. (2007). *Models and methods in social network analysis*. New York, NY: Cambridge University Press.

Chartrand, G. (1977). *Introductory graph theory*. New York, NY: Dover.

Cook, D. J., & Holder, L. B. (2007). *Mining graph data*. Hoboken, NJ: Wiley-Interscience.

Doyle, S. (2007). The role of social networks in marketing. *Journal of Database Marketing & Customer Strategy Management, 15*(1), 60–64. doi:10.1057/palgrave.dbm.3250070

Dulio, D., Skinner, R., & Masket, S. (2009). 527 committees and the political party network. *Conference Papers -- Midwestern Political Science Association*, 1.

Erdos, P., & Renyi, A. (1960). On the evolution of random graphs. *Publications of the Mathematical institute of Hungarian Academy of Sciences, 5,* 17-61.

Fearon, C., Ballantine, J., & Philip, G. (2010). Understanding the role of electronic trading and inter-organisational cooperation and coordination. *Internet Research, 20*(5), 545–562. doi:10.1108/10662241011084095

Hafner-Burton, E. M., & Montgomery, A. H. (2006). The new power politics of international organizations: Social structural inequality in the international system. *Conference Papers -- American Political Science Association*, (pp. 1-35).

Lin, T. S., Yao, Y. Y., & Zadeh, L. A. (2002). *Data mining, rough sets and granular computing*. Heidelberg, Germany: Physica-Verlag.

Maldonado, N. (2010). Connect and promote. *Career World, 38*(5), 26–29.

Mizoguchi, K. (2009). Nodes and edges: A network approach to hierarchisation and state formation in Japan. *Journal of Anthropological Archaeology, 28*(1), 14–26. doi:10.1016/j.jaa.2008.12.001

Mote, J. E., Jordan, G., Hage, J., & Whitestone, Y. (2007). New directions in the use of network analysis in research and product development evaluation. *Research Evaluation, 16*(3), 191–203. doi:10.3152/095820207X235746

Nair, H. S., Manchanda, P., & Bhatia, T. (2010). Asymmetric social interactions in physician prescription behavior: The role of opinion leaders. *JMR, Journal of Marketing Research, 47*(5), 883–895. doi:10.1509/jmkr.47.5.883

Newman, M., Barabási, A. L., & Watts, D. J. (2006). *The structure and dynamics of networks.* Princeton, NJ: Princeton University Press.

Ortiz-Arroyo, D., & Akbar Hussain, D. M. (2008). An information theory approach to identify sets of key players in social networks. *Proceedings of EuroISI 2008, First European Conference on Intelligence and Security Informatics*, December 3-5th, Ebjerg Denmark, (pp. 15-26).

Pedrycz, W., & Gomide, F. (2007). *Fuzzy systems engineering: Toward human-centric computing.* New York, NY: John Wiley & Sons.

Popp, R. L., & Yen, J. (2006). *Emergent Information Technologies and enabling policies for counter-terrorism.* Hoboken, NJ: John Wiley & sons. doi:10.1002/047178656X

Scott, J. (2000). *Social network analysis.* Los Angeles, CA: SAGE Publishers.

Solomonoff, R., & Rapoport, A. (1951). Connectivity of random nets. *The Bulletin of Mathematical Biophysics, 13*, 107–117. doi:10.1007/BF02478357

Wasserman, S., & Faust, K. (1994). *Social network analysis: Methods and applications.* New York, NY: Cambridge University Press.

Watts, D. J., & Strogatz, S. H. (1998). Collective dynamics of 'small world' networks. *Nature, 393*, 440–442. doi:10.1038/30918

Yager, R. R. (1988). On ordered weighted averaging aggregation operators in multi-criteria decision making. *IEEE Transactions on Systems, Man, and Cybernetics, 18*, 183–190. doi:10.1109/21.87068

Yager, R. R. (1992). Applications and extensions of OWA aggregations. *International Journal of Man-Machine Studies, 37*, 103–132. doi:10.1016/0020-7373(92)90093-Z

Yager, R. R. (1996). Quantifier guided aggregation using OWA operators. *International Journal of Intelligent Systems, 11*, 49–73. doi:10.1002/(SICI)1098-111X(199601)11:1<49::AID-INT3>3.3.CO;2-L

Yager, R. R. (2006). Some learning paradigms for granular computing. *Proceedings of the IEEE International Conference on Granular Computing*, Atlanta, (pp. 25-29).

Yager, R. R. (2008). Intelligent social network analysis using granular computing. *International Journal of Intelligent Systems, 23*(11), 1196–1219. doi:10.1002/int.20314

Yager, R. R. (2010a). Concept representation and database structures in fuzzy social relational networks. *IEEE Transactions on Systems. Man & Cybernetics: Part A, 40*(2), 413–419. doi:10.1109/TSMCA.2009.2036591

Yager, R. R. (2010b). Associating human-centered concepts with social networks using fuzzy sets. In Furht, B. (Ed.), *Handbook of social network technologies and applications* (*Vol. 3*, pp. 447–467). doi:10.1007/978-1-4419-7142-5_21

Zadeh, L. A. (1983). A computational approach to fuzzy quantifiers in natural languages. *Computers & Mathematics with Applications (Oxford, England), 9*, 149–184. doi:10.1016/0898-1221(83)90013-5

Zadeh, L. A. (1996). Fuzzy logic = computing with words. *IEEE Transactions on Fuzzy Systems*, *4*, 103–111. doi:10.1109/91.493904

Zadeh, L. A. (1998). Some reflections on soft computing, granular computing and their roles in the conception, design and utilization of information/intelligent systems. *Soft Computing - A Fusion of Foundations. Methodologies and Applications*, *2*(1), 23–25. doi:doi:10.1007/s005000050030

Zadeh, L. A. (1999). Outline of a computational theory of perceptions based on computing with words. In Sinha, N. K., & Gupta, M. M. (Eds.), *Soft computing and intelligent systems* (pp. 3–22). Boston, MA: Academic Press. doi:10.1016/B978-012646490-0/50004-4

Zadeh, L. A. (2006). Generalized theory of uncertainty (GTU)-principal concepts and ideas. *Computational Statistics & Data Analysis*, *51*, 15–46. doi:10.1016/j.csda.2006.04.029

Zadrozny, S., de Tré, G., de Caluwe, R., & Kacprzyk, J. (2008). An overview of fuzzy approaches to database querying. In Galindo, J. (Ed.), *Handbook of research on fuzzy information processing in databases* (*Vol. 1*, pp. 34–54). Hershey, PA: Information Science Reference. doi:10.4018/978-1-59904-853-6.ch002

ENDNOTES

[1] In this work we shall use the term graph and network, more precisely social or relational network synonymously

[2] More formally we can view U as a set whose elements are all the subsets of V consisting of two elements.

Chapter 3
Fuzzy Dynamic Groups:
Measures and Implications
for Television Audiences

José-Domingo Mora[1]
University of Massachusetts-Dartmouth, USA

ABSTRACT

Television audiences have been shown to be a mixture of lone individuals and groups of viewers, with groups contributing at least 50% of total ratings. Viewing with others also makes the experience more enjoyable and has important effects on cognitive processing of programs and advertisements. A major problem for researchers and managers is that groups of viewers are dynamic entities difficult to define or measure. This study frames groups of television viewers as fuzzy sets and presents fuzzy measures of group size and composition. The effects of these characteristics on individual consumption of television are assessed using statistical models, which incorporate the arithmetic forms of the proposed measures.

INTRODUCTION

Human groups, small and large, change over time. For instance, consumers in a target market may change their attitudes towards brands as they become acquainted with the marketing mixes of competing products, and as they consider other consumers' opinions and behaviours. Similarly,

DOI: 10.4018/978-1-4666-0095-9.ch003

friends in a group visiting a theme park may change their views on specific attractions as the group becomes, simultaneously, a decision-making unit and the social context in which these attractions are experienced. Consumers in a target market may become older, move up (or down) the social ladder or gradually drift apart from preferred brands. In the theme park example, one of our friends might desert from the group at some point of the visit, which may alter the way the remaining members make decisions and, eventually, the rides they choose to try.

The examples above illustrate how time affects groups of consumers in two fundamental ways: (a) the characteristics of individuals in the group change; and, (b) the individual memberships in the group may change as well, sometimes because of changes in individual characteristics, sometime because behavioural affiliation (being *in* the group) ceases. That is, the sets "consumers in target market X" and "friends visiting theme park Y" are crisp only when considered at an instant dt and will not necessarily be the same at a future instant $dt+\tau$, where τ might be measured in seconds, days or years. Each of these two aspects introduces fuzziness in the definition of a group when this group is considered over a long enough period of time. Such groups will be called *dynamic* groups.

This chapter deals with aspect (b) of dynamic groups; it considers fuzziness introduced in membership by changes in behavioural affiliation over a period of time. In the application presented, these groups of consumers are the members of a family who are watching a television program at home. Groups of television viewers are affiliation groups actually *consuming* a product, very much like that group of friends at the theme park in the example above. As previously discussed, at instant dt the set of television viewers in this household could be defined without hesitation, but during an interval with a given duration some of the family members may watch the program during the whole interval while others may watch just a fraction.

How can such a group of viewers be defined and measured? This is a relevant question as cumulative evidence has revealed that television audiences are indeed clustered structures where lone individuals and groups coexist (e.g. Robertson, 1979; Lull, 1982; Schmidt, Woolf & Anderson, 2003). Furthermore, group consumption of television programs has a number of interesting effects on cognition and affect which in turn interact with how viewers experience, process and categorize programs and advertisements.

This chapter introduces a fuzzy approach to defining and measuring dynamic groups in the context of television audiences. A discussion of theoretical and empirical antecedents sets the scene to introducing this conceptualization and to developing measures of two important group characteristics: size and composition. The proposed measures are then applied to data from a commercial people-meter panel of television audience measurement operating in Mexico.

GROUPS, FAMILIES AND TELEVISION

Adamowicz, Hanemann, Swait, Johnson, Layton, Regenwetter et al. (2005) summarize the conclusions of an interdisciplinary symposium on family groups as follows: "Households may differ from groups that have been typically used in group research, which suggests the need for specially focused research efforts on household decision making. Group decision-making has been most often studied in the laboratory using ad-hoc groups that do not have a common history and future". They also pointed to some useful future research directions, among them the influence of group size and composition on family decision-making.

The literature on group decision making is ample and diverse; it comprehends contributions in econometrics (e.g. Browning & Chiappori, 1998; Cherchye, De Rock & Vermeulen, 2002; Bourguignon, Browning & Chiappori, 2010) game theory (e.g. Raiffa, 2002; Bacharach, 2006) which have been extended to incorporate the dynamic effects of repeated games (e.g. Andreoni & Miller, 1993); as well as social psychology (as reviewed by Hinsz, Tindale & Volrath, 1999; and, Kerr & Tinsdale, 2004); social choice theory (e.g. Craven, 1992); and, management science (as reviewed, for instance, by O'Leary-Kelly et al., 1994; and, Leask & Parker, 2006). Fuzzy methods have been use as well in the study of group decision making (e.g. Tanino, 1984; Kacprzyk, 1986; Herrera, Herera-

Viedma & Verdegav, 1996; Bordogna, Fedrizzi & Pasi, 1997; Pawlak, 2007) although applied to shared cognition and information processing, not to defining and operationalizing groups of decision makers.

Building on Steckel, Corfman, Curry, Gupta, Shanteau et al. (1991) the marketing literature on group decision making published in the last three decades can be viewed as split in two major streams:

1. Studies of heuristics for the aggregation of individual preferences into group decisions (e.g. Arora & Allenby, 1999).
2. Studies of group decision processes using experimental (e.g. Corfman & Lehman, 1987), quasi-experimental (e.g. Su, Fern & Ye, 2003) or statistical modeling approaches (e.g. Aribarg, Arora & Bodur, 2002.)

What the streams of literature i. and ii. have in common is that they both assume groups as cognitive structures, a theoretical standpoint later formalized by Hinsz, Tindale and Volrath (1997). Although contrasting in principle, these two major streams complement each other and a few studies assume both simultaneously (e.g. Chandrashekaran et al., 1996).

Scholars in social psychology have long struggled with a more fundamental question: Are groups equal to or else more than the sum of individual behaviours? In other words, are groups a level of analysis worth considering? One major theoretical perspective frames groups as interacting individuals (Rabbie, Schot & Visser, 1989) thus reducing group phenomena to a sum of interpersonal influences stemming from one-on-one behavioural interactions. A second, widely accepted perspective is *social identity theory* (Tajfel & Turner, 1979; Turner, Hogg, Oakes, Reicher & Wetherell, 1987) which states that an individual defines her self-identity over a continuum whose extremes are group identity and individual identity. The repertoires of individual

behaviours change along this continuum, as the individual perceives him or herself as either part of a group or as an autonomous agent. As opposed to the behavioural interactions perspective, social identity theory frames groups as distinct entities where processes other than one-on-one behavioural interactions take place and, thus, frames group processes as a level of analysis in its own right. The social identity paradigm incorporates behavioural interactions as the relational choice when individual identity prevails while providing a locus for the cognitive view of groups on the opposite side of the continuum.

In the communication literature, a specific stream has looked into groups of family member watching television programs. This stream was pioneered by Lull (1978, 1980, 1982) who proposed a framework of Social Uses of Television emphasizing the sharing of television viewing by family members as an important locus for a number of social behaviours. Two recent contributions by Yang, Narayan and Assael (2006) and Yang, Zhao, Erdem and Zhao (2010) in the marketing literature assume the competing behavioural interactions perspective. Both studies assess the interdependence between individual preferences for television programs among different family members using statistical models. Yang et al. (2006) show that mutual influences between wives and husbands are positive regardless of whether these influences derive from interactions while watching or else from interactions in any other occasions. Interdependence as captured by Yang et al. (2010) is narrowed down to the specific behavioural interactions that take place while watching television but it is still restricted to interactions between pairs of viewers. That is, this research does not address the problem of how groups affect the outcomes of television viewing, let alone the problem of what are the antecedents of group consumption of television programs.

A recent contribution by the author of this chapter (Mora, 2010) introduces a measure of degree of group viewing and uses statistical models to show that program type and demographics predict this behaviour. Findings indicate that group viewing accounts for 50% of television consumption in prime time; that individuals in groups watch longer than lone individuals; and, that mutual influences while watching are far more important than interpersonal interactions outside the group of viewers, i.e. in all other occasions around the clock. The measure used in this research is called index of shared viewing (ISV). As $ISV \in [0,1]$ this measure is actually a degree of agglomeration of viewers which is fuzzy in nature. Some limitations of this measure stem from the fact that it is independent of group size. For instance, $ISV_{h,p} = 0.75$ for program p watched in household h, means that in such a household this program was watched by three quarters of a group of any size. For a program of duration equal to one hour, a group of three people could have watched 45 minutes together while only a lone viewer was present during the initial 15 minutes. The same value for this index would result if, instead of two people, only one person joined the lone viewer after the first 15 minutes of the program, i.e. a group of size two watched the program during the last 45 minutes.

In sum, group size and group composition remain important but still largely unexplored factors in the broader research agenda proposed by Adamowicz et al (2005) and, more specifically, in the context of television viewing.

GROUP SIZE AND TV CONSUMPTION: AN EMPIRICAL STUDY

Despite the exponential growth in Internet users over the last decade and the wealth of possibilities the web has brought about for consumers and marketers alike, its prospects as an advertising medium are considerably less brilliant. The very large number of websites and the lack of a reliable third party assessment of website metrics are just two of several major constraints. Simultaneously,

broadcast television has introduced a number of innovative formats in the past decade while satellite and cable services have taken choice to the hundreds of channels as costs of producing and editing broadcast-grade programs have plummeted. People meter panels have managed to catch up with audience fragmentation and new measurement technologies will further these capabilities (e.g. the portable people meter). As a result, the dollar amount of advertising investment in television is still one order of magnitude larger than Internet's (Vranika, 2010; *AdvertisingAge*, 2006) which makes the study of television audiences highly relevant for media, advertising agencies and manufacturers.

Research in mass communications, using a variety of self-report, observational and "mass-observation" methods, has shown that television viewers tend to watch in groups; and, that family decisions about television programs are largely mediated by social processes (Lull, 1982; Lee & Lee, 1995; Schmitt et al., 2003). A limited number of estimates at different points in time and geography indicate that group viewing is quantitatively important (Robertson, 1979; Mora, 2010). In a recent, extensive report in *The Economist*, Budd (2010) reviews evidence mainly from commercial research and concludes that watching with others is a primary motivation to turn the TV set on.

Group consumption of mediated contents is managerially relevant for several reasons. First, because consuming in groups interacts with the cognitive processing of advertisements. For instance, Puntoni & Tavassoli (2007) show that exposure in a social context enhances the recall of advertisements which portray products as socially desirable objects. Furthermore, as watching with others improves the mood of family members (Lull, 1980; Csikszentmihalyi & Kubey, 1981) it is likely that the processing of advertisements will benefit from the cognitive spill-over of enhanced affect. Second, there are indications of a relationship between group viewing and engagement with advertisements (*Thinkbox*, 2009). This is a particularly relevant finding as more engaged viewers surf channels less frequently (e.g. Krugman, Cameron & McKearney White, 1995) and pay more attention to commercial advertisements (Tavassoli et al., 1995). As social context enhances the entertainment experience and provides clues for advertisement processing, the commercial value of an audience should be a function not just of its size and demographics but also of its degree of agglomeration and the distribution of group sizes.

Hypotheses and Research Question

Group size and composition are important properties as they affect several aspects of group decision making, as it has been well established in the literature (Kerr & Tindale, 2004; Adamowicz et al., 2005). Some contributions in the specific domain of television audiences provide basis to formulate hypotheses on the relationship of these two characteristics and individual consumption.

In a direct antecedent to the present study, Mora (2010) finds that individuals in groups watch longer than lone viewers, but larger group sizes have no additional effect on individual viewership. As these conclusions were drawn from a sample of 15-minute intervals, not from a sample of full television programs, it should be expected that the effects at the program level change. Time increases the probability of viewers dropping out from groups and, thus, should reduce the average individual viewership and, consequently, group size. Although the evidence presented earlier suggests that watching with others increases individual enjoyment of television programs no evidence supports that this is a linear effect; on the contrary, commercial researchers report that optimal levels of engagement with television programs are achieved in groups of just two individuals (*Thinkbox*, 2009). Thus, although there are no bases to speculate what group size maximizes individual viewing time, it is reasonable at this point to posit that

H1: *Group size has a convex (inverse-u) effect on individual consumption of television programs.*

The effects of group composition on individual viewership have been tested to a very limited extent. Yang et al. (2006) show that viewership of the partner increases individual viewerships of wives and husbands, and that these effects are asymmetrical: wives' preferences influence husbands' more than husbands' preferences influence wives'. Mora (2010) shows that when this endogenous relationship between individual viewerships is simultaneously considered with the presence of the partner while watching, the presence of the partner yields all other sources of mutual influences irrelevant. Nevertheless, the direction and asymmetry of the partner's presence effects remain the same. Therefore,

H2: *Presence of the partner increases individual consumption of wives and husbands.*

H3: *The effects of the presence of the wife on the viewership of the husband are larger than those in the opposite direction.*

As previously stated, these relationships have not been tested so far outside the parental couple. Therefore,

RQ1: *What are the effects of children's presence on the individual consumptions of wives and husbands?*

Fuzzifying Dynamic Groups

As dynamic groups of viewers change over the duration of program episode p, each individual i in household h has a degree of membership $\mu_p(i_{h,p})$ in the group of viewers watching p. Given the set H_h of all individuals living in household h, the group of viewers of p can be defined as the fuzzy set

$$G_{h,p} = \{(i_{h,p}, \mu_p(i_{h,p})): i_{h,p} \in H_h\} \tag{1}$$

Under this conceptual approach, group size is equivalent to the cardinality of $G_{h,p}$,

$$G_{h,p} = \sum_{i_{h,p} \in H_h} \mu_p(i_{h,p}) \qquad (2)$$

An algebraic operationalization of (2) is now introduced. Group size will remain constant in a segment s of duration π, assuming π is small enough. The viewership of individual i during s is,

$$v_{i,h,p,s} = t_{i,h,p,s} / \pi_{p,s} \qquad (3)$$

where $t_{i,h,p,s}$ is the total minutes i watched in a segment of the program episode p of duration $\pi_{p,s}$. Now, suppose that $N>1$ viewers are watching p in household h. As $\pi_{p,s}$ is small enough, the probability that at least one viewer watched the whole segment is large; and, all individual viewerships tend to overlap. Thus, the joint "viewing session" of the N individuals lasts for as long as the longest individual viewership and thus, the *degree of presence* of individual i in the group, which we will call *number of equivalent viewers* (*NEV*) is simply defined as,

$$NEV_{i,h,p,s} = \frac{v_{i,h,p,s}}{\max(v_{1,h,p,s}, \ldots, v_{N,h,p,s})}. \qquad (4)$$

Conceptually,

$$NEV_{i,h,p,s} \equiv \mu_{p,s}(i_{h,p,s}), \qquad (5)$$

where $\mu_{s,p}$ is the membership function for interval s of program p, as it was defined in (2) at the program level. Also, from (2) it follows that total group size during s is

$$NEV_{h,p,s} = \sum_{i=1}^{N} NEV_{i,h,p,s} \qquad (6)$$

Substituting (4) in (6) we get the full form at the segment level,

$$NEV_{h,p,s} = \frac{\sum_{i=1}^{N} v_{i,h,p,s}}{\max(v_{1,h,p,s}, \ldots, v_{N,h,p,s})}. \qquad (7)$$

This measure can be aggregated at the program episode level, as follows:

$$NEV_{h,p} = \frac{\sum_{s=1}^{S} NEV_{h,p,s}}{S} \qquad (8)$$

where S is the number of segments in p. As the number of individuals joining or deserting from a group increases with time, $NEV_{h,p}$ is fuzzier than $NEV_{h,s,p}$. Figure 1 illustrates the definition of $NEV_{h,s,p}$.

$NEV_{h,p}$ can be used as a continuous variable in any statistical model. The validity of (8) is conditional on measurement issues: if individual viewerships are observed at short enough segments s, then (8) holds true. Finally note that, conceptually,

$$NEV_{h,p} \equiv \sum_{i_{h,p} \in H_h} \mu_p(i_{h,p}) \qquad (9)$$

Group composition will now be considered under the same fuzzy approach. Group composition is a multidimensional construct reflecting the proportion of specific types of individuals in the group. For instance, in a family household, these types of individuals can be wife, husband or children. Thus, each element in the fuzzy set of television viewers $G_{h,p}$ is at the same time an element in the set R_r of all individuals playing role r in the set of all households in the audience, $H=\{H_h\}$. Also, the set of all role sets is $R=\{R_r\}$.

Thus, $G_{h,p}$ in (1) can be re-defined in terms of its composition —as opposed to its size— using

$\mu'_{r,h,p}$, the *average degree of presence* in the group of viewers of each role $r \in R_r$, as follows:

$$G_{h,p} = \bigcup_{r=1}^{R} \{(i_{h,p}, \mu'_{r,h,p}(i_{h,p})) : i_{h,p} R_r\} \qquad (10)$$

where R is the total number of roles and,

$$\mu'_{r,h,p} = \frac{\sum_{i_{h,p} \in R_r} \mu_p(i_{r,h,p})}{N_{h,p}} \qquad (11)$$

Where $N_{h,p}$ is the number of viewers of program p in household h, regardless of role; and, $\mu_p(i_{r,h,p})$ is the membership function in the group of viewers watching program p, as defined in (1) but restricted to the individuals playing family

role r. Algebraically, $G_{h,p}$ can be represented by a *composition vector*, $g_{h,p}$, of R elements, such that,

$$g_{h,p} = (r_{1,h,p}, ..., r_{R,h,p}) \qquad (12)$$

where, for the $N_{r,h,p}$ individuals playing role r in household h, we have that the degree $r_{r,h,p}$ of presence of group viewers in the set R_r is given by,

$$r_{r,h,p} = \frac{\sum_{r=1}^{N_r} v_{r,h,p}}{N_{r,h,p}} \equiv \mu'_{r,h,p}. \qquad (13)$$

Figure 1. Definition of NEV$_{h,s,p}$

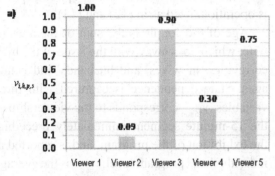

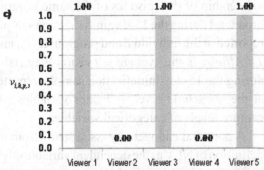

Distribution of viewerships	a)	b)	c)
$v_{1,h,p,s}$	1.00	0.75	1.00
$v_{2,h,p,s}$	0.09	0.07	0.00
$v_{3,h,p,s}$	0.90	0.68	1.00
$v_{4,h,p,s}$	0.30	0.23	0.00
$v_{5,h,p,s}$	0.75	0.56	1.00
$\sum v_{i,h,p,s}$	3.04	2.28	3.00
$\max(v_{1,h,p,s} ... v_{n,h,p,s})$	1.00	0.75	1.00
$NEV_{h,p,s}$	3.04	3.04	3.00

If each viewer watched random fractions of intervals as in graph a) the measure proposed in equation (7) would yield "one" individual plus several "fractions" of individuals, a group size equal to 3.04, as shown on column a) on the bottom right table. This measure holds if proportionality across individual viewerships holds but viewership is smaller (graph b) and column b)) which might affect the reliability of the measure. The actual distribution of viewerships at the segment level, as illustrated in c) does away with this issue: At the 15-minute segment length, groups are highly crisp (see text) but get fuzzier as the measure is aggregated at the program episode level (Figure 4).

Model Specification

The dependent variable individual viewership, $v_{i,h,p} \in [0,1]$ and it is not a probability but a degree of consumption. In addition to that, $v_{i,h,p}$ has an unknown distribution. Thus, a quasi-likelihood (QL) semi-parametric method is well-suited for parameter estimation. A model with a generalized linear model (GLM) form is estimated following Wedderburn's (1974) algorithm which is based on a GLM-specific modification of the Newton-Gauss method. QL estimation is widely used in biological and medical research. This model departs from past models predicting individual consumption of television programs, which have assumed a normal distribution for that dependent variable.

A variance vs. mean scatter plot of $v_{i,h,p}$ for wives and husbands, and a regression analysis on that same data showed a linear relationship, thus leading to the variance function,

$$\mathbf{V}(E[v_{i,h,p}]) = E[v_{i,h,p}] \qquad (14a)$$

and, to the choice of the logarithmic link function

$$E[v_{i,h,p}] = \exp(X_{i,h,p}'\boldsymbol{\beta}_d) \qquad (14b)$$

where $X_{d,i,p}$ is a matrix of exogenous predictors which include the proposed measures of Cardinality and Fuzziness, and $\boldsymbol{\beta}_d$ is a vector of coefficients. The dependent variables, viewership of wives and husbands, are operationalized as in equation (3) as proportions of the total duration of the program in minutes, as follows:

$$v_{r,h,p} = \frac{\sum_{s=1}^{S} t_{r,h,p,s}}{\sum_{s=1}^{S} \pi_{p,s}}, \qquad (15)$$

where suffix r substitutes for i, indicating an individual-role level measure.

Group size is operationalized as *NEV* as in equation (7). It is assumed that the 15-minute segment reported in the dataset is short enough to ensure that full overlapping of individual viewerships during that segment. This assumption is supported by the fact that in a sample of 150,000 segments of 15 minutes watched for at least one minute in a 10-day period, at least one viewer ended up watching the full segment in 96.7% of these segments. Thus, consistent with the empirical modelling literature using data from the USA (e.g. Rust & Alpert, 1984; Shachar & Emerson, 2000) this study finds that watching full 15-minute intervals is an almost ubiquitous behaviour in Mexico as well. Nevertheless, as detailed in upcoming sections, *NEV* values become smaller, i.e. groups become fuzzier, as segments are aggregated into programs [equation (8)] possibly due to desertion of group members after the first program segment. Following H1, *NEV* is inserted in the model in quadratic form. Group composition is operationalized as in (12) and (13).

Age of the couple is the sum of the ages of wife, which does away with the issue of the high correlation of wives' and husbands' individual ages. State dependence is captured with three variables: $v_{15\text{min}}$ corresponds to the viewership of the 15-minute segment immediately preceding the exhibition of the program, and is reported at individual and program level; $v_{\text{past\_e}}$ is the average viewership of the episodes of the same program broadcast during the 15-day initialization sample, reported at the individual and program level; and, *TV Affinity* is the average television viewership during the 15-day initialization sample, reported at the household level. Indicator variables will capture levels of categorical variables.

A potential endogeneity issue stems from the definition of NEV as the dependent variable might be present in either or both the numerator and the denominator [equation (7)]. We address this issue by using instrumental variables to estimate the values for NEV. The possible endogeneity between individual viewerships of wives and husbands is disregarded based on Mora (2010) who showed that the presence of the partner while watching explains practically all mutual influences between wives and husbands. That is, an exogenous variable accounting for the presence of the partner while watching will capture all mutual influences. This finding is extended as an assumption to the viewership of children in relation to each of the parent's.

Data

The dataset used for this study was collected by Ibope-AGB Mexico (IAM), a joint venture of Ibope (Brazil), Grupo Delphi (Mexico) and Nielsen Media Research. IAM has been operating the electronic people-meter panel in Mexico since 1996; this operation is the largest among all Spanish-speaking countries in the world, and it undergoes several yearly audits by local industry organizations, AGB Italia, and Ernst & Young.

The people meter technology consists of a large set of microcomputers installed on top of each of the many television sets in a sample of many households. These microcomputers record the channels which the set is tuned in, the time the set remains tuned in and the (pre-assigned) codes of the individuals that report being watching. The latter is made possible by a specific remote, different from the regular TV remote control, which serves the sole purpose of registering individuals as they sit before the TV set. A small electronic screen attached to the microcomputer displays the message "Who is watching?" every other minute while the TV set is on as a way of preventing under-reporting of viewers.

The panel of Mexican households is made up by more than 2,400 units and more than 9,500 individuals –the actual number fluctuates each day due to the dynamics of panel rotation and operational issues, but it is kept well over a pre-agreed minimum. The sampling design is stratified-probabilistic with over-representation of upper socio-economic strata; daily data are statistically representative of the urban Mexican population, and they are reported at lower levels of aggregation using several segmentation criteria. Number of minutes watched by each individual is reported at the 15-minute segment level.

Besides standard demographic segments, this dataset provides two particularly appealing segmentation schemes: by geography –i.e. Mexico City, Monterrey, Guadalajara, and a composite of 28 smaller cities called Provinces; and by psychographic group –a total of fourteen groups nested in three gender-age segments. The psychographic characterization of the panellists was developed by Marketing Trends (MT), a firm of Grupo Delphi, through a national study named "Psychotrends". In this study, MT used clustering methods to create psychographic segments that are consistent over time (Marketing Trends, 2004). This main study is updated every two years, and it consists of a lengthy questionnaire applied to a randomized quota sample of 4,400 households in 27 cities, including Mexico City, Guadalajara, Monterrey, and 24 of IAM's small cities composite. To enable IAM to characterize its panellists under this framework, MT developed a shorter diagnostic inventory using the items that explain most of the variance in their final set of clusters.

IAM's panel participants are characterized at the individual level by age, gender, and psychographic type –all other demographics are shared with other members of the household, e.g. SES and Region. Two role variables are used to characterize those adult individuals with major responsibilities: (a) the head of the household, who is defined as the person who other dwellers recognize as the main decision maker; and, (b) the housewife, who is recognized as the person who is responsible for grocery shopping, cleaning (whether she or he performs it or not) and everyday decisions. In the total sample, almost 70% of the households reported having a male playing the role of the head and a woman in the role of the housewife; around 20% reported having a single woman in the role of head and housewife; and, around 10% were a variety of single-headed households.

This dataset allows for the identification of individual viewerships and roles, as in equation (1) and to further specify indicator variables in the proposed model as follows: Lone Couple (vs. base case, Couple with Children), Pyschographic Type of the Wife (4 levels, base case Traditionalists), Psychographic Type of the Husband (4 levels, base case Passives), Geography (3 levels, base case Monterrey) and Program Genre (9 levels, base case Newscasts). The ordinal variable Socio-Economic Status is also included (3 levels, base case Lower).

Sample

The estimation sample is made up by five different weekdays sampled from five different weeks within the period January-February 2006. The time slot reported in the sample is "prime time" Monday to Friday, which runs from 7:00 pm to 11:00 pm. The households selected for this study were those reporting a male head and a female housewife; we will refer to them for the remainder of the paper simply as head and wife. It is assumed that the head and the wife form a couple either married or not. Further, households with adults other than the housewife-head couple were excluded in order to reduce noise introduced by households with more than two adults and, possibly, more complex decision rules.

Only time segments with viewership of national broadcast television larger than zero are part of the sample, i.e. channels 2, 5, 7, 9 and 13, as program descriptions for pay and local free systems are not available. The final sample consists of one or more episodes of 31 programs watched by 775 households. The total sample size is 11,109 episode-households. Figure 2 summarizes the composition of the estimation sample and Figure 3 presents its continuous variables. A second sample comprising the 15 days immediately before the first estimation week was created in order to calculate

the state dependence variables, as explained in the next section.

Figure 4 shows the distribution of $NEV_{h,p}$ as a histogram. As stated earlier, the proposed measure becomes considerably fuzzier as it is aggregated over the time segments making up a program. Fractions of groups on Figure 1 add up to 65.2% while crisp groups represent 34.8% (assuming that fuzzy groups whose $NEV_{h,p}$ add up to an integer percentage figure are negligible). When $NEV_{h,p}$ is averaged over a period of five days to yield $avgNEV_{h,p}$, fractional groups add up to 72.6% while crisp groups represent 27.4%. The variable $avgNEV_{h,p}$ is the variable used as a predictor in model estimation.

Results and Discussion

Figures 5 and 6 summarize fit statistics and parameter estimates for three models predicting, respectively, viewership of wife and viewership of husband. Models are labelled from 1 to 3 in both tables to signal identical model specifications across tables. A "w" next to the model number on Figure 5 indicates that it has been estimated with viewership of wives as the dependent variable. An "h" next to the model number on Figure 6 indicates estimates for husbands. The fit statistics are the deviance, an analogous of the unexplained variance in linear regression; and, McFadden's R^2, an analogous of R^2 in linear regression, which we adjust to account for the number of predictors.

The quadratic form of NEV yields better fit in models 2w and 2h as compared to the linear form of NEV in models 1w and 1h, which supports H1. Introducing the average viewership of husbands, wives and children as operationalizations of Group Composition improves the fit of models 3w and 3h respect to size-only models 3b and 4b. Furthermore, as predicted by H2, the presence of the partner has a positive effect on the viewership of both husbands and wives; and, as predicted by H3, such influences are asymmetrical with wives

Figure 2. Sample composition (%)

Socio-Economic Status	
Upper/Mid-Upper	20.5
Middle	18.9
Mid-Low	30.8
Low	29.9
	100.0

Psychographic types - Wives	
Sophisticates	20.3
Traditionalists	9.3
Materialists	16.2
Mommies	25.3
Dreamers	29.0
	100.0

Geography	
Mexico City	31.9
Provinces	28.5
Guadalajara	21.0
Monterrey	18.6
	100.0

Psychographic types - Husbands	
Reflexives	19.9
Pragmatists	19.9
Passives	16.5
Jetsetters	25.4
Self-centered	18.5
	100.0

influencing husbands more than husbands influencing wives.

Figure 7 shows that the convex effects predicted in H1 translate into a positive contribution to viewership of the wife by lone viewing and by groups of two viewers; nil contribution by groups of three viewers; and, negative contribution by groups size four and larger. Among husbands, positive contributions of group viewing extend to groups of four family members and, interestingly, the maximum contribution to husband's

Figure 3. Statistics for continuous variables

a) Means and standard deviations

	Mean	SD
$V_{wife,h,p}$	0.202	0.287
$V_{husb,h,p}$	0.134	0.244
Couple Age	0.298	0.458
$NEV_{h,p}$	1.599	0.952

b) Correlations

	$V_{wife,h,p}$	$V_{husb,h,p}$	Age of Couple	$NEV_{h,p}$
$V_{wife,h,p}$	1.0000	0.3023	0.0168	0.2614
		<.0001	0.0764	<.0001
$V_{husb,h,p}$		1.0000	0.0777	0.2923
			<.0001	<.0001
Age of Couple			1.0000	-0.0773
				<.0001
$NEV_{h,p}$				1.0000

p-values underneath correlation values

Figure 4. Proportions of group sizes as NEV$_{h,p}$

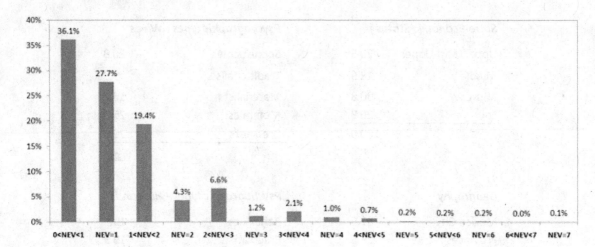

individual viewership seems to be achieved by groups of 2 to 3 viewers.

Consistent with past research, lone couples tend to watch more television than couples with children when group composition is not considered; when group composition is considered, this positive effect turns slightly negative (on wives, 3w) or at least modestly positive (on husbands, 3h). Consistent with past research considering viewership of the partner (Yang et al., 2006; Mora, 2010) age of the couple has a negative effect on individual viewership of both wives and husbands (models 3w and 3h).

Psychographic groups are overall more important predictors of individual viewership among husbands than among wives in the full models (3w and 3h). Interestingly, the psychographics of the wife have a remarkably larger importance on husband's viewership than the almost nil influence of husband's psychographics on wife's viewership. This is consistent with H3.

Higher Socio-economic Status presents remarkably small estimates in all models. Again, the inclusion of group characteristics in the model, especially group size, should explain the differ-

ences. Lower strata households are usually lager than higher strata households and this had been offered as a partial explanation to the negative effects of Socio-Economic Status on individual viewing, together with possession of more TV sets and higher penetration of pay TV in higher strata. These results indicate that the size of the household accounts for most of those effects.

All geographic regions increase individual viewership of wives compared to Guadalajara, consistent with the lower ratings this city has traditionally contributed to the national average in Mexico (Jara & Garnica, 2009). This relationship reverses among husbands but that is unlikely to compensate for the larger effect of the increased wives' viewership in Guadalajara, as the wives consume more television than husbands (see Figure 2).

Eight of the nine program genres positively affect viewership of wives, which is intuitively correct as the base case is newscasts. Among husbands, as it should be expected, several genres reduce viewership respect to newscasts. The estimates for Telenovelas are interesting as they are either negative or else small across models,

Figure 5. Standardized estimates for models prediction viewership of wives

		Model 1w		Model 2w		Model 3w	
	Deviance=	2,557		2,518		2,510	
	Adj. McFadden's R^2=	0.4017		0.4108		0.4125	
		Estimate	Pr(>|t|)	Estimate	Pr(>|t|)	Estimate	Pr(>|t|)
	(Intercept)	-2.1199	<.0001	-2.1426	<.0001	-2.1311	<.0001
Group Size	$avg\,NEV$	-0.1446	<.0001	0.2619	<.0001	0.1859	<.0001
	$avg\,NEV^2$			-0.3905	<.0001	-0.3405	<.0001
Group Composition	$V_{husband}$					0.0537	<.0001
	$V_{children}$					0.0212	0.0821
Couple Characterisics	Couple Age	-0.0576	<.0001	-0.0542	<.0001	-0.1791	<.0001
	Lone couple	0.3563	<.0001	0.3651	<.0001	-0.0564	<.0001
Psychographic Types Wives (Base: Traditionalists)	Sophisticates	-0.0422	0.3167	-0.0131	0.7564	0.3471	<.0001
	Dreamers	0.0881	0.0265	0.1118	0.0051	-0.0119	0.7776
	Materialists	0.0507	0.1869	0.0734	0.0573	0.1186	0.0030
	Mommies	-0.0077	0.8324	0.0138	0.7070	0.0718	0.0625
Psychographic Types Husbands (Base: Passives)	Jetsetters	0.0234	0.5308	0.0357	0.3407	0.0152	0.6788
	Self centered	0.0375	0.2966	0.0378	0.2931	0.0360	0.3362
	Reflexives	0.0730	0.0374	0.0689	0.0496	0.0361	0.3148
	Pragmatists	0.0460	0.1886	0.0464	0.1866	0.0686	0.0499
Socio-Economic Status (Base: Lower)	Upper/Upper-Middle	0.0316	0.3668	0.0348	0.3210	0.0513	0.1434
	Middle	0.0681	0.0407	0.0789	0.0180	0.0368	0.2936
	Lower Middle	0.0290	0.3064	0.0506	0.0757	0.0836	0.0121
Geography (Base: Guadalajara)	Mexico City	0.1253	0.0002	0.0807	0.0162	0.0571	0.0450
	Provinces	0.1638	<.0001	0.1252	0.0003	0.0871	0.0094
	Monterrey	0.1522	<.0001	0.1196	0.0016	0.1301	0.0001
Program Genre (Base: Newscasts)	Telenovelas	-0.1157	0.0102	-0.0955	0.0344	0.1314	0.0005
	Magazines	0.3050	<.0001	0.3152	<.0001	-0.1094	0.0161
	Contests	0.1443	0.3885	0.1927	0.2509	0.3058	<.0001
	Cartoons	0.8437	<.0001	0.8613	<.0001	0.1948	0.2444
	Reality TV	0.4468	0.0022	0.4301	0.0032	0.8240	<.0001
	US-made Comedy	1.2347	<.0001	1.2556	<.0001	0.3879	0.0079
	US-made Drama	0.3607	0.0382	0.3493	0.0453	1.2213	<.0001
	Mexican sitcom	0.2540	0.0003	0.2405	0.0007	0.3515	0.0434
	Mexican_series	-0.0305	0.7535	-0.0088	0.9284	0.1915	0.0075
Channel (Base: Channel 13)	Channel 2	0.1826	<.0001	0.1804	<.0001	-0.0249	0.7986
	Channel 5	-1.0632	<.0001	-1.0667	<.0001	0.1683	<.0001
	Channel 9	-0.5365	<.0001	-0.5439	<.0001	-1.0538	<.0001
	Channel 7	-0.6504	<.0001	-0.6459	<.0001	-0.5505	<.0001
State Dependence	V_{15min}	0.6259	<.0001	0.6228	<.0001	-0.3405	<.0001
	V_{past_e}	0.4133	<.0001	0.3832	<.0001	0.6231	<.0001
	TV Affinty	-0.1838	<.0001	-0.1621	<.0001	0.3835	<.0001

Figure 6. Standardized estimates for models prediction viewership of husbands

		Model 1h		Model 2h		Model 3h	
	Deviance=	2,231		2,156		2,135	
	Adj. McFadden's R^2=	0.4185		0.4382		0.4434	
		Estimate	Pr(>|t|)	Estimate	Pr(>|t|)	Estimate	Pr(>|t|)
	(Intercept)	-2.3216	<.0001	-2.2917	<.0001	-2.2360	<.0001
Group Size	$avg\,NEV$	-0.1465	<.0001	0.5496	<.0001	0.4525	<.0001
	$avg\,NEV^2$			-0.6299	<.0001	-0.5512	<.0001
Group Composition	v_{wife}					0.1276	<.0001
	$v_{children}$					-0.0274	0.0932
Couple Characterisics	Couple Age	0.0125	0.4067	0.0304	0.0451	-0.1272	<.0001
	Lone couple	0.5077	<.0001	0.5126	<.0001	0.0322	0.0342
Psychographic	Sophisticates	-0.1575	0.0021	-0.1584	0.0022	0.4460	<.0001
Types Wives	Dreamers	-0.1048	0.0287	-0.0985	0.0405	-0.1715	0.0009
(Base: Traditionolists)	Materialists	0.0479	0.2818	0.0225	0.6141	-0.1041	0.0303
	Mommies	-0.1259	0.0034	-0.1308	0.0024	0.0071	0.8738
Psychographic	Jetsetters	0.0918	0.0468	0.1124	0.0157	-0.1374	0.0014
Types Husbands	Self centered	0.0605	0.1735	0.0513	0.2505	0.1185	0.0108
(Base: Passives)	Reflexives	0.1160	0.0056	0.1189	0.0047	0.0733	0.1010
	Pragmatists	0.0449	0.3000	0.0645	0.1393	0.1373	0.0011
Socio-Economic	Upper/Upper-Middle	0.0321	0.4558	0.0230	0.5949	0.0861	0.0487
Status	Middle	-0.0688	0.1046	-0.0826	0.0527	0.0257	0.5521
(Base: Lower)	Lower Middle	-0.0759	0.0280	-0.0438	0.2082	-0.0970	0.0232
Geography	Mexico City	-0.0381	0.3153	-0.1401	0.0003	-0.0474	0.1733
(Base: Guodolojoro)	Provinces	-0.0276	0.4694	-0.1172	0.0025	-0.1605	<.0001
	Monterrey	-0.1609	0.0007	-0.2536	<.0001	-0.1336	0.0006
Program Genre	Telenovelas	-0.3095	<.0001	-0.3135	<.0001	-0.2669	<.0001
(Base: Newscosts)	Magazines	0.1476	0.0184	0.1503	0.0169	-0.3645	<.0001
	Contests	-0.6110	0.0025	-0.4871	0.0162	0.1290	0.0398
	Cartoons	0.5445	<.0001	0.5583	<.0001	-0.5146	0.0110
	Reality TV	0.2911	0.0198	0.2650	0.0348	0.5074	<.0001
	US-made Comedy	0.8150	<.0001	0.8545	0.0000	0.2260	0.0717
	US-made Drama	0.0067	0.9714	-0.0233	0.9009	0.7998	<.0001
	Mexican sitcom	0.1653	0.0388	0.1315	0.1017	-0.0358	0.8482
	Mexican_series	-0.1918	0.1377	-0.1895	0.1446	0.0388	0.6360
Channel	Channel 2	0.2132	<.0001	0.2266	<.0001	-0.2326	0.0735
(Base: Channel 13)	Channel 5	-0.9463	<.0001	-0.9516	<.0001	0.2051	<.0001
	Channel 9	-0.4007	<.0001	-0.3991	<.0001	-0.9206	<.0001
	Channel 7	-0.1291	0.0814	-0.1126	0.1311	-0.3970	<.0001
State Dependence	v_{15min}	0.6904	<.0001	0.6817	<.0001	-0.5512	<.0001
	v_{past_e}	0.3651	<.0001	0.2984	<.0001	0.6729	<.0001
	TV Affinty	-0.1741	<.0001	-0.1107	<.0001	0.2853	<.0001

Figure 7. Effects of group size on individual viewerships of wives and husbands

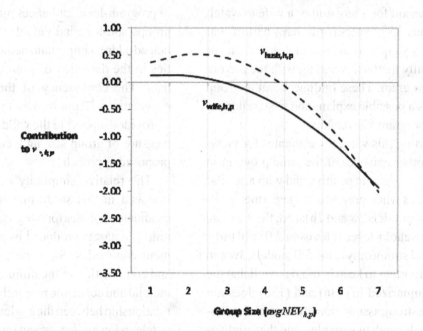

Note: Non-standardized parameters were used to generate this graph.

contrary to past research considering only joint viewing of wives and husbands. Telenovelas are the Latin American version of soap operas: highly emotional, melodramatic serials, although with duration limited to 80 to 100 episodes. Ethnographic research (Barrios, 1986) has revealed potentially important *social uses* (Lull, 1980) of this genre in at least some families. Again, controlling for group characteristics produces the surprisingly negative estimates respect to Newscasts among husbands, and smaller than any other genre among wives. These findings indicate that social uses of these programs (e.g. conversational entry, agenda for talking) may explain viewership of Telenovelas rather than individual tastes. These results may have important implications for broadcasters around the globe as this specific television program genre is one of the most popular in the world.

Estimates for Channel 2 are positive and significantly different from those for Channel 13 in models not considering group composition, consistent with the position of these two competitors

in the Mexican market. Considering group composition obliterates this difference among wives while turning it slightly negative among husbands. This shift indicates an interaction between brand (channel) and occasion (watching with a significant other) which has been well documented in the marketing literature. A similar effect happens for Channel 5 among wives. The remaining channels, 7 and 9, show negative estimates, consistent with their market shares.

The state dependence variables show some interesting patterns. In contrast with past research, which has found consistently large effects of past viewing on future viewership (e.g. Rust & Alpert, 1984; Shachar & Emerson, 2000; Goetler & Shachar, 2001) the estimate for viewership of the previous 15-minute segment, v_{15min}, turns negative when group composition is included in models 3w and 3h. It seems that in models 2w and 2h the effects of the prospect of watching with others the upcoming program had been hidden behind the viewership of the previous segment. As the estimates for children are negative, it seems that the very reason for a husband or a wife to watch the previous 15 minutes (or at least part of that segment) is simply to tune-in in preparation for what actually matters: watching with the partner the next program. These findings point to group viewing as a possible explanation to state dependence of program viewership.

Supporting this view, the estimates for viewership of other episodes of the same program in the past, v_{past_e}, remain positive and with a similar magnitude as when presence of the partner is not considered (models 2w and 2h); and, the estimate for the household-level Television Affinity turns positive and strong only in the full models, 3w and 3h. It is important to keep in mind as well that the model summarized in (13a) and (13b) does not impose the strong assumption of a normal distribution on the dependent variables, and that might as well help explain the differences in estimates on Figures 5 and 6 respect to the literature.

CONCLUSION AND FUTURE RESEARCH

This research presents an assessment of the effects of *dynamic groups* characteristics on *individual* behaviour in a non-experimental setting which, to the best of the author's knowledge, is one of the few available in the literature. The effects of group composition on individual behaviour are probably mediated by group processes as variations in group composition are indeed changes in the family roles present in the group, which should affect the way individuals relate to each other (e.g. Corfman & Lehman, 1987; Yang et al., 2010). Variations in group size may as well alter the decision-making heuristics and choices (e.g. Grofman, Feld & Owen, 1984; Sorkin, Hayes & West, 2001).

Fuzzy sets provide accurate representations of program-level audiences made up by dynamic groups and lone individuals. This approach has helped address important methodological difficulties in the detection of groups on people-meter data. The consistency of the results with the expectations formalized as hypotheses 1, 2 and 3 provides support to the validity of the proposed measure of group size and, consequently, to the proposed approach.

The relative simplicity of the measures introduced in this study makes them interesting candidate variables for integration in the overnight ratings datasets produced by audience measurement companies. Such measures of group size and composition to the minute may enable commercial and academic researchers to elucidate the relationship between the agglomeration structures of television audiences and ratings. Furthermore, advertising researchers may investigate the effects of these important group characteristics on post-hoc campaign metrics such as advertisement recall and attitudes towards brands.

REFERENCES

Adamowicz, W., Hanemann, M., Swait, J., Johnson, R., Layton, D., & Regenwetter, M. (2005). Decision strategy and structure in households: A "Groups" perspective. *Marketing Letters*, *16*(3), 387–399. doi:10.1007/s11002-005-5900-6

Age, A. (2006). *Fact pack: 4th Annual guide to advertising and marketing*. Retrieved from http://adage.com/images/random/FactPack06.pdf

Andreoni, J.A., & Miller, J. H. (1993). Rational cooperation in the finitely repeated prisoner's dilemma: Experimental evidence. *The Economic Journal*, *103*(418), 570–585. doi:10.2307/2234532

Bacharach, M. (2006). *Beyond individual choice: Teams and frames in game theory* (Gold, N., & Sugden, R., Eds.). Princeton, NJ: Princeton University Press.

Barrios, L. (1988). Television, telenovelas and family life in Venezuela. In Lull, J. (Ed.), *World families watch television*. Newbury Park, CA: Sage.

Bordogna, G., Fedrizzi, M., & Pasi, G. (1997). A linguistic modeling of consensus in group decision making based on OWA operators. *IEEE Transactions on Systems, Man, and Cybernetics. Part A, Systems and Humans, 27*(1), 126–132. doi:10.1109/3468.553232

Bourguignon, F., Browning, M., & Chiappori, P. (2009). Efficient intra-household allocations and distribution factors: Implications and identification. *The Review of Economic Studies, 76*(2), 503–528. doi:10.1111/j.1467-937X.2008.00525.x

Browning, M., & Chiappori, P. A. (1998). Efficient intra-household allocations: A general characterization and empirical tests. *Econometrica: Journal of the Econometric Society, 66*(6), 1241–1278. doi:10.2307/2999616

Budd, J. (2010, May 1-7). Changing the channel: A special report on television. *The Economist,* 148-160.

Cherchye, L., De Rock, B., & Vermeulen, F. (2007). The collective model of household consumption: A Nonparametric characterization. *Econometrica: Journal of the Econometric Society, 75*(2), 553–574. doi:10.1111/j.1468-0262.2006.00757.x

Corfman, K. P., & Lehmann, D. R. (1987). Models of cooperative group decision-making and relative influence: An experimental investigation of family purchase decisions. *The Journal of Consumer Research, 14*(1), 1–13. doi:10.1086/209088

Craven, J. (1992). *Social Choice*. Cambridge, UK: Cambridge University Press. doi:10.1017/CBO9780511521911

Csikszentmihalyi, M., & Kubey, R. (1981). Television and the rest of life: A systematic comparison of subjective experience. *Public Opinion Quarterly, 45*(3), 317. doi:10.1086/268667

Goettler, R. L., & Schachar, R. (2001). Spatial competition in the network television industry. *The Rand Journal of Economics, 32*(4), 624–656. doi:10.2307/2696385

Grofman, B., Feld, S. L., & Owen, G. (1984). Group size and the performance of a composite group majority: Statistical truths and empirical results. *Organizational Behavior and Human Performance, 33*(3), 350–359. doi:10.1016/0030-5073(84)90028-X

Herrera, F., Herrera-Viedma, E., & Verdegay, J. L. (1996). A model of consensus in group decision making under linguistic assessments. *Fuzzy Sets and Systems, 78*(1), 73–87. doi:10.1016/0165-0114(95)00107-7

Hinsz, V. B., Tindale, R. S., & Vollrath, D. A. (1997). The emerging conceptualization of groups as information processes. *Psychological Bulletin, 121*(1), 43–64. doi:10.1037/0033-2909.121.1.43

Jara, J. R., & Garnica, A. (2009). *Medición de audiencias de televisión en México (Measuring television audiences in Mexico)*. Mexico: Grupo Editorial Patria.

Kacprzyk, J. (1986). Group decision-making with a fuzzy linguistic majority. *Fuzzy Sets and Systems, 18*(2), 105–118. doi:10.1016/0165-0114(86)90014-X

Kerr, N. L., & Tindale, R. S. (2004). Group performance and decision making. *Annual Review of Psychology, 55*, 623–655. doi:10.1146/annurev.psych.55.090902.142009

Krugman, D. M., Cameron, G. T., & McKearney White, C. (1995). Visual attention to programming and commercials: The use of in-home observations. *Journal of Advertising, 24*(1), 1–12.

Leask, G., & Parker, D. (2006). Strategic group theory: Review, examination and application in the UK pharmaceutical industry. *Journal of Management Development, 25*(4), 386–408. doi:10.1108/02621710610655846

Lee, B., & Lee, R. S. (1995). How and why people watch TV: Implications for the future of interactive television. *Journal of Advertising Research, 35*(6), 9–18.

Lull, J. T. (1978). Choosing television programs by family vote. *Communication Quarterly, 26*(4), 53–57. doi:10.1080/01463377809369314

Lull, J. T. (1980a). The social uses of television. *Human Communication Research, 7*(3), 319.

Lull, J. T. (1980b). Family communication patterns and the social uses of television. *Communication Research, 7*(3), 319. doi:10.1177/009365028000700303

Lull, J. T. (1982). How families select television programs: A mass-observational study. *Journal of Broadcasting, 26*, 801–811. doi:10.1080/08838158209364049

Lull, J. T. (Ed.). (1988). *World families watch television*. Newbury Park, CA: Sage.

Mora, J. D. (2010). *Understanding the social structure of television audiences: Three essays.* Doctoral dissertation, Simon Fraser University, Vancouver, BC.

O'leary-Kelly, A. M., Martocchio, J. J., & Frink, D. D. (1994). A review of the influence of group goals on group performance. *Academy of Management Journal, 37*(5), 1285. doi:10.2307/256673

Pawlak, Z., & Skowron, A. (2007). Rough sets and Boolean reasoning. *Information Sciences, 177*(1), 41–73. doi:10.1016/j.ins.2006.06.007

Puntoni, S., & Tavassoli, N. T. (2007). Social context and advertising memory. *JMR, Journal of Marketing Research, 44*(2), 284–296. doi:10.1509/jmkr.44.2.284

Rabbie, J. M., Schot, J. C., & Visser, L. (1989). Social identity theory: A conceptual and empirical critique from the perspective of a behavioural interaction model. *European Journal of Social Psychology, 19*(3), 171–202. doi:10.1002/ejsp.2420190302

Raiffa, H. with Richardson, J., & Metcalfe, D. (2002). *Negotiation analysis: The science and art of collaborative decision making.* Cambridge, MA: Harvard University Press.

Robertson, T. S. (1979). Parental mediation of television advertising effects. *The Journal of Communication, 29*(1), 12–25. doi:10.1111/j.1460-2466.1979.tb01678.x

Rust, R., & Alpert, M. (1984). An audience flow model of television viewing choice. *Marketing Science, 3*(1), 113–127. doi:10.1287/mksc.3.2.113

Schmitt, K. L., Woolf, K. D., & Anderson, D. R. (2003). Viewing the viewers: Viewing behaviors by children and adults during television programs and commercials. *The Journal of Communication, 53*(2), 265–281. doi:10.1111/j.1460-2466.2003.tb02590.x

Shachar, R., & Emerson, J. W. (2000). Cast demographics, unobserved segments, and heterogeneous switching costs in a television viewing choice model. *JMR, Journal of Marketing Research, 37*(2), 173–186. doi:10.1509/jmkr.37.2.173.18738

Sorkin, R. D., Hays, C. J., & West, R. (2001). Signal-detection analysis of group decision making. *Psychological Review*, 108(1), 183–203. doi:10.1037/0033-295X.108.1.183

Steckel, J. H., Corfman, K. P., Curry, D. J., Gupta, S., & Shanteau, J. (1991). Prospects and problems in modeling group decisions. *Marketing Letters*, 2(3), 231–240.

Su, C., Fern, E. F., & Ye, K. (2003). A temporal dynamic model of spousal family purchase-decision behavior. [JMR]. *JMR, Journal of Marketing Research*, 40(3), 268–281. doi:10.1509/jmkr.40.3.268.19234

Tajfel, H., & Turner, J. (1979). An integrative theory of intergroup conflict. In Austin, W. G., & Worchel, S. (Eds.), *The social psychology of intergroup relations*. Monterey, CA: Brooks-Cole.

Tavassoli, N. T., Schultz, C. J. II, & Fitzsimons, G. J. (1995). Program involvement: Are moderate levels best for ad memory and attitude toward the ad? *Journal of Advertising Research*, 35(5), 61–72.

Thinkbox. (2009, November 10). It ain't what you view, it's the way that you view it. Retrieved from http://www.thinkbox.tv/server/show/nav.854

Marketing Trends (2004). *Definición de estilos de vida* (Definition of lifestyles [in Mexico]) Electronic document.

Turner, J. C., Hogg, M. A., Oakes, P. J., Reicher, S. D., & Wetherell, M. S. (1987). *Rediscovering the social group: A self-categorization theory*. Oxford, UK: Blackwell.

Vranika, S. (2010, September 23) Nielsen testing a new web-ad metric. *The Wall Street Journal*, p. B8.

Wedderburn, R. W. M. (1974). Quasi-likelihood functions, generalized linear-models, and Gauss-Newton method. *Biometrika*, 61(3), 439–447.

Yang, S., Narayan, V., & Assael, H. (2006). Estimating the interdependence of television program viewership between spouses: A Bayesian simultaneous equation model. *Marketing Science*, 25(4), 336–349. doi:10.1287/mksc.1060.0195

Yang, S., Zhao, Y., Erdem, T., & Zhao, Y. (2010). Modeling the intrahousehold behavioral interaction. [JMR]. *JMR, Journal of Marketing Research*, 47(3), 470–484. doi:10.1509/jmkr.47.3.470

KEY TERMS AND DEFINITIONS

Endogenous Variable: In econometrics, any variable or parameter in a model that is correlated with the error term, which may happen due to a number of reasons. In the restricted context of this paper, endogeneity between viewership of the husband and viewership of the wife could stem from the correlation between these two variables, i.e. the wife likes the program because the husband likes it too and, thus, influences her in a number of ways.

Generalized Linear Model (GLM): A class of models comprehending linear and non-linear mathematical forms. In a GLM, the relationship between the dependent and the independent variables is "linearized" by predicting the former from a function of the linear form of the latter. Such function is called "link function". Nelder and Wedderburn (1972) formalized GLM to unify a family of models, including linear, logarithmic and logistic, for which a specific estimation method is applicable provided that the distribution of the dependent variable belongs in the "exponential family" of distributions which include the normal distribution. GLM considerably expanded the range of phenomena that could be predicted by statistical models by relieving researchers from the need to assume that the variables describing such phenomena are normally distributed.

Number of Equivalent Viewers (NEV): A fuzzy measure of group size calculated as the ratio of the summation of individual viewerships to the maximum viewership in the group.

Psychographics: Variables measuring interests, attitudes and opinions of consumers. Psychographic variables can be aggregated as indexes or else used in multivariate models to define homogeneous groups of consumers.

Quasi-Likelihood Estimation (QL): A semi-parametric estimation method introduced by Wedderburn (1974) which, remarkably, allows estimating a model with a GLM form only from the mean and the variance of the distribution of the dependent variable. That is, no assumptions on the distribution of the dependent variable are necessary.

State Dependence: When the value of a variable describing a specific behaviour, e.g. watching television, depends on a previous value of that very same variable. Past viewership of a television program is usually a strong predictor of future viewership of the same program.

Viewership: The fraction of a program or segment watched by an individual.

ENDNOTE

[1]   The author thanks IBOPE-AGB México for providing the data for this study.

Chapter 4
Using Case Data to Ensure 'Real World' Input Validation within Fuzzy Set Theory Models

Sara Denize
University of Western Sydney, Australia

Sharon Purchase
University of Western Australia, Australia

Doina Olaru
University of Western Australia, Australia

ABSTRACT

Fuzzy set theory models have considerable potential to address complex marketing and B2B problems, but for this methodology to be accepted, models require validation. However, there is relatively little detail in the literature dealing with validation of fuzzy simulation in marketing. This limitation is compounded by the difficulty of using case-based and qualitative evidence (data to which fuzzy models are well suited) when applying more general validation. The chapter illustrates a fuzzy model validation process using small-N cased based data and concludes with recommendations to assist researchers in validating their fuzzy models.

INTRODUCTION

Researching B2B marketing poses difficult issues, particularly when investigating business networks and their interactions. We are often faced with a small number of organizations (small-N) and a large number of variables, many of which are 'fuzzy'. For example, actors themselves

often take multiple roles such as manufacturer, new product developer, and information broker. Therefore, even classifying actors is problematic when using multivariate research techniques. Case study techniques overcome these issues as they allow for rich variable descriptions (Piekkari, Plakoyiannaki, & Welch, 2010). Yet, cases have disadvantages, notably the difficulty in conducting case comparisons or investigating multiple possible scenarios. Fuzzy set theory overcomes

DOI: 10.4018/978-1-4666-0095-9.ch004

many of these issues (Donzé & Meier, 2011). Yet, even though fuzzy set theory opens up new ways of investigating business networks, it can only be achieved if the fuzzy models that are used are validated (and verified) within real-world contexts.

Fuzzy set theory has not been used extensively within the marketing and management disciplines, with even less papers reporting model validation (and verification), despite its importance (Richiardi, Roberto, Saam, & Sonnessa, 2006). The diversity of views about validation processes has undoubtedly contributed to this omission. As Petty (2009, p. 40) observes, "the practice of verification and validation is as varied as the subjects of the model involved". In the social sciences, various authors have documented the difficulties associated with this task observing that the context to be modeled is usually large and complex with "only a small number of observable instances and data sufficiently detailed for validation" (Petty, 2009, p. 140).

Previous literature highlights the need to develop a suite of "best practices" to validate and verify computational simulation models (Louie & Carley, 2008; Richiardi, et al., 2006; Wilensky & Rand, 2007; Windrum, Fagiolo, & Moneta, 2007), yet given the unique characteristics of fuzzy set theory some of these "best practices" cannot be applied in their current form. Reporting validation and verification practices is critical if fuzzy set theory models are to be accepted by the wider academic community and their findings used by practitioners (Louie & Carley, 2008; Maguire, McKelvey, Mirabeau, & Öztas, 2006). This chapter outlines a process for business marketers to validate their fuzzy set theory models (at least in part).

The validation process we describe has a number of advantages for fuzzy set theory modelers, in that it: (1) allows model builders to develop the fuzzy rule based system without working from a full factorial set of rules, thus improving validation efficiencies; (2) checks for consistency and coverage of the fuzzy rule based system improving

model sufficiency; and (3) validates the simulation model within real world data sets. We note that working from the full factorial set of rules is extremely resource demanding and that model builders must still complete a validation process to compare to real world data.

The chapter begins by reviewing general processes of verifying and validating models and goes on to identify techniques and methods that are particularly relevant for fuzzy set theory models. We then consider how researchers can establish the extent to which their model fits the "real-world" and contribute to the discourse on model validation by illustrating a process that uses case-based evidence. Here we focus on the use of linguistic information, consisting of nuances and variation, in fuzzy simulation methods. Fuzzy set theory is well suited to dealing with the ambiguity and natural language used in this type of data (Donzé & Meier, 2011). The case describes the innovation and commercialization processes for various photovoltaic technologies and focuses on a lead group of researchers who have impacted the development of solar technologies on the world stage. We conclude the chapter with insights and recommendations for researchers when embarking on the validation process.

BACKGROUND

Verifying and validating simulation models is essentially an exercise in comparisons. In the broadest sense, researchers must compare the model and its outputs to the 'real world' system it represents. Modelers make comparisons at critical points and it is these comparisons that modelers describe as verification and validation (Louie & Carley, 2008; Petty, 2009) and are outlined in Figure 1.

As shown in Figure 1, modeling systems comprise of: a simuland ('real world' system); a set of requirements (what the model aims to achieve); a conceptual model (specifies the key

Figure 1. Comparisons in verification, validation and accreditation (adapted from Petty, 2010, p. 333)

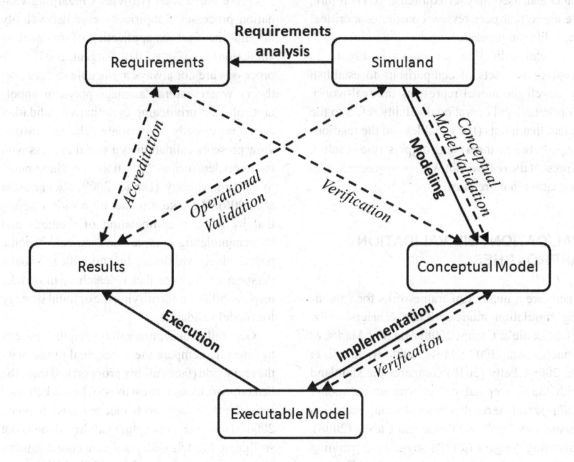

parts and their relation to each other); an executable model (which when executed produces results); and the results (generated by the executable model). The solid lines connecting the parts of the system are the steps of model development, while the dashed lines show the verification and validity steps that allow comparisons with the real-world context.

Before exploring model validation, we briefly discuss verification and accreditation, neither of which are the focus of this chapter. For a detailed discussion see Petty (2010). Model verification checks the conceptual model performs according to initial specifications, and that the executable model works as anticipated by the conceptual model. Verification approaches depend on the type of modeling tools used and include static

methods such as multivariate data analysis and cause-effect graphing and dynamic methods such as comparison testing (Petty, 2010) and docking (Axtell, Axelrod, Epstein, & Cohen, 1996; Maguire, et al., 2006). When undertaking dynamic verification, the modeler compares multiple models of the same simuland and the extent to which the results converge provides a degree of confidence that the models perform according to conceptual specifications.

Accreditation is a decision that the model produces results that perform as required (Petty, 2010). In military or commercial contexts, models perform a specific purpose and the chief operating officer or user makes this decision. However, a great deal of the modeling undertaken by researchers in marketing is not applied and researchers rather than users may set requirements. Therefore, we argue that peer review constitutes a critical accreditation process.

Model validation (as shown in Figure 1) involves two sets of comparisons to establish how well the model represents the real-world. Conceptual and operational validity refers to the extent that inputs (the variables and the relationships between them) and outputs (the results), represent the real-world. We now consider model validation in more detail.

VALIDATION AND VALIDATION APPROACHES

There are a number of frameworks for validating simulation models (Klein & Herskovitz, 2005; Louie & Carley, 2008; Midgley, Marks, & Kunchamwar, 2007 ; Moss, 2008; Richiardi, et al., 2006). Petty (2010) compares the simuland with the conceptual model (*conceptual model validity)* and the results obtained during execution (*operational validity)*. Louie and Carley (2008), following Sargent (2004), suggest determining data appropriateness, accuracy and sufficiency *(data validity)*. Richiardi et al. (2006) present a contrasting view and consider five different types of validity. Other authors recommend assessing necessary and sufficient conditions (Häge, 2007); internal validation and parallel validation using multiple measures (Verkuilen, 2005); replicative, predictive, and structural validity (Troitzsch, 2004) as well as more generally comparing the model to the simuland and other well validated models (Edmonds, 2003). Validity is assessed using different techniques and no consensus exists as to what validity is or how it is determined (see Louie & Carley, 2008; Midgley, et al., 2007; Petty, 2010; and Sargent, 2004 for examples of validation techniques). In this chapter we take the view that validity is the extent to which the model inputs and outputs represent the real-world.

There are at least two views regarding validation processes. Empiricists establish validity through the rigorous application of quantitative validation tools (Petty, 2010; Sargent, 2004). Such processes are not always applicable to fuzzy set theory where natural language plays an important role and privileging quantitative validation is not necessarily appropriate. The contrasting view presents validation as a social process with the modelers using "intuition" or "judgment" to confirm validity (David, 2009; Richiardi, et al., 2006). We take a moderate position noting that by using a combination of methods and by accumulating comparisons, models become progressively validated. In line with the social perspective we note that researchers must take responsibility for identifying the optimal strategy for model validation.

Generally, conceptual validity requires experts to carefully compare the conceptual model with the real world (face validity process) and track the behavior of elements to establish whether behavior is similar to the real world (trace analysis) (Sargent, 2004). However, conceptual validity alone is not sufficient. Models with good conceptual validity may not perform and models with limited conceptual validity may provide excellent representations of the real world (Küppers & Lenhard, 2005).

Comparing model results with the real world requires data sufficiency and this is at the heart of the validation problem for marketers. Louie and Carley (2008) highlight that favoring statistical and quantitative procedures for operational validity is common (see Law & Kelton, 1999). Yet quantitative data is not always available or even necessary when conducting fuzzy set theory simulation. Using validation tools with limited data has lower statistical power and "carr(y)ies the least weight in convincing others that the model is valid" (Louie & Carley, 2008, p. 252). If the simuland is not observable, operational validity can be extrapolated by exploring model behavior using sensitivity analysis and comparing to other models (Sargent, 2004). Calibrated grounding can also establish model validity with limited data (Schreiber & Carley, 2007). This technique uses a two-step approach, grounding the model using empirical data and then internally calibrating model processes to reflect the simuland.

Assessing Validity in Fuzzy Set Models

External evidence is used when specifying set membership and set relations, as well as making judgments about set membership, allowing real world calibration and "well-constructed fuzzy sets" (Ragin, 2008, p. 71). In the social sciences external frameworks often use case-based data (Kvist, 2007) and modeling processes involve repeated and sustained comparisons between theory, empirical evidence, and the conceptual and executable models. Building fuzzy models is a process of continuously striving for greater validity through constant comparisons rather than only assessing validity as the last step.

Determining empirical support for set relations and membership functions is a component of validation and considers the consistency and coverage of set relations, as well as the calibration of membership functions (Kvist, 2007; Ragin, 2000, 2008; Verkuilen, 2005). Consistency is the extent to which cases with the same set relations configuration share the same outcomes and determines the necessary conditions for a specific outcome. Coverage describes the extent that an outcome is "explained" by a configuration set and provides the researcher with an understanding of the "relevance of the necessary condition" (Ragin, 2008, p. 44). Calibration is the process of formally describing the set membership function and matching it to an external standard. Thus, calibrated fuzzy sets enable specification of whether a case is in (or not in) a set and allows exploration of how particular conditions impact outcomes (Ragin, 2008; Smithson & Verkuilen,

2006). By considering each of these processes it is possible to make assertions regarding the validity of the model.

The options available for assessing validity in fuzzy set models are often limited. This is because the empirical data used in fuzzy set modeling may be case-based with qualitative constructs and small-N sample sizes. Strategies that may be used in these situations can include:

- *Sensitivity analysis* and *comparison testing* (Sargent, 2004);
- *The Turing test* where validity is established when it is not possible to distinguish between real world behavior and that generated by the model (Petty, 2010; Sargent, 2004);
- *Predictive validation* where model outputs are compared to empirical real world data (generally graphical comparisons for small-N cases, but they may include confidence intervals and statistical tests) (Petty, 2010; Sargent, 2004).

The use of fuzzy models is relatively limited in marketing with even fewer papers discussing validity treatments. Much of the work illustrates possible uses of fuzzy methods (Meier & Werro, 2007; Shipley, Korvin, & Omer, 1996). Some discuss model development processes and validity improvements (see for example, Häge, 2007; Verkuilen, 2005). Only a few describe both rigorous model development processes and validity assessment (for example, Olaru & Smith, 2005; Streit & Borenstein, 2009). Both of these researchers use graphic comparison methods of outputs against real world values. Olaru and Smith (2005) resolve the limited data problem using a hold-out sample, making visual comparisons and producing "hit ratios" (of correct classification). We will now illustrate a predictive validity process (as categorized by Petty (2010)) using case based linguistic data. Linguistic data is commonly used within the business marketing domain but there is limited discourse on the use of this data within simulation validation processes.

SIMULATION CONTEXT

This section provides details of the simulation context, viz. the simuland, the conceptual model and case data used in the validation process.

The Simuland and the Conceptual Model

The fuzzy modeling process begins by specifying the simuland and the model requirements (to facilitate subsequent accreditation). We are interested in the emergent processes in innovation networks and what combinations of network characteristics contribute to innovation success. These are questions of significance for marketing researchers as existing explanations for innovation success have been incomplete, particularly for discontinuous radical innovation (Elfring & Halsink, 2003; Ferguson, Paulin, Möslien, & Müller, 2005; Möller, Rajala, & Svahn, 2005; Walter, Auer, & Ritter, 2006).

The conceptual model was established based on previous literature briefly summarized in Table 1. The model comprises the following variables: actors and the interactions between them; the resources they control in the network (including social capital, knowledge and access to complementary innovations); and the broader environmental context.

Access to capital, knowledge and commercialization experience are critical to innovation development (Pittaway, Robertson, Munir, Denyer, & Neely, 2004). Two types of knowledge (product and process) have a direct impact on the development of the innovation. Complementary products or technologies are also necessary for innovation commercialization and access to these complementary resources is linked to innovation

success (Fershtman & Kamien, 1992). Social capital positively impacts information flow and network innovativeness (Pittaway, et al., 2004; Trippl & Tödtling, 2007). Financial backers or manufacturers supply resources and refresh capital through successful innovations (considerably increasing knowledge and skills). Environment munificence moderates innovation adoption and diffusion. Network innovation is the resulting increase in resources throughout the network (financial and knowledge). This paper describes a validation process and will not justify the conceptual model.

Selecting the Case Study

Innovation processes occur within business networks where case methodologies allow researchers to explore process flows at the network level. Therefore, the decision concerning case selection is important. For this project the case selection decision criteria include:

- The importance of radical innovation rather than incremental innovation in creating business network dynamics with rapid change;
- 'Green' energy is a topical industry and generates interest throughout the community and the government policy sector;
- Access to organizations allowing the researchers to conduct interviews; and
- A large amount of secondary data to triangulate the interviews.

The case selected describes the innovation of thin-film crystalline silicon on glass (CSG) photovoltaic (PV) solar cells during the period 1985-2008 in Australia (and internationally as the case develops). Thin-film CSG technology enables the production of robust solar cells, which during pre-production testing set international benchmarks for solar conversion efficiency. The case considers the innovation and commercialization story from the

Table 1. Conceptual model variables

Variable	Definition	Levels
Focal actor	Organization or individual with the following role or roles: manufacturer; research and development; and financial backer	Individual variable - Manufacturer; Research and Development; Financial backer
Number of Actors in the Network by Type • number Manufacturers • number RDs • number Financial Backers	Number of actors by type in proportion to the total number of actors in the network	Network variable – few, medium, high
Financial Resources (Jayanthi, Roth, Kristal, & Venu, 2009)	Monetary resources accessed to finance innovation	Individual variable – relative finances accumulated/ lost since previous episode – low, medium, high
Product Knowledge Resource (Ford & Saren, 2001)	Specialized product development knowledge	Individual variable – relative knowledge development of focal actor – low, medium, high
Process Knowledge Resource (Ford & Saren, 2001)	Specialized manufacturing process knowledge	Individual variable – relative knowledge development of focal actor – low, medium, high
Uniqueness of Knowledge	Relevance and uniqueness of knowledge resource to obtain advantage	Individual variable – low, medium, high
Complementary Products (Sengupta, 1998; Staudenmayer, Tripsas, & Tucci, 2005)	Products that improve the value of the focus innovation within the product system	Network variable – low, medium, high
Social Capital (Nahapiet & Ghoshal, 1998)	Ability of organization to access present and future network resources	Network variable – relationship capital developed within the broader network – low, medium, high
Environmental Munificence (Koka, Madhavan, & Prescott, 2006)	Amount of resources available to the organization from the environment	Network variable – low, medium, high
Changes in Financial Resources		Network output variable – negative, minimal positive, high positive
Changes in Knowledge Resources		Network output variable – low, medium, high

perspective of three main actors, two businesses (Pacific Solar P/L, CSG Solar Australia P/L) and a University (University of New South Wales). The case begins during the pre-innovation period and looks at precursor technology and ends when businesses who bought the CSG technology ceased operations at the end of 2008. This case "fits" the simulation context—it is a radical innovation, and the case provides information on each of the target variables for the simulation model.

Empirical data was publicly available and includes various reports and case summaries published by government/s, government departments, journals, press releases, popular media reports and company websites. Employing search strategies for maximum output is crucial to generate outputs of sufficient variety. Documents ranging from research reports and journal articles describing the technology to reports and information that described aspects of the innovation process, the actors and activities are necessary for producing a holistic case. Data was filtered to exclude material that exclusively focused on the technology and the science (compared to the innovation process) as it did not relate to the research focus. For example, excluded data described the types of experiments conducted, the chemical processes used to create the thin film etc. In this context, details of the technology were only relevant to the extent that it could be used to assess the "novelty" of the innovation.

Case Summary

Throughout the case description references to source documents are provided in square brackets, viz, [ETS018] is a report on the commercialization of photovoltaic research in Australia by Muriel Watt for a government department in 2003 and is provided in Table 4 (see Appendix). Modified narrative event sequencing (Buttriss & Wilkinson, 2006) was used to identify critical points in the history of the focal case. Critical events are shown below and provide a framework for constructing a story around the focal case.

A leading Australian university (UNSW) develops CSG technology through an established research group that had previous successes in earlier technologies [ETS025]. The research group establishes an international reputation in PV technologies and successfully obtains financial funding (Australian Research Council ARC) to establish a research centre—the Centre for Photovoltaic Devices and Systems (1991-1994) [ETS024]. The Centre had an operational pilot line for the fabrication of buried contact solar cells and generates royalties through licensing agreements with BP Solar Pty Ltd [ETS018]. During 1992, Unisearch Pty Ltd (wholly owned by UNSW) commences marketing of buried contact cells creating a strong revenue stream for further building their research output, including work on CSG thin film technologies. The snapshot for this early pre-innovation network is shown in Figure 2 and displays the major players from 1985 to 1994.

During this pre-innovation period centre researchers (Professor Martin Green, Dr. Stuart Wenham and Dr. Zhengrong Shi, among others) make gradual improvements of thin film PV technologies optimizing procedures for the fabrication of CSG PV cells (for which proof of

concept had previously been established) [ETS024]. In 1995 a spin-off company (Pacific Solar Pty Ltd) commences operations and is jointly owned by Unisearch Ltd (30%) UNSW and Pacific Power [ETS023].

During this same period the research group at the University of New South Wales becomes a special research centre funded by the ARC. Pacific Solar P/L maintains strong links with the researchers by engaging the Centre for contract research and seconding staff to assist with developmental research [ETS025]. This first stage in the development of the thin-film CSG PV technology is shown in Figure 3.

Recognizing that complimentary technologies are essential for commercialization, Pacific Solar establish a wholly owned subsidiary to develop a low cost modular inverter [ETS017] which proves to be crucial in creating a revenue stream. Inverter sales initially compliment the first generation buried cell solar panels made by BP solar. Figure 4 shows the development of the early commercialization network.

Pacific Power (a state owned utility company) funding is crucial for the early commercialization of the CSG technology but is stopped in 2001. By 2001, Pacific Solar needs further capital to fund the ongoing development and commercialization of the CSG technology. Eurosolare SpA (a subsidiary of the Italian energy conglomerate Eni SpA) purchased a 25% holding in Pacific Solar. At the time Eurosolare SpA had 5 MW operating capacity and the investment was viewed as strategically significant [ETS012]. Not only did Eurosolare SpA become the European distributor for the modular inverter [ETS035], but the investment provides important public confirmation of Eni SpA's interest in environmentally sustainable energy solutions [ETS012]. Figure 5 shows the network for ongoing commercialization of the CSG technology.

In 2001 one of the key research team members (Shi) leaves the UNSW and his role in Pacific

Figure 2. Pre-innovation network (1985-1994)

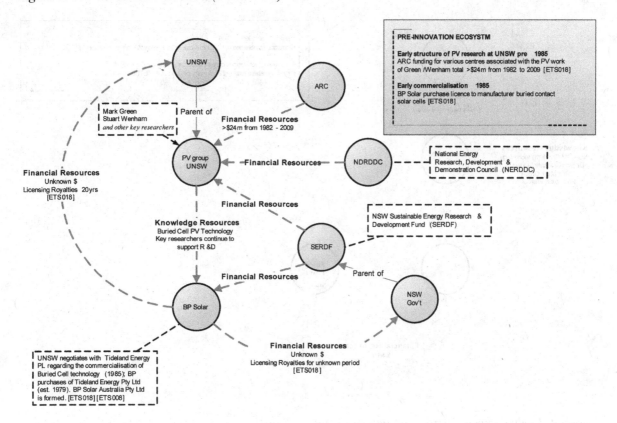

Solar and establishes what is today one of the world's largest manufacturers (Suntech) of solar panels [ETS001]. Commercialization work continues at Pacific Solar, however, it is becoming clear that considerable further investment is necessary to fully commercialize the technology. In 2004 Pacific Solar sold the technology rights to CSG Solar P/L. David Hogg, (previously from Unisearch Ltd and the Managing Director at Pacific Power) joins CSG Solar P/L as part of the management team. Over twenty former employees of Pacific Solar own substantial shares in the new company. Shortly after joining CSG Solar P/L, Hogg moves to Germany taking up a senior management position in the parent company. This final "mature" commercialization network is shown in Figure 6.

A consortium of European investors, who were themselves either directly involved in solar cell production or interested in sustainable energy production, backs CSG Solar AG. The company has financial support from Land Saxony-Anhalt (local government) and from the European Union European Funds for Regional Development (EFRE) [ETS003]. CSG Solar AG continues the development of the thin-film technology and by 2006 commences mass production of thin-firm CSG cells and reaches the milestone of 24/7 production in 2007 [ETS004]. By 2008 the company is producing 13 MW per annum [ETS039]. However, by the end of the year the company closes the manufacturing plant and lays off a substantial proportion of their workforce [ETS045].

Figure 3. Development network (1995 – 1996)

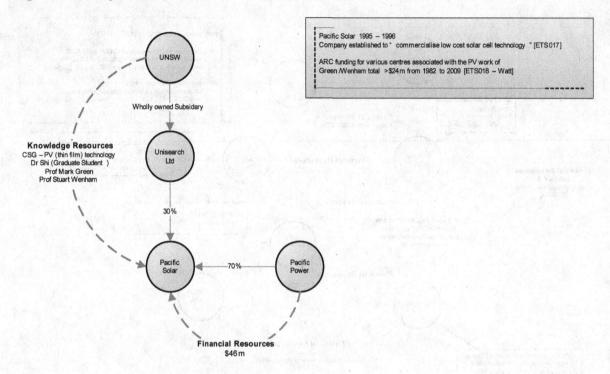

Figure 4. Early commercialization 1 network (1996 – 2000)

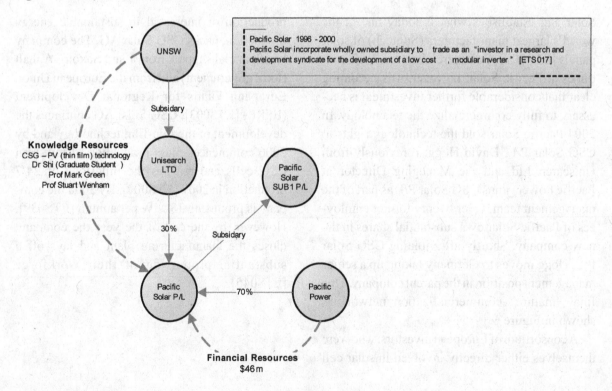

Figure 5. Early commercialization 2 network (2000 – 2001)

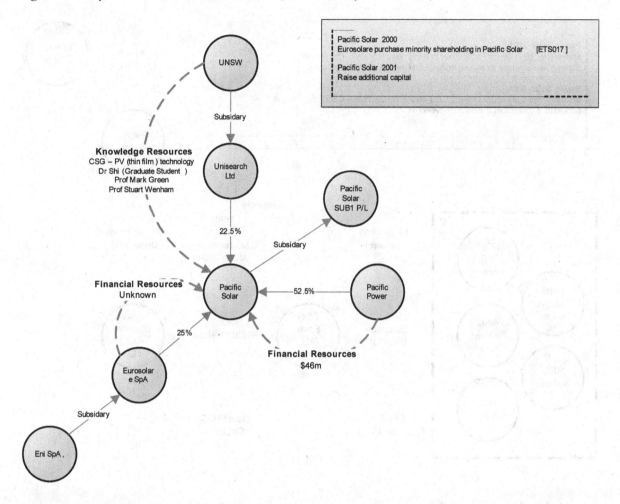

ILLUSTRATING A VALIDATION PROCESS

Given the lack of discussion concerning validating fuzzy set theory models, a flow chart is developed for this project. The flow chart (Figure 7) provides an overview of the fuzzy model development process, highlighting the points for assessing model validity (shown in grey).

Although the figure implies a highly ordered sequential process, experience indicates many recursive processes inevitably occur. These are shown as feedback loops and in order to improve clarity they are simplified. We show the fuzzy modeling process in three main steps: (1) identi-

fication of the variables' domains and description *(deriving the fuzzy inputs)*; (2) extraction of the initial set of rules *(deriving rules)*; and (3) review and refinement of the fuzzy-rule based system (FRBS) *(reviewing and refining the FRBS)*. In this part of the process, attention is directed to improving the validity of the model (rather than assessing validity). At the end of this three step process we demonstrate how operational validity can be assessed using statistical techniques. We now consider Figure 7 in more detail.

Before the first step, the case was analyzed for the critical events described in the previous section. Critical events were identified when radical change occurred in the innovation network and

Figure 6. Mature commercialization 3 network (2001 – 2008)

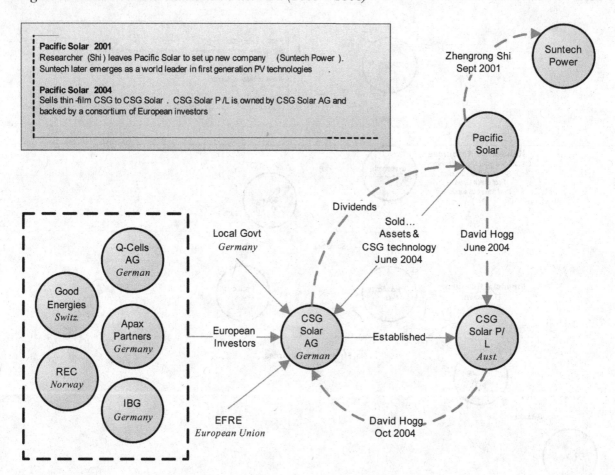

coincided with large capital investments, players entering or leaving the network and/or commercialization of technology. In developing the five critical events researchers considered which variables played an important role in the innovation process. At the same time, the case data was analyzed using content analytic approaches as described by Luna-Reyes and Anderson (2003) and Streit and Borenstein (2009) where coding corresponds to the model variables. Case analysis permitted the researchers to make a preliminary assessment of conceptual validity by considering the alignment between the conceptual model and the case data. With fuzzy models it is not possible to fully assess conceptual validity until the FRBS is specified (step 3), as illustrated the validation

process produces successively more granulated descriptions of the case data enabling progressively more detailed comparisons between the case and the conceptual model to be made. The researchers made the preliminary determination that the model demonstrated the potential for conceptual validity.

Step 1: Deriving Fuzzy Inputs

A number of scenarios are developed from each critical event. A scenario describes a critical event from the perspective of a focal actor. For example scenario three, given in Table 4, shows the pre-innovation network from the perspective of the photovoltaic group at UNSW. Each scenario is

Figure 7. The development of the fuzzy model, specifying set membership, assessing consistency and coverage of set relations, calibration of membership functions and assessing validity

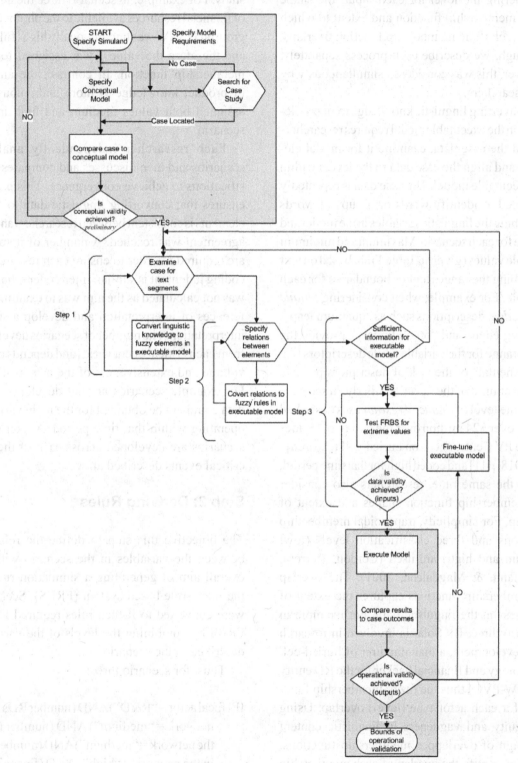

analyzed to derive fuzzy inputs. This involves considering the level for each input, the shape of the membership function and extent to which each level of the membership function overlaps. Although, we describe each process separately, however, this was considered simultaneously by the researchers.

Converting linguistic knowledge to fuzzy elements in the executable model requires researchers to read the case data, examine it for model elements and align the case data to the levels within the executable model. The case data is repeatedly inspected to identify words or groups of words describing the linguistic variables in the model and is done for each scenario. Maximum and minimum variable values (given in Table 1) are based on text describing the ranges and/or boundaries for each variable. For example, when considering *unique knowledge,* descriptions such as "quantum leap", "leading edge" and "revolutionary" provide the upper range for the variable while descriptors like "incremental" or the lack of descriptors provide the lower limit of the range. Similarly, in scenario three, the level of *financial resources* is described as "... over $24 million over the past two decades [to the PV Centre focus on buried-cell research]" [ETS018, p 11] and coded high for that time period.

At the same time, researchers also consider the membership function shapes and extent of overlap. For simplicity, trapezoidal membership functions and three classification levels (low; medium and high) are used (Cordón, Herrera, Hoffmann, & Magdalena, 2001). The overlap of membership functions captures the extent of fuzziness in the linguistic data. For example in scenario three, BP Solar is involved in research and development, a manufacturer of buried-cell technology and financial backer for the RD entity (UNSW-PVC) thus the fuzzy membership functions for each actor type (level) overlap. Using ambiguity and vagueness in linguistic content as a sign of overlapped membership functions, we then specify the overlap of each membership function. A membership value of 1 was allocated

when crisp information was available in the case study. For example, in scenario three the amount of financial resources available to the photovoltaic group at UNSW was unequivocally high (fully in) and therefore the value 1 was assigned for this membership function. In contrast, the amount of product knowledge is more ambiguous and assigned both values medium and high in this scenario.

Each researcher independently analyzes scenarios and then discusses and compares classifications to achieve convergence. This process ensures that converting linguistic data to fuzzy elements is consistent between researchers and that agreement was reached. A number of iterations are required in order to ensure each researcher's coding judgment is similar. Inter-coder reliability was not calculated as the aim was to examine differences of interpretation and develop a shared interpretation. The number of scenarios developed from each critical event varies and depends on the volume and extensiveness of the data available. For example scenarios are not developed were data could not be obtained for the main variables operating within that time period. A total of 21 scenarios are developed across each of the five critical events described above.

Step 2: Deriving Rules

The objective this step to define the relations between the variables in the scenario with the overall aim of generating a simulation rule for the fuzzy-rule based system (FRBS). Scenarios were converted to if-then rules required for the FRBS by combining the levels of the variables described in the scenario.

Thus, for scenario three:

IF (focal actor = "R&D") AND (number RDs in the network = "medium") AND (number Ms in the network = "medium") AND (number FBs in the network = "high") AND (financial resources = "high") AND (product knowledge resources = "medium") AND (uniqueness of knowledge = "medium") AND (process knowledge resources = "medium") AND (complementary products = "medium") AND (social capital = "medium") AND (environmental munificence = "low") THEN changes in knowledge resources [OR financial resources] = "medium".

Each scenario generates at least two fuzzy rules and therefore, two records in the fuzzy-rule based system (one rule for each output variable). If there are multiple levels for the input and output variables in the conceptual model, multiple rules are generated for each scenario. This is illustrated in scenario three where multiple levels are assigned for six input variables (for example, as mentioned previously process knowledge is ambiguous and has two levels) thus, the FRBS includes 64 individual rules to describe this scenario ($2^6=64$).

Step 3: Reviewing and Refining the FRBS

We review and refine the FRBS by addressing both consistency and coverage of the FRBS more formally (Ragin, 2000, 2008). Although the consistency and coverage of the FRBS was considered simultaneously we discuss each refinement process separately, first addressing coverage and then the consistency of the FRBS.

Our model is complex with eleven input variables in different combinations. We begin by simplifying the FRBS to facilitate the assessment coverage (and consistency). This is accomplished using multidimensional scaling (MDS), first to group input variables and then to identify the white spots where rule coverage is incomplete. The first MDS adequately describes the variable space (Stress = 0.0387 and RSQ=0.992) and combines the eleven input variables to create five variable clusters:

- Structure of the network – number of each type of actor (R&D, M, and FB)
- Knowledge resources (product/innovation and processes) as well as complementary products,
- Social capital and environmental munificence,
- Financial resources, and
- Knowledge uniqueness.

The correlations between input variables, given in the Appendix (Table 6), support the MDS clustering, providing additional evidence that the five variable clusters could be used for further analysis. Also variable clusters make some empirical sense with themes such as: network structure; innovation resources; network resources and radicalness of the innovation.

Having simplified the data, we then used MDS to assess the coverage of the FRBS. The second MDS analysis had equally good measures of fit (S-Stress = 0.0213; Tucker's coefficient of congruence =0.996) and offers researchers a variety of data presentation approaches. We use scatter plots to visualize the "white spots" in the FRBS (21 scenarios and 722 rules), where coverage is inadequate. Figure 8 shows the scatter plots between the grouped variables.

To interpret the scatter plots, each diagram is reviewed to assess the distribution of coverage. Scatter diagrams should have a random distribution. Figure 8 illustrates that *knowledge uniqueness* does not vary and that coverage is incomplete. However, we note that this is not surprising because the case involves a radical innovation where knowledge uniqueness is inevitably high. We also note that there is less variability in the FRBS for *environmental munificence* and *social capital*. In the case, social capital is high because the central actors are fairly constant and have strong relatively stable relationships. Furthermore, although the environmental conditions change, they do so quite slowly. An example of a scatter diagram with good coverage is *knowledge resources/complementary products* and *financial resources.*

Figure 8 provides an initial overview of possible coverage problems. To develop a more detailed understanding of possible coverage problems we use a series of scatter plots for individual variables. These individual scatter plots revealed a number of areas where coverage could be improved, namely:

- Low number of RDs and low social capital,
- Low number of M and high munificence of the environment,
- High level of process knowledge and medium/high uniqueness of knowledge,
- High level of process knowledge, high complementary products and low level of munificence and low/medium level of social capital.

Prior to conducting further analysis, we address the coverage problems by carefully re-examining the case data for new scenarios. During this refining stage a further seven scenarios relevant to the scope of the model were added. The final study uses 28 scenarios as the basis of rule development. The data was re-analyzed using the procedure described above and noted that, by including additional rules, data coverage improved. Table 2 provides the relative frequency of the each variable in the final fuzzy model (28 scenarios with 874 rules).

Table 2 shows an unbalanced design (for example, there are fewer manufacturers and fewer scenarios with high levels of process knowledge and complementary products). However, this is consistent with the literature for radical innovation and with this type of disruptive technology as there are inevitably fewer manufacturers and corresponding lower levels of process knowledge and complementary products (naturally this is different today but during the case period this pattern was evident). The unbalanced design is

also expected when infeasible combinations of inputs are discarded from the FRBS – an advantage of the empirical derivation process used.

Despite the data limitations, we conclude that there is sufficient case data to describe the conceptual model. Thus, the preliminary determination regarding acceptable conceptual validity can be confirmed. We note the specific boundary, that conceptual validity has been established for "radical or disruptive" innovation contexts. Further consideration is required to extend the application of this model beyond this specific context.

As we have noted, while examining the FRBS for coverage we simultaneously considered its consistency. We now describe this process in more detail. Consistency is established when a series or conditions are met in the FRBS. Specifically, (1) the same sets of input values cannot result in completely different outputs; (2) infeasible combinations should not occur; (3) the model should produce meaningful results even when run with extreme values provided they are within the FRBS boundaries; and (4) the model should fail (execution halt) when run with extreme values just outside the FRBS boundaries.

The first two consistency checks are completed using a range of inspection strategies. For example, we examined groups of similar input combinations and the corresponding output value by inspecting the rules spreadsheet using filters in excel. We also inspected the multivariate outlier points on scatter plots for grouped input variables (using MDS as described above). Outliers may involve infeasible combinations (for example, rules where Financial Backers have no financial resources). Correlations between input and output variable were also used to evaluate consistency. The FRBS may be regarded inconsistent when correlations between input and output variables are not significant. These preliminary checks did not reveal any problem with consistency in the FRBS.

We also evaluated consistency by running the model and testing its behavior under a range of

Figure 8. Assessing coverage of the rule space for groups of input variables (preliminary FRBS with 21 scenarios and 722 rules)

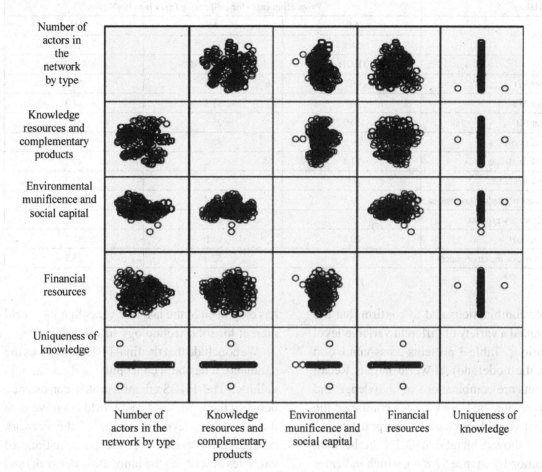

extreme conditions. We developed feasible input data which was just inside and just outside the model boundaries. First, input data was randomly generated to reflect established input ranges and according to the non-parametric correlations presented in the Appendices (Table 6). Out of range input data was adjusted to just exceed the limits of input ranges and correlations. As anticipated the model failed to execute when out-off-domain values where used. The model ran successfully and produced the expected responses (outcomes) as judged by the researchers. This provided further evidence confirming the consistency of the FRBS.

Summarizing Operational Validity

After reviewing and refining the fuzzy rules based system (step 3) it is possible to demonstrate the extent to which the fuzzy model results correspond to the real-world case data and assess the bounds of operational validity. This is accomplished by executing the model with both case input data and randomly generated input data (created along the lines described in step 3 using the established input ranges and according to the non-parametric correlations presented in the Appendices (Table 6)). Prior to using the randomly generated data, each record was reviewed by the researchers to remove

Table 2. Proportion of records from the case obtained for each input variable (n=874)

Input variables	Proportion cases for calibrating fuzzy inputs (%)		
	FB	M	RD
1. Focal actor			
	54.5	17.6	27.9
Variables	HIGH	MEDIUM	LOW
2a. Number RD	46.7	31.4	22.0
2b. Number M	6.9	31.8	61.3
2c. Number FB	30.0	25.6	44.4
3. Financial resources	29.5	38.0	32.5
4. Product knowledge	17.2	33.2	49.7
5. Process knowledge	6.9	20.8	72.3
6. Uniqueness of product knowledge	30.4	25.4	44.2
7. Complementary products	6.9	22.6	70.5
8. Social capital	20.8	65.0	14.2
9. Munificence of the environment	11.4	52.9	35.7

infeasible combinations and to confirm that the data included a variety of different variable/level combinations. Table 3 presents cross-tabulation results of the model and real-world outputs. Recall that outputs are combinations of knowledge and financial resources. Here we have combined the two output variable for ease of interpretation.

Table 3 shows a hit ratio of 93.7% (higher than classification by chance 57.8%), which indicates this is good consistency between the model output and the real-world situation and good alignment between the operational model and the simuland. Thus, operational validity is confirmed.

This determination notwithstanding, the result also highlights the data requirements for further model refinement. For example, the model does not have rules, which reflect highly successful innovation outcomes (e.g., high increases in the network resources – both knowledge and in particular increases in financial resources). This can be attributed to the limited commercial success achieved by the participants in the innovation network. This seems to be quite typical for innovation radical technology, which often does not achieve full commercialization until much later in technology development cycle. For example, it

has only been in the last five years that the world market for solar technology has flourished.

We conclude that the final FRBS describes the simuland, it has both conceptual and operational validity. The FRBS, demonstrates consistency between the model and real-world data. We note that there is uneven coverage of the network configuration spaces (i.e. the combinations of variables describing the innovation network) and possible omissions of behavioral rules for those configurations. Thus, although the model provides an adequate description of networks involved in "radical or disruptive" innovation, it cannot be applied beyond these "boundaries". Further efforts to calibrate the model for other contexts including using cases describing other radical innovations particularly those with commercial success overcomes the uneven coverage.

DISCUSSION

Fuzzy models allow researchers to systematically explore ambiguity and complexity in marketing systems and handle linguistic inputs to develop different insights from case-based and qualita-

Table 3. Cross tabulation of observed and predicted fuzzy output

Observed output	Predicted fuzzy output			
	Low	Medium	High	Percent Correct
Low	455	10	0	97.8%
Medium	21	125	4	83.3%
High	0	6	34	85.0%
Overall Percentage	72.7%	21.5%	5.8%	93.7%

tive data. However, to gain acceptance within the research community, improvements in communicating model development processes and validity assessments are required. This chapter focuses on these issues and illustrates validation processes that can be used. From these processes the researchers learnt a number of valuable lessons listed below:

Lesson 1: Careful Case Selection to Enable Model Building, Calibration, Verification, and Validation

Modeling requires sufficiently detailed evidence and preferably longitudinal data to provide enough scenarios for model 'training' and 'testing'. We use a rich evolving case where detailed documentation is available to assess variable relationships. As the focal company is a university (public organization), the requirement for transparency and open documentation ensures much of the information is publicly available. Private research organizations without the same transparency/public accountability requirements make such documentation difficult to obtain.

Lesson 2: Do not Rely on one Type of Information Source

The focus on discourse is very important because adjectives used within the case material provide important criteria for considering fuzzy classification levels. Data collection should draw from multiple sources to ensure that the discourse is descriptive enough to include numerous adjectives. For example media reports and company press releases often use more descriptive discourse than journal articles and government reports. Yet, a mixture of both is required to give the holistic picture and allow case triangulation.

Lesson 3: Balance Team Homogeneity against the Need to Maintain Richness in Interpretation

Reaching convergence on subjective assessment is confounded by the (in)compatibility of language between diverse team members requiring development of shared meanings between team members. Greater team homogeneity would facilitate this process however this may limit the richness of the ideas which is the strength fuzzy models that should be retained.

Lesson 4: Use Hybrids/ Combinations of Methodologies and not Undervalue the Subjective Assessments

Given the nature of fuzzy modeling, classical data validation processes are insufficient and therefore multi-method validation processes are required. Within the suite of validation processes the requirement to incorporate qualitative data along with expert knowledge means that both empirical and subjective processes need to work together.

Lesson 5: Resource Saving in the Validation Process

The full factorial design for the conceptual model has 177,147 combinations of inputs or rules. Researchers using a full-factorial design would need to simplify this large number of rules by examining and eliminating unviable rules. However, realistic rules may be deleted and unrealistic rules may be included in such an elimination process. In contrast, the validation process used here efficiently produces a FRBS system comprising 874 rules that are based on real world data. Further we note that by assessing the consistency and coverage of the FRBS we are able to establish the boundaries of model validity. We argue that this approach enables researchers to identify a compact and more general set of rules without the excessive effort required to trim down a full factorial set of combinations for unbelievable situations.

Lesson 6: Coverage and Consistency

Ensuring coverage and consistency of set relations with real-world data is critical if trust is to be developed in using fuzzy set theory models (Kvist, 2007; Ragin, 2000, 2008). This paper describes a process that researchers can use to investigate whether there fuzzy models meet the requirements of coverage and consistency. Given that many fuzzy models investigate complex phenomena the ability to obtain real-world quantitative data is not always possible. The process described in this paper outlines a credible process for investigating coverage and consistency that does not privilege quantitative data over qualitative data. Both types of data can be used in the process described. Using MDS to assess consistency and coverage gives an unbiased process of assessment rather than subjective assessment by the researchers involved. The process illustrated allows reviewers of fuzzy set theory models confidence that consistency and coverage can be assessed and improved by researchers.

Although we highlight six important lessons, readers need to be aware that their fuzzy models may have different optimal validation strategies depending on the research focus and data available. These lessons are not final as further refinement of different validation processes will improve model development. For example sensitivity analysis will also improve operational validity.

CONCLUSION

Further improvements in validation processes are important if fuzzy set theory model development is to be become a more prominent tool within marketing research. Future avenues to take our validation processes include considering other innovation contexts such as incremental innovation. We note that these innovation networks are very different and that the combinations of variables may not be consistent with the current model. Yet, given the flexibility of fuzzy system we don't expect the model output to vary. Another avenue to further improve validation processes is to conduct sensitivity analysis on the variables and analyze whether outputs dramatically change.

In conclusion, we highlight the importance of developing a validation strategy for model developers and the importance of articulating model validation processes for improving wider acceptance of fuzzy set theory models within the marketing discipline. We demonstrate the application of a validity building and accessing methodology, it is possible to establish a set of relevant inferred inductive behavioral rules (using case-based data) and which when converted into fuzzy rules, could validly reproduce the real-world system. Using linguistic data, rather than quantitative data, works towards the strength of fuzzy set models, that is, ambiguity and incorporating natural language and we would recommend other researchers also consider these validation processes.

REFERENCES

Axtell, R., Axelrod, R., Epstein, J. M., & Cohen, M. D. (1996). Aligning simulation models: A case study and results. *Computational and Organizational Organization Theory, 1*(2), 123–141. doi:10.1007/BF01299065

Buttriss, G., & Wilkinson, I. F. (2006). Using narrative sequence methods to advance international entrepreneurship theory. *Journal of International Entrepreneurship, 4*, 157–174. doi:10.1007/s10843-007-0012-4

Cordón, O., Herrera, F., Hoffmann, F., & Magdalena, L. (2001). Genetic fuzzy systems: Evolutionary tuning and learning of fuzzy knowledge bases. In *Advances in fuzzy systems - Applications and theory*, (p. 488).

David, N. (2009). Validation and verification in social simulation: Patterns and clarification of terminology, In Squazzoni, F. (Ed.), *Epistemological aspects of computer simulation in the social sciences* (*Vol. 5466*, pp. 117–129). Berlin, Germany: Springer. doi:10.1007/978-3-642-01109-2_9

Donzé, L., & Meier, A. (2011). Applying fuzzy logic and fuzzy methods to marketing, In Meier, A., & Donzé, L. (Eds.), *Fuzzy methods for customer relationship management and marketing: Applications and classification*. Hershey, PA: IGI Global.

Edmonds, B. (2003). Towards an ideal social simulation language, In Simão Sichman, J., Bousquet, F., & Davidsson, P. (Eds.), *Multi-Agent-Based Simulation II* (*Vol. 2581*, pp. 105–124). Berlin, Germany: Springer. doi:10.1007/3-540-36483-8_8

Elfring, T., & Halsink, W. (2003). Networks in entrepreneurship: The case of high-technology firms. *Small Business Economics, 21*, 409–422. doi:10.1023/A:1026180418357

Ferguson, R. J., Paulin, M., Möslien, K., & Müller, C. (2005). Relational governance, communication and the performance of biotechnology partnerships. *Journal of Small Business and Enterprise Development, 12*(3), 395–408. doi:10.1108/14626000510612303

Fershtman, C., & Kamien, M. I. (1992). Cross licensing of complementary technologies. *International Journal of Industrial Organization, 10*(3), 329–348. doi:10.1016/0167-7187(92)90001-F

Ford, D., & Saren, M. J. (2001). *Managing and marketing technology*. London, UK: Thompson.

Häge, F. M. (2007). Constructivism, fuzzy sets and (very) small-N: Revisiting the conditions for communicative action, *Journal of Business Research, 60*(5), 512–521. doi:10.1016/j.jbusres.2007.01.009

Jayanthi, S., Roth, A., Kristal, M., & Venu, L. (2009). Strategic resource dynamics of manufacturing firms. *Management Science, 55*(6), 1060–1076. doi:10.1287/mnsc.1090.1002

Klein, E. E., & Herskovitz, P. J. (2005). Philosophical foundations of computer simulation validation. *Simulation & Gaming, 36*, 303–329. doi:10.1177/1046878104273437

Koka, R., Madhavan, R., & Prescott, J. (2006). The evolution of inter-firm networks: Environmental effects on patterns of network change. *Academy of Management Review, 33*(3), 721–737. doi:10.5465/AMR.2006.21318927

Küppers, G., & Lenhard, J. (2005). Validation of simulation: Patterns in the social and natural sciences. *Journal of Artificial Societies and Social Simulation, 8*(4), 3.

Kvist, J. (2007). Fuzzy set ideal type analysis. *Journal of Business Research, 60*(5), 474–481. doi:10.1016/j.jbusres.2007.01.005

Law, A. M., & Kelton, D. W. (1999). *Simulation modeling and analysis*. New York, NY: McGraw-Hill.

Louie, M. A., & Carley, K. M. (2008). Balancing the criticisms: Validating multi-agent models of social systems. *Simulation Modelling Practice and Theory*, *16*, 242–256. doi:10.1016/j.simpat.2007.11.011

Luna-Reyes, L. F., & Andersen, D. L. (2003). Collecting and analyzing qualitative data for system dynamics: methods and models. *System Dynamics Review*, *19*(4), 271–296. doi:10.1002/sdr.280

Maguire, S., McKelvey, B., Mirabeau, L., & Öztas, N. (2006). Complexity science and organization studies, In Clegg, S., Hardy, C., Nord, W., & Lawrence, T. (Eds.), *Handbook of organization studies* (pp. 164–214). London, UK: Sage.

Meier, A., & Werro, N. (2007). A fuzzy classification model for online customers. *Informatica*, *33*, 175–182.

Midgley, D., Marks, R., & Kunchamwar, D. (2007). Building and assurance of agent-based models: An example and challenge to the field. *Journal of Business Research*, *60*(8), 884–893. doi:10.1016/j.jbusres.2007.02.004

Möller, K., Rajala, A., & Svahn, S. (2005). Strategic business nets—Their type and management. *Journal of Business Research*, *58*, 1274–1284. doi:10.1016/j.jbusres.2003.05.002

Moss, S. (2008). Alternative approaches to the empirical validation of agent-based models. *Journal of Artificial Societies and Social Simulation*, *11*(1), 5.

Nahapiet, J., & Ghoshal, S. (1998). Social capital, intellectual capital, and the organizational advantage. *Academy of Management Review*, *23*, 242–266.

Olaru, D., & Smith, B. (2005). Modelling behavioural rules for daily activity scheduling using fuzzy logic. *Transportation Journal*, *32*(4), 423–441.

Petty, M. D. (2009). Verification and validation, In Sokolowski, J. A., & Banks, C. M. (Eds.), *Principles of modeling and simulation: A multidisciplinary approach* (pp. 121–149). Hoboken, NJ: John Wiley & Sons Inc.

Petty, M. D. (2010). Verification, validation and accreditation, In Sokolowski, J. A., & Banks, C. M. (Eds.), *Modeling and simulation fundamentals: Theoretical underpinnings and practical domains* (pp. 325–372). New Jersey: John Wiley & Sons. doi:10.1002/9780470590621.ch10

Piekkari, R., Plakoyiannaki, E., & Welch, C. (2010). 'Good' case research in industrial marketing: Insights from research practice. *Industrial Marketing Management*, *39*(1), 109–117. doi:10.1016/j.indmarman.2008.04.017

Pittaway, L., Robertson, M., Munir, K., Denyer, D., & Neely, A. (2004). Networking and innovation: A systematic review of the evidence. *International Journal of Management Reviews*, *5/6*(3&4), 137–168. doi:10.1111/j.1460-8545.2004.00101.x

Ragin, C. C. (2000). *Fuzzy-set social science*. Chicago, IL: University of Chicago Press.

Ragin, C. C. (2008). *Redesigning social inquiry: fuzzy sets and beyond*. Chicago, IL: University of Chicago Press.

Richiardi, M., Roberto, L., Saam, N., & Sonnessa, M. (2006). A common protocol for agent-based social simulation. *Journal of Artificial Societies and Social Simulation*, *9*(1).

Sargent, R. G. (2004). *Validation and verfication of simulation models*. Paper presented at the 36th Winter Simulation Conference, Washington, DC, USA.

Schreiber, C., & Carley, K. M. (2007). *Agent interactions in construct: An empirical validation using calibrated grounding.* Paper presented at the 2007 BRIMS Conference, Norfolk.

Sengupta, S. (1998). Some approaches to complementary product strategy. *Journal of Product Innovation Management, 15*(4), 352–367. doi:10.1016/S0737-6782(97)00106-9

Shipley, M. F., Korvin, A. D., & Omer, K. (1996). A fuzzy logic approach for determining expected values: A project management application. *The Journal of the Operational Research Society, 47*(4), 562–569.

Smithson, M., & Verkuilen, J. (2006). *Fuzzy set theory: Applications in the social sciences (vol. no. 07/147).* Thousand Oaks, CA: Sage Publications.

Staudenmayer, N., Tripsas, M., & Tucci, C. (2005). Interfirm modularity and its implications for product development. *Journal of Product Innovation Management, 22*(4), 303–321. doi:10.1111/j.0737-6782.2005.00128.x

Streit, R. E., & Borenstein, D. (2009). Structuring and modeling data for representing the behavior of agents in the governance of the Brazilian financial system. *Applied Artificial Intelligence, 23*, 316–345. doi:10.1080/08839510902804796

Trippl, M., & Tödtling, F. (2007). Developing biotechnology clusters in non-high technology regions—The case of Austria. *Industry and Innovation, 14*(1), 47–67. doi:10.1080/13662710601130590

Troitzsch, K. G. (2004). *Validating simulation models.* Paper presented at the 18th European Simulation Multiconference. Retrieved from http://citeseerx.ist.psu.edu/viewdoc/summary?doi=10.1.1.143.6554

Verkuilen, J. (2005). Assigning membership in a fuzzy set analysis. *Sociological Methods & Research, 33*, 462–496. doi:10.1177/0049124105274498

Walter, A., Auer, M., & Ritter, T. (2006). The impact of network capabilities and entrepreneurial orientation on university spin-off performance. *Journal of Business Venturing, 21*, 541–567. doi:10.1016/j.jbusvent.2005.02.005

Wilensky, U., & Rand, W. (2007). Making models match: Replicating an agent-based model. *Journal of Artificial Societies and Social Simulation, 10*(4), 1–22.

Windrum, P., Fagiolo, G., & Moneta, A. (2007). Empirical validation of agent-based models: Alternatives and prospects. *Journal of Artificial Societies and Social Simulation, 10*(2), 8.

KEY TERMS AND DEFINITIONS

Accreditation: The decision that a fuzzy simulation is able to perform the tasked it was designed to accomplish.

Conceptual Model: A description that specifies the key parts of the simulation and their relation to each other.

Conceptual Validity: The degree to which the conceptual model accurately reflects the simuland (real-world system).

Executable Model: A simulation model (using rules in fuzzy simulations) which when executed produces results.

Operational Validity: The degree to which the executable model produces results that reflect the simuland (real-world system).

Verification: An evaluation to determine if the conceptual model performs according to initial specifications, and that the executable model works as anticipated by the conceptual model.

APPENDIX

Table 4. Bibliography of case references

ETS001: Arise the sun king, *Sydney Morning Herald (SMH),* 12 September 2006
ETS003: Building on experience, *CSG Solar website,* Retrieved May 2008 from www.csgsolar.com.
ETS004: CSG Solar AG expands it workforce and moves to 24/7 operation, *CSG Solar press release,* 16 April 2007, Retrieved May 2008 from www.csgsolar.com.
ETS012: Eni increases its stake in the Australian Pacific Solar strengthening its presence in the renewable resources sector, *Eni press release,* 7 March, 2001. Retrieved May 2008 from www.eni.it.
ETS017: Pacific Power, *Auditor-General's Report to Parliament 2001,* NSW Government 2001.
ETS018: Watt, M (2003). *The commercialisation of photovoltaics research in Australia,* A report for Science and Innovation Mapping, Department of Education Science and Training, Australia.
ETS023: Preliminary Figures 2006, *Q-Cells AG presentation.* Retrieved May 2008 from www.q-cells.com.
ETS024: *1992 Annual Report,* Centre for Photovoltaic Devices and Systems, University of New South Wales, Australia.
ETS025: 1996 Annual Report, Photovoltaics Special Research Centre, University of New South Wales, Australia.
ETS035: Aussie solar system makes European debut, Pacific Solar press release, 25 October 2001, Retrieved May 2008 from www.ferret.com.au.
ETS039: Turning visions into reality, *CSG Solar website,*www.csgsolar.com, accessed May 2008
ETS045: Blue Square Energy Blues, Gunther Porfolio, 9 January 2009. Retrieved April 2010 from http://guntherportfolio.com.

Table 5. Classification of text elements, membership functions, evidence from the case (scenario three – during the pre-innovation network)

ACTORS -->	R&D:UNSW-PVC, BPS Manufacturer [Buried Cell] BPS FB: ARC, NERDDC, NSW SERDF, BPS

Variable	Membership Function	Exemplar Descriptors	Scenario 3 UNSW-PVC 1985-1994 [Buried-Cell]	Senario 3 Linguistic Membership Value	Scenario 3 Degree Of Membership
Focal actor (Main role)	**CRISP VALUES** 1=FB; 2=M; 3=RD **RANGES** {1, 2.2) = FB; (1.3, 2.7) = M; (1.8, 3} = RD	Use actual organization perspective	[3] R&D	3	1
Number of R&D	**RANGES** [0,1.2) = LOW (0.6, 2.4) = MED (1.8, 3] = HIGH	Used actual number	[MEDIUM - HIGH] 2	MEDIUM HIGH	0.60 0.72
Number of manufacturers	**RANGES** [0, 1) = LOW (0.6, 2.1) = MED (1.5, 3] = HIGH	Used actual number	[MEDIUM] 1	MEDIUM	1
Number of financial backers	**RANGES** [0, 2) = LOW (1, 5) = MED (4, 10] = HIGH	Used actual number	[HIGH] 4 - 7	HIGH	1

continued on following page

Table 5. Continued

Variable	Membership Function	Exemplar Descriptors	Senario 3 UNSW-PVC 1985-1994 [Buried-Cell]	Senario 3 Linguistic Membership Value	Scenario 3 Degree Of Membership
Financial resources (amount)	**RANGES** [0, 1.5) = LOW (0.4, 2.2) = MED (1.8, 3] = HIGH	Used actual investment: In this time period funding ranged from NEGLIGIBLE to PEAK VALUE of $24m	**[HIGH]** **[GENERAL]** Development and demonstration of a new PV technology past the initial research phase to a stage where commercialisation might be considered requires substantial investment. [ETS018, p21]; **[GENERAL]** ARC funding for fundamental research has been critical to the generation of new PV ideas and technologies.[ETS018, p21]; **[BURIED CELL]**... over $24 million over the past two decades [to the PV Centre focus on buried-cell research],... [ETS018, p 11]; **[BURIED CELL]** The initial idea for the laser grooved buried grid cell came out of ARC funded, research at the UNSW PV Centre. Further development of the idea was supported by funding from NERDDC and the NSW SERDF. [ETS018, p 16];	HIGH	1
Product Knowledge Resource (amount)	**RANGES** [0, 0.9) = LOW (0.6, 2.4) = MED (1.8, 3] = HIGH	LOWER: Small team, narrow focus, Incremental HIGHER: Critical Mass, Expertise, Patent Application	**[MED-HIGH]** **[GENERAL]**... a precursor to successful research outcomes has been the establishment of critical masses of research expertise and necessary infrastructure at Australian universities. [ETS018, p21]; **[NEW]** A new generation of double-sided bifacial buried contact solar cells designed for operation under about 3 suns' concentration is being developed for use within these modules and roof tiles. [ETS024, p25]; **[BURIED CELL]**... Incremental improvements in present cell technology to bring both laboratory and commercial practice closer to basic performance limits... [ETS024, p4];	MEDIUM HIGH	0.50 0.50

continued on following page

Table 5. Continued

Variable	Membership Function	Exemplar Descriptors	Senario 3 UNSW-PVC 1985-1994 [Buried-Cell]	Scenario 3 Linguistic Membership Value	Scenario 3 Degree Of Membership
Process Knowledge Resource (amount)	RANGES [0, 0.9) = LOW (0.6, 2.4) = MED (1.8, 3] = HIGH	LOWER: Upgrading, Incremental, Problems HIGHER: Major, Significant, New	[LOW-MEDIUM] [PROCESS] A major development for the buried contact solar cell during 1992 has been the development of a high speed multibladed dicing wheel saw capable of scribing the groove for a large area buried contact solar cell in only a few seconds. [ETS024, p25]; [INCREMENTAL]...upgrading the pilot line allowed research activities... [ETS024, p24];	LOW MEDIUM	0.33 0.33
Uniqueness of Knowledge	RANGES [0, 1.1) = LOW (0.6, 2.1) = MED (1.75, 3] = HIGH	LOWER: Not mentioned, Incremental, No change HIGHER, Groundbreaking, Break through, Quantum Leap, Revolutionary	[MEDIUM] [NEW] A new generation of double-sided bifacial buried contact solar cells designed for operation under about 3 suns' concentration is being developed for use within these modules and roof tiles. [ETS024, p25]; [INCREMENTAL] incremental improvements to present bulk silicon technology [ETS024, p6]	MEDIUM	1
Complementary Products	RANGES [0, 0.4) = LOW [0.25, 0.75) = MED [0.6, 1] = HIGH	LOWER: Upgrading, Incremental, Problems, New (to the team) HIGHER: Major, Significant	[LOW - MEDIUM] [COMPLEMENTARY]...A new area of work was the development of static concentrators for incorporation into either roof tiles or photovoltaic modules, in such a way as to enable them to behave equivalently to conventional flat plate photovoltaic modules.[ETS024, p25]	LOW MEDIUM	0.30 0.30
Social Capital	RANGES [0, 1.2) = LOW (0.75, 2.25) = MED (1.5, 3] = HIGH	LOWER: No relationships, Limited flows HIGER: Successful, Established	[MEDIUM] [GENERAL] Successful research teams typically generate output higher than that indicated by their individual efforts. Establishment of successful research teams is dependent of the relationships between researchers and takes time.[ETS018, p21] *Evidence from annual reports suggests that by 1994 longstanding relationship with BP Solar and its precursor Tideland Energies*	MEDIUM	1

continued on following page

Table 5. Continued

Variable	Membership Function	Exemplar Descriptors	Senario 3 UNSW-PVC 1985-1994 [Buried-Cell]	Senario 3 Linguistic Membership Value	Scenario 3 Degree Of Membership
Environmental Munificence	**RANGES** [0, 0.4) = LOW (0.2, 0.8) = MED (0.6, 1] = HIGH	LOWER: Limited, Small market, Resource constraints HIGHER: Favourable, Support, High Demand	**[LOW-MED]** **[GENERAL]** PV research has been supported over the past two decades by various government research, development and commercialisation programs, although there has been no overall PV strategy for Australia. [ETS018, p4]	LOW MEDIUM	0.30 1.00
Changes in Knowledge Resources	**RANGES** [0, 1) = LOW (0.4, 1.6) = MED (1.2, 2] = HIGH	LOWER: Not mentioned, Incremental, No change, No revenue HIGHER, Groundbreaking, Break through, Quantum Leap, Revolutionary; Royalties, Profit	**K[MED]; S{LOW-MEDIUM]** **[1992]** Associate Director, Dr. Stuart Wenham and Director, Professor Martin Green were awarded the 1992 CSIRO Medal for researchers external to the CSIRO for the invention, development and commercialization of the buried contact solar cell. [ETS024, p47]; **[GENERAL]** Successful PV commercialisation offers good rewards to researchers and universities, in terms of royalties or shareholder returns, which can be ploughed back into further research. However, these might take a long time (10 years or more) to emerge. [ETS018, p15]. **[GENERAL]** With these unfavourable market conditions, PV is not yet a highly profitable technology [ETS018, p24]; **[BURIED CELL]** A licence fee and royalties will also be paid to UNSW until 2005. The university uses royalties [from Buried Cell technology] to fund infrastructure requirements, since these are often difficult to fund via research grants. [ETS018, p16]; This represents a significant improvement on the previously highest recorded efficiency of 17% achieved by the University of New South Wales in 1988. [ETS024, p25]	MEDIUM	1

continued on following page

Table 5. Continued

Variable	Membership Function	Exemplar Descriptors	Senario 3 UNSW-PVC 1985-1994 [Buried-Cell]	Senario 3 Linguistic Membership Value	Scenario 3 Degree Of Membership
Changes in Financial Resources	**RANGES** [-1, 0.2) = LOW [-0.4, 1.4) = MED [0.8, 2] = HIGH	LOWER: Not mentioned, Incremental, No change, No revenue HIGHER, Groundbreaking, Break through, Quantum Leap, Revolutionary; Royalties, Profit	**K[MED]; S{LOW-MEDIUM]** **[1992]** Associate Director, Dr. Stuart Wenham and Director, Professor Martin Green were awarded the 1992 CSIRO Medal for researchers external to the CSIRO for the invention, development and commercialization of the buried contact solar cell. [ETS024, p47]; **[GENERAL]** Successful PV commercialisation offers good rewards to researchers and universities, in terms of royalties or shareholder returns, which can be ploughed back into further research. However, these might take a long time (10 years or more) to emerge. [ETS018, p15]. **[GENERAL]** With these unfavourable market conditions, PV is not yet a highly profitable technology [ETS018, p24]; **[BURIED CELL]** A licence fee and royalties will also be paid to UNSW until 2005. The university uses royalties [from Buried Cell technology] to fund infrastructure requirements, since these are often difficult to fund via research grants. [ETS018, p16]; This represents a significant improvement on the previously highest recorded efficiency of 17% achieved by the University of New South Wales in 1988. [ETS024, p25]	LOW MEDIUM	0.20 0.25

Table 6. Non-parametric correlations between input variables

	Actor type	Number RD	Number M	Number FB	Financial resources	Product knowledge	Process knowledge	Knowledge Uniqueness	Complementary products	Social capital	Environmental Munificence
Focal actor	1										
Number RDs	.554**	1									
Number Ms	.387**	.608**	1								
Number FBs	.555**	.544**	.711**	1							
Financial resources	-0.036	-.210**	-0.051	-0.022	1						
Product knowledge	.623**	.512**	.412**	.475**	-0.015	1					
Process knowledge	.567**	.391**	.534**	.550**	.184**	.527**	1				
Uniqueness of knowledge	.480**	.343**	.161**	.211**	-.491**	.467**	0.038	1			
Complementary products	.382**	.239**	.326**	.345**	0.077	.647**	.516**	.256**	1		
Social capital	.169**	-0.01	.115*	.095*	.381**	.321**	.385**	-0.081	.440**	1	
Environmental Munificence	.095*	.166**	.227**	.244**	.211**	.264**	.321**	-.119*	.328**	.517**	1

** significant at 0.01 level; * significant at 0.05 level.

Section 2
Customer Relationship Management and Web Analytics

Chapter 5
Fuzzy Clustering of Web User Profiles for Analyzing their Behavior and Interests

Stanislav Kreuzer
Goethe University, Germany

Natascha Hoebel
Goethe University, Germany

ABSTRACT

One of the keys to building effective e-customer relationships is an understanding of consumer behavior online. However, analyzing the behavior of customers online is not necessarily an indicator of their interests. Therefore, building profiles of registered users of a website is of importance if it goes beyond collecting obvious information the user is willing to give at the time of the registration. These user profiles can contribute to the analysis of the users' interests. Important tools for the analysis are data-mining techniques, for example, the clustering of collected user information. This chapter addresses the problem of how to define, calculate, and visualize fuzzy clusters of Web visitors with respect to their behavior and supposed interests. This chapter shows how to cluster Web users based on their profile and by their similar interests in several topics using the fuzzy and hybrid CORD (Clustering of ORdinal Data) clustering system, which is part of the Gugubarra Framework.

INTRODUCTION

Companies today operate in an increasingly competitive environment. Therefore, finding and retaining customers is a critical factor for most businesses offline and online. One of the keys to building effective e-customer relationships is an

DOI: 10.4018/978-1-4666-0095-9.ch005

understanding of user behavior online (Turban et al., 2004). However, analyzing the behavior of users online is not necessary an indicator of their interests.

Content providers compete for the user's attention, and at the same time, they have to convince their customers to keep using specific content sources or e-services. When exploring the Internet marketplace, various strategies can be observed for attracting new customers or maintaining a "significantly sized" customer base that may generate revenue directly through payments or indirectly through advertisements (Shapiro & Varian, 1998).

Efficient optimization of a service or resource of any kind requires a quantitative survey and assessment of its usage. Data-mining techniques can achieve remarkable results in extracting essential information from such seemingly amorphic data. Clustering algorithms have evolved greatly since the development of data-mining technologies in terms of significance, performance and quality. In particular, when taking into account the constantly growing number of modern clustering algorithms, research on the usability and adaptivity of data seems inevitable in a practical environment. It is clear that an efficient solution to all clustering problems cannot be achieved by one algorithm.

Consequently, it is necessary to expand the field of research to a set of partial solutions. Therefore, we introduced our fuzzy clustering approach named CORD (Clustering of Ordinal Data) at the 6th International Conference on Web Information Systems and Technologies in 2010. It was published by INSTICC Press in (Hoebel & Kreuzer, 2010) and online by SciTePress.

CORD was designed to support the analysis of web site users' interests. Clustering web users by their behavior can also be useful for measuring "trends" in a web community and for electronic customer relation management or e-CRM, namely in the process of building long-term relationships and increasing e-customer loyalty, which is the degree to which a web customer will stay with a specific vendor or a brand (Turban et al., 2004).

As with all clustering algorithms, CORD must deal with the issue of distance computation for the observed elements. Most of the known approaches focus on *numerical data* that allows measuring the distance by arithmetic operations, for example, using a Euclidean or chi-squared distance metric. Others focus on *categorical data* (Gan et al., 2005; Huang, 1997; Parmar,

2007) and measure the distance by counting the number of different attribute values. This metric is known as the Hamming distance in information theory. The focus of the CORD approach is to efficiently cluster large amounts of *ordinal data*, which, unlike pure categorical data, possesses an inherent order.

The CORD approach combines modifications of three modern clustering approaches to create a hybrid solution that is able to efficiently process very large sets of ordinal data.

The algorithm *An Extension of Self-organizing Maps to Categorical Data* (NCSOM) by Chen and Marques (2005) is hereby used for a rough pre-clustering. NCSOM improves the result of the clustering task by helping in the decision process of choosing how many centroids/clusters should be used and where the k-centroids should be placed.

The main clustering task utilizes a k-modes algorithm and its *fuzzy set extension* described by Kim et al. (2004) in *Fuzzy Clustering of Categorical Data using Fuzzy Centroids*.

Finally to deal with large amounts of data, the BIRCH algorithm described by Zhang et al. (1996) in *BIRCH: An Efficient Data Clustering Method for Very Large Databases* was adapted to ordinal data.

Combining these approaches, the resulting system is able to extract efficiently significant information even from very large datasets, as this is the case when millions of web user profiles are stored.

The next section describes our motivation and the ordinal data of the web user profiles that are clustered with CORD. It introduces the ordinal scale of interest, which is the basis for the ability to associate an interpretation to each cluster. Section 3 describes the theoretical background and related work. The CORD clustering approach is described in section 4. The GUI of the Gugubarra Framework (the tool that uses CORD) is shown in section 5, focusing on the visualization of the fuzzy centroids. The chapter ends with further research issues and conclusions.

MOTIVATION: USER PROFILES AND SCALE OF INTEREST

The current developments of internet technologies create new opportunities for web content providers while increasing the available options for web users. In this dynamic environment, understanding of the users' behavior and interests is pivotal for the online business strategies. As the amount of users grows exponentially with the continuous development of internet market scenarios, relying on individual feedbacks is nowadays by no means enough to put up a successful and customer-aligned business strategy. A similar environment can be found in the fields of modern customer relation management and market research. An efficient way to analyze and identify customer needs is the key to a successful alignment. The CORD clustering is part of the Gugubarra Framework that supports web site owners in the environment of customer interest identification and analysis. Gugubarra is the Aboriginal name for the Kookaburra bird and not an acronym. The tool was implemented in a project at the Goethe University of Frankfurt that aims at understanding the interests of registered users of a web site by evaluating their behavior and actions performed while visiting the site. The project focuses on calculating different kinds of user profiles for web site visitors. The fuzzy CORD approach was designed to create an appropriate solution for clustering and visual analyzing of large amounts of user profiles. This should help in understanding user behavior and in personalizing advertisements.

Building profiles of registered users of a web site, as in the case of a portal, is important if it goes beyond collecting the obvious information the user is willing to give at the time of the registration.

To measure the supposed "interests" of web users, the concept of *non-obvious user profiles (NOPs)* was introduced. The user's NOP is inferred by the user's behavior in one or more sessions on the web site. A NOP represents the interests of one user in different topics. It is a vector associated to one user with numerical weight values between *0* and *1* for each topic. For further details, refer to (Hoebel et al., 2006).

To recognize changes in users' interests, it is not necessary to distinguish between weight values such as *0.3* and *0.35*. In addition, a numerical value is not very meaningful.

Therefore, these values can be mapped to a so-called scale of interest, as described in the following. The *scale of interest* classifies the values in a human understandable form in ordinal categories. An example for a scale of interest is *no*, *little*, *strong*, or *total* interest.

For using CORD, the website owner can choose a value for the parameter *g*, which indicates how fine the owner would like to differentiate in the interest scale. In other words, the parameter *g* defines the granularity in the interest scale. The range of the non-obvious profile weights, i.e., the range between *0* and *1,* is split into *g* intervals, each corresponding to one ordinal value.

The mapped intervals can have the same size (see Figure 1a) or not when calculated by a split-function (see Figure 1b). A known ordinal scale is the Richter magnitude scale, which is based on a logarithmic function.

The scale can be visualized with a gray scale (see Figure 1d) or with colors that correspond to the gray scale (see Figure 1c, but note that the colors throughout this chapter are only shown in the digital version of this chapter).

The mapping of the NOP value to the ordinal value is visualized with the following example. Supposed we define a scale using *g=3* with intervals having roughly the same size. This results in the following three intervals and mapping:

- **Strong:** includes the NOP values between *0.67-1.00*.
- **Medium:** includes the NOP values between *0.34-0.66*.
- **Little:** includes the NOP values between *0.00-0.33*.

Figure 1. Scale of interest examples

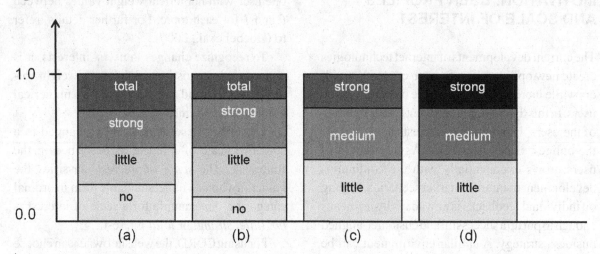

Defining the scale of interest is key for the clustering. The Gugubarra approach is flexible and gives the owner of a web site the possibility to tune the clusters. In particular, by choosing different g values and choosing an appropriate split-function, he can define the correspondence between various values of the interest scale. The split-function does not necessarily have to be linear. The definition of the split-function is application dependent, reflects the requirements of the application, and, of course, influences how users are clustered in the end. On the basis of this *ordinal* scale of interest, it is possible to associate a meaning to each cluster, as shown in section 4.

Sometimes profiles are stored in a scale of interest right from the start. This is especially valid for another kind of profile, which is the *user feedback profile*. Several web sites allow or ask their users to give feedback on their interests, hobbies or opinions about a product or the site itself. A user feedback can then be given on a scale of interest over a number of topics. The reply can then be stored in a feedback profile. To better understand users, it can be of interest to cluster across this feedback (i.e., what the user tells about his interest) and the NOP (i.e., what he is supposed to be interested in, by analyzing his

click streams). Thereby the data must have the same cardinality and scale.

The utilization of the NOP approach opens up several interesting possibilities, for example the ability to cluster or group visitors of a web site with "similar" interests and then offer them personalized e-services.

In most research done until now, web users are clustered by their click streams or by their visited pages. By using the NOP approach, we have the ability to cluster web users by looking at the content of the web pages and the users' interests in several topics related to the pages. For further details, refer to (Hoebel et al., 2006).

BACKGROUND

CORD is a hybrid clustering algorithm based on three modern clustering algorithms. Before going into a detailed description of the CORD approach, we will therefore provide a brief overview of the theoretical foundations behind those three algorithms and the modifications applied to them to make CORD work efficiently. The chapter ends with related work on clustering categorical data and on clustering web users.

Fuzzy Centroids: The Fuzzy k-Modes Extension

The kernel of CORD consists of a modified and optimized implementation of the fuzzy k-Modes algorithm extension for categorical data described by Kim et al. (2004).

The fundamental idea of the basic k-Modes algorithm is to form k centroids, each consisting of a constellation of values for each of the available attributes in the dataset. These constellations are then iteratively modified with respect to the mean of all the records (a record is in our case a user profile) to which they are the most similar. The algorithm tries to come to a stable result, where no more changes in any record's centroid membership (definition see below) are recorded. The fuzzy k-Modes algorithm introduced by Huang et al. (1997) extends the basic operation of k-Modes by saving the degree to which a record belongs to a certain centroid. This step makes this information available in subsequent iterations, so that membership decisions of records can be calculated more exactly. Additionally, the fuzzy extension to the fuzzy k-Modes algorithm uses fuzzy sets as centroids to overcome the information loss that occurs in subsequent iterations of the normal fuzzy k-Modes due to the fact that the centroids are integers, which enforces "hard" membership decisions. The fuzzy sets allow the algorithm to build on information from the previous iterations when choosing the centroids in the current iteration. In this way, the center of a cluster can be calculated more accurately.

The *fuzzy centroid* $\tilde{Z}$ is hereby defined as a tuple $\tilde{Z} = \left(\tilde{z}_1, ..., \tilde{z}_r \right)$ of r fuzzy attributes, each of the form $\tilde{z}_i = \left\{ \left(a_{i,1}, w_{i,1} \right), ..., \left(a_{i,n_i}, w_{i,n_i} \right) \right\}$, where $a_{i,j}$ is the attribute value of one of r attributes A_i, $w_{i,j}$ is the correspondent confidence degree of $a_{i,j}$ for being chosen as the centroid's value of A_i and $1, ..., n_i$ is the cardinality of the i-th attribute A_i. The confidence degree for each attribute value of each of the r attributes A_i of a centroid is determined by the records belonging to the corresponding cluster of the centroid (except for the nonexistent attribute values, which remain 0 all the time).

Looking closely at the definition of such a centroid, one can discover the stochastic $r \times n^*$ matrix $[w]$ formed from the degrees $w_{i,j}$ of r attributes A_i with each A_i having up to n^* degrees $w_{i,j}$, one for each attribute value $a_{i,j}$. The cardinality n^* denotes the maximum cardinality of the r attributes A_i. Furthermore, the definition of a stochastic matrix dictates $\sum_{j=1}^{n^*} w_{i,j} = 1$ for the sum of the degrees w_i of each attribute A_i. Attributes with a cardinality smaller than n^* will have a grade of zero for the grades $w_{i,j}$ of their non-existing attribute values.

An analogous definition can be given for the stochastic $n \times k$ *membership matrix* $[\mu]$, which denotes the degree of membership of each of the n records to each of the k centroids or their clusters, respectively. The degree of membership of a record to a centroid is hereby computed using a distance measure $d\left(\tilde{Z}, X \right) = \sum_{i=1}^{r} \delta \left(\tilde{z}_i, x_i \right)$, where $\tilde{Z}$ denotes one of the k centroids, X denotes one of n records in the data set and $\delta \left(\tilde{z}_i, x_i \right) = \sum_{t=1}^{n^*} \tau \left(a_{i,t}, x_i \right)$, with $\tau \left(a_{i,t}, x_i \right)$ being equal to $w_{i,t}$ if and only if w_i is equal to the value $a_{i,t}$; otherwise, it is zero. This distance measure computes the distance of a record to the target centroid by summarizing the degrees of importance for the values of each of the attributes of X as given in the centroid matrix $[w]$ of the target centroid.

With these definitions in mind, it is now possible to define the iterative step of the algorithm as well as its stop condition. A transition or a step of the algorithm can now be defined as follows:

$$\mu_{i,j}(t+1) = \left(\sum_{l=1}^{k} \left(\frac{d(\tilde{Z}_i, X_j)}{d(\tilde{Z}_l, X_j)} \right)^{\frac{1}{m-1}} \right)^{-1}.$$

The parameter m > 1 hereby controls the fuzziness of the computation. The bigger m is chosen, the more fuzzy the computation will be. For an m≈1 most of the entries of the membership matrix [μ] will be very close to 1, in case of m > 1 they will differ more or less according to the size of m. Afterwards, the centroid matrices $[w]_i$ for all of the k centroids can be updated as follows:

$$w_{i,j} = \sum_{l=1}^{n} \gamma(\tilde{z}_i, x_l) \text{ with } \gamma(\tilde{z}_i, x_l) = \mu_{i,l}^m$$

if and only if $a_{i,j}$ is equal to $x_{l,i}$, which is the i-th attribute value of x_l. The iterative step $\mu_{i,j}(t)$ as well as the update of the centroid matrices $[w]_i$ afterwards can now be repeated. Each iteration of these two steps tries to optimize the centroid matrices and by doing this approximates an optimal solution. The quality of the approximation of the centroid matrices can be checked by computing a mean distance of all records to each of the centroids weighted by the grade of membership of each record to the target cluster (centroid). This is done by an objective function:

$$J([\mu], \tilde{Z}) = \sum_{i=1}^{k} \sum_{j=1}^{n} (\mu_{i,j})^m d(\tilde{Z}_i, X_j).$$

This objective function is computed at the very end of an iteration. As long as the result of the objective function is monotonically decreased in each iteration of the algorithm, this means that the mean weighted distance is reduced and a more optimal solution for the cluster centroids is found. An optimal solution for the fuzzy centroids is reached and the computation can be stopped, if a succeeding result is bigger or equal to its predecessor.

BIRCH: Efficient Clustering of VLDB Databases

The BIRCH (**B**alanced **I**terative **R**educing and **C**lustering using **H**ierarchies) algorithm was introduced by Zhang et al. (1996) and is a well-known hierarchical clustering method for very large databases. The focus of this algorithm is efficiency. Therefore, it is specially crafted to process and cluster the whole dataset with one run through at most, keeping every piece of information about the dataset in fast memory (RAM). The information collected by the algorithm is organized in a height balanced tree structure, which is called a *CF*-tree or cluster feature tree. Each leaf of this *CF*-tree consists of a set of cluster features. Each cluster feature can be seen as a summary of a subset of records in the dataset, which only saves the information about the computed center of the records in its subset. This task can be accomplished with a simple average or median computation for numeric records. In the case of categorical or ordinal data, the center of a *CF*-Feature can be defined as a record having a minimal distance to all records in the same subset. A distance measure for this task can be naively defined for two records x_i and x_j as

$$d(x_i, x_j) = \sum_{k=1}^{n} \tau(x_{i,k}, x_{j,k}), \text{ with } \tau(x_{i,k}, x_{j,k}) \text{ be-}$$

ing equal to one if and only if the attribute value $x_{i,k}$ is equal to the attribute value $x_{j,k}$; otherwise, it is zero. In the section below, we will define a more sophisticated distance measure, which is optimized for handling data of an ordinal scale of interest.

After having passed through the complete dataset once (at most), the algorithm returns a summarized representation of the dataset in the leaves of its cluster feature tree held in memory. These leaves can then by processed efficiently using an arbitrary clustering algorithm of one's own choice.

NCSOM: Self-Organizing Maps for Categorical Data

The NCSOM algorithm, introduced by Chen and Marques (2005), is an extension of the Self-Organized Map (SOM) algorithm for categorical data and builds upon the artificial neural networks described by Teuvo Kohonen. The data structure of the NCSOM algorithm is a rectangle shaped two-dimensional network of n neurons and has the same number of neurons on all of its sides. Each neuron has a randomly initialized r-dimensional reference vector $m_i = \left[m_{i,1}, \ldots, m_{i,r} \right]$, where r denotes the number of attributes of records in the dataset. During an iteration of the algorithm, these reference vectors change dynamically, adapting to the records being processed as well as to the vectors of their neighbor neurons. The result of these iterations is a map of neurons, where neurons with vectors similar to one another are grouped together. This map can be visualized graphically in a way, where groups of similar neurons are partitioned into clusters by lines of surrounding neurons that are not similar to those in the group. The algorithm demands no knowledge of the underlying data and is able to determine a global optimum of the cluster partition.

A Distance Metric for Ordinal Data

The motivation for a specific metric is the observation that the ordinal attributes of user profiles all have the same cardinality and scale of attribute values. Using the scale of interest as a domain results in having comparable attributes with the same context and symbolism, namely the users' interests in different topics. Implementing text-based distance metrics is not appropriate because the label letters themselves do not hold any distance information. Distance metrics for numerical data cannot be applied to this problem domain, as the ordinal data cannot be target to mathematical operations such as addition or subtraction, thus making ordinal data not convertible to a numerical scale. Ordinal data only offer information about the ordering of elements, whereas the distance between such elements is not defined and has not to be the same between various neighboring elements. This point is the central matter for this research field and is discussed in statistics. Podani has discussed this issue for Braun-Blanquet dominance: *"it is inappropriate to analyse Braun-Blanquet abudance/dominance data by methods assuming that Euclidean distance is meaningful"* (Podani, 2005, p. 497). Distance metrics for categorical data could be applied to this problem domain, as can be seen in various clustering algorithms such as CACTUS, ROCK or STIRR. However, it seems insufficient because ordinal data can offer more information (e.g., the ordering) than simple categorical data. The attribute values of the scale of interest in our problem domain are ordered and are assumed to be quasi-equidistant. For two independent ordinal attributes A and B, each having different amounts of attribute values, one can not say that the distance between two neighboring attribute values of A is the same as the distance of two neighboring attribute values of B. This could not be true even if these ordinal attributes were not fully independent since A and B have different amounts of attribute values and therefore are of different granularity. In our problem domain, we deal with users' interests in different topics, which indeed are all measured with the same granularity. As these attributes all do represent an amount of interest, they are all measured in the same way by each individual, although one can not say, that each individual has the same understanding of the difference between two neighboring attribute values. Nevertheless, the interesting point is that even if the perception of difference varies from individual to individual, each individual does measure different interests in the same scale. These facts in combination allow for the assumption of equidistance to be made. The additional benefit of this assumption can be best explained by an example. If one uses the Hamming distance for categorical data, the distance between the ordinal categories *little* and *strong* is equal to the distance between the categories *little* and *medium*. With our proposed distance measure $d(X,Y)$ below, the first distance is higher than the second. This result makes sense because the exact distance between each of the categories does not play a large role in measuring the overall distance. What does play a large role is the fact that there is one category between *little* and *strong*, whereas between *little* and *medium,* there is none (see Figure 1d). This thinking is a logical procedure any human repeats in everyday life, where exact measuring is unavailable.

In stating this assumption, the number of categories between two attribute values can now be taken into account. The distance measure $d(X,Y)$ for two records X and Y of a dataset N can now be defined in the following way:

$$d(X,Y) = \sum_{i=1}^{r} \delta(x_i, y_i) \text{ with}$$

$$\delta(x_i, y_i) = \begin{cases} 0 & if\ (x_i = y_i) \\ \|Rank(x_i) - Rank(y_i)\| & else \end{cases}$$

Rank(x_i) denotes the position of the category for the *i*-th attribute x_i of record *X* in the order of an ordinal scale of interest. A distance of $d(X,Y)$ = 1 for two records means that the two differ from each other by only one ordinal attribute value, and the differing categories are ordered next to each other on the ordinal scale. This value is the smallest distance two ordinal records can have. The next higher distance value is 2; thus, the distance concept is discrete. This distance metric can now be applied to distance calculations in various clustering algorithms. In our case, we applied this

form of distance measurement to all stages of the CORD algorithm.

Related Work in Different Areas

Clustering Categorical Data

Categorical data play an important role in the area of log file analysis. Data extracted from log files can contain a variety of attributes such as timestamps, IP addresses, URLs, page impressions, language codes, country codes, and strings of browser names. Most of this data have categorical domains. In the area of *clustering categorical data*, several algorithms have been presented. However, there are fewer methods for handling the special case of ordinal data, as the NCSOM does. For completeness, we give in the following section a short summary of the algorithms that cluster categorical data.

The k-Modes algorithm (Huang, 1997) ranks among other well-known algorithms and is a modification of the k-means introduced by MacQueen (1967) and its k-means variant (Anderberg, 1973).

The GKMODE (Gan et al., 2005) is an evolutionary algorithm that is able to find a global optimum, which is different from the k-Modes algorithm. GKMODE was developed as a mixture of the k-modes (Huang, 1997) and the GKA algorithm (Krishna & Murty, 1998).

The CLICKS algorithm (Zaki et al., 2005) summarizes the dataset as a k-partite graph and mines the maximal k-partite cliques, which correspond to the clusters. The categorical values of a domain are used to build the nodes of the graph.

The MMR algorithm (Parmar et al., 2007) is a relatively new procedure for clustering categorical data and is based on the *rough set concept* described by Pawlak (1997). The *rough set concept* is used for the representation of uncertain or incomplete information, which is based on the formation of equivalence relations and equivalence classes in the input data. This procedure is used by MMR, which finds clusters with the rough membership function.

Different clustering methods are based on the idea of co-occurrence or a neighborhood of values in the dataset, e.g., CACTUS (Ganti et al., 1999), ROCK (Guha et al., 1999), and STIRR (Gibson et al., 1998).

Our distance measure for categorical data is different from those proposed, as defined in CACTUS, ROCK, STIRR and K-modes. A further similarity measurement for categorical attributes was suggested by Nambiar and Kambhampati (2005). The similarity between two values binding a categorical attribute is measured as the percentage of distinct attribute-value pairs (AV-pair) common to both. An AV-pair can be visualized as a selection query that binds only a single attribute.

Clustering Web Users

In the area of *clustering web users*, taking into account non-obvious profiles as described in this chapter is a new approach.

Most of the related methods cluster users on the basis of sequences of visited pages (click-streams) and often also without inclusion of the *time* spent on each page (Fu et al., 1999), (Hay et al., 2001). In our approach, the relative time spend on the page is taken into account in the computation of the NOPs.

In some related methods (Fu et al., 1999), (Hay et al., 2001), (Wang et al., 2004), (Wang & Zaïane, 2002), users are clustered over sequences of pages without looking at the *content* of the pages. Fu et al. (1999) assume a semantic structure of a web site in folders.

In contrast, Banerjee and Ghosh (2001) include the time in a similarity function. During the view of a click stream, Banerjee and Ghosh look for the longest common subsequence in a path. They construct a graph with these paths, which is then divided into partial graphs (clusters) with a partitioning procedure.

Hay et al. (2001) also compute the similarity of the navigation paths. The fewer insert, delete and rearrange operations that are necessary to change one sequence into another, the more similar two sides are. The users are then grouped with a hierarchical cluster procedure (Ward's procedure). Unfortunately, it is not possible to determine whether two pages are equal based on the meaning of their content.

Manco et al. (2003) use a cosine measure to compute the similarity of two pages. In addition, the TF-IDF measure is used, which regards all relevant word trunks. Then the users are grouped after the similarity of their sequences of visited pages are determined and with consideration of their behavior, e.g., the duration on the visited page. They use a graph partitioning procedure similar to Mobasher et al. (2002) and Shahabi et al. (1997), which both use a java applet for data collection. They represent a web site as a graph. The graph vertices are pages, and the edges are links between the pages. The users are clustered by their navigation path, which is regarded here as a link sequence and by the time spent on this path. The link sequences are clustered with the assistance of a cosine measure and the k-means algorithm.

Q. Wang et al. (2004) use a combination of a k-means with a minimum spanning tree algorithm for clustering. The users are grouped here as in (Shahabi et al., 1997) on the basis of their clicked links or on the basis of their visited pages. For the algorithm, a semantic structure of the web site is also necessary, as in (Fu et al., 1999).

Wang and Zaïane (2002) compute the similarity of two web pages based on their URL; consequently, as in (Fu et al., 1999), a semantically structured web site in folders is required. They then compute the similarity of two click streams (best matching of two sessions). With the help of the TURN algorithm, the sessions and thus the users are clustered.

Xiao et al. (2001) cluster users based on their similarity, which can be determined with different measures. One way is to only consider which sites were or were not visited. Another way is to include the frequency of visits to each site into this measure.

Another measure defined in (Shahabi et al., 1997) is based on the order of the pages, and they introduced a matrix-based clustering method. Kim and Chan (2008) built a so-called *user interest hierarchy* with a divisive hierarchical clustering method. In this way, important words from the pages the user has visited are filtered and stored in one cluster. These data are divided by the algorithm into a tree structure. However, a grouping of the users is not carried out.

Other Areas of Related Work

Several algorithms have been proposed in the area of *clustering large datasets*, such as BIRCH and CLARANS (Clustering Large Applications based on RANdom Search). Before BIRCH was introduced by Zhang et al. (1996), CLARANS, which was developed by Ng and Han (1994), was presented at VLDB '94. CLARANS identifies candidate cluster centroids through the analysis of repeated random samples from the original data.

There are *specialized fields*, e.g., multi-relational data clustering. Yin and Han proposed CrossClus (Yin et al., 2007), which clusters data stored in multiple relational tables based on user guidance and multi-relational features. This algorithm requires the help of the user, which is the person who wants to cluster the elements.

Clustering can be applied to various domains and issues, e.g., in (Aggarwal et al., 2006), the k-anonymity (a technique to preserve privacy in data) is treated as a special clustering problem, called r-cellular clustering. Aggarwal et al. (2006) handle categorical attributes by representing them as *n* equidistant points in a metric space.

Hybrid Systems are used in various research fields, e.g., in the Web area, Hybrid Recommender Systems that combine information filtering and collaborative filtering techniques were defined

(Burke, 2002). Helmer (2007) proposed a hybrid approach to measure the similarity of semi-structured documents based on entropy. Kossmann et al. (2002) use a hybrid approach to find the Skyline, i.e., a set of interesting points from a potentially large set of data.

FUZZY CLUSTERING OF WEB USER PROFILES USING CORD

The word *hybrid* originates from the Greek language and means bundling, crossing or mixture. A hybrid is the combination of two or more different things and is aimed at achieving a particular objective. In this case, a hybrid concept is used to cluster large amounts of ordinal data.

The *first phase* of the concept processes the whole dataset once to create a summary of its most distinctive features that is small enough to be held in main memory. For this phase, we utilize a modification of the BIRCH algorithm. The main task of the first phase is not to do any clustering but merely to summarize the incoming data by merging the most similar records to groups or Cluster Features. This way the most distinctive features are maintained.

The clustering task of the *main phase* does not operate on bare dataset records; instead, it uses the results from the BIRCH phase as input. The Cluster Features are now treated as dataset records, the advantage in the main phase is the ability to work solely with the much faster main memory. As the data on which the clustering algorithm of the main phase has to operate is mostly based on summaries and averaged values, an algorithm which is based solely on hard decisions (only yes/no decisions) could have its difficulties to recognize the best solution. This could result in alternating cluster formations in succeeding iterations which are unable to form a stable optimum. Therefore the fuzzy k-Modes algorithm with a fuzzy centroid extension is used in the main task. Its use in this phase has the advantage, that soft decisions can be made in each iteration retaining as much information as possible about the history of the computation. The fuzzy k-Modes algorithm with a fuzzy centroid extension applies these soft decisions to the membership of records to a cluster, as well as to the composition of the cluster centroid itself resulting in a more precise inspection of the dataset terrain and a more effective search for an optimal solution.

A *preliminary data analysis phase* can be placed before the main clustering task to review the structure of the summary produced in the first phase and to manually optimize the initialization of the main phase by choosing the initial cluster centers as well as their amount. A modification of the NCSOM algorithm is used here for creating a similarity map, where the best places for initial cluster centers can be seen and picked visually. Again, the Cluster Features from the result of the first phase are treated as simple dataset records and fed into the NCSOM algorithm as input.

The results of the main clustering phase, which consist of k matrices $w_{i,j}$ of weights for each of the k clusters, can then be stored efficiently. Moreover, the ability to save the weight matrices allows the main clustering task to be paused and resumed. A refinement from a previous result can then be performed in the same way, which allows the use of the old result as initialization, so that the clustering does not have to be restarted completely.

Optimizing Fuzzy k-Modes with Fuzzy Centroids for Implementation

The fuzzy k-Modes algorithm with its fuzzy centroid extension, as introduced by Kim et al. (2004), cannot be efficiently implemented the naive way; however, with some optimizations to its iteration cycle, it can be implemented efficiently. When clustering very large datasets, the main goal is efficiency, which leads to considering more than just theoretical time complexities. In this case, a naive implementation of the algorithm needs at least 3 iterations through a set of N elements

for a dataset with N records to complete one of its iteration cycles. This estimate is based on the observation that each iteration cycle consists of at least 3 steps, and each one of them requires a run through either the source dataset or a generated set of N entries. Furthermore, these 3 steps have to be run in a specific order because they all rely on the results from each other. These steps are

1. Compute / update the objective function $J\big([\mu], \tilde{Z}\big)$,
2. Compute / update the record to cluster membership matrix $[\mu]$ and
3. Compute / update the fuzzy centroid matrix $[w]$.

In addition, in the case of a very large dataset, each iteration cycle of the algorithm needs to swap the very large $n \times k$ membership matrix $[\mu]$ to disk, which generates an additional write and a consequent read cycle of the same cardinality as the dataset. Given the assumption that the data in the dataset and the entries generated for the membership matrix $[\mu]$ are approximately the same size, these accesses require 5 iterations through a very large dataset.

We aim to implement this algorithm with only one iteration through the dataset per iteration cycle. This goal can be accomplished by parallelizing the computations of all of the 3 steps of the cycle. This modification does not affect the functionality of the algorithm but does decrease the computation time. Beginning with the step of updating the membership matrix $[\mu]$ and comparing it to the update of the centroid matrix, one can see that the computation of a row of matrix $[\mu]$ for one record of the dataset can directly be followed by a computation of an update for matrix $[w]$. The latter update is possible because it consists of a sum of partial results, with each of them consisting of calculations performed for a single record. This same approach applies to the last of the 3 steps – the calculation of the objective function. This

Listing 1. Optimized implementation of the fuzzy k-Modes algorithm

```
1 void modifiedFuzzyCentroids (intk) {
2 W1 = W2 = {Wj}, j = 1,...,k ;
3 M = μ [ x ][ y ], x = 1,..., n, y = 1,..., k ;
4 obj0 = obj1 = 1;
5 iN=0;
6
7 for (Wj ∈ W1, j = 1,...,k) {
8 Wj = initializeFuzzyCentroid (j);
9 }
10 while (obj0 < obj1 && iN < maximumCount){
11 obj0 = obj1;
12 obj1=0;
13 for (Xi ∈ N, i = 1,...,n) {
14 μ[ i ] = computeMembershipMatrixRow(W1, Xi, obj1);
15 W2 = updateFuzzyCentroids(μ[ i ], W2, Xi) ;
16 }
17 switchPlaces(W1, W2);
18 iN++;
19 }}
```

step can also be split up such that its computation can be described as a sum of partial results from calculations per record and is thus not dependant on the whole computed result from the contributing steps but rather is able to compute a partial result with each record processed and sum these results up to a complete result.

The modified version of the algorithm can be seen in *Listing 1*. After having initialized the k fuzzy centroids (lines 7-9), the iteration starts by computing a row of the membership matrix M as well as a partial result for the objective function to be summed up in $obj1$ from the centroid matrix set (or array) W_1 and each of the records X_i from

Listing 2. Modified distance metric for the fuzzy k-Modes algorithm

```
1 d computeDistance (Xi ∈ N, Wl ∈ W) {
2 d = 0 ;
3
4 for (i = 1,...,r) {
5 for (j = 1,..., ni){
6 d += | xi − ai,j | * Wl [ i ][ j ] ;
7 }
8 }
9 return d ;
10 }
```

the dataset N (line 14). The computed matrix row for X_i is then sequentially fed into the update of the centroids (line 15), which again generates a partial result that is summed up in W_2 as the iteration progresses through the dataset (lines 13-16). Swapping the matrix sets W_1 and W_2 (line 17) is necessary because the algorithm needs a fully computed centroid matrix set from its previous iteration for its calculations while it places the partial results of these calculations in the "spare" matrix (W_1 or W_2). The algorithm finishes when one of the stop conditions (line 10) is triggered.

The previously discussed distance metric for ordinal data has to be modified to be implemented in this algorithm. The modification can be seen in *Listing 2*. The distance between a record X_i and a centroid confidence matrix W_l can be calculated as a sum of distances between the category values of each of the r attributes of X_i and all of the categories for the corresponding attributes of the centroid matrix W_l weighted by the confidence degree of these categories to form the center of the centroid. This distance metric is used to compute a distance row of the membership matrix [μ], which is presented in *Listing 3*. This task is accomplished by first calculating the distances of X_i to all of the k centroids (lines 5-6), which is followed by a computation of the matrix row and objective function with the pre-computed distance values (lines 7-9). After computing an updated membership matrix row, the next step is the computation of the partial results for the update of the k centroids.

A suitable implementation of this process is given in *Listing 4*. Given the membership matrix row μ, the set of centroid confidence matrices W and the record X_i corresponding to the computed μ, the function computes and appends new partial results to the set W. After the update of the centroids, the $W_j \in W$ will not follow the limitations of a stochastic matrix anymore. Individual entries can and eventually will contain values greater than one. To resolve this issue, each of the k cen-

Listing 3. Calculation of a membership matrix row and objective function

```
1  μ getMatrixRow (W, Xi ∈ N, cost) {
2  μ = (μ1,…,μk);
3  d = (d1,…,dk);
4
5  for (Wj ∈ W, j = 1,…,k) {
6  dj = getDistance (Wj, Xi); }
7  for (Wj ∈ W, j = 1,…,k) {
8  μ[j] = 1 / power (dj / sum(dj), 1 / (m − 1));
9  cost += μj*dj; }
10 return μ;
11 }
```

Listing 4. Fuzzy centroid confidence degree calculation

```
1  W updateCentroids (μ, W, Xi ∈ N) {
2  for (Wj ∈ W, j = 1,…,k) {
3  for (i = 1,…,r, xi ∈ X) {
4  wj,i += power(μ[j], m); }}
5  return Wl;
6  }
```

troids has to be normalized at the end of each iteration cycle. This step ensures that every new cycle starts with a strictly stochastic matrix and that the whole process does not diverge toward infinity, eventually killing all computations with buffer overflow errors. Looking at these optimizations as a whole, one can note an improvement in execution time by a factor of at least 3. The distance measure presented in *Listing 2* thereby helps to achieve a crisper result in less time. In an environment like VLDB, where every single run of an algorithm is a cost-intensive task, this optimization can have a large impact. However, the real bottleneck remains unsolved. In general, the vast amount of data in VLDB databases is not the right kind of input for an iterative algorithm like fuzzy k-Modes or k-Modes. To tackle this problem, we will use the BIRCH algorithm to drastically decrease the amount of data without losing the distinctive features of the information contained in a dataset.

Increasing Processing Speed with the BIRCH Approach

The BIRCH algorithm is an incremental and hierarchical clustering algorithm for very large databases. This algorithm in its raw form can cluster multi-dimensional metric data points and attempts to produce the best possible clustering using a given set of resources such as memory.

Chiu et al. (2001) introduced an approach based on BIRCH. This extended approach uses a distance measure based on maximum likelihood estimation for mixed numerical and categorical data. The BIRCH algorithm is used as a preprocessor to create a feasible dataset for the second step of the algorithm. As the main goal of our work is to further optimize the processing of very large amounts of ordinal data, we likewise need to modify and implement the BIRCH concept as a preprocessor stage. The BIRCH algorithm builds so-called cluster features into a cluster feature tree. Each cluster feature or CF is initialized with one record as a centroid. Other records will be absorbed as long as they are similar to the centroid to a certain degree, which is defined by a suitable distance metric. A parameter T controls the distance interval size (radius) within which records get absorbed by the corresponding CF. With the previously defined distance metric for ordinal data, we can now modify the BIRCH algorithm to process ordinal data. The parameter T now defines how many attribute values can differ between a centroid of the CF and a neighboring record and still be considered a part of the subset represented by this CF. Keeping only the centroids of each CF ensures that the size of the dataset decreases while keeping distinctive features of information in the dataset intact as they are the features that are likely to differ the most. If the size of the CF tree exceeds during execution the provided memory limit, the tree must be reduced. Here the T parameter is used. As the parameter T increases, the CFs of the old tree leaves are inserted into a new tree. Due to the now larger radius, as controlled by T, some of the

CFs of the old tree are absorbed by other CFs in the new tree. The tree becomes smaller, but also a bit more blurry. This effect can be positive as it effectively eradicates outliers because they disappear in the crowd. This approach is implemented for the first phase of CORD, providing its result as input to be clustered by the modified fuzzy k-Modes algorithm described earlier.

The result from BIRCH can also be processed by an in-between phase, as described in the following section. This new phase is used to increase the quality of a cluster analysis with the fuzzy k-Modes algorithm by helping to identify adequate initial centroids.

Increasing Quality with NCSOM

Before the output of the modified BIRCH algorithm, which is in the form of a summary of the dataset, can be clustered by the fuzzy k-Modes algorithm, the number k of centroids has to be selected and properly initialized. This phase is crucial for the quality of the final result. There are several automatic approaches for this initialization step, including setting the k centroids to random values and taking the top k most common patterns in the dataset. We will handle both the correct choice of the parameter k and the proper initialization of the k centroids by introducing another algorithm – NCSOM. The NCSOM algorithm is based on self-organized maps by T. Kohonen (2001) and does not require any information about the dataset to compute a globally optimal clustering result. As a representative of SOM algorithms, the NCSOM algorithm can be described in two ways – as an *offline* and an *online* algorithm. The advantage of the *online* version of the algorithm is its ability to work on data from a dataset without knowing its size. The downside of this version is its impact on quality. The *offline* or *batch* version of the algorithm must know the dataset as a whole to be able to process it, but in return, it produces results of better quality because

it can better optimize the computation. We will concentrate on the *offline* version of the algorithm because we always have the whole dataset ready and are primarily concerned with achieving the best result possible.

The *offline* algorithm creates a two-dimensional map of neurons, each of which consists of a reference vector. The positions of these neurons, which are described by their reference vectors, are random at the beginning of the procedure and are grouped closer to each other depending on their distance as determined by a distance metric. The degree to which the vectors are able to change during iteration i is controlled by a function $\delta(i)$, which is a monotonic decreasing function of the maximum number of iterations. The degree of changeability is then, in most cases, described as an exponential decreasing function of the value of $\delta(i)$ in each iteration of the algorithm. The distance between neighboring vectors can be illustrated on a grayscale similarity map image. With increasing distance between vectors of each two neurons, the color of the pixel on the similarity map corresponding to the distance of these two neurons gets darker. Groups of similar neurons can be then identified as bright areas on the similarity map (see Figure 2). If a neuron from the center of such a bright area is chosen to represent a centroid, its reference vector will be a good choice for a centroid of the records represented by this area. This representation thus not only assists in finding the number k of centroids that exist in the clustering structure but is also helpful in specifying the initial centroid allocation for a following cluster analysis.

As the NCSOM algorithm normally operates on numeric data only, it must be modified to be able to process ordinal data. As before, we again applied our previously discussed distance measure to the algorithm. The resulting implementation of the distance measure is analogous to that of the Fuzzy k-Modes algorithm.

Figure 2. Similarity map

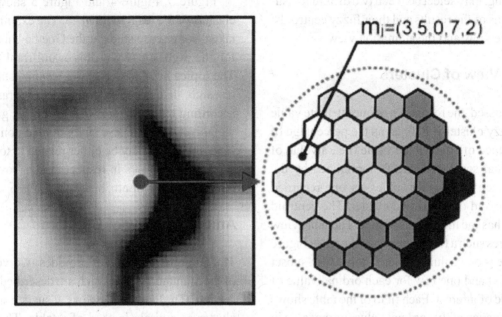

$m_j = (3,5,0,7,2)$

An important factor of the algorithm is the network size. The computation time of the algorithm is quadratic with respect to the neuronal net side length. The best case run time is approximately at least *maxIterations* * *n* for *n* records in a dataset because the algorithm always use a maximum number of steps. However, in this case, the dataset has to be read only once per iteration.

THE GUGUBARRA FRAMEWORK AND THE VISUALIZATION OF FUZZY CLUSTERS AND THEIR CENTROIDS

The fuzzy CORD approach is tested in a case study at the Goethe University for the web site www.dbis.cs.uni-frankfurt.de as part of the Gugubarra Framework. The visualization of fuzzy centroids is described in this section on the basis of the study results.

The *Gugubarra Framework* is an independent software but open to communicated with Content-Management-Systems (CMS). Its version 3.0 is in the prototype test stage and consists of two applications: the *Gugubarra Designer* and the *Gugubarra Analyzer*. Each is composed of different components, which are implemented in Java and PHP. The Gugubarra Designer runs on the server machine of the web site and is a part of a CMS, e.g., a plug-in for the *Joomla!* CMS. Here, the web site owner or editor can add topics and actions to the content via a web browser. The result is stored in XML metadata files together with the log files of the user sessions. The owner or analyzer can then use the Gugubarra Analyzer to calculate, store, and cluster the NOP profiles. Further information on the architecture, implementation and snapshots are reported in (Hoebel, 2011).

The Gugubarra Analyzer is implemented in Java. The web interface was built using Tapestry 5.1 and JavaFX 1.2. With the Gugubarra Analyzer, the stored non-obvious and feedback profiles of the web users can be clustered with CORD. Each time the algorithm is processed, a result is stored in the database. Each result may be selected, and its clusters can be visualized. The user, who is analyzing, may select between two different visualizations of the results and their fuzzy centroids: the table view and the animation view.

Table View of Clusters

As discussed, the resonance of one attribute value in a fuzzy cluster is defined as the percentage of appearance of an attribute value (i.e., a value of an ordinal scale of interest) normalized by the appearance of all other values for one regarded attribute and one regarded cluster. The centroid always has the highest resonance. The table view visualizes such a fuzzy cluster, as shown in Figure 3. There is one column for each topic (or a subset of topics) and one row for each ordinal value of the scale of interest. Each field of the table shows the resonance of this ordinal value for the topic in the visualized cluster. Thus, the higher the resonance is, the darker is the gray color of the field. This feature is comparable to the gray scale, as discussed in the "Motivation" section.

The centroid is marked with a red border. For example, the centroid of the cluster shown in Figure 3 has a resonance of 99% for a medium interest in the topic of teaching and 97% for a high interest in the topic of exams. This feature makes the advantage of the fuzzy centroids with an ordinal scale apparent. The scale automatically gives a cluster interpretation or meaning that labels the group of users in this cluster. For example, the cluster of Figure 3 represents a group of people, where the majority seem to have a medium interest in teaching.

Figure 3, Figure 4 and Figure 5 show the 3 clusters of the result with *id=3*. The example was taken from a case study at the Goethe University for the web site www.dbis.cs.uni-frankfurt.de. The topics here are: teaching, exams, start-ups, research, databases, e-commerce, programming according to the lectures offered of this group at the university. In a case study of an e-commerce field, the topics may be either related to topics or classify the visitors in respect to their loyalty or other behaviors or attributes.

Animated View of Clusters

The Gugubarra Analyzer provides two versions of the animated view, which are described in this section. The animated views visualize a fuzzy cluster as a circle instead of a table. The circle does not immediately show all the information regarding the cluster. Instead, there is a legend and mouse-over tool tips that provide detailed information. The radius size of each cluster correlates to the number of users in relation to other clusters. However, the radius is restricted by a minimum and maximum size.

The topics are arranged on the outside of each cluster circle in a clockwise direction starting at 12 o'clock. The field of the table view is a small colored circle inside the fuzzy cluster. We also name it "field" in the following. The fields of one column, i.e., one topic, are placed radically inside the cluster. With default settings, only 3 fields of one topic are visualized. Figure 6 and Figure 7 show the two animated views for the cluster

Figure 3. Graphical tabular representation of the centroid of the 1st fuzzy cluster of three in total

	Teaching	Exams	Start-Ups	Research	Databases	E-Commerce	Programming
high	0%	97%	0%	2%	0%	0%	0%
medium	99%	0%	0%	0%	97%	0%	0%
small	0%	0%	0%	0%	0%	0%	0%
MISSING VALUE	0%	2%	100%	98%	3%	100%	100%

Figure 4. Graphical tabular representation of the centroid of the 2nd fuzzy cluster of three in total

	Teaching	Exams	Start-Ups	Research	Databases	E-Commerce	Programming
high	37%	68%	95%	95%	37%	100%	100%
medium	37%	21%	5%	5%	11%	0%	0%
small	26%	11%	0%	0%	53%	0%	0%
MISSING VALUE	0%	0%	0%	0%	0%	0%	0%

Figure 5. Graphical tabular representation of the centroid of the 3rd fuzzy cluster of three in total

	Teaching	Exams	Start-Ups	Research	Databases	E-Commerce	Programming
high	0%	0%	0%	7%	0%	0%	0%
medium	30%	0%	0%	0%	0%	0%	0%
small	23%	23%	0%	0%	0%	0%	0%
MISSING VALUE	46%	77%	100%	93%	100%	100%	100%

with *id=1*, according to Figure 4. The difference between the two versions is described below.

The fields are colored differently than the fields of the table view. The colors are used to create a more attractive view then the table view.

The order and the color of the fields vary according to the version of the animated view.

These are the only differences between the two versions. The two animated views - and their implementation of field order and color - are described in the following section:

Scale of Interest View

The *scale of interest view* is strongly connected to the *table view*. As in the table view, the fields are arranged in the order of their scale of the interest value; see the example in Figure 6. The scale of interest value for each topic decreases from the

Figure 6. The scale of interest animated view: Shades refer to the resonance scale

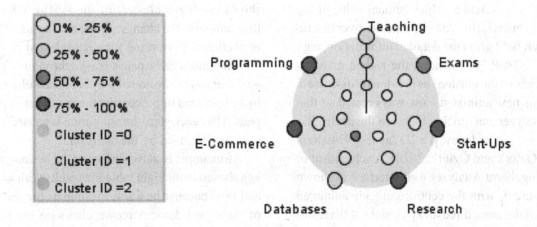

outside to the inside of the fuzzy cluster. The highest scale of interest, e.g. "high", is placed on the border of the circle. The size of each field correlates to the scale of interest value, i.e., bigger circles have a higher interest value.

Because the resonance is not apparent from the order, it is visualized through the color of the fields. A legend/caption defines which color refers to which percentage range of resonance. To obtain the exact percentage, a mouse-over tool tip on each field gives the detailed information, e.g., "high, 37%." Furthermore, the legend gives an overview of the clusters. For example, the legend in Figure 6 describes that the shown yellow fuzzy cluster has an *id=1*.

Centroid Outside View

This view arranges the fields in the order of their resonance; see Figure 7. The resonance of the ordinal value for each topic decreases from the outside to the inside of the fuzzy cluster. As a result, the centroid value of each topic is always on the outside. All fields that are placed on the border of the cluster together make up the centroid. In addition, the size of each field correlates to the resonance value, i.e., bigger circles have a higher resonance.

Because the scale of interest value is not apparent from the order, it is visualized through the colors of the fields. A legend/caption defines which color refers to which ordinal value of the scale of interest. In addition, a mouse-over tool tip on each field gives the detailed information, e.g., "high, 37%." Furthermore, the legend gives an overview of the clusters, as previously discussed.

This new animated view was created so that the analyzer can quickly focus on the centroid.

The animated view is a 2D JavaFX visualization (Öztürk and Öztürk, 2010). A screenshot of the Gugubarra Analyzer web interface is shown in Figure 8, with the centroid outside animated view of the same three fuzzy clusters of the result

with *id=3*, which was introduced in the previous section.

The distance between the clusters is related to one center cluster. The greater the centroid distance between a cluster and the center cluster is, the greater the visualized distance between these two clusters. However, to maintain a feasible and user-friendly view, the distance is restricted to a pre-defined minimum and maximum distance. The cluster chosen as the center cluster may be changed by the analyzer.

Animation of Cluster Changes over Time

The fuzzy clusters belonging to one result are a snap-shot of a certain data constellation. Clusters are dynamic and time-variant, as the users' interests and behaviors may change over time. As a result, certain users might not belong to the same cluster of user interest permanently, and they will migrate to another cluster.

To study these cluster changes, the Gugubarra Analyzer visualizes the motion of a web user through the clusters over time. The moment when the user changes the clusters between two results is shown in Figure 8.

To see the animated movements, the analyzer has to choose two or more results from a table. Then he may start the animation, which successively processes the selected results. The program shows the fuzzy clusters of the first result and then animates the changes to the next result. This animation is performed for each selected result. An animation can be paused (asynchronous). The analyzer has the option of playing the results step by step instead of processing the result list in one pass. After each step, the animation is paused and may be continued by the analyzer.

An example is shown in Figure 8. The analyzer has chosen in the right table the results with *id=1* and *id=3* because he wants to compare the results of these two days. After he clicks on the play button, the animation processes the results. The

Figure 7. The centroid outside animated view: Shades refer to the scale of interest

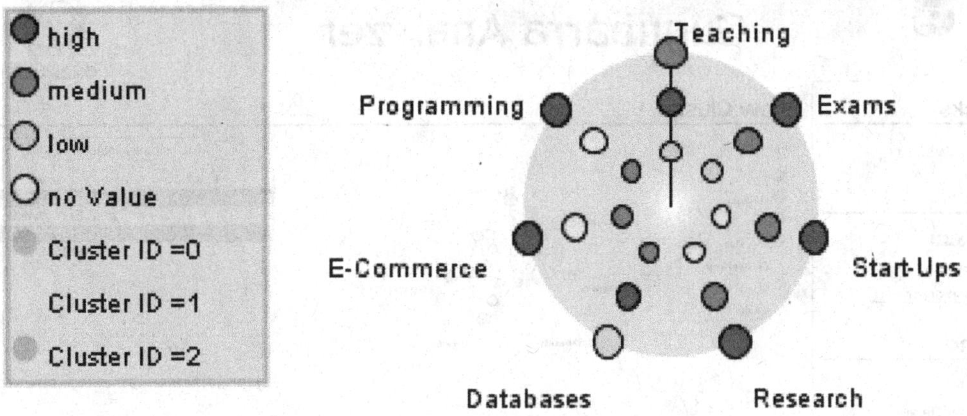

animation first shows the fuzzy clusters resulting from *id=1*. Then it moves the clusters to their new position of result *id=3*.

Afterwards, the animation shows the changes of the clusters (Figure 8) by moving the users from their old cluster to their new cluster. Consequently, small circles, which represent the users, are shifted from one cluster to another. The small circles contain the labels of the number of users that change the cluster. In the example, the users are moved in groups of at most five.

Beyond that, the colors of the small circles are interpolated to demonstrate the flowing transition of users from the old cluster to the new cluster. In addition, a connection channel between the clusters appears to underline the effect of the migration. Additionally, the cluster size may change according to its number of users. The cluster either is made smaller or larger depending on whether users moved to another cluster or were added to the current cluster.

Finally, the topics and field colors are updated to show the resulting clusters of *id=3*.

FUTURE RESEARCH DIRECTIONS

The next version of the Gugubarra Analyzer may provide a third animated view. The view can present a cluster as a multi-vector line graph, known as kiviat graph or spider diagram, which goes back to Georg von Mayr (1877). A design of a kiviat graph for a fuzzy cluster is shown in Figure 9. Each line would represent an ordinal value of the scale of interest. The cross-over of the line with the black topic line reflects the resonance value. If the cross-over is more to the outside, the resonance is higher. A cross-over on the border of the cluster is therefore equivalent to 100% resonance.

Future user tests will show the usability of the different fuzzy centroid views and focus on which views are more intuitive, preferred by analyzers, or easier to understand.

Another topic of research we plan to investigate in the future is analyzing "trends" for a web user community and, when possible, making "forecasts" of the pattern of interest of the web community.

The current version of the Gugubarra Analyzer provides a bar-chart view on the changes of an individual only. A new module should measure "trends" to give an overview of the changes from

Figure 8. The animated scale of interest view of the result with id=3

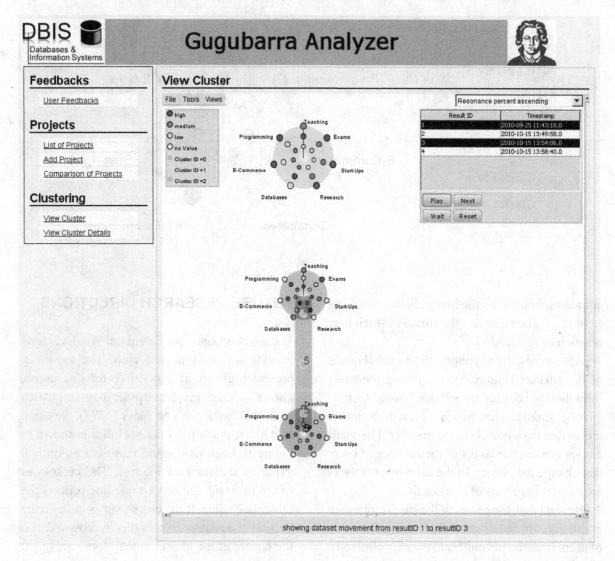

the past to the present in the whole community. It should provide statistical results in addition to the animated view, e.g.:

- "In the last week, there was a strong increase in interest in the topic *Programming*".
- "80% of all visitors have a current stable interest in the topic *Start-Ups*".
- "More than 50% of all visitors interested in *Programming* also showed an interest in *Databases*".

We are also interested in using clusters for predictions. A "forecast" should make an assumption on how the clusters and the interests will change from the present to the future, e.g., "In the next weeks there will be a strong increase of interest in the topic *Start-Ups*".

Showing "trends", predicting "forecasts" and generating targeted e-services will be the focus of future publications.

Figure 9. The design for a multi-vector line graph

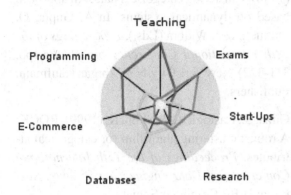

CONCLUSION

This chapter presented a hybrid fuzzy clustering approach and its application for clustering ordinal data in the field of web-usage-mining. This hybrid clustering approach can be effectively used to cluster and analyze large sets of feedback data rendering it particularly useful for the analysis and recognition of user interests and behavior in various environments. Especially when the emphasis lies on more than the classical CRM, the ability to track changing customer interests effectively over time and to react to changing demands arising from changed customer interests in time is an effective way to optimize one's offerings according to the current market situation.

Furthermore the chapter described a practical example, the Gugubarra Analyzer, and how it uses CORD to cluster web users based on their non-obvious and feedback profiles. It described how the results can be visualized and tracked over time effectively without restarting the whole process from the beginning.

SOM- and k-Means-based clustering algorithms are already being used to cluster *numerical data*. This chapter presented an efficient and scalable means to process *ordinal data*, including

large sets, in similar ways. NCSOM is helpful for finding the initial position and number of centroids.

We described an efficient way of extending and implementing the fuzzy k-modes algorithm, so that results may be saved and be resumed or refined instead of being processed each time from the beginning. This procedure is especially helpful in the field of mining large amounts of slowly changing web-usage data.

A simple and efficient modification of the BIRCH algorithm for processing ordinal data was implemented. The implementation of BIRCH can be used as an efficient preliminary phase for both Fuzzy k-Modes with Fuzzy Centroids and NCSOM. Both algorithms benefit from this co-operativity, as their iterative computations can be done on data that is fully held in main memory.

All three algorithms use a distance measure for ordinal data that is based on the considerations and definitions in the section "A Distance Metric for Ordinal Data". This procedure minimizes errors and inaccuracies when linking the different phases of the hybrid system to each other.

However, each of the implemented algorithms can be executed independently or in a different order than the one proposed here. The BIRCH phase, for example, is not necessary when clustering small data sets.

Once web users are clustered by their profiles, the information may be used for targeted offerings, i.e., personalized information or services for web users, if and only if they are requested.

REFERENCES

Aggarwal, G., Feder, T., & Kenthapadi, K. (2006). Achieving anonymity via clustering. *Proceedings of the 25th ACM SIGMOD-SIGACT-SIGART Symposium on Principles of Database Systems* (pp. 153-162). Chicago, IL: ACM Press.

Anderberg, M. R. (1973). *Cluster analysis for applications*. New York, NY: Academic Press.

Banerjee, A., & Ghosh, J. (2001). Clickstream clustering using weighted longest common subsequences. *Proceedings of the Web Mining Workshop at the 1st SIAM Conference on Data Mining* (pp. 33-40). Chicago, IL, USA.

Burke, R. (2002). Hybrid recommender systems: Survey and experiments. *User Modeling and User-Adapted Interaction, 12*(4), 331–370. doi:10.1023/A:1021240730564

Chen, N., & Marques, N. C. (2005). *An extension of self-organizing maps to categorical data. Progress in Artificial Intelligence*. Berlin, Germany: Springer Verlag.

Chiu, T., Fang, D., Chen, J., Wang, Y., & Jeris, C. (2001). A robust and scalable clustering algorithm for mixed type attributes in large database environment *Proceedings of the 7th ACM SIGKDD* (pp. 263-268). San Francisco, CA: ACM Press.

Fu, Y., Sandhu, K., & Shih, M.-Y. (1999). Fast clustering of Web users based on navigation patterns *Proceedings of the World Multiconference on Systemics, Cybernetics, and Informatics (SCI/ISAS '99)* (vol. 5, pp. 560-567). Orlando, Florida, USA.

Gan, G., Yang, Z., & Wu, J. (2005). A genetic k-modes algorithm for clustering categorical data. In Li, X., Wang, S., & Dong, Z. Y. (Eds.), *Advanced data mining and applications* (*Vol. 3584*, pp. 195–202). Springer Verlag. doi:10.1007/11527503_23

Ganti, V., Gehrke, J., & Ramakrishnan, R. (1999). CACTUS - Clustering categorical data using summaries. *Proc. of the 5th ACM SIGKDD International Conference on Knowledge Discovery and Data Mining (KDD '99)* (pp. 73-83). San Diego, CA: ACM Press.

Gibson, D., Kleinberg, J. M., & Raghavan, P. (1998). Clustering categorical data: An approach based on dynamical systems. In A. Gupta, O. Shmueli, & J. Widom (Eds.), *Proceedings of the 24th International Conference on VLDBs* (pp. 311-322). New York City, NY: Morgan Kaufmann Publishers.

Guha, S., Rastogi, R., & Shim, K. (1999). ROCK: A robust clustering algorithm for categorical attributes. *Proceedings of the 15th International Conference on Data Engineering*. Sydney, Australia: IEEE Computer Society.

Hay, B., Wets, G., & Vanhoof, K. (2001). Clustering navigation patterns on a website using a sequence alignment method. *Proceedings of the 17th International Joint Conference on Artificial Intelligence* (pp. 1-6). Seattle, Washington, USA.

Helmer, S. (2007). Measuring the structural similarity of semistructured documents using entropy. *Proceedings of the 33rd International Conference on VLDBs* (pp. 1022-1032). Vienna, Austria: ACM Press.

Hoebel, N. (2011). *User interests and behavior on the Web: Measurements and framing strategies*. Dissertation submitted to Johann Wolfgang Goethe-University. Frankfurt, Germany.

Hoebel, N., Kaufmann, S., Tolle, K., & Zicari, R. V. (2006). The design of Gugubarra 2.0: A tool for building and managing profiles of Web users. In T. Nishida, Z. Shi, U. Visser, X. Wu, J. Liu, B. Wah, W. Cheung & Y.-M. Cheung (Eds.), *Proceedings of the 2006 IEEE/WIC/ACM International Conference on Web Intelligence* (pp. 317--320). Washington, DC: IEEE Computer Society.

Hoebel, N., & Kreuzer, S. (2010). CORD: A hybrid approach for efficient clustering of ordinal data using fuzzy logic and self-organizing maps. In J. Filipe & J. Cordeiro (Eds.), *Proceedings of the 6th International Conference on Web Information Systems and Technologies (WEBIST '10)*. Valencia, Spain: INSTICC Press.

Huang, Z. (1997). A fast clustering algorithm to cluster very large categorical data sets in data mining. *Workshop on Research Issues on Data Mining and Knowledge Discovery (DMKD '97)* (pp. 1-8). Tucson, Arizona, USA.

Kim, D.-W., Lee, K. H., & Lee, D. (2004). Fuzzy clustering of categorical data using fuzzy centroids. *Pattern Recognition Letters*, *25*(11), 1263–1271. doi:10.1016/j.patrec.2004.04.004

Kim, H. R., & Chan, P. K. (2008). Learning implicit user interest hierarchy for context in personalization. *Applied Intelligence*, *28*(2), 153–166. doi:10.1007/s10489-007-0056-0

Kohonen, T. (2001). *Self-organizing maps* (3rd ed.). Springer Verlag.

Kossmann, D., Ramsak, F., & Rost, S. (2002). Shooting stars in the sky: an online algorithm for skyline queries. *Proceedings of the 28th International Conference on VLDBs* (pp. 275-286). Hong Kong, China: Morgan Kaufmann Publishers.

Kreuzer, S. (2008). *Driving the ordinal scale - Moderne Algorithmen zum Einsatz im Data-Mining Bereich*. Frankfurt: Goethe University.

Krishna, K., & Murty, M. N. (1999). Genetic K-means algorithm. *IEEE Transactions on Systems, Man, and Cybernetics. Part B, Cybernetics*, *29*(3), 433–439. doi:10.1109/3477.764879

MacQueen, J. B. (1967). Some methods for classification and analysis of multivariate observations. In L. M. Le Cam & J. Neyman (Eds.), *Proceedings of the 5th Berkley Symposium on Mathematical Statistics and Probability* (vol. 1, pp. 281-297). Berkeley, CA: University of California Press.

Manco, G., Ortale, R., & Sacca, D. (2003). Similarity-based clustering of Web transactions. *Proceedings of the ACM Symposium on Applied Computing* (pp. 1212-1216). Melbourne, FL: ACM Press.

Mayr, G. v. (1877). *Die Gesetzmäßigkeit im Gesellschaftsleben*. Oldenbourg.

Mobasher, B., Dai, H., Luo, T., & Nakagawa, M. (2002). Discovery and evaluation of aggregate usage profiles for Web personalization. *Data Mining and Knowledge Discovery*, *6*(1). doi:10.1023/A:1013232803866

Nambiar, U., & Kambhampati, S. (2005). Answering imprecise queries over web databases. *Proceedings of the 31st International Conference on VLDBs*. Trondheim, Norway: ACM Press.

Ng, R. T., & Han, J. (1994). Efficient and effective clustering methods for spatial data mining. *Proceedings of the 20th International Conference on VLDBs* (pp. 144-155). Santiago, Chile: Morgan Kaufmann Publishers.

Öztürk, B., & Öztürk, M. (2010). *Visualisierung von Clustern*. Frankfurt, Germany: Goethe University.

Parmar, D., Wu, T., & Blackhurst, J. (2007). MMR: An algorithm for clustering categorical data using rough set theory. *Data & Knowledge Engineering*, *63*(3), 879–893. doi:10.1016/j.datak.2007.05.005

Pawlak, Z. (1997). Rough set approach to knowledge-based decision support. *European Journal of Operational Research*, *99*(1), 48–57. doi:10.1016/S0377-2217(96)00382-7

Podani, J. (2005). Multivariate exploratory analysis of ordinal data in ecology: Pitfalls, problems and solutions. *Journal of Vegetation Science*, *16*(5), 497–510. doi:10.1111/j.1654-1103.2005.tb02390.x

Shahabi, C., Zarkesh, A. M., Adibi, J., & Shah, V. (1997). Knowledge discovery from users Web-page navigation. *Proceedings of the 7th International Workshop on Research Issues in Data Engineering, RIDE '97: High Performance Database Management for Large-Scale Applications* (pp. 20-29). Birmingham, UK: IEEE Computer Society.

Shapiro, C., & Varian, H. R. (1998). *Information rules: A strategic guide to the network economy.* Boston, MA: Harvard Business School Press.

Wang, Q. M., Dwight, J., & Edwards, H. K. (2004). Characterizing customer groups for an e-commerce website. *Proceedings of the 5th ACM Conference on Electronic Commerce (EC '04)* (pp. 218-227). ACM Press.

Wang, W., & Zaiane, R. O. (2002). Clustering Web sessions by sequence alignment. *Proceedings of the 13th International Workshop on Database and Expert Systems Applications (DEXA '02)* (pp. 394-398). Aix-en-Provence, France: IEEE Computer Society.

Xiao, J., Zhang, Y., Jia, X., & Li, T. (2001). Measuring similarity of interests for clustering Web-users *Proceedings of the 12th Australasian Database Conference* (pp. 107-114). Gold Coast, Australia: IEEE Computer Society.

Yin, X., Han, J., & Yu, P. S. (2007). CrossClus: User-guided multi-relational clustering. *Data Mining and Knowledge Discovery, 15*(3), 321–348. doi:10.1007/s10618-007-0072-z

Zaki, M. J., Peters, M., Assent, I., & Seidl, T. (2005). CLICKS: An effective algorithm for mining subspace clusters in categorical datasets. *Proceedings of the 11th ACM SIGKDD* (pp. 736-742). Chicago, IL: ACM Press.

Zhang, T. R., Ramakrishnan, R., & Livny, M. (1996). BIRCH: An efficient data clustering method for very large databases. In H. V. Jagadish & I. S. Mumick (Eds.), *Proceedings of the ACM SIGMOD* (pp. 103-114). Montreal, Canada: ACM Press.

KEY TERMS AND DEFINITIONS

Cluster Visualization: The visualization of data collected into a cluster, which represents and summarizes the corresponding data in an efficient way.

Clustering: The assignment of a set of observations (elements) into subsets called clusters so that elements in the same cluster are similar to each other and less similar to elements of other clusters.

Fuzzy Centroid: A centroid is an element that represents the combination of values that is the closest to the average of all the observations in a cluster. Fuzzy denotes that the values of this combination are fuzzy.

Hybrid Algorithm: An algorithm formed by combining several different algorithms (and possibly technologies) to a new solution with unique features and capabilities.

Ordinal Data: A data type for values that can be counted and arranged with respect to an ordering but cannot be the target of mathematical operations such as addition or subtraction as the distance between them is not defined.

User Profile Analysis: The analysis of user profiles, including usage statistics and other behavioral data for each user.

VLDB: Very Large Data Bases.

Web Mining: The application of data-mining techniques to discover informational patterns in data acquired from the web.

Chapter 6
Using a Fuzzy-Based Cluster Algorithm for Recommending Candidates in E-Elections

Luis Terán
University of Fribourg, Switzerland

Andreas Ladner
Institut de Hautes Études en Administration Publique, Switzerland

Jan Fivaz
University of Bern, Switzerland

Stefani Gerber
University of Bern, Switzerland

ABSTRACT

The use of the Internet now has a specific purpose: to find information. Unfortunately, the amount of data available on the Internet is growing exponentially, creating what can be considered a nearly infinite and ever-evolving network with no discernable structure. This rapid growth has raised the question of how to find the most relevant information. Many different techniques have been introduced to address the information overload, including search engines, Semantic Web, and recommender systems, among others. Recommender systems are computer-based techniques that are used to reduce information overload and recommend products likely to interest a user when given some information about the user's profile. This technique is mainly used in e-Commerce to suggest items that fit a customer's purchasing tendencies. The use of recommender systems for e-Government is a research topic that is intended to improve the interaction among public administrations, citizens, and the private sector through reducing information overload on e-Government services. More specifically, e-Democracy aims to increase citizens' participation in democratic processes through the use of information and communication technologies. In this chapter, an architecture of a recommender system that uses fuzzy clustering methods for e-Elections is introduced. In addition, a comparison with the smartvote system, a Web-based Voting Assistance Application (VAA) used to aid voters in finding the party or candidate that is most in line with their preferences, is presented.

DOI: 10.4018/978-1-4666-0095-9.ch006

1 MOTIVATION

The rapid increase of information on the Internet is currently a key issue when one is looking for relevant information. In the political sector, the amount of available information about candidates and political parties is also drastically increasing. This is becoming a significant issue for voters when they face election processes that require them to select their representatives from a big list of candidates since, in many cases, the candidates are relatively unknown to their constituents.

In this chapter, the use of recommender systems for eElections is presented as an alternative to solve the problems of information overload.

Recommender systems are computer-based techniques that attempt to present information about products that are likely to be of interest to a user. This technique is mainly used in eCommerce in order to provide suggestions on items that a customer is, assumable, going to like.

Yager (2003) distinguishes between recommender systems and targeted marketing by considering that a recommender system is a "participatory" system in which the user intentionally provides information about his preferences. In a targeted marketing effort, the recommendation is based on extensional information, which is nothing but information predicated upon the actions or past experiences with respect to specific objects.

A recommender system for eCommerce specifies two basic entities, which include the user (i.e., customer) and the item (i.e., product). The main goal of this type of recommender system that is used in eCommerce is to basically increase the sales of products. The main problems of recommender systems, according to Vozalis et al. (2003), include the following:

- **Quality of Recommendations:** The information received from a recommender system must be reliable; for that reason, recommender systems should minimize the number of false positive results (i.e., the products that the customer does not like).

- **Sparsity:** A recommendation system is related to the number of recommendations made by customers. The sparsity problem of recommender systems emerges when the number of rated items is small compared to the total number of items, which leads to weak recommendations since the recommender systems are based on similarities between individuals.

- **Scalability:** Increasing the number of users and products elevates the cost in terms of computations in recommender systems.

- **Lost of Neighbor Transitivity:** The correlations between users cannot be expressed unless they have purchased and rated common items.

- **Synonymy:** Recommender systems generally cannot link products with different names that belong to the same category.

- **First Rater Problem:** A product cannot be recommended unless another customer has previously rated it.

- **Unusual User Problem:** This problem refers to users who cannot define their opinion about a product. This causes inconsistent recommendations.

The most-used techniques in recommender systems are based on collaborative filtering technologies according to Guo et al. (2007) and Sarwar et al. (2001). They include collaborative filtering algorithms that are memory-based (i.e., user-based) and model-based (i.e., item-based).

- **Memory-based collaborative filtering algorithms:** These techniques are based on the computation of "neighborhood formation" that uses the user-item matrix R, which contains the ratings of items by users (users are not required to provide their opinion on all items). This may cause the previously mentioned problem of sparsity.

The most common techniques used to reduce the effect of sparsity consist of default voting, preprocessing using averages, the use of filterbots, and the use of dimensionality reduction techniques.

- **Model-based collaborative filtering algorithms:** The model-based (i.e., item-based) collaborative filtering algorithm uses the set of items that the active user u_a has ranked to compute the similarities between this item and a target item (i_j) and to select the n most similar items. In order to compute similarities between items i_i and i_j, model-based techniques isolate the users that have rated both items.

According to Yager (2003), recommender systems, which are used in eCommerce, can be classified as "targeted marketing" since they use information that is based on the actions or past experiences of users. The accuracy of the recommendation in this type of method depends directly on users' participation. In targeted marketing, the main objective of the recommendation is to increase the margin of sales by recommending products that the users are likely to find appealing.

Given that we focus on recommender systems, which could contribute to improved democratic processes in eGovernment, the definition of Yager (2003) for recommender systems is used in this chapter with the assumption that, in eGovernment systems, the users are willing to participate in the process of providing information about their preferences.

2 ELECTRONIC GOVERNMENT AND ELECTRONIC DEMOCRACY

The European Commission (2010) refers the term *eGovernment* to the use of information technologies to improve the interaction between public administrations, citizens, and the private sector. Three types of relationships are defined for eGovernment: Administration-to-citizens (A2C), Administration-to-Business (A2B), and Administration-to-Administration (A2A).

Meier (2009) describes an eGovernment framework developed at the University of Fribourg that consists of three levels: Information and Communications, Production, and Participation. It is shown in Figure 1(a).

The lowest level provides information and communication for eGovernment. It focuses on the design of communal Web portals. The second level consists of the actual public services (e.g., electronic procurement, taxation, and electronic payments, among others). The third level refers to citizen participation. This chapter focuses on the participation level; more specifically, eDemocracy.

The term *eDemocracy* refers to the use of information and communication technologies that enable citizens to exercise their rights and fulfill their obligations in the information and knowledge society in a time- and place-independent manner.

In his work, Meier (2009) mentions the importance of citizen participation in eDemocracy (e.g., eElection and eVoting). Meier defines the term *eDiscussion* as a stage where citizens could know more about the candidates or the subject in a voting process. It uses information and communication technologies, such as forums, decision aids, and subscription services, among others, to aid voters in making decisions.

In the same way, once an eVoting or eElection process has been completed, Meier defines the term *ePosting* as another stage that is required on eDemocracy. This stage facilitates the publication of results, and it gives voters the possibility to open discussion channels about the process. Figure 1(b) shows the stages of eVoting and eElection as part of a process chain.

In this chapter, a fuzzy recommender system (FRS) for eElections introduced by Terán et al. (2010) is used. The FRS provides a user-friendly bi-dimensional interface, which can help voters to establish the most similar candidates according

Figure 1. e-Government framework

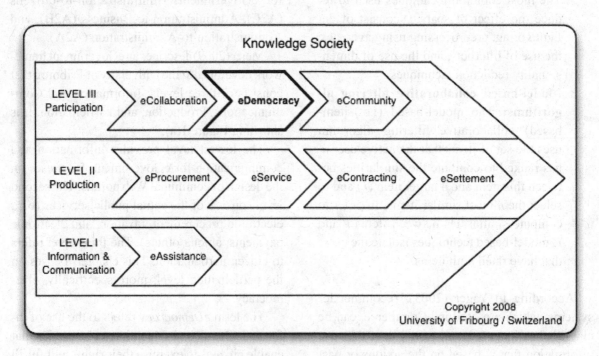

(a) Knowledge Society

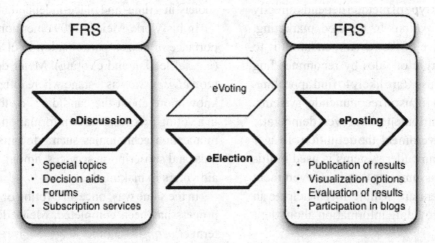

(b) Stages of eVoting and eElection as part of a Process Chain

to their preferences and tendencies. Figure 1(b) shows that the FRS could also be employed on eDiscussion as an add-on tool so that users may become better acquainted with the candidates who are involved in an election. Different types of tools similar to the FRS have been used in different countries. In this chapter, a Web-based application called *smartvote*, which has been used in Switzerland since 2003, is described.

In addition, Figure 1(b) shows that the FRS could also be used on ePosting as an add-on tool to analyze the congruence between pre- and post-election periods. This tool could help citizens to improve what is described in the work of Meier (2009) as "public memory" and to enhance the so-called "political controlling." In the work of Schwarz et al. (2010), an analysis of congruence in the Swiss lower house between 2003 and 2009 indicates that 85% of elected authorities voted in the parliament according to what they claimed on *smartvote* when they where candidates. The FRS could be used with the approach proposed by Schwarz et al. (2010) in which 34 *smartvote* questions came up in the parliament. For that reason, an appropriate design of the questions used to generate candidates' profiles is extremely important if analysis of congruence is required. In this chapter, the generation of profiles is not covered; rather, it is only assumed that such a profile can be generated and evaluated by using the FRS for both pre- and post-election periods.

Finally, according to Yager (2003) and with the assumption that users are willing to collaborate in providing information about their preferences, recommender systems that are used in eDemocracy are classified as "participatory" systems. These types of recommender systems are suitable for the one-and-only item, according to Guo et al. (2007), where the *recommendation target* is a unique item/event. Examples of one-and-only items include the sale of a house, trade exhibitions, elections, voting, and community building efforts, among others, where recommendations make no use of past actions since these events occurred only once.

3 SMARTVOTE: A VOTING ADVICE APPLICATION

3.1 About Smartvote

The amount of data available on the Internet is growing exponentially and creating what can be considered an almost infinite and ever-evolving network with no discernable structure. This phenomenon not only affects our daily lives, but it also has an important impact on politics and electoral campaigns. In the work of Fivaz et al. (2010), clear evidence of the increasing popularity of Voting Advice Applications (VAAs)[1] is shown. In this work, Fivaz et al. (2010) describe the use of the *smartvote* (2010) project, which is an online VAA for local, cantonal, and national elections in Switzerland

smartvote was developed in 2002 and 2003 by the Swiss non-profit organization Politools[2]. The core of *smartvote* is the issue-matching module. A couple of months before an election, all candidates receive the *smartvote* questionnaire, either by e-mail or post, and they are asked to mark their responses and return it. The 2007 questionnaire consisted of more than 70 questions on the most important political issues (e.g., "Do you think that nuclear power plants should be shut down?"). The possible answers are "yes," "rather yes," "rather no," and "no". Candidates do not have the possibility to opt out. They must answer all questions and confirm their answers before they are saved in the *smartvote* database.

About two months before the election, the *smartvote* Web site is made accessible to the voters and leads them through three steps in order to arrive at their individual voting recommendation. First, voters must specify their political profile. They are asked to answer the same questionnaire that the candidates completed, but they can choose between a "deluxe version" that consists of all questions and a "rapid version" that only includes 36 questions. Unlike the candidates, the voters have also a "no answer" option if they wish to leave out a number of questions, and they can weigh the answers according to the level of importance that the issues hold for them. The Web site provides voters with additional background information, including pros and cons for each question. Second, voters have to select the constituency for which they want to receive a voting recommendation, and they must also decide whether they wish to receive a voting recommendation on the individual candidate or party level. Third, *smartvote* compares the voters' answers with the answers of parties or candidates, including the voters' weighting factors. As a result, the voters receive voting recommendations in the form of individualized "matching lists" with a decreasing ranking of parties or candidates according to their match to the voters' answers (see Figure 2(a))

The Web site also provides visualizations for political profiles:

- The *smartmap* shows political positions in a two-dimensional coordinate system, where the North-South axis represents a liberal-conservative tendency, and the West-East axis represents a left-right tendency. Figure 2(b) shows an example of *smartmap* in which the dots represent a

specific candidate and the colors signify political parties.

- The *smartspider* expresses the strength of attitudes and positions of political candidates based on themes. The *smartspider* has eight axes that are oriented from the perspective of their content to areas of Swiss politics. Figure 2(c) shows an example of a *smartspider* that indicates the political tendencies of a specific candidate and the voter.

- Additionally, *smartvote* offers a comprehensive database of all candidates that consists of a political profile, information about their political careers and agendas, details about their education, professional and family backgrounds, as well as links

Figure 2. Smartvote system outputs

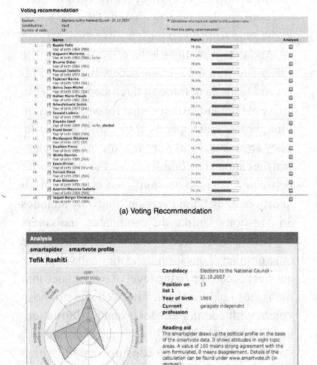

(a) Voting Recommendation

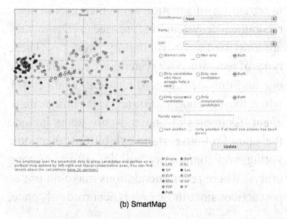

(b) SmartMap

(c) SmartSpider

(d) Candidate Profile

to their personal Web sites and video files. Figure 2(d) shows an example of this type of output.

3.1.1 Participation

smartvote went online for the first time in June 2003 at the start of the national election campaign. Slightly more than 50% of the candidates participated and answered the questionnaire. In the following years, *smartvote* offered its services to several dozen of cantonal and local elections. With every election that it covered, the Web site could increase its popularity and gain more media partners to the extent that, in 2007, *smartvote* was considered a regular part of the electoral campaign. More than 30 media partners (e.g., print media as well as TV and radio broadcasters) supported *smartvote* and integrated the tool and its analyses, such as the *smartspider* graphs of important candidates, into their own news coverage. Due to the cooperation with media partners, *smartvote* present both on- and offline via the media. With regard to this broad coverage it is not surprising that, in the 2007 elections, the number of participating candidates increased considerably: Out of the 3,100 candidates, 85% revealed their political preferences by answering the *smartvote* questionnaire. The program's use by voters also increased. The number of generated voting recommendations grew from 255,000 in 2003 to nearly one million in 2007.

3.1.2 Impacts on Voters' Decision-Making

After the 2007 national elections, a survey among *smartvote* users was conducted. Among other aspects, this survey data allows a look at the impact *smartvote* has had on voters and their decision-making process. Initial analysis of this data showed that its users regarded *smartvote* as an important channel of information (Fivaz & Felder, 2009).

In actuality, they regarded *smartvote* as their most important source of information (see Figure 3).

Furthermore, Ladner et al. (2010) found evidence, based at the same survey data, that *smartvote* also directly affected voters' decisions: 67% of the *smartvote* users stated that the voting recommendation that they received influenced their electoral choice. This finding is supported by additional evidence. Ladner et al. (2010) could also show that among *smartvote* users, the amount of swing-voters, or those who voted for a different party than in the previous elections, is significantly higher than among voters who did not use *smartvote*. However, since these are only initial results, they should be treated with caution. Nevertheless, they clearly indicate that the *smartvote* voting recommendation does affect the electoral decision. Thus, it is very important to take a closer look at the applied methods for calculating *smartvote's* data.

3.2 Smartvote Profile Generation

smartvote's recommendations are based on the similarities that exist between voters and candidates. In a first step, candidates and voters must specify their own political profiles through their responses on a questionnaire, which consists of 60-80 questions regarding political issues. The *smartvote* questionnaire can be divided into groups of questions that each addresses a specific political field. The *smartvote* questionnaire defines two types of questions:

- **Standard Questions,** which are related to the acceptance or rejection of a specific political issue.
- **Budget Questions**, which inquire whether you would spend more or less in certain areas.

Figure 3. Importance of media and campaigning

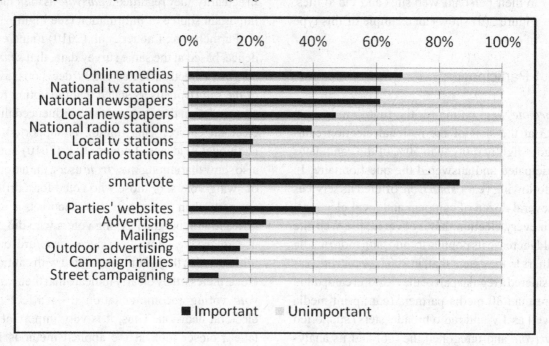

3.3 Smartvote Match Points Computation

To generate its recommendations, the *smartvote* system uses a statistical method to compute the "match points" by using equation (1):

$$MP_i(v,c) = 100 - |a_{iv} - a_{ic}| + b \qquad (1)$$

where $MP_i(v,c)$ represents the number of points of agreement (i.e., match points), a_{ic} and a_{iv} represent the numerical answers given by voter *v* and candidate *c* to questions *i*, and *b* represents a bonus which applies if, and only if, we are in the presence of a perfect match ("Yes-Yes" and "No-No" combinations).

The next step in the matching calculations is to take into account the relevance that each voter gives to each question. All the questions also have a weighting, which consist of "+", "=", and "-." Depending on the weighting assigned by the voter, the corresponding match points are multiplied by

the factors 2, 1, or 0.5 (weighting value "+" corresponds to factor value 2, weighting value "=" corresponds to factor value 1, and weighting value "-" corresponds to factor value 0.5), as shown in equation (2):

$$MP_i(v,c,w) = (100 - |a_{iv} - a_{ic}| + b) \times w_i \qquad (2)$$

where w_i is the weighting value that citizen *c* gives to a given questions *i*. A matching value, which is the percentage between voter *v* and candidate *c*, is calculated using equations (3) and (4),

$$MP(v)_{Max} = \sum_{i=1}^{n} a_{iv} \times w_i \qquad (3)$$

where $MP(v)_{Max}$ is the theoretical maximum possible match score, which depends only on the answers and weights of voter *v*.

$$MP(v,c,w) = \frac{MP(v,c,w)}{MP(v)_{Max}} \times 100 \qquad (4)$$

where $MP(v,c,w)$ represents the matching value as the percentage between voter v and candidate c.

smartvote can also be used in order to generate recommendations by full lists; in this case, the matching values are computed by using the mean average of all candidates on the list.

3.4 Smartvote Recommendation Output

The output that relevant for this article is the voting recommendations shown in Figure 3(a), which provides a list of candidates that are closest to the voter's political profile. The voting recommendations can be displayed either by candidate or full list.

3.5 Symmetry Problem

There is a drawback in using *smartvote's* matching point computation. Known as "the symmetry problem," this challenge can be illustrated with the following example:

Two individuals, p_1 and p_2, both answer the *smartvote* questionnaire as both voters v_1 and v_2 and candidates c_1 and c_2, respectively. The responses to all of their questions as candidate and voter are the same for p_1 and p_2. Assume that the answer to a specific question of p_1 is "Yes" (score = 100), and p_2 is "Probably Yes" (score = 75).

The relation between pairs $v_1 - c_2$ and $v_2 - c_1$ are

$$MP(v_1, c_2) = \frac{100 - |100 - 75|}{150} = 0.5$$

$$MP(v_2, c_1) = \frac{100 - |100 - 75|}{100} = 0.75$$

As it is shown, the computation of matching points depends on the maximum possible match score, which, in turn, depends on the answer that is provided by the voter.

4 FUZZY-BASED CLUSTER ALGORITHM FOR RECOMMENDIND E-ELECTIONS

Although collaborative filtering-based approaches are more widely used, they are only suitable in the repeat-appeared scenario, which is described by Vozalis (2003). As mentioned in section 2.2, recommender systems for eGovernment must also be suitable in the one-and-only items scenario, in which the *recommendation target* is a unique item/event (i.e., a voter v wants to receive a recommendation of n candidates that are close to his preferences in an election E).

In the voting/election scenario, the recommendation makes no use of past events, given the fact that candidates could be different for each election or they could change their political orientation.

Furthermore, in the recommendation generation, it is necessary to define the elements needed and the output of the system that is developed. As mentioned previously, a recommender system that is used on eElections must be able to recommend a list of n candidates close to the preferences of a specific voter.

In this chapter, a fuzzy-based cluster algorithm for recommending in eElections that was introduced by Terán et al. (2010) is presented. It provides information about the closest candidates to a voter and the distribution of political parties that are organized in fuzzy clusters.

In the section 4.1, the basic concepts of fuzzy logic, fuzzy sets and fuzzy clustering are introduced. Section 4.2 shows the architecture of the fuzzy recommender systems (FRS) and their components, which are better described in sections 4.3 (fuzzy interface), 4.4 (fuzzy profile), 4.5 (recommendation engine), and 4.6 (recommendation output).

4.1 Fuzzy Logic, Fuzzy Sets, and Fuzzy Clustering

Fuzzy logic is a multi-value logic that allows a better understanding of the result of a statement that, in real life, is more approximate than precise. In contrast with "sharp logic," in which the results of a statement are binary ("true or false," "one or zero"), fuzzy logic admits a set of truth-values in the interval [0,1]. Fuzzy logic is derived from the fuzzy set theory that was introduced by Zadeh (1965) in which a fuzzy set is determined by a membership function with a range of values between 0 and 1. Zadeh (1965) provides a definition of fuzzy sets, which is shown below:

Definition 1. A fuzzy set is built from a reference set that is called the universe of discourse. The reference set is never fuzzy. Assuming $U = \{x_1, x_2..., x_n\}$ as the universe of discourse, then a fuzzy set A ($A \subset U$) is defined as a set of ordered pairs: $\{(x_i, \mu_A(x_i))\}$, where $x_i \in U$, $\mu_A: U \rightarrow [0,1]$ is the membership function of A and $\mu_A(x) \in [0,1]$ is the degree of membership of x in A.

Fuzzy clustering is an unsupervised learning task, which aims to decompress a set of objects into "clusters" based on similarities, where the objects belonging to the same cluster are as similar as possible. In sharp clustering, each element is associated with just one cluster.

The main algorithms used to generate clusters are c-means (sharp clustering) and fuzzy c-means (fuzzy clustering). The fuzzy recommender system that is proposed in this chapter uses the fuzzy c-means algorithm explained below.

The c-means algorithm that was originally proposed by Bezdek (1981) is a method of cluster analysis, which aims to partition n observations into c clusters. Each observation belongs to one and only one cluster. Fuzzy c-means (FCM) is an extension of the c-means algorithm, which allows gradual membership of data points to clusters with different degrees of membership according

to the fuzzy set theory introduced by Zadeh (1965). Thus, fuzzy c-means defines a given set of samples $X = \{x_1, x_2,...,x_n\}$, a set of clusters Y_i ($\{i=1,...,c\}$ and $\{2 \leq c < n\}$), and a $c \times n$ fuzzy partition matrix $U=[u_{ij}]$. The membership degree u_{ij} of an observation x_i in a cluster Y_i is such that $u_{ij} = \mu_{\Gamma_i}(x_j) \in [0,1]$.

A probabilistic cluster partition defined by the constraints in (5) and (6) guarantees that clusters are not empty, and that the sum of the membership for each x is equal to 1.

$$\sum_{j=1}^{n} u_{ij} > 0, \forall i \in \{1,...,c\} \tag{5}$$

$$\sum_{i=1}^{c} u_{ij} = 1, \forall j \in \{1,...,n\} \tag{6}$$

Thus, the FCM algorithm is based on minimization of an objective function shown in (7),

$$J_m = \sum_{i=1}^{c} \sum_{j=1}^{n} u_{ij}^m \| x_j - y_i \|^2 \tag{7}$$

where x_j is the j-th of d-dimensional measured data, y_i is the d-dimensional center of cluster i, m is any real number greater than 1 (m determines the level of fuzziness, and $m=2$ is a typical value that is used), and $\| * \|$ is any norm that expresses the similarity between any measured item and the cluster center.

In (7), $Y=[y_i]$ is a matrix of cluster centers ($i=\{1,...,c\}$).

The membership function u_{ij} and the center y_i of clusters are computed in order to take the derivative of the objective function J_m with respect to the parameters to optimize equal to zero, and, taking in to account constraint (6), equations (8) and (9) are obtained.

$$u_{ij} = \frac{1}{\sum_{l=1}^{c} \frac{\| x_j - y_i \|}{\| x_j - y_l \|}^{\frac{2}{m-1}}} \qquad (8)$$

$$y_i = \frac{\sum_{j=1}^{n} u_{ij}^m x_j}{\sum_{j=1}^{n} u_{ij}^m} \qquad (9)$$

The FCM algorithm is a two-step iterative process that is defined as follows: First, set the input variables c, m, and ε (ε is a termination criteria, and normally $\varepsilon \in [0,1]$). Second, set an iteration number $k=0$. Third, randomly generate a matrix of cluster centers $Y^{(k)}$. Then, given the initial matrix $Y^{(k)}$, compute the fuzzy partition matrix $U^{(k)}$.

Finally, using a repeat-until loop, update $Y^{(k+1)}$ using $U^{(k)}$, then update $U^{(k+1)}$ using $Y^{(k+1)}$. The process is repeated until the termination criterion is reached ($|U^{(k+1)} - U^{(k)}| \leq \varepsilon$). The termination criteria could also be a predefined number of iterations. The FCM algorithm is defined in Table 1.

The outputs of the modified FCM are a fuzzy partition matrix $U^{(k+1)}$, which contains the membership degree of each element x_j, and a matrix of cluster centers $Y^{(k+1)}$.

Table 1. FCM Algorithm

```
Input: c, m, ε
Output: U^(k+1), Y^(k+1)
1: Set iteration number: k ← 0
2: Generate matrix of cluster centers: Y^(k) ← random
3: Compute U^(k) ← Y^(k)
4: repeat
5: Update Y^(k+1) ← U^(k)
6: Update U^(k+1) ← Y^(k+1)
7: until |U^(k+1) - U^(k)| ≤ ε
8: return U^(k+1), Y^(k+1)
```

4.2 Architecture

The recommendation process is divided into three steps. In the first step, the voters and candidates must create their profiles by using a fuzzy interface, which is described in greater detail in the following section, to be stored in a database.

In the second step, once all necessary profiles have been created, the user selects the recommendation target and the type of output (i.e., the top-N recommendation or fuzzy cluster analysis). In the final step, once the recommendation engine has computed all information, the user receives the recommendation in the pre-established format. The architecture of the FRS is presented in Figure 4(a). Each element is discussed in depth in the following sections.

4.3 Fuzzy Interface

The fuzzy interface is comparable to the *smartvote* interface that is used by candidates and voters to complete a questionnaire regarding political issues (each question has different possible responses). In spite of the flexibility provided by the *smartvote* interface, it can be considered a sharp interface. For this reason, and to guarantee flexibility, a convenient tool is used to determine the level of agreement, disagreement, and relevance for each specific question. Figure 4(b) shows an example of the fuzzy interface.

4.4 Fuzzy Profile

In the work of Terán et al. (2010), in order to generate a recommendation, the voters and candidates have to generate a profile that describes their preferences. A profile representation called a "fuzzy profile (FP)" is proposed. The FP, a multi-dimensional Euclidean space, is defined by:

$$FP_i = (fpc_{i1},...,fpc_{in})$$

Figure 4. Fuzzy-based cluster algorithm for recommending candidates in e-elections

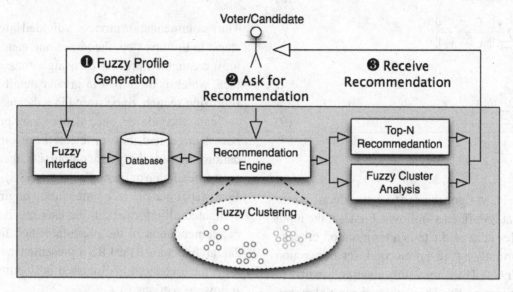

(a) Fuzzy-based Recommender System Architecture

ENVIRONMENT, TRANSPORT ENERGY	Tendency			No Answer	Relevance		
	Disagree	Indifferent	Agree		-	=	+
3 Should the protection provisions of wolves be relaxed?	100 50	0	50 100	◎	100 50	0	50 100

(b) Fuzzy Interface

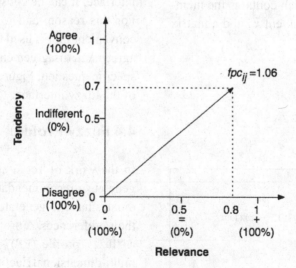

(c) Fuzzy Profile Component Computation

where FP_i is the FP vector of user i, and fpc_{ij} is the j-th fuzzy profile component (fpc).

Each fpc is equal to the norm of a multi-dimensional Euclidean space defined by:

$$fpc_{ij} = \| (q_{ij1}, ..., q_{ijl}) \| = \sqrt{\sum_{k=1}^{l} q_{ijl}^2}$$

where fpc_{ij} is the j-th fuzzy profile component of FP_i, and q_{ijk} is the k-th component of fpc_{ij}.

To illustrate the use of a FP, a *smartvote* profile instance of user i (FP_i) that is composed by n questions ($FP_i = (fpc_{i1}, ..., fpc_{in})$) is used. Each question has two components: "tendency" and "relevance" (q_{ij1} and q_{ij2}), where:

$$fpc_{ij} = \| (q_{ij1}, q_{ij2}) \| = \sqrt{q_{ij1}^2 + q_{ij2}^2}.$$

Figure 4(c) shows the results of the fuzzy profile component (fpc) for a general question in the *smartvote* system.

4.5 Recommendation Engine

The FRS is based on the generation of a fuzzy cluster, as shown in Figure 4(a). Once the FP is generated, the next step is to ask for a recommendation. At this point, the user selects a particular event and the type of recommendation (top-N recommendation or fuzzy clustering analysis). The request is sent to the recommendation engine, which processes the query.

To provide a graphical representation of the results that users can easily analyze, the recommendation engine transforms the high-dimensional space of FP to a bi-dimensional space, which reduces the complexity of data analysis. The recommender engine uses a mapping method that was originally proposed by Sammon (1969), which is described in more detail in below.

4.5.1 Sammon Mapping

Clustering-based data mining tools are becoming popular because they are able to "learn" the mapping of functions and systems or explore structures and classes in the data. Sammon's mapping technique attempts to preserve the inter-pattern distances. It is a well-known technique that is used to transform a high-dimensional space (n-dimensions) to a space with lower dimensionality (q-dimensions) by finding N points in the q-dimensional space.

Denoting the distances between two different points x_i and x_j ($i \neq j$) in the original space as d_{ij}, and the distance between points y_i and y_j in the mapped space as d_{ij}', then the mapping becomes a minimization problem of the called Sammon's stress E, as defined in equation (10)

$$E = \frac{1}{\lambda} \sum_{i=1}^{N-1} \sum_{j=i+1}^{N} \frac{(d_{ij} - d_{ij}')^2}{d_{ij}}, \lambda = \sum_{i=1}^{N-1} \sum_{j=i+1}^{N} d_{ij} \tag{10}$$

In order to minimize E, Sammon applied a steepest descent technique in which the new y_{i_l} at iteration $t + 1$, is given in equation (11)

$$\dot{y}_{i_l}(t+1) = y_{i_l}(t) - \alpha \left[\frac{\frac{\partial E(t)}{\partial y_{i_l}(t)}}{\frac{\partial^2 E(t)}{\partial^2 y_{i_l}(t)}} \right] \tag{11}$$

where $y_{i_l}(t)$ is the l-th coordinate of point y_i in the mapped space, α is a constant that is empirically computed to be $\alpha \approx 0.3$ or 0.4. The partial derivatives in (1) are given by:

$$\frac{\partial E(t)}{\partial y_{i_l}(t)} = -\frac{2}{\lambda} \sum_{k=1,k \neq i}^{N} \left[\frac{d_{ki} - d_{ki}'}{d_{ki} d_{ki}'} \right] (y_{i_l} - y_{k_l})$$

Figure 5. Illustration of Sammon mapping

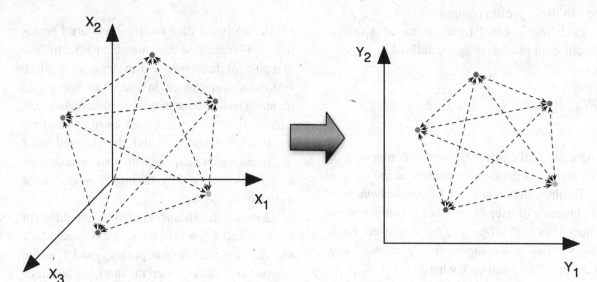

$$\frac{\partial^2 E(t)}{\partial^2 y_{i_i}(t)} = -\frac{2}{\lambda} \sum_{k=1, k \neq i}^{N} \frac{1}{d_{ki} d_{ki'}} \left[(d_{ki} - d_{ki'}) - \left(\frac{(y_{i_i} - y_{k_i})^2}{d_{ki'}} \right) \left(1 + \frac{d_{ki} - d_{ki'}}{d_{ki}} \right) \right]$$

Figure 5 provides an illustration of Sammon mapping from a three-dimensional space to a bi-dimensional space.

This chapter focuses on the Sammon mapping method for the visualization of the clustering results, which preserves inter-pattern distances. Nevertheless, there are three problems that must be taken into account when the Sammon mapping technique is used. They are:

- The prototypes of clusters are usually not known a-priori, and they are calculated along with the partitioning of the data. These prototypes can be vectors that are dimensionally equal to the examined data points, but they also can be defined as geometrical objects (i.e., linear or non-linear subspaces or functions). Sammon mapping is a projection method that is based on the preservation of the Euclidian inter-point distance norm, so it can be only used by clustering algorithms that are calculated with this type of distance norm. As mentioned in section 4.2.3, fuzzy profiles are defined to be a multidimensional Euclidean space, which fulfills the required condition of the Sammon mapping technique.

- The Sammon mapping algorithm forces one to find, in a high n-dimensional space, N points in a lower q-dimensional subspace, such these inter-point distances correspond to the distances measured in the n-dimensional space. This causes a computationally expensive algorithm, since every iteration step requires the computation of N (N−1)/2 distances.

- Finally, this gradient-descent method has the possibility of reaching a local minimum in the error surface, while searching for the minimum of E, so experiments with different random initializations are necessary. In order to avoid this problem, the initialization is estimated using the principal component analysis (PCA) technique, which maps the data points into a lower dimensional space. The PCA technique is described in the following section.

4.5.2 Principal Component Analysis

The PCA technique, which was introduced by Karl Pearson in 1901, involves a mathematical procedure that transforms a number of (possibly) correlated variables into a (smaller) number of uncorrelated variables called principal components. The first principal component accounts for as much of the variability in the data as possible, and each succeeding component accounts for as much of the remaining variability as possible. The main objectives of PCA are:

- To identify new meaningful underlying variables.
- Discover or reduce the dimensionality of the data set.

The mathematical background lies in "eigen analysis:" The eigenvector associated with the largest eigenvalue has the same direction as the first principal component. The eigenvector associated with the second largest eigenvalue determines the direction of the second principal component.

In this chapter, we used the second objective. In that case, the covariance matrix of the data set, which is also called the "data dispersion matrix, is defined as follows:

$$\mathbf{F} = \frac{1}{N}\left(\mathbf{x}_k - \mathbf{v}\right)\left(\mathbf{x}_k - \mathbf{v}\right)^T$$

where $\mathbf{v} = \overline{\mathbf{x}}_k$ is the mean of the data set. N is equal to de number of objects in the data set.

The PCA technique is based on the projection of correlated high-dimensional data onto a hyper-plane. This mapping uses only the first few q nonzero eigenvalues and the corresponding eigenvectors of the covariant matrix is defined as:

$$\mathbf{F}_i = U_i \Lambda_i U_i^T$$

The covariant matrix $\mathbf{F}_i$ is decomposed to the matrix Λ_i that includes the eigenvalues $\lambda_{i,j}$ of $\mathbf{F}_i$ in its diagonal in decreasing order, and to the U_i matrix that includes the eigenvectors that correspond to the eigenvalues in its columns.

The vector $\mathbf{y}_{i,k} = \mathbf{W}_i^{-1}(x_k) = \mathbf{W}_i^T(x_k)$ is a q-dimensional reduced representation of the observed vector x_k, where the weight matrix $\mathbf{W}_i$ contains the q principal orthonormal axes in its column $\mathbf{W}_i = U_{i,q}\Lambda_{i,q}^{\frac{1}{2}}$.

4.5.3 Fuzzy Cluster Analysis

Once the FP is mapped to a low-dimensional space, FRS generates fuzzy clusters by using the fuzzy c-means algorithm (refer to section 4.1), which requires two main inputs: the number of clusters and a random matrix of cluster centers. For this reason, prior knowledge of the dataset is required. In the eElection scenario, FRS considers the number of clusters to be equal to the number of political parties.

The second input that is required by the fuzzy c-means algorithm is the matrix of initial centers, which is generated randomly. Consequently, the algorithm may converge to a local minimum, given the random nature of the algorithm.

To avoid this problem, a modified version of the FCM algorithm is introduced by Terán et al. (2010). It initializes the matrix of centers with a random member of each political party. The initialization process is based on two assumptions: First, the cluster formation relies on the existence of political parties. Second, the members of political parties have the same ideology according to the ACE project (2006). The modified FCM is presented in Table 2.

The outputs of the modified FCM are a fuzzy partition matrix $U^{(k+1)}$ that contains the membership degree of voters and candidates with respect

Table 2. FCM Modified

Input:c, m, ε
Output: $U^{(k+1)}, Y^{(k+1)}$
1: Set iteration number: $k \leftarrow 0$
2: for $i=1$ to c do
3: $y_i \leftarrow$ random member from P_i
4: end for
5: Compute $U^{(k)} \leftarrow Y^{(k)}$
6: *repeat*
7: Update $Y^{(k+1)} \leftarrow U^{(k)}$
8: Update $U^{(k+1)} \leftarrow Y^{(k+1)}$
9: *until* $|U^{(k+1)} - U^{(k)}| \leq \varepsilon$
10: *return* $U^{(k+1)}, Y^{(k+1)}$

to each cluster, and a matrix of cluster centers $Y^{(k+1)}$.

4.5.4 Top-N Recommendation

The top-N candidates similar to voter v are generated by using the bi-dimensional fuzzy profile. The distances of all candidates, with respect to voter v, are computed and the N closest candidates are displayed.

The similarity percentage $(S_{vc_i}(\%))$ of a voter v and the i-th candidate (c_i) is computed using the most distant candidate (d_{max}) as reference. The computation of similarity percentage is shown in equation (12),

$$S_{vc_i}(\%) = 100 - (\frac{100 \times d_{vc_i}}{d_{max}}) \qquad (12)$$

where d_{vc_i} is the distance between voter v and the i-th candidate.

The outputs of this algorithm are the n closest candidates and their similarity percentage with respect to voter v.

4.6 Fuzzy Recommender System Recommendation Output

The objective of the FRS for eElections is to assist voters in making decisions by providing them with information about the candidates that are close to their preferences and tendencies, which could help to improve democratic processes.

Although collaborative filtering-based approaches are more widely used than fuzzy methods, they are only suitable in the repeat-appeared scenario. The recommender systems for eGovernment must also be suitable in the one-and-only items scenario, where the recommendation target is a unique item/event.

In the work of Terán et al (2010), a FRS prototype (FRSP) has been developed to display the results of a recommendation. FRSP has the following input variables: number of clusters (political parties), top-N candidates, total number of candidates, number of questions, number of components of each question, and voter responses. FRSP uses the typical parameters of a fuzzy c-means algorithm (m=2, and ε=1×10^{-4}) and Sammon mapping algorithm (PCA is used as initialization method, total iterations = 500, and relative tolerance =1×10^{-9}).

The recommendation process is given in three steps. First, voters and candidates must create their fuzzy profiles by using a fuzzy interface. The fuzzy interface is a convenient tool that is used to determine the level of agreement/disagreement and relevance of specific questions found in the voter/candidate profiles.

In the work of Terán et al. (2010), the FP of candidates is randomly generated by assuming the answer of candidates and voters. In this chapter, the displayed results correspond to the answers of candidates and voters provided by the *smartvote* (2010) project to the Swiss national elections in 2007. The dataset contains the answers of 257 candidates to the two chambers of the Swiss parliament (i.e., the National Council and the Council of States), who responded to the 73 questions on the *smartvote* questionnaire. The results that are presented in this chapter consider only the voters who answered the complete questionnaire on order to provide a better accuracy of results. The candidates, who are a part of the dataset, belong to the following political parties:

- Central Democratic Union
- Christian Democratic Party
- Christian-Social Party
- Evangelical Party
- Federal Democratic Union
- Green Party
- Independent Citizens Movement
- Labor Party
- Left Alternative
- Liberal Movement Ecology
- Liberal Party
- Opening Movement
- Radical Democratic Party
- Social Democratic Party
- Swiss Democrats

The recommendation engine used by the FRS transforms multi-dimensional fuzzy profiles into bi-dimensional profiles by implementing the Sammon mapping technique, which attempts to preserve inter-pattern differences, and the PCA technique for the initialization.

The FRS shown in this chapter has two graphical interfaces: the fuzzy cluster analysis graphical interface (FCAGI) and the top-N recommendation graphical interface (TNRGI), which are described in the following sections.

On both graphical interfaces: FCAGI and TNRGI, candidates and the voter are represented using different geometric figures in different colors and orientations. Each political party has a center, this is represented by a geometric figure with the same shape and color of the figures representing the candidates belonging to that political party. The percentage of closeness of a voter to the centers of each political party is presented as percentage and it is placed next to each center of clusters.

The results of the experiments that are presented in the following sections have to be interpreted as mentioned.

4.6.1 Fuzzy Clustering Analysis Graphical Interface (FCAGI)

The FCAGI displays, in a bi-dimensional map, the locations of a voter and the candidates (which are labeled according to their political parties), the clusters that are generated according to each political party, and the percentage of the closeness of voter to each cluster. The FCAGI gives voters the possibility to analyze different political parties and topics by using checkboxes (refer to Figure 6).

The fuzzy cluster analysis is computed by applying the bi-dimensional fuzzy profile. The fuzzy clusters are generated by using a modified version of the fuzzy c-means algorithm with two main inputs: the number of clusters and a random matrix of cluster centers. The number of clusters is equal to the number of political parties, and the random matrix of cluster centers is computed by taking a random member of each political party.

Figure 6(a) shows the FCAGI of a *smartvote* dataset voter by taking into account all of the political parties and topics. The results that are displayed show that candidates, who belong to the same political parties, are located close to each other and tend to form clusters in most cases.

Another interesting result is that some candidates are closest to political parties other than the one that they belong to. This result clearly shows that, even though candidates belong to a political party, they do not necessarily think in the same manner, which was an expected result.

A second experiment presented in this chapter uses the fifth-closest political parties to the same voter used in the experiment that is shown in Figure 6(a). The closest political parties shown in Figure 6(a) are:

- Radical Democratic Party (56% of proximity)
- Swiss Democrats (14% of proximity)

Figure 6. fuzzy clustering analysis graphical interface (FCAGI)

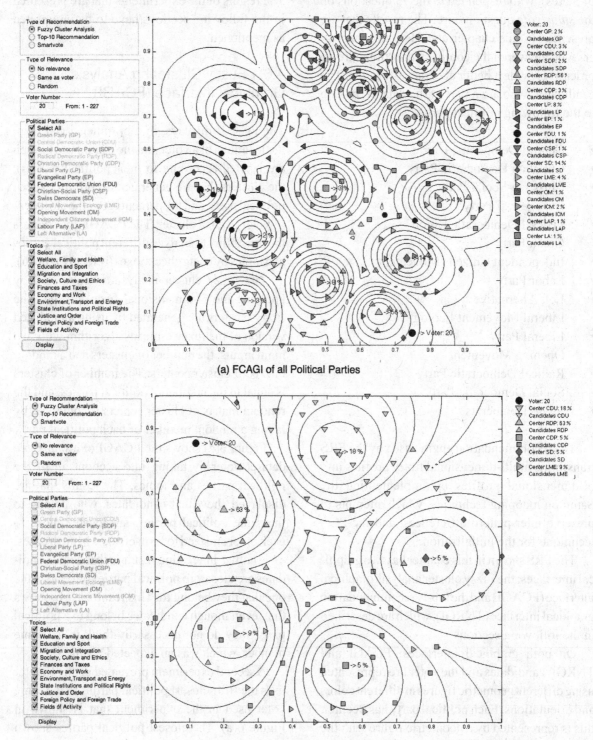

(a) FCAGI of all Political Parties

(b) FCAGI of closest Political Parties to voter

- Liberal Party (8% of proximity)
- Liberal Movement Ecology (4% of proximity)
- Christian Democratic Party (3% of proximity)

Figure 6(b) shows the FCAGI of a *smartvote* dataset user by taking into account all of the topics and the five closest political parties.

The displayed results indicate the formation of clusters. In this experiment, it is also clear that some candidates apparently belong to different political parties. It is possible to explain this observation by realizing that the candidates who belong to a political party do not necessary think in the same manner.

4.6.2 Top-N Recommendation Graphical Interface (TNRGI)

The TNRGI displays the location of a voter, candidates (labeled by political parties), the clusters generated according to each political party, together with a percentage of closeness of the voter to each cluster, and the N-closest candidates labeled with the percentage of proximity to the voter.

The top-N candidates that are similar to voter v are generated by using the bi-dimensional fuzzy profile. The distances of all candidates, with respect to voter v, are computed and the N closest candidates are displayed.

In order to generate the top-N candidates and similarity percentages, the FRSP computes a vector of distances between the voter and all candidates by using the normalized FP.

Figure 7 shows the results of an experiment by using the closest political parties of the voter that were used in previous experiments and shown in Figure 6(b).

5 DISCUSSION

5.1 Issues, Controversies, and Problems

In this chapter, the FRS that was introduced by Terán et al. (2010) is presented. The results shown are using real data that was provided by the *smartvote* project in the Swiss national elections, 2007. Although the obtained results were as expected, there are still some drawbacks that must be taken into account. These drawbacks are related to the generation of profiles, initialization of cluster centers, and the scenario in which the majority of members of each political party do not belong to the same cluster.

Generation of profiles: The fuzzy profile proposed by Terán et al. (2010) considers a multidimensional Euclidean space, which is equal for both voters and candidates. In the case of *smartvote*, the candidates' questionnaire differs from the one that is used by the voters since they can also provide a weighing value to each question.

Initialization of cluster centers: The computation of the centers proposed by Terán et al. (2010) uses a modified version of the fuzzy c-means algorithm, which considers the initial centers by evaluating a random member of the political party. As is shown in Figure 5, the FRSGI displays the locations of politicians in a bi-dimensional space where it is evident that, in some cases, the members of a political party could belong to a cluster that differs from the one that corresponds to his/her political party.

The majority of members do not belong to a cluster: The number of members of a political party must be taken into account for the computation of cluster centers. The fuzzy c-means algorithm moves the centers on each iteration, but it does not consider the case where the majority of members are outside the cluster to which they

Figure 7. Top-N recommendation graphical interface (TNRGI) of closest political parties to voter

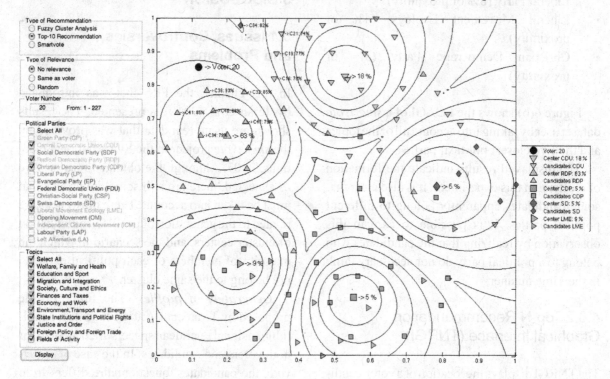

belong; otherwise, there could be the case where the majority of members of a political party are outside their own cluster. This case could be presented when having a political party with a small number of members. The fuzzy c-means algorithm moves the center of all clusters until the stop criteria be reached without considering the case when the center of a cluster was moved far away from their members.

5.2 Solutions and Recommendations

In order to overcome the problems mentioned in previous section, the following solutions are proposed.

Generation of profiles: To avoid the problem that arises when using the data provided by *smartvote* (2010) to evaluate the FRS, due to the lack of weighing the values in the questionnaire of candidates, three solutions were proposed:

- Not to take the voter relevance
- Consider that the relevance of voters is equal to relevance of the candidates
- Assume the random relevance of candidates

The first solutions provide results, but the main problem of this approach is the omission of the information that is provided by voters. In the second and third solutions, we are assuming the candidates' answers, which accomplish nothing except adding noise to our results. These options were implemented and evaluated in the FRS that is presented in this chapter.

Computation of cluster centers: As mentioned in previous section, the initialization proposed by Terán et al. (2010) could lead to be in presence of local minimum in the case that the member which was selected as random is located far away of the cluster where the other members of the political party belongs to.

This scenario could be given since that politicians who belong the same political party do not necessarily think in the same manner. In order to avoid this problem, the initialization centers are computed with the mean value of all members of each political party. In this chapter, the FRS was evaluated by using the proposed initialization method.

The majority of members do not belong to a cluster: To avoid the situation in which the majority of members do not belong to the same cluster, it is recommended that stop criteria be added when the majority of members of a political party are out of each cluster. The FRS presented in this chapter does not consider this final recommendation. Therefore, this recommendation should be considered In future research and evaluation.

6 OUTLOOK

It should be noted that, although the prototype is used for eElections, it could be applied for other domains, such as community building and public memory, among others.

In the case of "public memory," as described in Meier (2009), past behaviors could be taken into account by using voting records to assess the claims of elected authorities prior to the elections, or in the case of candidates who were previously elected. Thus, past behaviors can be used as more reliable profile information.

In the work of Schwarz et al. (2010), an evaluation of congruence of pre-election statements on *smartvote's* voting advice application and post-election behavior in the Swiss lower house between 2003 and 2009 can be found. In this work, the evaluation is conducted by taking 34 questions from the *smartvote* questionnaire were subsequently voted on in the parliament. The results show an 85% political congruence (i.e., acting in accordance to the positions that were revealed in the *smartvote* questionnaire before the election).

In future research, the FRS could also be used to analyze whether the candidates really acted as they claimed. The FRS could display their location in the bi-dimensional map as candidates and how they behave while they were elected authorities to allow voters to easily understand politicians' behavior.

The FRS has to be evaluated and compared by using different methods for dimensionality reduction and clustering algorithms such as:

- Kmeans (clustering algorithm)
- Gustafson-Kessel Algorithm (clustering algorithm)
- Gath-Geva Algorithm (clustering algorithm)
- Lineal Discrimination Analysis (dimensionality reduction)
- Multidimensional Scaling (dimensionality reduction)
- Fuzzy Sammon Mapping (dimensionality reduction)

Once the FRS has been evaluated and compared with other methods and algorithms, the evaluation of the fuzzy interface, FRSGI, and TNRGI must be made. It is important to evaluate how the users of such system react when using the proposed tool in order to evaluate and improve it before putting it in production.

In future research, the FRS could be also used in so-called community building. The main idea is that when voters have filled their profiles, this information could be used for creating communities, which share similar political points of view. The same idea could be used when creating discussion forums, in which the creator of a forum topic could include only those citizens who are close to him, which could generate more constructive debates that can easily end up in consensus.

7 CONCLUSION

In this chapter, the FRS for eElections used in eGovernment proposed by Terán et al. (2010) is presented. The main objectives of FRS are to increase citizens' participation, and to provide more information to citizens about candidates, which could possibly improve democratic processes.

The recommender system approach differs from collaborative filtering methods in that they are based on past experiences. It is also suitable in the one-and-only scenario in which events such as voting and election processes occur only once.

Another important feature that is introduced in the proposed recommendation system is the fuzzy clustering analysis. It provides a graphical representation of political parties distributed in clusters, helping citizens to analyze politician's behavior according to similarities among them.

Fuzzy clustering analysis differs from classic clustering (i.e., sharp clustering) in that the observations belong to one, and only one, cluster. Moreover, classic clustering makes no use of gradual membership.

The main differences between the proposed recommender system and the *smartvote* system are the computation of similarities and the way that recommendations are displayed to users.

The *smartvote* system computes similarities that are based on "match points" (section 3.1), and the recommendations are displayed as a list of the closest candidates with a percentage of similarity.

The FRS computes similarities based on distances in a high-dimensional space. In addition, it computes fuzzy clusters based on the number of political parties, which are part of an eElection process (section 5.1) where candidates and voters are described in a finest granularity and can belong to several clusters.

The recommendations in the FRS are displayed in a bi-dimensional space, which includes the percentage of similarity of the *n*-closest candidates. Therefore, relationships to closest "neighbors" can be derived and analyzed.

8 REFERENCES

Bezdek, J. C. (1981). *Pattern recognition with fuzzy objective function algorithms*. New York, NY: Plenum Press.

European Commission. (2010). *ICT for government and public services*. Retrieved September 10, 2010, from http://ec.europa.eu/information_society/activities/egovernment/index_en.htm

Fivaz, J., & Felder, G. (2009). Added value of e-democracy tools in advanced democracies? The voting advice application *smartvote* in Switzerland. In Shark, A. R., & Toporkoff, S. (Eds.), *Beyond Egovernement–Measuring performance: A global perspective* (pp. 109–122). Washington, DC: Public Technology Institute and ITEMS International.

Guo, X., & Lu, J. (2007). Intelligent e-government services with personalized recommendation techniques. *International Journal of Intelligent Systems, 22*, 401–417. doi:10.1002/int.20206

Ladner, A., Fivaz, J., & Pianzola, J. (2010). *Impact of voting advice applications on voters' decision-making*. Paper presented at the Conference on Internet, Politics, Policy 2010: An Impact Assessment. Oxford.

Meier, A. (2009). *E-democracy & e-government*. Berlin, Germany: Springer.

Mobashe, R., Burke, R., & Sandvig, J. (2006). *Model-based collaborative filtering as a defense against profile injection attacks*. Paper presented at the 21st National Conference on Artificial Intelligence (AAAI'06), Boston, Massachusetts.

Pearson, K. (1901). Principal components analysis. *The London. Edinburgh and Dublin Philosophical Magazine and Journal, 6*, 566.

Project, A. C. E. (2006). *Roles and definitions of political parties*. Retrieved September 10, 2010, from http://aceproject.org/ace-en/topics/pc/pca/pca01/pca01a

Sammon, J. W. (1969). A nonlinear mapping for data structure analysis. *Journal IEEE Transactions on Computers, 18*, 401–409. doi:10.1109/T-C.1969.222678

Sarwar, B., Karypis, G., & Konstan, J. (2001). *Item-based collaborative filtering recommendation algorithms*. Paper presented at the 10th International World Wide Web Conference, China, Hong Kong.

Schwarz, D., Schädel, L., & Ladner, A. (2010). Pre-election positions and voting behavior in Parliament: Explaining positional congruence and changes among Swiss MPs. *Journal Swiss Political Science Review, 16*(4), 533–564. doi:10.1002/j.1662-6370.2010.tb00440.x

Smartvote. (2010). Retrieved September 10, 2010, from http://www.smartvote.ch/

Terán, L., & Meier, A. (2010, september). *A fuzzy recommender system for e-election*. Paper presented at the International Conference on Electronic Government and the Information Systems Perspective (EGOVIS 2010), Bilbao, Spain.

Valente de Oliveira, J., & Witold, P. (Eds.). (2007). *Advances in fuzzy clustering and its applications*. West Sussex, England: Wiley. doi:10.1002/9780470061190

Vozalis, E., & Margaritis, K. (2003). *Analysis of recommender systems' algorithms*. Paper presented at the Sixth Hellenic European Conference on Computer Mathematics and its Applications (HERCMA 2003), Athens, Greece.

Yager, R. (2003). Fuzzy logic methods in recommender systems. *International Journal of Fuzzy Sets and Systems, 136*, 133–149. doi:10.1016/S0165-0114(02)00223-3

Zadeh, L. (1965). Fuzzy sets. *Journal of Information and Control, 8*, 338–353. doi:10.1016/S0019-9958(65)90241-X

KEY TERMS AND DEFINITONS

eGovernment: The use of information technologies and knowledge in the internal processes of government and the delivery of products and services of the state to citizens and industry.

eDemocracy: The use of information and communication technologies to enable citizens to exercise their rights and fulfill their obligations in the information and knowledge society in a time- and place-independent manner.

Fuzzy Cluster Analysis: A method used by the fuzzy recommender system to display, in a bi-dimensional map, the locations of a voter and candidates, as well as the clusters that are generated according to each political party.

Fuzzy Interface: A graphical interface used by candidates and voters in the fuzzy recommender system to complete a questionnaire regarding political issues.

Fuzzy Profile: A multi-dimensional Euclidean space used by the fuzzy recommender system to general profiles of candidates and voters.

Fuzzy Recommender System: An application that is used to recommend candidates who are close to voters' preferences and tendencies in an eElection process.

Top-N Recommendation: A display of the location of voters and candidates, and the clusters that are generated according to each political party, together with a percentage of closeness of voters to each cluster, and the N-closest candidates labeled with the percentage of proximity to the voter.

ENDNOTES

1   Examples of VAA's: Who do I vote for? (www.whodoivotefor.co.uk), Kieskimpas (www.kieskompass.nl), Project Vote Smart (www.vote-smart.org), Glassboth (www.glassboth.org), On the Issues (www.ondthe-

issues.org), Openpolis (www.openpolis.it), Manobalsas (www.manobalsas.lt), smart-vote Ottawa (www.smartvoteottawa.ca), Political Compass (www.politicalcompass.org), EU-Profiler (www.euprofiler.eu),

Niqash(www.nicahs.org), and Wahlkabine (www.wahlkabine.at), Politikkabine (www.politikkabinne.at).

2   *Politools* is a private association in Bern: www.politools.net

Chapter 7
Fuzzy Online Reputation Analysis Framework

Edy Portmann
University of Fribourg, Switzerland

Tam Nguyen
National University of Singapore, Singapore

Jose Sepulveda
National University of Singapore, Singapore

Adrian David Cheok
National University of Singapore, Singapore

ABSTRACT

The fuzzy online reputation analysis framework, or "foRa" (plural of forum, the Latin word for marketplace) framework, is a method for searching the Social Web to find meaningful information about reputation. Based on an automatic, fuzzy-built ontology, this framework queries the social marketplaces of the Web for reputation, combines the retrieved results, and generates navigable Topic Maps. Using these interactive maps, communications operatives can zero in on precisely what they are looking for and discover unforeseen relationships between topics and tags. Thus, using this framework, it is possible to scan the Social Web for a name, product, brand, or combination thereof and determine query-related topic classes with related terms and thus identify hidden sources. This chapter also briefly describes the youReputation prototype (www.youreputation.org), a free Web-based application for reputation analysis. In the course of this, a small example will explain the benefits of the prototype.

INTRODUCTION

The Social Web consists of software that provides online *prosumers* (combination of *pro*ducer and con*sumer*) with a free and easy means of interacting or collaborating with each other. Consequently,

DOI: 10.4018/978-1-4666-0095-9.ch007

it is not surprising that the number of people who read Weblogs (or short blogs) at least once a month has grown rapidly in the past few years and is likely to increase further in the foreseeable future. Blogging gives people the ability to express their opinions and to start conversations about matters that affect their daily lives. These conversations strongly influence what people think about companies and what products they purchase. The influence of these conversations on potential purchases is leading many companies to strategically conduct blogosphere scanning. Through this scanning, it is possible to identify conversations that mention a company, a brand, the name of high-profile executives, or particular products. Through participation in the conversations, the affected parties can improve the company's image, mitigate damage to their reputation posed by unsatisfied consumers and critics, and promote their products.

To proactively shield their reputation from damaging content, companies increasingly rely on online reputation analysis. Because consumer-created Web sites (such as blogs) have enhanced the public's voice and made it very simple to make articulated standpoints and, given the advances and attractiveness of search engines, these analyses have recently become more important. They can map opinions and influences on the Social Web, simultaneously determining the mechanisms of idea formation, idea-spreading, and trendsetting. In light of these factors, the intention of the foRa framework is to let communications operatives search the Social Web to find meaningful information in a straightforward manner. The term *foRa* originates from the plural of *forum*, the Latin word for marketplace. Thus, the foRa framework allows an analysis of reputation in online marketplaces and provides communications operatives—i.e., the companies concerned with reputation management—with an easy-to-use dashboard. This dashboard, which is an interactive user interface, allows the browsing of related topics.

This chapter is organized into six subchapters:

- The first subchapter—*Background*— provides the reader in four sections with definitions and discussions of the topic: the first section states the paradigms of the

Social Web with respect to electronic business; the second section introduces Web search engines and their Web agents; the third section introduces the overall approach to overcome the gap between inexplicit humans and explicit machines; the last section illustrates a visual approach as a link between humans and machines. All of the sections of this subchapter, likewise, incorporate literature reviews.

- The second subchapter—*The Use of Search Engines for Online Reputation Management*—comprises two sections: the first explains reputation management and the second discusses online reputation analysis.

- The third subchapter—*The Fuzzy Online Reputation Analysis Framework*—demonstrates the whole chapter's underlying foRa framework. In doing so, the first section illustrates the framework briefly; the second section explains the building of the fuzzy grassroots ontology; the third section reveals the selection of its ontology storage system; and the fourth section presents the reputation analysis engine.

- The fourth subchapter—*YouReputation: A Reputation Analysis Tool*—presents the youReputation prototype. To provide the readers not only with an abstract framework but also an easy-to-use tool, the building of the *youReputation* (combination of *your* and *reputation*) prototype is also described.

- The fifth subchapter—*Future Research Directions*—discusses further emerging trends and promising fields of study.

- The last subchapter—*Conclusion*—summarizes the key aspects developed and suggests possible further improvements of the presented framework.

BACKGROUND

To explain the advantages of the framework, this subchapter illustrates the underlying fields of study. The first section introduces electronic business and explains the paradigms of the Social Web. Because the framework collects tags from folksonomies by dint of Web agents, the second section provides an overview of the functionalities of Web agents. The third section reveals the metamorphoses from folksonomies to ontologies. The fourth and last section aims to introduce interactive knowledge visualization as Topic Maps.

Electronic Business in the Social Web

In 1972, McLuhan and Nevitt predicted that, with technology, the consumer would increasingly turn into a producer and that the role of producers and consumers would begin to blur and merge. From this concept, the term *prosumer* was coined to express the mutual roles of producer and consumer in online relationships (McLuhan & Nevitt, 1972). As individuals become involved in online processes, their role shifts from passive to active. Thus, *social software* has created a new generation of consumers who are far more interested in companies and products than were the consumers of the past. Social software commonly refers to media that facilitate interactive information-sharing, interoperability, user-centered design, and collaboration. In contrast to erstwhile Web sites where users were limited to passive content browsing, a *social Web site* gives users the freedom to enter a conversation and, thus, to interact or collaborate with others. Examples range from folksonomies, mashups, social networking, and video sharing sites to Web applications, blogs, and wikis (O'Reilly, 2005).

Most online prosumers know the structure of the *Social Web* well, so they share their experiences with companies, brands, products, and services online. Social software is shifting the way in which people communicate by giving them the opportunity to contribute to discussions about anything. Social Web sites are amplifying voices in marketplaces and exerting far-reaching effects on the ways in which people buy. As a result, these Web sites have implications for companies and should be taken seriously while doing (electronic) business.

According to Meier and Stormer (2009), electronic business is defined as the exchange of services with the help of media to achieve added value. In electronic business companies, both public institutions and individuals can be prosumers, and the relationship therein generates added value for all involved. This relationship may take the form of either a monetary or an intangible contribution. A central need of an electronic business is to appropriately manage its relationships with consumers (Bruhn, 2002). As the Social Web is not moderated or censored, individuals can say anything they want, whether it is good or bad. This freedom indicates the need to manage relationships with consumers by carefully watching and, if necessary, interacting with them in an appropriate way (Scott, 2010). Because there are plenty of examples of how not to interact, this communication with consumers should be carefully considered and relinquished to communications operatives to optimize business relationships (Portmann, 2008). Increasingly, companies are looking to gain access to conversations and to take part in the dialogue. This strategy can be integrated into a customer relationship management (CRM) strategy for managing and nurturing the company's interactions with its stakeholders. In electronic business, cautious monitoring of the company's reputation in online marketplaces should be considered.

Now that we have introduced the prosumer paradigm, one can easily imagine the flood of information produced by all of them. Therefore, the next section briefly introduces the concept of Web agents and search engines.

Finding Appropriate Information in the Social Web

A *Web agent* is a program that accumulates information from the Web in an automated and methodical fashion. Primarily, Web agents are used to create a copy of visited sites for later processing by a search engine that allows fast and sophisticated searches. Hence, the Web agent initially starts with a list of sites to visit. While the agent visits this list, it identifies sources in the site and subjoins them into a crawl frontier list. Sources from the crawl frontier list are visited recursively in accordance with a set of conventions.

Using a Web agent, a *Web search engine (WSE)* stores information on the visited Web sites. The information of each site is analyzed, and the results of the analysis are stored and indexed for rapid searching later. Based on an index, a WSE later provides a listing of best-matching Web sites according to a search query. Since Manning et al. (2008), this process has become an accepted standard for information searches and an often-visited source of information-finding. WSEs typically present their results in a single list, called a hit list. The hits can consist of images, text, Web sites, and auxiliary types of documents such as multimedia files (Baeza-Yates & Ribeiro-Neto, 2011).

The foRa framework rests upon the principles of WSEs and Web agents. Based on a search query, our query engine connects to queries with underlying Web content. An important point is that, even though millions of hits may be found by WSEs, some sites may be more relevant, popular, or authoritative than others (Baeza-Yates & Ribeiro-Neto, 2011). A possible means of sorting the found Web sites is by exploring the associations between objects that provide different types of relationships and that are not apparent from isolated data. These analyses have increasingly been applied by search engines to provide a relevance rating.

Today, most search engines apply common operators to specify a search query, but some engines provide an advanced feature that allows for a definition of the distance between topics. In a similar manner, foRa finds and provides better results. Based on the built-in query engine, the framework employs methods to rank the results according to several different factors.

After we have demonstrated the functionality of Web agents and search engines, we now introduce a concept to minimize the gap between humans and machines: in the Social Web, human-made taxonomies can be collected and retooled into machine-understandable ontologies by Web agents. This is the topic of the following section.

From Folksonomies to Fuzzy Ontologies

About three millennia ago, the ancient Assyrians annotated clay tablets with small labels to make them easier to tell apart when they were filed in baskets or on shelves. The idea survived into the twentieth century in the form of the catalog cards that librarians used to record a book's title, author, subject, etc. before library records were moved to computers (Gavrilis et al., 2008). The actual books constituted the data; the catalogue cards comprised the metadata. Metadata in the Social Web are called *tags*: non-hierarchical keywords assigned to a piece of information, such as a uniform resource locator (URL), a picture, or a movie (Smith, 2008; Troncy et al., 2011). According to Peters (2009), the outcomes of collaboratively creating and manipulating tags to annotate and categorize content are *folksonomies* (a blend of *folk* and *taxonomy*). Tags are generally chosen informally and personally by a creator or by viewers (depending on the system used to describe the item) to aid searching. For this reason, tags are simple to create but generally lack a formal grounding, as intended by the *Semantic Web* (Voss, 2007). Through tags, value is added by structuring the information and ranking it in order of relevance to ease query searches, as outlined by Agosti (2007).

In the framework, folksonomies are used as a starting point to harvest collective knowledge, which is then normalized and converted into a machine-understandable ontology. This conversion marks a transition from a human-oriented Social Web to a machine-oriented Semantic Web; because both concepts are joined, it is labeled the *Social Semantic Web* (Breslin et al., 2009; Blumauer & Pellegrini, 2009). An *ontology* is a design model for specifying the world that consists of a set of types, relationships, and properties. According to Gruber (1993), an ontology is a *"formal, explicit specification of a shared conceptualization."* Ontologies offer a common terminology, which can be used to model a domain. A domain comprises the types of objects and concepts that exist and their properties and relations.

Through harvesting tags from folksonomies, a tagspace (a set of associated tags with related weights) is created in which semantic closeness is represented by distance. To achieve an allied tagspace (where all harvested tags are related to each other), it is essential to establish tags and their relationships to each other (Kaser & Lemire, 2007). As Hasan-Montero and Herrero-Solana (2006) suggested, the easiest way to find the similarity between two tags is to count the number of co-occurrences, i.e., the number of times the two tags are allocated to the same source. However, there are other measurements to establish similarity, such as locality-sensitive hashing (where the tags are hashed in such a way that similar tags are mapped to the same set with a high probability) and collaborative filtering (where several users define tags and their relations jointly). Each of these methods produces relationships among tags, and each offers a semantically-consistent picture in which nearly all of the tags are related to each other to some degree (Setsuo & Suzuki, 2008).

At present, our intention for the Semantic Web is to amend the bottom-up attempt of the Social Web in a top-down manner (Cardoso, 2007). The fundamental aim is a stronger knowledge representation, as can be achieved with folksonomies, for example. *Fuzziness* can overcome the gap between folksonomies and ontologies because fuzziness corresponds to the way in which humans think (Werro, 2008) and it is, thus, suitable for characterizing vague information and helps to more efficiently handle real-world complexities. One possible way to use these advantages is through *fuzzy clustering algorithms*, which allow modeling of the uncertainty associated with vagueness and imprecision through mathematical models (Oliveira & Pedrycz, 2007; Bezdek et al., 2008).

To build the ontology, the tagspace will first be clustered with random initialization by a fuzzy clustering algorithm into pre-computed classes (Portmann & Meier, 2010). Thus, the number of classes can be determined by various methods. In the section about the fuzzy grassroots ontology, a simple method is explained. Because this is fuzzy clustering, it is possible for each tag to belong to one or more classes with different degrees of membership. Thus, it is possible that linguistic issues such as homographs, homophones, and synonyms, as well as their overlaps, can be identified. For example, because every tag can belong to different classes, it is possible that the tag *"bow"* can belong to either the class *"ship"* or the class *"weapon."* Because the harvested tags will be normalized, it is, furthermore, possible to spot homophones such as *"bow"* and *"bough"* (Figure 1).

The creation of an ontology is an iterative process where the first node in the hierarchy is stored in a *knowledge database* and the process is repeated. To complete an ontology of the created first-nodes, they are clustered again into pre-computed classes, making it possible to get a second-step, followed by a third-step hierarchy, and so forth. During this iterative process, all of the built hierarchies—now called ontologies—are collected and stored in a knowledge database by an ontology tool. Using this established ontology, it is possible for both humans and machines to recognize dependencies. For example, by trailing up a *"watercraft"* ontology, it is feasible to deduce

Figure 1. A fragment of an ontology

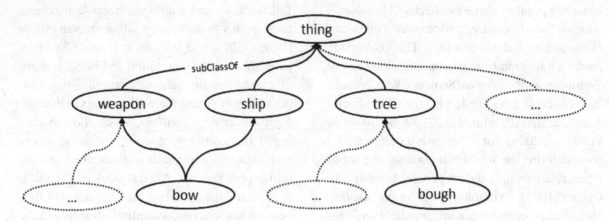

that "*boats*" are related to "*ships*." Furthermore, it is possible to recognize that, besides "*watercrafts*," there are also "*aircrafts*," for example.

Now that we have demonstrated the automatic processing of folksonomies to ontologies, we want to show how the machine-oriented ontologies can be easily made available to humans again. Therefore, the next section introduces interactive visualization techniques to let humans experience these ontologies.

Ontology-Based Knowledge Representation as Interactive Topic Maps

Visualization techniques should empower people to spot patterns in Web data, identify areas that need additional analysis, and make sophisticated decisions based on these patterns (Zudilova-Seinstra et al., 2008). The human capability to converse, communicate, reason, and make rational decisions in an environment of imprecision, uncertainty, incomplete information, and partial truth will be supported by this visualization. The manner in which people experience and interact with visualizations affects their understanding of the data; people benefit from the ability to visually

manipulate and explore. Visual interaction can support gut instincts and provide an instrument to both substantiate theses and support viewpoints.

Besides mere visualization, an interesting feature of this method is the ability to discover hotspots through an interactive possibility. To increase the ability to explore the data (and thus, to better understand the results), an effective integration of the *visualization* and *interaction applications* is important. According to Ward et al. (2010), interactive visualization can be used at each step of knowledge discovery, such as the process of automated data mining for characterizing patterns in the data. Nevertheless, the field of analyzing data to identify relevant concepts, relations, and assumptions, combined with the conversion of data into machine language, is known as *knowledge representation* (Van Harmelen et al., 2007; Weller, 2010). Because knowledge is used to achieve intelligent behavior, the fundamental goal of knowledge representation is to present data in a manner that will facilitate reasoning; here, knowledge representation and reasoning are seen as two sides of the same coin. In the field of artificial intelligence, problem-solving can be simplified by an appropriate choice of knowledge representation (Agosti et al., 2009; Sirmakessis,

2005). Presenting data in the right way makes certain problems easier to solve. On the one hand, our ontology provides machines with a general knowledge of vague human concepts and, on the other hand, the ontology-based, interactive visualization of this knowledge through Topic Maps helps people to find related patterns. Importantly, for a straightforward search of a company's online reputation, this interactive visualization can be used as a starting point; the similar topics and tags are visualized closer and the more dissimilar topics and tags are placed farther apart.

Within the framework, a dashboard is used to visualize topics and tags using *interactive Topic Maps*. These maps rely on a formal model that subsumes those of traditional identification guides (such as indexes, glossaries, and thesauri) and extends them to cater to the additional complexities of digital information. Interactive Topic Maps are also an international standard technology for qualifying knowledge structures (Pepper, 2010). They provide a way to visualize how a topic is connected to other topics. Based on these maps, the findability of information is improved. Related tags are displayed using interactive Topic Maps, enabling a communications operative to find related tags by browsing. The topic contains a set of related tags presented on the screen and allows the clicking of any tag that appears around the topic. Comparable to Zadeh's (2010) z-mouse, the dashboard allows the user to zoom in and out (akin to the zooming function in Google Maps) to find related topics and associated tags for a stated query. Hence, this interactive visualization helps to identify the previously unknown but related topics and tags and to thereby gain new knowledge.

The next subchapter introduces the use of Web search engines for online reputation management. It is shown why reputation management is such an important point in doing business in the Social Semantic Web.

THE USE OF SEARCH ENGINES FOR ONLINE REPUTATION MANAGEMENT

The practices of monitoring, addressing, or mitigating search engine results pages or mentions in social media are summarized as online reputation management (ORM). The first section of this subchapter gives a short introduction into reputation management, both online and general. The second section illustrates the necessity of online reputation analysis, a reputation management task that is conducted by communications operatives.

Online Reputation Management

Shakespeare defined reputation as the *"purest treasure mortal times afford,"* Abraham Lincoln labeled it a *"tree's shadow,"* and Benjamin Franklin pointed out that *"it takes many good deeds to build a good one, and only one bad to lose it."* Because of reputation, companies and other institutions have failed or succeeded. *Reputation* can be defined as a social evaluation of a group of entities toward a person, a group of people, or an organization regarding a certain criterion. More simply, reputation is the result of what you do, what you say, and what other people say about you (Gaines-Ross, 2008). Although reputation is built upon trust, in turn, trust is an outcome of a sound reputation; these two concepts form a symbiotic relationship to each other (Picot et al., 2003; Ebert, 2009; Klewes & Wreschniok, 2009). Chun (2005) considered a company's reputation to be a synoptic standpoint of the perceptions held by all of the germane stakeholders of a company, that is, what communities, creditors, consumers, employees, managers, the media, and suppliers believe that the organization stands for and the associations they make with it. A sound reputation sustainably strengthens a company's position in the struggle for profitable clients in the hunt for talent and in its affiliations with stakeholders.

Reputation management, if it is to evolve as a prevailing business task, rests on the basis of public relations (PR). In the Social Web, its form and character encompasses social media and such communication platforms as personal computers, laptops, and mobile phones (Phillips & Young, 2009). Companies with stronger positive reputations are able to attract more and better customers; their customers are more loyal and buy broader ranges of products and services. Because the market believes that these companies will deliver sustained earnings and future growth, they have higher price-to-earnings ratios, higher market values, and lower costs of capital. Moreover, in an economy where 70% to 80% of equity is derived from intangible assets that are difficult to assess, companies are particularly vulnerable to anything that damages their reputation (Eccles et al., 2007). Reputation management is becoming a paradigm in its own right as a consistent way of looking at a company and at its business performance. As an aid for communications operatives, a number of ORM applications already exist, but only some of them are free and only a handful deal with reputation analysis (Gunelius, 2010). In the literature, several approaches have described how to identify reputation; most of them rely on the management task of reputation analysis (Fombrun & Wiedmann, 2001; Eisenegger & Imhof, 2007; Ingenhoff & Sommer, 2008). Nevertheless, the significance of these analyses is critical considering that a negative search engine result will often be clicked first when listed with a company's Web site. An instrument to measure the information on a company's reputation is *reputation analysis*. Reputation analysis involves scanning and monitoring reputation data. Therefore, the next section inducts the reader in reputation analysis in more depth.

Online Reputation Analysis

With its emphasis on influencing search engine results to protect a company, *online reputation analysis* can be viewed as a field that relates to other areas of online marketing, such as word-of-mouth marketing (WOMM), search engine optimization (SEO), and PR. An organization must present the same message to all of its stakeholders to convey coherence, credibility, and ethics. Communications operatives can help to build this message by combining the vision, mission, and values of the company. Corporate communication can be both internal (e.g. employees and stakeholders) and external (e.g. agencies, channel partners, media, government, industry bodies and institutes, educational institutes, and the general public) (Röttger, 2005). According to Van Riel and Fombrun (2007), corporate communication is the set of activities required to manage and orchestrate all of the internal and external communications, which are aimed at creating favorable starting points with the stakeholders on whom the company depends. It consists of the accumulation and dissemination of information with the common goal of enhancing the organization's ability to retain its license to operate.

Hence, as reported by Ingenhoff (2004), the goal of *scanning* for a company's reputation, on the one hand, is the early detection of changes in the environment of the company that may affect or restrict the company's scope. On the other hand, new sectors can be detected through scanning. To position itself as an expert and opinion leader and to realize new opportunities, the company can occupy these new sectors. Another goal of this approach is to evaluate the reputations of competitors; occasionally, a competitor will launch an unknown product or a new production method that can be detected through scanning. Nevertheless, a challenge of reputation scanning is the prevention of flooding caused by vast amounts of data. Issues must be summarized into manageable topics, and their changes must be surveyed in the ensuing permanent *monitoring* to avoid surprises. Monitoring is a method of reputation analysis that is equivalent to scanning but watches a selected range of topics.

Though most executives know the value of their own reputations, it is also not uncommon for companies to hire professionals to manage their reputation risks. According to Eccles et al. (2007), effectively managing reputational risk involves assessing the company's reputation among stakeholders, evaluating the company's real character, closing reputation-reality gaps, monitoring changing beliefs and expectations, and placing a particular executive in charge of these tasks. The assignment of this executive typically consists of tracking the actions of an entity and the opinions of other entities about those actions, reporting on the actions and opinions, and reacting to the report, creating a feedback loop.

Now that we have demonstrated all important background information for our framework, we present in the ensuing subchapter the foRa framework.

THE FUZZY ONLINE REPUTATION ANALYSIS FRAMEWORK

The foRa framework permits searching of the Social Web to find reliable information on reputation. Using this framework, it is possible to scan the Web according to a query to determine topic classes with related tags and, thus, to identify hidden information. The first section provides an overview of the framework, followed by an explanation of the three main parts of the framework. The second section explains the creation of the fuzzy grassroots ontology. The third section describes the storage of the established ontology with ontology tools. The fourth section presents the reputation analysis engine.

Component Overview

As discussed, ORM deals with monitoring, addressing, or mitigating mentions in social media. It grew out of the perception of the significant influence that a Web search could have on business and the desire to change unpleasant results. Herein, we intend to illustrate our approach for reputation analysis in the Social Web. The foRa framework consists of three main parts: a fuzzy grassroots ontology where collected data will be converted into an ontology, an ontology storage system for the established ontology, and a reputation analysis engine where a communications operative can identify reputation information using a dashboard (Figure 2).

Figure 2 indicates the alternating roles of prosumers with the arrow around the framework. The topmost layer in our framework includes the producer role and illustrates, thereby, a part of the Social Web. However, the Social Web also contains the consumer role of consuming, for instance, annotation and Web sources. Therefore, this layer should be pictured as steadily moving from the producer to the consumer role. The bottommost layer illustrates the components of the Semantic Web stack used by the framework; this layer does not involve prosumer roles because it is not comprised of the whole stack. The middle layer illustrates the structure of the framework.

The next section presents the core of the foRa framework, the fuzzy grassroots ontology (in Figure 2, abbreviated with "FGO"). As already envisaged, this fuzzy grassroots ontology marks the handover of vague, human-created knowledge to machines.

The Fuzzy Grassroots Ontology

The fuzzy grassroots ontology comprises three elements. The first element is a *Web agent* that constantly crawls the Social Web, looking for tags and the underlying Web sites. In fact, the fuzzy grassroots ontology relies on not one but several

Figure 2. The foRa framework architecture

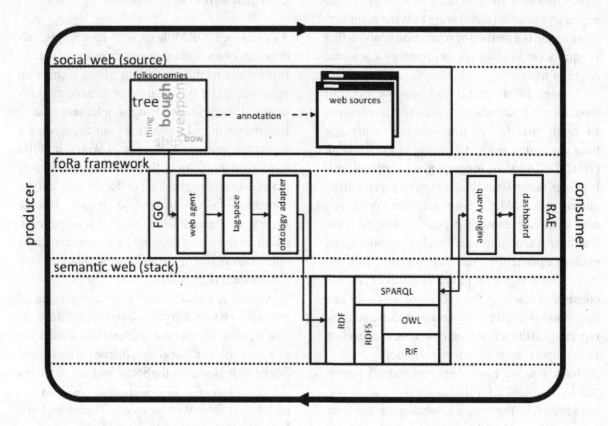

Web agents. Agents identify all tagged sources and subjoin them into a crawl frontier list. During this process, the tags are normalized and the underlying sources are ranked.

The second element is the creation and plotting of the *tagspace*. The previously collected and normalized tags are linked to each other using a metric function, and distance metrics identify the distance between each two individual tags. After this step, all of the tags are linked to each other and plotted onto a tagspace, which is the input for the ontology adaptor.

The *ontology adaptor* separates the plotted tagspace into hierarchies of classes with the help of Bezdek's (1981) FCM (fuzzy c-means) algorithm. To build our ontology, we clustered the tagspace with random initialization using FCM. The tag nearest to the center names the class, and the other tags—including the eponym itself—are

stored in this class by name and the membership degree for belonging to the class.

Web agents first used collected tags from folksonomies to establish a fuzzy grassroots ontology. In this sense, the ability to find high-quality sources is important for overcoming information overload. Collaborative filtering, or recommender systems, can identify high-quality sources that utilize individual knowledge. One known algorithm that has proven to be successful in automatically identifying high-quality sources within a hyperlinked environment is Kleinberg's (1998)*Hyperlink-Induced Topic Search (HITS)* algorithm. HITS starts with a small root set of documents and moves to a larger set T by adding up documents that link to and from the documents in the root set. The goal of the algorithm is to identify hubs (i.e., documents that link to numerous high-quality documents) and authorities (i.e., documents that are linked from numerous high-quality documents). The hyperlink structure of the documents in T is given by the adjacency matrix A, where A_{ij} denotes whether there is a link from document d_i to document d_j. Using this matrix A, a weighting algorithm constantly updates the hub weight and authority weight for each document until the weights converge. Essentially, the hubs and authorities are the documents with the biggest values in the main eigenvectors of A^TA and AA^T, respectively. HITS is used by the framework to rank all of the Web sites in combination with their identified tags according their relevance. Later, during a search, these ranked sources are then displayed according to various context dimensions.

A well-known problem with folksonomies is that typing errors can occur because there is no editorial supervision and people choose their own tags to annotate Web sources. This problem leads to overlapping but only slightly related terms in the underlying ontology. Certainly, it can be assumed that a search system can find relevant information despite misspelling in tags because queries could contain the same mistakes, but the necessity of a fault-tolerant treatment of queries soon becomes clear. According to Lewandowski (2005), one has to distinguish between different types of typing error strategies, such as dictionary-based and statistical approaches. Dictionary-based approaches compare entered query terms with a dictionary and if the dictionary does not cover the query term, they search for similar terms. Statistical methods refer misspellings with no or only a few hits to the most commonly used similar syntax. To determine phonetic similarity, tags will be reduced to a code that is able to conform to similar tags. A well-known basic example for the English language is the Soundex algorithm for indexing names by sound (Russell, 1918; Russell, 1922). Algorithm 1 illustrates the method of Russell's Soundex algorithm. The goal of this method is to encode homophones to the same representation so that they can be matched, despite their minor differences in spelling. The algorithm mainly encodes consonants; a vowel will not be encoded unless it is the first letter.

A major advantage of the utilization of a Soundex algorithm is that the correctly spelled ontology terms can be used as auto-completion and auto-suggestion while the user is typing search terms into the dashboard.

However, after all of the tags have been collected and normalized, they need to be sorted. Because our Web agents are constantly crawling through the Web, this sorting process must be periodically repeated.

The tagspace is a representation of a consistent picture and serves as the input for the ontology adaptor. Several steps are required to plot the tagspace from the found tags. The first step is to

Algorithm 1. Soundex algorithm

---

1. Capitalize all of the letters in the word and drop all of the punctuation marks.
2. Retain the first letter of the word.
3. Change all occurrence of the letter:
  "A," "E,"I," "O," "U," "H," "W," "Y,"→0
4. Replace consonants with digits as follows:
  "B," "F," "P," "V,"→1
  "C," "G,"J," "K," "Q," "S," "X," "Z,"→2
  "X," "Z,"→3
  "L,"→4
  "M," "N,"→5
  "R,"→6
5. Collapse adjacent identical digits into a single digit of that value.
6. Remove all non-digits after the first letter.
7. Return the starting letter and the first three remaining digits. If needed, append zeroes to make it a letter and three digits.

---

define the relationship of the various found tags. To define these relationships, variations of the Minkowski metric are normally used:

$$d_M(j,k) = \left(\sum_{i=1}^{n} \left| x_{ji} - x_{ki} \right|^p \right)^{1/p} \quad (1)$$

Here, $d_M(j,k)$ denotes the distance of the objects j and k, x_{ji} and x_{kj} the value of the variable i for the object j and $k(j = 1,2,...,n)$, and $p(\geq 1)$ the Minkowski constant. The critical factor in this equation is to obtain the constant p, which defines the Minowski metric. A simple Minkowski metric-based coefficient that can be used to measure the semantic correlation between tags is the Jaccard similarity coefficient $d_J(A,B)$. Let A and B be the sets of resources characterized by two tags. Relative co-occurrence is ascertained with the following formula:

$$d_J(A,B) = \frac{|A \cap B|}{|A \cup B|} \quad (2)$$

That is, relative co-occurrence is identical to the partition among the amount of resources in which tags co-occur and the amount of resources in which either of the two tags appear. This collection method causes tags to become united and offers a semantically consistent picture in which nearly all of the tags are related to each other.

This semantically consistent picture is referred to as the tagspace.

To begin the point representation, it is necessary to set a limitation for the tagspace. The plotting algorithm starts with a number of seed points (Algorithm 2). Some seed points will be referred from the seeds, but they are limited to a certain depth. Child point locations are computed based on Bourke's (1997) algorithm, which calculates the intersection of two or three circles.

After the found and normalized tags have been united, assorted, and plotted into a tagspace, a machine-understandable ontology can be established. The algorithm allocates the position of each point in the tagspace. Based on this algorithm, we can easily show the necessary points in the selected region, which is very effective for supporting a zoom function. Another parameter to take into account is the constant variability of the underlying data. We are familiar with the idea that data are at fixed values to be analyzed, but here, they are constantly moving around. In fact, they change every second, hour, or week. This consideration is legitimate because most data come from the real world, where no absolutes exist. The trends or demands of the Web can change dramatically. To interact with *live data*, we need to continually update the data and distance among the tags in the tagspace. As a result, the plotting algorithm described above is able to provide a good perspective on moving data.

Algorithm 2. Plotting the points

---

1. Create the point list from a number of seeds with a predefined depth and select one source point.

2. Select each point in the list except the selection point.

3. Calculate the plotted points that are within a given distance to the selected point.

4. Check the number of plotted points that have a relationship with the current point.

   a. If no plotted points are detected, then draw the current point with a random position.

   b. If there is one plotted point detected, then draw the current point with the same y but with an x value that is calculated to fit the distance.

   c. If there are two plotted points detected, then draw the current point as one of the two intersections point of two circles whose centroids and radii are the two plotted points and their distances to the current point, respectively.

   d. If there are three plotted points detected, then draw the current point as the intersection of the three circles whose centroids and radii are the three plotted points and their distances to the current point, respectively.

5. Return to Step 2 for the next point.

The ontology adaptor can be described as follows. All n tags plotted in the tagspace will be sorted by the fuzzy c-means (FCM) algorithm (Algorithm 3). This algorithm attempts to split a limited collection of elements

$$X = \{x_1, \ldots, x_n\} \subseteq \mathbb{R}^n$$

into an assortment of c fuzzy classes according to a specified condition. Assigning cluster numbers c ex ante is a common problem in clustering. In this case, to roughly define the number of clusters, we use the following rule:

$$c \approx \sqrt{n/2} \tag{3}$$

In fuzzy clustering, each point has a degree of belonging to a class using fuzzy logic rather than belonging to one particular class. Thus, points on the edge of a class may participate to a less significant degree than points in the center of a class. The degree of membership is u_{ik} in the interval $[0..1]$. The greater u_{ik} is, the stronger the membership of an element x_k to the class i will be. Hence, for each point x, there is a coefficient denoting participation at the kth level $u_k(x)$. Thus, the FCM algorithm is based on the minimization of an objective function:

$$J_{(U,V,X)} = \sum_{i=1}^{c} \sum_{k=1}^{n} \left(u_{ik}\right)^m d^2 \left(v_i, x_k\right) \tag{4}$$

where m is the weighting exponent (or fuzzifier), u_{ik} is the membership degree of element x_k to class i, and $d(v_i, x_k)$ is the distance of x_k to v_i, represented by the prototype v_i. Characteristically, the sum of all of the coefficients $u_k(x)$ is defined as 1:

$$\forall_x \left(\sum_{k=1}^{c} u_{ik}(x) = 1 \right) \tag{5}$$

By FCM, the focal point of a class is the average of all of the points, each weighted by its amount of belonging to the class:

$$v_i = \frac{\sum_x u_{ik}(x)^m x}{\sum_x u_{ik}(x)^m} \tag{6}$$

The amount of belonging is associated with the inverse of the distance to the heart of the class:

$$u_{ik}(x) = \frac{1}{d(v_i, x_k)} \tag{7}$$

After the coefficients are normalized and fuzzified with a true parameter m(>1), their sum is 1. In other words, the weighting exponent is adjusted with parameter m. This leads to:

$$u_{ik}(x) = \frac{1}{\sum_j \left(\frac{d\left(v_i, x_k\right)}{d\left(v_j, x_k\right)} \right)^{2/(m-1)}} \tag{8}$$

For m equal to 2, this method is the same as normalizing the coefficients linearly so that their sum is equal to 1. When m is close to 1, the class center closest to the point is given a considerably larger weight relative to the others.

Step 5 of Algorithm 3 is necessary because the terms can belong to more than one class (by drawing on the FCM algorithm). Nevertheless, using the proposed method, a model can be derived with several classes that the term belongs in to a certain degree, dependent on the degree of membership. By Step 4, the procedure is repeated until we have a class with a single tag in it; this tag forms the tip of the hierarchy. Figure 3 graphically indicates how the conversion of tags to ontologies is executed. Starting from the left, the algorithm splits the tagspace using FCM, denoted according to the mathematical perspec-

Algorithm 3. Fuzzy C-means algorithm

1. Select an amount of classes withFormula (3)above.
2. Assign coefficients randomly to each point in the classes.
3. Reiterate until the algorithm has converged (that is, the adjustment of the coefficients between two iterations is no more than ε, a given sensitivity boundary value):
    a. Calculate the centroid for each class, usingFormula (6)above.
    b. For each point, compute its coefficients within the class, usingFormula (8)above.
4. Reiterate Steps 1 to 3 for every class until there is only one term left in the class.
5. Concatenate all of the same terms together.

tive. The ontological perspective shows the classification of tag A (eponym of the class A). The relationship (along with the distance) to the other classes (B, C, D, etc.) and also to the tags of each class is stored in the ontology storage system.

However, the hierarchy of all of the classes is stored using the ontology tool, so we obtain several hierarchies that are jointly called ontology. The ranked Web sites that belong to the single tags are stored separately but linked to the ontology.

Figure 3. Schematic representation of the ontology-building process

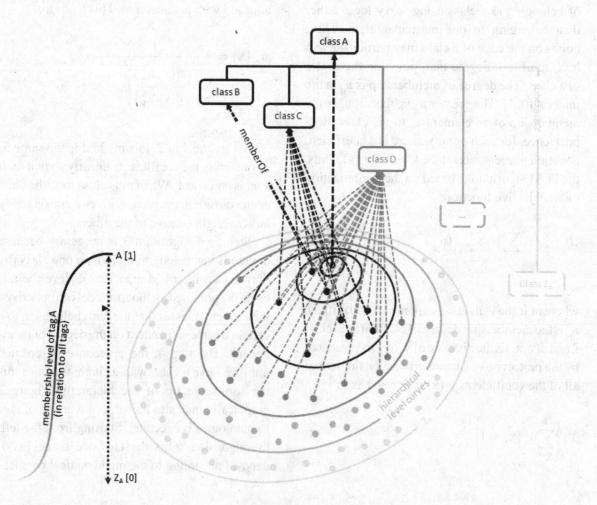

The created fuzzy grassroots ontology now needs to be stored with an adequate ontology tool. Therefore, the next section presents several recent ontology tools. Since we do not implement such an ontology tool by ourselves but rely on the World Wide Web Consortium (W3C) recommendations, this ensuing section reveals also our selection of an ontology tool to store and process the fuzzy grassroots ontology in an effective manner.

The Ontology Storage System

Several Semantic Web or ontology tools have recently been developed. In this section, we analyze and classify the most important of these tools. Many available applications are academic prototypes, meaning that most of the implementation in the query language aims to support but not to provide the necessary programming and administrative abilities to make them operational within a real working environment. Besides the emerging commercial software that supports ontology, an increasing number of ontology applications boost the advancement of ontology storage and query support. In this section, we compare the most common ontology tools. Accordingly, we select the most attractive ontology tool and corresponding query language for our framework. Table 1 lists different ontology tools according to various categories.

The latest versions of the different tools introduced in Table 1 is given in brackets after each tool's name and a brief sketch of each presented category (cat.) is given in alphabetical order below:

- *Ontology API (Application Programming Interface: OA)* is a set of classes for manipulating ontology information, for example, adding or removing classes, properties, relationships, or individuals. The alignment API is an implementation for expressing and sharing ontology alignments.
- *Ontology Editors (OE)* are applications designed to assist knowledge engineers or domain experts in the creation or manipulation of ontologies. They often express ontologies in one of several ontology languages and propose graphical design environments and interfaces for implementing reasoners. Some of these applications are able to export their output to other languages.
- *Ontology Storage (OS)* can handle a large number of connections. Some prominent systems include RDFStore, Jena, and Sesame (Rohloff et al., 2007). The storage is also an ontology server that is used at design, commit, and runtime. Ontologists use this server to develop ontologies. There are various ways to store ontologies; there are database management systems such as PostgreSQL or MySQL and in-memory or distributed data systems such as Common Object Request Broker Architecture (CORBA). Each system has its own advantages and disadvantages.
- *Topic Map Engine (TM)* provides a comprehensive API to allow programmers to create, modify, and query Topic Map structures.

The necessity for ontology-building, annotating, and integrating storage and learning tools is indisputable. Additionally, human information consumers and Web agents must use and query ontologies and the resources committed to them, creating a further need for ontologies and querying tools. However, the context of storing and querying knowledge has changed due to the wide acceptance and use of the Web as a platform for communicating knowledge. In the past few years, the number of ontology query languages has increased rapidly. Depending on the input data, different query languages are needed. Furthermore, not all ontology tools support all kinds of input data and query languages. Table 2 shows a classification of the most prominent query languages. Currently, efforts are being made to define languages for the

Table 1. List of ontology tools

Tool	Cat.	Note
AllegroGraph RDFStore (4.2)	*OS*	*AllegroGraph RDFStore is a modern, high-performance, persistent RDF graph database. AllegroGraph uses disk-based storage, enabling it to scale to billions of triples while maintaining superior performance. Allegro-Graph supports SPARQL, RDFS++, and Prolog reasoning from numerous client applications; (http://www.franz.com/agraph/allegrograph).*
COE (5.0)	*OE*	*COE is a project whose goal is to develop an integrated suite of software tools for constructing, sharing, and viewing OWL-encoded ontologies based on CmapTools, concept-mapping software used in educational settings, training, and knowledge capturing. Concept maps provide a human-centered interface to display the structure, content, and scope of an ontology; (http://www.ihmc.us/groups/coe).*
HOZO (5.2.30)	*OE*	*Hozo is an ontology editor with multi-window functions, globalization support, zooming (Concept Map), and other functions to make the editor more user-friendly; (http://www.hozo.jp).*
Jena (2.6.4)	*OA OE OS*	*Jena is a Java framework for building Semantic Web applications. It provides a programmatic environment for RDF, RDFS and OWL, and SPARQL and includes a rule-based inference engine; (http://jena.sourceforge. net).*
KAON (1.2.9)	*OS*	*KAON is an ontology management infrastructure targeted for business applications. It includes a comprehensive tool suite allowing easy ontology creation and management. Persistence mechanisms of KAON are based on relational databases; (http://sourceforge.net/projects/kaon).*
Major-ToM (2.0)	*TM*	*The Merging Topic Maps Engine (MaJorToM) project was founded to develop a lightweight, merging, and flexible Topic Maps engine satisfying different business use cases. The engine provides a couple of new features listed above to other engines based on Topic Maps API version 2.0; (http://code.google.com/p/ma-jortom).*
Networked Planet (1.3)	*TM*	*The Networked Planet Web3 Platform is a complete solution for creating, organizing, and publishing structured semantic data. The Web3 platform stores and manages data in a schema-less data store, allowing complete flexibility in the shape of the data stored; (http://www.networkedplanet.com/Products/Web3).*
OBO-Edit (2.1.11)	*OE*	*OBO-Edit, an open-source ontology editor written in Java, is optimized for the OBO biological ontology file format. It features an easy-to-use editing interface, a simple but fast reasoner, and powerful search capabilities. OBO-Edit was developed by the Berkeley Bioinformatics and Ontologies Project and is funded by the Gene Ontology Consortium; (http://oboedit.org).*
Ontopia (5.1.3)	*TM*	*Open-source tools for building, maintaining, and deploying Topic Maps-based applications; (http://www. ontopia.net).*
OWL-API (3.2.2)	*OA*	*The OWL API is a Java API and reference implementation for creating, manipulating, and serializing OWL Ontologies; (http://owlapi.sourceforge.net).*
Protégé (4.1)	*OA OE*	*Protégé is a free, open-source ontology editor and knowledge base framework. The Protégé platform supports two main ways of modeling ontologies via the Protégé-Frames and Protégé-OWL editors. Protégé ontologies can be exported into a variety of formats, including RDF(S), OWL, and XML Schema. Protégé is based on Java, is extensible, and provides a plug-and-play environment that makes it a flexible base for rapid prototyping and application development; (http://protege.stanford.edu).*
REDLAND (1.0.13)	*OS*	*Redland, a set of free software C libraries supporting RDF, providing storage for graphs in memory and persistently with Sleepycat/Berkeley DB, MySQL 3-5, PostgreSQL, AKT Triplestore, SQLite, files, or URIs. It supports multiple syntaxes for reading and writing RDF as RDF/XML, N-Triples and Turtle Terse RDF Triple Language, RSS, and Atom syntaxes via the Raptor RDF Syntax Library and querying with SPARQL and RDQL using the Rasqal RDF Query Library; (http://librdf.org).*
Ruby Topic Maps (2.0)	*TM*	*Ruby Topic Maps (RTM) is a Topic Maps engine for the Ruby programming language. It can be used alone or together with other frameworks such as Ruby on Rails; (http://rtm.topicmapslab.de).*

continued on following page

Table 1. Continued

Tool	Cat.	Note
Semantic Studio (1.7)	OE	Semantic Studio is an ontology development tool with presentations in various formats, including visual presentation and persistence into semantic repositories, file systems, or databases. It allows the development of ontologies by using different presentations, among which there is an inner kernel presentation on which all other presentations are based. In our terms, all presentations are re-presentations of the kernel presentation. The kernel presentation is close to the "in-memory" model of Jena, but it differs in many respects, which we regard as further abstraction from presentation details; (http://www.w3.org/2001/sw/wiki/Semanticstudio).
Sesame (2.0)	OS	Sesame is a Java framework for storing, querying, and inferencing for RDF. It can be deployed as a Web server or used as a Java library. Features include several query languages (SeRQL and SPARQL), inferencing support, and RAM, disk, or RDBMS storage; (http://sourceforge.net/projects/sesame).
SOFA-API (0.3)	OA	SOFA (Simple Ontology Framework API) is an open-source project aimed at the development of an integral software infrastructure and a common development platform for various ontology-oriented and ontology-based software applications; (http://sofa.projects.semwebcentral.org).
tinyTiM (2.0)	TM	A very small and easy-to-use Topic Map engine implementing the TMAPI interfaces; (http://tinytim.source-forge.net)
TRIPLE	OS	TRIPLE is an RDF query, inference, and transformation language for the Semantic Web; (http://triple.semanticweb.org)

Semantic Web. The goal of these languages is to represent Web information so it is understandable and accessible to a machine. In addition, it should also be guaranteed that these languages have enough expressive power to represent the rich semantics of real-world information. They should also be efficient enough to be processed by a machine. All of the languages are based on eXtensible Markup Language (XML). According to Anoniou and Van Harmelen (2008), some of these languages are very successful, such as Resources Description Framework (Schema)

Table 2. The classification of selected query languages

Data	Query Lang.	Note	Supported by
XML	XQuery, XPath, XPointer	Query languages for XML data sources.	AltovaXML, SAXON
RDF	SPARQL	SPARQL is a recursive acronym for SPARQL Protocol and RDF Query Language. As implied by its name, SPARQL is a general term for both a protocol and a query language.	AllegroGraph Prova, RDFStore, SparqlOwl, etc.
	RDQL	Query language for RDF in Jena models.	Jena; Sesame
OWL	OWL-QL	The Joint US/EU ad hoc Agent Markup Language Committee is proposing an OWL query language called OWL-QL.	Bossam, FaCT++, Hoolet, KAON2, SHER
	SQWRL	Semantic Query-Enhanced Web Rule Language (SQWRL, pronounced "squirrel") is a SWRL-based language for querying OWL ontologies. It provides SQL-like operations to retrieve knowledge from OWL.	Protégé-OWL
SWRL	SWRL	SWRL is a rules-language that combines OWL with Rule Markup Language (RuleML).	Bossam, KAON2, Pellet, Protégé-OWL, RacerPro
	DLP	Description logic programs (DLPs) are another proposal for integrating rules and OWL. Compared with description logic programs, SWRL takes a diametrically opposed integration approach. DLP is the intersection of Horn logic and OWL, whereas SWRL is (roughly) the union of them.	KAON

(RDF(S)) and Web Ontology Language (OWL); these languages are recommended by the W3C. Table 2 reveals the established query languages according to the underlying data.

At this point our focus was mainly to demonstrate the application of RDF triples and accordingly we abstained from trying a Topic Map engine. Instead, for our implementation of the youReputation prototype, we used AllegroGraph's RDF-Store, which is a modern, high-performance, persistent RDF graph database. It uses disk-based storage, enabling it to scale to billions of triples while maintaining superior performance. Additionally, it supports SPARQL, RDFS++, and Prolog reasoning from numerous client applications. In a future revision of this prototype, the Topic Map engines should necessarily be evaluated again

After we have presented the creation and management of our fuzzy grassroots ontology, we show in the following section the dashboard for the human-computer interface and its query engine, together called the reputation analysis engine (in Figure 2, abbreviated as "RAE").

The Reputation Analysis Engine

This system consists of two parts: the dashboard and the query engine. The *dashboard* is a user interface designed so that its text can easily be read; it is the part of the framework communication that operatives interact with. The second and equally important part of the system is the *query engine,* with which automatically presented queries are created after first use. Every interaction initiated by the communication operatives on the dashboard-visualized Topic Map prompts the query engine to provide a new SPARQL query to find the related topics and tags within the ontology storage system. Once the related topics and tags have been located, the query engine also provides the dashboard with the stored and ranked underlying Web sites.

The dashboard is the main visualization of the system (Figure 4). It provides a Topic Map that conveys information such as topics and the relationships between topics. Topic Maps are standardized and similar to the concepts of mind maps or concept maps in many respects (Pepper, 2010). Topic Maps can also be expressed using XML. However, one difference between the Resource Description Framework (RDF) and a Topic Map is that the latter is centered on topics while the former is centered on resources. The RDF data model is based upon the idea of making statements about Web resources in the form of subject-predicate-objective expressions; known as triples. Topic Maps are not limited to triples, and they represent information using a topic (representing any concept), association (representing hyper-graph relationships between topics), and occurrences (representing information resources). Furthermore, while RDF directly annotates resources, Topic Maps create a semantic network layer—a *virtual map*—above the information resources, leaving the information resources unchanged. Topic Maps explicitly support the concept of identity merging between multiple topics or Topic Maps. Furthermore, because ontologies are Topic Maps themselves, they can also be merged, allowing the automated integration of information from diverse sources into a coherent new Topic Map. The visualization not only shows Topic Maps that were inducted from search results but also more valuable information, such as the different layers (multi-level) that can be viewed by zooming in.

The first time the dashboard is used, users do not need to modulate any settings (such as weight K) but only feed the search field box with a name, product, brand, or combination thereof. Instead, the interactive visualization should intuitively lead users to their desired Web sources. Based on the query engine, the dashboard provides a suggested indicator to the user. In other words, a weight K is not set manually but automatically by the framework; however, an operative may change the predicted weight ($K \geq 0.8$) by using the

Figure 4. The appearance of the interactive dashboard: The topic map (left) and the hit lists (right).

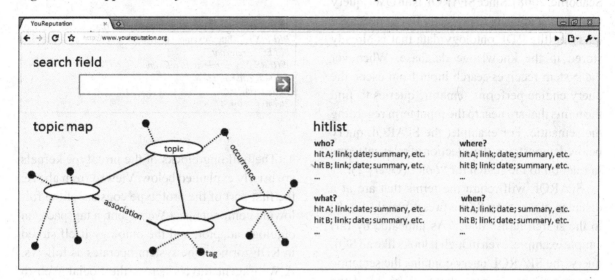

mouse scroll wheel on the Topic Map. Using clicking, zooming in and out, and dragging and dropping, the user can evaluate an entered search term on the Topic Map of the dashboard; i.e., the user can adjust K implicitly. Furthermore, the visual displays hits in different context dimensions, allowing the gaining of further knowledge not only about the entered search term but also about who said what and how influencing this person is.

The Topic Map helps to identify search results by topics that communications operatives can focus on to find exactly what they are looking for or to discover unexpected relationships between items. Tags visualized farther away from a topic belong to it at a less significant level than do the tags that are closer; the same applies to the relationship of the topic itself. Nevertheless, each time the user clicks on the interactive Topic Map, the missing parts of the maps are downloaded from servers and inserted into the dashboard.

A smart representation of the topic-corresponding hits can support further insights. A good way to present hits are Dey and Abowd's (2000)*four w's* (*who*, *what*, *where*, and *when*) as the minimal context dimensions to display. Using this method,

the different characteristics of social media can help to distinguish these dimensions; some are of greater value in achieving such a distinction, others less. A microblogging service, for instance, is a great tool for finding very recent information; it answers the when question. Social networks could become a tool for information on who, and wikis may be used to answer who, what, when, and where. As a tool for discussion, blogs might not just answer the questions of who, what, when, and where; they could also be used as an information tool to learn about the background of an issue and to analyze why (Hächler, 2010). Splitting hits, with respect to their origin, into context dimensions allows an intuitive interaction with a different kind of social media.

The query engine is an introduction into how a user-provided query can be enriched using ontology. However, to query ontology data, we need to use a query language. As more data is being stored in RDF formats— friend of a friend (FOAF) and really simple syndication (RSS) are two examples that can rest on it—a need has arisen for a simple way to locate specific information. SPARQL, as a powerful query language, fills that niche, making it easy to find data in RDF (Prud'hommeaux &

Seaborne, 2008). Since SPARQL is an OWL query language, it appears to perfectly fit our needs for querying the RDF ontology data that is already stored in the knowledge database. Whenever the system receives search input from users, the query engine performs semantic queries to find the terms that are near to the input term regarding the semantic. For example, the SPARQL query below demonstrates the selection of relevant terms in relation to the search for "*bow*" (Query 1).

SPARQL will return the terms that are at a distance closer than 8 (the preset weight for K) to the search term "*bow*." As indicated by this simple example, even though it looks like an SQL query, the SPARQL query contains the semantic meaning. Depending on the proximities of the Web-agent-collected terms in the fuzzy grassroots ontology, this search will envisage, for example, the topics "*ship*" and "*weapon*" on the Topic Map.

To provide the readers not only with an abstract framework but also with an easy-to-use tool, the next subchapter showcases the youReputation prototype, a free Web-based reputation analysis tool.

YOUREPUTATION: A REPUTATION ANALYSIS TOOL

For a short demonstration of the foRa framework features, our youReputation prototype scanned data from the social bookmarking service Delicious (www.delicious.com) and the microblogging platform Twitter (www.twitter.com). The prototype provided the results regarding the input, computed a reputation with the relevant information, and converted the valuable information into an ontology. The goal of youReputation is to provide a reputation result based on the search input. The results include relevant terms and links to Web sites that correspond to a term that the user wants to evaluate. The data crawled from Delicious and Twitter was processed, clustered, and converted to an ontology. Figure 5 indicates the kernel of the youReputation prototype.

Query 1. Selecting relevant terms

```
PREFIX dc: <http://purl.org/dc/elements/1.1/>
PREFIX ns: <http://example.org/ns#/>
SELECT ?relevant
WHERE { ?x ns:relevant ?relevant.
FILTER ?distance < 8.
?x dc:term ?term.
?term = "bow"}
```

The building blocks of the prototype kernels are briefly explained below. Viewed from above, the first part of the prototype consists of the following components: a Web agent, a tagspace, an ontology adaptor, and the ontology itself stored in RDF format. The system operates as follows. A Web agent travels across the Social Web to collect information. Heterogeneous data must be adjusted before storing. Noise data (i.e., advertisements, banners, footers, etc.) are removed. The remaining data (i.e., tags from Delicious or Twitter) are normalized and stored. Then, the ontology adaptor converts the raw data from the Web agents into an ontology. After conversion, the ontologies can be queried using SPARQL, which runs the queries on the RDF/OWL data.

Seen from below, the second part of the prototype consists of the following components: a dashboard; a query engine; the Semantic-Web-stack-based components SPARQL, OWL, RDFS, Rule Interchange Format (RIF); and an RDF-based semantic ontology. Although originally envisioned as a rules layer for the Semantic Web, in reality, the design of RIF is based on the observation that there are many rules languages in existence and what is needed is to exchange rules between them. RIF is not used by the youReputation prototype, but it could be integrated to personalize the ranking hits; in a possible later extension of youReputation to a system with login functionality, it would be feasible to analyze user behavior and accordingly favor the ranking of found sources. RDFS is an extensible knowledge representation language intended to structure RDF resources and provide the basic elements for the description of

Figure 5. The youReputation prototype kernel

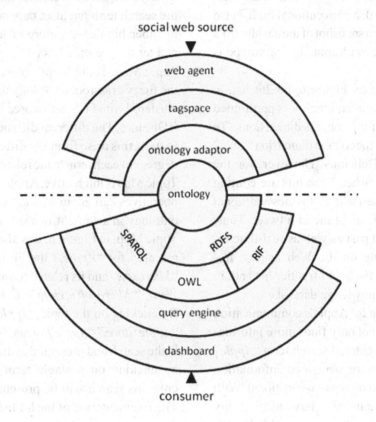

ontologies. Many RDFS components are included in OWL, a family of knowledge representation languages for authoring ontologies. The language is characterized by formal semantics and by RDF/XML-based serializations for the Semantic Web and has especially attracted academic, medical, and commercial interest. Through SPARQL, the semantic ontology can be grasped. It was standardized by the RDF data access working group of the W3C and later became an official recommendation. The query engine supports the query process using SPARQL.

Whenever the user inputs search text, the query engine attempts to find relevant terms by querying the ontology base. The dashboard as a visualization tool is responsible for showing these results as a Topic Map that indicates the relationship between tags and their information. Then, the system retrieves the stored URL related to the tag

to provide the relevant information. Retrieved hits are also presented on the dashboard according to the context dimensions.

To explain the benefits of the youReputation prototype, let's introduce a small example. The problem with new and previously unobserved information on the Web is that the relationship between terms and topics is not precisely known. Thus, we assume that a communication operative at Apple Inc., a multinational corporation that designs and markets computer electronics, is asked to analyze the corporation's online reputation, so Apple's communication operative decides to give our prototype a chance and, hence, makes use of the youReputation prototype. For that purpose, the communication operative enters the search term *"Apple"* in the search field box on the start page. On the left side of the dashboard, immediately, the visualized ontology (meaning all Apple-related topics and terms) appears. Moreover, on the right side of the dashboard, a conventional hit list also appears. In Figure 6, a snapshot of the dashboard's Apple search of the youReputation prototype is presented.

As demonstrated by Figure 6, the hit list, in reality, is not very conventional; it is partitioned into the presented four context dimensions. To illustrate, the hits for the context dimension "what" are coming from Delicious. However, for the context dimension "when," the hits are coming from Twitter because Twitter provides additional data such as the date and time of a tweet. Thus, it is possible to find past as well as real-time information depending on the Web agents' frequency of updating the crawl frontier list and, in doing so, also the knowledge database.

The consequence for Apple's communication operative is that he not only finds more information concerning his entered search term "*Apple*" but also receives more structured information (based on the context dimension partitions). With a conventional Boolean search, he would find only information containing the term "*Apple*". In contrast, youReputation enables him to find not only the search term but also, depending on the fuzzy membership degree, more or less-related topics and terms, presented as an appealing interactive Topic Map. Topic Maps are generated based on the fuzzy grassroots ontology that is the tagspace clustered with FCM and stored in AllegroGraph's RDFStore. The different distances from the topic to the terms arise from the different membership degrees of each term to the related topic. Since this Topic Map is interactive, Apple's communication operatives can zoom in and out and browse the ontology in a straightforward way. Based on the Topic Map, in Figure 6, it is also noted that, after a search for "*Apple*," the business competitors "*Microsoft*" and its related terms (e.g. "*Microsoft Word*," "*Microsoft update*," etc.) also can be found. By clicking on the topic "*Apple*," all terms (e.g. "*Apple Store*," "*Apple Forum*," etc.) are included in the search and presented in the hit list, whereas, by clicking on a single term (e.g. "*iPhone*"), only this search will be presented in the hit list. The fragmentation of the hit list according to the

Figure 6. A snapshot of the youReputation prototype dashboard

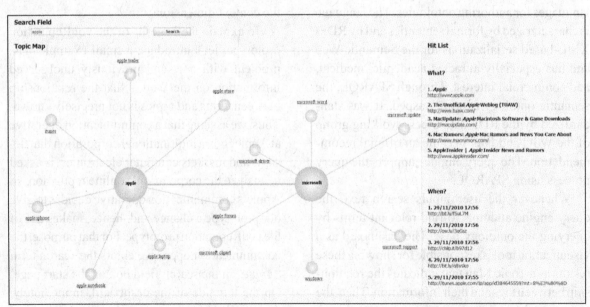

context dimensions helps to better structure his located information.

Having presented our foRa framework, including the associated youReputation prototype, the next subchapter discusses universal future research directions for the Social Semantic Web.

FUTURE RESEARCH DIRECTIONS

There have been several attempts to help not only online reputation analysis but also all kinds of WSEs to overcome keyword search. Through recent evolutions in Social Web technologies resulting in easy-to-use tools, users continually bustle in today's Web and create a quickly growing volume of data (O'Reilly & Battelle, 2009). This situation implies that the productivity of WSEs should increase. With tagging, an early limitation of current WSEs is redressed because people can label and find content themselves. Current reputation analysis relies heavily on customer surveys, although online reputation analysis tools, such as Actionly (www.actionly.com), BackType (www.backtype.com), Engagor (www.engagor. com), Radian6 (www.radian6.com), and ReputationDefender (www.reputationdefender.com), try to provide insights into a firm's Social Web prestige in an interactive style. Because most communications operatives are not familiar with the optimal wording of search queries (which requires the use of SPARQL), new search forms should be developed.

Solutions to overcome these limitations include the so-called QA (question-answering) systems (Zadeh, 2006). For instance, Wolfram Alpha's system (www.wolframalpha.com) is capable of handling user requests concerning measurements, but it is not able to understand the semantics behind user queries. The engine achieves nothing beyond the tasks at which machines are known to excel, manipulating numbers and symbols. A

promising way to overcome these limitations is the *computing with words (CWW)* paradigm (Zadeh, 1996). Formulated in 1996 as a methodology in which the objects of computation are words and propositions drawn from natural language, such as, for example, *"high tree"* or *"a tree has many boughs."* Unlike a classical logical approach, CWW provides a much more expressive language for knowledge representation and, consequently, for reasoning. Because fuzziness is ubiquitous and essential for humans, CWW offers a new perspective for improving human-machine interactions (Zadeh, 2004). According to Hagras (2010), CWW relates to developing intelligent systems that are able to receive perceptions and propositions drawn from natural language as input words and then produce a decision or output based on these words. According to Guadarrama (2010), CWW can be used in knowledge representation, learning, and programming. Our interactive visualization of the ontology as Topic Maps is a first effort to represent world knowledge (Craven et al., 2000).

It is a long way toward an *intelligent Web*, as Spivack (2009) outlined. A first step in this direction will be to integrate natural language into the Web to achieve a real Semantic Web (Zadeh, 2009; Zadeh, 2010). The CWW paradigm can be used for this task. Thus, future communications operatives will be able to use natural language to search for online reputation information. In an intelligent Web, it will be possible to ask questions and receive context-dependent answers. There are several emerging technologies meant to overcome further challenges toward a true intelligent Web, such as the *Web of things* model (interconnection of all types of devices through Web standards), *machine translation* (the translation of text or speech from one natural language to another), *machine vision* (the recognition of objects in an image and the ability to assign properties to those objects to make them machine-readable), *structured storage* (which does not require fixed table schemas), and *quantum computing* (which will be able to solve certain types of problems much faster than any current computers).

In conclusion, the next subchapter discusses once more the overall coverage of this chapter and closes with concluding remarks.

CONCLUSION

The proposed approach attempts to establish a knowledge representation for reputation analysis through Topic Maps (which are a standard for the representation and exchange of knowledge) with an emphasis on the findability of information. So far, a few WSEs have relied on clustering content into different classes, but none of them have been able to understand or process intuitive and human-oriented Web queries based on linguistic terms or expressions. Visualized interactive Topic Maps can help find similar linguistic terms clustered around a topic. The interactive visualization of these maps is a first step that was established solely to augment user understanding, but, in the future, maps underlying semantic ontologies ought to be enhanced to knowledge bases to allow the machines to reason using the user's vague natural language expressions. Based on this knowledge base, a future WSE that is able to understand natural language queries could be established.

This chapter provided a foundation for further analysis of a reputation system, the foRa framework, and the youReputation prototype. We studied the development and analysis of reputation systems and developed methodologies to address some of the fundamental definitions, such as the Semantic Web, ontologies, and fuzzy clustering algorithms. Our prototype was designed to be simple and easily extensible. The introduced framework is an approach for communications operatives to gain deeper insights into the reputation of a company in online media. Because the boundaries in fuzzy classification systems are not rigorous, it is possible to find more and higher-quality results. As

revealed here, the found hits can be presented in an understandable way using an appropriate form of splitting into context dimensions according to their origin. This system allows communications operatives to successfully interact with different kinds of social media. Among other things, the prototype is intended to illustrate the possibilities provided by the vast amount of recent Social Web data. Therefore, it simulates only a few aspects of the foRa framework. Developing the youReputation prototype according to the framework with a prototyping method has the benefit of allowing us to obtain feedback from users during the development process.

Strictly following the methods of prototyping and to increase comprehension, we always used the simplest formulas and algorithms to highlight our ideas in this chapter. Furthermore, we believe that this system represents a good starting point to develop other kinds of social semantic software. However, we will continue to experiment with variations of more advanced formulas and algorithms. For example, we will evaluate whether there are potentially superior measures to the Jaccard similarity measurement. Further experimental tests include comparisons with commonly used non-metric measurements: the Dice, the Kulczynski, the Russel and Rao, Simple Matching, and the Tanimoto coefficient. Additionally, Kleinberg's HITS algorithm will be tested against other comparable algorithms: Google's PageRank, Marchiori's Hyper Search, and Yahoo's TrustRank. Using a variety of Soundex algorithm derivatives, such as Daitch–Mokotoff, fuzzy Soundex, Metaphone and Double Metaphone, New York State Identification and Intelligence System (NYSIIS), and the Reverse Soundex algorithm, we expect further improvements of our prototype. Although we focused here on the English language, semantic ontologies for other languages could be established through the same methods with adapted language-relevant algorithms (e.g., the "Kölner phonetic" for the German language). Another essential evaluation will be to weigh the FCM algorithm against other comparable fuzzy clustering algorithms, such as fuzzy self-organizing maps (FSOMs), fuzzy clustering by local approximation of memberships (FLAME), Gath-Geva, and Gustafson-Kessel.

Another important point for further reputation analysis should be the analysis of word-inherent positive or negative connotations to automatically categorize found Web sources; this objective could, potentially, be based on fuzzy techniques. With further involvement of the previously discussed context dimensions, the influence of different Social Web prosumers can be elicited. In addition, the patterns of interaction with our dashboard displayed by communications operatives can be used as a springboard to affect the future ranking of documents, producing a more personalized outcome.

REFERENCES

Agosti, M. (2007). *Information access through search engines and digital libraries*. Berlin, Germany: Springer.

Anoniou, G., & Van Harmelen, F. (2008). *A Semantic Web primer*. Cambridge, MA: MIT Press.

Baeza-Yates, R., & Ribeiro-Neto, B. (2011). *Modern information retrieval: The concepts and technology behind search*. New York, NY: Addison-Wesley Educational Publishers.

Bezdek, J. C. (1981). *Pattern recognition with fuzzy objective function algorithms*. New York, NY: Plenum Press.

Bezdek, J. C., Keller, J., Krisnapuram, R., & Pal, N. R. (2008). *Fuzzy models and algorithms for pattern recognition and image processing*. New York, NY: Springer.

Blumauer, A., & Pellegrini, T. (2009). *Social Semantic Web: Web 2.0 - Was nun?* Berlin, Germany: Springer.

Bourke, P. (1997). *Intersection of two circles*. Retrieved November 30, 2010, from http://local.wasp.uwa.edu.au/~pbourke/geometry/2circle/

Breslin, J. G., Passant, A., & Decker, S. (2009). *The Social Semantic Web*. Berlin, Germany: Springer. doi:10.1007/978-3-642-01172-6

Bruhn, M. (2002). *Relationship marketing: Management of customer relations*. Essex, UK: Financial Times.

Cardoso, J. (2007). The Semantic Web vision, where are we? *IEEE Computer Society*, *22*(5), 22–26.

Chun, R. (2005). Corporate reputation: Meaning and measurement. *International Journal of Management Reviews*, *7*(2), 91–109. doi:10.1111/j.1468-2370.2005.00109.x

Craven, M., DiPasquo, D., Freitag, A., McCallum, T., Mitchell, K., & Nigam, S. (2000). Learning to construct knowledge bases from the World Wide Web. *Artificial Intelligence*, *118*(1–2), 69–113. doi:10.1016/S0004-3702(00)00004-7

Dey, A. K., & Abowd, G. D. (2000, April). *Towards a better understanding of context and context-awareness*. Paper presented at the CHI 2000 Workshop on the What, Who, Where, When, Why and How of Context-Awareness, Hague, Netherlands.

Ebert, T. (2009). *Trust as the key to loyalty in business-to-consumer exchanges: Trust building measures in the banking industry*. Wiesbaden, Germany: Gabler. doi:10.1007/978-3-8349-8307-7

Eccles, R. G., Newquist, S. C., & Schatz, R. (2007). Reputation and its risks. *Harvard Business Review*, *85*(2), 104–114.

Eisenegger, M., & Imhof, K. (2007). Das Wahre, das Gute und das Schöne: Reputations-Management in der Mediengesellschaft. *Fög discussion paper 2007-0001*. Retrieved November 30, 2010, from http://www.foeg.uzh.ch/staging/userfiles/file/Deutsch/f%C3%B6g%20discussion%20papers/2007-0001_Wahr_Gut_Schoen_2007_d.pdf

Fombrun, C. J., & Wiedmann, K. P. (2001). Reputation quotient. Analyse und Gestaltung der Unternehmensreputation auf der Basis fundierter Erkenntnisse. *Schriftenreihe Marketing Management*, 1-52.

Gaines-Ross, L. (2008). *Corporate reputation: 12 steps to safeguarding and recovering reputation*. Hoboken, NJ: John Wiley & Sons.

Gavrilis, C., Kakali, C., & Papatheodoro, C. (2008). Enhancing library services with Web 2.0 functionalities. In Christensen-Dalsgaard, B. (Eds.), *ECDL 2008, LNCS 5173* (pp. 148–159). doi:10.1007/978-3-540-87599-4_16

Gruber, T. R. (1993). A translation approach to portable ontology specifications. [Knowledge Systems Laboratory.]. *Technical Report KSL*, *92*(71), 199–220.

Guadarrama, S. (2010). Guadarrama on CWW. In Mendel, J. (Ed.), *What computing with words means to me* (pp. 24–25). IEEE Intelligence Magazine.

Gunelius, S. (2010). *Blogging all-in-one for dummies*. Indianapolis, IN: John Wiley & Sons.

Hächler, L. (2010). *Web 2.0 and 3.0: How online journalists find relevant and credible information*. Unpublished Master thesis, University of Fribourg, Fribourg, Switzerland.

Hagras, H. (2010). Hagras on CWW. In Mendel, J. (Ed.), *What computing with words means to me* (pp. 24–25). IEEE Intelligence Magazine.

Hasan-Montero, Y., & Herrero-Solana, V. (2006). Improving tag-clouds as a visual information retrieval interfaces. *Proceedings of International Conference on Multidisciplinary Information Sciences and Technologies*.

Ingenhoff, D. (2004). *Corporate issues management in multinationalen Unternehmen: Eine empirische Studie zu organisationalen Strukturen und Prozessen*. Wiesbaden, Germany: VS Verlag für Sozialwissenschaften.

Ingenhoff, D., & Sommer, K. (2008). The interrelationships between corporate reputation, trust and behavioral intentions. A multi-stakeholder approach. *58th Annual Conference of the International Communication Association (ICA)*, (pp. 21-27). Montreal, Canada

Kaser, O., & Lemire, D. (2007). *Tag-cloud drawing: Algorithms for cloud visualization*. Banff: Electronic Edition.

Kleinberg, J. (1998). Authoritative sources in a hyperlinked environment. In *9th ACM-SIAM Symposium on Discrete Algorithms*, (pp. 1-33). Odense, Denmark.

Klewes, J., & Wreschniok, R. (2009). *Reputation capital: Building and maintaining trust in the 21st century*. Berlin, Germany: Springer.

Lewandowski, D. (2005). *Web information retrieval: Techniken zur Informationssuche im Internet*. Düsseldorf, Germany: Deutsche Gesellschaft f. Informationswissenschaft u. Informationspraxis.

Manning, C. D., Raghavan, P., & Schütze, H. (2008). *Introduction to information retrieval*. New York, NY: Cambridge University Press.

McLuhan, M., & Nevitt, B. (1972). *Take today: The executive as dropout*. New York.

Meier, A., & Stormer, H. (2009). *eBusiness & eCommerce: Managing the digital value chain*. Berlin, Germany: Springer.

O'Reilly, T. (2005). *What is Web 2.0? Design patterns and business models for the next generation of software*. Retrieved November 30, 2010, from http://oreilly.com/web2/archive/what-is-web-20.html

O'Reilly, T., & Battelle, J. (2009). *Web squared: Web 2.0 five years on, special report*. Retrieved November 30, 2010, from http://www.web2summit.com/web2009/public/schedule/detail/10194

Oliveira, J. V., & Pedrycz, W. (2007). *Advances in fuzzy clustering and its applications*. West Sussex, UK: John Wiley & Sons. doi:10.1002/9780470061190

Pepper, S. (2010). Topic maps. In *Encyclopedia of Library and Information Sciences*. Retrieved November 30, 2010, from http://www.google.ch/url?sa=t&source=web&cd=1&sqi=2&ved=0CCMQFjAA&url=http%3A%2F%2Fwww.ontopedia.net%2Fpepper% 2Fpapers%2FELIS-TopicMaps.pdf&rct=j&q= pepper%20topic%20maps&ei=aF7uTKjoHYiSswavzpT-Cg&usg=AFQjCNFolzoDB1u5NNgkRRbRi9itkEaJnA&sig2=cmLGL3R5x6CubvBQfKmnmA&cad=rja

Peters, I. (2009). *Folksonomies: Indexing and retrieval in the Web 2.0*. Berlin, Germany: Saur.

Phillips, D., & Young, P. (2009). *Online public relations: A practical guide to developing an online strategy in the world of social media*. London, UK: Kogan Page Limited.

Picot, A., Reichwald, R., & Wigand, R. T. (2003). *Die grenzenlose Unternehmung: Information, Organisation und Management*. Wiesbaden, Germany: Gabler Verlag.

Portmann, E. (2008). *Informationsextraktion aus Weblogs*. Saarbrücken, Germany: VDM.

Portmann, E., & Meier, A. (2010). A fuzzy grassroots ontology for improving weblog extraction. *Journal of Digital Information Management, 8*(4), 276–284.

Prud'hommeaux, E., & Seaborne, A. (2008). *SPARQL query language for RDF*. W3C Recommendation 15 January 2008. Retrieved November 30, 2010, from http://www.w3.org/TR/rdf-sparql-query/

Rohloff, K., Dean, M., Emmons, I., Ryder, D., & Summer, J. (2007). An evaluation of triple-store technologies for large data stores. *Proceedings of the 2007 OTM Confederated International Conference on the Move to Meaningful Internet Systems*.

Röttger, U. (2005). Kommunikationsmanagement in der Dualität von Struktur. *Medienwissenschaft Schweiz/Science des Mass Média Suisse, 1*(2), 12-19.

Russel, R. C. (1918). *US patent 1261167, 1918*.

Russel, R. C. (1922). *US patent 1435663, 1922*.

Scott, D. M. (2010). *The new rules of marketing and PR: How to use social media, blogs, news releases, online video, and viral marketing to reach buyers directly*. New Jersey: John Wiley & Sons.

Setsuo, A., & Suzuki, E. (2008). *Discovery science: 7th International Conference, DS 2004, Padova, Italy, October 2-5, 2004*. Berlin, Germany: Springer.

Sirmakessis, S. (2005). *Knowledge Mining: Proceedings of the NEMIS 2004 Final Conference*. Berlin, Germany: Springer.

Smith, G. (2008). *Tagging. People-powered metadata for the Social Web*. Berkeley, CA: New Riders.

Spivack, N. (2009). *The evolution of the Web: Past, present, future*. Retrieved November 30, 2010, from http://www.novaspivack.com/uncategorized/the-evolution-of-the-web-past-present-future

Troncy, R., Huet, B., & Schenk, S. (2011). *Multimedia semantics: Metadata, analysis and interaction*. New Jersey: John Wiley & Sons. doi:10.1002/9781119970231

Van Harmelen, F., Lifschitz, V., & Porter, B. (2007). *Handbook of knowledge representation.* New York, NY: Elsevier.

Van Riel, C. B. M., & Fombrun, C. (2007). *Essentials of corporate communication: Implementing practices for effective reputation management.* Abingdon, UK: Routledge. doi:10.4324/9780203390931

Voss, J. (2007). Tagging, folksonomy & co - Renaissance of manual indexing? *Proceedings of the International Symposium of Information Science,* (pp. 234–254).

Ward, M., Grinstein, G. G., & Keim, D. (2010). *Interactive data visualization: Foundations, techniques, and applications.* Natick, MA: Transatlantic Publishers.

Weller, K. (2010). *Knowledge representation in the Social Semantic Web.* Berlin, Germany: de Gruyter Saur.

Werro, N. (2008). *Fuzzy classification of online customers.* Retrieved November 30, 2010, from http://ethesis.unifr.ch/theses/downloads.php?file=WerroN.pdf

Zadeh, L. A. (1996). Fuzzy logic = Computing with words. *IEEE Transactions on Fuzzy Systems, 4*(2), 103–111. doi:10.1109/91.493904

Zadeh, L. A. (1999). From computing with numbers to computing with words – From manipulation of measurements to manipulation of perceptions. *IEEE Transactions on Circuits and Systems: Fundamental Theory and Applications, 45*(1), 105–119. doi:10.1109/81.739259

Zadeh, L. A. (2004). A note on Web intelligence, world knowledge and fuzzy logic. *Data & Knowledge Engineering, 50,* 291–304. doi:10.1016/j.datak.2004.04.001

Zadeh, L. A. (2006). From search engines to question answering systems – The problems of world knowledge, relevance, deduction and precisiation. In Sanchez, E. (Ed.), *Fuzzy logic and the Semantic Web* (pp. 163–210). Elsevier. doi:10.1016/S1574-9576(06)80011-0

Zadeh, L. A. (2009). Toward extended fuzzy logic—A first step. *Fuzzy Sets and Systems, 160*(21), 3175–3181. doi:10.1016/j.fss.2009.04.009

Zadeh, L. A. (2010, July). *Precisiation of meaning: Toward computation with natural language.* Presented at the IEEE 2010 Summer School on Semantic Computing, Berkeley, CA.

Zudilova-Seinstra, E., Adriaansen, T., & van Liere, R. (2008). *Trends in interactive visualization: State-of-the-art survey.* Berlin, Germany: Springer.

KEY TERMS AND DEFINITIONS

Folksonomy: Is a system of classification derived from the practice and method of collaboratively creating and managing tags to annotate and categorize content; this practice is also known as collaborative tagging, social classification, social indexing, and social tagging.

Interactive Visualization: Is a branch of graphic visualization in computer science that involves studying how humans interact with computers to create graphic representations of information.

Ontology: Provide criteria for distinguishing various types of objects (e.g. concrete and abstract, existent and non-existent, real and ideal, independent and dependent) and their ties (relations, dependences and predication). Within computer science the term stands for a design model for specifying the world that consists of a set of types, relationships and properties.

Reputation Analysis: Is a reputation management task conducted by communications operatives and consist of the process of tracking an entity's actions and other entities' opinions about those actions; reporting on those actions and opinions; and reacting to that report creating a feedback loop.

Search Engine: Is an instrument intended to search for information on the Web. The search results are typically presented in a single list and are generally called hits. The information can consist of images, text, Web pages, and auxiliary types of documents.

Semantic Web: Describes methods and technologies to allow machines to understand the meaning—or semantics—of information on the Web. According to the original vision, the availability of machine-readable metadata would enable automated agents and other software to access the Web more intelligently.

Social Semantic Web: Subsumes developments in which social interactions on the Web lead to the creation of explicit and semantically rich knowledge representations. The Social Semantic Web can be seen as a Web of collective knowledge systems, which are able to provide useful information based on human contributions and which get better as more people participate. The Social Semantic Web combines technologies, strategies and methodologies from the Social and the Semantic Web.

Social Web: Describes how people socialize or interact with each other throughout the Web as a medium with easy-to-use software.

Topic Map: Is a standardized format of representation and interchange of knowledge, with an emphasis on the findability of information.

Chapter 8
Fuzzy Target Groups in Analytic Customer Relationship Management

Michael Kaufmann
Swiss Mobiliar Insurance & Pensions, Switzerland

Cédric Graf
ITpearls AG, Switzerland

ABSTRACT

Scoring models yield continuous predictions instead of sharp classifications. Scoring customers for profitability, loyalty, or product affinity corresponds to an inductive fuzzy classification: The model represents a continuous membership function mapping the set of customers into the fuzzy set of interesting customers – the fuzzy target group. This chapter presents a method for membership function induction based on normalized likelihood ratios. Applications of this method are proposed for selection, visualization, and prediction in the field of analytics in general, and for customer profiling, target group definition and customer scoring specifically for analytic customer relationship management. A real world case study is described. Furthermore, an implementation of the proposed method, developed at the research center for fuzzy marketing methods (FMsquare[1]), is presented.

INTRODUCTION

Management Summary

In this Chapter, the application of analytics (quantitative decision support) to customer relationship management (CRM) is discussed. It is shown how three analytic techniques, selection (find-ing relevant attributes), visualization (plotting relevant associations) and prediction (estimating relevant class membership) help increase success of CRM-based marketing activities. Furthermore, it is shown how inductive fuzzy logic techniques provide a technical means to support these three types of analyses, and a prototype implementation is presented.

DOI: 10.4018/978-1-4666-0095-9.ch008

The benefit of analytic CRM is its *focusing on relevant information in order to increase efficiency*. Selection, visualization and prediction can help optimize efficiency of CRM and Marketing resource investment by *quantitative decision support*. The fuzzy logic method presented in this chapter, *inductive fuzzy classification (IFC)*, is a research approach which can be applied to support decisions in CRM-based marketing either in a human oriented or automated approach. Its benefit is (1) a selection *and relevance filtering* algorithm which works for both numeric and symbolic data; (2) a standardized semantically *intuitive visualization* technique for human decision makers; and (3) a method *to increase predictive accuracy* of existing models by transforming enterprise information into the fuzzy domain.

The basic idea is to compute fuzzy membership degrees to desirable targets from existing data (likelihood-based inductive approach). The resulting models, called *membership functions*, can be used in targeted database marketing in order to identify relevant customer attributes regarding a target such as product affinity; to plot the corresponding data-based target associations of relevant customer attributes in two dimensions; and *to improve campaign response rates* and maximizing efficacy of predictive models by transforming customer attributes into membership degrees to target likelihood. Specific visual examples can be found in Figures 2, 3, and 5. The section Case Study shows a real world instance.

Fuzziness

The world is not just black and white: Sometimes, statements are in-between true and false. This gradual concept of truth is the basis for fuzzy logic or approximate reasoning, as proposed by Zadeh (1975) and Bellman & Zadeh (1977). Fuzzy Logic, based on the concept of fuzzy sets introduced by Zadeh (1965) allows propositions with a gradual truth value and thus supports approximate reasoning, gradual and soft consolida-

tion and non-exclusive classification. Fuzziness is an imprecision of boundaries, of concepts that are not clearly defined. Fuzzy logic provides a mathematically precise definition of fuzzy concepts, if those concepts are ordinal, by assigning a gradual membership degree to its elements. Fuzzy propositions lead to fuzzy classes, which allow gradual, fuzzy class boundaries. Fuzzy classification is a method for imprecise data consolidation, where the degree of membership in classes is gradual (Del Amo, Montero, & Cutello, 1999). The application of fuzzy classification to analytical customer relationship management (aCRM) has the advantage of precisiation of fuzzy concepts (Zadeh, 2008, p. 14) in the context of decision support for direct customer contact (Werro, 2008). This precisiation can be achieved by inducing membership functions to fuzzy target classes (Setnes, Kaymak, & van Nauta Lemke, 1998).

Analytics

Analytics is *the method of logical data analysis*[2]. According to Zimmermann (1997), data analysis is the *search for structure in data.* The more data is available, the more complex it becomes to find relevant information. Consequentially, enterprises analyze their data in order to gain useful insights. *Business Analytics* is defined as "a broad category of applications and techniques for gathering, storing, analyzing and providing access to data to help enterprise users make better business and strategic decisions (Turban, Aronson, Liang, & Sharda, 2007, p. 256).

The ability of enterprises to analyze the potentially infinite space of available data– their capacity of business analytics – is a major competitive advantage. Companies that use analytics as key strategies are called analytics competitors by Davenport (2006). They can differentiate themselves through a better customer understanding in a time when products and technologies are becoming more and more comparable. Analytics competitors apply predictive modeling to a wide

Figure 1. Inductive fuzzy classification for individual marketing

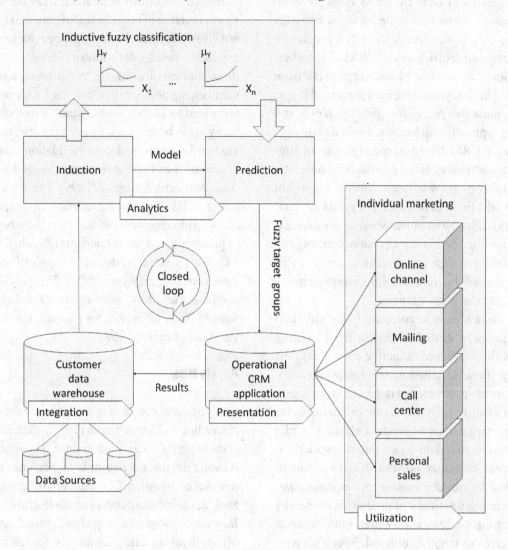

range of fields such as customer relationship management, supply chain management, pricing, and marketing. Their top management understands and advocates that most business functions can benefit from quantitative optimization. In fact, business analytics can be applied to almost any area that concerns an enterprise:

- **Customer relationship management (CRM):** Prediction of the most appropriate customer relationship activity
- **Web Analytics:** Optimization of the website according to click stream analysis

- **Compliance:** Prediction of illegal behavior such as fraud or money laundering
- **Risk Management:** Prediction of credit worthiness
- **Strategic Management:** Visualization of customer profiles for product or market strategies
- **Marketing:** Prediction of customer product affinity

In 2002, *comprehensibility* and *integration* were identified as the driving force of emerging trends in business analytics (Kohavi, Rothleder, &

Figure 2. Example of attribute ranking for the German credit data

Attribute	Correlation of NLR with target
Checking status	0.379304635
Credit history	0.253024544
Duration	0.235924759
Purpose	0.190281416
Savings status	0.189813415
Credit amount	0.184522282
Housing	0.173987212
Property magnitude	0.157937117
Age	0.136176815
Employment	0.128605942
Personal status	0.093525855
Installment commitment	0.091375548
Other payment plans	0.079139824
Foreign worker	0.077735317
Job	0.061875096
Other parties	0.060046535
Own telephone	0.051481771
Existing credits	0.042703728
Residence since	0.034584104
Num. dependents	0.007769441

Figure 3. Visualization of a relevant attribute and its association with the target as an inductive membership function

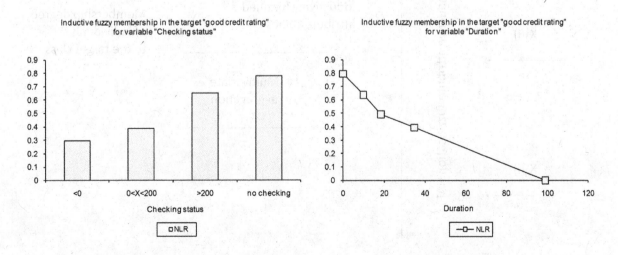

Simoudis, 2002). Today, good business analytics is either comprehensible *or* integrated: Human decision makers need interpretable, visual or textual models in order to understand and apply analytic insights in their daily business. Contrarily, information systems demand machine readable, integrated automated interfaces from analytic applications to operational systems in order to apply scorings or classifications in automated processes.

Insights from analytics are traditionally presented to human decision makers as tables and graphics. Today, more and more analytic results are loaded automatically from analytic systems into operational systems, a concept which is called *integrated analytics*. Those systems can automate certain decision processes, or display analytic insights to users of operational systems. In aCRM, scorings such as cross selling ratings can be transferred directly into the operational CRM application, where they are presented to sales representatives. Certain CRM decisions can

be automated, such as choosing an individualized advertisement message in the online channel (Kaufmann & Meier, 2009). The process of integrated analytics can be described in five steps. Firstly, analytic data is collected form different sources. Secondly, a predictive model is induced from the data, either in a supervised form using a target variable, or in an unsupervised form of clustering or association analysis. Thirdly, a prediction, classification or score is assigned to the original data based on the induced model. For example, a loyalty or churn prediction is assigned to every customer record based on a predictive model calculated by analysis of past churns. Fourthly, these predictions are transmitted to the operational systems, where they are applied to decision support. Finally, outcomes of decision support – for example, sales decisions and actions – are fed back into the analytic data pool for meta-analysis and iterative optimization.

Figure 4. Proposed schema for likelihood-based IFC for prediction

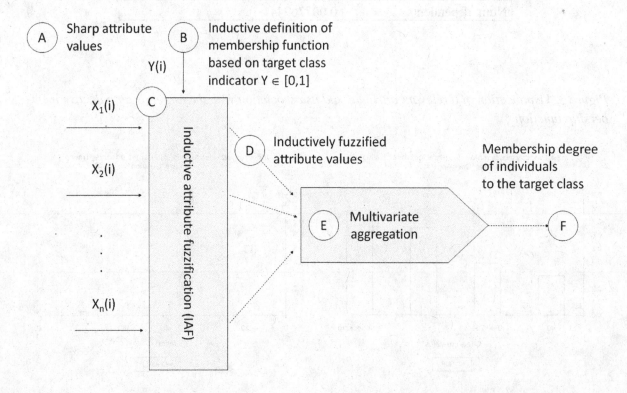

Figure 5. Schema of a fuzzy customer profile based on IFC-NLR, together with two instances presented by Kaufmann (2009)

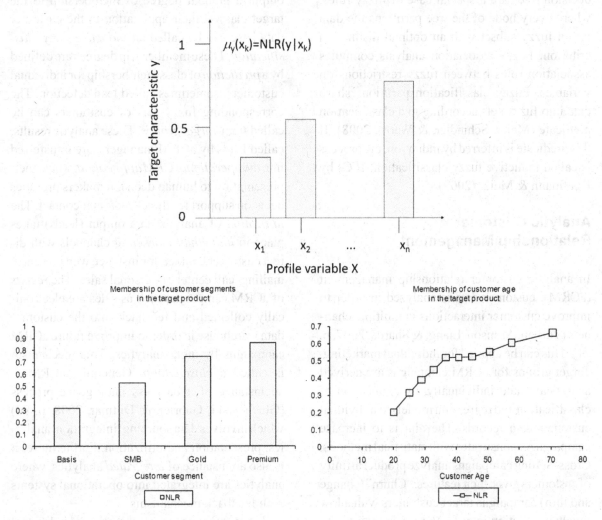

Fuzzy Data Analysis

Application of fuzzy logic techniques to analytics is called fuzzy data analysis. This permits gradual relationships between data and predictions. The application of fuzzy logic to analytics is appropriate when there is fuzziness in the data, the prediction target, or in the association between the two (Zimmermann, 1997). The advantage of fuzzy classification methods is that the class boundary is not sharp: Patterns detected by fuzzy data mining provide soft partitions of the original data. Furthermore, an object can belong to several

classes with different degrees of membership (Zimmermann, 2000).

Two main advantages of fuzzy logic techniques that are pointed out by Hüllermeier (2005) are the elimination of certain threshold effects because of gradual, soft data partitioning, and the comprehensibility and *interpretability* of resulting models containing linguistic terms. Hüllermeier (2005) discusses possible fields of application of fuzzy set theory to data mining: Fuzzy cluster analysis partitions a set of objects into several fuzzy sets with similar properties in an unsupervised manner. Learning of fuzzy rules computes decision rules with fuzzy propositions. Fuzzy decision trees are a special case of fuzzy rules, where every node of the tree partitions the data into a fuzzy subset with an optimal distinction criterion. Fuzzy association analysis computes association rules between fuzzy restrictions on variables. Fuzzy classification partitions sharp data into fuzzy sets according to a classification predicate (Meier, Schindler, & Werro, 2008). If this predicate is inferred by induction, the process is called inductive fuzzy classification (IFC) by Kaufmann & Meier (2009).

Analytic Customer Relationship Management

In analytic customer relationship management (aCRM), customer data is analyzed in order to improve customer interactions in multiple channels (Turban, Aronson, Liang, & Sharda, 2007, p. 71). This can be applied for individual marketing. Target groups for aCRM campaigns are derived analytically and individually, by application of classification and regression models to individual customer data records. The aim is to increase campaign response rates with statistical methods. Cross-Selling campaigns analyze product affinity of customers given their features. "Churn" (change and turn) campaigns target customers with a low loyalty prediction in order to re-gain their trust.

Figure 1 illustrates a schematic information system that can enable aCRM processes. In contemporary enterprises, due to intensive application of computing machinery and electronic data bases in business processes, there exist large amounts of possibly useful customer data in various software applications that can serve as *data sources* for aCRM. The heterogeneity of data storage implies a necessity for data *integration* before they can be analyzed. A system that automates this task is called a *customer data warehouse* (Inmon, 2005). Based on this integrated data pool, *analytics* provides *inductions* of predictive *models* for desirable customer classes such as product

purchase, profitability or loyalty. If these models output a gradual degree of membership to the target classes, their application to the customer data base can be called an *inductive fuzzy classification*. These membership degrees are defined by a *prediction* of class membership for individual customers, sometimes called lead detection. The corresponding fuzzy sets of customers can be called *fuzzy target groups*. These analytic results, called leads by aCRM managers, are transferred into the *operational CRM application*, where their presentation to human decision makers provides decision support for direct customer contact. The *utilization* of analytic data output (leads) takes place in *individual marketing* channels with direct customer contact, for instance web presence, mailing, call center or personal sales. The *results* of aCRM campaigns such as sales are electronically collected and fed back into the customer data warehouse in order to improve future aCRM campaigns by meta-analytics. This mechanism is called a *closed loop*. Generally, aCRM is an instance of a business intelligence process (Gluchowski, Gabriel, & Dittmar, 2008, p. 90) which involves data sourcing, integration, analytics, presentation and utilization. Furthermore, it is also an instance of *integrated* analytics, where analytics are integrated into operational systems with feedback mechanisms.

In comparison to mass marketing, in individual marketing every customer is provided with the advertisement that fits best whenever the customer is identified. Especially when customer databases such as a customer data warehouse are present, an individual customer scoring is possible: The customer's target membership score is used to assign an individual advertisement message to each customer. These messages are delivered electronically via customer relationship management application to individual marketing channels. Campaign target groups are individualized. All customers in the target groups are known individually and are contacted directly.

APPLICATION OF INDUCTIVE FUZZY CLASSIFICATION TO ANALYTICS

The understanding of inductive fuzzy classification in the presented research approach is an inductive *gradual* ranking of individuals (Zimmermann, 2000, p. 223). In many interpretations, the induction step consists of learning *fuzzy rules* (Wang & Mendel, 1992), (Roubos, Setnes, & Abonyi, 2003), (Dianhui, Dillon, & Chang, 2001), (Hu, Chen, & Tzeng, 2003). In the present approach, fuzzy classification is understood more generally as inducing *membership functions* to fuzzy classes, and assigning individuals to those classes. In general, a membership function can be any function mapping into the interval between one and zero. Consequently, inductive fuzzy classification (IFC) is defined as the process of *assigning individuals to fuzzy sets whose membership function is generated from data so that the membership degrees provide support for an inductive inference.*

An inductive fuzzy class y' provides a predictive model μ for membership in a class y. This model is represented by an inductive membership function for y', which maps from the universe of discourse U into the interval between zero and one (Formula 1).

$$\mu_{y'}(i) : U \rightarrow [0,1] \qquad (1)$$

Consider the fuzzy classification predicate P(i,y):= "i is likely a member of y". This is a fuzzy proposition (Zadeh, 1975) as a function of i and y which indicates that there is inductive support for the conclusion that an individual i belongs to a class y. The truth function τ of this fuzzy propositional function can be defined by the membership function of an inductive fuzzy class. Thus, P(i,y) is a fuzzy restriction on U defined by $\mu_{y'}$ (Formula 2).

$$\tau(i \text{ is likely a member of } y) := \mu_{y'}(i) \qquad (2)$$

In practice, any function that assigns values between zero and one to data records can be used as a fuzzy restriction. The aim of inductive fuzzy classification is to calculate a membership function to a fuzzy set of likely members in the target class. Hence, any type of classifier with a normalized numeric output can be viewed as an inductive membership function to the target class, or as a truth function for the fuzzy proposition P(i,y).

State of the art methods for inductive fuzzy classification in that sense include linear regression, logistic regression, naïve Bayesian classification, neural networks, fuzzy classification trees and fuzzy rules. These are classification methods yielding numerical predictions that can be normalized in order to serve as a membership function to the inductive fuzzy class y':= { i ∈ U | i is likely a member of y }.

The basic idea of inductive fuzzy classification based on normalized likelihood ratios (IFC-NLR) is to transform inductive support of target class membership into a membership function with the following properties: The higher the likelihood of i ∈ y in relation to i ∉ y, the greater the degree of fuzzy inductive membership of i in y'. For an attribute X, the NLR function calculates a membership degree of a value x ∈ dom(X) in the predictive class y', based on the likelihood of target class membership. The resulting membership function is defined as a relation between all values in the domain of the attribute X and their normalized likelihood ratio (NLR).

The likelihood ratio (Hawthorne, 2008) represents a numeric degree of support for one of two opposite hypotheses. It is defined as the ratio between the likelihood L(y | x) of the hypothesis that an individual i is an element of the target class y and the opposite hypothesis L(¬y | x) that i is not an element of the target class, given the evidence that the attribute X of this individual has the value x, denoted by X(i) = x. These likelihoods are calculated on the basis of the available data as conditional relative frequencies (Formula 3).

$$L(y \mid x) := p(X(i) = x \mid i \in y):$$
$$= \frac{\mid \{i \in U \mid X(i) = x \wedge i \in y\} \mid}{\mid \{i \in U \mid i \in y\} \mid} \tag{3}$$

$$L(\neg y \mid x) := p(X(i) = x \mid i \notin y):$$
$$= \frac{\mid \{i \in U \mid X(i) = x \wedge i \notin y\} \mid}{\mid \{i \in U \mid i \notin y\} \mid}$$

By inductive logic, following the principle of likelihood (Hawthorne, 2008), the ratio between the two likelihoods is an indicator for the degree of support for the inductive conclusion that i ∈ y given the evidence that X(i) = x.

In order to transform the likelihood ratio into a fuzzy set membership function, it can be normalized in the interval between zero and one. Luckily, for every ratio R = A/B, there exists a normalization N = A/(A+B) having the following properties:

• N is close to zero if R is close to zero
• N is equal to 0.5 if and only if R is equal to 1
• N is close to 1 if R is a large number

This kind of normalization is applied to the aforementioned likelihood ratio in order to derive the normalized likelihood ratio function (NLR). Accordingly, the membership μ of an attribute value x in the target class prediction y' is defined by the corresponding NLR, as formalized by Formula 4.

$$\mu_{y'}(x) := NLR(y \mid x) = \frac{L(y \mid x)}{L(y \mid x) + L(\neg y \mid x)} \tag{4}$$

Alternatively, two likelihoods can be compared by a normalized difference, as shown by Formula 5. In that case, the membership function is defined by a normalized likelihood difference (NLD), and its application for classification is called induc-

tive fuzzy classification by normalized likelihood difference (IFC-NLD). In general, IFC methods based on normalized likelihood comparison can be categorized by the abbreviation IFC-NLC.

$$\mu_{y'}(x) := NLD(y \mid x) = \frac{L(y \mid x) - L(\neg y \mid x) + 1}{2} \tag{5}$$

If the target class is fuzzy, for example because the target variable is gradual, the likelihoods are calculated by fuzzy conditional relative frequencies based on fuzzy set cardinality (Dubois & Prade, 1980). Therefore, the formula for calculating the likelihoods is generalized in order to be suitable for both sharp and fuzzy characteristics. Thus, in the general case of variables with fuzzy truth values, the likelihoods are calculated as defined by Formula 6.

$$L(y \mid x) := \frac{\sum_{i=1}^{n} \mu_x(i) \mu_y(i)}{\sum_{i=1}^{n} \mu_y(i)}$$

$$L(\neg y \mid x) := \frac{\sum_{i=1}^{n} \mu_x(i)(1 - \mu_y(i))}{\sum_{i=1}^{n} (1 - \mu_y(i))} \tag{6}$$

Accordingly, the calculation of membership degrees using the NLR function (Formula 4) works for both categorical and fuzzy target classes and for categorical and fuzzy analytic variables. For numerical attributes, the attribute values can be discretized using quantiles, and a piecewise linear function can be approximated to average values in the quantiles and the corresponding NLR, as proposed by Kaufmann (2011). A membership function for individuals based on their attribute values can be derived by aggregation, as explained in the following section on prediction.

The presented IFC method provides a means for computing inductive membership functions for a target class. These membership functions can be visualized. Furthermore, they can be used for inductive fuzzification of attributes, which can be applied for attribute selection and for improving predictive models. Thus, the proposed IFC methods can be applied in the following areas of data analysis:

- **Selection:** Attributes can be scored by the correlation of automatically generated inductive membership degrees with a binary or fuzzy target class in order to select relevant attributes.
- **Visualization:** Induced membership functions can serve as human-readable diagrams of association between analytic and target variables using a plot of automatically generated membership functions.
- **Prediction:** Data sets used for prediction can be inductively fuzzified by transforming the original data into inductive target membership degrees, which can improve the correlation of predictions with the actual class membership.

Selection

In practice, there is an abundance of data available. The problem is to find relevant attributes for a given data mining task. Often, thousands of variables or more are available. Most machine learning algorithms are not suited for such a great number of inputs. Also, human decision makers need to know which ones of those customer attributes are relevant for their decisions. Therefore, the most relevant attributes need to be selected before they can be used for visualization or prediction.

In order to find relevant attributes for predicting a target class y, an attribute selection method can be derived from membership functions induced by inductive fuzzy classification, using the method proposed in the previous section. All possible analytic variables can be ranked by the correlation coefficient of their normalized likelihood ratio (NLR) with the target variable. For every attribute X_k, the membership function in the predictive

target class y' denoted by $\mu_{y'}(X_k)$ is computed. The membership in target y is indicated by a Zadehan variable Y, which is a variable with a domain of fuzzy truth values in the interval between zero and one. Then, the Pearson sample correlation coefficient (Weisstein, 2010) between the NLR based membership degrees and the Zadehan values of Y is calculated. Thus, the relevance of an attribute X_k regarding target y is defined as the correlation of its inductive fuzzification with the target variable (Formula 7). The most relevant variables are the ones with the highest correlation.

$$relevance(X_k) := corr(\mu_{y'}(X_k), Y) \qquad (7)$$

The fuzzification of analytic variables prior to attribute relevance ranking has the advantage that all types of analytic variables, linguistic, categorical, Boolean, Zadehan and numeric variables, can be ranked using the same measure. Choosing correlation as a measure of association with the target has the advantage that it is a standard aggregate in the SQL language, and thus readily available in major database systems.

To illustrate the proposed method, the attributes of the German credit data[3] are ranked regarding the target class of customers with a good credit rating (Figure 2). Those attributes have been inductively fuzzified with normalized likelihood ratios. The Pearson coefficient of correlation between the resulting membership degrees and the Boolean target variable "good credit rating" has been calculated. One can see that for a credit rating, checking status, credit history or duration of customer relationship are quite correlated attributes, whereas for example the number of existing credits is less relevant.

This kind of attribute selection can be used as an input for visualization and prediction. If a target class is defined, the relevant correlated variables can be identified. A visualization of five to ten most relevant variables give good insights about associations in the data.

Visualization

The IFC-NLR method can be applied to create visualizations of associations between an analytic variable (a factor) and a class (a target). A visualization of variable association is a human-readable presentation that allows the reader to see the distribution of target likelihood in tabular form or as a graph.

Using inductive fuzzy classification for visualization, the table consists of relations between factor values and normalized target likelihood ratios, and the graph results in a plot of the inductive membership function. For categorical factors, the graph is a bar chart. For numerical factors, the membership function is plotted as a continuous line. The advantage of this method is that the notion of membership of a factor X in a target Y is semantically clear and intuitively understandable by readers. Furthermore, the semantics of the normalized likelihood ratio function is mathematically clearly defined.

As an example, for two variables from the German credit dataset, Checking status and Duration, the inductive fuzzy membership function in the target class of customers with a good credit rating can be visualized as shown in Figure 3. This graphic can be interpreted as follows: Customers without checking account or with a balance of more than 200 are more likely to belong to a good credit history than not. Customers with a negative balance are more likely to belong to bad credit rating. For the duration of the credit (in months), the shorter the duration is, the higher the likelihood of good credit history. Credits with duration of more than 19 months have a higher likelihood to belong to a bad credit history, and accordingly the normalized likelihood ratio is less than 0.5.

Prediction

A method for the application of likelihood-based IFC to prediction has been studied by Kaufmann and Meier (2009). The basic idea is to create a multivariate inductive model for target class membership by a combination of inductively fuzzified attributes derived by membership function induction. The proposed approach for application of likelihood-based IFC to prediction consists of a univariate inductive fuzzification of analytic variables prior to a multivariate aggregation. This has the advantage that non-linear associations between analytic variables and target membership can be modeled by an appropriate membership function. As presented in Figure 4, the following steps are applied in order to derive an inductive membership degree of an individual i in the prediction y' for class y based on the individual's attributes:

- **A:** The raw data consists of sharp attribute values.
- **B:** An inductive definition of the membership function for the attribute values in the predictive fuzzy class y' is calculated using the previously described IFC-NLC methods.
- **C:** The attribute values are fuzzified using the derived membership functions from step B. This step is called inductive attribute fuzzification (IAF), defined as supervised univariate fuzzy classification of attribute values.
- **D:** After that, the data set consists of fuzzified attribute values in the interval [0,1] indicating the inductive support for class membership.
- **E:** The several fuzzified analytic variables are aggregated into a membership degree of individuals in the predictive class. This can be a simple conjunction or disjunction, a fuzzy rule set, or a statistical model derived by supervised machine learning algorithms such as logistic or linear regression.
- **F:** This results in a multivariate membership function that outputs an inductive membership degree for an individual i in class y, which represents the resulting prediction.

Empirical tests (Kaufmann, 2011) have shown that using the proposed method of inductive attribute fuzzification prior to application of conventional machine learning algorithms significantly improves the average correlation between prediction and target. For binary target variables, a combination of IAF with a normalized likelihood ratio (NLR) and the subsequent application of a logistic regression turned out to be optimal. For numerical targets, a simple fuzzification by normalization of the target and an IAF using a normalized likelihood difference (NLD) as input to the calculation of a regression tree has shown to be optimal.

However, this improvement by IAF can be shown only in average prediction correlation. There are instances of data where the application of IAF lowers the predictive performance. Therefore, an IAF is worth a try, but it has to be tested whether in the given data domain it really improves the prediction or not. IAF provides a tool for fine-tuning predictive modeling, but answering the question about the best classification algorithm in a specific context takes place in the data mining process in which the algorithm with the best results is selected (Küsters, 2001).

MEMBERSHIP FUNCTION INDUCTION FOR ANALYTIC CRM

The general application of IFC-NLC to the field of analytics for selection, visualization and prediction can be applied to analytic CRM. Three applications are proposed. Visualizations of induced membership functions of customer characteristics in CRM targets provide fuzzy customer profiles. Furthermore, membership function induction (MFI) allows fuzzy definitions of target groups based on customer characteristics. Finally, scoring methods can represent membership functions to fuzzy target groups defined as fuzzy sets of customers to which every individual customer has a degree of membership.

Customer Profiling

The aim of a customer profile is to make associations between customer characteristics and target classes of interesting customers with desirable features understandable to marketing decision makers. The question is which customer features are associated with the target. A customer profile visualizes the likelihood of target class membership given different values of an attribute, in order to show relevant features that distinguish the target class from the rest of the customers. In the context of CRM, there are several target customer classes that are interesting for profiling:

- **Product affinity:** Customers that have bought a given product
- **Profitability:** Customers that are profitable to the enterprise
- **Recency:** Customers that are active buyers because they have recently bought a product
- **Frequency:** Customers that buy frequently
- **Monetary value:** Customers that generate a high turnover
- **Loyalty:** Customers that have used products or services for a long period of time
- **Credit worthiness:** Customers that pay their bills promptly

A customer profile for the mentioned target customer classes should answer the question: What distinguishes customers in this class from other customers? Thus, the association between class membership and customer attributes is analyzed. The customer attributes that can be evaluated for target likelihood include all of the aforementioned characteristics, and additionally socio-demographic data, geographic data, contract data, and transaction behavior recorded in operational computer systems such as CRM interactions and contacts in direct marketing channels.

If one looks more closely at the target customer classes, one can see that these classes are fuzzy.

For example, to generate a "high turnover" is a fuzzy proposition, and the corresponding customer class is not sharply defined. Of course, one could discretize the class using a sharp boundary, but this does not reflect reality in an appropriate manner. Therefore, it is proposed to visualize fuzzy customer classes as fuzzy sets with membership functions.

In order to generate customer profiles based on a target class and the relevant customer attributes, the method of membership function induction by normalized likelihood ratios presented in the previous sections can be applied. It is proposed to select the relevant customer attributes first, using the method described above. After that, the relevant attributes are called profile variables. For a profile variable X, the values $x_k \in dom(X)$ are called profile characteristics. They are assigned an inductive membership degree for the predictive target class y' defined by $\mu_{y'}(x_k) := NLR(y \mid x_k)$. A plot of the corresponding membership function represents a visual fuzzy customer profile for variable X, as illustrated by Figure 5.

Two instances of a fuzzy customer profile using normalized likelihood ratios is shown in Figure 5, where the customers of investment funds products of a financial service provider are profiled by customer segment and customer age. The interpretations of the graphs is that customers above the age of 50 and customers in the segments Gold and Premium are more likely to buy investment funds than the average customer.

A fuzzy customer profile derived with the IFC-NLR method creates a visual image of the customer class to be analyzed by showing degrees of membership of customer features in the target characteristic. Marketing managers can easily interpret the resulting reports.

Fuzzy Definition of Target Groups

Marketing target groups can be defined by on typical characteristics of existing product users. This method is based on analysis of existing customer data in the information systems of a company, which is an instance of secondary market research. The data of customers that are product users (the test group) is compared to the data of customers that do not use the product (the control group). The attributes separating test and control group most significantly are used to define the target group of potential customers. These attributes are the most selective ones. Accordingly, the target group is derived inductively by similarity to the set of existing product users. As an example, a customer profile could show that customers between 30 and 40 years of age in urban areas are twice as likely to be product users as other customers. In that case, the target group for this particular product could be defined accordingly.

Analytic target group definitions are based on a set of customer characteristics. However, these characteristics differ in relevance. Thus, the set of relevant customer characteristics for a product target group is a *fuzzy set* because the boundary between relevant and non-relevant characteristics is gradual. The corresponding membership degree can be precisiated by a relevance or selectivity metric. It is proposed to use a normalized likelihood ratio as a measure of selectivity.

The likelihood of product usage u_P for product P given that a customer record i in the existing customer database d has characteristic c can be computed accurately as a sampled conditional probability $p(c \mid u_P)_d$, defined as the number of product users that have this feature, divided by the number of product users (Formula 8). In this formula, $c(i)$ and $u_P(i)$ are truth values that indicate presence or absence of a customer characteristic and the usage of the product.

$$p(c \mid u_P)_d := \frac{\mid \{i \in d \mid c(i) \wedge u_P(i)\} \mid}{\mid \{i \in d \mid u_P(i)\} \mid} \quad (8)$$

This product usage likelihood can be compared to the likelihood $p(c \mid \neg u_P)_d$ of the opposite hypothesis that a customer is not a product user, given characteristic c, calculated as the number of non-users of the product that have characteristic c divided by the total number of non-users (Formula 9).

$$p(c \mid \neg u_P)_d := \frac{|\{i \in d \mid c(i) \wedge \neg u_P(i)\}|}{|\{i \in d \mid \neg u_P(i)\}|} \quad (9)$$

As explained above, the likelihood ratio is a measure for comparison of two hypotheses. Thus, the selectivity of a customer characteristic c can be expressed by the ratio between the likelihood of product usage, given c, and likelihood of product non-usage, given c (Formula 10). This ratio can be normalized, as formalized by Formula 11.

$$LR(u_P \mid c)_d := \frac{p(c \mid u_P)_d}{p(c \mid \neg u_P)_d} \quad (10)$$

$$NLR(u_P \mid c)_d := \frac{p(c \mid u_P)_d}{p(c \mid u_P)_d + p(c \mid \neg u_P)_d} \quad (11)$$

Finally, the selectivity of characteristic c expressed as a normalized likelihood ratio represents an inductive degree of membership of this characteristic in the fuzzy target group definition for product P. An inductive fuzzy target group definition t based on analysis of database d is a fuzzy set of customer features, and its membership function is defined by the corresponding NLR (Formula 12).

$$\mu_t(c)_d := NLR(u_P \mid c)_d \quad (12)$$

A customer characteristic may or may not be defined by a granular attribute value. Characteristics can also be computed by functional combination of several basic attribute values. Furthermore, the customer characteristic indicator $c(i)$ can indicate a fuzzy truth value in the interval [0,1] if the corresponding characteristic

c is a fuzzy proposition such as "high turnover". In that case, the definition of the NLR for fuzzy truth values from the previous section can be applied. However, the aim of analytic target group definition is to find or construct optimal defining target customer characteristic indicators with the highest possible degree of membership in the target group definition. These indicators can be constructed by logical connections or functions of granular customer characteristics.

This kind of analytic target group definition is a conceptual one, suited for presentation to human decision makers, because it is intuitively understandable. It results in a ranking of customer characteristics that define typical product customers. However, for integrated analytics in analytic CRM, a scoring approach is more promising, because it yields better response rates, although the resulting models may be less comprehensible.

Fuzzy Target Groups Based on Customer Scoring

In analytic customer relationship management (aCRM), each customer is targeted not only directly, but also individually with an advertisement message, decision or activity. The behavior of an organization towards an individual customer is analytically customized according to the customer's classification, and customers with different characteristics are targeted with different behavior. Individual customers are assigned a score for different CRM targets based on a predictive multivariate model. IFC methods can be applied to customer data for individual marketing in order to calculate *a predictive scoring model* for product usage. This model can be applied on the data to *score customers for their product affinity*, which corresponds to an inductive fuzzy classification of customers, where the predictive model is a multivariate membership function.

An aim of customer analytics is the application of prediction to the selection of a target group with likelihood to belong to a given class of customers. For example, potential buyers or credit worthy payers can be selected by applying data analysis to the customer database. This is done either by *segmentation* or *scoring* (Sousa, Kaymak, & Madeira, 2002). By applying a segmentation approach, sharp sets of customers with similar characteristics are calculated. Those segments have a given size. For individual marketing, a scoring approach is more promising, where every customer is assigned a score predicting a likelihood of response. The score is calculated by application of a predictive multivariate model with numeric output, such as neural networks, linear regression, logistic regression or regression trees. When a numeric score can be normalized, it represents a membership function to a fuzzy set of customers with a high response likelihood - *the fuzzy target group* - to which every customer has a degree of membership. This scoring process can be applied for every product. Thus, for every individual customer the degree of membership to all possible cross selling target groups is known, and in direct customer contact the customer can be assigned the advertisement message with the highest score.

There are different methods for fuzzy customer scoring. For example, fuzzy clustering for product affinity scoring was presented by Setnes, Kaymak, & van Nauta Lemke (1998), where the reason for using fuzzy systems instead of neural networks is declared as the *comprehensibility* of the model. Kaufmann & Meier (2009) evaluated a supervised fuzzy classification approach for prediction using a combination of NLRs with an algebraic disjunction. In the present approach, a hybrid method between fuzzy systems and statistical modeling is proposed for prediction (as explained above), using univariate inductive membership functions for improving the target correlations of logistic regressions or regression trees. However, all inductive scoring methods that yield a numeric value representing response likelihood can be normalized in order to represent a membership function to a fuzzy set of custom-

ers, and can therefore be categorized as inductive fuzzy classification.

A classical sharp CRM target group $T \subset C$ is a subset of all customers C defined by a target group definition t: $T := \{i \in C \mid t(i)\}$. In the case of scoring methods for target selection, the output of the model application is numeric, and can be normalized in the interval $[0,1]$ to represent a membership function. In that case, the target group is a fuzzy set T', and the (normalized) customer score is a membership function $\mu_{T'}: C \rightarrow [0,1]$. This score is defined by a predictive model M as a multivariate combination of n customer attributes $X_1, ..., X_n$, as shown in Formula 13.

$$\mu_{T'}(i) := M(X_1(i), ..., X_n(i)) \qquad (13)$$

Because T' is a fuzzy set, it has to be *defuzzified* when a campaign requires a binary decision. For example, the decision about contacting a customer by mail has to be sharp. An alpha-cut of the fuzzy set allows the definition of individual marketing target groups of optimal size regarding budget and response rate, and leads to a sharp target group T_α, as formalized in Formula 14.

$$T_\alpha := \{i \in C \mid \mu_{T'}(i) \geq \alpha\} \qquad (14)$$

For individual marketing, the fuzzy target group membership degrees are predictive scores that are processed via the customer relationship management (CRM) system, which dispatches them to the distribution channel systems for mapping customers to individualized advertisement messages. In all computer supported channels with direct customer contact, inbound or outbound, as soon as the customer is identified, a mapping can be calculated to the product to which the customer has the highest score. Based on that, the advertisement message is chosen. In the online channel, logged in customers are displayed individual advertisement banners. Customers are sent individual letters with product advertisement. And in the call center and in personal sales, if the customer can be identified, the agent can try cross-selling for the next best product.

Case Study

Let us consider a specific example, as published by Kaufmann and Meier (2009). In 2008, PostFinance ltd, the financial service provider of the Swiss Post, intended to improve marketing efficiency by quantitative decision support. They only wanted to contact customers with personal advertisement messages who are *really* interested in their Investment Funds (IF) product, because anything else is a waste of resources of both the company and their customers. In order to do so, Mr. Kaufmann, data warehouse analyst at PostFinance, run a selection algorithm on the customer database, with sales of Investment Funds as target variable. Based on existing contact, sales and customer information, he identified seven relevant customer attributes that distinguish interested customers from others most significantly:

- Customer Segment
- Number of products
- Age
- Overall balance
- Customer group
- Balance on private account
- Loyalty

Mr. Kaufmann computed a predictive numerical model IFM which assigned a numerical value to every customer record based on the record's attribute values for customer segment, number of products, overall balance, loyalty, customer group, balance on private account and age.

IFM : customer segment

$\times$number of products

$\times$overall balance

$\times$loyalty   (15)

$\times$customer group

$\times$balance on private account

$\times$age $\rightarrow [0,1]$

Now, Mr. Kaufmann had identified a *fuzzy target group* for the company's product IF, with an inductive membership function μ to the inductive fuzzy class IF' of customers i likely to buy that product (Formula 16).

$$\mu_{IF'}(i) := IFM(\text{customer segment}(i),$$
$$\text{number of products }(i),$$
$$\text{overall balance }(i), \text{loyalty }(i),$$
$$\text{customer group }(i),$$ (16)
$$\text{balance on private account}(i),$$
$$\text{age}(i)) \in [0,1]$$

In fact, this target group was a *fuzzy set* of customer records, each with a membership degree between one and zero. With this information, Mrs. Gartenmann, online channel manager at PostFinance, could implement an analytic CRM campaign in order to contact individual customers with high response likelihood online. The sales results after three months showed a significant improvement of advertisement conversion in comparison to random selection.

SOFTWARE IMPLEMENTATION

The IFC-NLR data mining methodology introduced by Kaufmann & Meier (2009) has been implemented by Graf (2010) as a supervised attribute filter in the WEKA machine learning workbench (Hall, Frank, Holmes, Pfahringer, Reutemann, & Witten, 2009). The aim of this implementation is to enable the use of IFC-NLR in a typical data mining process. This IFC-Filter allows the evaluation of the algorithm. In this section, WEKA is presented, and the software implementation is described. A description of the functionality of the algorithm will give the necessary background. A use case of the IFC-Filter in a data mining process will be presented, and a user's guide will introduce the application of the software.

Software use Case

WEKA can be used for data mining in order to create predictive models based on customer data. The IFC-Filter can facilitate visualization of the association between customer characteristics and the target class, and it can improve predictive performance of customer scoring by transforming attribute values into inductive fuzzy member-

ship degrees, as explained above. Thus, it can perform membership function induction (MFI) and inductive attribute fuzzification (IAF), as shown in Figure 6.

The IFC-Filter transforms sharp input data into membership degrees which indicate the inductive support for the conclusion that the data record belongs to the target class. In order to do so, first, membership functions are induced from data and optionally displayed to the screen. Then, these functions are applied to fuzzify the original attributes. Visualization and Prediction based on the concepts of MFI and IAF are two main use cases for the IFC-Filter software in the data mining process.

In order to visualize associations between variables, inductive membership functions can be plotted with the method IFC-NLR described earlier. Thus, for every analytic variable, a function mapping from the variable's domain into a degree

Figure 6. Software architecture of the IFC-Filter

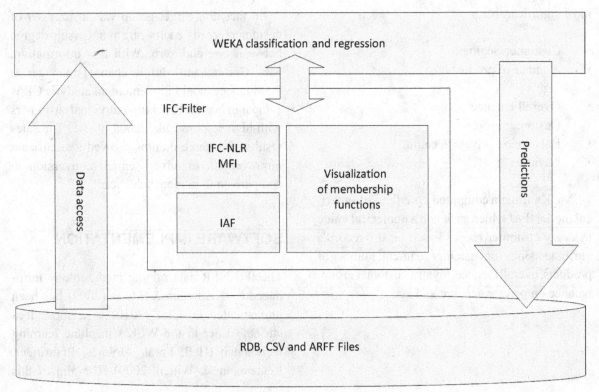

of membership in the inductive fuzzy target class is displayed graphically. This plot gives intuitive insights about associations between attribute values and the target class.

For prediction, the transformation of crisp attribute values into inductive membership degrees can enhance the performance of existing classification algorithms. The IFC-Filter transforms the original attribute values into inductive membership indicating target class likelihood based on the original value. After that, a classical prediction algorithm such as logistic regression can be applied to the transformed data and to the original data in order to compare the performance. It is possible that IAF improves prediction. If that is the case, IAF data transformation can be applied to huge data volumes in relational databases using the SQL code generated by the IFC-Filter.

User's Guide

The software is available for download[4] in source and binary format for researchers and practitioners for experimenting and practicing inductive fuzzy classification. To make your initiation to it as smooth as possible we provide here a short tutorial to use the IFC-filter software:

- To start the application you can simply double click the file weka.bat. It is configured to be initialized with 2 GB RAM. You can change this setting by modifying the parameter -Xmx2024m. Java Version 6 is required.
- The simplest way to use the filter is to use the *KnowledgeFlow* button on the appearing GUI Chooser. There you have the possibility to load knowledge flow schemes in the left upper corner. Five of them are already prepared. You find them in the directory *Scheme* and in the sub directory *DB*. The scheme in the *DB-folder* contains a Database Loader which is configured for an Oracle XE database which can be

downloaded free of charge. The other four schemes in the *Scheme*-folder contain data loader for ARFF file formats. The data for them are in the directory called *Data*.

- By right clicking the data loader a menu appears in which you can choose *start loading*. This will activate the data mining algorithm. The results can be seen in the text viewer component of the scheme. Right click the text viewer after the algorithm has completed and choose *show result*.
- The graphical component of the filter can be activated by right clicking the IFC-Filter component in the flow. This can be done with a right click on the component, by choosing *configure* and setting the *IFCWindow* parameter to true.

The Knowledge Flow allows the interconnection of elements such as filters classifiers and clustering in a graphical interface. The knowledge flow window contains the following main components: The tool bar provides a choice of different components which can be dragged and dropped into the knowledge flow layout. The knowledge flow layout gives the opportunity to assemble WEKA components into a data flow in order to test, evaluate and perform data mining methods. The status and log panel supports the monitoring of the data mining process. The forth component contains buttons for clearing, saving or loading knowledge flow layouts. Figure 7 shows an example of a knowledge flow using a linear regression with IFC-Filter executed in parallel to the linear regression without IFC-Filter. The following paragraphs explain the corresponding data flow in detail.

First, a data source is attached to the Knowledge Flow. For data contained in WEKA ARFF files, this is done with the *ArffLoader* which can be found in the *DataSource section* of the tool bar. *DatabaseLoader* is also a possible option if the data resides in a relational database.

Figure 7. Knowledge flow with IFC-Filters

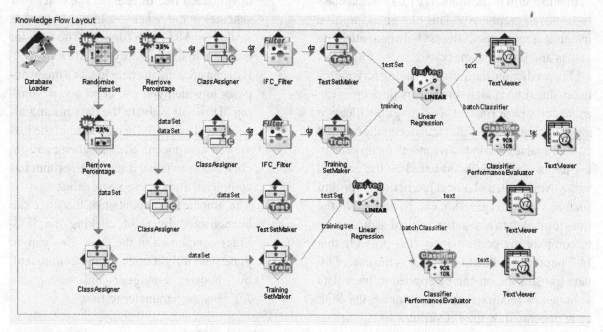

After that, training and test sets are generated. To achieve this, the source data is separated into two random data sets. For this purpose, the *Randomize* filter and the *RemovePercentage* filter can be applied, which can be found in the *Filter* toolbar. The *Randomize* filter blends the instances of a data set randomly. The *RemovePercentage* filter removes a percentage of the data set. By clicking with the right mouse button on the *RemovePercentage* icon, a configuration menu appears. Two parameters can be modified: the parameter *percentage* determines the percentage of the data set which will be removed; the parameter *InvertSelection* defines whether the data removal begins at the top or the bottom of the data. It is proposed to set *invertSelection* to true and percentage to 33% for training data, and to set *InvertSelection* to false and *percentage* to 66% for test data. The resulting two randomly split data sets can be used for evaluating the performance of predictive models. The class label of the data set is defined with a *ClassAssigner*. In order to apply the *IFC_Filter node*, it is put between *ClassAssigner* and *TestSetMaker* or *TrainingSetMaker*.

The nodes *TestSetMaker* and *TrainingSetMaker* define which part of the data split is used for training and which one for testing.

The configuration of the *IFC_Filter* can be performed by clicking with the right mouse button on the symbol of the *IFC_Filter* in the Knowledge Flow layout. In the appearing menu, *configure* can be chosen. This will open the configuration frame for the filter. The activation of the graphical illustration of the results of the *IFC_Filter* can be activated by setting *IFCWindow* to true. The field *classValue* allows choosing the target variable if the class of the data set is categorical. Accepted values are "first", "last", or a numerical value which represents the position of the target variable. If the class is binary, this selection is not supported. The parameter *percentageOfDataSet* defines the percentage of the data dataset contained in a quantile at which the iteration of the algorithm is stopped. This function gives the possibility to compensate for over fitting. The parameter *targetType* gives a choice between categorical or binary target variables as output of the algorithm. In order to apply algorithms that require categorical class labels, the target type is set to categorical. For algorithms with numerical or binary target variables such as linear regression, the target type is set to binary.

Finally, the training and test datasets serve as input into a classifier node, which calculates a predictive model and computes predictions for the test set. In one case, the data is inductively fuzzified using an IFC filter, and in the second case, regression is applied directly to the original data. *ClassifierPerformanceEvaluator* compares the predictions and the actual values in the test set in order to assess the predictive performance for both variants. Finally, the results are output in a *TextViewer*.

Visualization of Membership Functions

As proposed in the section on application of inductive fuzzy classification to analytics, the IFC-Filter can visualize membership functions that indicate target membership likelihoods. Figure 8 shows two screenshots of the membership function plots for the variables "Duration" and "Checking status" from the German Credit dataset. The IFC-Filter has the possibility to activate a frame containing a graphical illustration of the resulting membership functions. Each analytical variable is represented by a tab in this frame. The presentation of numerical analytical variables differs slightly from that of categorical analytical variables, because it presents a continuous membership function. An additional tab, the SQL Panel contains the membership functions of all analytic variables in SQL syntax.

As shown in Figure 8, the illustration of numerical analytical variables consists of four fields. The first field is a table containing the normalized likelihood ratios (NLR) with the corresponding quantiles and average quantile values (AQV). The second field shows a histogram containing the NLR and their corresponding AQV. The third field shows the membership function of the analytical

variable. The forth field shows the membership function in SQL syntax for this particular analytical variable which can be used directly in a relational database for fuzzy classification of variables.

The illustration of categorical analytical variables can be reduced to three fields. The first field is a table containing the NLR with the corresponding quantile and average value of the quantile. The second field shows a histogram containing the NLRs corresponding to the categorical values. The third field shows the membership function in SQL syntax.

The SQL-Panel displays a concatenation of the membership functions for all analytical variables that have been input for membership function induction by the IFC-Filter. This database script can be applied in a database in order to transform large database tables into inductive degrees of membership in a target class. This can improve the predictive quality of multivariate models.

CONCLUSION

Direct customer relations are central to every business activity. Today, software CRM systems support large organizations to relate to individual customers in a mass market. Data analysis on individual customers based on the available data can be applied for CRM in order to improve customer relationships. This kind of analytic CRM provides decision support to company representatives in marketing channels with direct customer contact for offers, underwriting, sales, communications, gifts and benefits.

For the analytics process step in aCRM, it is proposed to classify customers inductively and fuzzily in order to target individual customers with the right relationship activities. Firstly, the customers are *classified* by assigning them to different CRM targets (classes) such as product offers or promotional gifts. Secondly, this classification is done *inductively* by analyzing present data as

Figure 8. Visualization of membership functions with the IFC-Filter

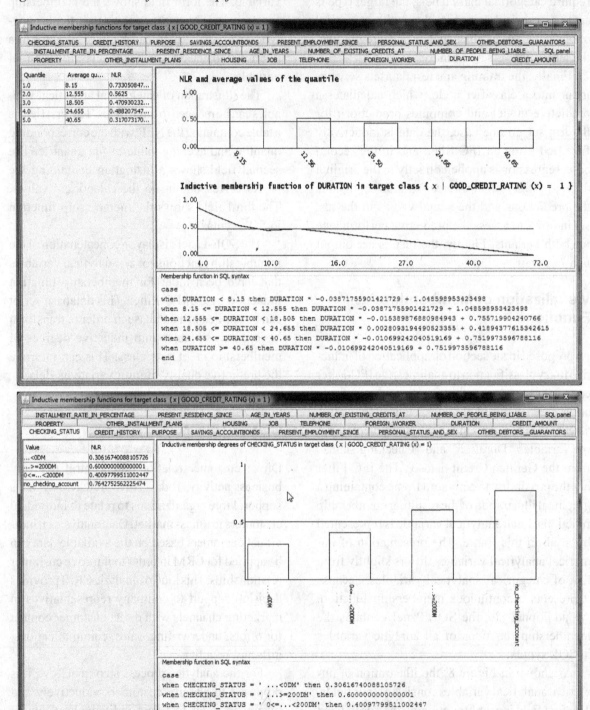

evidence for or against target membership based on customer characteristics. Thirdly, the assignment of individual customers to targets is *fuzzy* if the resulting classes have a gradual membership function. Finally, those inductive membership degrees to fuzzy CRM targets provide decision support by indicating the likelihood of desired response in customer activities based on customer characteristics. These membership functions can be used in analytics to select the most important characteristics regarding a target, for visualizing the relationship between characteristics and a target, and to predict target membership for individual customers.

The proposed method for membership function induction is based on calculating likelihoods of target membership in existing data. These likelihoods are turned into a fuzzy set membership function by comparison and normalization using a normalized likelihood ratio or a normalized likelihood difference. This algorithm has been implemented in the WEKA machine learning workbench as a supervised attribute filter, which inductively fuzzifies sharp data and visualizes the induced membership functions. This software can be downloaded for experimental purposes.

Sharp binary classification and segmentation lead to anomalies of threshold, and fuzzy classification provides a solution with gradual distinctions that can be applied to CRM, as pointed out by Werro (2008). Gradual customer partitioning has the advantage that the size of CRM target groups can be varied by choosing a threshold according to conditions such as budget or profitability. Of course, scoring methods for CRM are state of the art; additionally, the present approach suggests that fuzzy logic is the appropriate tool for reasoning about CRM targets, because they are essentially fuzzy concepts. Scoring provides a means for precisiation of this fuzziness, which provides numerical membership degrees of customers in fuzzy target groups.

The advantages of membership function induction for fuzzy classification of customers are

efficiency and precision. Firstly, membership functions to CRM targets can be derived automatically, which is an efficient way of definition. And secondly, those inferred membership functions are precise, because they indicate an objective, measurable degree of likelihood for target membership. Thus, the semantics of the membership function is clearly grounded.

In the presented method a transformation from probabilistic to fuzzy logic is achieved by precisiating the membership degrees to fuzzy concepts such as CRM targets using membership functions based on a measure of likelihood This blends the concepts of inductive and fuzzy logic. Fuzziness is an uncertainty of distinction, and likelihood is an uncertainty of conclusion. Fuzziness can be precisiated with membership functions, and likelihood can be precisiated by sampled conditional probabilities. The present approach suggests that there are fuzzy concepts such as CRM target groups that can be precisiated as a function of likelihoods.

Further research could investigate the use of fuzzy logic for optimizing cut-off points in CRM activities. Although scoring-based target groups are fuzzy, many (but not all) CRM activities are binary in nature. For this kind of decisions, fuzzy target groups need to be defuzzified by choosing a threshold. Thus, aCRM could be modeled as a fuzzy system including fuzzification, fuzzy rules and defuzzification, and appropriate measures for defuzzification in terms of fuzzy logic could be developed.

REFERENCES

Bellman, R. E., & Zadeh, L. A. (1977). Local and fuzzy logics. In Dunn, J. M., & Epstein, G. (Eds.), *Modern uses of multiple-valued logic*. Kluwer Academic Publishers. doi:10.1007/978-94-010-1161-7_6

Davenport, T. H. (2006, January). Competing on analytics. *Harvard Business Review*.

Del Amo, A., Montero, J., & Cutello, V. (1999). On the principles of fuzzy classification. *Proceedings of 18th North American Fuzzy Information Processing Society Annual Conf*, (pp. 675 – 679).

Dianhui, W., Dillon, T., & Chang, E. J. (2001). A data mining approach for fuzzy classification rule generation. *IFSA World Congress and 20th NAFIPS International Conference*, (pp. 2960-2964).

Dubois, D. J., & Prade, H. (1980). *Fuzzy sets and systems. Theory and applications*. Academic Press.

Gluchowski, P., Gabriel, R., & Dittmar, C. (2008). *Management Support Systeme und Business Intelligence*. Berlin, Germany: Springer Verlag.

Graf, C. (2010). *Erweiterung des Data-Mining-Softwarepakets WEKA um induktive unscharfe Klassifikation (Master's Thesis)*. Department of Informatics, University of Fribourg, Switzerland.

Hall, M., Frank, E., Holmes, G., Pfahringer, B., Reutemann, P., & Witten, I. H. (2009). The WEKA data mining software: An update. *SIGKDD Explorations*, *11*(1). doi:10.1145/1656274.1656278

Hawthorne, J. (2008). Inductive logic. In Zalta, E. N. (Ed.), *Stanford encyclopedia of philosophy*. Stanford, CA: The Metaphysics Research Lab, Stanford University.

Hu, Y., Chen, R., & Tzeng, G. (2003). Finding fuzzy classification rules using data mining techniques. *Pattern Recognition Letters*, *24*(1-3), 509–514. doi:10.1016/S0167-8655(02)00273-8

Hüllermeier, E. (2005). Fuzzy methods in machine learning and data mining: Status and prospects. *Fuzzy Sets and Systems*, 387–406. doi:10.1016/j.fss.2005.05.036

Inmon, W. H. (2005). *Building the data warehouse* (4th ed.). Wiley Publishing.

Kaufmann, M. (2009). An inductive approach to fuzzy marketing analytics. In M. H. Hamza (Ed.), *Proceedings of the 13th IASTED International Conference on Artificial Intelligence and Soft Computing,* Palma, Spain.

Kaufmann, M. (2011). *Inductive fuzzy classification for marketing analytics* (PhD Thesis, to appear). University of Fribourg, Switzerland.

Kaufmann, M., & Meier, A. (2009). An inductive fuzzy classification approach applied to individual marketing. *Proceedings of 28th North American Fuzzy Information Processing Society Annual Conference*.

Kohavi, R., Rothleder, N. J., & Simoudis, E. (2002). Emerging trends in business analytics. *Communications of the ACM*, *45*(8), 45–48. doi:10.1145/545151.545177

Küsters, U. (2001). Data Mining Methoden: Einordung und Überblick. In Hippner, H., Küsters, U., Meyer, M., & Wilde, K. (Eds.), *Handbuch Data Mining im Marketing - Knowledge Discover in Marketing Databases* (pp. 95–130). Wiesbaden, Germany: Vieweg GABLER.

Meier, A., Schindler, G., & Werro, N. (2008). Fuzzy classification of relational databases. In Galindo, M. (Ed.), *Handbook of research on fuzzy information processing in databases* (*Vol. II*, pp. 586–614). Information Science Reference. doi:10.4018/978-1-59904-853-6.ch023

Roubos, J. A., Setnes, M., & Abonyi, J. (2003). Learning fuzzy classification rules from labeled data. *Information Sciences—Informatics and Computer Science. International Journal (Toronto, Ont.)*, *150*(1-2).

Setnes, M., Kaymak, H., & van Nauta Lemke, H. R. (1998). Fuzzy target selection in direct marketing. *Proceedings of the IEEE/IAFE/INFORMS Conference on Computational Intelligence for Financial Engineering (CIFEr)*.

Sousa, J. M., Kaymak, U., & Madeira, S. (2002). A comparative study of fuzzy target selection methods in direct marketing. *Proceedings of the 2002 IEEE International Conference on Fuzzy Systems (FUZZ-IEEE '02).*

Turban, E., Aronson, J. E., Liang, T.-P., & Sharda, R. (2007). *Decision support and business intelligence systems*. New Jersey: Pearson Education.

Wang, L., & Mendel, J. (1992). Generating fuzzy rules by learning from examples. *IEEE Transactions on Systems, Man, and Cybernetics, 6*, 1414–1427. doi:10.1109/21.199466

Weisstein, E. W. (2010). *Correlation coefficient*. Retrieved from http://mathworld.wolfram.com/CorrelationCoefficient.html

Werro, N. (2008). *Fuzzy classification of online customers*. PhD Thesis. Fribourg, Switzerland: University of Fribourg.

Witten, I. H., & Eibe, F. (2005). *Data mining. Practical machine learning tools and techniques*. San Fancisco, CA: Elsevier.

Zadeh, L. A. (1965). Fuzzy sets. *Information and Control, 8*, 338–353. doi:10.1016/S0019-9958(65)90241-X

Zadeh, L. A. (1975). Calculus of fuzzy restrictions. In Zadeh, L. A., Fu, K.-S., Tanaka, K., & Shimura, M. (Eds.), *Fuzzy sets and their applications to cognitive and decision processes*. New York, NY: Academic Press.

Zadeh, L. A. (2008, August 11-22). Toward human level machine intelligence - Is it achievable? The need for a paradigm shift. *IEEE Computational Intelligence Magazine, 3*(3).

Zimmermann, H. J. (1997). Fuzzy data analysis. In Kaynak, O., Zadeh, L. A., Turksen, B., & Rudas, I. J. (Eds.), *Computational intelligence: Soft computing and fuzzy-neuro integration with applications*. Springer-Verlag.

Zimmermann, H. J. (2000). *Practical applications of fuzzy technologies*. Berlin, Germany: Springer Verlag.

KEY TERMS AND DEFINITIONS

Analytic Customer Relationship Management (aCRM): Quantitative decision support for direct customer interactions.

Fuzzy Target Group: Fuzzy set of customers targeted with an advertisement message or customer relationship activity, based on a defining membership function.

Inductive Attribute Fuzzification (IAF): Transformation of original attribute values into a degree of membership in the target class using an induced membership function.

Inductive Fuzzy Classification (IFC): Partitioning of individuals into fuzzy sets based on inductive inference.

Membership Function Induction (MFI): Derivation of fuzzy set membership functions based on evidence in the form of existing data.

Normalized Likelihood Comparison (NLC): Indication of the degree of discrepancy in likelihood of two opposite hypotheses, normalized in the interval between zero and one.

Normalized Likelihood Difference (NLD): Measure for the degree of inductive support for one of two opposite hypotheses, as a difference of evidence based hypothesis likelihoods, normalized in the interval between zero and one.

Normalized Likelihood Ratio (NLR): Measure for the degree of inductive support for one of two opposite hypotheses, as a ratio of evidence based hypothesis likelihoods, normalized in the interval between zero and one.

Zadehan Variable: A variable with a domain of numerical gradual truth values in the interval between zero and one, in analogy to a Boolean variable.

ENDNOTES

[1]   http://www.fmsquare.org (accessed 11.2010)

[2]   http://www.merriam-webster.com/diction-
ary/analytics (accessed 11.2010)

[3]   http://archive.ics.uci.edu/ml/datasets/
Statlog+(German+Credit+Data) (accessed
11.2010)

[4]   http://diuf.unifr.ch/is/ifc (accessed 11.2010)

Chapter 9
Web Analytics with Fuzziness

Darius Zumstein
University of Fribourg, Switzerland

ABSTRACT

In the Internet economy and information society, it has become an essential task of electronic business to analyze, to monitor, and to optimize websites and Web offers. Therefore, this chapter addresses the issues of Web analytics, which is defined as the measurement, collection, analysis, and reporting of Internet data for the purposes of understanding and optimizing website usage. After a short introduction, the second section defines Web analytics, describes benefits and problems of Web analytics, as well as different software architectures and products. Third, a controlling loop is proposed for Web content and Web user controlling in order to analyze Key Performance Indicators (KPIs) and to take website- and e-business-related actions. Fourth, different Web metrics and KPIs of information, transaction and communication are defined. Fifth, a fuzzy Web analytics approach is proposed, which makes it possible to classify Web metrics precisely into more than one class at the same time. Considering real Web data of the Web metrics page views and bounce rate, it is shown that fuzzy classification allows exact and flexible segmentation of Web pages or other objects and gradual rankings within fuzzy sets. In addition, the fuzzy logic approach enables Computing with Words (CWW), i.e. the perception-based, linguistic consideration of Web data and Web metrics instead of measurement-based, numerical ones. Web usage mining with inductive fuzzy classification and Web Analytics with Words (WAW) allows intuitive, human-oriented analyses, description, and reporting of Web metrics values in natural language.

1. WHY WEB ANALYTICS WITH FUZZINESS?

Since the development of the World Wide Web 20 years ago, corporate websites have become a crucial instrument of information, communication and transaction. With the growing importance of the web, the analysis, monitoring and optimization of a website and online marketing – Web Analytics (WA) – is now an important issue for both business practice and academic research.

DOI: 10.4018/978-1-4666-0095-9.ch009

According to a study of Forrester (2009), 74% of large enterprises agreed that web analytics is a technology they cannot do without. Consequently, it is not the question *if* companies do web analytics, but *how, why and what for*? Surprisingly, little academic and practical research has been done on web analytics so far to answer these and further research questions.

Today, many companies are using web analytics software like Google Analytics, Webtrends or Omniture to collect, store and analyze web data. These powerful tools provide dashboards and reports with many metrics to web analysts and managers, responsible for planning and decision-making about website-related activities. One problem of measurement-based reports is that all web metrics values, e.g. the number of page views, visits, visitors or conversion rates, are often raw numbers and therefore difficult to interpret. Another problem is that web data and metrics are usually reported, classified and evaluated in a sharp manner. This chapter proposes a fuzzy logic concept making it possible to classify web data and metrics fuzzily and to analyze and express their values with meaningful linguistic variables (i.e. words or word combinations).

After defining web analytics and its main benefits and problems, a web controlling framework with different levels is proposed in *section 3* as well as different steps and actions of web content and user controlling. *Section 4* explains various web and e-commerce metrics.

Section 5 exemplifies the fuzzy logic approach, showing how it can be used for classifying, describing and mining web data. In addition, the idea of web analytics with word and of fuzzy if-when rules for web analytics are shown. In the case study of *section 6*, real web data is classified fuzzily. Finally, *section 7* offers a conclusion and an outlook.

2. WEB ANALYTICS – AN OVERVIEW

2.1 Definition

According to the Web Analytics Association (WAA 2010), Web Analytics (WA) is defined as the measurement, collection, analysis and reporting of Internet data for the purposes of understanding and optimizing web usage. Inan (2009) considers web analytics as the study of user activities on a website in order to assure the site's performance, gain insights into the needs and wants of users' of the site and to identify areas that can be optimized. Weischedel et al. (2005) define WA as the monitoring and reporting of website usage so that enterprises can better understand the complex interactions between website visitor actions and website offers, as well as leverage insight to optimize the site for increased customer loyalty and sales. However, it is not only the website, web usage and sales which can be monitored, but also other objectives of a web presence (Zumstein & Meier 2010). Therefore, WA is defined as follows:

Definition 1 (Web Analytics): Web analytics is the measurement and analysis of web data to better understand website usage and user behavior as well as the definition and analysis of Key Performance Indicators (KPIs) in order to control the achievement of web-based goals and to optimize the website and electronic business, particularly electronic marketing and Customer Relationship Management (eCRM).

According to definition 1 in the broad sense of electronic business (compare Figure 1), WA goes further than just collecting and analyzing web data. First, WA can be understood as a *web controlling process* of defining, collecting, storing, preparing, measuring, analyzing and reporting web data, metrics, and KPIs. A web analytics system should not be an end in itself, but should help to measure and reach website or e-business related

Figure 1. Definition of Web analytics in the context of e-business. Source: (Meier & Zumstein 2010, p.6)

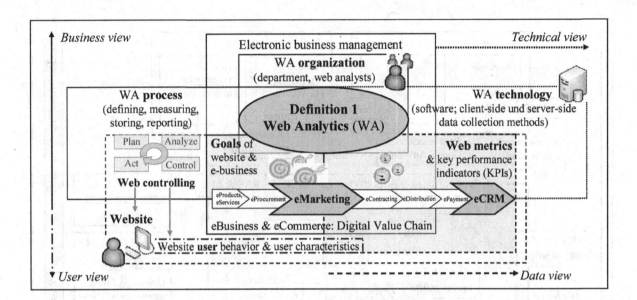

objectives, and to manage the *digital value chain* (Meier & Stormer 2009). In addition, WA should support management to take efficient and effective actions of e-marketing and eCRM.

2.2 Benefits of Web Analytics

The use and benefit of web analytics is manifolds and depends on the strategic objectives of a website. Generally speaking, the main benefits of web analytics are (compare also Figure 2):

1. **Analysis of website usage:** The analysis of website usage is necessary to know how many times website content has been accessed by visitors. Particularly, it shows trends in website usage.

2. **Measurement and achievement of website goals:** As mentioned in definition 1, WA helps to measure and achieve the objectives of a website, e.g. information, communication, transaction, lead generation or branding, by measuring different web metrics and KPIs discussed in section 4.

3. **Website optimization:** Based on the analyses of users' information accessing behavior, the *content* of a website can be aligned to the users' clicking, navigating and searching behavior. Moreover, website quality can be increased by analyzing the effects of the adaptions and improvements of the *navigation, structure, functionality, design and the usability* of the website (Palmer 2002).

4. **Visibility and search engine optimization:** WA is used to monitor the results of *Search Engine Optimization* (SEO) and *Search Engine Marketing* (SEM). Goal of SEO and SEM is to improve the visibility and rankings of web pages in search engines. Higher visibility relates strongly to website traffic (Drèze & Zufryden 2004). Web analytics tools reveal where, i.e. in which country or city, users are located, how they came to the website (e.g. using hyperlinks in search engines or external web pages) and they identify the *search or key words* used in search engines to find a web page.

Figure 2. Web analytics as an instrument of website and e-business analysis and controlling

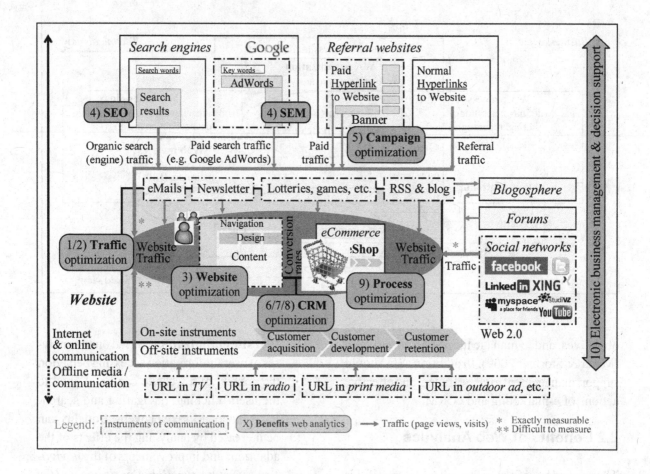

5. **Optimization of online marketing campaigns:** WA helps to measure the performance of the different on-site e-marketing instruments as *e-mails, newsletters, lotteries, games, blog entries or RSS feeds*, as well as off-site campaigns like *banner or keyword advertisements* (Hong 2007, Jackson 2009). WA allows comparing the effectiveness and efficiency of each e-marketing instrument to generate website traffic or online sales. For instance, it can be analyzed, how a blog entry or newsletter mailing performed, by tagging all links with JavaScript and measuring the clicks and conversion rates. In addition, e-marketing has indirect positive impact on a business more difficult to measure, e.g. reduced costs, added services or ease of information (Welling & White 2004).

6. **Visitor and customer orientation:** WA systems reveal the information (e.g. pages, files) or services (e.g. search function, forms, login, RSS feeds) accessed how often by users. Analyzing information demand, a high degree of *user orientation* – or customer centricity (Waisberg & Kaushik 2009) – is guaranteed, which is a precondition for electronic customer relationship management.

7. **Optimization of electronic Customer Relationship Management (eCRM):** A main reason to implement web analytics is the performance measurement of acquiring, developing and binding visitors and customers as well as to analyze and improve the output of eCRM (Econsultancy 2010). The success of *acquiring leads and customers* can be measured with different web metrics, e.g. the number of new visitors, leads or first time buyers. *Customer development and retention* is analyzed e.g. by the number of visits and purchases and the monetary value, i.e. order values and revenues. In addition, WA supports eCRM by *segmenting most valuable visitors or customers* (Sen et al. 2006) and by providing valuable data for *web usage mining* (see section 5.3).

8. **Profit optimization and competitive advantage:** In the context of electronic commerce, financial objective of WA is to reduce costs and to increase revenues and profits generated online, i.e. the maximization of online profitability and Return on Investment (ROI). Web controlling should measure the contribution of the website and online offers to the company's financial result. Finally, websites and e-business should build, secure and extend competitive advantages.

9. **Process optimization:** WA supports improving website-related and organizational business processes. Example is the design of *ideal order and payment processes* with low bounce rates.

10. **Management and decision support:** WA is used to plan, analyze and control strategic and operational objectives, which are connected with the website and e-business. It supports management to *legitimate website-related decision* based on facts and not on gut feeling. Therefore, a goal-oriented web performance measurement system facilitates *rational decision-making and performance-oriented management* of websites and e-business (Weischedel et al. 2005).

2.3 Problems of Web Analytics and Data Privacy

Beside the benefits, WA is also related with certain problems. For instance, analysts have difficulties to *interpret data values* or to make them actionable (Peterson 2005). Problems exist regarding *data quality*, e.g. measurement errors, or the *integration of data* in or from other information systems. In addition, it exists a *lack of standards* for web metrics or processes (Weischedel & Huizingh 2006) and it is difficult to find qualified specialists, to promote WA and to increase WA budget (Phippen et al. 2004).

However, the biggest problem in WA is data privacy. Privacy of Internet users is involved, if cookies, IP addresses or login data are used to identify or profile users and if web analytics tools track the interactions of visitors with websites. Visitor data, like preferred web pages, history of click behavior, location of access, browser settings and access data, is to keep secure and private. Data privacy becomes especially critical, if web or sales data are linked to *personal data* such as user IDs, name, e-mail, postal address or credit card number. Results of an empirical study of Zumstein et al. (2011) show that 16% of the Forbes 500 listed company websites *do not declare data collection practices at all*. Moreover, 35% do not declare the usage of cookies and 61% do not declare the recording of IP addresses. 91% of the websites do not name the web analytics system (provider) used to analyze web user behavior.

2.4 Software Architectures and Products

From a technical point of view, in web analytics it can be distinguished between four different approaches to collecting data: the analysis of log files (server-side data collection), page tagging (client-side data collection), the use of packet sniffing and reverse proxies. Following paragraphs focus on log files analysis and page tagging, because other methods are not often used in business practice.

Server-side data collection: In this method, data from log files are extracted and analyzed. Each time a web page is loaded in a browser, different data (e.g. user ID, user's IP address, requested files, referrer) are saved with a time stamp in the log file of a web server. The *advantage* of the log file analysis is that all requests and downloads of all files (e.g. text, PDF, pictures, audio or video files) from a web server are logged. However, a big *disadvantage* of log file analysis is that traffic on the website is not measured exactly because of the caching in web browsers and proxy servers. If a user clicks on the back button in the browser, already visited web pages are not reloaded from the server, but from the cache. Similarly, proxy servers buffer web pages, i.e. repeated page views are not recorded. Furthermore, all requests of search engines robots and crawlers distort the web statistics. Moreover, visitors cannot be identified distinctly, and user actions like mouse clicks or applications of new web technologies (like Flash or Ajax) are tracked neither. Finally, the extraction, preparation and analysis of log files can be complex and time-consuming. Given these problems, log file analysis has lost ground in recent years. Today, most tools are using page tagging, or a combination of the server- and client-side data collection, i.e. hybrid methods.

Client-side data collection: Using this method, a piece of JavaScript code is inserted in each web page (HTML page). If a page is loaded in the browser, the JavaScript is executed, and an invisible 1x1 pixel tag loaded, and all data regarding the page view and the visitor's actions is transmitted to a tracking server. Using cookies, data about each user and his sessions are recorded. Client-side WA solutions are mostly provided as Software as a Service (SaaS) by Application Service Providers (ASP). They have many *advantages*: First, all actions of users on a website are recorded in real time, i.e. all mouse clicks and all keyboard entries. Technical information about users is captured too: the size, resolution and colors of the monitor, type and language of the browser and operating system, and all plug-ins installed. Second, there is no caching in browsers or proxies, and the JavaScript is not read by search engine crawlers and robots. Finally, the tagging method can be implemented easily and no IT specialists are needed.

Despite of privacy issues, the client-side data collection method has become the *standard method* of web analytics. As a result, many different web analytics tools are available in the market. Web analytics software differs in their method, price and functionalities (compare table 1).

3. CONTROLLING LOOP FOR WEB ANALYTICS

3.1 Web Content Controlling and Web User Controlling

Web controlling as the management process of web analytics consists of the sub-steps *"plan"*, *"analyze"*, *"control" and "act"* (see definition 2). Objective of web controlling is the description of the state and development of website usage and e-business performance. Not only the management board, but also other stakeholders of the company, e.g. analysts, investors, business partners or suppliers, are interested to receive metrics and indicators on the non-monetary and monetary value creation of websites.

Web controlling focuses both on the analysis of website usage, i.e. web content controlling,

Table 1. Most used Web analytics systems. Source: adapted from (Meier & Zumstein 2010, p.16)

Provider/tool	URL	Method	Price segment	Operation
Piwik	www.piwik.org	page tagging	open source / free	internal
Open WA	www.openwebanalytics.com	page tagging	open source / free	internal
PageLogger	www.pagelogger.com	page tagging	open source / free	internal
Webalizer	www.webalizer.org	logfile analysis	open source / free	internal
AWStats	awstats.sourceforge.net	logfile analysis	open source / free	internal
Google Analytics	www.google.com/analytics	page tagging	free	hosted
Yahoo! Analytics	web.analytics.yahoo.com	page tagging	free	hosted
Clicky	www.getclicky.com	page tagging	free – lower price segment	hosted
Google Urchin	www.google.com/urchin	hybrid	lower price segment	internal
Etracker	www.etracker.com	page tagging	lower/middle price segment	hosted
Econda	www.econda.de	page tagging	lower/middle price segment	hosted
Coremetrics	www.coremetrics.com	page tagging	lower/middle price segment	hosted
Speed-Trap	www.speed-trap.com	page tagging	middle/higher price segment	hosted/internal
AT Internet	www.it-internet.com	page tagging	middle/higher price segment	hosted/internal
Webtrekk	www.webtrekk.de	page tagging	middle/higher price segment	hosted/internal
Unica	www.unica.com	page tagging	middle/higher price segment	hosted/internal
SAS WA	www.sas.com	page tagging	middle/higher price segment	hosted/internal
Nedstat	www.nedstat.com	page tagging	higher price segment	hosted/internal
Omniture	www.omniture.com	page tagging	higher price segment	hosted/internal
Webtrends	www.webtrends.com	page tagging	higher price segment	hosted/internal
Mindlab	www.mindlab.com	reverse proxy	higher price segment	internal

and on the analysis of user behavior, i.e. web user controlling (Zumstein & Meier 2010; see definition 3 and 4).

Web content controlling and web user content controlling can be considered as two sides of one medal.

Definition 2 (Web controlling): Web controlling is defined as the *planning, analysis and control* of website-related activities, processes, applications and services, as well as all actions of e-business and website management for the ongoing optimization of corporate performance.

Definition 3 (Web Content Controlling; WCC): Web content controlling is defined as the analysis and monitoring of *web usage and content demand* for optimizing the website and the online offer.

Definition 4 (Web User Controlling; WUC): Web user controlling is defined as the analysis of *website user behavior and characteristics* for optimizing user and online customer orientation, acquisition, retention and segmentation.

3.2 Web Controlling Loop

Figure 3 shows the closed loop for web controlling. To implement web analytics and web controlling effectively, management first has to define the website strategy and objectives on the strategic level, depending on the underlying *web-based business model* (number 1 in Figure 3).

Websites have different objectives, such as informing, communicating, branding, advertising, lead generating, selling, supporting, entertaining

Figure 3. Web controlling loop. Source: Adapted from (Meier & Zumstein 2010, p.10)

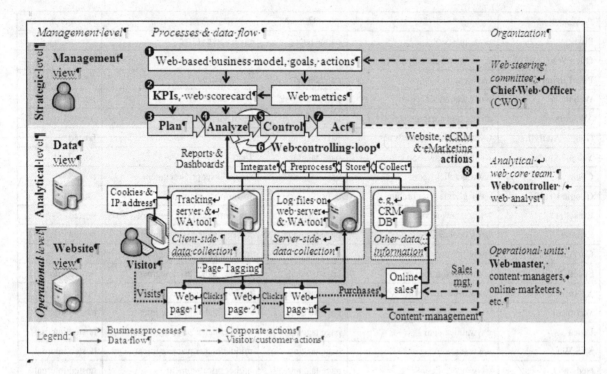

or community-building. Consequently, website success is always linked to the achievement of specific objectives and goals (Phippen et al. 2004, Bélanger et al. 2006). KPIs and web metrics are derived and defined according to the goals and sub-goals of the website (number 2 in Figure 3). Realistic target values of KPIs are *planed* in step 3. After collecting data on the data layer, using client- or server-side data collecting methods discussed above, web metrics are *analyzed and controlled* systematically in an ongoing closed-loop process of web controlling (step 4 and 5).

The web controlling loop (6) makes it possible to monitor website usage and the achievement of website goals and to analyze actual trends. The controlling loop also allows website managers to draw conclusions and to *(re)act* on an operational level (7). This is done by the means of different actions and activities of website management,

online marketing or eCRM (compare step 8 and section 3.3). Finally, a well implemented controlling loop permits website managers to allocate resources effectively.

However, business and data-related processes and the organization of web analytics are often cross-divisional and persons of different units work in interdisciplinary teams [Meier & Zumstein 2010]. On the strategic level, the *Chief Web Officer* (CWO) is the head of the web steering committee and implements the web-based business model and website strategy. The CWO is responsible for the website, its applications and services. On the analytical level, the *web controller* (web analyst) of the analytical web core team prepares and analyzes the data and metrics. On the operational level, the *web master*, content managers or other persons of the operational units are involved to administer and optimize the website.

3.3 Actions of Web Controlling

Possible actions of web controlling and electronic business are different in their nature and dependent of the website and its underlying web-based business model. However, content management, online marketing and eCRM are the most important domains of actions, since they are the central information and communication points of the website to the visitors or online customers.

Following examples illustrate some actions of web controlling. The different web metrics are defined and discussed in section 4.

Actions of content management:

- If the *bounce rate* of web page X is high, the *content* and/or hyperlinks of page X have to be adapted in order to reduce the bounce rate.
- If web page Y has *many page views* (i.e. Y belongs to the most visited web pages), the *content* has to be up-do-date and high in quality.
- If A, B and C are often entered *search words*, these search words have to be considered in the content and in the navigation of the website.
- If 80% of the visitors are coming from *English speaking* countries, content should be provided mainly in English language.

Actions of online marketing:

- If the *conversion rate* of product X is high, the online marketing *budget* (e.g. for Google AdWords) has to be augmented in order to increase sales of product X.
- If *newsletters* have higher conversion rates than ad banners, resources should be *invested* rather in sending newsletters than in ad banners.
- If *the abandonment rate* of the payment step in the order process is high,

the *payment process* (or the payment method) has to be analyzed and modified.

Actions of electronic customer relationship management:

- If *visitor X* visits the website regularly, then customer X has to be *animated* to interact and to buy.
- If *customer Z buys regularly* in the web shop, then his high loyalty could be *rewarded* by discounts.
- If the *number of online customers* is decreasing, then an *online marketing campaign* has to be launched to increase customer acquisition and retention.

4. WEB METRICS

4.1 Web Metrics of Web Content Controlling

A visitor can reach a website in different ways: either he enters the URL (Uniform Resource Locator) of the website directly in the address bar of the web browser, he is using a referred bookmark or he is referred by an external hyperlink from another website (compare Figure 4). Referrers are mostly search results of search engines like Google and paid or non-paid hyperlinks on external websites.

A visitor leaves the entry or *landing page* of a website, if he is not interested in the provided content. The *bounce rate* measures the share of such single page views. If the visitor is interested in the content and he clicks to a next page, a web page is called "sticky". Consequently, the page *stickiness* is the counterpart of the bounce rate (for the definition of the different web metrics see Table 2).

How visitors use a website is analyzed with different **web metrics**: The number of *page views* (page impressions), *visitors and visits* (sessions)

Figure 4. Metric model for Web content controlling. Source: adapted from (Zumstein 2010, p. 284)

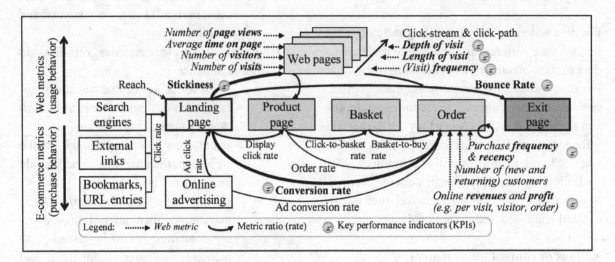

are standard metrics of web analytics (Sterne 2002, Kaushik 2010, Clifton 2010). In addition, the *average time on page*, *depth of visits* (i.e. the number of page views per visit) and the *length of visit* are further web metrics measured in most web analytics tools listed in Table 1. The most used *search words and phrases* in the search field of a website is particularly important information about the wants and demand of visitors.

If a corporate website is running a web shop, many other business relevant metrics are measured and monitored in electronic commerce (see Figure 4 and Table 2). Which service or product pages did (potential) customers view (so called *display click rate*)? Which products did they put often or seldom into the shopping cart (*click-to-basket rate*) and which items did they finally order (*basket-to-buy rate or order rate*)? The answers to these questions are important regarding the optimization of the website, the web shop and the product mix of a company. However, the most important KPI of e-commerce is the *conversion rate*, i.e. the share visitors who converted to customers by buying online.

In addition, it is an important task of e-business to analyze and monitor the total number and value of *product items* which customers ordered online in a certain period. This can be calculated both on an individual (single customer) or an aggregated level (customer segment or all customers). In addition, the number of orders and the *average order values* should be also calculated for both *new and returning customers*. In customer relationship management, the *number of repurchases* (purchase frequency) and *add-on selling* (i.e. cross-, up- and down-selling) are important. Revenues, costs and profits of online transactions, measured as a total or per visit, transaction, visitor or customer, are the most important financial indicators.

4.2 Web Metrics of Web User Controlling

Websites have become a crucial instrument of communication between Internet users and companies. However, it is a difficult task to measure the activities of communication with users by the means of metrics. Nevertheless, website operators do not know their visitors and customers personally and do not have many other possibilities than web analytics to assess the communication success of websites.

Table 2. Web metrics of information and transaction for Web controlling

Web metric	Definition
Page views	Number of page views (page impressions) of a web page accessed by a human visitor
Visits	A sequence of page views requests (a session) of a unique visitor without interruption
Visitors	Number of unique visitors (users) on a website
Time on page	The average length of time of all visitors spent on a single web page
Stickiness	The capability of a web page to keep a visitor on the website
Bounce rate	The percentage of single page view visits
Visit frequency	Number of visits, a visitor made on the website (loyalty indicator)
Visit recency	Number of days passed by, since a visitor last visit on the site
Length of visit	The average time of a visit, the visitors spent on the website
Depth of visit	Number of pages, the visitors visited during one visit
E-commerce metrics	
Conversion rate	Share of visitors who converts to customers (or doing another activity)
Ad conversion rate	Share of visitors, which clicked on a banner purchasing a product item
Display-click rate	Share of visitors, which viewed one or more product/service page(s)
Click-to-basket rate	Share of visitors, which put one or more product(s) in the shopping cart
Basket-to-buy rate	Share of visitors, which ordered the product(s) of the shopping basket
Order rate	Share of visitors, which viewed a product page and ordered the product
Repurchase rate	Share of online customers, who repurchase again on the website
Conversion rate	Share of visitors who converts to customers (or doing another activity)
Purchase recency	The length of time since the customers last purchase on the website
Purchase frequency	The number of customer's purchases on the website in a given period
Monetary value	Monetary value (revenues) of an online customer in a given period
Online costs	All costs related to an online transaction in a given period
Contribution margins	Contribution margin of an online customer in a given period
Online profit	Gross or net profit of an online customer in a given period
ROI	Return of Investment of the e-business and e-commerce
Number of customers	Absolute/relative number of online customers (customer base)

Analyst can evaluate the communication success of a website on the basis of the *number and quality of*

- *Contacts or requests* by contact forms, e-mail or call-back-buttons
- *Reactions or response* to personalized communication, e.g. on the website, in e-mails or newsletters
- *Registrations*, e.g. for login, newsletters, RSS feeds or downloads
- *Memberships,* e.g. in user groups, clubs or associations
- *Contributions, comments or ratings* on the website, in blogs, forums, wikis or in social networks.

Engaged visitors with a high degree of interactivity are called *online prosumers*. Online prosumers are *pro*ducers and con*sumers* at the same time (Meier & Stormer 2009). They are usually valuable users with high potential for online sales, but they also generate additional costs. However, an important objective of customer development is to bring as many persons of the target group to the website in order to convert them to online buyers and key online customers, or to regular customers, respectively. Web User Controlling monitors the number of surfers, prosumers, integrators (who are actively integrated into the digital value chain), buyers and key customers, as well as the effectiveness and efficiency to bind them.

In social commerce, not only technical interactivity with the website is important, but also personal interactivity, that means User Generated Content (UCG) on the website or in social media like Facebook, MySpace or Twitter.

5. WEB ANALYTICS WITH FUZZINESS

5.1 Limitations of Sharp Classification

All discussed web and e-commerce metrics in the previous sections have in common that they are usually *classified* and evaluated by human beings or computers in order to make business relevant statements and evaluations. In fact, data in web analytics and information systems are classified and handled generally in a sharp manner. That means that web metrics values are classified in a sharp way in classes with strictly defined boarders.

For example, in a sharp set (Figure 5a), the terms "few", "medium" or "many" page views of a web page can be either *true (1) or false (0)*. A value of 1 of the membership function μ (Y-axis in Figure 5a) means that the number of page views on the X-axis is corresponding to one single set. A value of 0 indicates that a given number of page views do not belong to one of the sets. The number of page views of a web page per day are defined as "few" between 0 and 32, 33 to 65 page views are "medium" and more than 66 are classified as "many" page views.

However, to classify page views – or any other web metric – sharply, is problematic as following example shows. If web page 1 has 65 page views, he is classified in the "medium" class, web page 2 with 70 has "many" page views. Although the two pages have been visited nearly the same way (page 2 visited only 5 times more often), they are assigned to two different sets, or classes respectively.

5.2 Fuzzy Classification of Web Metrics

The theory of fuzzy logic and fuzzy sets goes back to Lofti A. Zadeh in 1965. It takes the subjectivity, imprecision, uncertainty and vagueness of human thinking and language into account, and expresses it with mathematical functions (Zadeh 1965).

Figure 5. a) Sharp and b) fuzzy classification of the metric page views. Source: (Zumstein 2010, p.285)

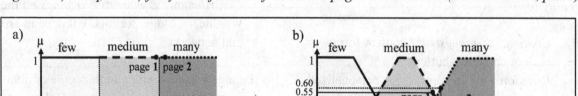

Figure 6. a) Two-dimensional sharp & b) fuzzy classification of the metrics page views and bounce rate. Source: adapted from (Zumstein 2010, p.285)

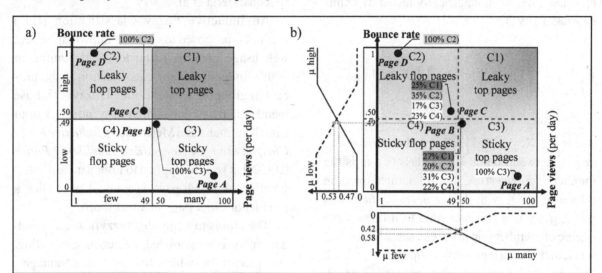

A fuzzy set can be defined formally as follows (Zimmermann 1991, Werro 2008, Meier et al. 2008):

if X is a set, then a fuzzy set A in X (A ⊂ X) is defined as

$$A = \left\{ (x_i, \mu_A(x_i)) \right\}$$

where $x_i \in X$, $\mu_A: X \rightarrow [0, 1]$ is the membership function of A and $\mu_A(x) \in [0, 1]$ is the membership degree of x in A. By defining fuzzy sets, there are continuous transitions between the terms "few", "medium" and "many" (compare Figure 5b). Fuzzily, page 1 is classified both as "medium" (0.55 resp. 55%) and "many" (0.45 resp. 55%). Web page 2 also belongs partly to two classes (60% to "many" and 40% to "medium") at the same time. Obviously, the fuzzy logic approach allows a more precise and fair classification, and the risk of misclassifications of web data can be reduced.

Now, an additional web metric (i.e. dimension), the *bounce rate*, is considered (Zumstein 2010, p.285f). Web page X has a "low" bounce rate and is therefore "sticky", if visitors view at least one other page (Y) after visiting page X. Page X has a "high" bounce rate if visitors leave the website immediately after viewing page X. As can be seen in Figure 6a, the two metrics "page views" and "bounce rate" define a two-dimensional matrix with four classes (sets): Class 1 (C1) is defined by a high bounce rate and many page views, while the pages in C2 – "leaky flop pages" – have high bounce rates and few views. Class C3 represents "sticky top pages", and pages in C4 are also sticky, but have few page views. Here too, the sharp classification of web pages is problematic: although web page C has almost the same values as page B, C is classified as a "leaky flop page", and B falls into the opposite group as a "sticky top page".

If a web analyst wants to identify all pages in C3, a sharp query will return page A and B, but not page C, although B and C are in very similar positions. In a fuzzy classification (Figure 6b), sharp boundaries disappear and pages can belong to more than one class. In the fuzzy classification, pages like B and C in the middle of the matrix, *belong to four classes at the same time*.

The basis for calculating the values for each class is the γ-operator in following equation. This algebraic product operator, known as "compensatory and", has been empirically tested by (Zimmermann 1991).

$$\mu_{Ai}\left(x\right) = \left[\prod_{i=1}^{m}\mu_i\left(x\right)\right]^{1-\gamma} \cdot \left[1 - \prod_{i=1}^{m}\left(1 - \mu_i\left(x\right)\right)\right]^{\gamma}$$

where $x \in X$, $\gamma \in [0, 1]$ and μ_i is the *membership degree* between 0 and 1 in a class (x); m is the number of *fuzzy sets* $A_1, \ldots, A_m$ defined over the reference set X with the *membership functions* $\mu_1, \ldots, \mu_m$; γ is a *constant* used to influence the degree of membership in the classes. The product is calculated with the membership degrees of each class and their complementary values $(1 - \mu_i(x))$.

For simplification, γ is now defined as 0 (so called minimum operator). For example, the membership degree of page B (in Figure 6b) in class C1 is calculated as follows:

$$C1 = \left(.58 \cdot .47\right)^{(1-0)} \cdot \left(1 - \left(\left(1 - .58\right) \cdot \left(1 - .47\right)\right)\right)^{0}$$
$$= .58 \cdot .47 \doteq .2726$$

Obviously, the definition of fuzzy sets allows gradual ranking within classes, and as a result, precise classifications of web metric values. In addition, data can be classified without loss of information.

Fuzzy classifications of KPIs like revenues and conversion rates are especially important, since their values usually have far-reaching consequences for businesses.

5.3 Web Usage Mining with Inductive Fuzzy Classification

Web usage mining is a data mining method to *recognize patterns in website navigation by website visitors* (Spiliopoulou 2000, Srivastava et al. 2000). A common web usage mining task is the analysis of associations between visited pages (Escobar-Jeria et al. 2007).

An Inductive Fuzzy Classification (IFC) method is proposed to discover knowledge about web usage patterns (Zumstein and Kaufmann 2009). Inductive fuzzy classification is the process of grouping elements into a fuzzy set whose membership function is inferred by induction from data (Kaufmann and Meier 2009). *Inductive Fuzzy Classification by Normalized Likelihood Ratios (IFC-NLR)* can be applied to infer a membership function of a web page in a target page (like a product or order page in a webshop).

The aim is to apply this fuzzyfication in web data analysis for knowledge discovery, reporting, and prediction, which has several advantages. First, most data mining methods are dichotomous in nature, especially classification. As proposed by Zimmermann (1997), fuzzy classification methods become appropriate when class membership is *supposed to be gradual*. Thus the advantage of fuzzy classification in web mining is the possibility to rank web pages by a gradual degree of membership in classes. Second, the results of knowledge discovery are often not directly understandable by human decision makers (Mobasher 1997). The advantage of fuzzy logic based methods is that the generated models (i.e. membership functions) are *easy to interpret*. In fact, using simple probabilistic measures with a clear semantic make the membership functions more understandable and suitable for human decision support (Zumstein and Kaufmann 2009, p.64).

For web usage mining it is interesting to know which *web pages* (page X) are visited together with a target page such as the *online shop* (target page Y). Therefore, a fuzzy classification for each web page is calculated with a degree of membership to the target page. That type of fuzzy classification indicates the degree of association in web usage between two web pages. To analyze the influence of an analytic variable X to a target variable Y in terms of fuzzy classification, the IFC-NLR method is applied to calculate the membership

Table 3. Example of visits of the web pages W2 and W3 and the online shop. Source: adapted from (Zumstein and Kaufmann 2008, p.65)

Web page W2 was visited	Online shop was visited		Web page W3 was visited	Online shop was visited	
	yes	no		yes	no
yes	345	234	yes	253	389
no	123	456	no	215	220
total	468	690	total	468	609

degree of values x ∈ dom(X) in the values y ∈ dom(Y). Thus, *the values of the target variable become fuzzy classes with a membership function* for the values of the analytic variable. To define this function, the IFC-NLR method proposes to calculate a *normalized Likelihood (L) ratio.*

$$\mu_y(x) := \frac{P(x \mid y)}{P(x \mid y) + P(x \mid \neg y)} = \frac{1}{1 + \dfrac{L(\neg y \mid x)}{L(y \mid x)}}$$

The equation shows the degree of membership of x in y. For example, the data presented in Table 3 is considered.

The fuzzy classification for page W2 as leading customers to the online shop is calculated as seen in Exhibit 1.

The inductive fuzzy classification of the web pages W2 and W3 shows that the visit of the online shop is more likely after a page view of web page W2 (0.68491) than after a page view of web page W3 (0.45839).

As a result, probabilistic induction facilitates identifying web pages that generate additional page views for the online shop. These insights can be applied to augment click rates (in Figure 4), online sales, i.e. high order and conversion rates, and to increase online revenues.

5.4 Definition of Fuzzy Concepts

Beside the gradual ranking within classes, the fuzzy logic approach makes it possible to work with *quantitative metrics*, i.e. hard facts like online revenues and *qualitative indicators*, i.e. soft criteria like user loyalty or engagement. In fact, the strength of the fuzzy logic approach is the possibility to define, model and use qualitative variables besides quantitative ones, which is not possible in binary computing.

In web analytics, fuzzy logic allows the definition of fuzzy concepts with fluent transitions (Fasel & Zumstein 2009). For example, the web analysts can define the fuzzy concepts "high traffic period", "above-average conversion rates", "strong customer loyalty" or "attractive web pages".

In fuzzy web analytics system, the web analyst may queries: give me…

- All web pages with "many page views" and "low bounces rates" (class C3 in Figure 6b)
- All web pages with "high conversion rates"

Exhibit 1.

$$\mu_{\text{online shop}}(W2) := \frac{1}{1 + \dfrac{P\left(W2 \text{ was visited} = yes \mid \text{online shop was visited} = no\right)}{P\left(W2 \text{ was visited} = yes \mid \text{online shop was visited} = yes\right)}} = \frac{1}{1 + \dfrac{\left(234 / 690\right)}{\left(345 / 468\right)}} = 0.68491$$

- The "most loyal customers" with high purchase frequency and high online revenues.

Applying the fuzzy logic to time constructs is especially suited. For example, it becomes not suddenly evening at 6 pm, or night at 10 pm, but human beings perceive a fluent transition between afternoon, evening and night (see Figure 7a). Different seasons do not start and end abruptly, and neither do seasonal variations, like the high season in winter tourism or in summer (see Figure 7b). Fuzzy time concepts are interesting for web analytics, since they allow new types of analysis. For example, the web analyst can query all web pages or visitors with many page views in high season or in the evening. With a sharp classification, all page views between 6 pm and 8 pm are displayed only, but arbitrarily not these at 5.59 or 8.01. With a fuzzy classification, already page views after 4 and until 10 pm are considered at a certain membership degree, or percentage, e.g. 50% afternoon and 50% evening at 5 pm in Figure 7a.

5.5 Web Analytics with Words

Sections 5.2, 5.3 and 5.4 explained that linguistic terms are used to describe membership functions of fuzzy sets in order to classify metrics more exactly and to define fuzzy concepts.

Moreover, the fuzzy logic approach makes it possible to describe, analyze and evaluate results and changes in web analytics using *human language*. In soft computing, this is called Computing With Words (CWW). According to the Task Force on Computer on Words, there exist different definitions what computing with words means (Mendel et al. 2010). Following the definition of Lofti A. Zadeh, "Computing with Words is a methodology for reasoning, computing and decision-making with information described in natural language" (Mendel et al. 2010, p.21) and the consideration of perception-based information (Zadeh 1999, 2001, 2004).

Consequently, Web Analytics with Words (WAW) is understood as a methodology for reasoning, computing and decision making of web usage or user data described in natural language. Since knowledge and experience of web analysts and managers is perceived and described in natural language, i.e. words and word combinations, the CWW approach is especially suited to analyze, describe, evaluate, report and communicate results and trends of web analytics with expressive words instead of meaningless data and numbers. In the words of Ronald Yager (Mendel et al. 2010, p.22): computing with words helps to manipulate and convert formal objects (i.e. web analytics data) into linguistic terms (i.e. website-related statements or recommendations) understandable to the human

Figure 7. Fuzzy time constructs: a) afternoon, evening and night and b) high season. Source: (Fasel & Zumstein 2009, p.281)

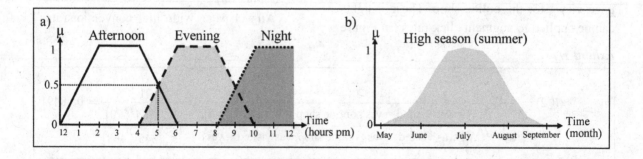

and to summarize large sets of data, in a way that a human can get a global understanding of the content of the web data. Thereby, It depends on the specific web analytics context and analysis case, how the *(re)translation processes and processing rules* are defined and implemented in order to transform web data into meaningful analysis and interpretation.

For instance, a web analytics tool reported 1'718 page views in June 2010 (see Figure 8 left). What does this measurement-based information say to the web analyst? Not much, as long as the analyst cannot compare this absolute number with a benchmark. If in July 2010 5'897 page views were recorded, the analyst perceives, understands or knows from comparison that the website had *much more* page views than the month before (compare Figure 8 on the right). If the number of visitors in-creased by 2.3% in 2010, the analyst might state that the number of visitors *"increased slightly"* in 2010. Many other examples of analysis show that humans have a perception-based rather than a measurement-based approach to interpreting, describing and communicating web data and information.

Web analytics tools report oodles of numbers, but web analysts often have difficulty interpreting

web data, recognizing trends and deriving useful conclusions.

However, in future, "intelligent" fuzzy web analytics systems could give meaningful answers to relevant business questions, which can be selected or formulated in natural language. To implement such an intelligent system, following stages can be formulated (compare Mendel et al. 2010, p.23):

- Codebook for Fuzzy Web Analytics
  1. Establish a web analytics vocabulary of words or an e-business and website management vocabulary in general.
  2. Collect the web data with client- or server-side data collection methods.
  3. Map the web data into a fuzzy set model for each web analytics with words by defining membership functions and linguistic terms for each web metric (as described in section 5.2/5.4)
- CWW/WAW Engine Implementation
  1. Develop or chose a WAW Engine used for web analytics, e.g. the fCQL toolkit (Werro 2007), a fuzzy data warehouse (Fasel & Shahzad 2010) or the spreadsheet program used in section 6.

Figure 8. Measurement-based and perception-based information about website traffic

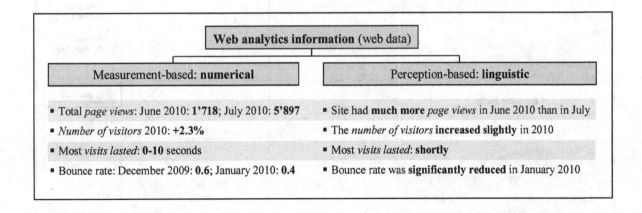

2. Implement a specific WAW Engine and formulate the input-output relations, for instance by modeling of the membership functions and γ-operator.

3. Map the fuzzy set outputs of the CWW Engine into recommendation, e.g. by defining fuzzy if-when-rules, discussed in the following section.

5.6 Definition of Fuzzy If-When-Rules for Web Analytics

Considering business relevant questions and web analyses, rules or recommendations regarding content, marketing or customer management can be linked to web data analysis. **If-when rules** are derived from experience or know-how in web analytics and dependent on the context. As discussed in section 3.3, for web content management it could be stated: If the number of page views of web page X is "high", then the content manager should take care about the content quality of the page. Or the online marketer states: If the

conversion rate Y is "high", then we augment the e-marketing budget for Y".

Conventional if-then rules are based on a *sharp logic*. In the examples this means that the definition of "high" is strictly defined to a sharp class of web metric values. Defining fuzzy classes has now far-reaching implications for web analytics, if **fuzzy if-when rules** are defined: if the "if condition" is *partly true*, then the "then clause" is also partly true. Consequently, the definition of fuzzy classes and constructs enables a more smooth, precise and adequate definition of if-when rules.

6. CASE: FUZZY CLASSIFICATION OF REAL WEB DATA

To demonstrate the approach of fuzzy classification of web metrics, real web data is considered in this section. The web data has been collected with the client-side data collection method using Google Analytics[1] on the website of the Information Systems Research Group at the University of

Figure 9. Value distribution of the web metrics a) pages views and b) bounce rate and c) classification of 100 web pages of the IS research group website in a two-dimensional matrix[2]

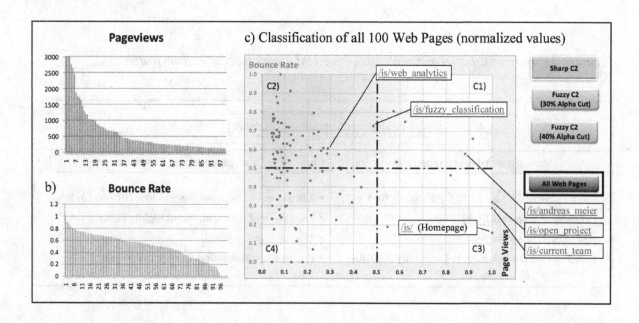

Figure 10. Sharp classification of class a) C2 and b) C3, fuzzy classification with an alpha cut of 30% for class c) C2 and d) C3 and an alpha cut of 40% for class e) C2 and f) C3

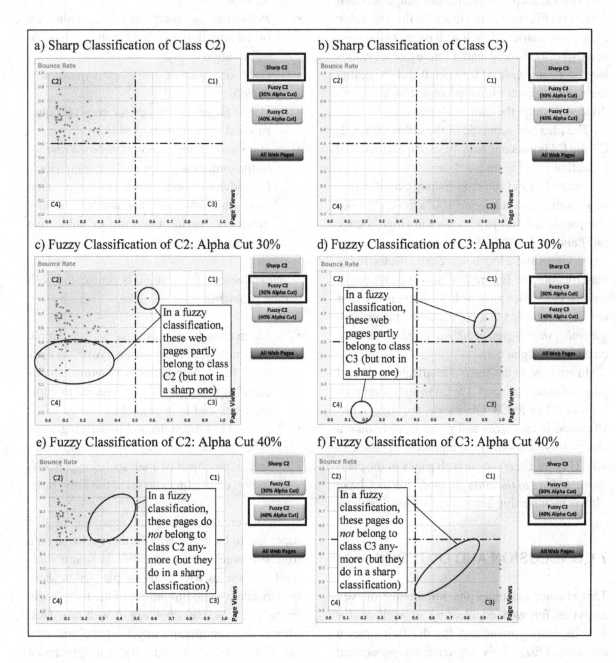

Fribourg, Switzerland. The raw data, details on the fuzzy sets and the calculation of the membership degrees with the γ-operator using Microsoft Excel® are available on the IS website.[2]

From the Google Analytics system, data of the two metrics page views and bounce rate has been selected from the 100 most visited web pages from May 2008 to mid December 2010. The values of the metric page views for the 100 pages vary between 127 and 3000 views (Figure 9a). The values of the bounce rate range between 0 and 1 (in Figure 9b). In Figure 9c, the data value of the two metrics of each web page is classified in a two-dimensional matrix. Note that all values have to be *normalized* between 0 and 1, i.e. that the value of each classified object in a class is divided through the sum of all classes.

The idea and semantic of the classes C1, C2, C3 and C4 is the same as in the example discussed in section 5.2 (Figure 6).

Figure 10a and 10b show a sharp classification of all web pages belonging 100% to C2 ("Leaky flop pages", i.e. few page views and a high bounce rate) and to C3 ("Sticky top pages", i.e. many pages views and a low bounce rate). In the fuzzy classification of Figure 10c and 10d, all pages are selected belonging with 30% to class C2 or to C3. That means that the classified pages have a *membership degree of 30%* or more to the class considered (alpha cut).

In contrast to the sharp classification, several pages of other classes (C1 & C4) also belong with 30% to C2 or to C3. Obviously, the fuzzy classification is less strict and more flexible than a sharp classification. If the alpha cut is raised to 40% (Figure 10e/f), some web pages of the class *do not belong to the class anymore*, i.e. they have a lower membership degree than 40% to this class.

7 CONCLUSION AND OUTLOOK

This chapter discussed the importance of web analytics for web engineering as well as for website management and for the first time, a conceptual fuzzy logic approach was introduced to web analytics.

Fuzzy web analytics has several advantages:

- *Precise classification* of objects in classes and a gradual ranking within classes, using the alpha cut, i.e. a certain membership

degree of the classified object to a specific fuzzy set
- *Reduction of complexity*, i.e. reduction of information overload without loss of information
- Use of *quantitative and qualitative variables*
- Use of *linguistic variables* (terms) for queries and computing with words
- *Human-oriented, perception-based and intuitive processing* of web data or metrics
- Consideration and mapping of *fuzzy if-then rules* and concepts that are intrinsically fuzzy, i.e. vague, uncertain or subjective per definition.

Nevertheless, fuzzy logic is confronted with certain problems:

- Sharp classification is usually clear, simple and straightforward for everyone. In contrast, fuzzy classification is *more complicated*, not as easy to understand, to communicate and to implement.
- Fuzzy classifications and underlying strategies can be confusing or even *contradictory*, if an object of analysis belongs to different, conflicting classes at the same time.

However, the conceptual approach of this paper has to be tested with further real web data from e-business and companies in future studies. Case studies with firms are planned to show the advantages and limitations of the fuzzy logic method in a business context of web analytics. Moreover, an empirical study using the structural equation modeling method will give insights about the use, benefits and problems of web analytics in business practice.

The research center Fuzzy Marketing Methods (www.FMsquare.org) is engaged with applications of fuzziness to different domains in information systems. It provides a number of open source prototypes, e.g. the fCQL (fuzzy Classification

Query Language) toolkit, which enables fuzzy queries and calculating membership degrees of data stored in MySQL databases.

REFERENCES

Bélanger, F., Fan, W., Schaupp, C., Krishen, A., Everhart, J., Poteet, D., & Nakamoto, K. (2006). Web site success metrics: Addressing the duality of goals. *Communications of the ACM, 49*(12), 114–116. doi:10.1145/1183236.1183256

Clifton, B. (2010). *Advanced Web metrics with Google analytics* (2nd ed.). New York, NY: Wiley.

Drèze, X., & Zufryden, F. (2004). Measurement of online visibility and its impact on Internet traffic. *Journal of Interactive Marketing, 18*(1), 20–37. doi:10.1002/dir.10072

Econsultancy. (2010). *Online measurement and strategy report 2010*, Retrieved June 7, 2010, from http://econsultancy.com

Escobar-Jeria, V. H., Martín-Bautista, M. J., Sánchez, D., & Vila, M. (2007). *Web usage mining via fuzzy logic techniques*. In P. Melin, O. Castillo, I. J. Aguilar, J. Kacprzyk, & W. Pedrycz (Eds.), 2007: *Lecture Notes In Artificial Intelligence, vol. 4529*, (pp. 243-252). New York, NY: Springer.

Fasel, D., & Shahzad, K. (2010). A data warehouse model for integrating fuzzy concepts in meta table structures. In *17th IEEE International Conference and Workshops on the Engineering of Computer-Based Systems*, IEEE Computer Society 2010, (pp. 100-109).

Fasel, D., & Zumstein, D. (2009). A fuzzy data warehouse approach for Web analytics. In *Proceedings of the 2nd World Summit on the Knowledge Society (WSKS)*, September 16-18, Crete, Greece.

Forrester Consulting. (2009). *Appraising your investments in enterprise Web analytics*. Retrieved June 7, 2011, from www.google.com/intl/en/analytics/case_studies/Appraising-Investments-In-Enterprise-Analytics.pdf

Fuzzy Marketing Methods. (2010). *Research center fuzzy marketing methods*, Retrieved June 11, 2011, from http://www.FMsquare.org

Hong, I. (2007). A survey of web site success metrics used by internet-dependent organizations in Korea. *Internet Research, 17*(3), 272–290. doi:10.1108/10662240710758920

Inan, H. (2010). *What is Web analytics?* Retrieved June 7, 2011, from http://hurolinan.com/index.php/category/what-is-web-analytics

Jackson, S. (2009). *Cult of analytics: Driving online marketing strategies using Web analytics*. Burlington, MA: Butterworth Heinemann.

Kaufmann, M., & Meier, A. (2009). An inductive fuzzy classification approach applied to individual marketing. In *Proceedings of the 28th North American Fuzzy Information Processing Society Annual Conference*, Ohio, USA.

Kaushik, A. (2009). *Web analytics 2.0 – The art of online accountability and science of customer centricity*. New York, NY: Wiley.

Meier, A., Schindler, G., & Werro, N. (2008). Fuzzy classification on relational databases. In Galindo, J. (Ed.), *Handbook of research on fuzzy information processing in databases* (*Vol. 2*, pp. 586–614). Hershey, PA: IGI Global. doi:10.4018/978-1-59904-853-6.ch023

Meier, A., & Stormer, H. (2009). *eBusiness & eCommerce – Managing the digital value chain*. Berlin.

Meier, A., & Zumstein, D. (2010). *Web analytics – Ein Überblick*. Heidelberg, Germany: Dpunkt Verlag. Retrieved from www.WebAnalyticsWebControlling.org

Mendel, J., Zadeh, L., Trillas, E., Lawry, J., Hagras, H., & Guadarrama, S. (2010). What computing with words means to me. *IEEE Computational Intelligence Magazine*, February, (pp. 20-26).

Mobasher, B. (2007). Web usage mining. In Liu, B. (Ed.), *Web data mining – Exploring hyperlinks, contents, and usage data*. New York, NY: Springer.

Palmer, J. (2002). Web site usability, design, and performance metrics. *Information Systems Research*, *13*(2), 151–167. doi:10.1287/isre.13.2.151.88

Peterson, E. (2005). *Web site measurement hacks*. New York, NY: O'Reilly.

Phippen, A., Sheppard, L., & Furnell, S. (2004). A practical evaluation of Web analytics. *Internet Research*, *14*, 284–293. doi:10.1108/10662240410555306

Sen, A., Dacin, P., & Pattichis, D. (2006). Current trend in Web data analysis. *Communications of the ACM*, *49*(11), 85–91. doi:10.1145/1167838.1167842

Spiliopoulou, M. (2000). Web usage mining for web site evaluation. *Communications of the ACM*, *43*, 127–134. doi:10.1145/345124.345167

Srivastava, J., Cooley, R., Deshpande, M., & Tan, P.-N. (2000). Web usage mining: Discovery and application of usage patterns from Web data. *ACM SIGKDD*, *1*(2), 1–12.

Sterne, J. (2002). *Web metrics*. New York, NY: Wiley.

Waisberg, D., & Kaushik, A. (2009). Web analytics 2.0: Empowering customer centricity. *Search Engine Marketing Research Journal*, *2*(1). Retrieved June 7, 2011, from: www.semj.org

Web Analytics Association. (2010). *Web Analytics Association*. Retrieved June 7, 2011, from www.webanalyticsassociation.org

Weischedel, B., & Huizingh, E. (2006). Website optimization with Web metrics: A case study. In *Proceedings of the 8th International Conference on Electronic Commerce* (ICEC'06), August 14-16, Fredericton, Canada, (pp. 463-470).

Weischedel, B., Matear, S., & Deans, K. (2005). The use of emetrics in strategic marketing decisions. *International Journal of Internet Marketing and Advertising*, *2*, 109–125. doi:10.1504/IJIMA.2005.007507

Welling, R., & White, L. (2006). Measuring the value of corporate web sites. *Journal of Internet Commerce*, *3*(3), 127–145. doi:10.1300/J179v05n03_06

Werro, N. (2008). *Fuzzy classification of online customers*. Dissertation, University of Fribourg, Retrieved June 7, 2011, from http://ethesis.unifr.ch/theses/downloads.php?file=WerroN.pdf

Zadeh, L. A. (1965). Fuzzy sets. *Information and Control*, *8*, 338–353. doi:10.1016/S0019-9958(65)90241-X

Zadeh, L. A. (1999). From computing with numbers to computing with words – From manipulation of measurements to manipulation of perceptions. *IEEE Transactions on Circuits and Systems*, *45*(1), 105–119.

Zadeh, L. A. (2001). A new direction in AI – Toward a computational theory of perceptions. *AI Magazine*, (Spring): 73–84.

Zadeh, L. A. (2004). A note on Web intelligence, world knowledge and fuzzy logic. *Data & Knowledge Engineering*, *50*, 291–304. doi:10.1016/j.datak.2004.04.001

Zimmermann, H.-J. (1991). *Fuzzy set theory and its applications*. London, UK: Kluwer.

Zimmermann, H.-J. (1997). Fuzzy data analysis. In Kaynak, O., Zadeh, L. A., Turksen, B., & Rudas, I. J. (Eds.), *Computational intelligence: Soft computing and fuzzy-neuro integration with applications*. New York, NY: Springer.

Zumstein, D. (2010). Web analytics – Analysing, classifying and describing Web metrics with fuzzy logic. In *6th International Conference on Web Information Systems and Technologies (WEBIST)*, April 7-10, Valencia, Spain, (pp. 282-290).

Zumstein, D., Drobjnak, A., & Meier, A. (2011). Data privacy in Web analytics – An empirical study and declaration model of data collection on websites. In *Proceedings of the 7th International Conference on Web Information Systems and Technologies (WEBIST)*, May 6-9 (2011), Noordwijkerhout, The Netherlands.

Zumstein, D., & Kaufmann, M. (2009). A fuzzy Web analytics model for Web mining. In *Proceedings of IADIS European Conference on Data Mining*, June 18-20, Algarve, Portugal.

Zumstein, D., & Meier, A. (2010). Web-controlling – Analyse und Optimierung der digitalen Wertschöpfungskette mit Web Analytics. In *Proceedings of the Multikonferenz Wirtschaftsinformatik (MKWI)*, February 23-25, Göttingen, Germany, (pp. 299-311).

ENDNOTES

[1] Google Analytics is a free web analytics tool, accessible under www.google.com/analytics

[2] For details on data and calculations see http://diuf.unifr.ch/is/web_analytics. Direct link to the Microsoft Excel® file: http://diuf.unifr.ch/is/userfiles/file/research/Fuzzy_Web_Analytics.xls (accessed the 7th of June 2011).

Section 3
Performance Analysis

Chapter 10
Fuzzy Data Warehouse for Performance Analysis

Daniel Fasel
University of Fribourg, Switzerland

Khurram Shahzad
Royal Institute of Technology (KTH), Sweden

ABSTRACT

The numeric values retrieved from a data warehouse may be difficult to interpret by business users, or may be interpreted incorrectly. Therefore, for more accurate understanding of numeric values, business users may require an interpretation in meaningful, non-numeric terms. However, if the transition between non-numeric terms is crisp, true values cannot be measured, and smooth transition between classes may not take place. To address that problem, the authors employ a fuzzy classification-based approach for data warehouse. For that, they present a fuzzy data warehouse modeling approach, which allows integration of fuzzy concepts without affecting the core of a classical data warehouse. The essence of the approach is that a meta-tables structure is added for relating non-numeric terms with numeric values. This enables integration of fuzzy concepts in dimensions and facts, while preserving the time-invariability of the data warehouse. Additional to that, the use of fuzzy approach allows analysis of data in both sharp and fuzzy manners. The proposed approach is demonstrated through a case study of a movie rental company.

INTRODUCTION

In enterprises, data is spread across a number of heterogeneous sources and is not available for analysis and decision-making. In order to analyze enterprise-wide data, data warehouses are

DOI: 10.4018/978-1-4666-0095-9.ch010

implemented (Chaudhuri, 1997) and data from transactional sources are transferred into it for analysis and decision making in enterprises to achieve competitive advantages.

Typically, output from data warehouse is a set of numeric values (called fact) based on the input given to it in the form of dimensions (Inmon, 2005).

These numeric values can be difficult to understand or can be interpreted differently by different users, which could lead to different decisions. Consider the example of a movie rental company, in which movies are in service for a certain period of time. Given the movie discarding principle, discard old movies, there is a possibility that different users or a single user (at different occasions) may end up discarding movies after different years of service. A solution to this problem is adding linguistic terms and explicit classification of movies into new and old movies. Figure 1(a) shows the classification of movies in accordance with the given principle i.e. a movie is considered as new if its service time is less than 10 year and old if its service time is 10 or more years. This manner of classification is called crisp classification.

If the classification between linguistic terms is crisp, true values cannot be measured and smooth transition between classes cannot take place (Fasel, 2010). The movie classification example discussed above, does not offer smooth transition between classes (new and old) i.e. a movie in service for 9 years 365 days is new and the one in service for 9 year 366 days is old, although the difference is only 1 day. To understand the inability of crisp approaches to measure true values, consider another example of movie classification. This classification is based on the content of a movie, using the linguistic terms humorous, love story and war movie. Given a movie, that has both humorous and love story content mixed in some ratio, it is not possible to classify it correctly using the crisp approach. To address the discussed problems, a fuzzy approach has been used to classify values using linguistic terms. Figure 1(b) shows the smooth classification of movies into humorous, love story and war movie using a fuzzy based approach.

In this chapter, a fuzzy data warehouse modeling approach is discussed, which allows integration of fuzzy concepts as meta-tables without affecting the core of a classical data warehouse. The essence of the approach is that a meta-tables structure is added to data warehouse for classification, which enables integration of fuzzy concepts in dimensions and facts, while preserving the time-invariability of the data warehouse. Also in this chapter, we present a method, which includes some guidelines that can be used to convert a classical warehouse into a fuzzy data warehouse. The key benefit of integrating fuzzy concepts is that it allows analysis of data in both sharp and fuzzy manners. In addition to that, the aggregation, propagation of fuzzy concepts and typical operations of a classical data warehouse are discussed for the fuzzy data warehouse. The use of the proposed approach is demonstrated through a case study of a movie rental company and the benefits of integrating fuzzy concepts in performance analysis are illustrated.

The rest of chapter is organized as follows, a brief overview of basic concepts given in the *basic concepts* section. We review relevant work in the *existing approaches of fuzzy data warehouse* section. The proposed approach fuzzy classification is given in *Fuzzy Data Warehouse – integrating fuzzy concepts in meta-tables structure* section. Also, this section contains classification of fuzzy concepts. A method for converting a classical data warehouse to fuzzy data warehouse is presented in *method for modeling Fuzzy Data Warehouse* section. Operations on fuzzy data warehouse are defined in *operations, aggregation and propagation of fuzzy concepts* section and the demonstration of the proposed approach is depicted in *a case study in performance analysis of a movie rental company* section.

BASIC CONCEPTS

Data warehouse (DWH) has been defined by a number of authors, however Inmon's definition has received most reception over the years. According to Inmon (2005), 'a data warehouse is a subject oriented, non volatile, integrated and time variant data in favor of decision making'.

Figure 1. Sharp and fuzzy classification

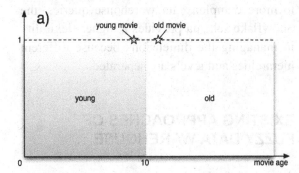 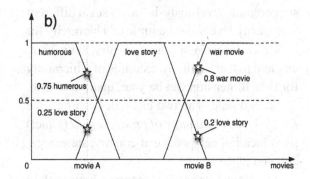

Introduced in mid 90s, data warehouse has been widely adapted in several sectors and successful implementations have been reported in healthcare, agriculture, engineering, banking sector, building construction and businesses in order to enhance the analytical capabilities of enterprises.

Figure 2 shows the architecture of a classical data warehouse. Transactional sources act as a data source for data warehouse, however the data stored in transactional system is not optimized for analysis and decision making (Kimball, 2008). Therefore, data from transactional sources is extracted, transformed into a form that is compatible with warehouse after removing inconsistencies and loaded in data warehouse for further usage.

As shown in Figure 2, data warehouse can further be used for analysis using tools like OLAP and mining to identify patterns for forecasting.

In contrast to classical databases in which entities and their relationships are modeled, in data warehouse, the values (key business metrics) that are critical for a business and the different aspects that can be used to analyze those values are modeled in a multidimensional way. Critical values are generally numeric values and are called facts. Examples of facts are quantity of products sold and amount of profit earned. Aspects are the different perspective that can be used for analysis of facts and are called dimensions.

Figure 2. Architecture of data warehouse adapted from (Chaudhuri, 1997)

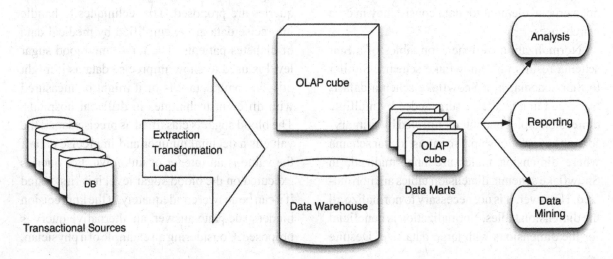

Dimensions can be organized as hierarchies to support multilevel analysis – analyses at different granularity levels. An example of a hierarchy for a location dimension can be country, state, area, city and place. Similarly, example of a hierarchy for time dimension can be year, quarter, month, week, and date. The two examples can be used for analyses of *quantity of products sold* (a fact) from location perspective at country, state, area, city and place levels.

The logical structure of data warehouse called dimensional schema (sometimes referred to as multidimensional schema) has two major types, Star and Snowflake schema (Kimball, 2008). This classification is based on the difference in quantity and types of dimensions and facts.

Star Schema has one fact table surrounded by multiple dimension tables and in each dimension only one dimension table exists. Dimension and fact tables are interconnected by a primary - foreign key relationship. It has to be noted that in Star schema, dimension tables are not normalized. The advantage of unnormalized dimension tables lies in the query performance of the data warehouse. Due to unnormalized tables expensive and complex joins over dimension hierarchies can be omitted. As dimension tables in general only consume about 5% of the data storage in a data warehouse and dimension updates are handled centralized (Pederson, 2001), normalization is not a crucial element for data consistency in data warehouses.

Normalization of dimension tables of a Star schema results in a Snowflake schema. Similar to Star schema, in a Snowflake schema data is organized in a fact table surrounded by multiple dimension tables and interconnected by primary-foreign key relationship. In contrast to Star schema where dimension tables are unnormalized, in Snowflake schema, dimension tables are normalized. However, it is not necessary to normalize all the dimension tables. Normalization is beneficial for the dimensions with large data size. Despite

the fact that normalized dimension tables leads to more complex data warehouse queries, the Snowflake schema provides a higher flexibility in managing the dimensions because different hierarchies and levels are separated.

EXISTING APPROACHES OF FUZZY DATA WAREHOUSE

A number of efforts have been reported to integrate fuzzy logic with data warehouse. The related work for this study has been divided into two categories followed by a brief discussion. These categories are: 1) data warehouse approach for handling imprecise data, 2) approaches for implementing fuzziness into data warehouse.

Data Warehouse Approaches for Handling Imprecise Data

Pedersen, Jensen and Dyreson (1999) described techniques for handling imprecise data in OLAP systems. Imprecise data, as defined by Motro and Smets (1997), is a special kind of imperfect data by which the accuracy of data is fuzzy. Pedersen et al. (1999) have suggested to test if imprecise data is involved in the query process. In that case, it is checked if the imprecise data is still precise enough to answer the query. Otherwise, alternative queries are proposed. The techniques to handle imprecise data are exemplified by medical data of diabetes patients. The long time blood sugar level is used to show imprecise data as it might miss in some data sets or it might be measured with different techniques in different hospitals. The blood sugar is classified as precise data if the value is a decimal number and imprecise data if the value is an integer or unknown. For queries executed on the blood sugar level it is first tested if it can be answered adequately. If the imprecision hinders adequate answer, an alternative query is proposed. Considering an example of a physician, who wants to know all persons having a blood sugar level between 5.4 and 6.2. If the query is executed on person data sets that have imprecise blood sugar level measures, the system might propose a query like all persons having a blood sugar level between 5 and 7 instead.

This approach does not directly integrate fuzzy logic into data warehouses but fuzzy classification of imprecise data might facilitate querying such a data warehouse. An alternative solution to proposing new query is to classify blood sugar level with a fuzzy concept containing the linguistic terms low, middle and high. The physician can then execute query data by using the linguistic terms as: all persons with a high blood sugar level. The use of fuzzy data warehouse can therefore handle the imprecision of the data at the modeling level. A benefit of handling imprecision of data at modeling level is that the complexity of imprecise data is not passed to the user level.

Burdick, et al. (2007) proposed an OLAP model to handle both imprecise and uncertain data. This model uses probability distribution functions to handle uncertain qualitative information. An example provided is the problem of brake incidents of a specific car. For each car instance an additional category attribute brake is created that contains a two-tuple value holding the probability distribution of a brake incident. The attribute contains the probability for an incident and for no incident in the following form: <0.8, 0.2>, with a probability of 0.8 that no brake incident will happen. In another step of the approach Burdick describes characteristics for consistent aggregation and queries of such probability distribution in the OLAP cube.

Based on Kosko (1990) a probabilistic system can be represented by fuzzy theory. The likelihood that brakes are breaking can therefore be represented as fuzzy concept. In conclusion of that, imprecise and uncertain data as described by Burdick et al. (1990) can be interpreted by the fuzzy data warehouse model proposed in this study.

Approaches for Implementing Fuzziness into Data Warehouse

In the area of rules mining on data cubes Alhajj and Kaya (2003) proposed an implementation of a fuzzy OLAP cube in order to perform fuzzy association rules mining. The fuzzy OLAP cube contains the membership degrees of the fuzzy sets as measures. The actual measures of the data warehouse that should be mined are not included in the fuzzy OLAP cube. Based on the membership degrees, fuzzy association rules are applied. Alhaj and Kaya experimentally prove that this technique produces meaningful results with reasonable efficiency.

Our proposed fuzzy data warehouse approach allows executing fuzzy association rules mining directly as described by Alhajj and Kaya. In order to build the fuzzy sets the meta-table structures of fuzzy concepts can be used. Due to the ability to simultaneously query crisp and fuzzy data, we hypothesize that it is possible to combine fuzzy association rules mining and other data mining technique with less effort than it would be on the proposed OLAP cube by Alhajj and Kaya.

Delgado, et al. (2004) and Molina, et al. (2006) integrates fuzzy concepts directly in the dimension structure of a data warehouse. As an example, a dimension hierarchy over age is depicted. A set of age value {1,...,100} is aggregated over the two hierarchy paths age → legal age → all and age → group → all. The dimension attribute legal age has the instances yes and no, whereas, the dimension attribute group is a fuzzy concept with the linguistic terms young, adult and old as instances. Therefore, all the value instances of age are classified within the fuzzy concept groups. When navigating from age to groups the values in age are repartitioned into the linguistic terms based on their belonging to it. For example, the age value 25 might belong to young with a membership degree of 0.7 and to adult with a degree of 0.3. In this case a roll-up to the hierarchy level group would partition age

25 as 17.5 (0.7*25) to the instance young and 7.5 (0.3*25) to adult.

Schepperle, et. al. (2004) proposed a similar approach for integrating fuzzy concepts into dimension structures. Conditions for aggregation over fuzzy concepts in dimension structures are further discussed in detail. Based on the summarizability conditions of Lenz and Shoshani (1997), extended aggregation conditions are proposed. In essence, the extended conditions force the membership degrees of all linguistic terms to be normalized to 1. Additionally, they propose an extension of the Common Warehouse Meta-model (Medina and Trujillo, 2002) to cover imprecise data.

A drawback is the need to split the instance values according their membership degrees for aggregating. This is not possible for qualitative values like stores. Our approach assumes that fuzzy concept often integrates business terminology as linguistic variables. Business terminology is dependent on persons, departments and market situations and therefore changes more frequently than stored data. Based on this assumption, it takes extra effort to remodel the data warehouse whenever a change in fuzzy concepts occurs. Integrating fuzzy concepts in meta-tables and excluding them from the navigation paths allows a more stable model i.e. it is not needed to remodel data warehouse for each change in fuzzy concept. Furthermore, the membership degrees do not have necessarily to be normalized as normalization might also lead to loss of information.

Kumar, et. al. (2005) describes a fuzzy data warehouse approach for integrating fuzzy concepts on facts. The membership degrees are derived using the CLARANS (Ng and Hang, 1994) clustering algorithm. In Kasinadh and Krishna (2007) the same approach with multi-attribute summarization for calculating the membership degrees is used. Both approaches essentially integrate fuzzy concepts on facts and depict how to operate over them.

Pérez, et. al. (2007) proposes a fuzzy spatial data warehouse. The approach is exemplified for a data warehouse representing risk zones around a volcano. The dimensions space, theme and time in the model are extended with fuzzy concepts as a top level hierarchy element.

The solution from Pérez et al. is developed for a specific application of fuzzy concepts in data warehouses. It does not consider a general approach to integrate fuzziness in data warehouses. With the integration of fuzzy concept in meta-tables, as proposed here, the fuzzy spatial data warehouse from Pérez et al. and the integration of fuzziness on facts, as Kumar et al. propose, can be modeled. Additionally, this approach is much more generic and can be applied to other domains than just spatial data warehouses.

Sapir, et. al. (2008) defines a method for creating a fuzzy data warehouse. The method depicts how to integrate fuzzy concepts in dimension structures and facts. The fuzzy concepts are stored in additional tables. A fuzzy hierarchy is a hierarchy, in which the fuzzy concepts are directly bound into the dimension structure as similarly proposed by Delgado et al. (2004). To overcome the difficulty of aggregating over fuzzy concepts, bridge tables are used, as described by Kimball and Caserta (2004).

In contrast to our approach, only one table is used to store the linguistic terms and the corresponding membership degrees. The feature to define fuzzy concepts with more than one set of linguistic terms or multiple membership degrees for a linguistic term is lost when only using one table. The model of Sapir et al. (2008) has to introduce artificial bridge table for being able to consistently aggregating. Excluding fuzzy concepts in meta-tables omits the need of such artificial constructs and retains the time invariability as already stated for the approach of Delgado and al. (2004).

Feng and Dillon (2003) presented a framework for implementing fuzziness into data warehouse. The framework uses a three-layer model to describe the semantics of a fuzzy data warehouse. The first level contains aggregated views of sharp data collections as a set of cubes. These set of cubes are enriched in the second level with fuzzy concepts based on the aggregated facts in the cubes. In the third level, fuzzy concepts are introduced for dimensions of the cubes. Furthermore, operations on fuzzy data warehouse and an explanation how fuzzy concepts can be integrated in SQL query statements are discussed. This framework provides a complete overview on how to integrate fuzzy logic into data warehouses and Feng and Dillon manifest the validity of the framework with SQL extensions.

In conclusion, it can be stated that the fuzzy data warehouse model proposed in this chapter is generic enough to cover all the specific solutions discussed in literature and summarized above. The proposed meta-tables structure allows analyzing the data in the fuzzy data warehouse simultaneously crisp and fuzzy. Only the framework of Feng and Dillon provides this possibility too. But in contrast to the framework of Feng and Dillon, fuzzy concepts on facts and dimensions are not treated separately what makes our model less complex. Additionally, compared to most of the approaches the meta-model simplifies the integration and the aggregation of the fuzzy concepts. It has to be mentioned, that the approach in this chapter can be integrated in existing classical data warehouses by only adding two meta-tables per fuzzy concept. Therefore, it not only covers the solution proposed by previous authors but also allows integrating such solutions in existing data warehouses.

FUZZY DATA WAREHOUSE: INTEGRATING FUZZY CONCEPTS IN META-TABLES STRUCTURE

Our approach to address the problems described in the preceding section is based on integrating fuzzy concepts as a meta-tables structure, without affecting the core of a data warehouse. The proposed approach is more flexible as it allows integrating

and defining fuzzy concepts without the need for redesigning the core of a data warehouse. By using the fuzzy data warehousing approach, it is possible to extract and analyze the data simultaneously in a classical sharp and in a fuzzy manner. The purpose of this section is to present the meta-model of our fuzzy data warehouse and to characterize the different fuzzy concepts.

Modeling Fuzzy DWH: The Meta-Model and Definitions

According to Harel et. al. (2004), a meta-model defines the elements of a conceptualization, as well as their relationships. Figure 3 shows the meta-model of our proposed fuzzy data warehouse in which the right hand side shows the meta-model of classical data warehouse whereas the left hand side depicts how fuzzy concepts are integrated with classical data warehouse as a meta-tables structure.

The classical DWH model class in the meta-model refers to a data warehouse schema that is composed of one or more fact tables and two or more dimension tables. Where, a fact table is located at the center of a data warehouse model (surrounded by dimension tables) and it mainly captures measurements (facts) of a business process (Kimball, 2004) and relationship with dimension tables with the help of fact attributes. A fact attribute could be a measure or a key attribute (primary key and/or foreign key). A measure (a subclass of fact attribute) captures critical value about a business process e.g. number of customers, whereas a set of key attributes are used to capture relationship with dimension tables.

The numeric values of a classical data warehouse may be difficult to interpret by business users. One possible reason is that, business users are accustomed to their own vocabularies. In the absence of clearly defined vocabularies (for interpretation of numeric values in business terms) different users may end up interpreting the numeric values differently. Consider an example

Figure 3. Fuzzy data warehouse meta-model

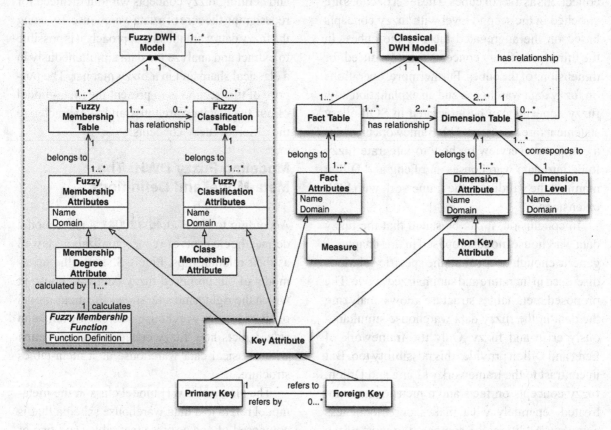

of customer age from the movie rental company's case in which age of customers varies from 15 to 60 years. In order to analyze the sales of movies across age-groups (like young, middle age, and old), a business user may consider a 20 year old customer as middle age whereas another user may consider the same customer as young. This makes the analysis error pruned.

For a more accurate and consistent interpretation (across different users) of numeric values, business users require an interpretation in meaningful non-numeric terms (vocabularies). For the customer age example consider that non-numeric values are {young age, middle age, old age} where crisp classification can be defined as,

- If customer age is < 15, Age group = young age

- If customer age is ≥15 and ≤ 40, Age group = middle age
- If customer age is > 40, Age group = old age

In the example a 15 and 40 year old customers have the same non-numeric value, although their age difference is 25 years. On the other hand, 14 and 15 year old customers have 1 year age difference but they have different non-numeric values. This is an example of a classification handled sharply, which does not allow a smooth transition between classes.

To address this problem, we propose the integration of fuzzy concepts as meta-tables structure. In order to integrate fuzzy concepts, it is required to identify the attribute that captures numeric values needed for interpretation of business users. Such an attribute is called target attribute. Formally it is defined as:

Definition 1 (Target Attribute): *A dimension attribute or a metric that is required to be classified fuzzily is called a target attribute (TA)*. Consider the example of customer age as a target attribute. As describe above, the attribute captures the age of customers who rent movies, where the value of age varies from 15 year to 60 years.

The *fuzzy DWH model* class in the meta-model refers to the fuzzy part integrated within a data warehouse. For each identified target attribute a fuzzy DWH model can be added. Therefore, a classical DWH model can have more than one fuzzy DWH model. For customer age (as target attribute) a fuzzy DWH model can be added. It could be the case that a user wants to classify movies by using linguistic terms like {new movie, recent movie, old movie}. In this case, a separate fuzzy DWH model can be added for classifying movies.

Under fuzzy classification, instances of an attribute TA are classified over a set (S) that is represented by a linguistic variable. The linguistic variable consists of a set of non-numeric terms called linguistic terms. For customer age, the linguistic variable is age group and the non-numeric values are {young age, middle age, old age}. Figure 3 shows the concepts and relationship between them. In fuzzy data warehouse, the linguistic terms are captured in an attribute called class membership attribute, represented by a subtype of fuzzy classification attribute. Formally it is defined as:

Definition 2 (Class Membership Attribute): *A class membership attribute (CMA) for a target attribute TA, represented by CMA(TA), is an attribute that has a set of linguistic terms to which the target attribute may belong*. The values of a CMA are a set of distinct fuzzy classes to which the target attribute may belong. In other words, for all possible values of a target attribute (domain of attribute) there is a corresponding CMA value. The values of CMA are the values of the set S.

For the example target attribute *customer age*, the class membership attribute becomes,

CMA(customer age) = CMA_AgeGroup,

and the values of class membership attribute becomes,

CMA_AgeGroup = {young age, middle age, old age};

In order to integrate fuzzy concept, a fuzzy classification table that captures the class membership attribute and identifier of the table values is also needed. A fuzzy DWH model may have more than one classification. Therefore, it can have multiple fuzzy classification tables. Formally, fuzzy classification table is defined as:

Definition 3 (Fuzzy Classification Table): *A table that consists of fuzzy classes and their unique identifiers is called fuzzy classification table (FCT)*. It is a two-attribute table that consists of an identity attribute and a class membership attribute, where the identity attribute is a unique identifier of the table values.

FCT (TA) = {Identifier, CMA(TA) } ;

FCT for target attribute *customer age* becomes,

FCT(customer age) = {AgeGroup_ID, CMA_Age Group} ;

In order to fuzzily relate the values of the target attribute TA with linguistics terms (captured by class membership attribute in fuzzy classification table), we use membership degree concept to calculate the degree of relation between values of target attribute and linguistic terms i.e. between age of customer and age group. Membership degree is defined as:

Definition 4 (Membership Degree): *It is the degree to which the values of a target attribute TA are related with linguistic terms over a set of [0, 1].* It is represented by MD. In our example of customer age, MD degree is the degree to which the age of a customer lets say 17 years is related with an age group.

In order to calculate MD of a target attribute that can vary from 0 to 1 we use a membership function, which is defined as:

Definition 5 (Membership Function): *A membership function of a target attribute TA is a function that is used to calculate the membership degree of a target attribute TA to a class membership attribute CMA.* It is represented by μ and the value ranges from 0 to 1. Formally,

$$\mu \ (TA) \in [0, 1].$$

For the target attribute customer age, a membership function can be defined to calculate the member degree for each instance of class membership attribute. A key benefit of using membership function is that it offers a smooth transition between different age groups over a set of [0,1]. The membership function for customer age is presented in Exhibit 1.

Similarly, a membership function for each instance of CMA (middle age and old age) can also be defined. The values (membership degree)

generated by membership function are captured as membership degree attributes in the fuzzy DW model represented by a sub-class of fuzzy membership attribute in the meta-model. Fuzzy membership degree attribute is defined as:

Definition 6 (Membership Degree Attribute): *A membership degree attribute MDA of a target attribute TA, is an attribute that has a set of membership degrees of the target attribute TA.* The value of a membership degree is calculated by a membership function and is represented by, $\mu(TA) = MD$; where MD is the membership degree of TA. For customer age, the membership degree attribute is MD_AgeGroup.

In order to relate fuzzy concepts and values in the data warehouse, a fuzzy membership table is needed that captures the information about identification of target attribute, identification of fuzzy classification table, and membership degree attribute. It is an intermediate table that relates fuzzy classification table with the part of classical data warehouse model, as shown in the meta-model. A fuzzy DWH model may have multiple membership tables. Formally, fuzzy membership table is defined as:

Definition 7 (Fuzzy Membership Table): *A table that stores the values representing the degree to which a value is related to a fuzzy class is called fuzzy membership table.* It is a table with four attributes: the identity attribute of the table, the identifier of the target attribute TA, the identifier of the fuzzy classification table FCT (T A) and membership degree attribute MDA for TA. Formally,

Exhibit 1.

μ_{young} (customer_age) = { if customer_age $\leq$ 15, MD_AgeGroup = 1
if customer_age $\geq$ 25, MD_AgeGroup = 0
else if MD_AgeGroup =(25- customer_age)/ (25-15) }.

FMT (TA) = {Identifier, Identifier of T A, Identifier of FCT (TA), MDA(TA) } ;

FMT for target attribute customer age becomes,

FMT(CustomerAge) = {ID, CustomerAge_ID, AgeGroup_ID, MD_AgeGroup} ;

The meta-model describes the relationship between different elements that a fuzzy data warehouse may contain. In addition to that, the cardinalities describe the way these elements can be related with each other. By using the meta-model the fuzzy concepts are rolled out of data warehouse and added as meta-tables structure.

Characterizing Fuzzy Concepts

In contrast to a transactional system, data in data warehouse is populated on regular bases, never deleted and rarely modified. The data size therefore grows steadily and it can be observed over the years that the value range also grows simultaneously. If the data size grows over the physical capacity of the storage system, it is necessary to partition the value ranges and to archive parts of it. Consider a movie rental company data warehouse that stores information about movies. It is likely that over time more movies and different genres are added. The data of old movies that are not anymore available in the stores are sorted out and archived separately. Considering this mechanisms, one can state that the value ranges of movies and genres are fluctuating over time.

Fuzzy concepts should be flexible in the sense that they should properly handle fluctuating value ranges. Depending on how the fluctuation should be handled, different fuzzy concept types can be defined. We characterize fuzzy concepts into three types based on the value range of the fuzzy concept: limited fuzzy concept, open ended fuzzy concept and adaptive fuzzy concept.

Limited fuzzy concept: This type of fuzzy concept does not consider values out of the value range for which it was initially defined. The lowest and highest values of the original value range define the minima and maxima point of the fuzzy concept. Afterwards, all new values that are out of this range are discarded. Figure 4 (a) exemplifies a fuzzy concept that is limited in its range. The lowest and highest class membership attribute (CMA) is limited with a maxima point and a minima point.

Formally, a limited fuzzy concept can be defined as a fuzzy concept for which the value range of the target attribute (TA) is limited with a minima (min) and maxima (max) point; $dom_{TA} = [min, …, max]$. In real world, it makes sense to use limited concept, if the value ranges have static lower and upper boundaries. This can be exemplified within an employee dimension and the fuzzy concept age. Considering that a company does not employ people younger than 18 and the age for retirement is 65, the fuzzy concept age with its classification attributes young age, middle age and old age will have 18 as minima and 65 as maxima point.

Limited fuzzy concept has lower computation cost for the membership degree attribute because it has to be calculated only for values between the minima and maxima point. The fuzzy membership table does not necessarily grow linear to the target attribute table and therefore it might reduce the size of the meta-tables structure in the data repository. In contrast, the classification only covers a restricted range. If the value range fluctuates the limited fuzzy concept can only cover a part of the data. Consequently, it affects the quality of classification in a negative way.

Open ended fuzzy concept: A possibility to overcome this limitation is to remove the minima and maxima points and leave the fuzzy concept with open ends. Instead of minima and maxima points, knee points are defined. Each value beyond a knee point will fully belong to the class membership attribute in which the corresponding knee point is located. With this characteristic the fuzzy concept will always cover the whole value

Figure 4. Fuzzy concepts

a) Limited Fuzzy Concept

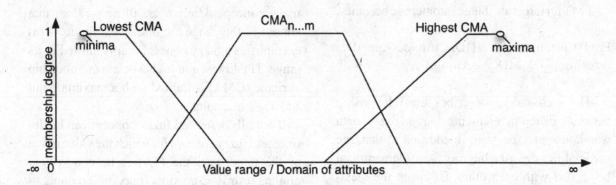

b) Open ended Fuzzy Concept

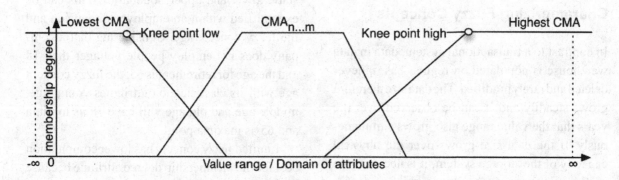

c) Adaptive Fuzzy Concept

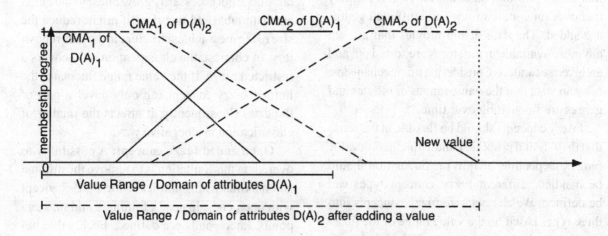

range. Figure 4 (b) describes the open ended fuzzy concept and shows that beyond the two knee points the possible belonging to the corresponding class membership attribute is always 1.

In practice, a limited fuzzy concept can be defined as a fuzzy concept ($\{CMA_{\_low}, ..., CMA_{\_high}\}$) for which the measured value range of the target attribute (TA) is infinite. Value instances below the lower knee point (LK) fully belong to the lowest class membership attribute (CMA) and value instances above the higher knee point (HK) fully belong to the highest CMA. Formally,

$$dom_{TA} = [-\infty, ..., +\infty] \wedge x_{low}, x_{high} \in TA \wedge$$
$$x_{low} < LK \wedge HK < x_{high} \wedge \mu_{CMA\_low}(x_{low}) = 1 \wedge$$
$$\mu_{CMA\_high}(x_{high}) = 1$$

For illustration of the open ended fuzzy concept the customer dimension with fuzzy classification age can be used. In contrast to the age of employees a customer is not limited in age but most of the time between the age of 14 and 50. Therefore, a lower knee point can be chosen at the age of 20 and a higher knee point at the age of 40. This knee points will define that every customer under 20 fully belongs to the class membership attribute young and every customer older than 40 fully belongs to the class membership attribute old. Following the discussed classification, a client with age 65 fully belongs to old age CMA. This type of fuzzy concept allows classifying all the clients, even if the age of a customer is outside the initial distribution of client age.

In contrast to the limited fuzzy concept, the open ended fuzzy concept requires as many data tuples in the fuzzy membership table as the Cartesian product of the class membership attribute and the target attribute. For every new value, the membership degrees are calculated and thus the computation cost increases as compared to the limited fuzzy concept. On the other hand, this concept covers all possible values of a value range. It is important to note that the classification and

knee points have to be defined in a way that the distribution of the values in the different class membership attributes correspond to the initial desired meaning of the fuzzy concept. This adequate definition is a general difficulty for fuzzy concepts and has to be handled by the designer of the fuzzy concepts. If it is not addressed properly and for instance the knee points are chosen to close together, it is likely that values can be easily classified to either the lowest or highest class membership attribute.

Adaptive fuzzy concept: In cases when it is not possible to predict the boundaries or the distribution of the value range at the time of defining a fuzzy concept, we propose the use of adaptive fuzzy concept. This type of fuzzy concept is not defined with fix points as knee points or minima and maxima points. The class membership attributes (CMA) are relative to the value range and cover a percentage of the value range instead of a defined subset of values. Due to relative behavior of the adaptive fuzzy concept, it can support fluctuating set of fuzzy concept and automatically adapts itself to changed value ranges. Figure 4 (c) shows a fuzzy concept with initial class membership attributes CMA_1 and CMA_2 based on the value range $D(A)_1$. Instead of defining the membership functions for the CMA's on absolute sets, they are defined as a percentage of $D(A)_1$. In the example, CMA_1 is covering 80% of the $D(A)_1$ starting from the lowest value instance. Similarly, CMA_2 can also be defined. When a new value outside of the value range $D(A)_1$ is stored, the value range grows to $D(A)_2$. Due to its relativity property, the fuzzy concept automatically adjusts to the new value range.

Formally, a limited fuzzy concept is a concept, which is defined relative to value range of the target attribute (TA). Consider the example of a company that uses revenue as its measure in the fact table and applies a fuzzy concept with the class membership attributes high, middle and low to classify revenue. Over time the revenue might grow and there is a possibility that company faces losses during some periods. In order to cover this fluctuation of the value range, the fuzzy concept can be defined as adaptive fuzzy concept. According to adaptive fuzzy concept, for every new value of target attribute the membership function checks whether it is within the defined value range or not. In case it is outside the value range, it is checked if the value range should be adapted to the value or not. If the value is an outlier it will still get classified based on the old value range and will therefore belong fully to one of the class membership attributes on the outside (low or high). If the value range gets modified every membership degree attribute in the membership table, including the new value, will be recalculated based on the new value range.

Adaptive fuzzy concepts have the disadvantage that they might be sensitive on outlier values. Therefore, it is necessary to define countermeasures for outlier values in the membership functions. A possible way to define a countermeasure is to calculate the standard deviation and discard values with high variance. If the value range is changed all the existing membership degree attributes are recalculated. For traceability it might be necessary to archive the old membership degrees. Given that membership degrees change frequently, it is likely that the adaptive fuzzy concept may lead to substantial increase in data warehouse size.

A METHOD FOR MODELING FUZZY DATA WAREHOUSE

In this section we present a method that can guide modelers to model fuzzy data warehouse without deep knowledge of fuzzy logic. Later, this method is used to develop fuzzy data warehouse model for the movie rental case. The input to the method is a classical data warehouse model and the output is a fuzzy data warehouse model. It is a two-step method, in the first step elements of classifica-

tion are defined and in the second step the fuzzy data warehouse is build. Figure 5 shows the tasks within each step and the order in which they are performed. The details of the steps are as follows:

Defining Classification Elements

The purpose of this step is to define classification elements that are used in the second step to build the fuzzy data warehouse model. It involves three tasks, identify target attribute, identify linguistic term and define membership function. The details are as follows:

First Task: The *first task* is to identify what should be classified i.e. to identify the target attribute (represented by TA), which contains the values that are aimed to be classified fuzzily. This is done by taking into account the end-user input. In the simplest case, one target attribute is identified. For the movie rental case, consider the example of customer age as a target attribute.

Second Task: The *second task* is to determine how the values of identified target attribute should be classified i.e. to identify the set of linguistics terms (also called fuzzy classes) that are used for classification of instances of a target attribute. Repeat this task for all target attributes. It is represented by iterative loop 1 in Figure 5. There are two possibilities here:

Case 1 - Distinct Linguistic Terms: It is the simplest case in which the linguistic terms are distinct i.e. there is a single set of linguistic terms. Formally,

TA instance : Fuzzy Classes (1)   (1)

For the customer age example consider the following set of linguistic terms {young age, middle age, old age}.

Case 2 - Different Linguistic Terms for a Target Attribute: It is a case in which there is more than one set of linguistic terms to classify instances of target attributes. In this case, instances of the target

Figure 5. A graphical overview of the method for modeling fuzzy data warehouse

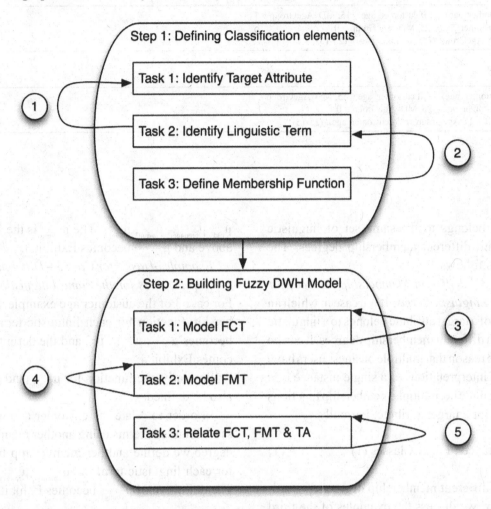

attribute belong to more than one set of linguistic term as identify by business users. Formally,

TA instance (1): Fuzzy Classes (M)

For the customer age example consider that the following two sets of linguistic terms are identified. These sets are {young age, middle age, old age} and {teenager, adult, senior}. The linguistic terms that already exist in a classical data warehouse model can be used for classifying instances of target attribute. It could also be the

case that the classes does not exist in the classical data warehouse model i.e. the user can identify new classes.

Third Task: The *third task* is to define a membership function (represented by μ) for each value of linguistic term. As discussed above, the membership function is used to determine membership degree. It is done in such a way the values can be determined over a scale of 0 to 1. Repeat the task for each identified linguistic term. It is represented by iterative loop 2 in Figure 5. It could be the case that for different users a target

Exhibit 2.

μ_{young} (customer_age) = { if customer_age $\leq$ 15, MD_AgeGroup = 1
    if customer_age $\geq$ 25, MD_AgeGroup = 0
else if MD_AgeGroup =(25- customer_age)/ (25-15)}.

Exhibit 3.

$\mu_{teenager}$ (customer_age) = { if customer_age $\leq$ 15, MD_AgeGroup = 1
    if customer_age $\geq$ 25, MD_AgeGroup = 0
    else if MD_AgeGroup =(25- customer_age)/ (25-15)}$_\wedge$

attribute belongs to the same set of linguistic terms with different membership degrees. The case is as follows:

Case 3 – Different Membership Degrees for the same Linguistic Terms: It is a case in which an instance of a target attribute belongs to a linguistic term with different membership degrees. It can be due to the reason that multiple business users have different interpretations of a single instance of a target attribute i.e. multiple membership functions are used for a target attribute. Formally,

TA – instance : Fuzzy Classes (1)   (1)

but with different membership degrees.

Below, we discuss the examples of the third task for each case:

Example of task 3 for Case 1 – Distinct linguistic terms. For the *customer age* example, a membership function is defined for each linguistic term i.e. μ_{young}, μ_{middle}, μ_{old} e.g. the μ_{young} becomes Exhibit 2.

Example of task 3 for Case 2 – Different Linguistic Terms for a Target Attribute. For case 2 of the *customer age* example, a membership function is defined for each linguistic term i.e. μ_{young}, μ_{middle},

μ_{old}, $\mu_{teenager}$, μ_{adult}, μ_{senior}. The μ_{young} is the same as above and $\mu_{teenager}$ becomes Exhibit 3.

Example of task 3 for Case 3 – Different Membership Degrees for the same Linguistic Terms. For case 3 of the customer age example, a membership function for each linguistic term of set becomes μ_{young}, μ_{middle}, μ_{old} and the definition becomes Exhibit 4.

Similarly, the function for μ_{middle} and μ_{old} can also be defined.

In order to relate the customer age with the same linguistic terms using another membership degree we define another membership function for each linguistic term i.e. μ_{young1}, $\mu_{middle1}$, μ_{old1}. The definition of μ_{young1} becomes Exhibit 5.

Building Fuzzy Data Warehouse Model

The purpose of this step is to employ the identified classification elements for building a fuzzy data warehouse model. It involves three tasks, create fuzzy classification table, create fuzzy membership table and relate tables. The details are as follows:

First Task: The *first task* towards building a fuzzy data warehouse model is to model a fuzzy

Exhibit 4.

μ_{young} (customer_age) = {if customer_age $\leq$ 15, MD_AgeGroup = 1
if customer_age $\geq$ 25, MD_AgeGroup = 0
else if MD_AgeGroup =(25- customer_age)/ (25-15)}

Exhibit 5.

$$\mu_{young1} (customer\_age) = \{ \text{if } customer\_age \leq 20, MD\_AgeGroup = 1$$
$$\text{if } customer\_age \geq 40, MD\_AgeGroup = 0$$
$$\text{else if } MD\_AgeGroup = (40- customer\_age)/ (40-20)\}.$$

classification table for each set of linguistic terms. As describe in section *modeling fuzzy DWH: the meta-model and definitions*, it is a two-attribute table in which one attribute is the identifier of the table and second attribute is the class membership attribute. The values of class membership attribute are the values of the linguistic variable (also referred as linguistic terms). As stated above the task should be repeated for each set of linguistic terms, which is represented by the self-loop 3 in Figure 5.

Second Task: The *second task* in building a fuzzy data warehouse model is to create fuzzy membership tables. As describe in the *modeling fuzzy DWH: the meta-model and definitions* section, it is a four attribute table in which the first attribute is the identifier of the table, the second attribute is the identifier of the target attribute, the third attribute is the identifier attribute of FCT and the fourth attribute is the membership degree attribute for the target attribute. The values of membership degree attribute are calculated by membership functions, as identified above.

For the cases described above, we present some guidelines for the first and the second task, which are as follows:

Case 1 - Distinct Linguistic Terms: It is the simplest case in which there is a single set of linguistic terms with no repetition between them. For this case, define a membership degree attribute (MDA) and a class membership attribute (CMA) for a target attribute, as given below:

TA (1): (1) MDA; MDA (1): (1) CMA

Guideline 1: Add a fuzzy classification table (*FCT*) and a fuzzy membership table (*FMT*) for target attribute TA, as given below:

Dimension/Fact (1): (1) FMT and FMT (1): (1) FCT

For the customer age example, there is one distinct set of linguistic terms i.e. {young age, middle age, old age}. Therefore, by following guideline 1, add a FCT(customer age) = {AgeGroup_ID, CMA_AgeGroup} and a FMT(customer age) = {MembershipID, AgeGroup_ID, CustomerAge_ID, MDA_AgeGroup}.

Case 2 – Different Linguistic Terms for a Target Attribute: It is a case in which there is more than one set of linguistic terms. For this case, define multiple membership degree attributes (MDA) and multiple class membership attributes (CMA) for a target attribute, where one membership degree attribute corresponds to a class membership attribute, as given below.

TA (1): (M) MDA and MDA (1): (M) CMA

Guideline 2.1: If an instance of a TA belongs to multiple fuzzy classes but with the same membership degree, add M number of FCTs and a FMT, where M is the number of distinct set of linguistic terms.

Guideline 2.2: If an instance of a TA belongs to more than one fuzzy classes with different membership degrees, add M number of FCTs and FMTs, as given below, where M is the number of distinct set of linguistic terms. Self-loop 3 and 4 respectively in Figure 5 represents the addition of M number of FCTs and FMTs.

Dimension/Fact (1): (M) FMT and FMT (1): (M) FCT

For the customer age example, there are two distinct sets of linguistic terms i.e. {young age, middle age, old age} and {teenager, adult, senior}. Therefore, following guideline 2.1 add FCT1(customer age) = {AgeGroup1_ID, CMA_AgeGroup} and FCT2(customer age) = {AgeGroup2_ID, CMA_AgeGroup}, one for each set. Also, add a FMT(customer age) = {MembershipID, AgeGroup1_ID, AgeGroup2_ID, CustomerAge_ID, MDA_AgeGroup}.

Case 3 – Different Membership Degrees for the same Linguistic Terms: It is a case in which target attributes belong to a linguistic term with different degrees. For this case, define multiple membership degree attributes (MDA) and a class membership attribute (CMA) for a target attribute, as given below.

TA (1): (M) MDA and MDA (M): (1) CMA

Guideline 3: If an instance of a TA belongs to a fuzzy class but with multiple membership degrees, add a FCT and M number of FMTs, as given below, where M is the number of distinct membership degrees.

Dimension/Fact (1): (M) FCT and FMT (M): (1) FCT

For the customer age example, there is one set of linguistic terms i.e. {young age, middle age, old age}, however different membership functions for different users are defined. Therefore, following guideline 3 add a FCT(customer age) = {AgeGroup_ID, CMA_AgeGroup}, a FMT1(customer age) = {MembershipID, AgeGroup_ID, CustomerAge_ID, MDA1_AgeGroup} and FMT2(customer age) = {MembershipID, AgeGroup_ID, CustomerAge_ID, MDA2_AgeGroup}.

Third Task: The *third task* is to relate each FMT and FCT with the 'to be classified' table i.e. the table that contains the target attribute. For that, add a foreign key relation FMT(Identifier of TA) = TA(Identifier) to relate the TA table with the FMT table. Second, add a foreign key relation FMT(Identifier of FCT) = FCT (Identifier) to relate each FCT and FMT. This task is similar for all three cases.

OPERATIONS, AGGREGATION AND PROPAGATION OF FUZZY CONCEPTS

Classical Data Warehouse Operations

E. F. Codd introduced Online Analytical Processing (OLAP) in 1993 as a database-processing category (Codd, Codd, & Smalley, 1993). According to Codd, OLAP optimizes database processing for the analysis in regard of business data and processes. In essence, the data (to analyze) is organized in the form of a multidimensional data model that is today commonly known as OLAP cube. For analyzing multidimensional data structures the specialized operators drill-down, roll-up, slice and dice are described by Codd et al. (1993). In a further step, Agrawal, Gupta and Sarawagi (1997) and Vassiliadis (1998) defined algebraic operations on multidimensional cubes. Each operation is applied on a cube that is representing a collection of data in a multidimensional space and produces as output another cube. A cube C can be defined as a 3-tuple,

$$C = <D, M, R>,$$

where D is the set of dimensions, M is the fact and R is the representation of the data collection of the combination of D and M. R further contains information about the representation of the data collection such as order by and grouping operations.

Inspired by the operations of Agrawal et al. (1997) roll-up, drill-down, slice and dice are explained next and it is further shown how to apply these operators in a fuzzy data warehouse.

The *roll-up* operation consolidates the values of a dimension hierarchy to a value on the next higher level. Therefore, this operation is used to navigate a dimension upwards. For the dimension store a roll-up operation is executed when the dimension level store is aggregated to the next higher level city. It can be seen as an operation on a base cube (C) that results in another cube (C_a) on a higher hierarchy level of the dimension. In order to merge from one cube to another over one dimension (D), a function (f_D) defining how the dimension instances are aggregated and a function (f_m) defining how the facts are aggregated have to be specified. Formally,

$$\text{roll-up}(C, D, f_D, f_m) = C_a.$$

The revenue of January 2009 might be $m_C(\text{January } 2009) = 8,000.$ and December 2009 $m_C(\text{December } 2009) = 5,000.$ The function f_m is defined as a summation and therefore the revenue of 2009 is calculated as $m_{Ca}(2009) = 8,000 + 5,000 = 13,000.$ In this example, the function f_D defines that January 2009 and December 2009 belongs to year 2009.

In the data warehouses modeled using a Star or Snowflake scheme the function f_D is implicitly given by the data structure of the dimension tables. The function f_m has to be specified explicitly in the query statement during the analysis of the data or in the data warehouse meta scheme.

The *drill-down* operation is used to navigate from top to bottom in a dimension and is the opposite operation of roll-up. For being able to perform a drill-down it has to be known in advanced how the value instances are compound from the lower hierarchy instances. Considering the example of yearly revenue, the revenue of the year 2010 can not drilled-down to monthly revenue, if the revenue of every month in 2010 is not known in detail. Otherwise, one can decompose the revenue of 2010 in infinite ways. A roll-up operation

defining the aggregation functions and the value instances on the higher hierarchy level has to be executed before a drill-down operation. Hence, the drill-down operation can be considered as a binary operation. Formally, a drill-down operation can be written as:

$$\text{drill-down}(C_a, D, f_D^{-1}, f_m^{-1}) = C,$$

where, $C_a = \text{roll-up}(C, D, f_D, f_m).$

The *slice* operation extracts a subset of values based on one or more dimensions using a dimension attribute to define the subset (OLAP Council, 1995). In the multi dimensional space of a data warehouse this corresponds to cutting out a slice from a data cube. In order to exemplify, the dimension store can be sliced using the value 2010 for the attribute year in the dimension time. This will extract the revenue of all stores that exist in 2010 and all the cities in which a store exists at this time. A slice operation can formally be defined as,

$$\text{slice}(C, d_m) = C_s,$$

where $d_m \in \text{dom}(D_m)$ and $D_m \in D.$

d_m is the instance value of a dimension D_m defining the slice. For extracting the revenues of all the stores in 2010 as described in the example above, the slice operation is as follows:

$$\text{slice}(C = < D = \{\text{store, year}\}, M = \text{revenue}, R>, \text{year} = 2010) = C_s.$$

Extracting a subset of values based on more than one dimension using more than one dimension attribute to define the subset is called a dice. Dice is therefore an extended version of the slice operation as it is a slice with multiple slicers. Slicers in a dice are combined using the logical operations AND, OR or NOT. The dice operation can formally be defined as an extended slice operation:

$$\text{dice}(C, \{d_m, \ldots, d_k\}, \{f_m, \ldots, f_{k-1}\}) = C_d$$

where, $\forall$ $(d_m,...,d_k)(d_m \in dom(D_m) \wedge ... \wedge d_k \in dom(D_k))$, $\{D_m,...,D_k\} \in D$ and $\forall(x \in \{m,...,k-1\})$ $(f_x \in \{AND, OR, NOT\})$.

$\{d_m,...,d_k\}$ is a set of dimension instances that are the slicers for the operation. The set $\{f_m,...,f_{k-1}\}$ are the logical operators that combine the slicers.

An example for a dice operation might be a sub-cube representing revenues of all the clients in all the stores in the city Fribourg in the year 2010. The dice operation is presented as follows:

dice(C= <D={client, store, client}, M = revenue, R>,{city="Fribourg", year=2010}, {AND}).

Summarization to Guarantee Consistent Aggregations

A data warehouse uses summarization functions for the aggregation of facts over the dimensions. Depending on dimensional relations, hierarchical structures can be complex and if the summarization of the data is inconsistent, the result set of the corresponding operations is erroneous. Rafanelli and Shoshani (1990) defined a framework called summarizability that describes characteristics for consistent aggregations. The framework is based on earlier discussions about operations in statistical databases (Shoshani, 1982). Based on Rafanelli and Shoshani (1990), Lenz and Shoshani (1997) defined the necessary conditions to guarantee summarizability in OLAP cubes. Data summarization and the dimension structures have to fulfill these conditions in order to provide consistent aggregations.

The first condition for summarizability states that aggregations of elements over a dimensional structure always form disjoint subsets. Considering the example that a dimension store aggregates all stores of a movie rental company into cities, a store is located in only one city at a time to fulfill the disjointness in summarizability.

In addition to disjointness, summarizability defines the condition of completeness. In order to fulfill this characteristic, all stores must be located in one of the cities. Therefore, it is not be possible that one of the stores is not considered in the aggregation operation to the next higher dimension level city.

The last condition of the summarizability is the type compatibility. Lenz and Shoshani (1993) defined different types of facts, which characterize the behavior of the aggregation of these facts over dimension hierarchies. The types of values are categorized in: flow, stock and value per unit type. The type flow can be aggregated by a summation function (SUM). For the type value per unit the SUM aggregation is never allowed. The stock type can be aggregated with SUM as long it is not aggregated over the time dimension. Aggregations by average (AVG), minima (MIN), maxima (MAX) and count (COUNT) functions are allowed for all types.

The store dimension aggregates store's revenues into city revenue with a summation function. Store revenues are of type flow and the combination with SUM is therefore a valid aggregation according to Lenz and Shoshani (1993). A nonvalid combination would be the aggregation of movies in stock over the time dimension, using a summation function. Doing so, the amount of movies in stock will be daily summed up to a movie stock at the end of the month. In reality, the movie stock at the end of the month is only as big as the stock at the last day of the month and not the sum of all days.

In order to be a fully functional data warehouse the fuzzy data warehouse should support the basic OLAP operators with respect to the summarizability. As the fuzzy data warehouse includes the classical data warehouse as a subset, all operations for crisp data are supported in the fuzzy data warehouse. In extension to the operations on crisp data, operations on fuzzy concepts are further discussed in this section.

Aggregation and Propagation of Fuzzy Concepts

In order to discuss OLAP operations on fuzzy concepts, at first it should be analyzed how fuzzy concepts can be aggregated in general. An aggregation in a classical data warehouse is the combination of a set of values in order to represent them in a more dense way. The operation for combining the values is a summation function in regard to the summarizability. For exemplification, the roll-up operation aggregates values of the fact on a specific dimension hierarchy level to a higher level. When aggregating fact revenue, the summation function can be SUM. In order to operate on fuzzy concepts, values of the membership degree attributes can be aggregated.

The movie rental company measures the surface of every store in square meters. A fuzzy concept with the linguistic terms small, moderate and big is attached to the target attribute store size in the store dimension in order to classify the stores based on the surface of stores. The stores are aggregated into cities. There is a possibility to apply fuzzy concept on city i.e. to classify city. With the aggregated fuzzy concept, city can be classified based on the overall surface of stores. To consolidate the membership degree attributes of the value instances on store into a single value instance on city, an additional aggregation function for the membership degrees should be defined. In the case of surface, the arithmetic average of the membership degree attributes of each class membership attribute can be used to generate the corresponding membership degree attributes for the cities. Figure 6 exemplifies the aggregation of the fuzzy concept 'surface' from 'store' to 'city'. Store A and B are aggregated into city Fribourg. Their surfaces, 20 and 35 square meters respectively, are aggregated to 27.5 square meters in city Fribourg using an average function. Both stores have a membership degree represented by μ for the linguistic terms of the fuzzy concept surface in Figure 6. The membership degrees of the city Fribourg are calculated using the arithmetic average of the membership degrees of store A and store B. For example, the membership degree of the class membership attribute small for the city Fribourg is calculated as follows: $\mu_{small}(55) = (\mu_{small}(20) * 20 + \mu_{small}(35) * 35) / 55$. Similarly, the membership degrees for the linguistic terms big and middle can be calculated.

Aggregation of fuzzy concept may not be semantically correct in all cases. A fuzzy concept for revenue of products may be semantically incorrect to aggregate based on the membership degrees. For example, the movie rental company has 20 independent movies from a single producer and 1 blockbuster movie in their portfolio for rent. The rent of the blockbuster is 2 times as expensive as an independent movie. All the rents of the movies are classified using a fuzzy concept revenue with the linguistic terms low, middle and high. The overall revenue of the blockbuster movie is classified as high. The independent movie revenue is classified as low. When aggregating the movies to producer hierarchy level a summation of the revenue of all movies is calculated to retrieve the overall revenue of the movie producer companies. The revenue of the independent movie producer is almost the same amount as for the blockbuster producer. In this case, it is semantically incorrect to aggregate the membership degree attributes of all the single movie instances to producer level. For the independent movie producer the classification would lead to low revenue because an arithmetic average of 20 times low revenue returns still low revenue. Similarly, the revenue for blockbuster producer results in high revenue. Consequently, the revenues are very close to each other but classified completely different. It can be said that aggregation of fuzzy concept are only semantically correct, if the initial target attributes and the target attributes, on which the aggregated fuzzy concepts are applied on, have the same value range. This is always the case, when the initial target attributes are ag-

Figure 6. Aggregation of a fuzzy concept

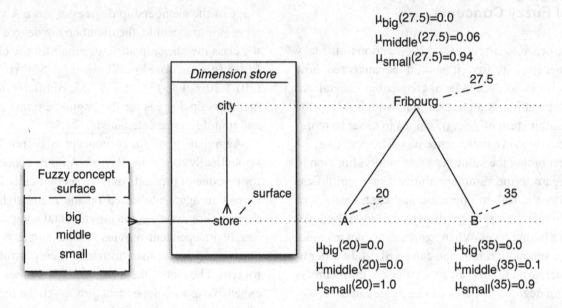

gregated using a summation function other than SUM.

When aggregation leads to incorrect classification, propagation of the fuzzy concept can be used. In contrast to the aggregation, the propagation of a fuzzy concept is not an operation based on the instances of the fuzzy concept. The linguistic variable, its terms and the membership functions are redefined on a new target attribute. The membership functions can be adapted to a new value range and the classification is correct even if the value range changes. The propagated and the original fuzzy concept might be considered as two different concepts. Nevertheless, the classification realized with the concepts is the same and the propagated fuzzy concept has to be seen as a variant of the original fuzzy concept.

The fuzzy concept revenue can be propagated to the hierarchy level producer. To do so, a variant of the concept including the fuzzy classification table and the fuzzy membership table must be defined on producer level. The target attribute for this fuzzy concept is the producer revenue. The producer revenue is still aggregated from movie revenue but the membership degrees

are calculated from the producer instance itself and are not aggregated. Both movie producer companies are now classified quite close to each other as only the overall revenue is taken into consideration i.e. not with how many movies the revenue is produced. Figure 7 exemplifies the propagation of the fuzzy concept revenue from the dimension hierarchy movie to producer. Each independent movie (Inde 1, …, Inde 20) is rented several times. For every rent a new instance of 5 money units for fact revenue is stored in the fact table. The total revenue for a movie is the sum of all the revenues obtained by renting the movies. Each movie has a membership degree for each linguistic term in the fuzzy concept movie revenue (μ_{high}, μ_{middle}, μ_{low}) as shown in Figure 7 under the fact instances. All independent movies fully belong to low revenue in this example. For the producer hierarchy level the movies are aggregated to independent movie producer (Inde Prod) and the fuzzy concept is propagated (dashed fuzzy concept producer revenue). The producer revenue, which is the sum of all movies revenues, is classified according to the propagated fuzzy concept. Hence, the membership degrees on the

Figure 7. Propagation of a fuzzy concept

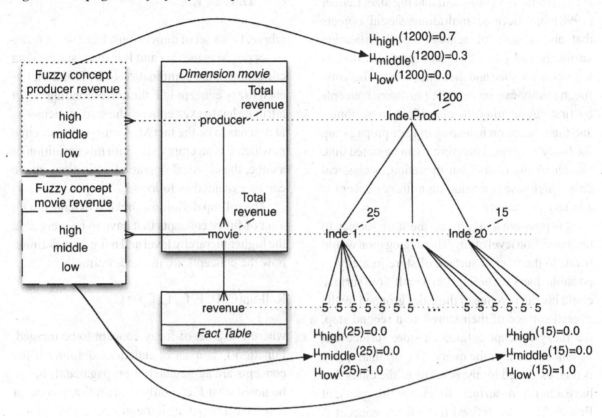

different hierarchy levels are independent to each other and get defined by the fuzzy concept on the corresponding hierarchy level.

The decision, if a fuzzy concept should be propagated, aggregated or both, is a complex task and depends on the nature of the target attribute and the semantic meaning of the classification. In general, the modeler of the fuzzy concept should consider different aspects. The most important aspect is to check if the fuzzy concept retains its semantic correctness on other hierarchy levels. For instance, a limited fuzzy concept might not be propagated if all the new values are outside the defined value range; respectively the fuzzy concept has to be redefined. If the aggregation or the propagation of a concept makes sense is often not based on technical constraints but on the perception of the modeler how the fuzzy concept should classify target attributes.

Classical Data Warehouse Operations in a Fuzzy Data Warehouse

In a classical data warehouse approach the facts, which are of quantitative nature, are aggregated according to dimensions hierarchies. Fuzzy concepts are defined as additional information to either a fact or a dimension attribute on a hierarchy level and are of qualitative nature. Considering a fuzzy concept on a dimension attribute, it possesses the same characteristics as classification attributes (Lehner 1998) of the dimension attribute. A classification attribute is an element that provides additional information on a dimension hierarchy. For the dimension attribute store, the size of the surface is a classification attribute. Often, a target attribute of a fuzzy concept is a classification attribute, for example, the size of the surface that is classified fuzzily into small and big size. Lehner (1998) has defined multidimensional objects that are capable of aggregating classification attributes and takes them into consideration as segments for slice and dice operations. The same functionality can be extended to fuzzy concepts by first aggregating the classification attributes and then, based on it, aggregating or propagating the fuzzy concept. Therefore it can be stated that, similar to the drill-down operation, a classical data warehouse operation on a fuzzy concept is a binary operation.

It is possible to aggregate the store surface to the dimension level of city. This aggregation would result in the overall surface of store in a city. A possible query including the overall store surface could be: the revenue of the cities grouped by the overall surface of their stores. In a second step, the fuzzy concept defined on store surface can be embedded into the query. The original query is then extended to: the revenue of the cities that have a big store surface. To answer this query, at first it should be defined if the fuzzy concept is propagated or aggregated. In case of aggregating the fuzzy concept, the arithmetic average of the membership degrees of a linguistic term (Fasel, 2009) is considered to calculate the corresponding membership degree for the linguistic term on city. When propagating the fuzzy concept, the membership function definition and linguistic terms are applied to the city store surface. Subsequently, the aggregated overall store surface values on dimension city are classified fuzzily using the propagated concept. The propagation of the fuzzy concept can be depicted in three sub steps: defining the fuzzy concept for the new target attribute, aggregating the crisp elements, calculating the membership degree of the aggregated elements based on the propagated fuzzy concept.

In order to discuss the classical data warehouse operation for handling fuzzy concepts, the definition of a cube has to be extended. A fuzzy cube is a 4-tuple defined as

$$C = <D, F, M, R>,$$

where, D is a set of dimensions, F is a set of fuzzy concepts, M is the fact and R is the resulting data collection of the combination of D, F, and M. For each fuzzy concept in F the corresponding target attribute has to exist either in the set of dimensions D or it has to be the fact M. A crisp cube is a cube in which F is an empty set. With this definition of a cube, the classical operation definitions above can be extended as follows.

The roll-up definition above is extended with a set of fuzzy concepts that have to be merged to the higher hierarchy level and a function defining how the concepts are merged. Formally,

$$\text{Roll-up}(C, D, F, f_D, f_F, f_M) = C_a,$$

where F is a set of fuzzy concept to be merged. Function f_F is a set of functions defining if the concepts are aggregated or propagated. It has to be noted, that F can only contain fuzzy concept that have a target attribute in D or $f_M(M)$. If F is an empty set, this operation is a crisp roll-up operation on a fuzzy cube resulting in a crisp cube.

As stated in the classical data warehouse operations section, a drill-down operation is the reciprocal operation of a roll-up. Therefore the fuzzy drill-down operation can be defined as:

$$\text{Drill-down}(C, D, F, f_d^{-1}, f_F^{-1}, f_M^{-1}) = C_a,$$

where $C = \text{roll-up}(C_a, D, F, f_d, f_F, f_M)$.

In slice operation, a fuzzy concept defined on a dimension can be used as selection or the slicer itself. The slice operation in a fuzzy data warehouse can be defined as:

$$\text{Slice}(C, s_m) = C_s.$$

The slicer s_m is an instance of either a dimension in D or a fuzzy concept in F. If s_m is a slicer on a fuzzy concept it limit the cube based on a class membership attribute / linguistic term of the fuzzy concept. The result cube C_s is always the same type of cube, fuzzy or crisp, as the initial cube C.

To refine slices with fuzzy concepts as slicers the α-cut (Zimmermann, 1991), can be used. The α-cut defines the degree to which a value has to belong to a fuzzy concept. Adding a α-cut to the slice operation above would result in a slice operation where s_m defines the class membership attribute together with the corresponding α-cut.

For the dice operation the same characteristics for fuzzy concepts apply as for the slice operation. The only difference is that multiple slicers are executed connected to each other with a logical operator. Crips and fuzzy slicer can be combined with each other. The extended dice operation can be formally defined as:

$$Dice(C, \{s_m,\ldots,s_k\},\{f_m,\ldots,f_{k-1}\}) = C_d,$$

where the set $\{s_m,\ldots,s_k\}$ is a set with either crisp or fuzzy slicers and $\{f_m,\ldots,f_{k-1}\}$ is the set of functions combining the slicers.

A CASE STUDY IN PERFORMANCE ANALYSIS OF A MOVIE RENTAL COMPANY

This section presents a performance analysis case study of a movie rental company. In the first step, the movie rental company and its initial data warehouse are depicted. In the second step, fuzzy concepts are created using the methodology presented in the section, *a method for modeling fuzzy data warehouse*. It is then shown, how the fuzzy concepts improve the analysis of the data collection in the data warehouse.

The information about the movies for this case study was retrieved from the open movie database project using their open API (TMDb Inc., 2010).

The Movie Rental Company

The movie rental company is based in Switzerland, since 2005. The company has 29 stores spread across 20 cities. It offers a collection of 661 movies for rent. All stores are equipped with distribution machines beside the stores where customers can rent movies beside the opening hours. Each rented movie is recorded by one of the employees working in the corresponding store. Therefore, to each record of a rent-transaction, an employee is listed. The movie rental company has in total 50 employees. New movies are rented for 7 CHF a day and movies older than 1 year are rent for 5 CHF a day. Each customer is asked to rate the movie when he returns the rented movie. The rating information is capture in order to provide movie rating charts as a service to the customers.

To measure the performance of the business, the movie rental company has implemented a data warehouse. An important fact that the company uses to evaluate its performance is the revenue of every single rent. For each transaction, information about customer, movie, employee and type is captured. The type dimension captures the information whether it is a new movie or an old movie. The movie dimension aggregates movies into two hierarchy paths. One path aggregates producer and the other path aggregates category of the movie. Both hierarchy paths are multi-valued hierarchies. A movie can be produced by multiple studios and can be categorized into multiple genres. In many to many relations in dimension hierarchy structures, we use the concept of bridge tables proposed by (Kimball and Caserta, 2004). A bridge table contains key relations, as it is also the case for many to many relations in classical database modeling, and a weighting factor. The weighting factor is used for retaining consistent aggregations over these hierarchies. Additional to the fact revenue, the rating and rent duration are kept in the fact table. Figure 8 presents the snowflake scheme of the movie rental data warehouse. All the key attributes, primary and foreign

Figure 8. Snowflake scheme for the data warehouse

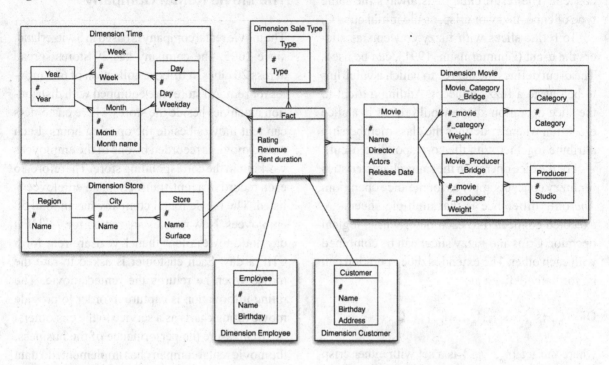

keys, are symbolized with a single #. The key attributes in the bridge tables are distinctively named to visualize the foreign key relation to the corresponding dimension attribute table.

By using the classical data warehouse shown in Figure 8, the movie rental company can analyze its performance in different aspects. For exemplification, the company might be interested in the overall revenues generated by new movies across different regions during 2010. This is a dice operation over a sub-cube visualizing the sum of the revenues grouped by regions. The slicers of the dice operation are executed on the dimension time (year = 2010) and the dimension type (type = 'new').

dice(<{region, time, type}, revenue, R>, {type="new", year=2010}, {AND}) = <{region, time, type}, revenue, R'>

The result set R' of the operation is shown in Table 1.

The movie rental company wants to analyze the revenue produced by movie producers. Movies from the 20 producers with the highest revenue are favorable for the company when choosing new movies for the portfolio. The revenues of movie producers should be divided with the weighting factor in the bridge table to give meaningful results. A notable amount of revenue is done with films that do not have an assigned producer studio. These revenues are summed into a virtual producer named as 'Not Known' and should not be considered in the result set. The slice operation for this analysis is

Slice(<producer, revenue, R>, producer <> "Not Known").

The final result set is shown in Table 2.

Table 1. Result set of dice operation: overall revenue of regions in 2010 of new movies

region	overall_revenue
German	2'209'734
French	1'595'097
Italian	291'681
Rhaeto-Romanic	142'812

Integration of Fuzzy Concepts in the Data Warehouse

Additional to the classical analysis in a data warehouse, the movie rental company needs the use of non- numeric terms. To do that, we employ integration of fuzzy concepts in the company's data warehouse. The details of the integrating fuzzy concepts are as follows:

Dimension Movie: The movies are classified into different genres. In the classical data warehouse a movie always belongs fully to a genre, which is represented in the hierarchy path from movie to category in the movie dimension. In reality, movies can often be categorized into several genres but it belongs more to one genre than to the other. For instance, the movie Star Wars can be classified in Science Fiction and Action, whereas it can be stronger classified in Science Fiction. The movie Spaceballs is a parody of Star

Table 2. Result set of slice operation: Revenue of movie producers

Studio	Revenue
Warner Bros. Pictures	3'331'127
Paramount Pictures	2'763'760
Universal Pictures	2'284'147
20th Century Fox	1'596'232
DreamWorks SKG	1'497'200
Walt Disney Pictures	1'480'180
Columbia Pictures Corporation	938'228
...	...

Wars and can be classified as Science Fiction and more strongly as Comedy.

Using the classification offered by classical data warehouse, the movie rental company cannot classify the movies asynchronous into different genres. Therefore, the company realizes the classification of the movies with a fuzzy concept. Based on the method presented in section *modeling fuzzy DWH: the meta-model and definitions*, the movie hierarchy is defined as a target attribute. The linguistic terms are the different genres to which movies can belong. These genres can be extracted from the dimension hierarchy category in the movie dimension. Following that, the membership function for each genre is defined. Because of the qualitative nature of the classification, the membership functions are discrete functions, respectively step functions (Meier, 2005), and a movie can belong to a genre with 5 different degrees i.e. $\mu_{genre} = [0, 0.33, 0.5, 0.66, 1]$. The company wants to classify every movie manually because it is not possible to derive the belonging to genre from existing data. Movies are attributes of the dimension movies and are not frequently changing in the fuzzy data warehouse. Therefore, it is feasible for the movie rental company to do once the effort of classifying all the movies manually.

After identifying target attribute, linguistic terms and their membership functions, the meta-tables structure for the fuzzy concept can be defined. In this case, one fuzzy classification table and one fuzzy membership table is created. The fuzzy classification table holds the genres as class membership attributes. The fuzzy membership table contains membership degrees for each target attribute corresponding to class membership attributes. The size of the fuzzy membership table is a Cartesian product of the movie table and fuzzy classification table.

By using the proposed approach, sharp classification of the movies is still maintained in the data warehouse, which makes it possible to analyze the classification in both ways, sharp and fuzzy. On the other hand, it is possible to remove the category table and the corresponding bridge table as the fuzzy concept is redundant to this dimension hierarchy path.

Dimension Customer: The movie rental company is interested in analyzing the revenue based on customer classifications in order to analyze how valuable are different customer groups for the company. A common classification is an ABC analysis in which customers realizing 80% of the revenue are classified as A category customers and all other customers are classified in B or C category. Most of the customers rent movies regularly and the achieved revenues per customer are close to each other. Therefore, the classical ABC analysis does not provide a satisfying classification. Using a fuzzy concept that classifies customers into good, moderate and bad customers is a more suitable classification. The fuzzy concept allows a more fine-grained classification of customers. After defining the customer table as target attribute and good, moderate and bad as linguistic terms, the membership functions should be defined. An adaptive fuzzy concept is used and the membership functions are defined as seen in Exhibit 6.

The base is calculated by subtracting the lowest revenue a customer realized from the highest revenue. The company calculates the membership degrees once i.e. at the time of creating the fuzzy concept. For properly classifying, the base and the membership degrees should be recalculated on a regular basis.

Additionally, the customers are classified according to their age for analyzing revenues based on customer age. The customers are hence classified with a fuzzy concept containing the linguistic terms old, middle and young. The target attribute is again the customer table in the customer dimension. The membership functions defined for classification are as presented in Exhibit 7.

This fuzzy concept can be characterized as an open ended fuzzy concept. All customers, older than 65 fully belong to the linguistic term old whereas customers, younger 20, fully belong to the linguistic term young. Although the age of the majority of customers lies between 20 and 65, it is still possible to classify customers older 65 or younger 20.

For building the two fuzzy concepts on customer dimension, two fuzzy classification tables and two fuzzy membership tables are created. The fuzzy classification tables hold the linguistic terms for each concept and the membership tables hold the corresponding membership degrees. Each fuzzy membership table will have the size of the Cartesian product of the fuzzy classification table and the customer table.

Fact Revenue: Furthermore, the movie rental company creates a classification on the revenue in the fact table. The revenue should be classified as high, middle and low revenue. For this case, the target attribute is in the fact table and the linguistic terms are high, middle and low. Renting a movie costs either 5 or 7 CHF a day. The revenue is defined by the cost of renting a movie times the renting duration. Therefore, the revenue is a discrete value and always a multiple of 5 or 7. An open ended fuzzy concept with discrete membership functions can be used in this case. The membership functions are defined as presented in Exhibit 8.

One fuzzy classification table and one fuzzy membership table is used to build this fuzzy concept in the fuzzy data warehouse.

Propagation of fuzzy concept revenue to movie dimension: A special case for fuzzy concepts on facts is the way to roll-up these concepts. The movie rental company likes to have revenues of the movies classified as good, middle and bad revenue. In order to reuse the fuzzy concept on the fact table the company can propagate the concept to the movie dimension. As discussed in section *aggregation and propagation of fuzzy concept*, usage of aggregation does not make sense in this case. For the propagation of the fuzzy concept, a new target attribute should be defined first, which

Exhibit 6.

base = highest_customer_revenue – lowest_customer_revenue
μ_{good} (customer_revenue) = { if customer_revenue ≥ 0.8 * base, $MD_{customer\_revenue}$ = 1
if customer_revenue ≤ 0.6 * base, $MD_{customer\_revenue}$ = 0
else $MD_{customer\_revenue}$ =
(customer_revenue – 0.6 * base) / (0.8 * base – 0.6 * base)}
$\mu_{moderate}$ (customer_revenue) = { if customer_revenue ≥ 0.8 * base, $MD_{customer\_revenue}$ = 0
if customer_revenue ≤ 0.2 * base, $MD_{customer\_revenue}$ = 0
if 0.4 * base ≤ customer_revenue ≤ 0.6 * base, $MD_{customer\_revenue}$ = 1
if 0.2 * base ≤ customer_revenue ≤ 0.4 * base, $MD_{customer\_revenue}$ =
(customer_revenue – 0.2 * base) / (0.4 * base – 0.2 * base)
else $MD_{customer\_revenue}$ =
(0.8 * base – customer_revenue) / (0.8 * base – 0.6 * base)}
μ_{bad} (customer_revenue) = { if customer_revenue ≥ 0.4 * base, $MD_{customer\_revenue}$ = 0
if customer_revenue ≤ 0.2 * base, $MD_{customer\_revenue}$ = 1
else $MD_{customer\_revenue}$ =
(0.4 * base – customer_revenue) / (0.4 * base – 0.2 * base)}

is the movie table in the movie dimension. The linguistic terms are the same as for the fact table fuzzy concept. The membership functions should be adapted to the movie dimension and are defined as presented in Exhibit 9.

For the propagation of the fuzzy concept, an additional fuzzy membership table should be created that interconnects the original fuzzy classification table and the movie table. The propagated fuzzy concept has the characteristic of an open ended fuzzy concept.

It has to be noted that the customer revenue fuzzy concept, discussed above for the customer dimension, cannot be propagated from the revenue fuzzy concept. The linguistic terms are not the same and therefore customer revenue is a distinct fuzzy concept.

Similarly, fuzzy concept for the fact rating and for the two dimensional attributes surface of stores and age of customers can be created. In a

next step, the data warehouse is extended with the meta-tables of the fuzzy concepts. In Figure 9 the fuzzy data warehouse scheme is presented including the meta-tables for all fuzzy concepts as shaded elements. For each fuzzy classification table (FCT) the key attribute is represented as # and the linguistic term are stored in the class membership attribute (CMA). In the fuzzy membership tables (FMT), the key attribute for the relation with FCT is represented as # CMA. Similarly, the key attribute for representing the relation to the target attribute is represented as # TA. The membership degrees are stored in the membership degree attribute (MDA). The propagations of the fuzzy concepts revenue and rating from the fact to the dimension movie are illustrated as dashed fuzzy membership tables and dashed relations. For simplicity, the dimensions, which do not have any fuzzy concept, are only depicted as boxes with the dimension name. The structures

Exhibit 7.

μ_{old} (customer_age) = { if customer_age ≥ 65, $MD_{customer\_age}$ = 1
if customer_age ≤ 40, $MD_{customer\_age}$ = 0
else $MD_{customer\_age}$ = (customer_age – 40) / (65 – 40)}
μ_{middle} (customer_age) = { if customer_age ≥ 65, $MD_{customer\_age}$ = 0
if customer_age ≤ 20, $MD_{customer\_age}$ = 0
if 30 < customer_age ≤ 40, $MD_{customer\_age}$ = 1
if 20 < customer_age ≤ 30, $MD_{customer\_age}$ = (customer_age – 20) / (30 – 20)
else $MD_{customer\_age}$ = (65 – customer_age) / (65 – 40)}
μ_{young} (customer_age) = { if customer_age ≥ 30, $MD_{customer\_age}$ = 0
if customer_age ≤ 20, $MD_{customer\_age}$ = 1
else $MD_{customer\_age}$ = (30 – customer_age) / (30 – 20)}

Exhibit 8.

μ_{high} (revenue) = { if revenue $\geq$ 25, $MD_{revenue}$ = 1
if revenue $\leq$ 14, $MD_{revenue}$ = 0
if revenue = 15, $MD_{revenue}$ = 0.33
if revenue = 20, $MD_{revenue}$ = 0.5
if revenue = 21, $MD_{revenue}$ = 0.66}
μ_{middle} (revenue) = { if revenue = 15, $MD_{revenue}$ = 1
if revenue = 21, $MD_{revenue}$ = 0.5
if 25 $\leq$ revenue $\leq$ 10, $MD_{revenue}$ = 0
if revenue = 14, $MD_{revenue}$ = 0.5}
μ_{low} (revenue) = { if revenue = 5, $MD_{revenue}$ = 1
if revenue = 7, $MD_{revenue}$ = 0.66
if revenue = 10, $MD_{revenue}$ = 0.33
if revenue $\geq$ 14, $MD_{revenue}$ = 0}

of these simplified dimensions are retained as shown in Figure 8.

Usage of the Fuzzy Data Warehouse

After creating the fuzzy data warehouse, the movie rental company has now a new set of performance measures for analyses purpose. This section describes how a selection of the fuzzy concepts can be used for performance analysis. Examples of the OLAP operations that include fuzzy concepts are depicted and the result set is presented.

Revenue of old customers: The movie rental company is interested in analyzing, how much revenue old customers generate. Therefore, a slice operation on the fuzzy data warehouse can be executed. In the operation, the fuzzy concept customer age is used as slicer. With a α-cut the result set of the slice operation can be further refined. The following slice operation is executed for this analysis.

slice(<customer, customer_age, revenue, R>, customer_age.old > 0.8)

The Table 3 shows the result set of the four first customers.

Revenue of customers grouped by fuzzy concept customer age: More interesting for the company is the distribution of revenues of movie rents by customers age. To answer this question, the company uses a roll-up operation in which the fuzzy concept customer age is the selection part of the query. In order to have a result that is consistent with the overall revenue, the membership degrees of old, middle and young for each target attribute instance has to be normalized to 1. Otherwise, the sum of the revenue of all linguistic terms will not correspond to the actual overall revenue. Similar, to a bridge table, the revenue of customers can then be distributed to the linguistic terms by taking the membership degree as weighting factor into account. The roll-up operation is given below:

roll-up(<customer, customer_age, revenue * MDA, R>, {}, customer_age, f_D, f_F, SUM)

The function f_D is implicitly defined in the data structure of the dimension customer and the properties in f_F have been defined during the modeling process of the fuzzy concept. The result set is presented in Table 4.

Revenue of small stores grouped by region in July and August 2010: The company also

Exhibit 9.

μ_{high} (movie_revenue) = { if movie_revenue $\geq$ 150,000, $MD_{movie\_revenue}$ = 1
if movie_revenue $\leq$ 80,000, $MD_{movie\_revenue}$ = 0
else $MD_{movie\_revenue}$ = (movie_revenue $-$ 80,000) / (150,000 $-$ 80,000)}
μ_{middle} (movie_revenue) = { if movie_revenue $\geq$ 150,000, $MD_{movie\_revenue}$ = 0
if movie_revenue $\leq$ 20,000, $MD_{movie\_revenue}$ = 0
if 60,000 $\leq$ movie_revenue $\leq$ 80,000, $MD_{movie\_revenue}$ = 1
if 20,000 $\leq$ movie_revenue $\leq$ 60,000, $MD_{movie\_revenue}$ =
(movie_revenue $-$20,000) / (60,000 $-$ 20,000)
else $MD_{movie\_revenue}$ = (150,000 $-$ movie_revenue) / (150,000 $-$ 80,000)}
μ_{low} (movie_revenue) = { if movie_revenue $\geq$ 60,000, $MD_{movie\_revenue}$ = 0
if movie_revenue $\leq$ 20,000, $MD_{movie\_revenue}$ = 1
else $MD_{movie\_revenue}$ = (60,000 $-$ movie_revenue) / (60,000 $-$ 20,000)}

Figure 9. Fuzzy data warehouse scheme for the movie rental company case study

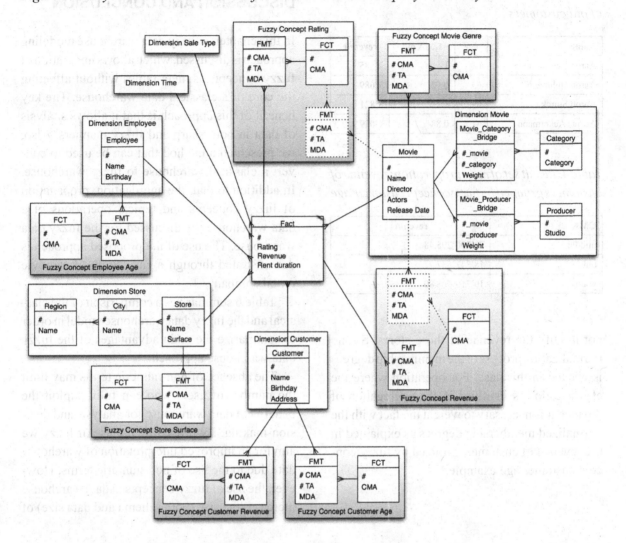

wants to analyze how much revenue small stores are producing. Therefore, the time frame July to August 2010 is chosen to reduce the size of the result set. For this analysis the following dice operation can be used:

dice(<{time, region, store}, {store_surface}, revenue, R>, {store_surface = small, year=2010, month=July, month=August}, {AND, AND, OR })

Only the revenue of the stores with a belonging to small store surface is aggregated to the dimension hierarchy level region. Hence, small store surface is a slicer of the dice operation. The other slicers are the time restriction July, August and 2010. A shortened result set of this dice operation is presented in Table 5.

Contrary to the roll-up operation of customer revenue grouped by customer age, the fuzzy concept in this dice operation is not involved in the summation process of revenue. It is only involved for selecting the concerned stores but does

Table 3. Result set of slicing operation: Revenue of old customers

Name	age	CMA old	revenue
Aaron Gehrhardt	68	1	7'585
Aaron Hohmann	63	0.92	7'689
Aaron Storck	69	1	3'821
Adrian Ackermann	62	0.88	4'059

Table 4. Result set of roll-up operation: revenue of customers grouped by fuzzy concept customer age

CMA	revenue
middle	21'700'295.48
old	18'347'537.72
young	10'710'068.80

not modify the revenue of those stores. So, no normalization process of the membership degrees is needed in this case. For operation where the classification is involved in the aggregation of the fact, it is necessary to weight the fact with the normalized membership degrees as explained in the revenue of customers grouped by fuzzy concept customer age example.

DISCUSSION AND CONCLUSION

In this chapter, a fuzzy data warehouse modeling approach is discussed, which allows integration of fuzzy concepts as meta-tables without affecting the core of a classical data warehouse. The key benefit of this approach is that it allows analysis of data in both sharp and fuzzy manners. Also, we presented a method that can be used to convert a classical warehouse to fuzzy warehouse. In addition to that, the aggregation, propagation of fuzzy concepts and typical operations of a data warehouse are discussed for the fuzzy data warehouse. The use of the proposed approach is demonstrated through a case study of a movie rental company.

Table 6 summarizes a comparison of the classical and the fuzzy data warehouse model in order to summarize the main advantages of the fuzzy data warehouse approach.

The absence of non-numeric terms may limit the number of users who can fully exploit the benefits of data warehouse for analysis and decision-making. By proposing the use of fuzzy we aim for an improved interpretation of warehouse data due to the use of non-numeric terms. However, the use of fuzzy concepts in data warehouse increases the size (both schema and data size) of

Table 5. Result set of dice operation: revenue of small stores grouped by region in July and August 2010

month in 2010	region	name	surface	CMA small	revenue
July	French	Store VER1	90	0.75	22'524
July	French	Store VER2	65	1	28'823
...	...	...	...	...	...
July	German	Store STG2	110	0.25	26'009
July	Italian	Store LUG2	95	0.63	27'167
August	French	Store NEU1	75	1	24'167
...	...	...	...	...	...
August	German	Store KÖ1	75	1	25'405
August	Italian	Store LUG2	95	0.63	26'254

Table 6. Comparison of classical and fuzzy data warehouse

Classical Data Warehouse	Fuzzy Data Warehouse
In a classical DWH, an instance cannot belong to more than one class at a time. Because of this, true values of the classification cannot be measured.	Classification of dimension attributes or facts in the Fuzzy DWH is done in a fuzzy manner, allowing values to belong to more than one class and the classification to be more accurate.
Qualitative interpretation of facts and dimension attributes is not supported in a classical DWH.	A Fuzzy DWH enables the use of non-numeric attributes. As a result, both qualitative and quantitative attributes can be used for analysis.
Decision-making processes are often involves business concepts. A classical DWH approach does not include any linguistic concept to interpret the data.	The definition of linguistic variables can be derived from the business environment. This reduces the effort of interpreting numeric values and facilitates decision-making processes.
Only crisp data is used for analysis and decision-making.	Both fuzzy and crisp data can be used for analysis and decision-making.
The classical schema consists of dimensions and facts.	A Fuzzy DWH schema consists of a classical schema together with fuzzy meta-tables called fuzzy classification table and fuzzy membership table.
In a classical DWH only extracted data (slices, dices, etc.) can be classified. The classification can therefore not be propagated on other hierarchy levels of dimensions.	In Fuzzy DWH, the fuzzy concepts can be propagated and/or aggregated over the dimensions in order to apply the classifications on other hierarchy levels.
The Retrieval of queries in a classical DWH is based on SQL in most cases.	A Fuzzy DWH can be queried on a linguistic level. For example, fCQL (Meier et. al. [10]) allows marketers to classify single customers or customer groups by classification predicates such as 'loyalty is high and turnover is large'.

warehouse. Also, it is expected that the increase in size of schema will have a negative effect on the performance of data warehouse i.e. an increase in execution cost of queries. A measurement of the change in cost however requires an experimental evaluation - it is a part of our future work.

From the study, we conclude the following, a) once implemented, the fuzzy approach offers interpretation of data in a more meaningful way, b) the approach offers an opportunity to support both fuzzy and crisp analysis at the same time, c) the developed method can be used to convert a classical data warehouse to a fuzzy data warehouse. Future work should include an evaluation of the affect of fuzzy approach on decision-making and an analysis of the impact of fuzzy concepts on the performance of query execution.

REFERENCES

Agrawal, R., Gupta, A., & Sarawagi, S. (1997). Modeling multidimensional databases. *Proceedings of the Thirteenth International Conference on Data Engineering*, (pp. 232–243).

Alhajj, R., & Kaya, M. (2003). Integrating fuzziness into OLAP for multidimensional fuzzy association rules mining. In *Proceedings of the Third IEEE International Conference on Data Mining*.

Burdick, D., Deshpande, P., Jayram, T., Ramakrishnan, R., & Vaithyanathan, S. (2007). OLAP over uncertain and imprecise data. *The VLDB Journal*, *16*(1), 123–144. doi:10.1007/s00778-006-0033-y

Chaudhuri, S., & Dayal, U. (1997). An overview of data warehousing and OLAP technology. *SIGMOD Record*, *26*(1), 65–74. doi:10.1145/248603.248616

Codd, E. F., Codd, S. B., & Smmalley, C. T. (1993). *Providing OLAP to user-analysts: An IT mandate*. Codd & Date Inc.

Delgado, M., Molina, C., Sanchez, D., Vila, A., & Rodriguez-Ariza, L. (2004). A fuzzy multidimensional model for supporting imprecision in OLAP. *2004 IEEE International Conference on Fuzzy Systems, 3*, (pp. 1331–1336).

Fasel, D. (2009). A fuzzy data warehouse approach for the customer performance measurement for a hearing instrument manufacturing company. In *Proceeding of Fuzzy Systems and Knowledge Discovery*. IEEE Explore. doi:10.1109/FSKD.2009.266

Fasel, D., & Shahzad, K. (2010). A data warehouse model for integrating fuzzy concepts in meta table structures. In *17th IEEE International Conference and Workshops on the Engineering of Computer-Based Systems*, (pp. 100–109). IEEE Computer Society.

Fasel, D., & Zumstein, D. (2009). A fuzzy data warehouse approach for web analytics. In M. D. Lytras, E. Damiani, J. M. Carroll, R. D. Tennyson, D. Avison, A. Naeve, … G. Vossen (Eds.), *Visioning and Engineering the Knowledge Society – A Web Science Perspective, Lecture Notes in Computer Science, volume 5736* (pp. 276–285). Springer.

Feng, L., & Dillon, T. S. (2003). Using fuzzy linguistic representations to provide explanatory semantics for data warehouses. *IEEE Transactions on Knowledge and Data Engineering, 15*(1).

Harel, D., & Rumpe, B. (2004). Meaningful modeling: What's the semantics of "semantics"? *Computer, 37*(10), 64–72. doi:10.1109/MC.2004.172

Inmon, W. H. (2005). *Building the data warehouse* (4th ed.). New York, NY: Wiley Publishing.

Kasinadh, D. P. V., & Krishna, P. R. (2007). *Building fuzzy OLAP using multi-attribute summarization*. International Conference on Computational Intelligence and Multimedia Applications.

Kimball, R., & Caserta, J. (2004). *The data warehouse ETL toolkit*. Wiley Publishing, Inc.

Kimball, R., Ross, M., Thornthwaite, W., Mundy, J., & Becker, B. (2008). *The data warehouse lifecycle toolkit* (2nd ed.). Wiley Publishing, Inc.

Kosko, B. (1990). Fuzziness vs. probability. *International Journal of General Systems, 17*(2), 211–240. doi:10.1080/03081079008935108

Kumar, K. V. N. N. P., Krishna, P. R., & Kumar De, S. (2005). Fuzzy OLAP cube for qualitative analysis. *Proceedings of ICISIP*.

Lehner, W. (1998). Modeling large scale OLAP scenarios. In *Advances in Database Technology – EDBT'98,* (vol. 1377, pp. 153–167). Springer.

Lenz, H.-J., & Shoshani, A. (1997). *Summarizability in OLAP and statistical data bases*. Statistical and Scientific Database Management.

Medina, E., & Trujillo, J. (2002). A standard for representing multidimensional properties: The common warehouse model (CWM). In Manolopoulos, Y., & Navrat, P. (Eds.), *Advances in Databases and Information Systems* (*Vol. 2435,* pp. 232–247). Lecture Notes in Computer Science Springer Verlag. doi:10.1007/3-540-45710-0_19

Meier, A., Werro, N., Albrecht, M., & Sarakinos, M. (2005). Using a fuzzy classification query language for customer relationship management. *Proceedings of the 31st VLDB Conference*.

Molina, C., Rodriguez-Ariza, L., Sanchez, D., & Vila, M. A. (2006). A new fuzzy multidimensional model. *IEEE Transactions on Fuzzy Systems, 14*(6), 897–912. doi:10.1109/TFUZZ.2006.879984

Motro, A., & Smets, P. (1997). *Uncertainty management in information systems: From needs to solutions*. Kluwer Academic Publishers. doi:10.1007/978-1-4615-6245-0

Ng, R., & Han, J. (1994). Efficient and effective clustering method for spatial data mining. In *Proceedings 1994 International Conference Very Large Databases*, (pp. 144–155).

OLAP Council. (1995). *OLAP and OLAP server definitions*. Retrieved from http://www.olapcouncil.org/research/resrchly.htm

Pedersen, T. B., & Jensen, C. S. (2001). Multidimensional database technology. *Computer, 34*(12), 40–46. doi:10.1109/2.970558

Pedersen, T. B., Jensen, C. S., & Dyreseon, C. E. (1999). *Supporting imprecision in multidimensional databases using granularities.* Eleventh International Conference on Scientific and Statistical Database Management.

Pérez, D., Somodevilla, M. J., & Pineda, I. H. (2007). *Fuzzy spatial data warehouse: A multidimensional model.* Eighth Mexican International Conference on Current Trends in Computer Science.

Rafanelli, M., & Shoshani, A. (1990). STORM: A statistical object representation model. *Statistical and Scientific Data Base Management Conference*, (pp. 14-29).

Sapir, L., Shmilovici, A., & Rokach, L. (2008). *A methodology for the design of a fuzzy data warehouse.* In Intelligent Systems, 2008. IS'08. 4th International IEEE Conference, volume 1.

Schepperle, H., Merkel, A., & Haag, A. (2004). *Erhalt von imperfektion in einem data warehouse.* Internationales Symposium: Data-Warehouse-Systeme und Knowledge-Discovery.

Shoshani, A. (1982). Statistical databases: Characteristics, problems, and some solutions. *Proceedings of the International Conference on Very Large Data Bases*, (pp. 208–222).

TMDb Inc. (2010). *The open movie data base project.* Retrieved November 21, 2010, from http://www.themoviedb.org/

Vassiliadis, P. (1998). Modeling multidimensional databases, cubes and cube operations. *Proceedings of the 10th International Conference on Scientific and Statistical Database Management.*

Zimmermann, H.-J. (1991). *Fuzzy set theory and its applications* (2nd ed.). Kluwer Academic Publishers.

KEY TERMS AND DEFINITIONS

Data Warehouse: Data storage optimized for decision making processes.

Fuzzy Classification: Classification of value based on fuzzy logic.

Fuzzy Concept: Definition and Implementation of linguistic variables in the data warehouse using meta-tables.

Fuzzy Data Warehouse: Extension of a data warehouse with meta-tables structure in order to implement fuzzy concepts.

Fuzzy Logic: Logic for mathematically describing imprecision and vagueness.

Linguistic Variable: A linguistic variable holding a set of linguistic terms, which fuzzy classifies a value range.

Meta-Model: Representation of a concept, its elements and their relations.

OLAP Cube and Operations: Online analytical processing; OLAP cube is a multidimensional representation of data; OLAP operations are predefined operations (roll-up, drill-down, slice, dice) for navigating an OLAP cube.

Chapter 11
A Fuzzy Logic Approach for the Assessment of Online Customers

Nicolas Werro
Swisscom AG, Switzerland

Henrik Stormer
Edorex Informatik AG, Switzerland

ABSTRACT

A key challenge for companies in the e-business era is to manage customer relationships as an asset. In today's global economy this task is becoming simultaneously more difficult and more important. In order to retain the potentially good customers and to improve their buying attitude, this chapter proposes a hierarchical fuzzy classification of online customers. A fuzzy classification, which is a combination of relational databases and fuzzy logic, allows customers to be classified into several classes at the same time and can therefore precisely determine the customers' value for an enterprise. This approach allows companies to improve the customer equity, to launch loyalty programs, to automate mass customization, and to refine marketing campaigns in order to maximize the customers' value and, this way, the companies' profit.

INTRODUCTION

The growing importance of e-business in today's economy forces enterprises to adapt their behaviour towards the different players in the market. This is particularly true for the customer relation-

ship management (CRM) as the traditional means based on human relationships are no longer available. In this area, the customer retention and the cross/add-on selling are special issues because the global economy enabled by the Internet allows, on the one hand, the companies to offer their

DOI: 10.4018/978-1-4666-0095-9.ch011

products or services worldwide and, on the other hand, also allows the customers to easily compare the different products/services and their prices.

This chapter proposes a new approach for managing customer relationships based on the customer equity principle by the means of a fuzzy classification (cf. Meier et. al. 2005). Unlike a sharp classification, a fuzzy classification allows elements to be classified in several classes at the same time. The notion of partial membership in the different classes provides more information by integrating the potential and the possible weaknesses of the classified elements. This approach can therefore precisely determine the customers' value according to an enterprise. In order to better retain the potentially good customers and to improve their buying attitude, the fuzzy classification approach can improve the customer equity, launch loyalty programs, automate mass customization and refine marketing campaigns. Other strengths of the fuzzy classification approach are the ability to work on a semantic level and the possibility of decomposing complex classifications into a hierarchy of classifications. The decomposition mechanism allows classifications to keep a small number of classes with a proper semantic even if many attributes are taken into account.

In practice, information systems are often based on very large data collections, mostly stored in relational databases. Due to an information overload, it is becoming increasingly difficult to analyze these collections and to generate marketing decisions (Edmunds and Morris 2000). In this context, a toolkit for the analysis of customer relationships which combines relational databases and fuzzy logic is proposed. Fuzzy logic, unlike statistical data mining techniques such as cluster or regression analysis, enables the use of non-numerical values and introduces the notion of linguistic variables. Using linguistic terms and variables results in a more human oriented querying process.

The proposed toolkit reduces the complexity of customer data and extracts valuable hidden information through a fuzzy classification. The main advantage of a fuzzy classification compared to a classical one is that an element is not limited to a single class but can be assigned to several classes. Furthermore, each element has one or more membership degrees which illustrate to what extend this element belongs to the classes it has been assigned to. The notion of membership gives a much better description of the classified elements and also helps to reveal the potential or the possible weaknesses of the considered elements.

In everyday business life, many examples can be found where fuzzy classification would be useful (Zadeh et al. 1997; Cox 1995). In CRM for instance, a standard classification would sharply classify customers of a company into a certain segment depending on their buying power, age and other attributes. If the client's potential of development is taken into account, the clients often cannot be classified into only one segment anymore, i.e. customer equity. Other examples are risk management in an insurance company or client's credit worthiness in a bank. In the last case, studies have shown that with a sharp classification, clients with almost similar risks were classified very differently. The opposite happened too, that is with clearly different properties the clients' overall judgment was very similar.

FUZZY CLASSIFICATION TOOLKIT

The proposed fuzzy classification toolkit is based on an extension of the Structured Query Language SQL. SQL is the standard for defining and querying relational databases. By adding to the relational database schema a context model with linguistic variables and fuzzy sets, the query language has to be extended. The proposed extension is the fuzzy Classification Query Language fCQL, described by Schindler (cf. Schindler 1998).

The classification language fCQL is designed in the spirit of SQL. Instead of specifying the attribute list in the select-clause, the name of the object column to be classified is given in the classify-clause. The from-clause specifies the considered relation, just as in SQL. Finally, the where-clause is changed into a with-clause which does not specify a predicate for a selection but a predicate for a classification. An example in CRM could be given as follows:

```
classify  Customer
from      CustomerRelation
with      Turnover is high and Pay-
          mentBehaviour is attrac-
          tive
```

This classification query would return the class C1 (Commit Customer). This class was defined as the aggregation of the terms 'high turnover' and 'attractive payment behaviour'. The chosen aggregation operator is the ?-operator which was suggested as compensatory and was empirically tested by Zimmermann and Zysno (cf. Zimmermann and Zysno 1980).

In this simple example, specifying linguistic variables in the with-clause is straightforward. However if customers are classified on three or more attributes, the capability of fCQL for a multi-dimensional classification space is increased. This can be seen as an extension of the classical slicing and dicing operators on a multidimensional data cube.

As noted above, the fuzzy classification is achieved by extending the relational database schema. This extension consists of meta-tables added to the system catalogue. These meta-tables contain the definition of the linguistic variables and terms, the description of the classes and all the meta-information regarding the membership functions. This approach is similar to the work done by Perez, et al. (2007).

FUZZY CUSTOMER CLASSES

Fuzzy Classification

In order to define classes in the relational database schema, we extend the relational model by a context model proposed by Chen (cf. Chen 1998). This means that to every attribute A_j defined by a domain $D(A_j)$, we add a context $K(A_j)$. A context $K(A_j)$ is a partition of $D(A_j)$ into equivalence classes. A relational database schema with contexts $R(A,K)$ is then the set $A=(A_1,...,A_n)$ of attributes with associated contexts $K=(K_1(A_1),...,K_n(A_n))$ (cf. Shenoi 1995).

To illustrate the fuzzy classification approach, a simple example of relationship management is used as a concrete fuzzy classification is presented later on. In this example, customers will be evaluated based on only two attributes turnover and payment behavior. In addition, these two qualifying attributes for customer equity will be partitioned into only two equivalence classes. The pertinent attributes and contexts for relationship management are:

- **Turnover in dollars per month:** The attribute domain is defined by [0, 1000] and is divided into the equivalence classes [0, 499] for low turnover and [500, 1000] for high turnover.
- **Payment behavior:** The domain of the attribute {in advance, on time, behind time, too late} has the two equivalence classes {in advance, on time} for an attractive payment behavior and {behind time, too late} for an unattractive one.

To derive fuzzy classes from sharp contexts, the qualifying attributes are considered as linguistic variables, and verbal terms are assigned to each equivalence class (cf. Zimmermann 1992). With the help of linguistic variables, the equivalence classes of the attributes can be described more intuitively (see Figure 1). In addition, every term

Figure 1. Linguistic variable turnover

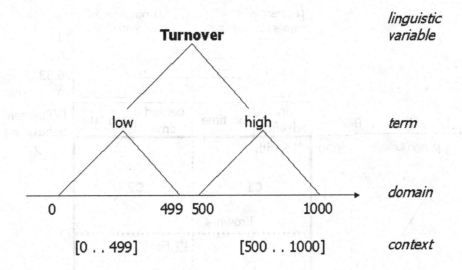

of a linguistic variable represents a fuzzy set. Each fuzzy set is determined by a membership function μ over the domain of the corresponding attribute (see Figure 2). The linguistic variables offer a more sensitive way to deal with numbers (cf. Mehta et al. (2009)

The definition of the equivalence classes of the attributes turnover and payment behavior determines a two-dimensional classification space shown in Figure 2. The four resulting classes C1 to C4 could be characterized by marketing strategies such as 'Commit Customer' (C1), 'Improve Loyalty' (C2), 'Augment Turnover' (C3), and 'Don't Invest' (C4).

With the context model, the usage of linguistic variables and membership functions, the classification space becomes fuzzy. This fuzzy partition has an important outcome, it implies the disappearance of the classes' sharp orders, i.e. there are continuous transitions between the different classes. This means that a customer can belong to more than one class at the same time and that his membership degrees in the different classes can be calculated. This precise information on the customers allows a company to correctly judge

its customers and to apply the customer equity by treating the customers according to their real value.

The selection of qualifying attributes, the introduction of equivalence classes and the choice of appropriate membership functions are important design issues. Database architects and marketing specialists have to work together in order to define an adequate fuzzy classification which will correctly express the company's viewpoint.

Customer Equity

Managing customers as an asset requires measuring and treating them according to their real value (cf. Blattberg et. al. 2001; Rust et. al. 2000). With sharp classes, i.e. traditional customer segments, this is not possible because all the elements within a class are treated the same way and there usually exists a strong discrepancy between the classes.

In Figure2 for instance, customers Brown and Ford have similar turnover as well as similar willingness to pay. However, Brown and Ford are treated differently: Brown belongs to the winner class C1 (Commit Customer) and Ford to the loser class C4 (Don't Invest). In addition, a traditional

Figure 2. Fuzzy classification with 4 example customers

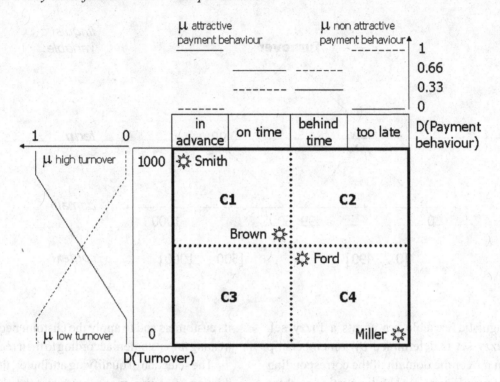

customer segment strategy treats the top rating customer Smith the same way as Brown, who is close to the loser Ford.

With a sharp classification, the following effects may happen:

- Customer Brown has no advantage of improving his turnover or his payment attitude as he already receives all the privileges of class C1.
- Brown may also be surprised and disappointed to be suddenly treated very differently if his turnover and payment behavior would slightly decrease.
- Customer Ford, who is a potentially good customer classified in the loser class, may find better opportunities elsewhere.
- More critical for the company is the fact that Smith, the most profitable customer, not being treated accordingly to his value could leave the company.

Those dilemmas can be adequately solved by the use of a fuzzy classification where the customers can belong to several classes. The notion of partial membership brings the disappearance of the sharp borders between the customer segments. Fuzzy customer classes better reflect the reality and allow companies to treat customers according to their real value. By driving the customer equity, a company can significantly improve the retention rate of potentially good to top customers.

Mass Customization

According to the customer equity principle, the fuzzy classification approach allows marketers to automate mass customization. Indeed the membership degrees of the customers in the different classes can precisely determine the privileges the customers deserve, for example a personalized discount reflecting their value for the enterprise (cf. Werro et. al. 2005). For that purpose, a discount rate can be associated with each fuzzy class: for instance C1 (Commit Customer) gets a discount rate of 10%, C2 (Improve Loyalty) a discount of 5%, C3 (Augment Turnover) 3%, and C4 (Don't Invest) 0%. The individual discount of a customer can then be calculated by the aggregation of the discount of the classes he belongs to in proportion to his membership degrees.

The top rating customer Smith belongs 100% to class C1 because he has the highest possible turnover as well as the best paying behavior; the membership of Smith in class C1 is written as Smith (C1:1.00). Customer Brown belongs to all four classes and is rated as (C1:0.28, C2:0.25, C3:0.25, C4:0.22). With a fuzzy classification, the customers of Figure 3 get the following discounts:

- Smith (C1:1.00, C2:0.00, C3:0.00, C4:0.00): 1.00*10% + 0.00*5% + 0.00*3% + 0.00*0% = 10%
- Brown (C1:0.28, C2:0.25, C3:0.25, C4:0.22): 0.28*10% + 0.25*5% + 0.25*3% + 0.22*0% = 4.8%
- Ford (C1:0.22, C2:0.25, C3:0.25, C4:0.28): 0.22*10% + 0.25*5% + 0.25*3% + 0.28*0% = 4.2%
- Miller (C1:0.00, C2:0.00, C3:0.00, C4:1.00): 0.00*10% + 0.00*5% + 0.00*3% + 1.00*0% = 0%

Using a fuzzy classification leads to a transparent and fair judgment: Smith gets the maximum discount and a better discount than Brown who belongs to the same customer class. Brown and Ford get nearly the same discount rate; they have comparable customer values although they belong to opposite classes. Miller, who sits in the same class as Ford, does not benefit from a discount.

Applying the customer equity with personalized discounts has two positive side effects apart being fair with the customers. The first one is to motivate all the customers to improve their buying attitude. For instance, with a sharp classification

the customer Brown, being in the best class, has no interest of improving his turnover or his payment behavior towards the company. With a fuzzy classification he can on the one hand get better privileges by improving his buying behavior and, on the other hand, he can concretely see his progression. The second side effect comes from the fact that only a small group of the customers in the winner class C1 (Commit Customer) gets the best discount. So if an enterprise gave 10% discount to all the customers in the sharp class C1, with a fuzzy classification it can offer to its very best customers a greater discount (20% for example) within the same discount budget. By treating accordingly the top customers, this approach strongly reinforces their loyalty towards the company.

Marketing Campaigns

Launching a marketing campaign can be very expensive. It is therefore crucial to select the most appropriate customers and then to be able to verify the impact of the marketing campaign in order to modify the target group or to improve the strategy. The fuzzy classification approach offers marketers convenient means for selecting customer subgroups and for measuring the efficiency of the marketing campaign.

One strategy example could be to select customers without payment problems and with a low turnover in order to propose them new or premium products. Using membership functions, a subset of customers in class C1 has been chosen. The application of membership functions allows marketers to dynamically modify the size of the target group in order to respect the available campaign budget. Modifying the size of the target group is also a valuable mean to increase or decrease the homogeneity between the targeted customers depending if the proposed products are very specific or intended for a large public (cf. Nguyen et. al. 2003).

Figure 3. Customer decomposition

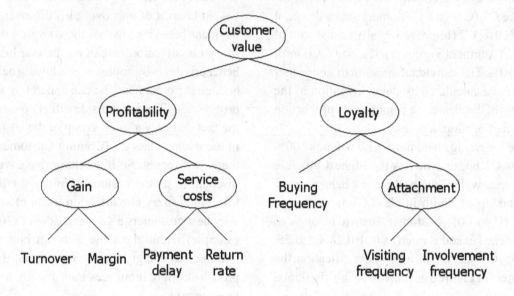

If the marketing campaign or a testing process has been launched, the fuzzy customer classes can be analyzed again. It is then possible to verify the impact of the campaign by measuring the new value of the targeted customers, i.e. if the target group has moved in the direction of class C1.

Based on the same principle, a fuzzy classification allows marketers to monitor the evolution of single customers through the classes. By comparing the value of a customer over time, it is possible to detect if this customer is increasing, maintaining or decreasing his value. Based on those observations, marketing actions can be taken on the customer level. The most pertinent application of the customers monitoring is the detection of churning customers. With the fuzzy classification approach, an automated trigger mechanism that supervises the customers' evolution based on several criteria can be easily implemented. If a good customer is suspected of having a churning behavior, an alert is sent to the marketing department which can take the appropriate action in order to retain this customer.

Web Analytics

The analysis of online customers compared to traditional ones has the advantage that a great deal of information about the customers' behavior is automatically logged in the system. If an electronic shop is considered, explicit and implicit information can be used for the analysis of the customer relationships. Explicit information is the data provided directly by the customer, like the product ratings, the forum entries and the orders, whereas implicit information is retrieved from his interaction with the system, e.g. the clickstream information. In order to analyze online customers the following information is available:

- **Orders:** The orders can determine the *turnover* and the *margin* of a customer as well as his *buying frequency*. Indirectly the *payment delay* and the *return rate* can also be identified.
- **Clickstream:** The clickstream information can establish the *visiting frequency*. Moe and Fader showed that people who

visited an online shop more frequently had a greater propensity to buy (cf. Moe and Fader 2004).

- **Product ratings:** The ratings of products can reveal the *involvement frequency*. Good ratings increase the selling of products and are the base for determining the taste of a customer, which can be used to recommend products (cf. Linden et al. 2003).

HIERARCHICAL FUZZY CLASSIFICATION

Customers can be classified based on many attributes. In the classification example shown in Figure 2, customers were only evaluated regarding the turnover and the willingness to pay. This simple example cannot be effective in real case applications. On the other hand a fuzzy classification with many linguistic variables and terms leads to a multidimensional classification space with a large number of classes. By combining all the available attributes, it may not be possible to extract a clear semantic for each resulting class. This problem, also true for sharp classifications, is partially resolved by the use of the fuzzy classes. By having a continuous transition between the classes, only few equivalence classes (linguistic terms) are required, reducing this way the number of final classes. The problem remains however for the number of dimensions (linguistic variables) which exponentially increases the number of classes. In order to keep a small number of classes with a proper semantic it is possible to decompose a complex fuzzy classification into a hierarchy of fuzzy classifications. By regrouping attributes of a given context in sub-classifications it is on the one hand possible to derive a precise definition of the classes and, on the other hand, to derive a new concept expressing a higher semantic than the basic attributes taken separately.

The decomposition principle also reduces the complexity of the initial problem allowing a better definition and optimization of the different fuzzy sub-classifications.

A good example of decomposition and a central perspective for a company is the customer loyalty. Many loyalty concepts have been proposed in the marketing literature. Harrison, for instance, proposes to express the customer loyalty based on two dimensions, the attachment and the buying behavior of the customers (cf. Harrison 2000). The resulting classification space contains four classes: class L1 (True Loyalty) is defined by a high attachment and many repurchases, class L2 (Latent Loyalty) is characterized by a high attachment but few repurchases, class L3 (Pseudo Loyalty) has many repurchases but a low attachment, and finally, class L4 (No Loyalty) has a low attachment and few repurchases.

The combination of the attributes attachment and buying behavior leads to the concept of customer loyalty which is a very important indicator for an enterprise. By assigning grades of loyalty to the fuzzy classes it is then possible to derive the grade of loyalty of the customers towards the company (i.e. the mass customization principle). The results of this fuzzy classification can either be queried normally, either be used in a higher-order fuzzy classification in order to build a hierarchy.

The decomposition principle allows marketers to merge given attributes in order to build more consistent and valuable concepts. Those concepts are then integrated as new dimensions in other fuzzy classifications. This mechanism leads to a hierarchy of fuzzy classifications. The decomposition principle can be achieved following a 'top-down' or a 'bottom-up' approach. For a fuzzy classification the 'top-down' approach means that the semantic of the desired final classes is already known. In this case, the dimensions which are defining the classes have to be determined. The dimensions can be concrete attributes or new concepts provided by sub-classifications. This process is repeated until all the fuzzy classifications are based on concrete attributes. The 'top-down' approach is particularly useful if the fuzzy classes have to be mapped with the terminology of the marketing department. The 'bottom-up' approach is more pragmatic by analyzing the available attributes and by combining them to create new concepts until the top fuzzy classification is achieved. This approach is meaningful if the top classification is not yet defined. In real cases, both approaches will often be used together due to the fact that the final classes defined with the 'top-down' approach will sometimes require attributes which are not available. Conversely, the 'bottom-up' approach often requires a marketing strategy in order to be successful.

Based on the above mentioned attributes and the decomposition principle, it is possible to build a hierarchical fuzzy classification of online customers (see Figure 3). The use of a hierarchical fuzzy classification for the analysis of customers allows marketers, on the one hand, to extract the precise value of the online customers and, on the other hand, to analyze the potential and the weaknesses of the classified customers in the different levels of the hierarchy. Indeed, each level of the hierarchy expresses a concept defined by a fuzzy classification; therefore it is possible to derive for every customer the appropriate marketing actions in order to augment their value. For instance, the marketing department can increase the profitability of the customers by analyzing them in the profitability sub-classification.

PRACTICAL EXAMPLE

The Kiel & Co Company

In order to get a representative case study, a partnership with a small-sized wholesaler company located in Bremen (Germany) has been created.

The Kiel & Co company is selling protective gear to business and private customers. Kiel & Co sells about 1'200 different products and its customer base were made up of around 6'000 customers. Within the customer base, 2'400 are active customers and from these around 200 are online customers. The average turnover per customer is approximately 500 Euro and the best customers can have a turnover up to 50'000 Euro. The products' margins can be very different depending on the product type but are comprised between 3% and 110%. However margins greater than 50% are rare and can be found only for very specialized products.

Even though most of the transactions still occur on the traditional channels, enough data could be collected in order to model a hierarchical fuzzy classification of their online customers. For the example, our selected customer profiles contain both online and off-line transactions. In contrast, their interaction profile (i.e. the visiting frequency) only reflects their online behavior. In order to derive the involvement attribute, Kiel & Co asked their customers to participate to an online survey for the evaluation of the firm's products and services. Note that for privacy reasons the customers have been anonymized.

In order to produce a faithful image of the customers, the following information is taken into account:

- **Transaction profile:** Out of the transaction profile, the turnover and the margin as well as the buying frequency of the customers can be derived. Indirectly, the payment delay and the return rate can also be extracted.
- **Interaction profile:** Based on the interaction profile, the visiting frequency can be established.

- **External data:** An online survey has been executed in order to determine the involvement frequency.

A Hierarchical Fuzzy Classification for the Customers of Kiel & Co

Based on the above-mentioned customer information, the presented hierarchical fuzzy classification can be modeled by the decomposition of two main perspectives: a financial perspective expressed by the concept of profitability and a relational perspective expressed by the concept of loyalty. Since the profitability concept shows the real contribution of the customers towards the company and that the loyalty concept is a strong indicator for predicting the future behavior of the customers, the combination of these two perspectives leads to the customer lifetime value concept.

The profitability concept representing the real contribution of the customers can be built based on the gain and the service costs concepts. On the one hand, the gain concept reflects the net income generated by the customers and can be derived from the turnover and the margin information. On the other hand, the service costs concept expresses the indirect costs incurred by the business relationship and is, for the Kiel & Co company, based on the payment delay and the return rate information.

The loyalty concept can be determined by a behavioral dimension (i.e. the repurchase rate) and an attitudinal dimension (i.e. the attachment level). The repurchase rate can be directly obtained from the buying frequency information. In contrast the attachment level is more complex to model. For instance, for Kiel & Co, the attachment concept has been modeled on the visiting frequency and on the involvement since users who visit an online shop frequently have a greater propensity to buy and that a social involvement can lead to a virtual community that increases the trust and the attachment towards the company.

Table 1 presents the selected customers as well as their respective information in order of decreasing turnover. Factory A has one of the highest turnover (58'300 Euro) with a comfortable margin of 14%. It visited the shop regularly (108 visits) and bought many items (65) which were paid within an average of 24 days. Constructor B has a relatively high turnover (15'073 Euro), a short payment delay of 11 days, however its margin, visiting and buying frequencies are much lower compared to Factory A's. Furthermore Constructor B returned 6% of its purchases. Factory C is another business customer with good visiting and buying frequencies (32 and 28) but with a relatively low turnover (6'967 Euro), a low margin (10%) and a long payment delay (26 days). Finally, Customer D, which is the only private customer in our test set, bought items for a value of only 673 Euro. His margin is however very high compared to the business customers (23%). Since private customers have to pay in advance, Customer D always has a payment delay of 0 day.

In contrast to all the other attributes, the involvement information is a qualitative attribute. As mentioned above, this attribute is based on the response to an online survey and is therefore derived from a general judgment as follows: customers who did not respond are given a "Bad" value; customers having partially filled the form are rated as "Average" whereas those who fully completed the survey have a "Good" involvement (see Table 2).

Based on the proposed hierarchical fuzzy classification, Kiel & Co is now able to derive for every online customer his customer lifetime value, his profitability level, his loyalty grade and so on. The potential and the possible weaknesses of the classified customers can therefore be precisely determined and analyzed in all levels of the hierarchy, based on either the resulting values of the modeled concepts or the semantics of the fuzzy classes they belong to.

Table 1. Customers and turnover

Customer	Turnover (in EUR)	Margin (in %)	Payment delay (in days)	Return Rate (in %)
Factory A	58000	14	24	0
Constructor B	15073	11	11	6
Factory C	6967	10	26	0
Customer D	673	23	0	0

Decomposition of the Profitability Concept

The definition of this fuzzy classification is achieved in three steps:

- First, the pertinent domain ranges have to be determined for the turnover and the margin attributes. Since the best Kiel & Co customers have a turnover of about 50'000 Euro, the domain of the attribute turnover is limited to the interval 0 to 50'000. This means that any customer having a greater turnover is classified with the maximum allowed value (i.e. 50'000 in this case). In a similar way, the margin domain range has been defined between 0 and 50 percent since most products lay in this interval.
- In a second step, based on the chosen domain definitions, the membership functions for the linguistic terms have to be defined. In this case study, all the membership functions are linear in order to be able to distinguish between all customers within the attributes' domain.
- Finally, the third step consists of assigning grades, i.e. gain grades, to the classes in order to be able to compute a gain value for each customer. For all the fuzzy classifications, the grades ranges from 0 to 100 and have been assigned linearly from the worst to the best class (see Figure 4).

Table 3 recapitulates the attributes values for turnover and margin and also indicates the gain value calculated by means of the personalized value.

Due to its maximal turnover and its good margin Factory A easily leads the gain concept with a personalized value of 79. The two other business partners are logically far behind, Constructor B being nevertheless better placed due to a much better turnover and a slightly bigger margin. Despite his tiny turnover, Customer D falls just behind Factory C since his excellent margin largely compensates his turnover.

The service costs concept reflects the indirect costs that the customers can generate by returning products and by not paying on time. The attribute return rate is the percentage of returned products; its domain has been limited to [0,10] as 10 percent is already a non-acceptable return rate for the Kiel & Co company. The payment delay attribute represents the average delay in days of a customer after the product has been shipped and

Table 2. Involvement information

Customer	Buying Frequency (frequency)	Involvement (frequency)
Factory A	65	108
Constructor B	12	25
Factory C	28	32
Customer D	11	12

Figure 4. Fuzzy classification of gain

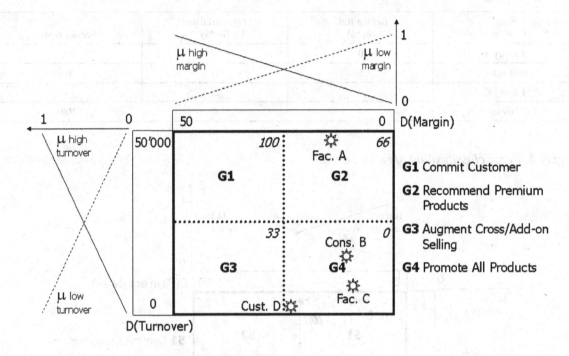

Table 3. Attributes values for turnover and margin

Customer	Turnover (in EUR)	Margin (in %)	Gain
Factory A	58000	14	79
Constructor B	15073	11	35
Factory C	6967	10	26
Customer D	673	23	21

has been defined over a domain ranging from 0 to 60. Note that the payment delay is typically an attribute which can be assessed using an overall judgment (i.e. a qualitative attribute) instead of numerical values.

Table 4 shows the service costs grades obtained based on the return rate and the payment delay values (cf. Figure 5). Note that in this case study 100 always refers to the best grade. In this classification, Customer D gets the best grade since he never returned articles and had to pay in advance according to the Kiel & Co policy. With also no return and an average payment delay, Factory A and C obtain the good personalized values of 85 and 84 respectively. Despite its relatively short

payment delay, Constructor B lags behind due to its high return rate.

The gain and service costs grades calculated in their respective fuzzy classification can now be used to define the profitability sub-classification. Since the grades for the gain and service costs concepts have both been defined on the interval [0,100], their domain definitions are logically identical.

Table 5 recalls the gain and service costs values and gives the profitability grades (cf. Figure 6). Having high gain and service costs grades, Factory A is largely ahead with a grade of 71. More surprising is the second place of Customer D with a personalized value of 56. Due to his outstanding

Table 4. Service costs grades

Customer	Return Rate (in %)	Payment delay (in %)	Service costs
Factory A	0	24	85
Constructor B	6	11	53
Factory C	0	26	84
Customer D	0	0	100

Figure 5. Fuzzy classification of service costs

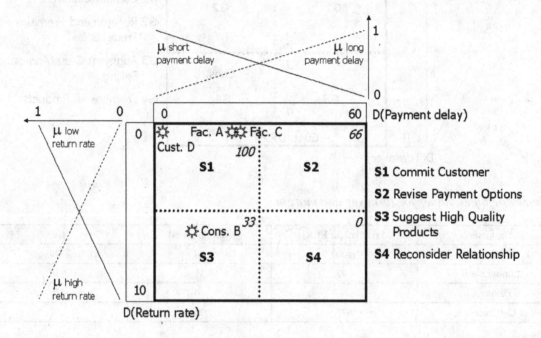

service costs performance, he can compensate his modest gain. Constructor B and Factory C get similar grades, Constructor B being ranked last due to its service costs problems.

Decomposition of the Loyalty Concept

The attachment concept can be defined in terms of visiting frequency and involvement. The involvement has a deeper meaning than the visiting frequency as sharing experiences denotes a greater attachment than just browsing an online shop. The involvement of the customers towards a company can be measured based on product ratings, forum

entries, online survey and all kinds of interactions showing an implication of the customers. Since Kiel & Co did not have enough product ratings available, the response rate to an online survey has been considered.

For the visiting frequency, the domain has been limited to the interval [0,120]. This definition comes from the observation that the best customers generally visit the shop every second working day. Thanks to its very high visiting frequency and having partially filled out the survey, Factory A gets the good grade of 70. Once again, Customer D arrives second with a score of 50 because he fully replied the questionnaire. Also, Constructor B and Factory C lay behind, Factory C having a

Table 5. Gain and service costs values

Customer	Customer Gain	Service costs	Profitability
Factory A	79	85	71
Constructor B	35	35	44
Factory C	26	84	48
Customer D	21	100	56

short lead due to its higher visiting frequency. The attachment decomposition is presented in Figure 7 and Table 6.

The loyalty sub-classification is defined by the dimensions buying behavior and attachment as proposed by Harrison (2000). In contrast to the attachment, the buying frequency or repurchases attribute can be directly derived from the order information. For Kiel & Co, the domain of the attribute buying frequency is the interval [0, 60] since good customers place around 60 orders per year.

The results of the loyalty sub-classification are shown in Table 7 (cf. Fig 8). Having an excellent buying frequency and a good attachment Factory A remains in the first position with a loyalty grade of

86. Then Factory C recovers the second place with a score of 43 having a higher buying frequency than Customer D and Constructor B. Customer D still has a slight advantage over Constructor B thanks to his attachment grade.

Customer Lifetime Value Classification

The top fuzzy classification expresses the concept of customer lifetime. It is based on the already defined concepts of customer profitability and loyalty. The profitability concept, which covers the financial context, is a major aspect as it expresses the real financial contribution of the customers towards the company. The loyalty concept, which

Figure 6. Fuzzy classification of profitability

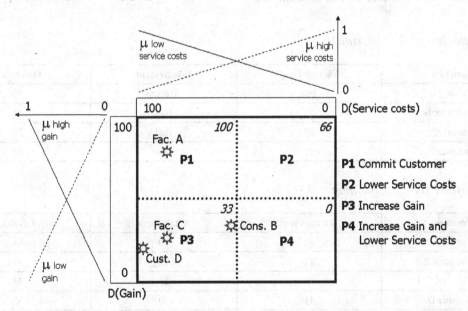

Figure 7. Fuzzy classification of attachment

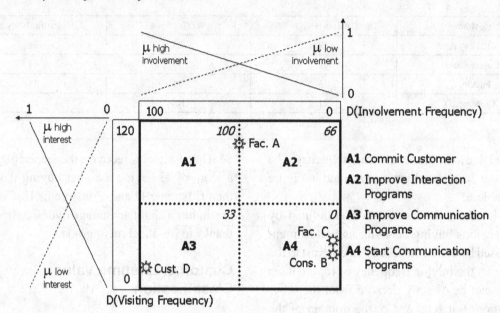

expresses the strength of the relationship between the customers and the enterprise, is a strong indicator of the customers' future buying behavior.

Table 8 shows the Customer lifetime value (CLV) of the selected customers (cf. Figure 9). Logically Factory A has the highest CLV (67) since it has a very good profitability and an excellent loyalty. The outsider of this assessment,

Customer D, takes the second place with a CLV of 49. Remember that Customer D could achieve a good profitability through a high margin, no article return and no delay in payment (by paying in advance). Finally Factory C has a better CLV than Constructor B since it has a slightly better profitability and a better loyalty.

Table 6. Attachment decomposition

Customer	Visiting Freq.	Involvement	Attachment
Factory A	108	Average	70
Constructor B	25	Bad	22
Factory C	32	Bad	25
Customer D	12	Good	50

Table 7. Loyalty sub-classification

Customer	Buying Freq.	Attachment	Loyalty
Factory A	65	70	86
Constructor B	12	22	30
Factory C	28	25	43
Customer D	11	50	35

Figure 8. Fuzzy classification of loyalty

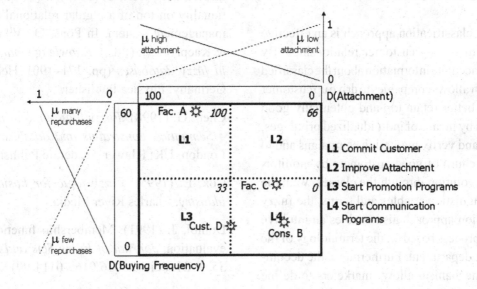

Table 8. Customer lifetime value (CLV)

Customer	Profitability	Loyalty	CLV
Factory A	71	87	67
Constructor B	44	30	42
Factory C	43	43	47
Customer D	35	35	49

Figure 9. Fuzzy classification of customer lifetime value

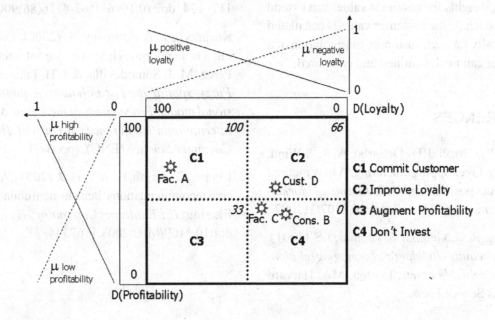

CONCLUSION AND OUTLOOK

The fuzzy classification approach is an effective mean for managing customer relationships. By providing accurate information about the classified elements, it allows companies to drive up customer equity, to better retain top and potentially good customers by means of individualized privileges, to launch and verify marketing campaigns and to avoid the churn of good customers by monitoring their evolution through the classes. With the help of linguistic variables and terms, the fuzzy classification approach also enables an intuitive querying process based on the terminology of the marketing department. Furthermore, the decomposition mechanism allows marketers to define hierarchies of fuzzy classifications in order to better model the reality and to apply appropriate marketing actions. All those tools help companies to maximize the value of their customers and, this way, their profits.

Online Shops typically have a lot of information about their customers that is usually automatically logged in the shop database. The chapter showed how this information could be used to automatically create a hierarchical fuzzy classification. Adding further customer information or using weights for customer values can extend the approach. If the customer value is calculated periodically for each customer, the evolution of a customer can be determined and compared.

REFERENCES

Arabie, P., Carroll, J. D., DeSarbo, W. S., & Wind, J. (1981). Overlapping clustering: A new method for product positioning. *JMR, Journal of Marketing Research, 18*, 310–317. doi:10.2307/3150972

Blattberg, R. C., Getz, G., & Thomas, J. S. (2001). *Customer equity - Building and managing relationships as valuable assets*. Boston, MA: Harvard Business School Press.

Bosc, P., & Pivert, O. (2000). SQLf query functionality on top of a regular relational database management system. In Pons, O., Vila, M. A., & Kacprzyk, J. (Eds.), *Knowledge management in fuzzy databases* (pp. 171–190). Heidelberg, Germany: Physica Publisher.

Chen, G. (1998). *Fuzzy logic in data modeling – Semantics, constraints and database design*. London, UK: Kluwer Academic Publishers.

Cox, E. (1995). *Fuzzy logic for business and industry*. Charles River Media.

Dombi, J. (1991). Membership function as an evaluation. *Journal of Fuzzy Sets and Systems, 35*, 1–21. doi:10.1016/0165-0114(90)90014-W

Edmunds, A., & Morris, A. (2000). The problem of information overload in business organisations: A review of the literature. *International Journal of Information Management, 20*(1), 17–28. doi:10.1016/S0268-4012(99)00051-1

Harrison, T. (2000). *Financial services marketing*. Essex, UK: Pearson Education.

Hruschka, H. (1986). Market definition and segmentation using fuzzy clustering methods. *International Journal of Research in Marketing, 3*(2), 117–134. doi:10.1016/0167-8116(86)90015-7

Kacprzyk, J., & Zadrozny, S. (2000). Data mining via fuzzy querying over the internet. In D. Perez, M. J. Somodevilla, & I. H. Pineda (Eds.). *Fuzzy spatial data warehouse: A multidimensional model, Proceedings of the Eighth Mexican International Conference on Current Trends in Computer Science* (ENC), (pp. 3-9).

Linden, G., Smith, B., & York, J. (2003). Amazon. com recommendations: Item-to-item collaborative filtering. *IEEE Internet Computing, 7*(1), 76–80. doi:10.1109/MIC.2003.1167344

Mehta, R. G., Rana, D. P., & Mukesh, A. Z. (2009). A novel fuzzy based classification for data mining using fuzzy discretization. *Proceedings of the WRI World Congress on Computer Science and Information Engineering*, (pp. 713-717).

Meier, A., Werro, N., Albrecht, M., & Sarakinos, M. (2005). Using a fuzzy classification query language for customer relationship management. *Proceedings of the 31st VLDB Conference*, Trondheim, Norway.

Moe, W. W., & Fader, P. S. (2004). Capturing evolving visit behaviour in clickstream data. *Journal of Interactive Marketing*, *18*(1), 5–19. doi:10.1002/dir.10074

Nguyen, P. T., Cliquet, G., Borges, A., & Leray, F. (2003). *L'opposition entre taille du marché et degré d'homogénéité des segments: Une approche par la logique floue* (Opposition between size of the market and degree of homogeneity of the segments: a fuzzy clustering approach). *Décisions Marketing*, *32*, 55–69.

Pons, O., Vila, M. A., & Kacprzyk, J. (Eds.). (2000). *Knowledge management in fuzzy databases* (pp. 211–233). Heidelberg, Germany: Physica Publisher.

Rust, R. T., Zeithaml, V. A., & Lemon, K. N. (2000). *Driving customer equity*. New York, NY: Free Press.

Schindler, G. (1998). *Fuzzy Datenanalyse durch Kontexbasierte Datenbankanfragen (Fuzzy data analysis through context-based database queries)*. Wiesbaden, Germany: Deutscher Universitäts-Verlag.

Setnes, M., & Kaymak, U. (2000). *Fuzzy modeling of client preference in data-rich marketing environments*. Research Paper ERS: ERS-2000-49-LIS, RSM Erasmus University.

Shenoi, S. (1995). Fuzzy sets, information clouding and database security. In Bosc, P., & Kacprzyk, J. (Eds.), *Fuzziness in database management systems* (pp. 207–228). Heidelberg, Germany: Physica Publisher.

Takahashi, Y. (1995). A fuzzy query language for relational databases. In Bosc, P., & Kacprzyk, J. (Eds.), *Fuzziness in database management systems* (pp. 365–384). Heidelberg, Germany: Physica Publisher. doi:10.1109/21.135699

Werro, N., Meier, A., Mezger, C., & Schindler, G. (2005). Concept and implementation of a fuzzy classification query language. *Proceedings of the International Conference on Data Mining, World Congress in Applied Computing*, Las Vegas.

Werro, N., Stormer, H., Frauchiger, D., & Meier, A. (2004). eSarine - A struts-based webshop for small and medium-sized enterprises. *Proceedings of the EMISA Conference - Information Systems in E-Business and E-Government*, Luxembourg.

Werro, N., Stormer, H., & Meier, A. (2005). Personalized discount - A fuzzy logic approach. *Proceedings of the 5th IFIP International Conference on eBusiness, eCommerce and eGovernment*, Poznan, Poland.

Zadeh, L. A., Bojadziev, G., & Bojadziev, M. (1997). *Fuzzy logic for business, finance and management (advances in fuzzy systems)*. World Scientific Publishing Company.

Zimmermann, H.-J. (1992). *Fuzzy set theory and its applications* (2nd ed.). London, UK: Kluwer Academic Publishers.

Zimmermann, H.-J., & Zysno, P. (1980). Latent connectives in human decision making. *Fuzzy Sets and Systems*, *4*, 37–51. doi:10.1016/0165-0114(80)90062-7

KEY TERMS AND DEFINITIONS

Customer Lifetime Value: The value of a customer containing all relevant parameters.

Customer Retention: The tie of a customer to a company.

Fuzzy Decomposition: A decomposition principle that is based on Fuzzy Logic.

Fuzzy Logic: The Fuzzy Logic definition has been created to create a reasoning that is approximate rather than accurate.

Marketing Campaign: An activity or set of activities used in marketing a product or service.

Online Shop: A shop that sells items electronically using the Internet.

Chapter 12
A Hybrid Fuzzy Multiple Objective Approach to Lotsizing, Pricing, and Marketing Planning Model

R. Ghasemy Yaghin
Amirkabir University of Technology, Iran

S.M.T. Fatemi Ghomi
Amirkabir University of Technology, Iran

ABSTRACT

Given high variability of demands, a manufacturer has to decide about the products' prices and lotsizing from a supplier. Due to imprecise and fuzzy nature of parameters such as unit costs and marketing function, a hybrid fuzzy multi-objective programming model including both quantitative and qualitative objectives is proposed to determine the optimal price, marketing expenditure, and lotsize. Considering pricing, marketing, and lotsizing decisions simultaneously, the model maximizes the profit, return on inventory investment (ROII) (as a financial performance criterion), and total customer satisfaction under general demand function with a time-varying pattern in fuzzy environment. After applying appropriate strategies to defuzzify the original model, the equivalent multi-objective crisp model is then transformed by a fuzzy goal programming method. A soft computing, particle swarm optimization (PSO) is applied to solve the final crisp problem. An industrial case study is provided to show the applicability and usefulness of the proposed model and solution method. Finally, concluding remarks are reported.

DOI: 10.4018/978-1-4666-0095-9.ch012

1. INTRODUCTION

Traditional inventory models focus on effective replenishment strategies and typically assume that a commodity's price is exogenously determined. In recent years, however, a number of industries have used innovative pricing strategies to manage their inventory effectively (Chen and Simchi-Levi, 2004). The benefits can be significant, including not only potential increases in profit, but also other improvements such as changes in demand levels or reduction in production variability, resulting in more efficient supply chains. For manufacturing industries, the coordination of price decisions with other aspects of the supply chain such as production and distribution is not only useful, but also essential. This integration of pricing, production and distribution decisions in retail or manufacturing environments is still in its early stages in many companies, but it has the potential to radically improve supply chain efficiencies in the same way as revenue management has changed airline, hotel and car rental companies (Chan et al., 2004).

The integration or coordination of production and marketing functions has been known to be crucial in practice for diminishing their conflicts and increasing a firm's profit by reducing opportunity losses incurred from separate or independent decision-making (Freeland, 1982; Kotler, 1971; Porteus and Whang, 1991; Kunreuther and Richard, 1971; Lee and Kim, 1993; Kim and Lee; 1998). One important area is joint pricing and lot sizing model (JPLM), which concerns simultaneous determination of an item's price and lot size or economic order quantity (EOQ) to maximize a firm's profit for constant but price-dependent demands over a planning horizon. Marketing expenditures which include the advertisement and promotion directly affect the demand of an item. The manufacturing companies increase the advertisement cost and give some advantages (like promotion and incentives) to their sales representatives according to their performances. The effort expended in marketing production is an important factor that is considered in JPLM. The marketing effort influences demand and, consequently, the firm profit. Marketing effort motivates sales and influences potential consumers with an immediate reason to buy (Huang and Li, 2001).

Traditionally, numerous papers have employed the profit maximization or cost minimization as their objective in designing and analyzing inventory models. Many researchers also optimized the inventory systems under return on investment (ROI) maximization. An inventory model using the criterion of ROI maximization is proposed by Schroeder and Krishnan (1976). Also, Rosenberg (1991) compares and contrasts profit maximization vs. return on inventory investment with respect to logarithmic concave demand functions. Otake et al. (1999) proposed an ROI maximization model with the lot size and setup cost reduction investment as the strategic joint decision variables. Otake and Min (2001) constructed and analyzed inventory and investment in quality improvement policies under ROI maximization. Recently, Li et al. (2008) constructed and analyzed inventory and capital investment in setup and quality under ROI maximization. Wee et al. (2009) proposed a joint replenishment model under profit and ROI maximization. Although the above researches are abundant, few studies have simultaneously considered profit and ROII maximization as performance criteria for the shortage constrained inventory model (Wee et al., 2009).

It is often difficult to determine the actual inventory parameters of the inventory problem. So the inventory cost parameters are assumed to be flexible, i.e., fuzzy in nature (Mandal et al., 2005). Due to the limitation on historical data, most of the input data and related parameters are not known with certainty because of incompleteness and/or unavailability of required data and expressed by imprecise terms (e.g., around $200). In addition, the decision maker (DM) often can not fit some probability distribution with certainty for uncertain parameters. The decisions made on the basis of stochastic models can only take the form of a distribution function, which can do little to help decision making in practical situations. However, such fuzziness in the critical data can not be represented in a deterministic or stochastic formulation and therefore the corresponding optimal results may not serve the real purpose of modeling. In reality, data on marketing expenditure are less readily available. Therefore, real-life scenarios require marketing parameters to be of imprecise type i.e. uncertainty is to be imposed in non-stochastic sense. Furthermore, a DM often has vague goals such as "This profit functions should be larger than or equal to a certain value." For such cases, fuzzy set theory and fuzzy mathematical programming methods should be used (Wee et al., 2009).

The aim of this paper is to propose a hybrid multi objective integrated pricing and lotsizing model in a fuzzy environment. The three important objective functions, i.e., profit, return on inventory investment (ROII) and a qualitative objective related to customer satisfaction (stated with linguistic terms) to find economic production quantity are considered. This area integrates three main decision criteria: profit, ROII and marketing-inventory model into a single model. Notably, in an inventory and marketing planning, objectives' goals, unit costs and marketing parameters, etc. are often assumed to be crisp and defined with certainty. But in practice, this is seldom the case so that the goals and parameters are normally vague and imprecise. Therefore, this paper presents a fuzzy multi objective programming method to capture this inherent fuzziness in the critical data and goals.

The reminder of this chapter is organized as follows. In the next section, the relevant literature is reviewed. Main focus of the chapter, problem description, assumptions and formulation are presented in Sections 3 and 4. Then, through applying efficient defuzzification strategy, the resultant equivalent crisp model is solved with fuzzy goal programming in Sections 5 and 6. Sections 7 and 8 present particle swarm optimization for solving final nonlinear optimization and case study example. Finally, Section 9 is devoted to concluding remarks and future research direction.

2. BACKGROUND

Several researchers have considered joint pricing and lotsizing models where demand depends on price or other factors over a planning horizon. For instance, Kim and Lee (1998) have determined the optimal values of selling price and order quantity in the fixed and variable capacity of a firm where demand is price-sensitive. Lee and Kim (1993) presented a model to determine optimal price, marketing expenditure, demand or production volume, and lot size for a firm. Their demand was sensitive to selling price and marketing expenditure. In the similar demand function, Lee (1993) introduced and compared the results obtained between models with and without discount for finding lot size and selling price. Esmaeili et al. (2009a and 2009b) have used similar approaches in a seller–buyer supply chain in two forms. In the first one, the buyer determined the lot size, while in the second form, the lot size is determined by the seller. Sadjadi et al. (2005) present a joint production, marketing and inventory model which determines the production lot size, marketing expenditure and product's selling price when demand and production have linear relationship. Abad (1988) considered a model where a supplier offers a discount to the retailers to obtain an optimal selling price and lot size for two classes of demand functions, iso-elastic and linear. Quantity discount is also considered by Lee (1993), Corbett and de Groote (2000) and

Esmaeili et al. (2007). Under a general demand function, Esmaeili (2009) used a new approach in JPLM including the marketing effort to increase profit for the manufacturer.

However, the primary concern on most of the previous inventory and marketing models focused on single objective. The assumption that firms always seek to maximize (or minimize) their profit (or cost) rather than making tradeoffs among multiple objectives has been criticized for a long time. The decision making situations become more complex and as the competitive environment develops, businesspersons are finding that they require deeming multiple objectives. Almost every imperative real world problem involves more than one objective. In the field of multiple objective inventory marketing research, Islam (2008) formulates a multi-objective marketing planning inventory model where the space capacity and the shortage are considered. He considered two objectives including total average inventory related cost and total additional cost. A multi-objective joint replenishment inventory model of deteriorating items is developed by Wee et al. (2009). Their model maximizes the profit and return on inventory investment (ROII) under fuzzy demand and shortage cost constraint. These studies on inventory planning did consider only marketing effort in order to determine order lot size without any consideration of pricing decisions.

The above mentioned works assume all required data can be precisely determined. In general, an inventory model involves "fuzziness" since the decision makers frequently use insufficient and imprecise data especially data on marketing environment are less sufficient due to the limitation on historical data and are typically fuzzy in nature. Moreover, it is often difficult to determine the actual inventory costs of the inventory problem. They fluctuate depending upon different aspects. So the inventory cost parameters are assumed to be flexible, i.e., fuzzy in nature (Mandal et al., 2005). Also, in the inventory planning context, various fuzzy models have been developed to determine ordering decisions among them we can refer to Mandal et al. (2005). Sadjadi et al. (2010) proposed a possibilistic geometric model for pricing and marketing planning and designed a fuzzy logic controller where demand and order lot-size are functions of price and marketing expenditures.

3. MAIN FOCUS OF THE CHAPTER

3.1. Issues, Controversies, Problems

In light of the lack of research dealing with multi-objective marketing inventory planning in joint pricing and lotsizing models, we developed a novel fuzzy multi objective integrated pricing and lotsizing decisions under a general demand function. Recently, due to the phenomenon of product life cycle, demand pattern plausibly is assumed to be time dependent in inventory literature. The proposed demand can have a general function with a time-varying pattern. To the best of our knowledge, there is no research work integrating hybrid multi objective optimization in joint pricing and lotsizing literature in a fuzzy environment. Hybrid means that it includes both quantitative and qualitative objectives. Wee et al. (2009) mentioned few papers have simultaneously considered profit and ROII maximization as performance criteria for inventory control and this unexplored area is important and interesting. Therefore, we consider a multi objective model including profit, ROII (as quantitative objectives) and also customer satisfaction (as a qualitative objective) maximization and develop a comprehensive hybrid fuzzy multi-objective model to determine the joint pricing, lotsizing and marketing plan of the manufacturer which hereafter is called the H-FMOJPLM model.

3.2. Solutions and Recommendations

The main contributions of this chapter can be summarized as follows. First, it introduces a novel fuzzy multi-objective model for jointly making some major inventory marketing decisions for manufacturer. Second, under the finite replenishment rate, we propose fuzzy general demand function with time-varying pattern. Third, using ROII maximization as a financial performance criterion, our area integrates three main decision criterions: profit, ROII and marketing-inventory model into a single model. Fourth, by including both qualitative and quantitative objectives, the implicit opinions of decision makers are complied as well. Fifth, customer satisfaction is involved by linguistic terms in the proposed model. Sixth, a soft computing, particle swarm optimization (PSO), is applied to solve the final crisp non-linear problem.

Totally, the proposed methodology could be used by manufacturing industries dealing with pricing and inventory decisions and trying to perfect science of marketing management.

4. PROBLEM DEFINITION AND FORMULATION

Various notations and their definitions used in proposed H-FMOJPLM are as follows:

4.1. Decision Variables and Input Parameters

P Selling price (decision variable)

M Marketing expenditure per unit (\$/unit) (decision variable)

T Duration of inventory cycle/cycle time (decision variable)

λ Production time in time cycle T

k_0 Setup cost (\$/setup)

R Production rate for the item (units/period)

$\tilde{c}_0$ Production cost per unit (\$/unit)

$\tilde{c}_h$ Holding cost per unit (\$/per unit)

$\tilde{c}_p$ Purchasing price per unit (\$/unit)

$I(t)$ Net inventory level at time t

$g(.)$ Consumer demand

$B(M)$ Marketing function; for notational simplicity, we use B and B(M) interchangeably

$D(P)$ Demand rate (units/period); for notational simplicity, we use D and D(P) interchangeably

$f(t)$ Demand rate at time t

M^{max} Maximum allowed total marketing cost

4.2. Assumptions

The main assumptions and characteristics used in H-FMOJPLM are as follows:

- There is a single product in the system.
- Inventory shortages are not allowed.
- The planning horizon is infinite.
- The replenishment rate is finite and more than the demand rate.
- The product is not perishable.
- The maximum marketing cost is limited.
- Demand is applied by a general function of price that is not specific, such as the models proposed by Kim and Lee (1998), Lee (1993) and Abad (1988).
- It is assumed that marketing effort is a function of marketing expenditure similar to Huang and Li (2001) and Esmaeili (2009) with fuzzy parameters.
- Demand response curve is an improved version of the general demand function proposed by Esmaeili (2009) and can be affected by price, marketing expenditure and time.
- Due to incompleteness and/or unavailability of required data over the life cy-

Figure 1. The membership function of trapezoidal fuzzy number $\tilde{a}$

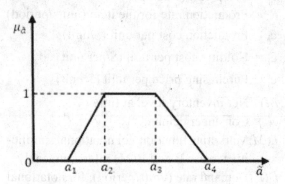

Figure 2. Graphical representation of inventory model over time

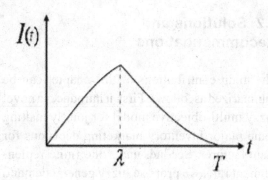

cles, critical parameters (such as unit costs and marketing inputs) are imprecise (fuzzy) in nature. Furthermore, the pattern of triangular or trapezoidal fuzzy numbers is adopted to represent each fuzzy parameter. Figure 1 presents a trapezoidal fuzzy number $\tilde{a} = (a_1, a_2, a_3, a_4)$. The parameters of $\tilde{a}$ are estimated by the decision maker. Noteworthy, for $a_2 = a_3$, a triangular fuzzy number could be obtained.

The net inventory system of a manufacturer discussed here is depicted graphically in Figure 2. The net inventory system can be achieved through the following computations:

4.3. Proposed Demand Function

There are many forms of demand functions. Marketing expenditures and pricing are the two familiar and mostly applying tools which can change the market demands considerably. Marketing expenditures which include the advertisement and promotion directly affect the demand of an item. The manufacturing companies increase the advertisement cost and give some advantages (like promotion and incentives) to their sales representatives according to their performances.

Various demand functions affected by price and advertising have been proposed to estimate the future demands.

If customers' willingness to pay does not increase over time, retailers can enhance their sales with price reduction and marketing tools. Various demand functions affected by price and marketing expenditures have been proposed to estimate the future demands. In reality, the demand may also vary with product life cycle duration. The assumption of a constant demand rate is usually valid in the maturity stage (Dye and Hsieh, 2010). Here, we propose the consumer demand function as follows:

$$g(t, P, M) = D(P)B(M)f(t) \qquad (1)$$

where $f(t)$ is a positive and continuous function of time, $D(P)$ is any non-negative, continuous, convex, decreasing function of the selling price and $B(M)$ is a positive and continuous function of marketing expenditure. In other words, the demand is defined as a function of price (P), marketing expenditure (M) with time-varying pattern. The proposed demand function has a general function in this approach. Moreover, marketing effort is allowed to be independent of selling price function. The marketing effort as a separated function is a function of marketing expenditure and has an effect on the demand. Utilizing a multiplicative effect by price and marketing expenditure to model consumer demand was seen in the literature (e.g. Esmaeili, 2009). Marketing effort is considered according to the following equation with fuzzy parameters: where

$$B(M) = \tilde{k} - e^{-\tilde{\beta}M} \qquad (2)$$

$\tilde{k}$ and $\tilde{\beta}$ are the scaling constants for marketing function. The assumption of a constant demand rate is usually valid in the maturity stage (Dye and Hsieh, 2010). In reality, the demand may vary with product life cycle. Therefore, the proposed demand function reflects demand feature of product life cycle by $f(t)$. The required parameters of demand function can be easily estimated by regression analysis.

During the production run $[0,\lambda)$ the rate of inventory increase is the production rate minus the consumer demand.

$$\frac{\partial I(t)}{\partial t} = R - D(P)B(M)f(t) \qquad (3)$$

with the boundary condition $I(0) = 0$. When no production in $[\lambda,T]$, the inventory decreases due to the demand.

$$\frac{\partial I(t)}{\partial t} = -D(P)B(M)f(t) \qquad (4)$$

with the boundary condition $I(T) = 0$. If $f(t) = e^{-\theta t}$, the sales trend over product life cycle is characterized by the positive value of θ which represents downward demand rate over time and exponential obsolesce factor. Therefore, the solutions of differentials (3) and (4) are respectively given by

$$I(t) = \int (R - D(P)B(M)f(t))dt, \qquad I(0) = 0 \; t\epsilon[0,\lambda) \qquad (5)$$

$$I(t) = \int (-D(P)B(M)f(t))dt, \qquad I(T) = 0, \; t\epsilon[0,\lambda) \qquad (6)$$

From (5) and (6), we have

$$I(t) = Rt - \frac{1}{\theta}D(P)B(M)\left(1 - e^{-\theta t}\right), \qquad t \in [0,\lambda) \qquad (7)$$

$$I(t) = \frac{1}{\theta}D(P)B(M)\left(e^{-\theta t} - e^{-\theta T}\right), \qquad t \in [\lambda,T] \qquad (8)$$

4.4. Mathematical Model

4.4.1. Objective Functions

The manufacturer's model is to determine P, M and T in a three-objective optimization manner: the total profit of manufacturer, the return on inventory investment (quantitative objectives) and service aspects of retailing (a qualitative objective).

4.4.1.1. Quantitative Objective Functions

The problem is to maximize the average profit objective of the manufacturer and return on inventory investment. The annual profit of model is expressed as manufacturer's profit = sales revenue– (production cost + marketing cost + ordering cost + holding cost) and return on inventory investment objective is defined as the ratio of the profit over the average investment. For inventory cycle of time span $[0,T]$, the following relations would be derived

The sales revenue is given by

$$\frac{1}{\theta} PD(P)B(M)\left(1-e^{-\theta T}\right) \tag{9}$$

The marketing cost is given by

$$\frac{1}{\theta} MD(P)B(M)\left(1-e^{-\theta T}\right) \tag{10}$$

The production cost is given by

$$\tilde{c}_0 R\lambda \tag{11}$$

The ordering cost is

$$k_0 \tag{12}$$

The holding cost is given by

$$
\begin{aligned}
\widetilde{c_h} \int_0^T I(t)\,dt &= \widetilde{c_h}\left(\int_0^\lambda I(t)\,dt + \int_\lambda^T I(t)\,dt\right) \\
&= \widetilde{c_h}\left[\frac{R}{2}\lambda^2 - D(P)B(M)\left(e^{-\lambda\theta}+\frac{\lambda}{\theta}-1\right)\right. \\
&\quad + D(P)B(M)(e^{-\lambda\theta}-e^{-\theta T}) \\
&\quad \left. + \frac{1}{\theta}D(P)B(M)e^{-\theta T}(\lambda-T)\right]
\end{aligned}
\tag{13}
$$

From Equations (9)–(13), the average profit, AP, is

$$
\begin{aligned}
\widetilde{AP}(T,P,M) = \frac{1}{T}\Bigg\{ &\frac{1}{\theta}PD(P)B(M)\left(1-e^{-\theta T}\right) - \tilde{c}_0 R\lambda \\
&- \frac{1}{\theta}MD(P)B(M)\left(1-e^{-\theta T}\right) - k_0 \\
&- \widetilde{c_h}\left[\frac{R}{2}\lambda^2 - D(P)B(M)\left(e^{-\lambda\theta}+\frac{\lambda}{\theta}-1\right)\right. \\
&\quad + D(P)B(M)\left(e^{-\theta\lambda}-e^{-\theta T}\right) \\
&\quad \left.\left. + \frac{1}{\theta}D(P)B(M)e^{-\theta T}(\lambda-T)\right]\right\}
\end{aligned}
\tag{14}
$$

The average inventory investment, AI, is

$$
\begin{aligned}
\widetilde{AI}(T,P,M) = \\
\frac{\tilde{c}_p}{T}\Bigg[&\frac{R}{2}\lambda^2 - D(P)B(M)\left(e^{-\lambda\theta}+\frac{\lambda}{\theta}-1\right) \\
&+ D(P)B(M)\left(e^{-\theta\lambda}-e^{-\theta T}\right) \\
&+ \frac{1}{\theta}D(P)B(M)e^{-\theta T}(\lambda-T)\Bigg]
\end{aligned}
\tag{15}
$$

Based on the classical inventory model described by Tersine (1994), λ is $D(P)B(M)(1-e^{-\theta T})/\theta R$. Then the return on inventory investment is

$$\widetilde{ROII}(T,P,M) = \widetilde{AP}(T,P,M) / \widetilde{AI}(T,P,M) \tag{16}$$

4.4.1.2. Qualitative Objective Function

A differentiation for manufacturers can be realized by their services, so that the service aspects of company are considered as the third objective here. Also, a comprehensive literature review provided by Mulhern (1997) concludes that very little research has addressed the service aspects of retailing. In this paper, by considering after sale services and on time delivery as two main criteria for customer satisfaction, the service-oriented retailing is addressed by a linguistic term similar to that of Jamalnia and Soukhakian (2009). Therefore, the qualitative objective is described as follows: customer satisfaction (CS) from the manufacturer about the mentioned issues should be "Rather High". More details related to mathematical modeling of this objective are given in subsection 6.1.

4.4.2. Model Constraints

Total marketing cost:

Table 1. Equation 19

$$
\begin{aligned}
\text{Max} \quad & \widetilde{AP}(T,P,M) = \frac{1}{T}\Bigg[\frac{1}{\theta}PD(P)B(M)\left(1-e^{-\theta T}\right) - \frac{1}{\theta}\tilde{c}_0 D(P)B(M)\left(1-e^{-\theta T}\right) \\
& -\frac{1}{\theta}MD(P)B(M)\left(1-e^{-\theta T}\right) - k_0 - \tilde{c}_h\Bigg[\frac{D^2 B^2(1-e^{-\theta T})^2}{2R\theta^2} \\
& -D(P)B(M)\Bigg(e^{-\frac{D(P)B(M)(1-e^{-\theta T})}{R}} + \frac{D(P)B(M)(1-e^{-\theta T})}{\theta^2 R} - 1\Bigg) \\
& +D(P)B(M)\Bigg(e^{-\frac{D(P)B(M)(1-e^{-\theta T})}{R}} - e^{-\theta T}\Bigg) \\
& +\frac{1}{\theta}D(P)B(M)e^{-\theta T}\Bigg(\frac{D(P)B(M)(1-e^{-\theta T})}{\theta R}-T\Bigg)\Bigg]\Bigg] \\[2mm]
\text{Max} \quad & \widetilde{ROII}(T,P,M) = \widetilde{AP}(T,P,M)\Bigg/\Bigg\{\frac{\tilde{c}_p}{T}\Bigg[\frac{D^2 B^2(1-e^{-\theta T})^2}{2R\theta^2} \\
& -D(P)B(M)\Bigg(e^{-\frac{D(P)B(M)(1-e^{-\theta T})}{R}} + \frac{D(P)B(M)(1-e^{-\theta T})}{\theta^2 R} - 1\Bigg) \\
& +D(P)B(M)\Bigg(e^{-\frac{D(P)B(M)(1-e^{-\theta T})}{R}} - e^{-\theta T}\Bigg) \\
& +\frac{1}{\theta}D(P)B(M)e^{-\theta T}\Bigg(\frac{D(P)B(M)(1-e^{-\theta T})}{\theta R}-T\Bigg)\Bigg]\Bigg\} \\[2mm]
\text{Max} \quad & CS \\[2mm]
\text{Subject to} \quad & \frac{1}{\theta}MD(P)B(M)\left(1-e^{-\theta T}\right) \le M^{max} \\
& T > 0 \\
& P,M \ge 0
\end{aligned}
$$

(19)

$$\frac{1}{\theta}MD(P)B(M)\left(1-e^{-\theta T}\right) \le M^{max} \qquad (17)$$

constraint (17) is the limitation of marketing cost.

Moreover, the non-negativity constraints of decision variables are as follow:

$$T > 0$$
$$P, M \ge 0 \qquad (18)$$

Finally, the proposed hybrid fuzzy multi-objective pricing and lotsizing model with total marketing cost constraint is formulated as presented in Table 1.

CS means customer satisfaction from the company attempts about the issues such as sale services and on time delivery.

5. FUZZY MATHEMATICAL ANALYSIS

With respect to the above-mentioned objective functions and constraints, we are dealing with a hybrid multi-objective possibilistic non-linear programming model. Some input parameters such as inventory costs and marketing parameters in marketing function may be ambiguous.

The fuzzy set theory and the possibility theory (Zadeh, 1978) may provide alternatives which are simpler and less data-demanding than the probability theory to cope with the uncertainties.

Before making a decision, decision-makers have to assess the alternatives with fuzzy numbers and rank them accordingly. It can be seen that ranking fuzzy numbers is a very important procedure in solving the fuzzy programming problem. In reality, decision-makers having different viewpoints will give different ranking outcomes under the same situation. Therefore, a number of methods have been proposed for ranking fuzzy numbers. A relatively simple computation and easily understood method proposed by Liou and Wang (1992) is considered in this paper such as related work Mandal et al. (2005).

Definition 5.1. (Dubois and Prade (1978)). A fuzzy number $\tilde{a}$ is a fuzzy set defined on the real line $\boldsymbol{R}$ whose membership function $f_{\tilde{a}}(x)$ has the following characteristics with $-\infty \leq \alpha \leq \beta \leq \gamma \leq \delta \leq \infty$:

$$f_{\tilde{a}}(x) = \begin{cases} f_{\tilde{a}}^{L}(x), & \alpha \leq x \leq \beta \\ 1, & \beta \leq x \leq \gamma \\ f_{\tilde{a}}^{R}(x), & \gamma \leq x \leq \delta \\ 0, & otherwise \end{cases}$$

where $f_{\tilde{a}}^{L} : [\alpha, \beta] \rightarrow [0,1]$ is the left membership function of fuzzy number $\tilde{a}$, continuous and strictly increasing in $[\alpha, \beta]$, and $f_{\tilde{a}}^{R} : [\gamma, \delta] \rightarrow [0,1]$ is the right membership function of fuzzy number $\tilde{a}$, continuous and strictly decreasing in $[\gamma, \delta]$..

Many different membership functions can be defined for fuzzy numbers that possess the abovementioned characteristics. Almost in fuzzy programming models, triangular and trapezoidal fuzzy numbers have been used.

Definition 5.2. Let $\tilde{a}$ be a fuzzy number with left membership function $f_{\tilde{a}}^{L}$ and right membership function $f_{\tilde{a}}^{R}$. The total expected value of $\tilde{a}$ with an index of optimism $\alpha \epsilon [0,1]$ is defined as

$$EV_{\alpha}(\tilde{a}) = \alpha EI(\tilde{a})^{R} + (1-\alpha) EI(\tilde{a})^{L} \qquad (20)$$

where $EI(\tilde{a})^{R}$ and $EI(\tilde{a})^{L}$ are the right and left expected values of $\tilde{a}$, respectively defined as

$$EI(\tilde{a})^{R} = \int_{\gamma}^{\beta} x f_{\tilde{a}}^{R}(x) dx \qquad (21)$$

$$EI(\tilde{a})^{L} = \int_{\gamma}^{\beta} x f_{\tilde{a}}^{L}(x) dx \qquad (22)$$

The parameter $\alpha \in [0, 1]$ reflects the decision maker's degree of optimism so that a larger value of α indicates a higher degree of optimism. More specifically, when $\alpha = 0, EV_{0}(\tilde{a}) = EI(\tilde{a})^{L}$ represents a pessimistic decision maker's viewpoint. For an optimistic decision-maker, we would have: $\alpha = 1$, $EV_{1}(\tilde{a}) = EI(\tilde{a})^{R}$. For a moderately optimistic decision-maker, with $\alpha = 0.5$, $EV_{0.5}(\tilde{a}) = (EI(\tilde{a})^{R} + EI(\tilde{a})^{L}) / 2$ (Li and Lai, 2001).

Therefore, to resolve the imprecise parameters in the mathematical model, the total expected value method with an index of optimism Li and Lai, (2001) and Mandal et al. (2005) is used for the defuzzification process and converting the fuzzy parameters into crisp numbers.

In addition, this model considers a qualitative objective (stated with linguistic terms) that decision makers may have. Qualitative objectives are usually stated by linguistic terms such as "Rather High" or "Very High". The concept of a fuzzy linguistic variable is very useful in dealing with the situations which are too complex or too ill-defined to be reasonably described in conventional quantitative expressions (Li and Lai, 2001). A linguistic variable can be regarded either as a variable whose value is a fuzzy number or as a variable whose values are defined in linguistic terms. We will use the triangular fuzzy numbers as membership functions of the qualitative objective to quantify it. More details of modeling the linguistic terms are given in subsection 6.1.

6. A FUZZY GOAL PROGRAMMING MODEL FOR H-FMOJPLM

There are several methods in the literature for solving multi-objective optimization models, among them, the fuzzy programming approaches are being increasingly applied. Fuzzy goal programming is the most common approach to solve such vector optimization problems enabling the DM to represent his/her fuzzy goals and reducing the equivalent multiple objective mathematical programming into a scalar (single objective) formulation. For example, a DM may feel that the goals should be "somewhat larger than g^{0}", "substantially less than g^{1}" or "around g^{2}", the vague goals.

In most literature on fuzzy goal programming for each objective, a deterministic model is independently solved and then the optimized values obtained to each goal are used as an aspiration level to define membership functions. Because our model includes qualitative objectives, it can not be solved before it is fuzzified. Therefore we use the decision maker's judgment to construct membership functions. We present qualitative objective in the fuzzy linguistic variable form where the fuzzy linguistic variable values are in a finite set of natural evaluation words or phrases such as good, high and etc. Distinct membership

functions are introduced for quantitative and qualitative objective functions. After that, the crisp multi objective non-linear programming model will be transformed to a hybrid fuzzy goal programming model.

6.1. Defining a Membership Function for the Qualitative Objective

We have one qualitative objective expressed with linguistic terms. We apply fuzzy number to represent linguistic variable. Many different membership functions can be defined for fuzzy numbers. A special example is the trapezoidal function (Figure 1).

Triangular and trapezoidal fuzzy numbers are symmetric and have unique maximum value in their membership functions degrees. These properties make them more suitable for fitness to linguistic terms features. In other words these properties help the triangular and trapezoidal fuzzy numbers to suitably explain treatment of linguistic variables (Jamalnia and Soukhakian, 2009).

This paper considers the linguistic value set $L=\{VL, L, RL, M, RH, H, VH\}$, where VL, L, RL, M, RH, H and VH denote Very Low, Low, Rather Low, Medium, Rather High, High and Very High, respectively. Figure 3 depicts membership functions for linguistic terms of qualitative objective - customer satisfaction from the manufacturer about the issues such as on time deliveries and after sale services should be "*Rather High*". It is assumed that customer satisfaction is in interval [0,100] in percentage and characterized by triangular fuzzy numbers as seen in Table 2.

Table 2. Triangular fuzzy numbers

$$VL = (0, 0, 10), \quad \mu_{VL}(x) = \begin{cases} \frac{1}{10}(10 - x) & 0 \leq x \leq 10 \\ 0 & otherwise \end{cases}$$

$$L = (5, 15, 25), \quad \mu_L(x) = \begin{cases} \frac{1}{10}(x - 5) & 5 \leq x \leq 15 \\ \frac{1}{10}(25 - x) & 15 \leq x \leq 25 \end{cases}$$

$$RL = (20, 30, 40), \quad \mu_L(x) = \begin{cases} \frac{1}{10}(x - 20) & 20 \leq x \leq 30 \\ \frac{1}{10}(40 - x) & 30 \leq x \leq 40 \end{cases}$$

$$M = (35, 50, 65), \quad \mu_M(x) = \begin{cases} \frac{1}{15}(x - 35) & 35 \leq x \leq 50 \\ \frac{1}{15}(65 - x) & 50 \leq x \leq 65 \end{cases}$$

$$RH = (60, 70, 80), \quad \mu_{RH}(x) = \begin{cases} \frac{1}{10}(x - 60) & 60 \leq x \leq 70 \\ \frac{1}{10}(80 - x) & 70 \leq x \leq 80 \end{cases}$$

$$H = (75, 85, 90), \quad \mu_H(x) = \begin{cases} \frac{1}{10}(x - 75) & 75 \leq x \leq 85 \\ \frac{1}{10}(90 - x) & 85 \leq x \leq 90 \end{cases}$$

$$VH = (90, 100, 0), \quad \mu_{VH}(x) = \begin{cases} \frac{1}{10}(x - 90) & 90 \leq x \leq 100 \\ 0 & otherwise \end{cases}$$

6.2 Defining Membership Functions for the Quantitative Objectives

In a fuzzy decision environment, the fuzzy goals are defined by their associated membership functions. A linear membership function is usually applied in practice (Yaghoobi and Tamiz, 2007). Here, the linear membership function is used as presented in Table 3. where AP^0 and $ROII^0$ are the lower tolerance limits for the fuzzy goals and $\mu_{\widetilde{AP}}$ and $\mu_{\widetilde{ROII}}$ indicate the achievement degree of the fuzzy goals. The above membership function is depicted in Figure 4.

Applying fuzzy non-linear programming method and using max–min as the operator, a max–min model for Problem (19) can be stated as presented in Table 4.

μ is the minimum of the membership values of the objectives and it is tried to maximize μ, the overall satisfactory level. More details about the above formulation can be found in fuzzy goal programming literature (e.g. Yaghoobi and Tamiz, 2007).

7. PARTICLE SWARM OPTIMIZATION

Particle swarm optimization (PSO) is an evolutionary algorithm introduced by Eberhart and Kennedy (1995). A study by Pilo et al. (2007) reflects that particle swarm optimization is exponentially growing. The particle swarm optimization is an algorithm for searching optimal solutions of complex problems through the interaction of individuals in a population of particles. Many researchers have widely applied PSO for solving optimization problems (e.g. Tsou, 2008; Dye and Hsieh, 2010; Zhao et al., 2010).

PSO is a form of swarm intelligence and is based on the simulation of the behavior of bird flocking or fish schooling. Assume that problem search space is d-dimensional. In PSO, at first a set of random particles (population) is initialized in the search space represented by a d-dimensional vector. In this algorithm, birds are particles and the position of each particle represents a potential solution to the problem. The performance of each solution is appraised with fitness function. In fact, every particle in the swarm is described by position and velocity. The velocity of each particle determines the change of its position and flying direction. To find the optimal solution, each particle regulates its flying according to its own flying experience (cognition part) and its companions' flying experience (social part). The first one is the previous best position of each particle and it is called pbest. The second one is the previous best position attained by any particle in swarm and it is called gbest. In

Figure 3. Membership functions for linguistic terms of qualitative service aspect of retailing objective-customer satisfaction

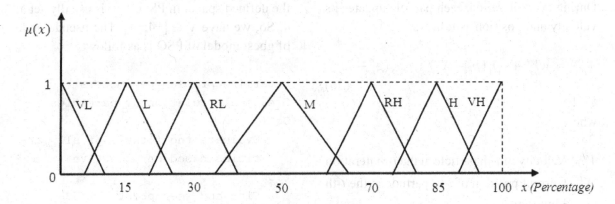

Table 3. Equations 23 and 24

$$\mu_{\widetilde{AP}}\big(AP(T,P,M)\big) = \begin{cases} 1, & AP(T,P,M) \geq AP^1 \\ \dfrac{AP(T,P,M) - AP^0}{AP^1 - AP^0}, & AP^0 \leq AP(T,P,M) \leq AP^1 \\ 0, & AP(T,P,M) \leq AP^0 \end{cases}$$

(23)

$$\mu_{\widetilde{ROII}}\big(ROII(T,P,M)\big) = \begin{cases} 1, & ROII(T,P,M) \geq ROII^1 \\ \dfrac{ROII(T,P,M) - ROII^0}{ROII^1 - ROII^0}, & ROII^0 \leq ROII(T,P,M) \leq ROII^1 \\ 0, & ROII(T,P,M) \leq ROII^0 \end{cases}$$

(24)

Figure 4. Linear membership function for the fuzzy profit and ROII objectives

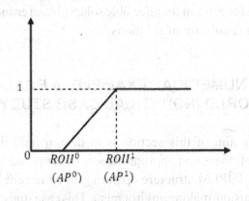

Table 4. Equation 25

Max	μ
Subject to	$\dfrac{AP(T,P,M) - AP^0}{AP^1 - AP^0} \geq \mu$
	$\dfrac{ROII(T,P,M) - ROII^0}{ROII^1 - ROII^0} \geq \mu$
	$\dfrac{1}{\theta} MD(P) B(M)\big(1 - e^{-\theta T}\big) \leq M^{max}$
	$0.1x - 6 \geq \mu$
	$8 - 0.1x \geq \mu$
	$T > 0$
	$P, M \geq 0$
	$\mu, x \geq 0$

(25)

other words, a particle moves towards its best previous position and towards the best particle. During every iteration, each particle updates its velocity and position as follows:

$$V_i^{t+1} = wV_i^t + c_1 r_1 (p_i^t - X_i^t) + c_2 r_2 (g_i^t - X_i^t)$$ (26)

where

V_i^t Velocity of i-th particle at the t-th iteration

X_i^t Current position of i-th particle at the t-th iteration

p_i^t Previous best position of i-th particle so far at the t-th iteration (pbest)

g_i^t Previous best position attained by any particle in swarm at the t-th iteration (gbest)

c_1, c_2 Positive constant weight factors

r_1, r_2 Uniformly distributed random numbers between 0 and 1

w Inertia weight

In fact, c_1 and c_2 are acceleration coefficients that determine the distance of the movement of each particle in a single iteration. These coefficients are based on the influence of cognition experience and social part. Usually, c_1 and c_2 are set in the range of [1.5,2.5]. So we set these coefficients at 2 to solve our problem.

The inertia weight controls the impact of the previous flight direction on current position and causes to convergence performance of the proposed algorithm. To reduce the influence of the inertia weight over the iterations, it is reduced by a linearly decreasing function as follows:

$$w = w_{max} - n / N(w_{max} - w_{min})$$ (27)

where w_{max} and w_{min} are the maximum and the minimum weight of inertia respectively, N is the maximum number of iterations and n is the current iteration.

The velocity of particles is limited to lie within $[-V_{max}, +V_{max}]$. This leads to particles just search the defined space. In PSO, V_{max} is usually set at 4. So, we have $V \in [-4,+4]$. The pseudo code of gbest model of PSO is as follows:

```
Determine problem parameters
Create a population of particles
Do {
    Evaluate the fitness of all par-
    ticles based on objective func-
tion
    Find and keep pbest
    Find and keep gbest
    Update the velocity of each par-
ticle
    Update the position of each par-
ticle
    } While [criteria are satisfied]
Return the best solution
```

It should be mentioned that we used penalty coefficients (pc) in each objective function to code our PSO algorithm. These coefficients reduce value of objective functions for infeasible solutions, and lead to omit the part of generated solutions that could not satisfy the marketing cost constraint. In fact these coefficients are weights of deviance from M^{max} according to marketing cost constraint for infeasible solutions and ensure the feasibility of solutions.

8. NUMERICAL EXAMPLE: A REAL-WORLD INDUSTRIAL CASE STUDY

The aim of this section is to demonstrate the usefulness and appropriateness of proposed H-FMOJPLM structure operating in an uncertain decision-making environment. This case study is originally motivated by the pricing and lotsizing problem of a company. The proposed fuzzy and crisp models are executed based on the firm's

Table 5. Parameters

$\widetilde{c}_0 = (4.8, 6.4, 8.5)$	$\widetilde{c}_h = (0.96, 1.32, 1.6)$	$\widetilde{c}_p = (7.65, 9.55, 12.7)$
$D(P) = (195 - 6.5P)^+$	$\widetilde{k} = (2.4, 2.8, 3, 3.5)$	$\theta = 1, M^{max} = 196$
$\widetilde{\beta}$ (0.26, 0.39, 0.48, 0.61)	$\alpha = 0.75$	$R = 110, k_0 = 438$

Table 6. Results of PSO algorithm

c_p	P	T	M	μ
(6,8.5,10.3)	19.65	0.99	0.15	0.962
(7.65,9.55,12.7)	20	0.99	0.31	0.629
(8.1,10.7,13)	22.09	0.10	0.27	0.47

data for a recent Iranian year, 1388 (2009–2010). As a real-world industrial case a data set is provided by a company in Iran to illustrate the applicability of proposed approach to practical marketing-inventory problems. This company manufactures a type of lock in Iran. Herein, to shorten the length of the paper, let the parameters of the problem be as presented in Table 5.

We let $(195 - 6.5P)^+$ denote the positive linear price sensitive demand. All of monetary data are expressed in ten thousand-Rial (Rial being the Iranian currency). It is noted that based on the available objective data as well as planners' knowledge, all of the imprecise data have been modeled as trapezoidal or triangular possibility distribution.

As stated earlier, in most literatures on fuzzy goal programming and fuzzy mathematical programming, first deterministic model is solved and then the solution values obtained to each goal are used as a benchmark to construct membership functions. Because our H-FMOJPLM model includes qualitative objectives, it can not be solved before it is fuzzified. Therefore we apply decision

maker's judgment to define membership functions of quantitative and qualitative objectives.

We should determine appropriate policy for P, T and M. We set our PSO parameters as follows: $V_{max} = 4$, $c_1 = 2$, $c_2 = 2$, $w_{max} = 1.2$, $w_{min} = 0.2$ and $N = 500$.

Solving the problem with PSO, the decision vector is <6,8.5,10.3>, i.e, $P = 19.65, T = 0.99, M = 0.15$, the final objective function (μ) is 0.962 and $x = 70.38$.

Based on the developed model, we expect that the increase in c_p leads to decrease in p. We benefited this fact to consider and evaluate the implemented PSO. So, we proposed two other hypothetical instances with different values of c_p. These problems are solved via our PSO. Table 6 presents the values of c_p and the results of PSO.

The results indicate the efficiency and suitable performance of implemented PSO algorithm.

9. CONCLUDING REMARKS

This paper attempts to formulate a hybrid fuzzy multi-objective pricing and lotsizing problem including both quantitative and qualitative objectives based on general demand function. In this formulation, fuzzy parameters and goals are represented by appropriate linear membership functions and after the defuzzification process, the equivalent crisp one is solved by a fuzzy goal programming method. We assumed that the demand function not only is sensitive to price and marketing expenditure but also fluctuates with time. Consequently, our model is also suitable for any product whose demand decreases with time such as PCs, mobile phones, etc. The area integrates three main decision criterions: profit, return on inventory investment and marketing-inventory model into a single model. A soft computing, particle swarm optimization (PSO), is used to solve the problem.

There are some directions for further research in this area. In some pricing and inventory decision making situations, life cycle of products is short and finite. Therefore, one of the main directions is to develop a finite planning horizon case of our proposed model. The study can be extended to consider other fuzzy mathematical programming-based approaches. It may occur that goal priorities also be imprecise or fuzzy. In addition, some or all of decision making variables and constraints can have special cases of fuzziness. One could add uncertainty to the mix as a stochastic demand function. Finally, the discussed problem could be generalized to allow for promotion or multiple demand classes in market segmentation.

REFERENCES

Abad, P. L. (1988). Determining optimal selling price and the lot size when the supplier offers all-unit quantity discounts. *Decision Sciences*, *3*(19), 622–634. doi:10.1111/j.1540-5915.1988.tb00290.x

Chan, L. M. A., Shen, Z. J. M., Simchi-Levi, D., & Swann, J. (2004). Coordination of pricing and inventory decisions: A survey and classification. In Simchi-Levi, D., Wu, S. D., & Shen, Z. J. M. (Eds.), *Handbook of quantitative supply chain analysis: Modeling in the e-business era* (pp. 335–392). Boston, MA: Kluwer Academic Publishers.

Chen, X., & Simchi-Levi, D. (2004). Coordinating inventory control and pricing strategies with random demand and fixed ordering cost: The finite horizon case. *Operations Research*, *52*(6), 887–896. doi:10.1287/opre.1040.0127

Corbett, C. J., & de Groote, X. (2000). A supplier's optimal quantity discount policy under asymmetric information. *Management Science*, *3*(46), 444–450. doi:10.1287/mnsc.46.3.444.12065

Dubois, D., & Prade, H. (1978). *Fuzzy sets and systems: Theory and applications*. New York, NY: Academic Press.

Dye, C. Y., & Hsieh, T. P. (2010). A particle swarm optimization for solving joint pricing and lot-sizing problem with fluctuating demand and unit purchasing cost. *Computers and Mathematics with Applications, 60*, 1895_1907.

Eberhart, R. C., & Kennedy, J. (1995). A new optimizer using particle swarm theory. In *Proceedings of the 6th International Symposium on Micro Machine and Human Science*, Nagoya, Japan, (pp. 39–43).

Esmaeili, M. (2009). Optimal selling price, marketing expenditure and lot size under general demand function. *International Journal of Advanced Manufacturing Technology*, *45*, 191–198. doi:10.1007/s00170-009-1952-8

Esmaeili, M., Abad, P. L., & Aryanezhad, M. B. (2009a). Seller–buyer relationship when end demand is sensitive to price and promotion. *Asia-Pacific Journal of Operational Research*, *26*(5), 605–621. doi:10.1142/S0217595909002353

Esmaeili, M., Aryanezhad, M. B., & Zeephong-sekul, P. (2009b). A game theory approach in seller-buyer supply chain. *European Journal of Operational Research, 195*, 442–448. doi:10.1016/j.ejor.2008.02.026

Esmaeili, M., Zeephongsekul, P., & Aryanezhad, M. B. (2007). A joint pricing and lot sizing models with discount: A geometric programming approach. *ANZIAM Journal, 49*, 139–154.

Freeland, J. R. (1982). Coordination strategies for production and marketing in a functionally decentralized firm. *ABE Transactions, 12*(2), 126–132.

Huang, Z., & Li, S. X. (2001). Co-op advertising models in manufacturer-retailer supply chains: A game theory approach. *European Journal of Operational Research, 135*, 527–544. doi:10.1016/S0377-2217(00)00327-1

Islam, S. (2008). Multi-objective marketing planning inventory model: A geometric programming approach. *Applied Mathematics and Computation, 205*, 238–246. doi:10.1016/j.amc.2008.07.037

Jamalnia, A., & Soukhakian, M. A. (2009). A hybrid fuzzy goal programming approach with different goal priorities to aggregate production planning. *Computers & Industrial Engineering, 56*(4), 1474–1486. doi:10.1016/j.cie.2008.09.010

Kim, D., & Lee, W. J. (1998). Optimal joint pricing and lot sizing with fixed and variable capacity. *European Journal of Operational Research, 109*(1), 212–227. doi:10.1016/S0377-2217(97)00100-8

Kotler, P. (1971). *Marketing decision making: A model building approach*. New York, NY: Holt, Rinehart & Winston.

Kunreuther, H., & Richard, J. F. (1971). Optimal pricing and inventory decisions for non-seasonal items. *Econometrica: Journal of the Econometric Society, 39*(1), 173–175. doi:10.2307/1909147

Lee, W. J. (1993). Determining order quantity and selling price by geometric programming optimal solution, bounds, and sensitivity. *Decision Sciences, 24*, 76–87. doi:10.1111/j.1540-5915.1993.tb00463.x

Lee, W. J., & Kim, D. (1993). Optimal and heuristic decision strategies for integrated production and marketing planning. *Decision Sciences, 24*(6), 1203–1213. doi:10.1111/j.1540-5915.1993.tb00511.x

Li, J., Min, K. J., Otake, T., & Voorhis, T. M. (2008). Inventory and investment in setup and quality operations under return on investment maximization. *European Journal of Operational Research, 185*, 593–605. doi:10.1016/j.ejor.2006.11.045

Li, L., & Lai, K. K. (2001). Fuzzy dynamic programming approach to hybrid multi objective multi stage decision making problems. *Fuzzy Sets and Systems, 117*, 13–25. doi:10.1016/S0165-0114(98)00423-0

Liou, T.-S., & Wang, M.-J. (1992). Ranking fuzzy numbers with integral value. *Fuzzy Sets and Systems, 50*, 247–255. doi:10.1016/0165-0114(92)90223-Q

Mandal, N. K., Roy, T. K., & Maiti, M. (2005). Multi-objective fuzzy inventory model with three constraints: A geometric programming approach. *Fuzzy Sets and Systems, 150*, 87–106. doi:10.1016/j.fss.2004.07.020

Mulhern, F. J. (1997). Retail marketing: From distribution to integration. *International Journal of Research in Marketing, 14*(2), 103–124. doi:10.1016/S0167-8116(96)00031-6

Otake, T., & Min, K. J. (2001). Inventory and investment in quality improvement under return on investment maximization. *Computers & Operations Research, 28*, 113–124. doi:10.1016/S0305-0548(00)00022-8

Otake, T., Min, K. J., & Chen, C. (1999). Inventory and investment in setup operations under return on investment maximization. *Computers & Operations Research, 26*, 883–899. doi:10.1016/S0305-0548(98)00095-1

Poli, R., Kennedy, J., & Blackwell, T. (2007). Particle swarm optimization: An overview. *Swarm Intelligence, 1*, 33–57. doi:10.1007/s11721-007-0002-0

Porteus, E. L., & Whang, S. (1991). On manufacturing/marketing incentives. *Management Science, 37*(9), 1166–1181. doi:10.1287/mnsc.37.9.1166

Rosenberg, D. (1991). Optimal price-inventory decisions profit vs ROII. *IIE Transactions, 23*, 17–22. doi:10.1080/07408179108963837

Sadjadi, S. J., Ghazanfari, M., & Yousefli, A. (2010). Fuzzy pricing and marketing planning model: A possibilistic geometric programming approach. *Expert Systems with Applications, 37*, 3392–3397. doi:10.1016/j.eswa.2009.10.009

Sadjadi, S. J., Orougee, M., & Aryanezhad, M. B. (2005). Optimal production and marketing planning. *Computational Optimization and Applications, 30*, 195–203. doi:10.1007/s10589-005-4564-8

Schroeder, R. G., & Krishnan, R. (1976). Return on investment as a criterion for inventory model. *Decision Sciences, 7*, 697–704. doi:10.1111/j.1540-5915.1976.tb00713.x

Tersine, R. J. (1994). *Principles of inventory and materials management* (4th ed.). NJ, USA: Prentice Hall PTR.

Tsou, C. S. (2008). Multi-objective inventory planning using MOPSO and TOPSIS. *Expert Systems with Applications, 35*, 136–142. doi:10.1016/j.eswa.2007.06.009

Wee, H., Lo, C., & Hsu, P. (2009). A multi-objective joint replenishment inventory model of deteriorated items in a fuzzy environment. *European Journal of Operational Research, 197*, 620–631. doi:10.1016/j.ejor.2006.08.067

Yaghoobi, M. A., & Tamiz, M. (2007). A method for solving fuzzy goal programming problems based on MINMAX approach. *European Journal of Operational Research, 177*, 1580–1590. doi:10.1016/j.ejor.2005.10.022

Zadeh, L. A. (1978). Fuzzy sets as a basis for a theory of possibility. *Fuzzy Sets and Systems, 1*, 3–28. doi:10.1016/0165-0114(78)90029-5

Zhao, L., Qian, F., Yang, Y., Zeng, Y., & Su, H. (2010). Automatically extracting T–S fuzzy models using cooperative random learning particle swarm optimization. *Applied Soft Computing, 10*, 938–944. doi:10.1016/j.asoc.2009.10.012

KEY TERMS AND DEFINITIONS

Fuzzy Optimization: Is a kind of optimization approach in a fuzzy environment.

Inventory: Materials and components that businesses hold in stock.

Linguistic Values: Is a term used in knowledge representation. It is simply knowledge from an expert(s) that contains no nominal value, just knowledge.

Marketing: Marketing's primary focus is to identify and satisfy customers in a way that helps build a solid and, hopefully, sustained relationship that encourages customers to continue doing business with the marketer.

Particle Swarm Optimization: Is a meta heuristics technique inspired by social behavior of bird flocking or fish schooling.

Pricing: Is the method a company uses to set the price its product. Pricing is one of the four aspects of marketing. The other three parts of the marketing mix are product management, promotion, and distribution.

Return on Inventory Investment: The ratio of profit to investment, and is a widely utilized economic performance measure dealing with finished goods inventories.

Section 4
Market Analysis

Chapter 13
A Fuzzy Segmentation Approach to Guide Marketing Decisions

Mònica Casabayó
ESADE-URL, Spain

Núria Agell
ESADE-URL, Spain

ABSTRACT

The aim of this chapter is to present a fuzzy segmentation model that combines statistical and Artificial Intelligence techniques to identify and quantify multifaceted consumers. One of the primary challenges faced by companies is getting to know their consumers. The latter are increasingly complex, versatile, ever-changing, and even contradictory; in other words, they are multifaceted. There is thus a need for techniques and tools to be able to segment this type of consumer in order to provide companies with the realistic information they need to make the appropriate marketing decisions. A real case study from the Spanish energy industry is included in this chapter to demonstrate the potential of the segmentation model being proposed.

1. INTRODUCTION

Consumers are complex. The marketplace is also complex and ambiguous. Moreover, the way consumers used to behave 50 years ago is completely different from that today. And the way they behave nowadays is likely to be different from how they will behave in the near future. A common challenge for companies is to understand how and why consumers act the way they do in order to make the appropriate marketing decisions.

In real life, when we ask an audience of marketing professionals whether consumers always behave the same way in different situations, the unanimous response is "No". When we ask if consumer motivations, preferences and attitudes

DOI: 10.4018/978-1-4666-0095-9.ch013

are static, they again coincide in saying "No". This "No" is also unanimous when we ask whether consumers always act in character.

Since Smith's definition of the market segmentation concept in 1956, it has been perceived as a conceptual model reflecting the way managers wish to see a given market (Wedel and Kamakura, 2002). Segmentation helps managers to understand this enormous variety of consumers. However, marketing managers understand that there are many different kinds of people displaying many different buying patterns and that market segmentation techniques haven't been of much help to these professionals (Yankelovich and Meer, 2006).

In general, when we segment individuals, we force them into a single segment category. If marketing professionals agree that this just does not reflect the world as consumers know it, why do we still do it?

Based on the fact that consumers behave not only differently but even often contradictorily, we need a fuzzy segmentation approach capable of capturing the consumer as he/she truly is: ambiguous, complex, plural and not black or white. The main purpose of this chapter, then, is to describe this innovative fuzzy segmentation model in detail. The major particularity of this multibehavioural model is its ability to interpret non-exclusive segments, enabling a clearer image of market realities and thus improving marketing managers' decision-making.

In order to achieve our purpose, we believe some previous points need to be considered:

- The subject of research has changed considerably in the last 50 years. This chapter describes the multifaceted consumer in the 21st century.
- Understanding consumers is the basis of marketing. Segmentation helps in this process. Therefore, we review the concept of market segmentation and its evolution.
- LAMDA, a fuzzy learning technique, is proposed and explained as an alternative

method to break with non-overlapping segmentation techniques.
- This innovative segmentation model is presented as a means to understand the multifaceted consumer.

Afterwards, the chapter invites the reader to examine a real business case in the Spanish energy industry from a multibehavioural perspective. Finally, conclusions are drawn and further research is suggested.

2. BACKGROUND

2.1 The Multifaceted Consumer: Making Decisions Based on a Multifaceted Subject of Analysis

The need to make decisions is a common characteristic shared by most companies. Nevertheless, the challenge resides in maximising success when choosing the best option from amongst possible alternatives. In this respect, the decisions that most directly affect corporate marketing departments are those related to the new 21st century consumer.

In the 1930s, a 25-year-old woman had a very clear notion of her role in the family, society and life, in general. There weren't many surprises in terms of her behaviour, habits or preferences. Today, however, we are faced with a consumer who is connected via new technologies, one who is demanding and informed and lives in an increasingly global setting. In this changing social context, then, it is surprising to find static, one-dimensional and/or predictable consumers. The great challenge faced by companies is developing new decision-making models for their marketing departments based on multiple realities and the consumers' versatile behaviour.

The new social context no longer offers clues based on the consumer's age. For example, a 16-year-old adolescent may be an avid consumer of products originally aimed at an adult target.

Conversely, a 43-year-old adult may dream of getting home from work to connect the PlayStation. A 60-year-old woman may want to feel and look young, while a 17-year-old girl may want her parents to pay for elective plastic surgery as soon as she turns eighteen. These very plausible scenarios also imply several contradictions: On the one hand, we have young adults and adolescents who want to grow up and become adults as soon as possible and, on the other, we have adults who want to remain eternally young.

Similarly, gender no longer seems to be a significant variable when attempting to understand consumers and better predict their behaviour. The traditional masculine roles are fading and vice versa.

The same is true of social class. How can we explain tourists who fly on low-cost airlines to stay at 5-star hotels? It's clear that consumers save and splurge at the same time depending on the product category and their tastes.

We also find this behavioural versatility in terms of consumer preferences. For example, we may prefer to have 300 friends in Facebook but we only have a direct relationship with 20. We may prefer organic and ecological food but on Sunday nights we eat a frozen pizza so as to not have to cook. Depending on the time and circumstances, we can prefer one brand of wine over another; we can choose one supermarket over another; our price sensitivity can vary; and we can be more open to recommending one product over another. The moment, the social context, the economic-political setting, our personal situation, our mood, etc., can all be variables influencing our daily habits. Logically, they not only affect us at the personal level or as citizens; they also affect us as consumers.

Carrying out research on this highly versatile and contradictory consumer is difficult. This is not, however, a new problem. For decades, the change in the information companies have had available has stimulated the creativity, flexibility, design, commercialisation and implementation of different data gathering, analysis and interpretation techniques and models. The greatest progress in market research techniques actually occurred between 1910 and 1920, when surveys were popularised to gather data. During the 1950s, quantitative methods became the protagonists. The 1990s, by contrast, were characterised as years of great technological innovation such as barcode scanners at points of sale, computer-assisted telephone interviews, remote data analyses, videoconference interviews, online surveys, etc. At the end of the 1990s, greater weight was given to ethnographic studies, consumer newspapers, blog and website analyses and data mining. These would lead the way for ethnography, neuromarketing, and Artificial Intelligence techniques, amongst others, at the start of the new millennium.

As an industry, market research has changed and adapted its methodologies and techniques in response to the consumers' increasing complexity. Now the challenge is to find new research methodologies that are capable of identifying, understanding and measuring the consumers' multibehavioural nature.

To summarise, consumers are neither static nor predictable. Understanding their behaviour and, more importantly, anticipating it are increasingly difficult. As such, if we want to reduce doubts when making marketing-related decisions, we need to have the appropriate dynamic and realistic tools. However, the most innovative technique is not always the most appropriate. Each methodology can be appropriate or not depending on the problem being researched. Clearly, some marketing decisions require static and concrete data while others, however, need analysis techniques which allow researchers to recognise and interpret reality just as it is: Ambiguous, versatile, uncertain and full of contradictions (Casabayó, 2010).

In the next section, we revise one of the primary problems found in marketing research: Market segmentation. We revise the leading segmentation techniques since their creation at the end of the 1950s and we present our segmentation technique, demonstrating its ability to realistically group and classify these multifaceted consumers.

2.2 Market Segmentation: From Smith (1965) to 2011

Segmentation, a concept which emerged in the late 1950s, is essentially a grouping task. Since its introduction by Smith (1956), recognising the existence of heterogeneity in the demand for goods and services, market segmentation has become a core concept in marketing theory and practice.

Based on the economic theory of imperfect competition, it is well established that markets and the customers who make up these markets are not homogeneous but heterogeneous in nature. Furthermore, even if a market can be partitioned into homogeneous segments, a list of criteria must be fulfilled for its effective segmentation: Measurability, relevance, accessibility, distinguishable nature, feasibility, inter-homogeneousity and intra-heterogeneousity. These traits have frequently been put forward as determining the effectiveness and profitability of marketing strategies (Loudon and Della Vita, 1993; Baker, 1988; Kotler, 2000).

Market segmentation does not have a unique, simple, and accepted definition. Despite the fact that the essence of grouping individuals is unquestionable, the concept of market segmentation itself has been understood in different ways. Frank, Massy and Wind (1972) and Assael and Roscoe (1976) were followers of Smith's conceptualization of market segmentation. Another way to perceive market segmentation is related to identifying homogeneous subgroups in a heterogeneous market (Johnson, 1971; Kotler, 2000). And, according to Luque (2000), segmentation has a double connotation: Segmentation as a strategy and as a technique. Therefore, it can be considered as both a strategic or an operational concept.

Independently of the point of view, it is important to note that segments are not physical entities that naturally co-exist in the marketplace; they are defined by researchers and practitioners to improve their ability to capture and serve their customers as best as possible. In other words, market segmentation is a theoretical marketing concept involving artificial groupings of consumers, constructed to help managers to make marketing decisions. Therefore, firms which can recognise the difference in consumer segments and develop the right offering for each of the segments have a competitive advantage (Kotler, 1989).

Despite the fact that classifying customers into groups might seem quite simple, there are multiple existing options to segment the market. In fact, the same market may be seen and grouped according to different criteria. Therefore, the identification of market segments is highly dependent on the bases for segmentation and the methods used to define them. The most important point is to be aware of the fact that the choice of these criteria may lead to different resulting segments. The same often occurs when choosing the segmentation technique (Frank *et al.*, 1972). And obviously, marketing decisions directly depend on the revealed outputs. According to McDonald and Dunbar (1995:1), "Market Segmentation is easy to understand once an organization has done it successfully! […] The problem is how to get there!"

Though there is no consensus on the definition of the market segmentation concept, the majority of proposed definitions in the literature coincide that it has at least one of the following goals (Casabayó, 2005):

1. Segmentation research consists of investigating the possible alternative bases for grouping segments. (At this point it is important to mention that markets are partitioned in our study on the basis of customer needs or characteristics, not on product factors).
2. Segmentation research is the study of alternative methodologies to find segments and evaluation criteria.

3. Segmentation research deals with the development of models to apply segmentation research findings to marketing decisions.

The goal of this chapter is not to find possible alternative criteria when partitioning segments. Independently of the selection criteria, as often occurs, one individual may belong to all the existing segments at the same time. Nevertheless, this chapter pursues the second goal above and inherent to segmentation research which consists of developing an alternative methodology to identify and measure the overlapping segments. The third goal is also pursued in this chapter as well. As mentioned previously, a fuzzy segmentation approach is developed and applied to a real marketing case. We describe these two goals in the next paragraphs.

3. PROPOSED SOLUTION

3.1 An Alternative Methodology: Evolving from Non-Overlapping Segmentation

For decades, though also questioned by some scholars (Ketchen and Shook, 1996; Punj and Steward, 1983), the cluster analysis technique has been the most widely used in market segmentation processes, with both academic and professional researchers trusting it to classify individuals. Cluster analysis is used to classify individuals or objects into a smaller number of mutually exclusive and exhaustive groups to ensure that there is as much similarity within groups and as much difference amongst groups as possible (Everitt, 1993).

Despite the fact that the cluster analysis technique has been mainly referred to in marketing literature as a descriptive method based on non-overlapping clustering, the use of applications based on overlapping or fuzzy clustering techniques has also increased since the 1980s (e.g., Arabie, 1977; Arabie *et al.,* 1981; Hruschka,

1986; Steenkamp and Wedel, 1992). Consequently, some authors have begun to differentiate between 3 categories of cluster analysis: Non-overlapping, overlapping and fuzzy clustering (Wedel and Kamakura, 2000).

Based on the multi-valued logic introduced by Lukasiewicz (Bergmann, 2008), the fuzzy set theory was introduced by Zadeh in 1965 (Zadeh, 1965). The main idea is to consider a fuzzy set as a group without a sharp boundary (Dubois and Prade, 1988), thus changing the membership function concept defined in classic sets theory as a binary assessment to a gradual function valued in the interval [0.1]. Zadeh's approach to fuzzy decision analysis (Zadeh, 1975) includes the concepts of fuzzy restrictions and fuzzy truth values that can be seen as elastic constraints on the values that may be assigned to a variable.

In keeping with this approach, fuzzy clustering was introduced based on the concept of fuzzy partition (Ruspini, 1969). It assumes that patterns or elements can belong to more than one cluster and it associates a membership value to each element in each of the segments. Different fuzzy clustering methodologies have been introduced during the last decades which allow us to assign membership values to patterns and to one or more clusters (Gath and Geva, 1989; Höppner *et al.*, 1999; Klawonn and Höppner, 2003).

The main difference between non-overlapping and overlapping or fuzzy clustering is the segment's external isolation. Whereas the first considers that every customer must belong to just one segment, the other two methods concur that each individual can belong to various segments. The main difference between the overlapping and fuzzy clustering techniques is that, although overlapping accepts this plural membership, fuzzy clustering analyzes the specific degree of membership of each individual to each segment or cluster. A graphic example is provided in Figure 1 to illustrate the main differences between the 3 types of cluster methods.

Figure 1. Graphic example of non-overlapping, overlapping and fuzzy clustering methods

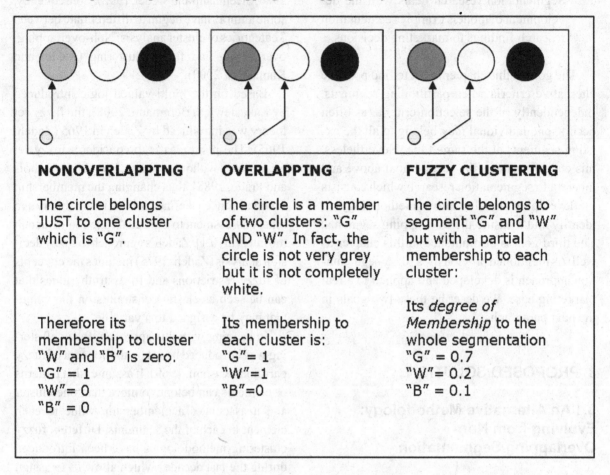

NONOVERLAPPING

The circle belongs JUST to one cluster which is "G".

Therefore its membership to cluster "W" and "B" is zero.
"G" = 1
"W"= 0
"B" = 0

OVERLAPPING

The circle is a member of two clusters: "G" AND "W". In fact, the circle is not very grey but it is not completely white.

Its membership to each cluster is:
"G"= 1
"W"=1
"B"=0

FUZZY CLUSTERING

The circle belongs to segment "G" and "W" but with a partial membership to each cluster:

Its *degree of Membership* to the whole segmentation
"G" = 0.7
"W"= 0.2
"B" = 0.1

The technique presented in this chapter is located between the overlapping and fuzzy clustering models. The differentiation point is that each individual's degree of membership to each cluster is considered separately. Therefore, the values of this membership do not have to add up to 1. This technique is described in detail in the next section.

While the concept of similarity between objects has usually been considered as the fundamental concept for individuals' recognition as members of a given cluster, in the methodology presented in this chapter, the concept of an individual's adequacy (or fit) to a given cluster is considered as a membership function to the whole cluster considered as a fuzzy set.

3.2. Description of the LAMDA Method: Theoretical Aspects

LAMDA (Logical Association in Multivariate Data Analysis) is a segmentation method based on fuzzy clustering (Höppner *et al*., 1999; Klawonn and Höppner, 2003). This methodology was developed in the late 80s by Aguilar-Matin (Aguilar-Martin and López de Mántaras, 1982; Aguado, 1988). LAMDA introduces the concept of an element's adequacy or fit to a cluster based on a fuzzy membership function defined in fuzzy sets (Aguilar-Martín and Piera, 1986).

To define this concept, it is assumed that each element is described by a set of descriptors (X1, X2,...Xn) which can be either quantitative or qualitative. Considering the marginal distribution of each variable in each of the clusters as Ci, a Marginal Adequacy Degree MADCi(Xj) can be computed for each descriptor j. This marginal adequacy represents the density or frequency with which the specific marginal observation appears in the cluster.

In fuzzy sets literature, t-norms, which are a generalization of (classical) set intersection, and t-conorms, which are a generalization of (classical) set union, are considered the basic operators to aggregate the partial information given by two fuzzy values (Dubois and Prade, 2003). T-norms and t-conorms are the only associative aggregation functions. These associative aggregation functions lead to n-ary aggregation functions by means of direct iteration in n arguments.

In some cases, they have also been considered hybrid connectives defined as a linear combination between a t-norm and its dual t-conorm (Zimmermann, 2010). The importance of these connectives is that they conform to the distinction between "and" and "or" aggregators and introduce a certain degree of compensation. The compensatory operators are considered to be more adequate in human decision-making (Zimmerman, 1987).

Thus, keeping the same notation L for the n-ary operator, the general expression of the hybrid connectives used in the LAMDA algorithm can be written in the following way and considering T as an n-ary t-norm and T* its n-ary dual t-conorm:

$$L = (1-\beta) \, T + \beta \, T^*.$$

As such, the β parameter is such that $\beta = 0$ represents the t-norm, T, for example, the Minimum, and $\beta = 1$ means the t-conorm, and T*, for example, the Maximum. This parameter will (inversely) determine the exigency level of the classification. We can thus call it tolerance. Some examples of t-norms currently used in the LAMDA algorithm are MinMax, Probabilistic, Frank and Lukasiewicz (Klir and Yuan, 1995).

In keeping with the above, in this paper fuzzy hybrid connectives, obtained as a linear combina-

tion of a t-norm and its dual t-conorm, are used to aggregate marginal adequacy functions and to allow for a Global Adequacy Degree GADCi (X) to be computed, such that:

GADCi(X) = L [MADCi(X1), MADCi(X2),…, MADCi(Xn)].

This degree of adequacy is calculated for each item and each segment considered, i.e., LAMDA gives us the adequacy or fit of each element to each segment separately. The assignment of a global adequacy degree for each individual to a class or segment is shown in Figure 2.

The learning process associated to LAMDA includes an estimation of the distribution function for each of the descriptors within each of the given segments. In addition, the algorithm keeps the observed kernel in every class, that is, a summary of the individuals that built the class. Nevertheless, whichever quantitative or qualitative distributions are assumed, the segmentation process always uses a recursive learning process. The algorithm automatically explores a set of hybrid connectives and the value for tolerance. The pair that gives the segmentation, in terms of frequency of success closer to the given one, is selected.

3.3 Advantages over Other Classification Techniques

The classification techniques usually applied in data mining have some serious drawbacks in spite of their important capabilities. LAMDA is an integrated approach that tries to combine these other techniques' strong points while avoiding their weaknesses.

The first approach to data mining and classification could, of course, be traditional statistical techniques, but they demand the user have thorough knowledge beforehand. Solid decisions imply a long and increasingly complex process in which every decision has to be justified and every

Figure 2. LAMDA architecture

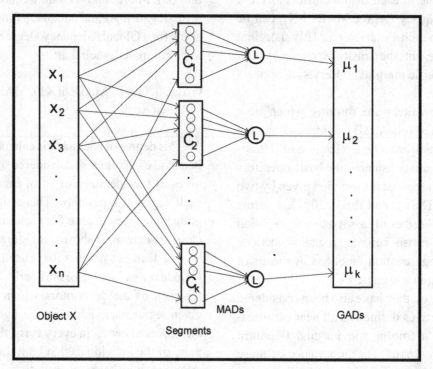

possibility explored. Marketing professionals need more user-friendly methods.

A second approach from the Artificial Intelligence field could be decision trees, but these algorithms only work on categorical data. In the numerical field, some techniques have been developed on unsupervised learning but they only cover the numerical variables and tend to be slow and complicated like traditional statistics.

Neural networks are the most popular approach to classification and data mining. Again, their self-learning capability for numerical problems can be amazing. But from a practical point of view, a particular network does not offer any guarantee of being able to learn how to solve a particular problem, nor do we know how long this learning can take. Even if they ultimately work, neural networks perform like "black boxes," and their decisions are difficult to understand from a human point of view.

In recent years, some variations on classical neural networks have been tried, including radial basis function networks, and some techniques have evolved from them, for example, Vector Support Machines. The latter algorithms perform numerical statistical searches in a more transparent way, but, again, there is a problem with complexity, and calculation can take too long.

Thus, there does not appear to be a technique capable of treating numerical and qualitative data at the same time, working automatically and efficiently while yielding easy-to-interpret results and performing supervised or unsupervised learning without changing its structure. LAMDA tries to do all these things.

- LAMDA deals with both quantitative and qualitative data. Traditional statistical methods usually replace qualitative variables with binary codes. However, these codes cannot be used to make any mathematical or statistical calculations that provide the user with worthwhile insights.

- The whole process is very intuitive, and the results are easily understood. The description of every class consists of a list of the observed modalities and their appearance frequencies for every qualitative descriptor. The quantitative descriptors for each class can be described by a variety of parameters, always including the observed average value.

- The process is sequential and incremental. This means that, unlike the case-based reasoning algorithms which need to keep vast amounts of data on the already processed individuals, LAMDA stores the present classes and deals only with the individual that is going to be classified. These characteristics make LAMDA faster than other classifying techniques and it requires less memory.

3.4 The Innovative Segmentation Model: From a Unibehavioural to a Multibehavioural Approach

The innovative segmentation model proposed in this chapter has a dual purpose: First, to contribute with a new segmentation approach which responds to the commercial need to interpret ambiguous market information as realistically as possible; its second purpose is to provide a market segmentation methodology which combines statistics and Artificial Intelligence. It is important to underscore at this point what we feel is the model's primary scientific contribution: The model allows us to *fuzzify* any segmentation obtained using the traditional statistical model. In other words, based on its initial (excluding) segmentation and its ability to learn, LAMDA allows us to capture and see the data's ambiguity and understand the total population as a whole from the point of view of each individual and each of the existing segments.

Consequently, the model provides non-exclusive segmentation which allows for a better conception of market reality and so enhances marketing managers' decision-making.

The fuzzy segmentation model, as illustrated in Figure 3, is divided into 4 parts: Data Collection, Analysis, Interpretation and Decision-making.

Data Collection is the first stage. The model can work with primary and/or secondary data at the same time. In other words, depending on the research problem, either the sample is collected or the whole customer database is selected for subsequent analysis.

Analysis is an important and pioneering part of this model as it combines the potentiality of two very important techniques such as cluster analysis and the LAMDA fuzzy learning technique. As mentioned previously, the LAMDA algorithm in the learning stage carries out an iterative search for the different connectives and tolerance and produces the most compatible segmentation possible through a cluster analysis.

The *interpretation* stage is another key part of the model. The cluster analysis technique carries out exclusionary segmentation whereby each individual from the sample is located in one and only segment. However, using LAMDA's interpretation, we can measure the ambiguity of the data. Every individual has as many associated values as resulting segments, and every value represents the adequacy degree for each initial cluster. Therefore, while the unibehavioural approach pushes each individual into one single segment, a fuzzy interpretation lets each individual belong to all the possible segments depending on his/her degree of fit to each. Extremes are still extremes, and a rigid consumer practically never behaves as a multifaceted consumer. But, in practice, the majority of consumers are not extreme, adopting a multibehavioural approach instead.

In the *decision-making* field, this fuzzy segmentation approach introduces a new way to understand data and thus has a direct affect on

Figure 3. Multibehavioural segmentation approach

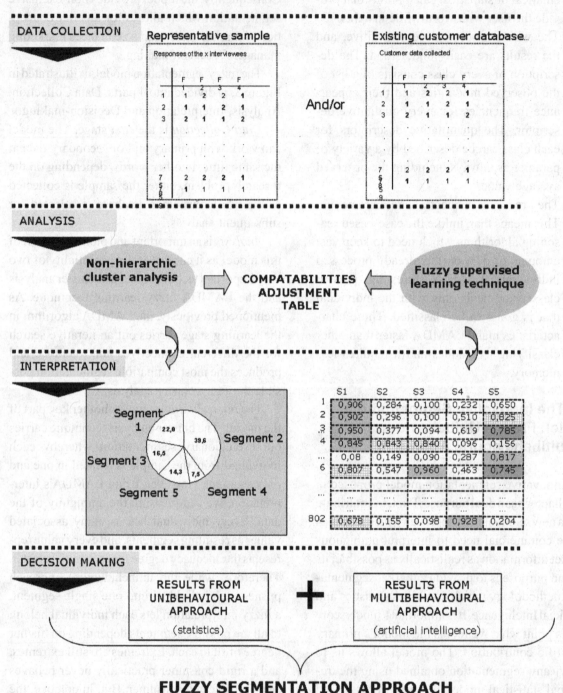

the result of any marketing actions (Casabayó and Martín, 2010). For instance, taking the unibehavioural approach, one particular multifaceted consumer would receive all the messages from the company addressed to the segment he/she belongs to but would not be told about any other products or services that the company addressed to another segment to which, in reality, he/she also belongs.

4. FIELD STUDY

A leading company in the Spanish energy sector became aware that segmenting the potential market by its corporate customers' demographic data (number of employees or type of business) or product characteristics (energy, eco-energy, etc.) and differentiating its offerings by adding features and functions (Christensen *et al.*, 2007) was not enough to cover the increasingly heterogeneous needs of its existing customers and capture new ones. Following up on the demand for energy from these clients, the company designed a motivational segmentation model for micro-SMEs related to their attitudes towards the sector.

4.1 Data Collection

Basic information for analysis was obtained by means of a qualitative research study consisting of personal interviews through a structured questionnaire with visual support. Interviews lasted approximately 45 minutes and were carried out on a total sample of 802 individuals from the universe studied. The margin of error for this representative sample size was +3.53%. Fieldwork was carried out in the first quarter of 2010.

Figure 4 describes the sample, which was weighted by type of company, defined by their activity, size and area based on 2009 National Classification of Economic Activities (NACE) data from the Spanish Statistics Institute (INE).

4.2 Analysis

Once the necessary data was collected, two segmentation techniques were used for our analysis. The first segmentation was carried out using the multivariate statistical method known as *non-hierarchical cluster analysis,* with free centres of gravity, while the second used LAMDA. Identifying the compatibility between the two techniques was key to interpret the results.

It should be noted that different segmentations could be obtained by using the LAMDA fuzzy technique, so measuring their degrees of compatibility implies choosing the most appropriate of these. As mentioned, these techniques come from different disciplines, statistics and Artificial Intelligence, respectively, with different requirements, models, and analysis and interpretation conditions, and they are, therefore, not directly comparable. Figure 5 details the result of this compatibility between the fuzzy segmentation model chosen and the segmentation obtained in Phase 1, indicating both the global compatibility and the compatibility for each class.

The compatibility between the two classifications is 92%. This means that 92% of the individuals in the sample are included in the same segment when comparing both (non-hierarchical and fuzzy segmentation techniques). As such, we can argue that there is a good match between the two and we can continue with the fuzzy segmentation process. This compatibility is calculated from the number of individuals in the same class, taking both classifications into consideration.

4.3 Interpretation

The non-hierarchical cluster identified 5 different segments regarding corporate clients' attitudes towards the energy market. Figure 6 reflects the distribution of these segments.

Figure 4. Representative sample

Business Type	802
Store	270
Bar	117
Restaurant	73
Office	177
Hairdresser	48
Other services	117
ZONE	**802**
Catalonia	198
East/south	253
Centre	200
North-east	151
No. of employees	**802**
No employees	379
From 1 to 5 employees	305
From 6 to 49 employees	118

However, is reality as fixed as that revealed by our results? From a practical point of view, is it possible for the same individual to belong to more than one segment? Therefore, is it possible for an "Optimistic/Receptive" segment member to sometimes think and act like a "Safety/Service" individual? Can the same individual have two or more different attitudes towards the energy market? By applying the artificial intelligence fuzzy learning technique (Aguilar-Martin and López de Mántaras, 1982; Aguilar-Martin and Piera, 1986; Aguado, 1998), we were able to add fuzziness

and its potential to the segmentation results obtained.

Starting from the idea that every individual has been placed into the segment where they have the maximum degree of adequacy, we can go on to examine those individuals with a value of over 90% of that maximum value in another segment. In cases where this coincidence occurs, we consider that these individuals belong to both segments. By using fuzzy segmentation, we want to check whether all the individuals in our sample have a clear and defined attitude or, conversely, if they include some fuzzy cases.

LAMDA defines the adequacy degree of an individual to a segment by means of a fuzzy aggregation function that is obtained through a linear combination of two fuzzy connectives. These fuzzy connectives are a t-norm and its associated t-conorm (Klir and Yuan, 1995) and correspond to the fuzzy translation of the classic logical connectives $\wedge$ (and) and $\vee$ (or) respectively.

As shown in Figure 7, the adequacy or degree of belonging of each individual in every segment was obtained in the first phase. With fuzzy segmentation, each individual presented an adequacy degree to each of the existing segments. The following illustration exemplifies 23 of the 802 individuals in the sample and their adequacy degrees to each segment. For example, individual number 3 is interesting. Although this client's maximum adequacy degree of 0.915 places him/her in the "Optimistic/Receptive" segment, this customer also presents an adequacy degree in the "Active/Exacting/High Value" segment, with a value of over 90% of its maximum. These values are too high for the individual client to be forced to belong to only the "Optimistic/Receptive" segment. Let's look at another example: Individual number 12. This client clearly presents a single attitude corresponding to the "Indignant/Show-off" segment, since the adequacy degrees of this individual client

Figure 5. Table of compatibilities

Sample= 802	Non-Hierarchical Cluster Segmentation						
Fuzzy Segmentation	Uninvolved Impassive	Active Exacting	Indignant Show-off	Optimistic Receptive	Safety Service	Fuzzy learning Tchque.	*Obtained*
Uninvolved Impassive	265	0	0	0	0	*265*	*33%*
Active Exacting High Value	8	167	0	4	0	*179*	*22%*
Indignant Show-off	14	7	114	5	0	*140*	*17%*
Optimistic Receptive	2	5	0	124	0	*131*	*16%*
Safety Service	10	8	0	2	67	*87*	*11%*
Non-Hierarchical Cluster Segmentation	*299*	*187*	*114*	*135*	*67*	92%	
Obtained:	*37%*	*23%*	*14%*	*17%*	*8%*		

to the other existing segments is never more than 50% of the maximum values.

Of the 802 individuals in our study, 558 (70%) only belong to a single segment. They, therefore, follow a single behavioural pattern. Of these 802 individuals, however, 244 (30%) belong to their own segment, but also reveal a high degree of adequacy (+90% of its maximum) to more than one segment. Using fuzzy segmentation lets us increase relevant information about individuals in the sample by 30% (see Figure 7). Figure 8

Figure 6. Segments obtained by non-hierarchical clusters

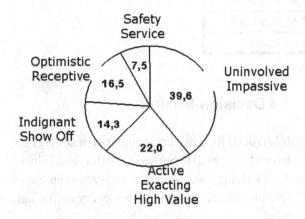

shows the number of micro-SMEs that, in addition to behaving in line with the main segment in which they are placed, also present other behavioural patterns. For example, of the total number of individuals with a maximum adequacy degree in the "Uninvolved/Impassive" segment (265), 218 only demonstrate 1 pattern (Uninvolved/Impassive). However, 44 present an adequacy degree of more than 90% of the maximum for two existing patterns, and 3 micro-SMEs behave according to 3 of the 5 segments defined. Of the "Active/Exacting/High Value" segment consisting of 179 micro-SMEs, 108 follow a single pattern, thus belonging to a single segment. Conversely, we find that the behaviour of 61 micro-SMEs falls into both "Active/Exacting/High Value" and another pattern, with an adequacy degree of over 90%.

In summary, 244 individuals reveal 2 or more patterns of behaviour.

Based on this information, our next objective is to identify and measure the plurality of individual behaviour in the 5 existing segments, that is, discover individuals' second or third patterns amongst those who present more than one pattern. Following the examples of "Uninvolved/Impassive" and "Active/Exacting/High Value", Figure 9

Figure 7. Adequacy degree of each individual in each segment. New focus in interpreting the results

	uninvolved	safety	active exacting	indignant	optimistic
1	0,906	0,284	0,100	0,232	0,650
6	0,902	0,296	0,100	0,510	0,825
10	0,950	0,377	0,094	0,619	0,785
11	0,845	0,084	0,707	0,096	0,156
14	0,817	0,149	0,090	0,287	0,817
16	0,807	0,547	0,096	0,463	0,745
17	0,702	0,801	0,206	0,098	0,409
19	1,000	0,099	0,452	0,133	0,654
21	0,991	0,094	0,440	0,098	0,726
24	0,678	0,155	0,098	0,428	0,204
26	0,903	0,750	0,503	0,432	0,099
27	0,904	0,098	0,605	0,098	0,743
29	0,817	0,521	0,643	0,143	0,098
30	0,920	0,199	0,514	0,559	0,318
33	0,876	0,097	0,837	0,181	0,169
38	0,811	0,200	0,067	0,495	0,796
39	0,945	0,100	0,527	0,094	0,652
41	1,000	0,450	0,181	0,238	0,620

	Maximum
	> 0.9* Maximum
	> 0.5* Maximum
	Not adequate

below details the behaviour of the 47 individuals who belong to both the "Uninvolved/Impassive" and other segments, and the 71 micro-SMEs which reveal both the "Active/Exacting/High Value" and other existing patterns, and so on, for each of the segments presented.

4.4 Decision-Making

It is crucial for a market segmentation strategy to have the potential to be used (Choffray and Lilien, 1978). Being able to carry out a fuzzy segmentation process that does not force every individual

Figure 8. Plurality of patterns per individual

Fuzzy Segmentation	No. of companies with 1 pattern	No. of companies with 2 patterns	No. of companies with 3 patterns	No. of companies with 4 and 5 patterns		NO. OF INDIVIDUALS / SEGMENT	Sample Univ.
Uninvolved Impassive	218	44	3	0	0	265	33.0%
	82%	17%	1%				
Active Exacting High Value	108	61	10	0	0	179	22.3%
	60%	34%	6%				
Indignant Show-off	106	28	6	0	0	140	17.5%
	76%	20%	4%				
Optimistic Receptive	61	66	4	0	0	131	16.3%
	47%	50%	3%				
Safety Service	65	21	1	0	0	87	10.8%
	75%	24%	1%				
General total	**558**	**220**	**24**	**0**	**0**	**802**	**100%**
	70%	27%	3%	0	0	100%	

in the sample to belong to only one segment but allows for any other real behaviours or patterns of behaviour to be identified and quantified is of great benefit to marketing professionals. It gives them a clearer vision of reality and helps them to be more accurate in their marketing actions.

Using "fuzziness" techniques when segmenting offers marketing professionals a specific value. Marketing departments can now decide which

customer acquisition actions are appropriate according to the customer's degree of plurality.

One of the greatest benefits of these techniques, although not used in this exercise, is being able to work with the whole population of individuals. By working with all of them (or the whole company database), individuals can be identified by name and surname, thus offering greater insights for targeting actions.

Figure 9. Identification of behavioural pluralities

	Uninvolved Impassive	Active Exacting	Indignant Show-off	Optimistic Receptive	Safety Service
Uninvolved Impassive	**218**	6	15	4	25
Active Demanding	4	**108**	26	33	18
Indignant Show-off	11	20	**106**	5	4
Optimistic	6	54	10	**61**	4
Safety	4	13	2	4	**65**

One of the main disadvantages of fuzzy segmentation is that the very duality that lets us consider the same individual within two different classes means we cannot consider global proportions or percentages. Interpretation has to be based on the proportion of individuals who are considered to belong to each segment. For instance, according to the non-hierarchical cluster method, 22% of individuals in the sample fall into the "Active/Exacting" segment, making this the second-largest segment in terms of the number of individuals. While we cannot reach this conclusion using fuzzy attitudinal segmentation, what we can see is that, amongst all the individuals, 33.9% are "Active/Exacting" (in first or second place), while 66.1% are not (See Figure 10).

It is important to bear in mind that statistics and Artificial Intelligence are highly complementary disciplines. A line of research is being pursued mainly in academic circles which aims to compare the two disciplines and measure their validity. Comparing apples with pears is never an easy task, but this is one clear example of the two being complementary. And the combination works.

5. CONCLUSION

Recently, we have seen a radical change in data analysis methods to explore similar problems to the one identified above. Currently, marketing managers have a wide range of segmentation techniques and models from which to choose. This is a new innovative segmentation approach that works mainly with huge, complex and different types of data. Advances in statistical analyses can now weigh various non-exclusive options simultaneously. Artificial Intelligence (AI) and, in particular, fuzzy logic techniques allow data to be analysed from a new perspective. Moreover, technological advances allow companies to gather large quantities of information about their customers, even if this data is often ambiguous and incomplete. AI techniques are increasingly capable of dealing with this type of information.

We no longer obtain a black and white picture of consumers and their membership in a given segment. Instead, the information gleaned from classifying data is used by the system to "learn" from the results before performing the next step in the process. This means that a firm can discover which multiple segments customers belong to and why. Thus, marketing managers can now identify changing price sensitivity and strong and weak consumers within time scales as short as a few days. This implies that one of the basic principles of segmentation theory – namely, homogeneous segments – has undergone a drastic change. The object of segmentation is no longer the customer, but rather his/her complex mix of behavioural patterns.

In most cases, the relationship between customers and a brand, a small shop or a retailer changes over time. The fuzzy segmentation approach takes this into account. The danger with the old approach was that consumer behaviour was treated as static, as if time, experience and situation made little difference. The solution is not to continually re-segment the market since this is unlikely to yield more reliable information. Instead, we need to introduce time-sensitive and situational factors. A way of doing this is to analyse customers' behaviour rather than the customers themselves. These behavioural patterns are not clear-cut, and, as such, analyses based on fuzzy logic allow these complex patterns to be defined. This means that the probability of belonging to a segment is now replaced by its adequacy/fit or how well it "matches" another segment. This principle questions the view that a customer who exhibits the preferences of a given segment cannot also simultaneously share completely different preferences of another customer segment. Thus, if a customer can behave differently according to

Figure 10. Complementariness between statistics and artificial intelligence to interpret the resulting data

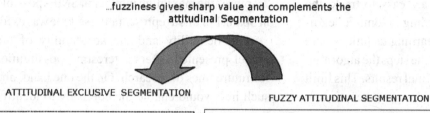

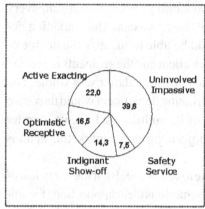

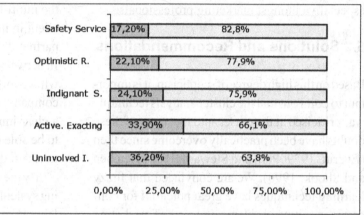

the situation, it seems likely that the concept of belonging to a single given group is incomplete. Hence, the idea of "matching" offers great value when it comes to assigning a behavioural pattern to each segment and analysing the extent to which that pattern matches the category.

5.1 Limits

Once the research community started to become aware of the potentiality of fuzzy logic techniques, several researchers, applying a combination of approaches, began publishing their work in different fields. As Flach (2001) states when analyzing the state of the art in machine learning, there is a clear trend in research combining approaches that were previously considered separate. Across the literature, a conclusion can be drawn that there is an increasing tendency to combine forms of machine learning and fuzzy logic. For instance, the number of publications that introduce fuzzy learning techniques from 2005 to 2010 is considerably higher than the number of publications

between 2000 and 1995, and so on. Despite the fact that there are few AI applications in marketing compared to fields in mainstream science, it is interesting to note that the majority of AI applications in the marketing literature are based on machine learning and fuzzy logic approaches. There are few publications found in the literature, however, and not all research projects use the same technique. For this reason, it should come as no surprise that one of the existing lines of research is orientated towards comparing the effectiveness of the techniques or demonstrating if learning techniques are more accurate than traditional statistical methods especially as regards market segmentation (Mazanec, 1992; Dasgupta, Dispensa and Ghose, 1997; Davies, Moutinho and Curry, 1996; Balakrishnan *et al.*, 1996; Setiono, Thong and Yap, 1998) and targeting (e.g., Tam and Kiang, 1992; Yoon, Swales and Margavio, 1993; Fish, Barnes and Aiken, 1995; Huang and Lippman, 1997).

That said, one of the greatest challenges faced in the AI field and, concretely, in terms of learning techniques, is managing its inherent "black box". While statistical methods are easy to track, the same cannot be said regarding automatic learning techniques. Existing learning techniques are incapable of showing us all the steps the algorithm takes before presenting its final results. This limit has and continues to provoke great scepticism, especially amongst marketing professionals.

5.2 Solutions and Recommendations

Based on this high degree of scepticism, it is important to point out that the cluster analysis technique was criticised at the outset, and that most of these doubts have been practically overcome since then (Everitt, 1979; Punj and Steward, 1993; Hetchen and Shook, 1996). We are convinced that fuzzy learning techniques have great potential for concrete marketing problems. In terms of marketing segmentation, we propose that combining different statistical and Artificial Intelligence techniques and tools offers great advantages. The important question is knowing how to correctly define the research problem, understanding the pros and cons of each existing technique, and designing a model that combines as many techniques as needed and allows for the same model to be constantly validated and updated because the reality being studied is ever-changing and complex.

5.3 Future Research Directions

Capturing new clients and retaining existing ones are two crucial objectives for marketing departments in companies that not only want to grow but want to be successful over the long term. The goal of the case study presented in this chapter served to segment the energy market in Spain in order to identify the primary types of corporate consumers and decide which represented the strategic segments for the company and on whom the company should focus its pertinent marketing

actions. Specifically, the goal of the study was to "capture" the maximum number of SMEs possible in Spain. For this a representative sample was used.

The flexibility and the adaptability of the model presented offers interesting possibilities for future lines of research. On the one hand, one such line would enable the company to identify the multi-behavioural profiles of each and every client in its database. As such, the marketing department would be able to identify the degree of fit between each client and the segments identified while working on the population as a whole. The company's marketing department would thus have a clear image of its multifaceted clients in order to be able to target appropriate marketing actions to retain them.

By the same token, we feel that the fuzzy learning system presented has clear applications for collaborative settings. Specifically, the methodology presented may be of interest for recommendation systems. The use of fuzzy segmentation in these systems would enable companies to identify different user groups with similar preferences. The use of the individual's adequacy or fit to each of the segments offers us a measure to be able to provide a good recommendation.

REFERENCES

Aguado, J. C. (1998). *A mixed qualitative-quantitative self-learning classification technique applied to simulation assessment in industrial process control.* PhD dissertation, Universitat Politécnica de Catalunya, Spain.

Aguilar-Martin, J., & López de Mántaras, R. (1982). The process of classification and learning: The meaning of linguistic descriptors of concepts. *Approximate Reasoning in Decision Analysis, 1982,* 165–175.

Aguilar-Martin, J., & Piera, N. (1986). Les connectifs mixtes: De nouveaux operateurs d'association des variables dans la classification automatique avec apprentissage. In Diday, E. (Eds.), *Data analysis and informatics* (pp. 253–265). North Holland Elsevier Science Publishers.

Arabie, P. (1977). Clustering representations of group overlap. *The Journal of Mathematical Sociology, 5*, 113–141. doi:10.1080/0022250X.1977.9989867

Arabie, P., Carroll, J. D., DeSarbo, W., & Wind, J. (1981). Overlapping clustering: A new method for product positioning. *JMR, Journal of Marketing Research, 18*(August), 310–317. doi:10.2307/3150972

Assael, H., & Roscoe, A. M. (1976). Approaches to market segmentation analysis. *Journal of Marketing, 40*, 67–76. doi:10.2307/1251070

Baker, M. J. (1988). *Marketing strategy and management*. New York, NY: MacMillan.

Balakrishnan, P. V. S., Cooper, M. C., Jacob, V. S., & Lewis, P. A. (1996). Comparative performance of the FSCL neural net and k-means algorithm for market segmentation. *European Journal of Operational Research, 93*, 346–357. doi:10.1016/0377-2217(96)00046-X

Bergmann, M. (2008). *An introduction to many-valued and fuzzy logic: Semantics, algebras, and derivation systems*. New York, NY: Cambridge University.

Casabayó, M. (2005). *Shopping behaviour forecasts: Experiments based on a fuzzy learning technique in the Spanish food retailing industry*. PhD. dissertation, The University of Edinburgh, UK.

Casabayó, M. (2010). El consumidor, en el punto de mira de las decisiones en márketing. *Harvard Deusto Marketing & Ventas, 98*, 40–44.

Casabayó, M., & Martín, B. (2010). *Fuzzy marketing, cómo comprender al consumidor camaleónico*. Barcelona, Spain: Deusto.

Choffray, J. M., & Lilien, G. L. (1978). A new approach to industrial market segmentation. *MIT Sloan Management Review, 19*(3), 17–29.

Christensen, C. B., Berstell, G., Anthony, S. D., & Nitterhouse, D. (2007). Finding the right job for your product. *MIT Sloan Management Review, 48*(3), 38–47.

Dasgupta, C. G., Dispensa, G. S., & Ghose, S. (1994). Comparing the predictive performance of a neural network model with some traditional market response models. *International Journal of Forecasting, 10*, 235–244. doi:10.1016/0169-2070(94)90004-3

Davies, F., Moutinho, L., & Curry, B. (1996). ATM user attitudes: A neural network analysis. *Marketing Intelligence & Planning, 14*(2), 26–32. doi:10.1108/02634509610110778

Dubois, D., & Prade, H. (1988). *Fuzzy sets and systems*. New York, NY: Academic Press.

Dubois, D., & Prade, H. (2003). A review of fuzzy set aggregation connectives. *Information Sciences, 36*(1-2), 85–121. doi:10.1016/0020-0255(85)90027-1

Everitt, B. S. (1979). Unresolved problems in cluster analysis. *Biometrics, 35*(March), 169–181. doi:10.2307/2529943

Everitt, B. S. (1993). *Cluster analysis*. New York, NY: John Wiley & Sons.

Fish, K. E., Barnes, J. H., & Aiken, M. W. (1995). Artificial neural networks - A new methodology for industrial market segmentation. *Industrial Marketing Management, 24*, 431–438. doi:10.1016/0019-8501(95)00033-7

Flach, P. A. (2001). On the state of the art in machine learning: A personal review. *Artificial Intelligence, 131*, 199–222. doi:10.1016/S0004-3702(01)00125-4

Frank, R. E., Massy, W. F., & Wind, Y. (1972). *Market segmentation*. Englewood Cliffs, NJ: Prentice Hall.

Gath, I., & Geva, B. (1989). Unsupervised optimal fuzzy clustering. *IEEE Transactions on Pattern Analysis and Machine Intelligence, 2*(7), 773–781. doi:10.1109/34.192473

Höppner, F., Klawonn, F., Kruse, R., & Runkler, T. (1999). *Fuzzy cluster analysis*. Chichester, UK: John Wiley & Sons.

Hruschka, H. (1986). Market definition and segmentation using fuzzy clustering methods. *International Journal of Research in Marketing, 3*, 117–134. doi:10.1016/0167-8116(86)90015-7

Huang, W. Y., & Lippman, R. P. (1997). Comparisons between neural net and conventional classifiers. *IEEE 1st International Conference on Neural Networks IV* (pp. 485-493).

Johnson, R. M. (1971). Market segmentation: A strategic management tool. *JMR, Journal of Marketing Research, 8*(February), 13–21. doi:10.2307/3149720

Ketchen, D. J., & Shook, C. L. (1996). The application of cluster analysis in strategic management research: an analysis and critique. *Strategic Management Journal, 17*(6), 441–458. doi:10.1002/(SICI)1097-0266(199606)17:6<441::AID-SMJ819>3.0.CO;2-G

Klawonn, F., & Höppner, F. (2003). What is fuzzy about fuzzy clustering? Understanding and improving the concept of the fuzzifier. In Berthold, M. R., Lenz, H. J., Bradley, E., Kruse, R., & Borgelt, C. (Eds.), *Advances in intelligent data analysis* (pp. 254–264). Berlin, Germany: Springer. doi:10.1007/978-3-540-45231-7_24

Klir, J. G., & Yuan, B. (1995). *Fuzzy sets and fuzzy logics: Theory and applications*. New Jersey: Prentice Hall.

Kotler, P. (1989). From mass marketing to mass customisation. *Planning Review, 17*, 10–13.

Kotler, P. (2000). *Marketing management*. New Jersey: Prentice-Hall.

Loudon, D. L., & Della Vitta, A. J. (1993). *Consumer behavior: Concepts and applications*. Singapore: McGraw-Hill.

Luque, T. (2000). Segmentación Jerárquica. In Luque, T. (Ed.), *Técnicas de análisis de datos en investigación de mercados* (pp. 347–382). Madrid, Spain: Pirámide.

Mazanec, J. A. (1992). Classifying tourists into market segments: A neural network approach. *Journal of Travel & Tourism Marketing, 1*(1), 39–59. doi:10.1300/J073v01n01_04

McDonald, M., & Dunbar, I. (1995). *Market segmentation*. Basingstoke, UK: MacMillan Press.

Punj, G., & Steward, D. W. (1983). Cluster analysis in marketing research: Review and suggestions for application. *JMR, Journal of Marketing Research, 20*, 134–148. doi:10.2307/3151680

Ruspini, E. (1969). A new approach to clustering. *Information and Control, 15*, 22–32. doi:10.1016/S0019-9958(69)90591-9

Setiono, R., Thong, J. Y. L., & Yap, C. S. (1998). Symbolic rule extraction from neural networks - An application to identifying organizations adopting IT. *Information & Management, 34*(2), 91–101. doi:10.1016/S0378-7206(98)00048-2

Smith, W. (1956). Product differentiation and market segmentation as alternative marketing strategies. *Journal of Marketing, 21*(July), 3–8. doi:10.2307/1247695

Steenkamp, J. B., & Wedel, M. (1992). Fuzzy cluster wise regression in benefit segmentation: Application and validation into its validity. *Journal of Business Research*, *26*(3), 237–249. doi:10.1016/0148-2963(93)90034-M

Tam, K. Y. (1994). Neural networks for decision support. *Decision Support Systems*, *11*, 389–392. doi:10.1016/0167-9236(94)90014-0

Wedel, M., & Kamakura, W. (2000). *Market segmentation: Conceptual and methodological foundations* (2nd ed.). Massachusetts, USA: Kluwer Academic Publisher.

Wedel, M., & Kamakura, W. (2002). Introduction to the special issue on market segmentation. *International Journal of Research in Marketing*, *19*(3), 181–183. doi:10.1016/S0167-8116(02)00075-7

Yankelovich, D., & Meer, D. (2006). Rediscovering market segmentation. *Harvard Business Review*, *24*(February), 122–131.

Yoon, Y., Swales, G., & Margavio, T. M. (1993). A comparison of discriminant analysis versus artificial neural networks. *The Journal of the Operational Research Society*, *44*(1), 51–60.

Zadeh, L. A. (1965). Fuzzy sets. *Information and Control*, *8*(3), 338–353. doi:10.1016/S0019-9958(65)90241-X

Zadeh, L. A. (1975). *Fuzzy sets and their applications to cognitive and decision processes*. New York, NY: Academic Press, Inc.

Zimmermann, H. J. (1987). *Fuzzy sets, decision making, and expert systems. International Series in Management Science Operations Research* (*Vol. 10*). Springer. doi:10.1007/978-94-009-3249-4

Zimmermann, H. J. (2010). Fuzzy set theory. *Wiley Interdisciplinary Reviews: Computational Statistics*, *2*(3), 317–332. doi:10.1002/wics.82

KEY TERMS AND DEFINITIONS

Adequacy Degree: The numerical value assigned to each individual with respect to each segment, indicating the degree to which said individual fits with the group or segment.

Fuzzy Clustering: A classification technique for individuals which uses its own fuzzy logic operators or rules; as a result, it obtains reveals different degrees of adequacy.

Fuzzy Learning Segmentation Technique: A method based on fuzzy logic operators which automatically permits defining population segments or classes automatically.

Learning Technique: A technique using iterative search tools which is capable of automatically obtaining pattern classifications.

Multibehavioural Segmentation: A segmentation model which enables us to identify, group and measure the multifaceted consumer.

Multifaceted consumer: A versatile and complex consumer who adapts his/her purchase and consumption habits and patterns depending on the occasion, even demonstrating paradoxical behaviour.

Chapter 14
Causal Recipes Sufficient for Identifying Market Gurus versus Mavens

Miri Chung
University of Rhode Island, USA

Arch G. Woodside
Boston College, USA

ABSTRACT

Prior research focusing on the market maven (MM) neglects to consider the possible existence of people who may represent an important source of marketplace information for MMs—the market guru (MG). A "market guru" is a consumer others frequently seek out for advice but who does not seek advice from others. In contrast to MG, a MM is a consumer who other consumers frequently ask for advice and who frequently seeks advice from others. This study raises the proposition that a greater share of MGs versus MMs are innovators, that is, individuals who rely on technical reports to become the first to adopt new products in her or his community. This study applies fuzzy-set qualitative comparative analysis (fs/QCA) to distinguish between MMs and MGs using multi-year data from a national U.S. omnibus survey. The findings support several propositions distinguishing MGs from MMs. MMs evaluate themselves as great influencers of consumers, highly sensitive to normative susceptibility, and possessing superior taste. However, MGs evaluate themselves exactly the opposite from MMs on these conditions.

INTRODUCTION

Consumer discussions with friends, family members, and acquaintances about what to buy, not to buy, and where to buy influence consumers' purchasing behavior (Chelminski & Coulter, 2006; Robertson & Kennedy, 1968; Feick & Price, 1987; Rogers, 1995). Therefore, understanding who diffuses market information and how market information flows are important for building and testing theories in consumer psychology.

Consumer behavior word-of-mouth research focuses mostly upon identifying a market in-

DOI: 10.4018/978-1-4666-0095-9.ch014

formation diffuser, that is, the "market maven". Market mavens (MMs) are "individuals who have information about many kinds of products, places to shop, and other facets of markets, and initiate discussions with consumers and respond to requests from consumers for market information" (Feick and Price 1987).

Because of MMs' expected influence occurs for many product and service categories, the empirical studies of market mavens traits are available in several disciplines – including consumer psychology, sociology, and marketing (Abratt, Nel, & Nezer, 1995; Belch, Krentler, & Willis-Flurry, 2005; Chelminski & Coulter, 2006; Ruvio & Shoham, 2007). The findings from these studies indicate that as important disseminators of general market knowledge, MMs are heavy information-seekers and want to possess market information to diffuse and generate social conversation (Walsh, Gwinner, & Swanson 2004). They tend to feel obligations with others involving marketplace issues and also to represent themselves to be important sources of general market information to other consumers (Clark & Goldsmith, 2005; Feick & Price, 1987).

Prior research focuses on maven's characteristics, however, neglects another potentially important segment of information diffusers, who may represent an important source of marketplace information to other consumers but do not seek out advice from other consumers and not involved in the marketplace socially. The study here identifies these consumers as "market gurus" (MGs).

In this study a "marketing guru" is a consumer others frequently seek out for advice but who does not seek advice from others. This definition appears to be the first to introduce "market guru" into the marketing and consumer research literatures. Developing theory about the antecedents associating with being a MG and confirming the existence of MGs among consumers were objectives for the present study. MMs' characteristics include possession of high amounts of market information; perform extensive search activities, and are female more often than male (Abratt, et al. 1995; Cal, 2004). These characteristics may apply only to MMs and not to MGs. MGs may be more likely to possess high amounts of technical versus market information; perform limited search activity, and may be males more than females.

Goldsmith, Flynn, and Goldsmith (2003) argue that MMs are likely to be distinct from other influencers, that is, innovators. Boone (1970) defines consumer innovators as persons who make innovative purchases without having to rely upon the experience of others. Although consumer innovators are likely to contribute to other consumers' needs about market information and likely to take new product risk (Robertson and Kennedy, 1968), they do not seek-out the advice of people regarding their purchasing. This characteristic represents MGs not seeking whereas MMs frequently seek other consumer to get and give advice.

However, the distinguishable causal recipes for MMs and MGs are ill-defined and heretofore are untested. Therefore this study examines the "distinguishability" of antecedent conditions for MGs versus MMs.

To identify distinguishable antecedent conditions of MGs versus MGs, this study uses a configurational method, fuzzy set qualitative comparative analysis (fs/QCA) (Ragin, 2000). The main reason to applying fs/QCA is that the method permits analyses of complex configurations of causal conditions as explanations of an outcome condition—and does so without assuming symmetric relationships among antecedents and outcomes. Unlike statistical methods that rely on matrix algebra, relying on Boolean algebra QCA methods explicitly consider alternative complex antecedent statements that are likely to associate with an outcome condition, that is, QCA calls attention to the frequent reality that more than one route (i.e., path) is sufficient and no one path is necessary to cause an outcome (see Ragin 1997).

Heretofore, the majority of studies examining maven's characteristic used regression based models (Engelland, Hopkins, & Larson 2001; Goldsmith, Clark, & Goldsmith 2006). Whereas regression analysis estimates the average effect of a predictor on outcome variable beyond all other predictors and assumes linear causation, fuzzy-set analysis assumes that each simple condition is neither necessary or sufficient in explaining an outcome (Katz, Vom Hau, & Mahoney, 2005; Ragin, 2000); fs/QCA allows the researcher to probe various links between configurations of antecedents and an outcome (Ragin, 2008b). By using fs/QCA, therefore, this study identifies unique configurations of conditions that associate with MGs versus MMs.

This article has the following organization. Following this introduction, section two describes MG theory and literatures about MMs and MGs. Section three describes the method and the dataset for the study. Section four describes antecedents for configural antecedent conditions and outcomes along with specific propositions for testing. Section five presents analyses and findings. Section six covers limitations and future directions for research.

MARKET MAVEN AND MARKET GURU

Because of MMs important role of interpersonal communication and dissemination of market information, scholars and marketers provide extensive descriptions of MMs (Walsh, et al. 2004). With increasing complexity and growing quantity of market information, MMs largely influence other consumers' purchase decision and behavior (Walsh, et al. 2004).

MMs seek market information aggressively. Price, Feick, & Guskey-Federouch (1988) describe MMs as "smart shoppers" because MMs tend to shop more organized and in planned ways using such as tools as shipping lists or coupons. Judging from results from Price, et al. (1988), MMs possess high amounts of information about shopping and are much involved thinking and actions relating to shopping. Since MMs have general information

such as prices, product quality, and variety (Slama & Williams, 1990), consumers seek to get marketplace information and knowledge from MMs.

MMs are perceived as heavy information diffusers. According to Feick and Price (1987), one reason why MMs want to possess market information is that they want to lead in social conversations. MMs feel obligated to be involved in the marketplace so that they can be informed what is happening in the marketplaces. MMs tend to initiate conversations and take special delight in interact with other consumers (Feick & Price 1987). Because an MM is likely to reveal themselves and have important role of transmitter of information, the MM is now an established and well documented leader of consumer followers (Goldsmith, et al., 2006; Ruvio & Shoham, 2007).

However, prior research focusing on MM's characteristics misses the possible existence of MGs. MGSs may be valuable diffusers of market information and are a source of general information to MMs but do not voluntarily reveal themselves unless consumers come to them for advice about products and brands. The original meaning of term "guru" is "heavy" or "weighty" and gurus well illustrate the belief certain persons have unique knowledge that may share with a limited number of other persons (Mlecko 1982).

According to the Spiritual Science Research Foundation (SSRF, 2010), the guru is the one who dispels the darkness of ignorance in man and bestows upon him experiences and knowledge. Gonda (1985) states, "It ["guru"] must primarily have described the man who on account of his special knowledge and function was held to be a bearer of power conspicuous by his prestige, 'weight', and influence." Also gurus have authority in the field but they gain insight and knowledge beyond people (SSRF 2010).

Taken together these features and modifying the original meaning of "guru", this study defines market gurus as people who dispels the darkness about a product-market through disseminating their insight, knowledge, and information regarding technical features, use, and benefits of products and services; MGs have authority to diffuse market information but differ from MMS in that MGs do not seek-out other consumers and initiate conversation with other consumers. Rather, market gurus tend to acquire market information not from consumers but from elsewhere (technical reports and brand websites versus social websites). Market gurus share market information without any expectation of receiving information from other consumers or that doing so will advance their social standings or reputations.

Property Space Analysis

Figure 1 is a "property-space" (Lazarsfeld 1937) cross-table that identifies MGs' and MMs' locations by two provisions relating to word-of-mouth information search. "Property-space analysis" includes the recognition the individuals exist theoretically at least in all possible conjunctive statements of two or more conditions. Both MM and MG includes the proposal that both MMs and MGs define themselves uniquely on the dimensions of receiving and giving information to other consumers. MMs are extreme in both seeking and giving information from/to other consumers. MGs are extreme in giving information to others but report very infrequent attempts in seeking information from others. Figure 1 includes property spaces for market followers (i.e., extreme seekers in combination with rarely giving information) and isolates (i.e., the combination of rarely seeking or giving product-market information to other consumers.

By showing the possible structure and components of a social system, property space analysis demonstrates how method (technique) can aid (as well as sometime impede) advances in theory (cf. Gigerenzer (2008). Locations in Figure 1 may reflect different theoretical positions in the innovation and diffusion literature (Rogers 1995) (see Exhibit 1).

Thus, coupling property space analysis with QCA permits a more complete study of all locations in the social structure involving the innovation of diffusions than considering only the antecedents and behavior of MMs. However, the objectives here are less ambitious; this chapter's objectives are to report the occurrence of MGs as well as MMs and to provide evidence of the causal recipes distinguishing MGs from MMs.

The percentages in the cells in Figure 1 show the distribution of consumers for all combinations of seeking and giving market information to other in national samples of U.S. consumers. The national samples are the "DDB Life Style" data, made available through the generosity of DDB Worldwide of Chicago, Illinois, who retain appropriate rights, including copyright, on these data, while allowing fair use for scholarly and academic research.

This data set covers 1975-1998 with a total unweighted sample size of 84,989 cases (Putnam 1995, 2000).

Among total number of consumers, proportions for market guru and market maven are extremely few in the DDB national samples; 1.4 percent refers to MGs and 0.6 percent refers to MMs. The property space analysis in Figure 1 reflects McClelland's (1996) proposal of the need to focus on extreme types of individuals (e.g., MGs and MMs) to control for noise in data.

Researches focusing on MM's role of information diffuser concentrate on behavioral and demographical characteristics. For example, research indicates that MMs are more likely to be female, relatively early to adopt new products, and to read variety of information sources such as all types of advertising, news, and magazines to gain general marketplace information (Abratt, et al., 1995), and then market mavens pass the information to consumers who want to listen (Feick and Price 1987). Since the combination of these traits may be about providing information and information seeking, MGs likely have some similar behavioral and demographical characteristics of MMs.

Figure 1. Property space configuration for market guru and market maven: Share of Americans in DDB Omnibus National Samples (1975-1998) (n = 84,989)

		Seek					
		-3	-2	-1	1	2	3
	-3	**isolates** 9.0%	4.0%	2.0%	2.4%	1.2%	**opinion followers** .6%
	-2	2.8%	5.7%	3.7%	4.1%	1.4%	.2%
	-1	2.3%	3.9%	6.1%	5.6%	1.7%	.4%
Come	1	3.2%	4.7%	6.3%	9.0%	3.5%	.5%
	2	1.2%	2.2%	2.6%	2.9%	1.7%	.5%
	3	**market guru** 1.4%	.6%	.8%	.8%	.7%	**market maven** .6%

Notes. Originally measured by 6-likert scale anchored by strongly disagree/strongly agree.
"Seek": I often seek out the advice of my friends regarding brands and products. "Come": My friends and neighbors often come to me for advice about products and brands.
Large central rectangle represents the majority of Americans who are not extreme in seeking or giving advice.

MGs want to gain general and new market information. Therefore MGs might search all types of market information sources and shop often. Also MGs are likely to diffuse their marketing information to MMs who seek-out MGs for advice about products and brands. Since females read magazine and are more involve in shopping for consumer products than males (Higie, Feick, & Price, 1987), MGs are also more likely to be female. As such, distinguishing between MMs and MGs through behavioral and demographical traits is unlikely. This study, therefore, suggests finding notable characteristics that are absent in the literature in the attempt to distinguish MGs from

Exhibit 1.

Social structure location (see Figure 1)	Innovation Stance
Market	guru Innovator
Market maven	Early adopter
Opinion Follower V	Very early majority
Isolates	Laggards

MMs. This study uses (fsQCA.com) to examine configurations of behavioral, demographics, and attitudes, interests, and opinions (AIOs) to identify MGs distinctly from MMs.

FUZZY SET QUALITATIVE COMPARARIVE ANALYSIS

Fuzzy-set QCA (Ragin 1987) is useful to testing causal conditions associating with particular outcomes. The method is useful for identifying sufficient, complex, causal conditions for an outcome (Katz, Vom Hau, & Mahoney, 2005; Ragin, 2000). Fuzzy set analyses allow cases to belong to varying degrees in multiple configurations (Ragin 2000). Through fs/QCA, this study expects to find accurate theoretical pathways that are sufficient for identifying MGs distinctly from MMs.

Since most research about MMs applies regression modeling (Engelland, et al., 2001; Goldsmith, et al., 2006), multiple and alternative configurations of conditions remain unreported until now. Just as there may be different combinations of conditions for MMs, there likely are different configurations of antecedents for MGs. The study here presumes that the factors leading to particular characteristic about information diffusers are the same for both market maven and market guru.

DATASET

This study uses the annual DDB datasets provided by DDB Needham's Life Style Survey. DDB dataset includes approximately 300 questionnaire items including demographics, consumption behaviors, and lifestyle attitudes, interests, and opinions (AIOs). The number of annual participants is about 3,000 during 1975 to 1999. This study here analyzes a subset of the 2,918 cases of the year 1997. The survey responses were available that include questions permitting the property-space analysis for the rationale in Figure 1 for just 1997.

Provision of market information is chosen for lifestyle antecedent condition. AIOs include possession of market information, search activities, shopping involvement, influence, and normative susceptibility. The items for analysis for each condition are developed from the annual DDB Needham Life Style Survey (see Table 1).

CAUSAL CONDITIONS AND FUZZY SET PROPOSITIONS

Market Mavens and Market Gurus

MMs maintain knowledge about brands across a wide range of products and services. MMs' brand awareness and product knowledge have been well established (Slama & Williams 1990). To get brand and product information, consumers want to hear endorsements from MMs.

With respect to information diffusion, MGs are also expected to have high brand awareness and information and are perceived by many consumers as valuable transmitters of information. However, whereas MMs enjoys initiate social discussions with consumers and gets information from consumers, MGs are unlikely to voluntarily approach consumers to get information and find insight and knowledge from other people (SSRF, 2010).

To examine memberships as a MM and MG, this study uses the following two items. "My friends and neighbors often come to me for advice about products and brands." "I often seek out the advice of my friends regarding brands and products". MMs have high membership with very high scores on both items whereas MGs have high membership with a very high score for first item and a very low score for second item.

Possession of Market Information

Possession of a variety of market information including new products that are especially useful for consumers is one of the salient traits of MMs (Abratt, et al., 1995). Feick and Price (1987) insist that MMs find out about new products and brands, across product categories because they are expected have more concerns about the marketplace generally than opinion followers. The characteristics of possession of market information may apply to MGs from the fact that consumers often come to them for advice about products and brands. To test the association of possession of market information with MMs and MGs, this study uses items from DDB dataset: "The latest fashion trends have bearing on what I wear." The proposition is that high scores of possession of market information indicates full membership as a MM and MG.

Table 1. Items for each antecedent condition

Condition		Symbol	Items
Outcome	Market Maven	Maven	My friends and neighbors often come to me for advice about products and brands. I often seek out the advice of my friends regarding brands and products
	Market Guru	Guru	My friends and neighbors often come to me for advice about products and brands, but I do not seek out the advice of my friends regarding brands and products
Lifestyle	Provision of Market Information	Provide	Wrote a letter to an editor of a magazine newspaper (frequency last 12 months)
Attitude, Interests, and Opinion (AIOs)	Possession of Market Information	Possess	The latest fashion trends have bearing on what I wear
	Search Activities	Search	I need to search (world, national, sports, etc.) everyday
	Shopping Involvement	Involve	Shopping is fun
	Influence	Influence	I am influential in my neighborhood
	Superior Taste	Superiority	I have much better tasted than most people
	Normative Susceptibility	Normative	The clothes I wear reflect who I am as a person
Demographic	Female	Female	Female respondent

Provision of Market Information

In the Feick and Price (1987) study, persons with a MM high score tend to provide information more frequently across product categories. Market mavens share and provide information through conversations with consumers or responding to requests for marketplace information. MMs like to initiate conversation (Chelminski and Coulter 2006).

Although MGs are unlikely to gain information from consumers and are unlikely to start a conversation voluntarily, MGs share every information about what they know about market knowledge without expectations and unconditionally. MGs' behavior of distributing information may be largely based on altruistic motives (S.S.R.F. 2010) and just for personal pleasure.

To examine relationship between provision behavior and information diffuser membership, this study uses the follow item, "Wrote a letter to an editor of a magazine or newspaper (frequency last 12 months)." As an important position of information diffuser, this study expects high frequency of provision of market information associating with high membership of MMs but not MGs because MMs seek-out contacts with others and MGs do not.

Search Activities

The MMs' and MGs' values come from useful market information and knowledge gained from frequent information seeking across products and experiences. Feick and Price (1987) propose that information diffuser's search behavior includes a variety of sources such as *Consumer Reports*, diverse forms of advertising, and general news. Kassarjian (1981) discusses the attention to advertising as indicators of the general information-diffuser concept. According to Higie, et al., (1987), MMs are particularly attentive to media.

The following item which represents search activities from DDB dataset, "I need to get the news every day." This study expects high score of news search activities with high membership of MGs and MMs because both are considered good sources of information by general consumers.

Shopping Involvement

Slama and Tashchian (1985) offer a purchasing involvement scale that measures the degree of enjoyment-of-shopping. Kassarjian (1981) discusses the interest in and the enjoyment of shopping as indicators of involvement concept. Feick and Price (1987) establish that the greater the enjoyment of shopping both generally the higher the MM score.

Therefore this study investigates the casual condition of shopping involvement and information diffuser membership by using follow item: "Shopping is fun." This study anticipates, similar to Feick and Price (1987)'s study, high membership of MMs associates with high score of shipping involvement more so than MGs membership. For MGs shopping is a means to an end more so than for MMs—MGs may shop for the sake of acquiring knowledge more so than for fun.

Gender

Traditionally, shopping is more a female than male responsibility in most cultures. Also females tend to be more involved with purchasing than males (Davis, 1971). According to Higie, et al. (1987), since women read more magazines and advertisements, women more than men are more likely to be MMs. This demographic characteristic may apply to MGs as well.

Although literature on the Hindu religion describes gurus as men (Mlecko, 1982), this study expects MGs to be females more than males since the market information is about products and brands not spiritual knowledge.

Self-Evaluation of Influence

MMs have general market information so consumers want to meet with a MM to get information and they are influenced by MMs (Elliott and Warfield, 1993; Williams and Slama, 1995). Also MMs want to influence consumers and reinforce their social image (Sundaram, Mitra, & Webster, 1998) so that marketers consider them as useful audiences. Usually MMs are already experts on many products and have high potential influence (Feick and Price, 1987). MMs tend to have greater confidence in word-of-mouth than commercial sources due to perceived credibility (Keller and Berry 2003) while MGs are likely to have greater confidence in commercial sources that MMs. Therefore MMs are likely to realize how much they affect consumers' purchasing decisions and MMs would evaluate their influencing power to be higher than MGs do.

MGs' sharing and seeking information is largely based on altruistic motives and own pleasure. Therefore MGs are unlikely to care much about how much they influence other consumers. Also MGs respond only when consumers come and want to listen and are unlikely to initiate meetings with consumers. MGs are unlikely to consider themselves to be highly influential broadly. This study uses the following item to examine self evaluation of influence. "I am influential in my neighborhood."

Normative Susceptibility

To effectively perform their role as a social communicator and influencer, MMs do not ignore what consumers want from them (Rogers, 1995). In other words, MMs are also influenced by consumers' expectations and social norms. The concept of normative susceptibility to interpersonal influence represents the MMs' psychological profile. Normative susceptibility is the tendency to satisfy the expectations of others (Burnkrant & Cousineau, 1975).

Bearden, Netemeyer, and Teel (1989) propose that the MM's social image increases when they confirm normative susceptibility in consumer contexts. The normative susceptibility of MMs especially includes the need to utilize products and the need to follow the expectations of others. This process likely leads toward a positive relationship between normative susceptibility to interpersonal influence and market mavenship (Steenkamp & Gielens, 2003).

However, MGs may not have a desire to be known or to become famous gurus (SSRF, 2010) and, therefore, they do not consume manifest a high normative susceptibility. Thus, MGs do not use products and brands to enhance their social image. Therefore this study expects a negative relationship between normative susceptibility and MG membership. The following item reflects normative susceptibility. "The clothes I wear reflect who I am as a person".

Superiority about Choice

MMs are responsive to requests of consumers and they perform well their role as an information diffuser. Also MMs feel comfortable with the unique role as a diffuser (Clark and Goldsmith, 2005). MMs likely know their high level of influence and enjoy their superiority and authority as sources of information. MMs recognize that other consumers consider MM's opinion and depend more on MMs' information rather than non-market mavens' opinions and information (Clark and Goldsmith, 2005). Therefore this study expects that MMs evaluate themselves to be better than other consumers in term of taste more so the MGs. MMs feel so because other consumers are more concerned with the MMs' choice than the choices and opinions of non-mavens.

Conversely, MGs consider themselves as messengers of information so they do not compare themselves and other consumers and focus on themselves. Therefore MGs are unlikely to feel superior in their choices and do feel uniqueness from other consumers.

To examine causal relationship of score of authority about choice and membership of MM and MG, this study uses the following item. "I have much better taste than most people"

CALIBRATION OF SCORES

Fs/QCA includes assigning a degree-of-membership to the antecedent conditions and outcome. To describe the degree of membership for a given case, fuzzy-set score needs to be generated by a calibration procedure. According to Ragin (2008a), fs/QCA uses Boolean set theory with membership scores falling between 0 and 1 for simple and combinatorial conditions. By permitting fuzzy-set membership scaling, partial membership can be employed so that loss of information can be minimized and accuracy of solutions can be maximized.

The "full membership" in a condition has a score of 1 and "mostly but not full membership" have close to 1 score such as 0.8 to 0.9. "Fully out" indicates non-membership and score is 0 and a score of 0.0 and 0.5 means "more or less out" or "mostly but not fully out."

The membership score 0.5 is known as the "crossover point", meaning the most ambiguousness score that is both not "in" and not "out" of the membership set. However, there is hard-and-fast no rule for calibration. Ragin (2008b) recommends that researcher calibrate fuzzy scores with social knowledge or own accumulated knowledge. The calibration for this study follows (Rihoux and Ragin, 2008). Following Fiss's (2009) suggestion, to avoid lose of cases information with fuzzy set score of zero, the analyses of the present study add a constant of 0.01 to zero membership scores. For establishing the fuzzy-set MM and MG, this study uses two items which are related concepts of MM and MG. By forming a cross-table (Table 2 and 3), this study assigns the qualitative breakpoints 0 (full out of set of market guru and market maven) and highly restrictive scores of.7 and.9 for mostly in memberships, and 1 (fully-in the sets of MM and MG).

Antecedent conditions measured by 6-point Likert scale are calibrated into six-value fuzzy set scores (Rihoux and Ragin, 2008) (see Table 4). For the condition of provision of market informa-

Table 2. Coding scheme fuzzy-set: Market maven

		Seek					
		-3	**-2**	**-1**	**1**	**2**	**3**
Come	-3	0.01	0.01	0.01	0.01	0.01	0.01
	-2	0.01	0.01	0.01	0.01	0.01	0.1
	-1	0.01	0.01	0.01	0.01	0.1	0.3
	1	0.01	0.01	0.01	0.1	0.3	0.7
	2	0.01	0.01	0.1	0.3	0.7	0.9
	3	0.01	0.1	0.3	0.7	0.9	1

Note. Originally measured by 6-point Likert scale anchored by strongly disagree/strongly agrees. "Seek": I often seek out the advice of my friends regarding brands and products. "Come": My friends and neighbors often come to me for advice about products and brands.

tion behavior, this study calibrates fuzzy-sets score by portion of total frequency (Table 5). Since Abratt, et al. (1995) describe females to be information diffusers, this study assigns full membership scores to females and zero membership scores to males (Table 6).

ANALYSIS

After calibration, the fs/QCA.com program permits the building "truth tables" to display all possible combinations of causal conditions and case distributions. The procedure of building a truth table is based on set-theory relations and connections between conditions. Some cases which have the same outcome shares for several

causal relevant conditions, called subset relation (Ragin 2000). The subset relation is, therefore, interpreted as sufficient for the outcome. Some cases that have the same outcome show other causally relevant conditions and are also interpreted as sufficient for the outcome (Ragin 2008a). Thus, fs/QCA allows researchers to find multiple pathways to an outcome (Epstein, Duerr, Kenworthy, & Ragin, 2008).

This study includes designing truth tables by selecting frequency thresholds of 1.0 and a consistency threshold of 0.8 since consistency values below 0.75 is considered substantially inconsistent (Ragin, 2005). Also the default consistency of fs/QCA is 0.8. The fs/QCA program produces the truth tables with eight antecedent conditions for both MMs (Table 7) and MGs (Table 8).

Table 3. Coding scheme fuzzy-set: Market guru

		Seek					
		-3	**-2**	**-1**	**1**	**2**	**3**
Come	-3	0.01	0.01	0.01	0.01	0.01	0.01
	-2	0.1	0.01	0.01	0.01	0.01	0.01
	-1	0.3	0.1	0.01	0.01	0.01	0.01
	1	0.7	0.3	0.1	0.01	0.01	0.01
	2	0.9	0.7	0.3	0.1	0.01	0.01
	3	1	0.9	0.7	0.3	0.1	0.01

Note. Originally measured by 6-pointg Likert scale anchored by strongly disagree/strongly agrees. "Seek": I often seek out the advice of my friends regarding brands and products. "Come": My friends and neighbors often come to me for advice about products and brands.

Table 4. Coding scheme fuzzy-set; provision of market information, possession of market information, shopping involvement, influence, normative susceptibility, superior taste

Fuzzy-set score	Original score (Likert scale)	Verbal label for Fuzzy set score
1	3	fully in
0.9	2	mostly but not fully in
0.7	1	more or less in
0.3	-1	more or less out
0.1	-2	mostly but not fully out
0.01	3	fully out

Table 5. Coding scheme fuzzy-set: Search activities

Original score (Frequency in Weeks)	Verbal label for Fuzzy set score	Fuzzy-set score
60	fully in	1.00
38	mostly but not fully in	0.75
18	more or less in	0.40
10	more or less out	0.20
6.5	mostly but not fully out	0.10
2.5	almost fully out	0.04
0	fully out	0.01

FINDINGS

This section presents the results of the necessary and the sufficient configurations for the market maven and market guru. The causal conditions are based on theoretical relations.

Necessary Conditions for the Outcome "Market Maven" and "Market Guru"

The necessary cause analysis examines each antecedent's necessity for the outcome to occur. According to Wagemann and Schneider (2007), an antecedent condition can be considered as necessary cause only when the consistency score is very high. Tables 9 and 10 show the results of the analysis of the necessary conditions for the MM and MG. As the consistency scores are not very high (i.e., less than 0.9), no simple (singular) antecedent condition can be considered necessary for the presence of MM and MG.

Parsimonious Solutions for the Outcome "Market Maven" and "Market Guru"

The analyses of parsimony solutions are important since they show the most simplified solutions

which support the basic antecedent conditions for membership in an outcome. Parsimony analysis takes out remainders, that is, configurations with no cases in the data set, so that logically simpler solutions are generated (Ochel & Rohwer, 2009). Parsimony solutions indicate the necessity of connected conditions since low coverage scores indicate triviality. Table 11 shows parsimony conditions for the MM membership. The causal combination of high provision of market information and female associates with high MM membership. Also MMs who have high membership tend to provide information as well as evaluate themselves as superior tasters. High provision of market information and high influence represent full MM membership. Given that parsimony solutions, every parsimony solution includes the provision of market information behavior. Since the provision of information behavior indicates the primary character of MMs as an information diffuser, the three parsimony solutions well represent the simple traits for MMs.

Table 6. Coding scheme fuzzy-set: Gender

Fuzzy-set score	original score	Verbal label for Fuzzy set score
1	Female	fully in
0.01	Male	fully out

Table 7. Truth table of all eight causal conditions for the outcome "market maven"

Possess	Provide	Female	Involve	Search	Normative	Superiority	Influence	Number	Maven	consist	pre	product
1	1	1	1	1	1	1	1	1	1	0.88	0.04	0.03
1	1	1	1	1	0	0	1	1	1	0.87	0.01	0.01
1	1	0	1	1	1	1	1	1	1	0.84	0.1	0.12
0	1	1	1	0	0	1	0	1	1	0.90	0.01	0.01
1	1	0	1	1	0	0	0	1	0	0.78	0.02	0.01
1	0	1	1	1	0	1	1	9	0	0.40	0.01	0.01
0	0	1	0	1	1	1	1	13	0	0.39	0.03	0.01
0	0	1	0	1	0	1	1	6	0	0.39	0.00	0.00
1	0	1	1	0	0	1	1	4	0	0.38	0.01	0.00
0	0	1	0	1	0	0	1	2	0	0.38	0.00	0.00
1	0	1	1	1	0	0	1	6	0	0.38	0.01	0.00
0	0	1	0	1	1	0	1	7	0	0.38	0.01	0.00
1	0	1	1	1	1	0	1	18	0	0.37	0.02	0.01
1	0	1	0	0	0	1	1	1	0	0.37	0.00	0.00
1	0	1	0	0	1	1	1	2	0	0.37	0.00	0.00
1	0	1	1	0	0	0	1	5	0	0.36	0.02	0.01
1	0	1	1	1	1	1	1	46	0	0.36	0.02	0.01
1	0	1	1	0	1	1	1	13	0	0.36	0.02	0.01
0	0	1	1	1	0	1	1	10	0	0.35	0.01	0.00

Table 8. Truth table of all eight causal conditions for the outcome "market guru"

Possess	Provide	Female	Involve	Search	Normative	Superiority	Influence	Number	Guru	consist	pre	product
1	1	1	1	1	1	1	1	1	1	0.92	0.13	0.12
1	1	1	1	1	0	0	1	1	1	0.90	0.04	0.04
0	1	1	1	0	0	1	0	1	1	0.87	0.02	0.02
1	1	0	1	1	0	0	0	1	1	0.90	0.17	0.14
1	1	0	1	1	1	1	1	1	0	0.79	0.08	0.06
1	0	1	0	1	0	1	1	6	0	0.44	0.01	0.00
0	0	1	1	1	0	1	1	9	0	0.44	0.02	0.01
1	0	1	0	1	0	0	1	2	0	0.44	0.00	0.00
1	0	1	0	1	1	1	1	13	0	0.43	0.03	0.01
1	0	1	0	0	0	1	1	1	0	0.43	0.01	0.00
1	0	1	0	1	1	0	1	7	0	0.43	0.01	0.00
1	0	1	0	0	1	1	1	2	0	0.43	0.01	0.00
0	0	1	1	1	1	1	1	46	0	0.43	0.07	0.03
1	0	1	1	1	0	1	1	10	0	0.42	0.02	0.01
0	0	1	1	1	0	0	1	6	0	0.42	0.00	0.00
1	0	1	1	0	0	1	1	4	0	0.42	0.00	0.00
1	0	1	1	0	1	1	1	13	0	0.42	0.02	0.01
1	0	1	0	0	1	0	1	5	0	0.42	0.02	0.01
1	0	1	0	0	0	0	1	5	0	0.41	0.01	0.00

Table 9. Analysis of the Necessary Conditions or the Outcome "Market Maven"

Condition tested	Consistency	Coverage
Possess	0.58	0.17
Provide	0.14	0.68
Female	0.58	0.09
Involve	0.81	0.13
Search	0.84	0.12
Normative	0.87	0.13
Superiority	0.82	0.1
Influence	0.74	0.18

Table 10. Analysis of the Necessary Conditions for the Outcome, "Market Guru"

Condition tested	Consistency	Coverage
Possess	0.49	0.22
Provide	0.10	0.73
Female	0.58	0.14
Involve	0.75	0.18
Search	0.81	0.17
Normative	0.82	0.18
Superiority	0.76	0.22
Influence	0.69	0.25

In Tables 11 to 14, the tilde symbol, "~" indicates "not in" the condition and a "~ condition" is calculated by 1 minus the membership value (e.g., "~ superior taste" = 1.0 – 0.20 = 0.80 for a score for superior taste equal to 0.20. The mid-level dot, "·", indicates the combination "and" for

a complex configuration (a causal recipe of two or more simple antecedent conditions).

The parsimony solution of MGs shows some opposite pathways from MMs (see Table 12). Similar with market maven, high provision of market information and female associates with high MG membership. However, high member-

Table 11. Three parsimony causal configurations of "market maven"

Parsimonious Causal Recipe	Coverage		Consistency
	Raw	Unique	
(a) Provide · Female	0.14	0	0.77
(b) Provide · Superiority	0.15	0	0.71
(c) Provide · Influence	0.15	0	0.74
Solution Coverage: 0.155			
Solution Consistency: 0.683			

Note: The frequency cutoff has been set at 1.00 and the consistency cutoff was 0.80.

Table 12. Four parsimony causal configurations of "market guru"

Parsimonious Causal Recipe	Coverage		Consistency
	Raw	Unique	
(a) Provide · Female	0.10	0.00	0.83
(b) Provide · ~Influence	0.10	0.00	0.75
(c) Provide · ~Superiority	0.10	0.00	0.76
(d) Provide · ~Normative	0.09	0.00	0.74
Solution Coverage: 0.107 Solution Consistency: 0.732			

Note: The frequency cutoff has been set at 1.00 and the consistency cutoff was 0.80.

ships of market gurus tend to provide market information but do not include themselves as strong influencers. Also high provision of market information but low normative susceptibility associates strongly with MG membership.

Finally, high membership of MG is likely to provide information but does not include themselves as possessing superior taste. All parsimonious solutions include MGs' aspect of information diffuser. Therefore this study identifies the four configurations of traits for MGs.

Sufficient (Intermediate) Solutions for the Market Maven Outcome

The analysis of intermediate conditions is based on supplied information about the connection between each causal condition and the outcome. In other words, the researcher designs the solution regarding how each causal condition should theoretically contribute to the outcome. A sufficient condition can produce a certain outcome

whereas a necessary condition must be present for an outcome to occur (Ragin, Rubinson, Schaefer, Anderson, Williams, & Giesel, 2008). Since MMs and MGs follow theoretical perspectives, examining sufficient solution is meaningful.

Table 13 displays the results of the analysis of the sufficient conditions for the outcome "market maven". Three intermediate solutions lead to a high MM membership: (1) a combination of female who evaluates herself as superior on taste, high shopping involvement, and high provision of market information; (2) female who thinks herself as heavy influencer to broad consumers, high search activities, high shopping involvement, high provision of market information and high possession of market information; and (3) high influence with superior taste, high normative susceptibility, high search activities and high shopping involvement with great provision and possession of market information.

The overall consistency of the solution is 0.76. This finding is an acceptable consistency level

Table 13. Three intermediate causal configurations of "market maven"

Intermediate Causal Recipe	Coverage		Consistency
	Raw	Unique	
(a) Superiority · Involve · Female · Provide	0.13	0.00	0.81
(b) Influence · Search · Involve · Female · Provide · Possess	0.13	0.00	0.86
(c) Influence · Superiority · Normative · Search · Involve · Provide · Possess	0.14	0.01	0.82
Solution Coverage: 0.148 Solution Consistency: 0.790			

Note: The frequency cutoff has been set at 1.00 and the consistency cutoff was 0.80.

Table 14. Three intermediate causal configurations of "market guru"

Intermediate Causal Recipe	Coverage		Consistency
	Raw	Unique	
(a) ~Influence · ~Normative · Involve · Female · Provide	0.08	0.00	0.87
(b) Search · Involve · Female · Provide · Possess	0.09	0.02	0.89
(c) ~Influence · ~Superiority · ~Normative · Search · Involve · Provide · Possess	0.08	0.01	0.85
Solution Coverage: 0.099 Solution Consistency: 0.808			

Note: The frequency cutoff has been set at 1.00 and the consistency cutoff was 0.80.

(Ragin 2005). This consistency indicates a 76% degree that the solutions as a whole are subsets of the outcome. Each solution also has relatively high consistency (i.e., 0.81, 0.86, and 0.82). Consequently, the subset relations are sufficient for a combination of characteristics of case aspects to the MM outcome.

The coverage of overall and each solution are relatively low. Coverage measures that how much complete solution can explain the memberships in the outcome (Ragin, et al., 2008). Therefore low coverage of results for this study indicates causal combination of MM's characteristics are very targeted—a few MMs are identifiable by each causal combination. However, the large sample size drives this low coverage finding. Since this study includes nearly 3,000 cases, the proportion of membership in the outcome explained by the complete solution is relatively low. The overall measured score is acceptable and worthy of interpretation.

Sufficient (Intermediate) Solutions for the Market Guru Outcome

The solutions for market gurus also generate insightful results. Three configurations have consistency scores for the MG outcome that are greater than Ragin's criterion of 0.8. Table 14 displays the intermediate solutions for MG membership.

The following three configurations reflect high MG membership: (1) a conjunction of females who evaluate herself as low influence to neighbor consumer, low normative susceptibility, high shopping involvement, and high provision of market information; (2) females who have high search activities, high shopping involvement, and high provision and possession of market information; and, (3) low influence with low self-evaluated superior taste, low normative susceptibility, high search activities and high shopping involvement with great provision and possession of market information to be important.

The overall consistency of the solution is 0.80 and each configuration consistency is higher than 0.85 score. These outcomes mean that all solutions help to explain the market guru outcome to a large extent. The subset relationships are sufficient for the combinations of antecedent conditions and MG membership. The coverages for the overall and each solution are relatively low; indicating that the proportion of complete solution explained by memberships of market guru is relatively low. However, this low coverage follows from the large sample size. Since the coverage measures the proportion score, such a large number of total cases can drive low proportions of the complete solutions. However, the overall results are worthwhile to interpret.

Examining theses configurations for market gurus and market mavens indicate that the results corroborate and extend the substantial body of prior research. The condition about information seeking and diffusion behavior applies to both by MGs and MMs. In the each combination, the five characteristics relating information seeking and diffusion, provision and possession of market information, search activities, shopping involvement, and female, shows expected results with high scores associating with high membership of each outcome. As the theory in this study expects, MMs and MGs have opposite psychological traits combination about social aspects.

CONCLUSION

The concept of market maven as an information diffuser is important for consumer research because of MMs' contributing role in describing patterns of adoption of innovations by consumers in the marketplace. However, prior research, which focuses on mavens' characteristics, neglects other important segments of consumers who are highly involved in the marketplace. The study here identifies the existence of such a marketplace influencers that we term, "market gurus."

This study examines the applicability of the characteristics of market mavens to market gurus and demonstrates the benefit of fs/QCA for testing theoretical combinations of antecedents that predict characteristics of market mavens and market gurus. Fs/QCA examines different combinations of causal conditions of information diffuser permitting this study to distinguish MGs from MMs.

The findings support the applicability of prior findings about MMs' characteristics to MGs. These characteristics are all about behavior of information seeking and diffusion, for example, possession and provision of market information, search activities, shopping involvement and gender. Therefore MGs do not distinguish themselves from MMs through these five traits since both market gurus and market mavens are similar on these external conditions. This study examine additional combinations including psychological antecedents, self evaluated influence, superiority taste, and normative susceptibility.

This study finds that MMs evaluate themselves as heavy influencers to consumers and are highly sensitive on normative susceptibility. Also MMs think they have superiority taste than most of people.

In contrast, MGs evaluate themselves as low influencers with non-superior tastes, and less sensitive to normative susceptibility. These relationships between outcome and psychological characteristics do not change with combination of additional antecedents such as information seeking and diffusing behavior. For the most parsimony and intermediate solutions, information seeking and diffusing behavior conditions provide positive explanations for both market guru and market maven, whereas psychological conditions display opposite causal combinations for explaining market gurus versus market mavens.

In addition, the general results support the conditions identified by the research model— a configurational approach helps to pinpoint more specific combinations of factors. For example, if a female has high self-evaluation score on superior taste and shopping involvement with heavy information provision, this female associates highly to the market maven outcome regardless of other conditions. If a female has low self-evaluation score on general influence and low normative susceptibility and shopping involvement with heavy information provision, she is representative of the market guru outcome. From these findings, this study provides useful model specifications and the analytic method indicates the need for testing differences between MMs and MGs using psychological characteristics.

LIMTATIONS AND FUTURE RESEARCH IMPLICATIONS

By taking psychological antecedents with a configurational approach, this study is able to describe the various pathways that consistently distinguish between MGs and MMs. Further, the study provides empirical evidence that MGs differ from MMs.

These findings beg the question of whether or not other psychological conditions with additional behavior and demographic conditions are useful for distinguishing MGs from MMs. Future research would benefit from focusing on ways in which the characteristics may need to be modified or refined to predict information diffusion more effectively.

Also the data used on this study are somewhat outdated. Using a similar analytic approach on more recent, less restricted, and representative samples of consumers would help to confirm or modify the current findings. This study does not include theory and empirical findings for opinion follower and laggards (as they appear in Figure 1). Certainly the study of combinations of antecedent conditions (i.e., causal recipes) for memberships in these two groups is worth doing. Such reporting is left for future research.

ACKNOWLEDGMENT

The authors thank the three double-blind reviewers for their insightful comments for improving this chapter. The authors thank Rama Krishna Kompella (University of Rhode Island) and Sereikhuoch Eng (University of Rhode Island) for their ideas and comments to the earlier drafts of the chapter. The authors alone are responsible for all limitations and errors that may relate to the study and the chapter.

REFERENCES

Abratt, R., Nel, D., & Nezer, C. (1995). Role of the market maven in retailing: A general marketplace influencer. *Journal of Business and Psychology, 10*(1), 31–55. doi:10.1007/BF02249268

Bearden, W., Netemeyer, R., & Teel, J. (1989). Measurement of consumer susceptibility to interpersonal influence. *The Journal of Consumer Research, 15*(4), 473–481. doi:10.1086/209186

Belch, M., Krentler, K., & Willis-Flurry, L. (2005). Teen internet mavens: Influence in family decision making. *Journal of Business Research, 58*(8), 569–575. doi:10.1016/j.jbusres.2003.08.005

Boone, L. (1970). The search for the consumer innovator. *The Journal of Business, 43*, 135–140. doi:10.1086/295260

Burnkrant, R., & Cousineau, A. (1975). Informational and normative social influence in buyer behavior. *The Journal of Consumer Research, 2*(2), 206–215. doi:10.1086/208633

Cal, Y. (2004). *The multicultural market maven: A market influencer for a diverse society*. Pullman, WA: American Academy of Advertising.

Chelminski, P., & Coulter, R. (2006). On market mavens and consumer self-confidence: A cross-cultural study. *Psychology and Marketing, 24*(1), 69–91. doi:10.1002/mar.20153

Clark, R., & Goldsmith, R. (2005). Market mavens: Psychological influences. *Psychology and Marketing, 22*(4), 289–312. doi:10.1002/mar.20060

Davis, H. (1971). Measurement of husband-wife influence in consumer purchase decisions. *JMR, Journal of Marketing Research, 8*(2), 305–312. doi:10.2307/3149567

Elliott, M., & Warfield, A. (1993). Do market mavens categorize brands differently? *Advances in Consumer Research. Association for Consumer Research (U. S.), 20*, 202.

Engelland, B., Hopkins, C., & Larson, D. (2001). Market mavenship as an influence of service quality evaluation. *Journal of Marketing Theory and Practice, 9*(1), 15–26.

Epstein, J., Duerr, D., Kenworthy, L., & Ragin, C. (2008). Comparative employment performance: A fuzzy-set analysis. In L. Kenworthy & A. Hicks, Basingstoke (Eds.), *Method and substance in comparative analysis* (pp. 67-90). London, UK: Palgrave Macmillan.

Feick, L., & Price, L. (1987). The market maven: A diffuser of marketplace information. *Journal of Marketing, 51*(1), 83–97. doi:10.2307/1251146

Fiss, P. C. (2009). *Practical issues in QCA*. Presentation at Academy of Management 2009. Retrieved from http://www-rcf.usc.edu/~fiss/QCA_PDW_2009_Fiss_Practical_Issues.pdf

Gigerenzer, G. (2008). *Rationality for mortals: How people cope with uncertainty*. Oxford, UK: Oxford University Press.

Goldsmith, R., Clark, R., & Goldsmith, E. (2006). Extending the psychological profile of market mavenism. *Journal of Consumer Behaviour, 5*(3), 411. doi:10.1002/cb.189

Goldsmith, R., Flynn, L., & Goldsmith, E. (2003). Innovative consumers and market mavens. *Journal of Marketing Theory and Practice, 11*, 54–65.

Gonda, J. (1985). *Change and continuity in Indian religion*. New Delhi, India: Pūsan & Sarasvatī.

Higie, R., Feick, L., & Price, L. (1987). Types and amount of word-of-mouth communications about retailers. *Journal of Retailing, 63*(3), 260–278.

Kassarjian, H. (1981). Low involvement: A second look. *Advances in Consumer Research. Association for Consumer Research (U. S.), 8*, 31–34.

Katz, A., Vom Hau, M., & Mahoney, J. (2005). Explaining the great reversal in Spanish America: Fuzzy-set analysis versus regression analysis. *Sociological Methods & Research, 33*(4), 539–573. doi:10.1177/0049124104266002

Keller, E., & Berry, J. (2003). *The influentials*. New York, NY: Free Press.

Lazarsfeld, P. F. (1937). Some remarks on the typological procedures in social research. *Festschrift fur Sozialforschung, 6*(1), 119–139.

McClelland, D. C. (1996). Does the field of personality have a future? *Current Directions in Psychological Science, 1*(1), 86–89.

Mlecko, J. (1982). The guru in Hindu tradition. *Numen, 29*(1), 33–61. doi:10.1163/156852782X00132

Ochel, W., & Rohwer, A. (2009). *Reduction of employment protection in Europe: A comparative fuzzy-set analysis*. Working Paper 2828, CESifo (Center for Economic Studies and IFO Institute for Economic Research) - IFO Institute for Economic Research.

Price, L., Feick, L., & Guskey-Federouch, A. (1988). Couponing behaviors of the market maven: Profile of a super couponer. *Advances in Consumer Research. Association for Consumer Research (U. S.), 15*(3), 354–359.

Putnam, R. D. (1995). Bowling alone: America's declining social capital. *Journal of Democracy, 6*(1), 65–78. Retrieved from http://xroads.virginia.edu/~HYPER/DETOC/assoc/bowling.htmldoi:10.1353/jod.1995.0002

Putnam, R. D. (2000). *Bowling alone: The collapse and revival of American community*. New York, NY: Simon & Schuster.

Ragin, C. (1987). *The comparative method: Moving beyond qualitative and quantitative methods*. Berkeley, CA: University of California Press.

Ragin, C. (1997). Turning the tables: How case-oriented methods challenge variable-oriented methods. *Comparative Social Research, 16*(1), 27–42.

Ragin, C. (2000). *Fuzzy-set social science*. Chicago, IL: University of Chicago Press.

Ragin, C. (2005). *From fuzzy sets to crisp truth tables*. Tucson, AZ: Department of Sociology, University of Arizona. Retrieved from http://www.compasss.org/files/WPfiles/Raginfztt_April05.pdf

Ragin, C. (2008a). Measurement versus calibration: A set-theoretic approach. In Box-Steffensmeiner, J., Brady, H., & Collier, D. (Eds.), *The Oxford handbook of political methodology* (pp. 174–188). New York, NY: Oxford University Press. doi:10.1093/oxfordhb/9780199286546.003.0008

Ragin, C. (2008b). Qualitative comparative analysis using fuzzy sets (fs/QCA). In Rihoux, B., & Ragin, C. C. (Eds.), *Configurational comparative analysis*. Thousand Oaks, CA: Sage Publications.

Ragin, C., Rubinson, C., Schaefer, D., Anderson, S., Williams, E., & Giesel, H. (2008). *User's guide to fuzzy-set/qualitative comparative analysis 2.0*. Tucson, AZ: Department of Sociology, University of Arizona.

Rihoux, B., & Ragin, C. (2008). *Configurational comparative methods: Qualitative comparative analysis (QCA) and related techniques*. Thousand Oaks, CA: Sage Publications, Inc.

Robertson, T., & Kennedy, J. (1968). Prediction of consumer innovators: Application of multiple discriminant analysis. *JMR, Journal of Marketing Research, 5*(1), 64–69. doi:10.2307/3149795

Rogers, E. (1995). *Diffusion of innovation*. New York, NY: The Free Press.

Ruvio, A., & Shoham, A. (2007). Innovativeness, exploratory behavior, market mavenship, and opinion leadership: An empirical examination in the Asian context. *Psychology and Marketing, 24*(7), 703–722. doi:10.1002/mar.20180

Slama, M., & Tashchian, A. (1985). Selected socioeconomic and demographic characteristics associated with purchasing involvement. *Journal of Marketing, 49*(1), 72–82. doi:10.2307/1251177

Slama, M., & Williams, T. (1990). Generalization of the market maven's information provision tendency across product categories. *Advances in Consumer Research. Association for Consumer Research (U. S.), 17*(1), 48–52.

Spiritual Science Research Foundation (SSRF). (2010a). *What is a guru?* Retrieved from http://www.spiritualresearchfoundation.org/articles/id/spiritualresearch/spiritualscience/guru

Spiritual Science Research Foundation (SSRF). (2010b). *Bridging the unknown worlds*. Retrieved from http://Www.Spiritualresearchfoundation.Org/Articles/Id/Spiritualresearch/Spiritualscience/Guru

Steenkamp, J., & Gielens, K. (2003). Consumer and market drivers of the trial probability of new consumer packaged goods. *The Journal of Consumer Research, 30*(3), 368–384. doi:10.1086/378615

Sundaram, D., Mitra, K., & Webster, C. (1998). Word-of-mouth communications: A motivational analysis. *Advances in Consumer Research. Association for Consumer Research (U. S.), 25*, 527–531.

Wagemann, C., & Schneider, C. (2007). *Standards of good practice in qualitative comparative analysis (QCA) and fuzzy-sets*. Technical, COMPASSS Working papers (WP 2007-51).

Walsh, G., Gwinner, K., & Swanson, S. (2004). What makes mavens tick? Exploring the motives of market mavens' initiation of information diffusion. *Journal of Consumer Marketing, 21*(1), 109–122. doi:10.1108/07363760410525678

Williams, T., & Slama, M. (1995). Market mavens' purchase decision evaluative criteria: Implications for brand and store promotion efforts. *Journal of Consumer Marketing, 12*(1), 4–21. doi:10.1108/07363769510147218

Compilation of References

Abad, P. L. (1988). Determining optimal selling price and the lot size when the supplier offers all-unit quantity discounts. *Decision Sciences*, *3*(19), 622–634. doi:10.1111/j.1540-5915.1988.tb00290.x

Abratt, R., Nel, D., & Nezer, C. (1995). Role of the market maven in retailing: A general marketplace influencer. *Journal of Business and Psychology*, *10*(1), 31–55. doi:10.1007/BF02249268

Adamowicz, W., Hanemann, M., Swait, J., Johnson, R., Layton, D., & Regenwetter, M. (2005). Decision strategy and structure in households: A "Groups" perspective. *Marketing Letters*, *16*(3), 387–399. doi:10.1007/s11002-005-5900-6

Age, A. (2006). *Fact pack: 4th Annual guide to advertising and marketing*. Retrieved from http://adage.com/images/random/FactPack06.pdf

Aggarwal, G., Feder, T., & Kenthapadi, K. (2006). Achieving anonymity via clustering. *Proceedings of the 25th ACM SIGMOD-SIGACT-SIGART Symposium on Principles of Database Systems* (pp. 153-162). Chicago, IL: ACM Press.

Agosti, M. (2007). *Information access through search engines and digital libraries*. Berlin, Germany: Springer.

Agrawal, R., Gupta, A., & Sarawagi, S. (1997). Modeling multidimensional databases. *Proceedings of the Thirteenth International Conference on Data Engineering*, (pp. 232–243).

Aguado, J. C. (1998). *A mixed qualitative-quantitative self-learning classification technique applied to simulation assessment in industrial process control*. PhD dissertation, Universitat Politécnica de Catalunya, Spain.

Aguilar-Martin, J., & López de Mántaras, R. (1982). The process of classification and learning: The meaning of linguistic descriptors of concepts. *Approximate Reasoning in Decision Analysis*, *1982*, 165–175.

Aguilar-Martin, J., & Piera, N. (1986). Les connectifs mixtes: De nouveaux operateurs d'association des variables dans la classification automatique avec apprentissage. In Diday, E. (Eds.), *Data analysis and informatics* (pp. 253–265). North Holland Elsevier Science Publishers.

Alhajj, R., & Kaya, M. (2003). Integrating fuzziness into OLAP for multidimensional fuzzy association rules mining. In *Proceedings of the Third IEEE International Conference on Data Mining*.

American Marketing Association. (2011). *Definition of marketing*. Retrieved May 25, 2011, from http://www.marketingpower.com/AboutAMA/Pages/Definitionof-Marketing.aspx

Anderberg, M. R. (1973). *Cluster analysis for applications*. New York, NY: Academic Press.

Andreoni, J. A., & Miller, J. H. (1993). Rational cooperation in the finitely repeated prisoner's dilemma: Experimental evidence. *The Economic Journal*, *103*(418), 570–585. doi:10.2307/2234532

Anoniou, G., & Van Harmelen, F. (2008). *A Semantic Web primer*. Cambridge, MA: MIT Press.

Arabie, P. (1977). Clustering representations of group overlap. *The Journal of Mathematical Sociology*, *5*, 113–141. doi:10.1080/0022250X.1977.9989867

Arabie, P., Carroll, J. D., DeSarbo, W. S., & Wind, J. (1981). Overlapping clustering: A new method for product positioning. *JMR, Journal of Marketing Research*, *18*, 310–317. doi:10.2307/3150972

Assael, H., & Roscoe, A. M. (1976). Approaches to market segmentation analysis. *Journal of Marketing, 40,* 67–76. doi:10.2307/1251070

Axtell, R., Axelrod, R., Epstein, J. M., & Cohen, M. D. (1996). Aligning simulation models: A case study and results. *Computational and Organizational Organization Theory, 1*(2), 123–141. doi:10.1007/BF01299065

Bacharach, M. (2006). *Beyond individual choice: Teams and frames in game theory* (Gold, N., & Sugden, R., Eds.). Princeton, NJ: Princeton University Press.

Baeza-Yates, R., & Ribeiro-Neto, B. (2011). *Modern information retrieval: The concepts and technology behind search.* New York, NY: Addison-Wesley Educational Publishers.

Baker, M. J. (1988). *Marketing strategy and management.* New York, NY: MacMillan.

Balakrishnan, P. V. S., Cooper, M. C., Jacob, V. S., & Lewis, P. A. (1996). Comparative performance of the FSCL neural net and k-means algorithm for market segmentation. *European Journal of Operational Research, 93,* 346–357. doi:10.1016/0377-2217(96)00046-X

Banerjee, A., & Ghosh, J. (2001). Clickstream clustering using weighted longest common subsequences. *Proceedings of the Web Mining Workshop at the 1st SIAM Conference on Data Mining* (pp. 33-40). Chicago, IL, USA.

Barabási, A. L., & Albert, R. (1999). Emergence of scaling in random networks. *Science, 286,* 509–512. doi:10.1126/science.286.5439.509

Bargiela, A., & Pedrycz, W. (2003). *Granular computing: An introduction.* Amsterdam, The Netherlands: Kluwer Academic Publishers.

Barrios, L. (1988). Television, telenovelas and family life in Venezuela. In Lull, J. (Ed.), *World families watch television.* Newbury Park, CA: Sage.

Bearden, W., Netemeyer, R., & Teel, J. (1989). Measurement of consumer susceptibility to interpersonal influence. *The Journal of Consumer Research, 15*(4), 473–481. doi:10.1086/209186

Bélanger, F., Fan, W., Schaupp, C., Krishen, A., Everhart, J., Poteet, D., & Nakamoto, K. (2006). Web site success metrics: Addressing the duality of goals. *Communications of the ACM, 49*(12), 114–116. doi:10.1145/1183236.1183256

Belch, M., Krentler, K., & Willis-Flurry, L. (2005). Teen internet mavens: Influence in family decision making. *Journal of Business Research, 58*(8), 569–575. doi:10.1016/j.jbusres.2003.08.005

Bellman, R. E., & Zadeh, L. A. (1977). Local and fuzzy logics. In Dunn, J. M., & Epstein, G. (Eds.), *Modern uses of multiple-valued logic.* Kluwer Academic Publishers. doi:10.1007/978-94-010-1161-7_6

Berge, C. (2001). *The theory of graphs.* New York, NY: Dover.

Bergmann, M. (2008). *An introduction to many-valued and fuzzy logic – Semantics, algebras, and derivation systems.* New York, NY: Cambridge University Press.

Bergmann, M. (2008). *An introduction to many-valued and fuzzy logic: Semantics, algebras, and derivation systems.* New York, NY: Cambridge University.

Bezdek, J. C. (1981). *Pattern recognition with fuzzy objective function algorithms.* New York, NY: Plenum Press.

Bezdek, J. C., Keller, J., Krisnapuram, R., & Pal, N. R. (2008). *Fuzzy models and algorithms for pattern recognition and image processing.* New York, NY: Springer.

Blattberg, R. C., Getz, G., & Thomas, J. S. (2001). *Customer equity – Building and managing relationships as valuable assets.* Boston, MA: Harvard Business School Press.

Blumauer, A., & Pellegrini, T. (2009). *Social Semantic Web: Web 2.0 - Was nun?* Berlin, Germany: Springer.

Bojadziev, G., & Bojadziev, M. (1997). *Fuzzy logic for business, finance, and management.* Singapore: World Scientific Publishing Co.

Bollobas, B. (2000). *Modern graph theory.* New York, NY: Springer.

Boone, L. (1970). The search for the consumer innovator. *The Journal of Business, 43,* 135–140. doi:10.1086/295260

Bordogna, G., Fedrizzi, M., & Pasi, G. (1997). A linguistic modeling of consensus in group decision making based on OWA operators. *IEEE Transactions on Systems, Man, and Cybernetics. Part A, Systems and Humans, 27*(1), 126–132. doi:10.1109/3468.553232

Bosc, P., & Kacprzyk, J. (Eds.). (1995). *Fuzzines in database management systems*. Heidelberg, Germany: Physica Publisher.

Bosc, P., & Pivert, O. (2000). SQLf query functionality on top of a regular relational database management system. In Pons, O., Vila, M. A., & Kacprzyk, J. (Eds.), *Knowledge management in fuzzy databases* (pp. 171–190). Heidelberg, Germany: Physica Publisher.

Bourguignon, F., Browning, M., & Chiappori, P. (2009). Efficient intra-household allocations and distribution factors: Implications and identification. *The Review of Economic Studies, 76*(2), 503–528. doi:10.1111/j.1467-937X.2008.00525.x

Bourke, P. (1997). *Intersection of two circles*. Retrieved November 30, 2010, from http://local.wasp.uwa.edu.au/~pbourke/geometry/2circle/

Breslin, J. G., Passant, A., & Decker, S. (2009). *The Social Semantic Web*. Berlin, Germany: Springer. doi:10.1007/978-3-642-01172-6

Browning, M., & Chiappori, P. A. (1998). Efficient intra-household allocations: A general characterization and empirical tests. *Econometrica: Journal of the Econometric Society, 66*(6), 1241–1278. doi:10.2307/2999616

Bruhn, M. (2002). *Relationship marketing: Management of customer relations*. Essex, UK: Financial Times.

Buckley, J. J., & Eslami, E. (2002). *An introduction to fuzzy logic and fuzzy sets*. Heidelberg, Germany: Physica Publisher.

Budd, J. (2010, May 1-7). Changing the channel: A special report on television. *The Economist*, 148-160.

Burdick, D., Deshpande, P., Jayram, T., Ramakrishnan, R., & Vaithyanathan, S. (2007). OLAP over uncertain and imprecise data. *The VLDB Journal, 16*(1), 123–144. doi:10.1007/s00778-006-0033-y

Burke, R. (2002). Hybrid recommender systems: Survey and experiments. *User Modeling and User-Adapted Interaction, 12*(4), 331–370. doi:10.1023/A:1021240730564

Burnkrant, R., & Cousineau, A. (1975). Informational and normative social influence in buyer behavior. *The Journal of Consumer Research, 2*(2), 206–215. doi:10.1086/208633

Buttriss, G., & Wilkinson, I. F. (2006). Using narrative sequence methods to advance international entrepreneurship theory. *Journal of International Entrepreneurship, 4*, 157–174. doi:10.1007/s10843-007-0012-4

Cal, Y. (2004). *The multicultural market maven: A market influencer for a diverse society*. Pullman, WA: American Academy of Advertising.

Cardoso, J. (2007). The Semantic Web vision, where are we? *IEEE Computer Society, 22*(5), 22–26.

Carrington, P. J., Scott, J., & Wasserman, S. (2007). *Models and methods in social network analysis*. New York, NY: Cambridge University Press.

Casabayó, M. (2005). *Shopping behaviour forecasts: Experiments based on a fuzzy learning technique in the Spanish food retailing industry*. PhD. dissertation, The University of Edinburgh, UK.

Casabayó, M. (2010). El consumidor, en el punto de mira de las decisiones en márketing. *Harvard Deusto Marketing & Ventas, 98*, 40–44.

Casabayó, M., & Martín, B. (2010). *Fuzzy marketing, cómo comprender al consumidor camaleónico*. Barcelona, Spain: Deusto.

Chamberlin, D. D., Astrahan, M. M., Eswaran, K. P., Griffiths, P. P., Lorie, R. A., & Mehl, J. W. (1976). A unified approach to data definition, manipulation, and control. *IBM Journal of Research and Development, 20*(6), 560–575. doi:10.1147/rd.206.0560

Chan, L. M. A., Shen, Z. J. M., Simchi-Levi, D., & Swann, J. (2004). Coordination of pricing and inventory decisions: A survey and classification. In Simchi-Levi, D., Wu, S. D., & Shen, Z. J. M. (Eds.), *Handbook of quantitative supply chain analysis: Modeling in the e-business era* (pp. 335–392). Boston, MA: Kluwer Academic Publishers.

Chartrand, G. (1977). *Introductory graph theory*. New York, NY: Dover.

Chaudhuri, S., & Dayal, U. (1997). An overview of data warehousing and OLAP technology. *SIGMOD Record, 26*(1), 65–74. doi:10.1145/248603.248616

Chelminski, P., & Coulter, R. (2006). On market mavens and consumer self-confidence: A cross-cultural study. *Psychology and Marketing, 24*(1), 69–91. doi:10.1002/mar.20153

Chen, G. (1998). *Fuzzy logic in data modeling – Semantics, constraints and database design*. London, UK: Kluwer Academic Publishers.

Chen, N., & Marques, N. C. (2005). *An extension of self-organizing maps to categorical data. Progress in Artificial Intelligence*. Berlin, Germany: Springer Verlag.

Chen, X., & Simchi-Levi, D. (2004). Coordinating inventory control and pricing strategies with random demand and fixed ordering cost: The finite horizon case. *Operations Research, 52*(6), 887–896. doi:10.1287/opre.1040.0127

Cherchye, L., De Rock, B., & Vermeulen, F. (2007). The collective model of household consumption: A Non-parametric characterization. *Econometrica: Journal of the Econometric Society, 75*(2), 553–574. doi:10.1111/j.1468-0262.2006.00757.x

Chiu, T., Fang, D., Chen, J., Wang, Y., & Jeris, C. (2001). A robust and scalable clustering algorithm for mixed type attributes in large database environment *Proceedings of the 7th ACM SIGKDD* (pp. 263-268). San Francisco, CA: ACM Press.

Choffray, J. M., & Lilien, G. L. (1978). A new approach to industrial market segmentation. *MIT Sloan Management Review, 19*(3), 17–29.

Christensen, C. B., Berstell, G., Anthony, S. D., & Nitterhouse, D. (2007). Finding the right job for your product. *MIT Sloan Management Review, 48*(3), 38–47.

Chun, R. (2005). Corporate reputation: Meaning and measurement. *International Journal of Management Reviews, 7*(2), 91–109. doi:10.1111/j.1468-2370.2005.00109.x

Clark, R., & Goldsmith, R. (2005). Market mavens: Psychological influences. *Psychology and Marketing, 22*(4), 289–312. doi:10.1002/mar.20060

Clifton, B. (2010). *Advanced Web metrics with Google analytics* (2nd ed.). New York, NY: Wiley.

Codd, E. F., Codd, S. B., & Smmalley, C. T. (1993). *Providing OLAP to user-analysts: An IT mandate*. Codd & Date Inc.

Cook, D. J., & Holder, L. B. (2007). *Mining graph data*. Hoboken, NJ: Wiley-Interscience.

Corbett, C. J., & de Groote, X. (2000). A supplier's optimal quantity discount policy under asymmetric information. *Management Science, 3*(46), 444–450. doi:10.1287/mnsc.46.3.444.12065

Cordón, O., Herrera, F., Hoffmann, F., & Magdalena, L. (2001). Genetic fuzzy systems: Evolutionary tuning and learning of fuzzy knowledge bases. In *Advances in fuzzy systems - Applications and theory*, (p. 488).

Corfman, K. P., & Lehmann, D. R. (1987). Models of cooperative group decision-making and relative influence: An experimental investigation of family purchase decisions. *The Journal of Consumer Research, 14*(1), 1–13. doi:10.1086/209088

Cox, E. (1995). *Fuzzy logic for business and industry*. Charles River Media.

Craven, J. (1992). *Social Choice*. Cambridge, UK: Cambridge University Press. doi:10.1017/CBO9780511521911

Craven, M., DiPasquo, D., Freitag, A., McCallum, T., Mitchell, K., & Nigam, S. (2000). Learning to construct knowledge bases from the World Wide Web. *Artificial Intelligence, 118*(1–2), 69–113. doi:10.1016/S0004-3702(00)00004-7

Csikszentmihalyi, M., & Kubey, R. (1981). Television and the rest of life: A systematic comparison of subjective experience. *Public Opinion Quarterly, 45*(3), 317. doi:10.1086/268667

Dasgupta, C. G., Dispensa, G. S., & Ghose, S. (1994). Comparing the predictive performance of a neural network model with some traditional market response models. *International Journal of Forecasting, 10*, 235–244. doi:10.1016/0169-2070(94)90004-3

Davenport, T. H. (2006, January). Competing on analytics. *Harvard Business Review*.

David, N. (2009). Validation and verification in social simulation: Patterns and clarification of terminology. In Squazzoni, F. (Ed.), *Epistemological aspects of computer simulation in the social sciences* (*Vol. 5466*, pp. 117–129). Berlin, Germany: Springer. doi:10.1007/978-3-642-01109-2_9

Davies, F., Moutinho, L., & Curry, B. (1996). ATM user attitudes: A neural network analysis. *Marketing Intelligence & Planning, 14*(2), 26–32. doi:10.1108/02634509610110778

Davis, H. (1971). Measurement of husband-wife influence in consumer purchase decisions. *JMR, Journal of Marketing Research, 8*(2), 305–312. doi:10.2307/3149567

Del Amo, A., Montero, J., & Cutello, V. (1999). On the principles of fuzzy classification. *Proceedings of 18th North American Fuzzy Information Processing Society Annual Conf*, (pp. 675 – 679).

Delgado, M., Molina, C., Sanchez, D., Vila, A., & Rodriguez-Ariza, L. (2004). A fuzzy multidimensional model for supporting imprecision in OLAP. *2004 IEEE International Conference on Fuzzy Systems, 3*, (pp. 1331–1336).

Dey, A. K., & Abowd, G. D. (2000, April). *Towards a better understanding of context and context-awareness*. Paper presented at the CHI 2000 Workshop on the What, Who, Where, When, Why and How of Context-Awareness, Hague, Netherlands.

Dianhui, W., Dillon, T., & Chang, E. J. (2001). A data mining approach for fuzzy classification rule generation. *IFSA World Congress and 20th NAFIPS International Conference*, (pp. 2960-2964).

Dombi, J. (1991). Membership function as an evaluation. *Journal of Fuzzy Sets and Systems, 35*, 1–21. doi:10.1016/0165-0114(90)90014-W

Donzé, L., & Meier, A. (2011). Applying fuzzy logic and fuzzy methods to marketing. In Meier, A., & Donzé, L. (Eds.), *Fuzzy methods for customer relationship management and marketing: Applications and classification*. Hershey, PA: IGI Global.

Doyle, S. (2007). The role of social networks in marketing. *Journal of Database Marketing & Customer Strategy Management, 15*(1), 60–64. doi:10.1057/palgrave.dbm.3250070

Drèze, X., & Zufryden, F. (2004). Measurement of online visibility and its impact on Internet traffic. *Journal of Interactive Marketing, 18*(1), 20–37. doi:10.1002/dir.10072

Dubois, D., & Prade, H. (1988). *Fuzzy sets and systems*. New York, NY: Academic Press.

Dubois, D., & Prade, H. (2003). A review of fuzzy set aggregation connectives. *Information Sciences, 36*(1-2), 85–121. doi:10.1016/0020-0255(85)90027-1

Dulio, D., Skinner, R., & Masket, S. (2009). 527 committees and the political party network. *Conference Papers -- Midwestern Political Science Association*, 1.

Dye, C. Y., & Hsieh, T. P. (2010). A particle swarm optimization for solving joint pricing and lot-sizing problem with fluctuating demand and unit purchasing cost. *Computers and Mathematics with Applications, 60*, 1895_1907.

Eberhart, R. C., & Kennedy, J. (1995). A new optimizer using particle swarm theory. In *Proceedings of the 6th International Symposium on Micro Machine and Human Science*, Nagoya, Japan, (pp. 39–43).

Ebert, T. (2009). *Trust as the key to loyalty in business-to-consumer exchanges: Trust building measures in the banking industry*. Wiesbaden, Germany: Gabler. doi:10.1007/978-3-8349-8307-7

Eccles, R. G., Newquist, S. C., & Schatz, R. (2007). Reputation and its risks. *Harvard Business Review, 85*(2), 104–114.

Econsultancy. (2010). *Online measurement and strategy report 2010*, Retrieved June 7, 2010, from http://econsultancy.com

Edmonds, B. (2003). Towards an ideal social simulation language. In Simão Sichman, J., Bousquet, F., & Davidsson, P. (Eds.), *Multi-Agent-Based Simulation II* (*Vol. 2581*, pp. 105–124). Berlin, Germany: Springer. doi:10.1007/3-540-36483-8_8

Edmunds, A., & Morris, A. (2000). The problem of information overload in business organisations: A review of the literature. *International Journal of Information Management, 20*(1), 17–28. doi:10.1016/S0268-4012(99)00051-1

Edvinsson, L., & Malone, M. S. (1997). *Intellectual capital – Realizing your company's true value by finding its hidden brainpower*. New York, NY: Harper Collins Publisher.

Eisenegger, M., & Imhof, K. (2007). Das Wahre, das Gute und das Schöne: Reputations-Management in der Mediengesellschaft. *Fög discussion paper 2007-0001.* Retrieved November 30, 2010, from http://www.foeg.uzh. ch/staging/userfiles/file/Deutsch/f%C3%B6g%20discussion%20papers/2007-0001_Wahr_Gut_Schoen_2007_d. pdf

Elfring, T., & Halsink, W. (2003). Networks in entrepreneurship: The case of high-technology firms. *Small Business Economics, 21,* 409–422. doi:10.1023/A:1026180418357

Elliott, M., & Warfield, A. (1993). Do market mavens categorize brands differently? *Advances in Consumer Research. Association for Consumer Research (U. S.), 20,* 202.

Engelland, B., Hopkins, C., & Larson, D. (2001). Market mavenship as an influence of service quality evaluation. *Journal of Marketing Theory and Practice, 9*(1), 15–26.

Epstein, J., Duerr, D., Kenworthy, L., & Ragin, C. (2008). Comparative employment performance: A fuzzy-set analysis. In L. Kenworthy & A. Hicks, Basingstoke (Eds.), *Method and substance in comparative analysis* (pp. 67-90). London, UK: Palgrave Macmillan.

Erdos, P., & Renyi, A. (1960). On the evolution of random graphs. *Publications of the Mathematical institute of Hungarian Academy of Sciences, 5,* 17-61.

Escobar-Jeria, V. H., Martín-Bautista, M. J., Sánchez, D., & Vila, M. (2007). *Web usage mining via fuzzy logic techniques.* In P. Melin, O. Castillo, I. J. Aguilar, J. Kacprzyk, & W. Pedrycz (Eds.), 2007: *Lecture Notes In Artificial Intelligence, vol. 4529,* (pp. 243-252). New York, NY: Springer.

Esmaeili, M. (2009). Optimal selling price, marketing expenditure and lot size under general demand function. *International Journal of Advanced Manufacturing Technology, 45,* 191–198. doi:10.1007/s00170-009-1952-8

Esmaeili, M., Abad, P. L., & Aryanezhad, M. B. (2009a). Seller–buyer relationship when end demand is sensitive to price and promotion. *Asia-Pacific Journal of Operational Research, 26*(5), 605–621. doi:10.1142/S0217595909002353

Esmaeili, M., Aryanezhad, M. B., & Zeephongsekul, P. (2009b). A game theory approach in seller-buyer supply chain. *European Journal of Operational Research, 195,* 442–448. doi:10.1016/j.ejor.2008.02.026

Esmaeili, M., Zeephongsekul, P., & Aryanezhad, M. B. (2007). A joint pricing and lot sizing models with discount: A geometric programming approach. *ANZIAM Journal, 49,* 139–154.

European Commission. (2010). *ICT for government and public services.* Retrieved September 10, 2010, from http://ec.europa.eu/information_society/activities/egovernment/index_en.htm

Everitt, B. S. (1979). Unresolved problems in cluster analysis. *Biometrics, 35*(March), 169–181. doi:10.2307/2529943

Everitt, B. S. (1993). *Cluster analysis.* New York, NY: John Wiley & Sons.

Fasel, D., & Shahzad, K. (2010). A data warehouse model for integrating fuzzy concepts in meta table structures. In *17th IEEE International Conference and Workshops on the Engineering of Computer-Based Systems,* (pp. 100–109). IEEE Computer Society.

Fasel, D., & Zumstein, D. (2009). A fuzzy data warehouse approach for Web analytics. In *Proceedings of the 2nd World Summit on the Knowledge Society (WSKS),* September 16-18, Crete, Greece.

Fasel, D. (2009). A fuzzy data warehouse approach for the customer performance measurement for a hearing instrument manufacturing company. In *Proceeding of Fuzzy Systems and Knowledge Discovery.* IEEE Explore. doi:10.1109/FSKD.2009.266

Fearon, C., Ballantine, J., & Philip, G. (2010). Understanding the role of electronic trading and inter-organisational cooperation and coordination. *Internet Research, 20*(5), 545–562. doi:10.1108/10662241011084095

Feick, L., & Price, L. (1987). The market maven: A diffuser of marketplace information. *Journal of Marketing, 51*(1), 83–97. doi:10:2307/1251146

Feng, L., & Dillon, T. S. (2003). Using fuzzy linguistic representations to provide explanatory semantics for data warehouses. *IEEE Transactions on Knowledge and Data Engineering, 15*(1).

Ferguson, R. J., Paulin, M., Möslien, K., & Müller, C. (2005). Relational governance, communication and the performance of biotechnology partnerships. *Journal of Small Business and Enterprise Development, 12*(3), 395–408. doi:10.1108/14626000510612303

Fershtman, C., & Kamien, M. I. (1992). Cross licensing of complementary technologies. *International Journal of Industrial Organization, 10*(3), 329–348. doi:10.1016/0167-7187(92)90001-F

Fish, K. E., Barnes, J. H., & Aiken, M. W. (1995). Artificial neural networks - A new methodology for industrial market segmentation. *Industrial Marketing Management, 24*, 431–438. doi:10.1016/0019-8501(95)00033-7

Fiss, P. C. (2009). *Practical issues in QCA*. Presentation at Academy of Management 2009. Retrieved from http://www-rcf.usc.edu/~fiss/QCA_PDW_2009_Fiss_Practical_Issues.pdf

Fivaz, J., & Felder, G. (2009). Added value of e-democracy tools in advanced democracies? The voting advice application *smartvote* in Switzerland. In Shark, A. R., & Toporkoff, S. (Eds.), *Beyond Egovernement–Measuring performance: A global perspective* (pp. 109–122). Washington, DC: Public Technology Institute and ITEMS International.

Flach, P. A. (2001). On the state of the art in machine learning: A personal review. *Artificial Intelligence, 131*, 199–222. doi:10.1016/S0004-3702(01)00125-4

Fombrun, C. J., & Wiedmann, K. P. (2001). Reputation quotient. Analyse und Gestaltung der Unternehmensreputation auf der Basis fundierter Erkenntnisse. *Schriftenreihe Marketing Management*, 1-52.

Ford, D., & Saren, M. J. (2001). *Managing and marketing technology*. London, UK: Thompson.

Forrester Consulting. (2009). *Appraising your investments in enterprise Web analytics*. Retrieved June 7, 2011, from www.google.com/intl/en/analytics/case_studies/Appraising-Investments-In-Enterprise-Analytics.pdf

Frank, R. E., Massy, W. F., & Wind, Y. (1972). *Market segmentation*. Englewood Cliffs, NJ: Prentice Hall.

Freeland, J. R. (1982). Coordination strategies for production and marketing in a functionally decentralized firm. *ABE Transactions, 12*(2), 126–132.

Fu, Y., Sandhu, K., & Shih, M.-Y. (1999). Fast clustering of Web users based on navigation patterns *Proceedings of the World Multiconference on Systemics, Cybernetics, and Informatics (SCI/ISAS '99)* (vol. 5, pp. 560-567). Orlando, Florida, USA.

Fuzzy Marketing Methods. (2010). *Research center fuzzy marketing methods*, Retrieved June 11, 2011, from http://www.FMsquare.org

Gaines-Ross, L. (2008). *Corporate reputation: 12 steps to safeguarding and recovering reputation*. Hoboken, NJ: John Wiley & Sons.

Gan, G., Yang, Z., & Wu, J. (2005). A genetic k-modes algorithm for clustering categorical data. In Li, X., Wang, S., & Dong, Z. Y. (Eds.), *Advanced data mining and applications* (*Vol. 3584*, pp. 195–202). Springer Verlag. doi:10.1007/11527503_23

Ganti, V., Gehrke, J., & Ramakrishnan, R. (1999). CACTUS - Clustering categorical data using summaries. *Proc. of the 5th ACM SIGKDD International Conference on Knowledge Discovery and Data Mining (KDD '99)* (pp. 73-83). San Diego, CA: ACM Press.

Gath, I., & Geva, B. (1989). Unsupervised optimal fuzzy clustering. *IEEE Transactions on Pattern Analysis and Machine Intelligence, 2*(7), 773–781. doi:10.1109/34.192473

Gavrilis, C., Kakali, C., & Papatheodoro, C. (2008). Enhancing library services with Web 2.0 functionalities. In Christensen-Dalsgaard, B. (Eds.), *ECDL 2008, LNCS 5173* (pp. 148–159). doi:10.1007/978-3-540-87599-4_16

Gibson, D., Kleinberg, J. M., & Raghavan, P. (1998). Clustering categorical data: An approach based on dynamical systems. In A. Gupta, O. Shmueli, & J. Widom (Eds.), *Proceedings of the 24th International Conference on VLDBs* (pp. 311-322). New York City, NY: Morgan Kaufmann Publishers.

Gigerenzer, G. (2008). *Rationality for mortals: How people cope with uncertainty*. Oxford, UK: Oxford University Press.

Gluchowski, P., Gabriel, R., & Dittmar, C. (2008). *Management Support Systeme und Business Intelligence*. Berlin, Germany: Springer Verlag.

Goettler, R. L., & Schachar, R. (2001). Spatial competition in the network television industry. *The Rand Journal of Economics, 32*(4), 624–656. doi:10.2307/2696385

Goldsmith, R., Clark, R., & Goldsmith, E. (2006). Extending the psychological profile of market mavenism. *Journal of Consumer Behaviour, 5*(3), 411. doi:10.1002/cb.189

Goldsmith, R., Flynn, L., & Goldsmith, E. (2003). Innovative consumers and market mavens. *Journal of Marketing Theory and Practice, 11*, 54–65.

Gonda, J. (1985). *Change and continuity in Indian religion.* New Delhi, India: Pūṣan & Sarasvatī..

Graf, C. (2010). *Erweiterung des Data-Mining-Softwarepakets WEKA um induktive unscharfe Klassifikation (Master's Thesis).* Department of Informatics, University of Fribourg, Switzerland.

Grint, K. (1997). *Fuzzy management – Contemporary ideas and practices at work.* New York, NY: Oxford University Press.

Grofman, B., Feld, S. L., & Owen, G. (1984). Group size and the performance of a composite group majority: Statistical truths and empirical results. *Organizational Behavior and Human Performance, 33*(3), 350–359. doi:10.1016/0030-5073(84)90028-X

Gruber, T. R. (1993). A translation approach to portable ontology specifications. [Knowledge Systems Laboratory.]. *Technical Report KSL, 92*(71), 199–220.

Guadarrama, S. (2010). Guadarrama on CWW. In Mendel, J. (Ed.), *What computing with words means to me* (pp. 24–25). IEEE Intelligence Magazine.

Guha, S., Rastogi, R., & Shim, K. (1999). ROCK: A robust clustering algorithm for categorical attributes. *Proceedings of the 15th International Conference on Data Engineering.* Sydney, Australia: IEEE Computer Society.

Gunelius, S. (2010). *Blogging all-in-one for dummies.* Indianapolis, IN: John Wiley & Sons.

Guo, X., & Lu, J. (2007). Intelligent e-government services with personalized recommendation techniques. *International Journal of Intelligent Systems, 22*, 401–417. doi:10.1002/int.20206

Hächler, L. (2010). *Web 2.0 and 3.0: How online journalists find relevant and credible information.* Unpublished Master thesis, University of Fribourg, Fribourg, Switzerland.

Hafner-Burton, E. M., & Montgomery, A. H. (2006). The new power politics of international organizations: Social structural inequality in the international system. *Conference Papers -- American Political Science Association,* (pp. 1-35).

Häge, F. M. (2007). Constructivism, fuzzy sets and (very) small-N: Revisiting the conditions for communicative action. *Journal of Business Research, 60*(5), 512–521. doi:10.1016/j.jbusres.2007.01.009

Hagras, H. (2010). Hagras on CWW. In Mendel, J. (Ed.), *What computing with words means to me* (pp. 24–25). IEEE Intelligence Magazine.

Hall, M., Frank, E., Holmes, G., Pfahringer, B., Reutemann, P., & Witten, I. H. (2009). The WEKA data mining software: An update. *SIGKDD Explorations, 11*(1). doi:10.1145/1656274.1656278

Harel, D., & Rumpe, B. (2004). Meaningful modeling: What's the semantics of "semantics"? *Computer, 37*(10), 64–72. doi:10.1109/MC.2004.172

Harrison, T. (2000). *Financial services marketing.* Essex, UK: Pearson Education Press.

Hasan-Montero, Y., & Herrero-Solana, V. (2006). Improving tag-clouds as a visual information re-trieval interfaces. *Proceedings of International Conference on Multidisciplinary Information Sciences and Technologies.*

Hawthorne, J. (2008). Inductive logic. In Zalta, E. N. (Ed.), *Stanford encyclopedia of philosophy.* Stanford, CA: The Metaphysics Research Lab, Stanford University.

Hay, B., Wets, G., & Vanhoof, K. (2001). Clustering navigation patterns on a website using a sequence alignment method. *Proceedings of the 17th International Joint Conference on Artificial Intelligence* (pp. 1-6). Seattle, Washington, USA.

Helmer, S. (2007). Measuring the structural similarity of semistructured documents using entropy. *Proceedings of the 33rd International Conference on VLDBs* (pp. 1022-1032). Vienna, Austria: ACM Press.

Herrera, F., Herrera-Viedma, E., & Verdegay, J. L. (1996). A model of consensus in group decision making under linguistic assessments. *Fuzzy Sets and Systems, 78*(1), 73–87. doi:10.1016/0165-0114(95)00107-7

Higie, R., Feick, L., & Price, L. (1987). Types and amount of word-of-mouth communications about retailers. *Journal of Retailing, 63*(3), 260–278.

Hinsz, V. B., Tindale, R. S., & Vollrath, D. A. (1997). The emerging conceptualization of groups as information processes. *Psychological Bulletin, 121*(1), 43–64. doi:10.1037/0033-2909.121.1.43

Hitzler, P., Krötzsch, M., & Rudolph, S. (2010). *Foundations of Semantic Web technologies*. Boca Raton, FL: Taylor and Francis Group.

Hoebel, N. (2011). *User interests and behavior on the Web: Measurements and framing strategies*. Dissertation submitted to Johann Wolfgang Goethe-University. Frankfurt, Germany.

Hoebel, N., & Kreuzer, S. (2010). CORD: A hybrid approach for efficient clustering of ordinal data using fuzzy logic and self-organizing maps. In J. Filipe & J. Cordeiro (Eds.), *Proceedings of the 6th International Conference on Web Information Systems and Technologies (WEBIST '10)*. Valencia, Spain: INSTICC Press.

Hoebel, N., Kaufmann, S., Tolle, K., & Zicari, R. V. (2006). The design of Gugubarra 2.0: A tool for building and managing profiles of Web users. In T. Nishida, Z. Shi, U. Visser, X. Wu, J. Liu, B. Wah, W. Cheung & Y.-M. Cheung (Eds.), *Proceedings of the 2006 IEEE/WIC/ACM International Conference on Web Intelligence* (pp. 317--320). Washington, DC: IEEE Computer Society.

Hong, I. (2007). A survey of web site success metrics used by internet-dependent organizations in Korea. *Internet Research, 17*(3), 272–290. doi:10.1108/10662240710758920

Höppner, F., Klawonn, F., Kruse, R., & Runkler, T. (1999). *Fuzzy cluster analysis*. Chichester, UK: John Wiley & Sons.

Hruschka, H. (1986). Market definition and segmentation using fuzzy clustering methods. *International Journal of Research in Marketing, 3*(2), 117–134. doi:10.1016/0167-8116(86)90015-7

Huang, W. Y., & Lippman, R. P. (1997). Comparisons between neural net and conventional classifiers. *IEEE 1st International Conference on Neural Networks IV* (pp. 485-493).

Huang, Z. (1997). A fast clustering algorithm to cluster very large categorical data sets in data mining. *Workshop on Research Issues on Data Mining and Knowledge Discovery (DMKD '97)* (pp. 1-8). Tucson, Arizona, USA.

Huang, Z., & Li, S. X. (2001). Co-op advertising models in manufacturer-retailer supply chains: A game theory approach. *European Journal of Operational Research, 135*, 527–544. doi:10.1016/S0377-2217(00)00327-1

Hüllermeier, E. (2005). Fuzzy methods in machine learning and data mining: Status and prospects. *Fuzzy Sets and Systems, 387–406*. doi:10.1016/j.fss.2005.05.036

Hu, Y., Chen, R., & Tzeng, G. (2003). Finding fuzzy classification rules using data mining techniques. *Pattern Recognition Letters, 24*(1-3), 509–514. doi:10.1016/S0167-8655(02)00273-8

Inan, H. (2010). *What is Web analytics?* Retrieved June 7, 2011, from http://hurolinan.com/index.php/category/what-is-web-analytics

Ingenhoff, D., & Sommer, K. (2008). The interrelationships between corporate reputation, trust and behavioral intentions. A multi-stakeholder approach. *58th Annual Conference of the International Communication Association (ICA),* (pp. 21-27). Montreal, Canada

Ingenhoff, D. (2004). *Corporate issues management in multinationalen Unternehmen: Eine empirische Studie zu organisationalen Strukturen und Prozessen*. Wiesbaden, Germany: VS Verlag für Sozialwissenschaften.

Inmon, W. H. (2005). *Building the data warehouse* (4th ed.). New York, NY: Wiley Publishing.

Islam, S. (2008). Multi-objective marketing planning inventory model: A geometric programming approach. *Applied Mathematics and Computation, 205*, 238–246. doi:10.1016/j.amc.2008.07.037

Jackson, S. (2009). *Cult of analytics: Driving online marketing strategies using Web analytics*. Burlington, MA: Butterworth Heinemann.

Jamalnia, A., & Soukhakian, M. A. (2009). A hybrid fuzzy goal programming approach with different goal priorities to aggregate production planning. *Computers & Industrial Engineering, 56*(4), 1474–1486. doi:10.1016/j.cie.2008.09.010

Jara, J. R., & Garnica, A. (2009). *Medición de audiencias de televisión en México (Measuring television audiences in Mexico)*. Mexico: Grupo Editorial Patria.

Jayanthi, S., Roth, A., Kristal, M., & Venu, L. (2009). Strategic resource dynamics of manufacturing firms. *Management Science, 55*(6), 1060–1076. doi:10.1287/mnsc.1090.1002

Johnson, R. M. (1971). Market segmentation: A strategic management tool. *JMR, Journal of Marketing Research, 8*(February), 13–21. doi:10.2307/3149720

Kacprzyk, J., & Zadrozny, S. (2000). Data mining via fuzzy querying over the internet. In D. Perez, M. J. Somodevilla, & I. H. Pineda (Eds.). *Fuzzy spatial data warehouse: A multidimensional model, Proceedings of the Eighth Mexican International Conference on Current Trends in Computer Science* (ENC), (pp. 3-9).

Kacprzyk, J. (1986). Group decision-making with a fuzzy linguistic majority. *Fuzzy Sets and Systems, 18*(2), 105–118. doi:10.1016/0165-0114(86)90014-X

Kaser, O., & Lemire, D. (2007). *Tag-cloud drawing: Algorithms for cloud visualization*. Banff: Electronic Edition.

Kasinadh, D. P. V., & Krishna, P. R. (2007). *Building fuzzy OLAP using multi-attribute summarization*. International Conference on Computational Intelligence and Multimedia Applications.

Kassarjian, H. (1981). Low involvement: A second look. *Advances in Consumer Research. Association for Consumer Research (U. S.), 8*, 31–34.

Katz, A., Vom Hau, M., & Mahoney, J. (2005). Explaining the great reversal in Spanish America: Fuzzy-set analysis versus regression analysis. *Sociological Methods & Research, 33*(4), 539–573. doi:10.1177/0049124104266002

Kaufmann, M. (2009). An inductive approach to fuzzy marketing analytics. In M. H. Hamza (Ed.), *Proceedings of the 13th IASTED International Conference on Artificial Intelligence and Soft Computing,* Palma, Spain.

Kaufmann, M. (2011). *Inductive fuzzy classification for marketing analytics* (PhD Thesis, to appear). University of Fribourg, Switzerland.

Kaufmann, M., & Meier, A. (2009). An inductive fuzzy classification approach applied to individual marketing. In *Proceedings of the 28th North American Fuzzy Information Processing Society Annual Conference*, Ohio, USA.

Kaushik, A. (2009). *Web analytics 2.0 – The art of online accountability and science of customer centricity*. New York, NY: Wiley.

Keller, E., & Berry, J. (2003). *The influentials*. New York, NY: Free Press.

Kerr, N. L., & Tindale, R. S. (2004). Group performance and decision making. *Annual Review of Psychology, 55*, 623–655. doi:10.1146/annurev.psych.55.090902.142009

Ketchen, D. J., & Shook, C. L. (1996). The application of cluster analysis in strategic management research: an analysis and critique. *Strategic Management Journal, 17*(6), 441–458. doi:10.1002/(SICI)1097-0266(199606)17:6<441::AID-SMJ819>3.0.CO;2-G

Kimball, R., & Caserta, J. (2004). *The data warehouse ETL toolkit*. Wiley Publishing, Inc.

Kimball, R., Ross, M., Thornthwaite, W., Mundy, J., & Becker, B. (2008). *The data warehouse lifecycle toolkit* (2nd ed.). Wiley Publishing, Inc.

Kim, D., & Lee, W. J. (1998). Optimal joint pricing and lot sizing with fixed and variable capacity. *European Journal of Operational Research, 109*(1), 212–227. doi:10.1016/S0377-2217(97)00100-8

Kim, D.-W., Lee, K. H., & Lee, D. (2004). Fuzzy clustering of categorical data using fuzzy centroids. *Pattern Recognition Letters, 25*(11), 1263–1271. doi:10.1016/j.patrec.2004.04.004

Kim, H. R., & Chan, P. K. (2008). Learning implicit user interest hierarchy for context in personalization. *Applied Intelligence, 28*(2), 153–166. doi:10.1007/s10489-007-0056-0

Klawonn, F., & Höppner, F. (2003). What is fuzzy about fuzzy clustering? Understanding and improving the concept of the fuzzifier. In Berthold, M. R., Lenz, H. J., Bradley, E., Kruse, R., & Borgelt, C. (Eds.), *Advances in intelligent data analysis* (pp. 254–264). Berlin, Germany: Springer. doi:10.1007/978-3-540-45231-7_24

Kleinberg, J. (1998). Authoritative sources in a hyperlinked environment. In *9th ACM-SIAM Symposium on Discrete Algorithms*, (pp. 1-33). Odense, Denmark.

Klein, E. E., & Herskovitz, P. J. (2005). Philosophical foundations of computer simulation validation. *Simulation & Gaming, 36*, 303–329. doi:10.1177/1046878104273437

Klewes, J., & Wreschniok, R. (2009). *Reputation capital: Building and maintaining trust in the 21st century*. Berlin, Germany: Springer.

Klir, J. G., & Yuan, B. (1995). *Fuzzy sets and fuzzy logics: Theory and applications*. New Jersey: Prentice Hall.

Kohavi, R., Rothleder, N. J., & Simoudis, E. (2002). Emerging trends in business analytics. *Communications of the ACM, 45*(8), 45–48. doi:10.1145/545151.545177

Kohonen, T. (2001). *Self-organizing maps* (3rd ed.). Springer Verlag.

Koka, R., Madhavan, R., & Prescott, J. (2006). The evolution of inter-firm networks: Environmental effects on patterns of network change. *Academy of Management Review, 33*(3), 721–737. doi:10.5465/AMR.2006.21318927

Kosko, B. (1990). Fuzziness vs. probability. *International Journal of General Systems, 17*(2), 211–240. doi:10.1080/03081079008935108

Kossmann, D., Ramsak, F., & Rost, S. (2002). Shooting stars in the sky: an online algorithm for skyline queries. *Proceedings of the 28th International Conference on VLDBs* (pp. 275-286). Hong Kong, China: Morgan Kaufmann Publishers.

Kotler, P. (1971). *Marketing decision making: A model building approach*. New York, NY: Holt, Rinehart & Winston.

Kotler, P. (1989). From mass marketing to mass customisation. *Planning Review, 17*, 10–13.

Kotler, P. (2000). *Marketing management*. New Jersey: Prentice-Hall.

Kotler, P., & Keller, K. L. (2006). *Marketing management*. Upper Saddle River, NJ: Pearson Prentice Hall.

Kreuzer, S. (2008). *Driving the ordinal scale - Moderne Algorithmen zum Einsatz im Data-Mining Bereich*. Frankfurt: Goethe University.

Krishna, K., & Murty, M. N. (1999). Genetic K-means algorithm. *IEEE Transactions on Systems, Man, and Cybernetics. Part B, Cybernetics, 29*(3), 433–439. doi:10.1109/3477.764879

Krugman, D. M., Cameron, G. T., & McKearney White, C. (1995). Visual attention to programming and commercials: The use of in-home observations. *Journal of Advertising, 24*(1), 1–12.

Kumar, K. V. N. N. P., Krishna, P. R., & Kumar De, S. (2005). Fuzzy OLAP cube for qualitative analysis. *Proceedings of ICISIP*.

Kunreuther, H., & Richard, J. F. (1971). Optimal pricing and inventory decisions for non-seasonal items. *Econometrica: Journal of the Econometric Society, 39*(1), 173–175. doi:10.2307/1909147

Küppers, G., & Lenhard, J. (2005). Validation of simulation: Patterns in the social and natural sciences. *Journal of Artificial Societies and Social Simulation, 8*(4), 3.

Küsters, U. (2001). Data Mining Methoden: Einordung und Überblick. In Hippner, H., Küsters, U., Meyer, M., & Wilde, K. (Eds.), *Handbuch Data Mining im Marketing - Knowledge Discover in Marketing Databases* (pp. 95–130). Wiesbaden, Germany: Vieweg GABLER.

Kvist, J. (2007). Fuzzy set ideal type analysis. *Journal of Business Research, 60*(5), 474–481. doi:10.1016/j.jbusres.2007.01.005

Ladner, A., Fivaz, J., & Pianzola, J. (2010). *Impact of voting advice applications on voters' decision-making*. Paper presented at the Conference on Internet, Politics, Policy 2010: An Impact Assessment. Oxford.

Lauterborn, R. (1990). New marketing litany – 4P's Passe, C-words take over. *Advertising Age, 1*, 26.

Law, A. M., & Kelton, D. W. (1999). *Simulation modeling and analysis*. New York, NY: McGraw-Hill.

Lazarsfeld, P. F. (1937). Some remarks on the typological procedures in social research. *Festschrift fur Sozialforschung, 6*(1), 119–139.

Leask, G., & Parker, D. (2006). Strategic group theory: Review, examination and application in the UK pharmaceutical industry. *Journal of Management Development, 25*(4), 386–408. doi:10.1108/02621710610655846

Lee, B., & Lee, R. S. (1995). How and why people watch TV: Implications for the future of interactive television. *Journal of Advertising Research, 35*(6), 9–18.

Lee, W. J. (1993). Determining order quantity and selling price by geometric programming optimal solution, bounds, and sensitivity. *Decision Sciences, 24*, 76–87. doi:10.1111/j.1540-5915.1993.tb00463.x

Lee, W. J., & Kim, D. (1993). Optimal and heuristic decision strategies for integrated production and marketing planning. *Decision Sciences, 24*(6), 1203–1213. doi:10.1111/j.1540-5915.1993.tb00511.x

Lehner, W. (1998). Modeling large scale OLAP scenarios. In *Advances in Database Technology – EDBT'98,* (vol. 1377, pp. 153–167). Springer.

Lenz, H.-J., & Shoshani, A. (1997). *Summarizability in OLAP and statistical data bases*. Statistical and Scientific Database Management.

Lewandowski, D. (2005). *Web information retrieval: Techniken zur Informationssuche im Internet*. Düsseldorf, Germany: Deutsche Gesellschaft f. Informationswissenschaft u. Informationspraxis.

Li, J., Min, K. J., Otake, T., & Voorhis, T. M. (2008). Inventory and investment in setup and quality operations under return on investment maximization. *European Journal of Operational Research, 185*, 593–605. doi:10.1016/j.ejor.2006.11.045

Li, L., & Lai, K. K. (2001). Fuzzy dynamic programming approach to hybrid multi objective multi stage decision making problems. *Fuzzy Sets and Systems, 117*, 13–25. doi:10.1016/S0165-0114(98)00423-0

Linden, G., Smith, B., & York, J. (2003). Amazon.com recommendations: Item-to-item collaborative filtering. *IEEE Internet Computing, 7*(1), 76–80. doi:10.1109/MIC.2003.1167344

Lin, T. S., Yao, Y. Y., & Zadeh, L. A. (2002). *Data mining, rough sets and granular computing*. Heidelberg, Germany: Physica-Verlag.

Liou, T.-S., & Wang, M.-J. (1992). Ranking fuzzy numbers with integral value. *Fuzzy Sets and Systems, 50*, 247–255. doi:10.1016/0165-0114(92)90223-Q

Loudon, D. L., & Della Vitta, A. J. (1993). *Consumer behavior: Concepts and applications*. Singapore: McGraw-Hill.

Louie, M. A., & Carley, K. M. (2008). Balancing the criticisms: Validating multi-agent models of social systems. *Simulation Modelling Practice and Theory, 16*, 242–256. doi:10.1016/j.simpat.2007.11.011

Lull, J. T. (1978). Choosing television programs by family vote. *Communication Quarterly, 26*(4), 53–57. doi:10.1080/01463377809369314

Lull, J. T. (1980a). The social uses of television. *Human Communication Research, 7*(3), 319.

Lull, J. T. (1980b). Family communication patterns and the social uses of television. *Communication Research, 7*(3), 319. doi:10.1177/009365028000700303

Lull, J. T. (1982). How families select television programs: A mass-observational study. *Journal of Broadcasting, 26*, 801–811. doi:10.1080/08838158209364049

Lull, J. T. (Ed.). (1988). *World families watch television*. Newbury Park, CA: Sage.

Luna-Reyes, L. F., & Andersen, D. L. (2003). Collecting and analyzing qualitative data for system dynamics: methods and models. *System Dynamics Review, 19*(4), 271–296. doi:10.1002/sdr.280

Luque, T. (2000). Segmentación Jerárquica. In Luque, T. (Ed.), *Técnicas de análisis de datos en investigación de mercados* (pp. 347–382). Madrid, Spain: Pirámide.

MacQueen, J. B. (1967). Some methods for classification and analysis of multivariate observations. In L. M. Le Cam & J. Neyman (Eds.), *Proceedings of the 5th Berkley Symposium on Mathematical Statistics and Probability* (vol. 1, pp. 281-297). Berkeley, CA: University of California Press.

Maguire, S., McKelvey, B., Mirabeau, L., & Öztas, N. (2006). Complexity science and organization studies. In Clegg, S., Hardy, C., Nord, W., & Lawrence, T. (Eds.), *Handbook of organization studies* (pp. 164–214). London, UK: Sage.

Maldonado, N. (2010). Connect and promote. *Career World, 38*(5), 26–29.

Manco, G., Ortale, R., & Sacca, D. (2003). Similarity-based clustering of Web transactions. *Proceedings of the ACM Symposium on Applied Computing* (pp. 1212-1216). Melbourne, FL: ACM Press.

Mandal, N. K., Roy, T. K., & Maiti, M. (2005). Multi-objective fuzzy inventory model with three constraints: A geometric programming approach. *Fuzzy Sets and Systems, 150*, 87–106. doi:10.1016/j.fss.2004.07.020

Manning, C. D., Raghavan, P., & Schütze, H. (2008). *Introduction to information retrieval*. New York, NY: Cambridge University Press.

Marketing Trends (2004). *Definición de estilos de vida* (Definition of lifestyles [in Mexico]) Electronic document.

Mayr, G. v. (1877). *Die Gesetzmäßigkeit im Gesellschaftsleben*. Oldenbourg.

Mazanec, J. A. (1992). Classifying tourists into market segments: A neural network approach. *Journal of Travel & Tourism Marketing, 1*(1), 39–59. doi:10.1300/J073v01n01_04

McClelland, D. C. (1996). Does the field of personality have a future? *Current Directions in Psychological Science, 1*(1), 86–89.

McDonald, M., & Dunbar, I. (1995). *Market segmentation*. Basingstoke, UK: MacMillan Press.

McLuhan, M., & Nevitt, B. (1972). *Take today: The executive as dropout*. New York.

Medina, E., & Trujillo, J. (2002). A standard for representing multidimensional properties: The common warehouse model (CWM). In Manolopoulos, Y., & Navrat, P. (Eds.), *Advances in Databases and Information Systems* (Vol. 2435, pp. 232–247). Lecture Notes in Computer Science Springer Verlag. doi:10.1007/3-540-45710-0_19

Mehta, R. G., Rana, D. P., & Mukesh, A. Z. (2009). A novel fuzzy based classification for data mining using fuzzy discretization. *Proceedings of the WRI World Congress on Computer Science and Information Engineering,* (pp. 713-717).

Meier, A., & Stormer, H. (2009). *eBusiness & eCommerce: Managing the digital value chain*. Berlin, Germany: Springer.

Meier, A., & Zumstein, D. (2010). *Web analytics – Ein Überblick*. Heidelberg, Germany: Dpunkt Verlag. Retrieved from www.WebAnalyticsWebControlling.org

Meier, A., Werro, N., Albrecht, M., & Sarakinos, M. (2005). Using a fuzzy classification query language for customer relationship management. *Proceedings of the 31st VLDB Conference.*

Meier, A. (2009). *E-democracy & e-government*. Berlin, Germany: Springer.

Meier, A., Schindler, G., & Werro, N. (2008). Fuzzy classification of relational databases. In Galindo, M. (Ed.), *Handbook of research on fuzzy information processing in databases* (Vol. II, pp. 586–614). Information Science Reference. doi:10.4018/978-1-59904-853-6.ch023

Meier, A., & Werro, N. (2007). A fuzzy classification model for online customers. *Informatica, 33*, 175–182.

Mendel, J., Zadeh, L., Trillas, E., Lawry, J., Hagras, H., & Guadarrama, S. (2010). What computing with words means to me. *IEEE Computational Intelligence Magazine,* February, (pp. 20-26).

Midgley, D., Marks, R., & Kunchamwar, D. (2007). Building and assurance of agent-based models: An example and challenge to the field. *Journal of Business Research, 60*(8), 884–893. doi:10.1016/j.jbusres.2007.02.004

Mizoguchi, K. (2009). Nodes and edges: A network approach to hierarchisation and state formation in Japan. *Journal of Anthropological Archaeology, 28*(1), 14–26. doi:10.1016/j.jaa.2008.12.001

Mlecko, J. (1982). The guru in Hindu tradition. *Numen*, *29*(1), 33–61. doi:10.1163/156852782X00132

Mobashe, R., Burke, R., & Sandvig, J. (2006). *Model-based collaborative filtering as a defense against profile injection attacks*. Paper presented at the 21st National Conference on Artificial Intelligence (AAAI'06), Boston, Massachusetts.

Mobasher, B. (2007). Web usage mining. In Liu, B. (Ed.), *Web data mining – Exploring hyperlinks, contents, and usage data*. New York, NY: Springer.

Mobasher, B., Dai, H., Luo, T., & Nakagawa, M. (2002). Discovery and evaluation of aggregate usage profiles for Web personalization. *Data Mining and Knowledge Discovery*, *6*(1). doi:10.1023/A:1013232803866

Moe, W. W., & Fader, P. S. (2004). Capturing evolving visit behaviour in clickstream data. *Journal of Interactive Marketing*, *18*(1), 5–19. doi:10.1002/dir.10074

Molina, C., Rodriguez-Ariza, L., Sanchez, D., & Vila, M. A. (2006). A new fuzzy multidimensional model. *IEEE Transactions on Fuzzy Systems*, *14*(6), 897–912. doi:10.1109/TFUZZ.2006.879984

Möller, K., Rajala, A., & Svahn, S. (2005). Strategic business nets—Their type and management. *Journal of Business Research*, *58*, 1274–1284. doi:10.1016/j.jbusres.2003.05.002

Mora, J. D. (2010). *Understanding the social structure of television audiences: Three essays.* Doctoral dissertation, Simon Fraser University, Vancouver, BC.

Moss, S. (2008). Alternative approaches to the empirical validation of agent-based models. *Journal of Artificial Societies and Social Simulation*, *11*(1), 5.

Mote, J. E., Jordan, G., Hage, J., & Whitestone, Y. (2007). New directions in the use of network analysis in research and product development evaluation. *Research Evaluation*, *16*(3), 191–203. doi:10.3152/095820207X235746

Motro, A., & Smets, P. (1997). *Uncertainty management in information systems: From needs to solutions*. Kluwer Academic Publishers. doi:10.1007/978-1-4615-6245-0

Mulhern, F. J. (1997). Retail marketing: From distribution to integration. *International Journal of Research in Marketing*, *14*(2), 103–124. doi:10.1016/S0167-8116(96)00031-6

Nahapiet, J., & Ghoshal, S. (1998). Social capital, intellectual capital, and the organizational advantage. *Academy of Management Review*, *23*, 242–266.

Nair, H. S., Manchanda, P., & Bhatia, T. (2010). Asymmetric social interactions in physician prescription behavior: The role of opinion leaders. *JMR, Journal of Marketing Research*, *47*(5), 883–895. doi:10.1509/jmkr.47.5.883

Nambiar, U., & Kambhampati, S. (2005). Answering imprecise queries over web databases. *Proceedings of the 31st International Conference on VLDBs*. Trondheim, Norway: ACM Press.

Newman, M., Barabási, A. L., & Watts, D. J. (2006). *The structure and dynamics of networks*. Princeton, NJ: Princeton University Press.

Ng, R. T., & Han, J. (1994). Efficient and effective clustering methods for spatial data mining. *Proceedings of the 20th International Conference on VLDBs* (pp. 144-155). Santiago, Chile: Morgan Kaufmann Publishers.

Nguyen, P. T., Cliquet, G., Borges, A., & Leray, F. (2003). *L'opposition entre taille du marché et degré d'homogénéité des segments: Une approche par la logique floue* (Opposition between size of the market and degree of homogeneity of the segments: a fuzzy clustering approach). *Décisions Marketing*, *32*, 55–69.

O'Reilly, T. (2005). *What is Web 2.0? Design patterns and business models for the next generation of software*. Retrieved November 30, 2010, from http://oreilly.com/web2/archive/what-is-web-20.html

O'Reilly, T., & Battelle, J. (2009). *Web squared: Web 2.0 five years on, special report*. Retrieved November 30, 2010, from http://www.web2summit.com/web2009/public/schedule/detail/10194

Ochel, W., & Rohwer, A. (2009). *Reduction of employment protection in Europe: A comparative fuzzy-set analysis*. Working Paper 2828, CESifo (Center for Economic Studies and IFO Institute for Economic Research) - IFO Institute for Economic Research.

OLAP Council. (1995). *OLAP and OLAP server definitions.* Retrieved from http://www.olapcouncil.org/research/resrchly.htm

Olaru, D., & Smith, B. (2005). Modelling behavioural rules for daily activity scheduling using fuzzy logic. *Transportation Journal, 32*(4), 423–441.

O'leary-Kelly, A. M., Martocchio, J. J., & Frink, D. D. (1994). A review of the influence of group goals on group performance. *Academy of Management Journal, 37*(5), 1285. doi:10.2307/256673

Oliveira, J. V., & Pedrycz, W. (2007). *Advances in fuzzy clustering and its applications.* West Sussex, UK: John Wiley & Sons. doi:10.1002/9780470061190

Ortiz-Arroyo, D., & Akbar Hussain, D. M. (2008). An information theory approach to identify sets of key players in social networks. *Proceedings of EuroISI 2008, First European Conference on Intelligence and Security Informatics*, December 3-5th, Ebjerg Denmark, (pp. 15-26).

Otake, T., & Min, K. J. (2001). Inventory and investment in quality improvement under return on investment maximization. *Computers & Operations Research, 28,* 113–124. doi:10.1016/S0305-0548(00)00022-8

Otake, T., Min, K. J., & Chen, C. (1999). Inventory and investment in setup operations under return on investment maximization. *Computers & Operations Research, 26,* 883–899. doi:10.1016/S0305-0548(98)00095-1

Öztürk, B., & Öztürk, M. (2010). *Visualisierung von Clustern.* Frankfurt, Germany: Goethe University.

Palmer, J. (2002). Web site usability, design, and performance metrics. *Information Systems Research, 13*(2), 151–167. doi:10.1287/isre.13.2.151.88

Parmar, D., Wu, T., & Blackhurst, J. (2007). MMR: An algorithm for clustering categorical data using rough set theory. *Data & Knowledge Engineering, 63*(3), 879–893. doi:10.1016/j.datak.2007.05.005

Pawlak, Z. (1997). Rough set approach to knowledge-based decision support. *European Journal of Operational Research, 99*(1), 48–57. doi:10.1016/S0377-2217(96)00382-7

Pawlak, Z., & Skowron, A. (2007). Rough sets and Boolean reasoning. *Information Sciences, 177*(1), 41–73. doi:10.1016/j.ins.2006.06.007

Pearson, K. (1901). Principal components analysis. *The London. Edinburgh and Dublin Philosophical Magazine and Journal, 6,* 566.

Pedersen, T. B., Jensen, C. S., & Dyreson, C. E. (1999). *Supporting imprecision in multidimensional databases using granularities.* Eleventh International Conference on Scientific and Statistical Database Management.

Pedersen, T. B., & Jensen, C. S. (2001). Multidimensional database technology. *Computer, 34*(12), 40–46. doi:10.1109/2.970558

Pedrycz, W., & Gomide, F. (2007). *Fuzzy systems engineering: Toward human-centric computing.* New York, NY: John Wiley & Sons.

Pepper, S. (2010). Topic maps. In *Encyclopedia of Library and Information Sciences.* Retrieved November 30, 2010, from http://www.google.ch/url?sa=t&source=web&cd =1&sqi=2&ved=0CCMQFjAA&url=http%3A%2F%2 Fwww.ontopedia.net%2Fpepper% 2Fpapers%2FELIS-TopicMaps.pdf&rct=j&q=pepper%20topic%20 maps&ei=aF7uTKjoHYiSswavzpT-Cg&usg= AFQjCN FolzoDB1u5NNgkRRbRi9itkEaJnA&sig2=cmLGL3R 5x6CubvBQfKmnmA&cad=rja

Pérez, D., Somodevilla, M. J., & Pineda, I. H. (2007). *Fuzzy spatial data warehouse: A multidimensional model.* Eighth Mexican International Conference on Current Trends in Computer Science.

Peters, I. (2009). *Folksonomies: Indexing and retrieval in the Web 2.0.* Berlin, Germany: Saur.

Peterson, E. (2005). *Web site measurement hacks.* New York, NY: O'Reilly.

Petty, M. D. (2009). Verification and validation. In Sokolowski, J. A., & Banks, C. M. (Eds.), *Principles of modeling and simulation: A multidisciplinary approach* (pp. 121–149). Hoboken, NJ: John Wiley & Sons Inc.

Petty, M. D. (2010). Verification, validation and accreditation. In Sokolowski, J. A., & Banks, C. M. (Eds.), *Modeling and simulation fundamentals: Theoretical underpinnings and practical domains* (pp. 325–372). New Jersey: John Wiley & Sons. doi:10.1002/9780470590621.ch10

Phillips, D., & Young, P. (2009). *Online public relations: A practical guide to developing an online strategy in the world of social media*. London, UK: Kogan Page Limited.

Phippen, A., Sheppard, L., & Furnell, S. (2004). A practical evaluation of Web analytics. *Internet Research, 14*, 284–293. doi:10.1108/10662240410555306

Picot, A., Reichwald, R., & Wigand, R. T. (2003). *Die grenzenlose Unternehmung: Information, Organisation und Management*. Wiesbaden, Germany: Gabler Verlag.

Piekkari, R., Plakoyiannaki, E., & Welch, C. (2010). 'Good' case research in industrial marketing: Insights from research practice. *Industrial Marketing Management, 39*(1), 109–117. doi:10.1016/j.indmarman.2008.04.017

Pittaway, L., Robertson, M., Munir, K., Denyer, D., & Neely, A. (2004). Networking and innovation: A systematic review of the evidence. *International Journal of Management Reviews, 5/6*(3&4), 137–168. doi:10.1111/j.1460-8545.2004.00101.x

Podani, J. (2005). Multivariate exploratory analysis of ordinal data in ecology: Pitfalls, problems and solutions. *Journal of Vegetation Science, 16*(5), 497–510. doi:10.1111/j.1654-1103.2005.tb02390.x

Poli, R., Kennedy, J., & Blackwell, T. (2007). Particle swarm optimization: An overview. *Swarm Intelligence, 1*, 33–57. doi:10.1007/s11721-007-0002-0

Pons, O., Vila, M. A., & Kacprzyk, J. (Eds.). (2000). *Knowledge management in fuzzy databases* (pp. 211–233). Heidelberg, Germany: Physica Publisher.

Popp, R. L., & Yen, J. (2006). *Emergent Information Technologies and enabling policies for counter-terrorism*. Hoboken, NJ: John Wiley & sons. doi:10.1002/047178656X

Porteus, E. L., & Whang, S. (1991). On manufacturing/marketing incentives. *Management Science, 37*(9), 1166–1181. doi:10.1287/mnsc.37.9.1166

Portmann, E. (2008). *Informationsextraktion aus Weblogs*. Saarbrücken, Germany: VDM.

Portmann, E., & Meier, A. (2010). A fuzzy grassroots ontology for improving weblog extraction. *Journal of Digital Information Management, 8*(4), 276–284.

Price, L., Feick, L., & Guskey-Federouch, A. (1988). Couponing behaviors of the market maven: Profile of a super couponer. *Advances in Consumer Research. Association for Consumer Research (U. S.), 15*(3), 354–359.

Project, A. C. E. (2006). *Roles and definitions of political parties*. Retrieved September 10, 2010, from http://aceproject.org/ace-en/topics/pc/pca/pca01/pca01a

Prud'hommeaux, E., & Seaborne, A. (2008). *SPARQL query language for RDF*. W3C Recommendation 15 January 2008. Retrieved November 30, 2010, from http://www.w3.org/TR/rdf-sparql-query/

Punj, G., & Steward, D. W. (1983). Cluster analysis in marketing research: Review and suggestions for application. *JMR, Journal of Marketing Research, 20*, 134–148. doi:10.2307/3151680

Puntoni, S., & Tavassoli, N. T. (2007). Social context and advertising memory. *JMR, Journal of Marketing Research, 44*(2), 284–296. doi:10.1509/jmkr.44.2.284

Putnam, R. D. (1995). Bowling alone: America's declining social capital. *Journal of Democracy, 6*(1), 65–78. Retrieved from http://xroads.virginia.edu/~HYPER/DETOC/assoc/bowling.htmldoi:10.1353/jod.1995.0002

Putnam, R. D. (2000). *Bowling alone: The collapse and revival of American community*. New York, NY: Simon & Schuster.

Rabbie, J. M., Schot, J. C., & Visser, L. (1989). Social identity theory: A conceptual and empirical critique from the perspective of a behavioural interaction model. *European Journal of Social Psychology, 19*(3), 171–202. doi:10.1002/ejsp.2420190302

Rafanelli, M., & Shoshani, A. (1990). STORM: A statistical object representation model. *Statistical and Scientific Data Base Management Conference*, (pp. 14-29).

Ragin, C. (2005). *From fuzzy sets to crisp truth tables*. Tucson, AZ: Department of Sociology, University of Arizona. Retrieved from http://www.compasss.org/files/WPfiles/Raginfztt_April05.pdf

Ragin, C. (1987). *The comparative method: Moving beyond qualitative and quantitative methods*. Berkeley, CA: University of California Press.

Ragin, C. (1997). Turning the tables: How case-oriented methods challenge variable-oriented methods. *Comparative Social Research*, *16*(1), 27–42.

Ragin, C. (2000). *Fuzzy-set social science*. Chicago, IL: University of Chicago Press.

Ragin, C. (2008a). Measurement versus calibration: A set-theoretic approach. In Box-Steffensmeiner, J., Brady, H., & Collier, D. (Eds.), *The Oxford handbook of political methodology* (pp. 174–188). New York, NY: Oxford University Press. doi:10.1093/oxfordhb/9780199286546.003.0008

Ragin, C. (2008b). Qualitative comparative analysis using fuzzy sets (fs/QCA). In Rihoux, B., & Ragin, C. C. (Eds.), *Configurational comparative analysis*. Thousand Oaks, CA: Sage Publications.

Ragin, C. C. (2008). *Redesigning social inquiry: fuzzy sets and beyond*. Chicago, IL: University of Chicago Press.

Ragin, C., Rubinson, C., Schaefer, D., Anderson, S., Williams, E., & Giesel, H. (2008). *User's guide to fuzzy-set/qualitative comparative analysis 2.0*. Tucson, AZ: Department of Sociology, University of Arizona.

Raiffa, H. with Richardson, J., & Metcalfe, D. (2002). *Negotiation analysis: The science and art of collaborative decision making*. Cambridge, MA: Harvard University Press.

Richiardi, M., Roberto, L., Saam, N., & Sonnessa, M. (2006). A common protocol for agent-based social simulation. *Journal of Artificial Societies and Social Simulation*, *9*(1).

Rihoux, B., & Ragin, C. (2008). *Configurational comparative methods: Qualitative comparative analysis (QCA) and related techniques*. Thousand Oaks, CA: Sage Publications, Inc.

Robertson, T. S. (1979). Parental mediation of television advertising effects. *The Journal of Communication*, *29*(1), 12–25. doi:10.1111/j.1460-2466.1979.tb01678.x

Robertson, T., & Kennedy, J. (1968). Prediction of consumer innovators: Application of multiple discriminant analysis. *JMR, Journal of Marketing Research*, *5*(1), 64–69. doi:10.2307/3149795

Rogers, E. (1995). *Diffusion of innovation*. New York, NY: The Free Press.

Rohloff, K., Dean, M., Emmons, I., Ryder, D., & Summer, J. (2007). An evaluation of triple-store technologies for large data stores. *Proceedings of the 2007 OTM Confederated International Conference on the Move to Meaningful Internet Systems*.

Rosenberg, D. (1991). Optimal price-inventory decisions profit vs ROII. *IIE Transactions*, *23*, 17–22. doi:10.1080/07408179108963837

Röttger, U. (2005). Kommunikationsmanagement in der Dualität von Struktur. *Medienwissenschaft Schweiz/Science des Mass Média Suisse*, *1*(2), 12-19.

Roubos, J. A., Setnes, M., & Abonyi, J. (2003). Learning fuzzy classification rules from labeled data. *Information Sciences—Informatics and Computer Science. International Journal (Toronto, Ont.)*, *150*(1-2).

Ruspini, E. (1969). A new approach to clustering. *Information and Control*, *15*, 22–32. doi:10.1016/S0019-9958(69)90591-9

Russel, R. C. (1918). *US patent 1261167, 1918*.

Russel, R. C. (1922). *US patent 1435663, 1922*.

Rust, R. T., Zeithaml, V. A., & Lemon, K. N. (2000). *Driving customer equity*. New York, NY: Free Press.

Rust, R., & Alpert, M. (1984). An audience flow model of television viewing choice. *Marketing Science*, *3*(1), 113–127. doi:10.1287/mksc.3.2.113

Ruvio, A., & Shoham, A. (2007). Innovativeness, exploratory behavior, market mavenship, and opinion leadership: An empirical examination in the Asian context. *Psychology and Marketing*, *24*(7), 703–722. doi:10.1002/mar.20180

Sadjadi, S. J., Ghazanfari, M., & Yousefli, A. (2010). Fuzzy pricing and marketing planning model: A possibilistic geometric programming approach. *Expert Systems with Applications*, *37*, 3392–3397. doi:10.1016/j.eswa.2009.10.009

Sadjadi, S. J., Orougee, M., & Aryanezhad, M. B. (2005). Optimal production and marketing planning. *Computational Optimization and Applications*, *30*, 195–203. doi:10.1007/s10589-005-4564-8

Sammon, J. W. (1969). A nonlinear mapping for data structure analysis. *Journal IEEE Transactions on Computers, 18*, 401–409. doi:10.1109/T-C.1969.222678

Sapir, L., Shmilovici, A., & Rokach, L. (2008). *A methodology for the design of a fuzzy data warehouse*. In Intelligent Systems, 2008. IS'08. 4th International IEEE Conference, volume 1.

Sargent, R. G. (2004). *Validation and verfication of simulation models*. Paper presented at the 36th Winter Simulation Conference, Washington, DC, USA.

Sarwar, B., Karypis, G., & Konstan, J. (2001). *Item-based collaborative filtering recommendation algorithms*. Paper presented at the 10th International World Wide Web Conference, China, Hong Kong.

Schepperle, H., Merkel, A., & Haag, A. (2004). *Erhalt von imperfektion in einem data warehouse*. Internationales Symposium: Data-Warehouse-Systeme und Knowledge-Discovery.

Schindler, G. (1998). *Fuzzy Datenanalyse durch Kontex-basierte Datenbankanfragen (Fuzzy data analysis through context-based database queries)*. Wiesbaden, Germany: Deutscher Universitäts-Verlag.

Schmitt, K. L., Woolf, K. D., & Anderson, D. R. (2003). Viewing the viewers: Viewing behaviors by children and adults during television programs and commercials. *The Journal of Communication, 53*(2), 265–281. doi:10.1111/j.1460-2466.2003.tb02590.x

Schreiber, C., & Carley, K. M. (2007). *Agent interactions in construct: An empirical validation using calibrated grounding*. Paper presented at the 2007 BRIMS Conference, Norfolk.

Schroeder, R. G., & Krishnan, R. (1976). Return on investment as a criterion for inventory model. *Decision Sciences, 7*, 697–704. doi:10.1111/j.1540-5915.1976.tb00713.x

Schwarz, D., Schädel, L., & Ladner, A. (2010). Pre-election positions and voting behavior in Parliament: Explaining positional congruence and changes among Swiss MPs. *Journal Swiss Political Science Review, 16*(4), 533–564. doi:10.1002/j.1662-6370.2010.tb00440.x

Scott, D. M. (2010). *The new rules of marketing and PR: How to use social media, blogs, news releases, online video, and viral marketing to reach buyers directly*. New Jersey: John Wiley & Sons.

Scott, J. (2000). *Social network analysis*. Los Angeles, CA: SAGE Publishers.

Sen, A., Dacin, P., & Pattichis, D. (2006). Current trend in Web data analysis. *Communications of the ACM, 49*(11), 85–91. doi:10.1145/1167838.1167842

Sengupta, S. (1998). Some approaches to complementary product strategy. *Journal of Product Innovation Management, 15*(4), 352–367. doi:10.1016/S0737-6782(97)00106-9

Setiono, R., Thong, J. Y. L., & Yap, C. S. (1998). Symbolic rule extraction from neural networks - An application to identifying organizations adopting IT. *Information & Management, 34*(2), 91–101. doi:10.1016/S0378-7206(98)00048-2

Setnes, M., & Kaymak, U. (2000). *Fuzzy modeling of client preference in data-rich marketing environments*. Research Paper ERS: ERS-2000-49-LIS, RSM Erasmus University.

Setnes, M., Kaymak, H., & van Nauta Lemke, H. R. (1998). Fuzzy target selection in direct marketing. *Proceedings of the IEEE/IAFE/INFORMS Conference on Computational Intelligence for Financial Engineering (CIFEr)*.

Setsuo, A., & Suzuki, E. (2008). *Discovery science: 7th International Conference, DS2004*, Padova, Italy, October 2-5, 2004. Berlin, Germany: Springer.

Shachar, R., & Emerson, J. W. (2000). Cast demographics, unobserved segments, and heterogeneous switching costs in a television viewing choice model. *JMR, Journal of Marketing Research, 37*(2), 173–186. doi:10.1509/jmkr.37.2.173.18738

Shahabi, C., Zarkesh, A. M., Adibi, J., & Shah, V. (1997). Knowledge discovery from users Web-page navigation. *Proceedings of the 7th International Workshop on Research Issues in Data Engineering, RIDE '97: High Performance Database Management for Large-Scale Applications* (pp. 20-29). Birmingham, UK: IEEE Computer Society.

Shapiro, C., & Varian, H. R. (1998). *Information rules: A strategic guide to the network economy*. Boston, MA: Harvard Business School Press.

Shenoi, S. (1995). Fuzzy sets, information clouding and database security. In Bosc, P., & Kacprzyk, J. (Eds.), *Fuzziness in database management systems* (pp. 207–228). Heidelberg, Germany: Physica Publisher.

Shipley, M. F., Korvin, A. D., & Omer, K. (1996). A fuzzy logic approach for determining expected values: A project management application. *The Journal of the Operational Research Society*, *47*(4), 562–569.

Shoshani, A. (1982). Statistical databases: Characteristics, problems, and some solutions. *Proceedings of the International Conference on Very Large Data Bases*, (pp. 208–222).

Sirmakessis, S. (2005). *Knowledge Mining: Proceedings of the NEMIS 2004 Final Conference*. Berlin, Germany: Springer.

Slama, M., & Tashchian, A. (1985). Selected socioeconomic and demographic characteristics associated with purchasing involvement. *Journal of Marketing*, *49*(1), 72–82. doi:10.2307/1251177

Slama, M., & Williams, T. (1990). Generalization of the market maven's information provision tendency across product categories. *Advances in Consumer Research. Association for Consumer Research (U. S.)*, *17*(1), 48–52.

Smartvote. (2010). Retrieved September 10, 2010, from http://www.smartvote.ch/

Smith, G. (2008). *Tagging. People-powered metadata for the Social Web*. Berkeley, CA: New Riders.

Smithson, M., & Verkuilen, J. (2006). *Fuzzy set theory: Applications in the social sciences (vol. no. 07/147)*. Thousand Oaks, CA: Sage Publications.

Smith, W. (1956). Product differentiation and market segmentation as alternative marketing strategies. *Journal of Marketing*, *21*(July), 3–8. doi:10.2307/1247695

Solomonoff, R., & Rapoport, A. (1951). Connectivity of random nets. *The Bulletin of Mathematical Biophysics*, *13*, 107–117. doi:10.1007/BF02478357

Sorkin, R. D., Hays, C. J., & West, R. (2001). Signal-detection analysis of group decision making. *Psychological Review*, *108*(1), 183–203. doi:10.1037/0033-295X.108.1.183

Sousa, J. M., Kaymak, U., & Madeira, S. (2002). A comparative study of fuzzy target selection methods in direct marketing. *Proceedings of the 2002 IEEE International Conference on Fuzzy Systems (FUZZ-IEEE '02)*.

Spiliopoulou, M. (2000). Web usage mining for web site evaluation. *Communications of the ACM*, *43*, 127–134. doi:10.1145/345124.345167

Spiritual Science Research Foundation (SSRF). (2010a). *What is a guru?* Retrieved from http://www.spiritualresearchfoundation.org/articles/id/spiritualresearch/spiritualscience/guru

Spiritual Science Research Foundation (SSRF). (2010b). *Bridging the unknown worlds*. Retrieved from http://Www.Spiritualresearchfoundation.Org/Articles/Id/Spiritualresearch/Spiritualscience/Guru

Spivack, N. (2009). *The evolution of the Web: Past, present, future*. Retrieved November 30, 2010, from http://www.novaspivack.com/uncategorized/the-evolution-of-the-web-past-present-future

Srivastava, J., Cooley, R., Deshpande, M., & Tan, P.-N. (2000). Web usage mining: Discovery and application of usage patterns from Web data. *ACM SIGKDD*, *1*(2), 1–12.

Staudenmayer, N., Tripsas, M., & Tucci, C. (2005). Interfirm modularity and its implications for product development. *Journal of Product Innovation Management*, *22*(4), 303–321. doi:10.1111/j.0737-6782.2005.00128.x

Steckel, J. H., Corfman, K. P., Curry, D. J., Gupta, S., & Shanteau, J. (1991). Prospects and problems in modeling group decisions. *Marketing Letters*, *2*(3), 231–240.

Steenkamp, J. B., & Wedel, M. (1992). Fuzzy cluster wise regression in benefit segmentation: Application and validation into its validity. *Journal of Business Research*, *26*(3), 237–249. doi:10.1016/0148-2963(93)90034-M

Steenkamp, J., & Gielens, K. (2003). Consumer and market drivers of the trial probability of new consumer packaged goods. *The Journal of Consumer Research*, *30*(3), 368–384. doi:10.1086/378615

Sterne, J. (2002). *Web metrics*. New York, NY: Wiley.

Streit, R. E., & Borenstein, D. (2009). Structuring and modeling data for representing the behavior of agents in the governance of the Brazilian financial system. *Applied Artificial Intelligence*, *23*, 316–345. doi:10.1080/08839510902804796

Su, C., Fern, E. F., & Ye, K. (2003). A temporal dynamic model of spousal family purchase-decision behavior. [JMR]. *JMR, Journal of Marketing Research*, *40*(3), 268–281. doi:10.1509/jmkr.40.3.268.19234

Sundaram, D., Mitra, K., & Webster, C. (1998). Word-of-mouth communications: A motivational analysis. *Advances in Consumer Research. Association for Consumer Research (U. S.)*, *25*, 527–531.

Tajfel, H., & Turner, J. (1979). An integrative theory of intergroup conflict. In Austin, W. G., & Worchel, S. (Eds.), *The social psychology of intergroup relations*. Monterey, CA: Brooks-Cole.

Takahashi, Y. (1995). A fuzzy query language for relational databases. In Bosc, P., & Kacprzyk, J. (Eds.), *Fuzziness in database management systems* (pp. 365–384). Heidelberg, Germany: Physica Publisher. doi:10.1109/21.135699

Tam, K. Y. (1994). Neural networks for decision support. *Decision Support Systems*, *11*, 389–392. doi:10.1016/0167-9236(94)90014-0

Tavassoli, N. T., Schultz, C. J. II, & Fitzsimons, G. J. (1995). Program involvement: Are moderate levels best for ad memory and attitude toward the ad? *Journal of Advertising Research*, *35*(5), 61–72.

Terán, L., & Meier, A. (2010, september). *A fuzzy recommender system for e-election*. Paper presented at the International Conference on Electronic Government and the Information Systems Perspective (EGOVIS 2010), Bilbao, Spain.

Tersine, R. J. (1994). *Principles of inventory and materials management* (4th ed.). NJ, USA: Prentice Hall PTR.

Thinkbox. (2009, November 10). It ain't what you view, it's the way that you view it. Retrieved from http://www.thinkbox.tv/server/show/nav.854

TMDb Inc. (2010). *The open movie data base project*. Retrieved November 21, 2010, from http://www.themoviedb.org/

Trippl, M., & Tödtling, F. (2007). Developing biotechnology clusters in non-high technology regions—The case of Austria. *Industry and Innovation*, *14*(1), 47–67. doi:10.1080/13662710601130590

Troitzsch, K. G. (2004). *Validating simulation models*. Paper presented at the 18th European Simulation Multiconference. Retrieved from http://citeseerx.ist.psu.edu/viewdoc/summary?doi=10.1.1.143.6554

Troncy, R., Huet, B., & Schenk, S. (2011). *Multimedia semantics: Metadata, analysis and interaction*. New Jersey: John Wiley & Sons. doi:10.1002/9781119970231

Tsou, C. S. (2008). Multi-objective inventory planning using MOPSO and TOPSIS. *Expert Systems with Applications*, *35*, 136–142. doi:10.1016/j.eswa.2007.06.009

Turban, E., Aronson, J. E., Liang, T.-P., & Sharda, R. (2007). *Decision support and business intelligence systems*. New Jersey: Pearson Education.

Turner, J. C., Hogg, M. A., Oakes, P. J., Reicher, S. D., & Wetherell, M. S. (1987). *Rediscovering the social group: A self-categorization theory*. Oxford, UK: Blackwell.

Valente de Oliveira, J., & Witold, P. (Eds.). (2007). *Advances in fuzzy clustering and its applications*. West Sussex, England: Wiley. doi:10.1002/9780470061190

Van Harmelen, F., Lifschitz, V., & Porter, B. (2007). *Handbook of knowledge representation*. New York, NY: Elsevier.

Van Riel, C. B. M., & Fombrun, C. (2007). *Essentials of corporate communication: Implementing practices for effective reputation management*. Abingdon, UK: Routledge. doi:10.4324/9780203390931

Vassiliadis, P. (1998). Modeling multidimensional databases, cubes and cube operations. *Proceedings of the 10th International Conference on Scientific and Statistical Database Management*.

Verkuilen, J. (2005). Assigning membership in a fuzzy set analysis. *Sociological Methods & Research*, *33*, 462–496. doi:10.1177/0049124105274498

Voss, J. (2007). Tagging, folksonomy & co - Renaissance of manual indexing? *Proceedings of the International Symposium of Information Science*, (pp. 234–254).

Vozalis, E., & Margaritis, K. (2003). *Analysis of recommender systems' algorithms*. Paper presented at the Sixth Hellenic European Conference on Computer Mathematics and its Applications (HERCMA 2003), Athens, Greece.

Vranika, S. (2010, September 23) Nielsen testing a new web-ad metric. *The Wall Street Journal*, p. B8.

Wagemann, C., & Schneider, C. (2007). *Standards of good practice in qualitative comparative analysis (QCA) and fuzzy-sets*. Technical, COMPASSS Working papers (WP 2007-51).

Waisberg, D., & Kaushik, A. (2009). Web analytics 2.0: Empowering customer centricity. *Search Engine Marketing Research Journal, 2*(1). Retrieved June 7, 2011, from: www.semj.org

Walsh, G., Gwinner, K., & Swanson, S. (2004). What makes mavens tick? Exploring the motives of market mavens' initiation of information diffusion. *Journal of Consumer Marketing, 21*(1), 109–122. doi:10.1108/07363760410525678

Walter, A., Auer, M., & Ritter, T. (2006). The impact of network capabilities and entrepreneurial orientation on university spin-off performance. *Journal of Business Venturing, 21*, 541–567. doi:10.1016/j.jbusvent.2005.02.005

Wang, Q. M., Dwight, J., & Edwards, H. K. (2004). Characterizing customer groups for an e-commerce website. *Proceedings of the 5th ACM Conference on Electronic Commerce (EC '04)* (pp. 218-227). ACM Press.

Wang, W., & Zaiane, R. O. (2002). Clustering Web sessions by sequence alignment. *Proceedings of the 13th International Workshop on Database and Expert Systems Applications (DEXA '02)* (pp. 394-398). Aix-en-Provence, France: IEEE Computer Society.

Wang, X. Ruan, D., & Kerre, E. E. (2009). *Mathematics of fuzziness – Basic issues*. Berlin, Germany: Springer Publisher.

Wang, L., & Mendel, J. (1992). Generating fuzzy rules by learning from examples. *IEEE Transactions on Systems, Man, and Cybernetics, 6*, 1414–1427. doi:10.1109/21.199466

Ward, M., Grinstein, G. G., & Keim, D. (2010). *Interactive data visualization: Foundations, techniques, and applications*. Natick, MA: Transatlantic Publishers.

Wasserman, S., & Faust, K. (1994). *Social network analysis: Methods and applications*. New York, NY: Cambridge University Press.

Watts, D. J., & Strogatz, S. H. (1998). Collective dynamics of 'small world' networks. *Nature, 393*, 440–442. doi:10.1038/30918

Web Analytics Association. (2010). *Web Analytics Association*. Retrieved June 7, 2011, from www.webanalyticsassociation.org

Wedderburn, R. W. M. (1974). Quasi-likelihood functions, generalized linear-models, and Gauss-Newton method. *Biometrika, 61*(3), 439–447.

Wedel, M., & Kamakura, W. (2000). *Market segmentation: Conceptual and methodological foundations* (2nd ed.). Massachusetts, USA: Kluwer Academic Publisher.

Wedel, M., & Kamakura, W. (2002). Introduction to the special issue on market segmentation. *International Journal of Research in Marketing, 19*(3), 181–183. doi:10.1016/S0167-8116(02)00075-7

Wee, H., Lo, C., & Hsu, P. (2009). A multi-objective joint replenishment inventory model of deteriorated items in a fuzzy environment. *European Journal of Operational Research, 197*, 620–631. doi:10.1016/j.ejor.2006.08.067

Weischedel, B., & Huizingh, E. (2006). Website optimization with Web metrics: A case study. In *Proceedings of the 8th International Conference on Electronic Commerce* (ICEC'06), August 14-16, Fredericton, Canada, (pp. 463-470).

Weischedel, B., Matear, S., & Deans, K. (2005). The use of emetrics in strategic marketing decisions. *International Journal of Internet Marketing and Advertising, 2*, 109–125. doi:10.1504/IJIMA.2005.007507

Weisstein, E. W. (2010). *Correlation coefficient*. Retrieved from http://mathworld.wolfram.com/CorrelationCoefficient.html

Weller, K. (2010). *Knowledge representation in the Social Semantic Web*. Berlin, Germany: de Gruyter Saur.

Welling, R., & White, L. (2006). Measuring the value of corporate web sites. *Journal of Internet Commerce, 3*(3), 127–145. doi:10.1300/J179v05n03_06

Werro, N. (2008). *Fuzzy classification of online customers.* PhD Thesis. Fribourg, Switzerland: University of Fribourg.

Werro, N., Meier, A., Mezger, C., & Schindler, G. (2005). Concept and implementation of a fuzzy classification query language. *Proceedings of the International Conference on Data Mining, World Congress in Applied Computing*, Las Vegas.

Werro, N., Stormer, H., & Meier, A. (2005). Personalized discount – A fuzzy logic approach. In *Proceedings of the 5th IFIP International Conference on eBusiness, eCommerce and eGovernment* (pp. 375-387). Poznan, Poland.

Werro, N., Stormer, H., & Meier, A. (2006). A hierarchical fuzzy classification of online customers. In *Proceedings of the IEEE International Conference on e-Business Engineering – ICEBE2006* (pp. 256-263). Shanghai, China.

Werro, N., Stormer, H., Frauchiger, D., & Meier, A. (2004). eSarine – A Struts-based webshop for small and medium-sized enterprises. In *Lecture Notes in Informatics EMISA2004 – Information Systems in E-Business and E-Government* (pp. 13-24). Luxembourg, Belgium.

Wilensky, U., & Rand, W. (2007). Making models match: Replicating an agent-based model. *Journal of Artificial Societies and Social Simulation, 10*(4), 1–22.

Williams, T., & Slama, M. (1995). Market mavens' purchase decision evaluative criteria: Implications for brand and store promotion efforts. *Journal of Consumer Marketing, 12*(1), 4–21. doi:10.1108/07363769510147218

Windrum, P., Fagiolo, G., & Moneta, A. (2007). Empirical validation of agent-based models: Alternatives and prospects. *Journal of Artificial Societies and Social Simulation, 10*(2), 8.

Witten, I. H., & Eibe, F. (2005). *Data mining. Practical machine learning tools and techniques.* San Francisco, CA: Elsevier.

Xiao, J., Zhang, Y., Jia, X., & Li, T. (2001). Measuring similarity of interests for clustering Web-users *Proceedings of the 12th Australasian Database Conference* (pp. 107-114). Gold Coast, Australia: IEEE Computer Society.

Yager, R. R. (2006). Some learning paradigms for granular computing. *Proceedings of the IEEE International Conference on Granular Computing*, Atlanta, (pp. 25-29).

Yager, R. (2003). Fuzzy logic methods in recommender systems. *International Journal of Fuzzy Sets and Systems, 136*, 133–149. doi:10.1016/S0165-0114(02)00223-3

Yager, R. R. (1988). On ordered weighted averaging aggregation operators in multi-criteria decision making. *IEEE Transactions on Systems, Man, and Cybernetics, 18*, 183–190. doi:10.1109/21.87068

Yager, R. R. (1992). Applications and extensions of OWA aggregations. *International Journal of Man-Machine Studies, 37*, 103–132. doi:10.1016/0020-7373(92)90093-Z

Yager, R. R. (1996). Quantifier guided aggregation using OWA operators. *International Journal of Intelligent Systems, 11*, 49–73. doi:10.1002/(SICI)1098-111X(199601)11:1<49::AID-INT3>3.3.CO;2-L

Yager, R. R. (2003). Fuzzy logic methods in recommender systems. *Fuzzy Sets and Systems, 136*, 133–149. doi:10.1016/S0165-0114(02)00223-3

Yager, R. R. (2008). Intelligent social network analysis using granular computing. *International Journal of Intelligent Systems, 23*(11), 1196–1219. doi:10.1002/int.20314

Yager, R. R. (2010a). Concept representation and database structures in fuzzy social relational networks. *IEEE Transactions on Systems. Man & Cybernetics: Part A, 40*(2), 413–419. doi:10.1109/TSMCA.2009.2036591

Yager, R. R. (2010b). Associating human-centered concepts with social networks using fuzzy sets. In Furht, B. (Ed.), *Handbook of social network technologies and applications* (*Vol. 3*, pp. 447–467). doi:10.1007/978-1-4419-7142-5_21

Yaghoobi, M. A., & Tamiz, M. (2007). A method for solving fuzzy goal programming problems based on MINMAX approach. *European Journal of Operational Research, 177*, 1580–1590. doi:10.1016/j.ejor.2005.10.022

Yang, S., Narayan, V., & Assael, H. (2006). Estimating the interdependence of television program viewership between spouses: A Bayesian simultaneous equation model. *Marketing Science, 25*(4), 336–349. doi:10.1287/mksc.1060.0195

Yang, S., Zhao, Y., Erdem, T., & Zhao, Y. (2010). Modeling the intrahousehold behavioral interaction. [JMR]. *JMR, Journal of Marketing Research*, *47*(3), 470–484. doi:10.1509/jmkr.47.3.470

Yankelovich, D., & Meer, D. (2006). Rediscovering market segmentation. *Harvard Business Review*, *24*(February), 122–131.

Yin, X., Han, J., & Yu, P. S. (2007). CrossClus: User-guided multi-relational clustering. *Data Mining and Knowledge Discovery*, *15*(3), 321–348. doi:10.1007/s10618-007-0072-z

Yoon, Y., Swales, G., & Margavio, T. M. (1993). A comparison of discriminant analysis versus artificial neural networks. *The Journal of the Operational Research Society*, *44*(1), 51–60.

Zadeh, L. A. (2008, August 11 - 22). Toward human level machine intelligence - Is it achievable? The need for a paradigm shift. *IEEE Computational Intelligence Magazine*, *3*(3).

Zadeh, L. A. (2010, July). *Precisiation of meaning: Toward computation with natural language.* Presented at the IEEE 2010 Summer School on Semantic Computing, Berkeley, CA.

Zadeh, L. A. (1965). Fuzzy sets. *Information and Control*, *8*(3), 338–353. doi:10.1016/S0019-9958(65)90241-X

Zadeh, L. A. (1975). Calculus of fuzzy restrictions. In Zadeh, L. A., Fu, K.-S., Tanaka, K., & Shimura, M. (Eds.), *Fuzzy sets and their applications to cognitive and decision processes*. New York, NY: Academic Press.

Zadeh, L. A. (1975). *Fuzzy sets and their applications to cognitive and decision processes*. New York, NY: Academic Press, Inc.

Zadeh, L. A. (1978). Fuzzy sets as a basis for a theory of possibility. *Fuzzy Sets and Systems*, *1*, 3–28. doi:10.1016/0165-0114(78)90029-5

Zadeh, L. A. (1983). A computational approach to fuzzy quantifiers in natural languages. *Computers & Mathematics with Applications (Oxford, England)*, *9*, 149–184. doi:10.1016/0898-1221(83)90013-5

Zadeh, L. A. (1996). Fuzzy logic = Computing with words. *IEEE Transactions on Fuzzy Systems*, *4*(2), 103–111. doi:10.1109/91.493904

Zadeh, L. A. (1998). Some reflections on soft computing, granular computing and their roles in the conception, design and utilization of information/intelligent systems. *Soft Computing - A Fusion of Foundations. Methodologies and Applications*, *2*(1), 23–25. doi:doi:10.1007/s005000050030

Zadeh, L. A. (1999). From computing with numbers to computing with words – From manipulation of measurements to manipulation of perceptions. *IEEE Transactions on Circuits and Systems*, *45*(1), 105–119.

Zadeh, L. A. (1999). Outline of a computational theory of perceptions based on computing with words. In Sinha, N. K., & Gupta, M. M. (Eds.), *Soft computing and intelligent systems* (pp. 3–22). Boston, MA: Academic Press. doi:10.1016/B978-012646490-0/50004-4

Zadeh, L. A. (2001). A new direction in AI – Toward a computational theory of perceptions. *AI Magazine*, (Spring): 73–84.

Zadeh, L. A. (2004). A note on Web intelligence, world knowledge and fuzzy logic. *Data & Knowledge Engineering*, *50*, 291–304. doi:10.1016/j.datak.2004.04.001

Zadeh, L. A. (2006). From search engines to question answering systems – The problems of world knowledge, relevance, deduction and precisiation. In Sanchez, E. (Ed.), *Fuzzy logic and the Semantic Web* (pp. 163–210). Elsevier. doi:10.1016/S1574-9576(06)80011-0

Zadeh, L. A. (2006). Generalized theory of uncertainty (GTU)-principal concepts and ideas. *Computational Statistics & Data Analysis*, *51*, 15–46. doi:10.1016/j.csda.2006.04.029

Zadeh, L. A. (2009). Toward extended fuzzy logic—A first step. *Fuzzy Sets and Systems*, *160*(21), 3175–3181. doi:10.1016/j.fss.2009.04.009

Zadeh, L. A., Bojadziev, G., & Bojadziev, M. (1997). *Fuzzy logic for business, finance and management (advances in fuzzy systems)*. World Scientific Publishing Company.

Zadrozny, S., de Tre, G., de Caluwe, R., & Kacprzyk, J. (Eds.). (2008). An overview of fuzzy approaches to flexible database querying. In J. Galindo (Ed.), *Handbook on research on fuzzy information processing in databases* (pp. 34-54, vol. 1). Hershey, PA: IGI Global.

Zaki, M. J., Peters, M., Assent, I., & Seidl, T. (2005). CLICKS: An effective algorithm for mining subspace clusters in categorical datasets. *Proceedings of the 11th ACM SIGKDD* (pp. 736-742). Chicago, IL: ACM Press.

Zhang, T. R., Ramakrishnan, R., & Livny, M. (1996). BIRCH: An efficient data clustering method for very large databases. In H. V. Jagadish & I. S. Mumick (Eds.), *Proceedings of the ACM SIGMOD* (pp. 103-114). Montreal, Canada: ACM Press.

Zhao, L., Qian, F., Yang, Y., Zeng, Y., & Su, H. (2010). Automatically extracting T–S fuzzy models using co-operative random learning particle swarm optimization. *Applied Soft Computing*, *10*, 938–944. doi:10.1016/j.asoc.2009.10.012

Zimmermann, H. J. (1987). *Fuzzy sets, decision making, and expert systems. International Series in Management Science Operations Research* (*Vol. 10*). Springer. doi:10.1007/978-94-009-3249-4

Zimmermann, H. J. (1997). Fuzzy data analysis. In Kaynak, O., Zadeh, L. A., Turksen, B., & Rudas, I. J. (Eds.), *Computational intelligence: Soft computing and fuzzy-neuro integration with applications*. Springer-Verlag.

Zimmermann, H. J. (2000). *Practical applications of fuzzy technologies*. Berlin, Germany: Springer Verlag.

Zimmermann, H. J. (2010). Fuzzy set theory. [John Wiley & Sons, Inc.]. *Wiley Interdisciplinary Reviews: Computational Statistics*, *2*(3), 317–332. doi:10.1002/wics.82

Zimmermann, H.-J. (1992). *Fuzzy set theory and its applications* (2nd ed.). London, UK: Kluwer Academic Publishers.

Zimmermann, H.-J., & Zysno, P. (1980). Latent connectives in human decision making. *Fuzzy Sets and Systems*, *4*, 37–51. doi:10.1016/0165-0114(80)90062-7

Zudilova-Seinstra, E., Adriaansen, T., & van Liere, R. (2008). *Trends in interactive visualization: State-of-the-art survey*. Berlin, Germany: Springer.

Zumstein, D. (2010). Web analytics – Analysing, classifying and describing Web metrics with fuzzy logic. In *6th International Conference on Web Information Systems and Technologies (WEBIST)*, April 7-10, Valencia, Spain, (pp. 282-290).

Zumstein, D., & Kaufmann, M. (2009). A fuzzy Web analytics model for Web mining. In *Proceedings of IADIS European Conference on Data Mining*, June 18-20, Algarve, Portugal.

Zumstein, D., & Meier, A. (2010). Web-controlling – Analyse und Optimierung der digitalen Wert-schöpfungskette mit Web Analytics. In *Proceedings of the Multikonferenz Wirtschaftsinformatik (MKWI)*, February 23-25, Göttingen, Germany, (pp. 299-311).

Zumstein, D., Drobjnak, A., & Meier, A. (2011). Data privacy in Web analytics – An empirical study and declaration model of data collection on websites. In *Proceedings of the 7th International Conference on Web Information Systems and Technologies (WEBIST)*, May 6-9 (2011), Noordwijkerhout, The Netherlands.

About the Contributors

Andreas Meier is Professor at the University of Fribourg (Switzerland) and head of the research center for Fuzzy Marketing Methods (www.FMsquare.org). His research interests include electronic business and government, information management, and data mining. He is a member of GI Europe, IEEE, and ACM. After studies at the Music Academy of Vienna he received a diploma in mathematics and a PhD in Computer Science from the Swiss Federal Institute of Technology (ETH) in Zurich. He was a system engineer at IBM, a researcher at the IBM research lab in California USA, a director at the international bank UBS, and a member of the executive board of the CSS insurance company before he joined the University of Fribourg.

Laurent Donzé is Professor of Statistics at the University of Fribourg (Switzerland). After his PhD in Econometrics at the University of Fribourg, he worked several years as research fellow on different projects in the field of applied statistics and econometrics. During this time, he completed his formation by studies in mathematics. In 1996, he was engaged as research fellow at the Swiss Federal Institute of Technology in Zurich (KOF ETH Zurich) and since 2002, he is teaching Statistics and Applied Econometrics at the University of Fribourg. His main research interests are in survey statistics, in measuring economic inequality and the impact of economic policy programs.

* * *

Núria Agell has been a Full Professor at ESADE since 2003 and Director of the ESADE Business School's PhD programme in Management Sciences since 2005. She was awarded a PhD in Mathematics from UPC for a dissertation on Qualitative Reasoning Modelling. She is the coordinator of the ESADE Research Group on Engineering Knowledge (GREC) and an active member of ARCA (Qualitative Reasoning Automatization and Applications). In October 2006, she was named President of the Catalan Association for Artificial Intelligence (ACIA). She is currently the leading coordinator of several publicly and privately-funded projects on the application of artificial intelligence to business, marketing, and finance.

Mònica Casabayó is currently in charge of the Consumer Behaviour and Market Research Area in ESADE's Department of Marketing Management. She is actively participating in a research project focused on the methodological aspects of marketing research, in particular the application of techniques from other disciplines (mainly Artificial Intelligence) to classical marketing problems, such as segmenting and forecasting consumer behaviour. In 2005 she was awarded a PhD by Edinburgh University's College of Humanities and Social Science. She won the "AI 2003 Best Poster Award" at the SGAI (International Conference on Innovative Techniques and Applications of Artificial Intelligence) held in Cambridge in December 2003. She has published in various national and international marketing journals. She has been an Associate Professor at ESADE since 2000.

Adrian David Cheok is Director of the Mixed Reality Lab, National University of Singapore. He is Associate Professor in the Department of Electrical and Computer Engineering. He became full Professor in Keio University, Graduate School of Media Design (Japan) in April 2008. He has previously worked in real-time systems, soft computing, and embedded computing in Mitsubishi Electric Research Labs (Osaka, Japan). He has been working on research covering mixed reality, human-computer interfaces, wearable computers and ubiquitous computing, fuzzy systems, embedded systems, and power electronics. He has successfully obtained funding for externally funded projects in the area of wearable computers and mixed reality from Nike, National Oilwell Varco, Defense Science Technology Agency, Ministry of Communications and Arts, National Arts Council, Singapore Science Center, and Hougang Primary School.

Miri Chung is currently a Doctoral student in Marketing at the University of Rhode Island. She received her BS in Education and Business Administration and M.S in Regional Information from Seoul National University. Her research interests are information diffusion, technology usage, and network effect on online. At the Association of Information Systems (AMICS 2006) Global Conference, one of her studies focusing on the empirical study of e-business was awarded the best paper of the year.

Sara Denize is a member of faculty and Associate Head of School at the University of Western Sydney and an affiliate of the Centre for Innovation and Industry Studies. Her research focuses on complexity in networks and interfirm relationships in a number of marketing settings.

Daniel Fasel is a PhD student at the Department of Computer Sciences at the University of Fribourg, Switzerland. He received his Masters of Arts in Information Systems and his Bachelor of Arts in Information Systems from the University of Fribourg. In addition to his studies, Daniel is employed as a System Engineer with the Department of Computer Science. He has four years of working experience in software engineering and quality management for a medical device manufacturing company. Daniel has published a number of research articles in the area of fuzzy logic and data warehousing.

Jan Fivaz (1974) is writing his PhD in Political Science at the Autonomous University Institute IDHEAP in Lausanne. He is also working as a Research Assistant at the University of Bern. His areas of research consist of electoral behavior, political parties, political representation, and e-Democracy. In 2009, he obtained a Master of Arts in History, Political Science, and Economics. Since 2003, he has been involved in the development of the voting advice application (VAA) smartvote.

Stefani Gerber (1981) is a scientific co-worker at the research project NCCR democracy. She obtained a Master of Computer Science in 2007 at the University of Bern. She has worked in the development of various Web applications, mostly in the context of political science and civic education. Her main interests are Web development, usability, accessibility, and surveys.

S.M.T. Fatemi Ghomi is a Professor in the Department of Industrial Engineering at Amirkabir University of Technology, Tehran, Iran. His research interests are in stochastic activity networks, production planning, scheduling, queuing theory, statistical quality control, and time series analysis and forecasting. He received his BS degree in industrial engineering from Sharif University, Tehran and the PhD degree in industrial engineering from University of Bradford, England.

Cédric Graf is a Software Developer at ITpearls in Switzerland. He achieved a Master's Degree in Computer Science at the University of Fribourg. For his Master's Thesis, he has developed the WEKA-implementation of the IFC-NLR methodology with the Information Systems Research Group. During his studies, he worked at UBS in the field of stock exchanges, asset reporting, security services, and market data systems for the division Wealth Management.

Natascha Hoebel, PhD, born 1977, studied computer science at the University of Applied Sciences in Frankfurt focusing on software engineering and business administration. Here she developed in her thesis a web application for the visualization of graph algorithms in the field of e-learning. 2000 to 2002, she worked as an web and application programmer at an e-commerce company. In 2003, she became a "Sun Certified Programmer for the Java 2 Platform." Since 2004, she has been a college Lecturer at the University of Applied Sciences and since 2005 Web project manager at Gaia Oasis. 2006 to 2011 she worked as a research assistant at the Goethe University of Frankfurt and optained her PhD. Her research interests include Web mining, new web media, consumer behavior, J2EE enterprise applications and data privacy.

Michael Kaufmann is working as a data architect at Swiss Mobiliar Insurance & Pensions in Switzerland since 2009, where he is responsible for data modeling and metadata management. He is external PhD Student in Computer Science with the Information Systems Research Group of Professor Andreas Meier at the University of Fribourg, Switzerland. After graduation in Computer Science with a Master's Degree in 2005, he worked as a data warehouse analyst at PostFinance, the financial service provider of the Swiss Post.

Stanislav Kreuzer, Dipl. Inf., born in 1982, studied Computer Science with a focus on Databases and Information Systems from 2002 to 2007 at the Goethe University in Frankfurt. In 2008, he wrote his diploma thesis about the theory and practical use of clustering algorithms and implemented a modern hybrid clustering system in Java. From 2000 to 2007, he worked as a Software Developer for an established software company. Since 2007, he has worked as an Analyst and Consultant for a leading business intelligence and market research provider in the healthcare sector. His research interests include Information Systems, data mining, clustering, J2SE/J2EE and J2ME applications, and Web development.

Andreas Ladner (1958) is Professor for Political Institutions and Swiss Public Administration at the Autonomous University Institute IDHEAP in Lausanne. His areas of research include political parties, municipalities, institutional change, and e-Democracy. He has conducted several major research projects on behalf of the Swiss National Science Foundation and authored books and articles on these topics. His latest book analyses the influence of municipal size on the quality of democracy in Swiss municipalities.

Ladner also leads a research project on the voting advice application (VAA), smartvote. He has been published in *International Political Science Review, the European Journal of Political Research, West European Politics, Electoral Studies and Party Politics*, among others. He also regularly comments on Swiss politics in the media.

José-Domingo Mora is an Assistant Professor of Marketing at the University of Massachusetts-Dartmouth. His research interests include media audiences, social influences and group processes, as well as statistical modeling. Dr. Mora holds a PhD in Marketing from Simon Fraser University; an MA in Communication Management from the University of Southern California; a BS in Biology and a BS in Communication, magna cum laude, from Universidad Central de Venezuela, Caracas. Prior to joining the doctoral program at SFU, Dr. Mora accumulated 16 years of industry experience working for consumer goods, petroleum, television, and audience measurement companies in Venezuela and Mexico.

Tam Nguyen is a PhD student and research member at Keio-NUS CUTE Center and Mixed Reality Lab of National University of Singapore. He has received his B.Sc. in Computer Science from the University of Sciences (Ho Chi Minh City, Vietnam) and M.Eng. in Computer Engineering from Chonnam National University (South Korea) in 2005 and 2009, respectively. His research interests include pervasive computing, embedded system, context reasoning, mixed reality, and human-computer interaction.

Doina Olaru is a Transport Engineer with academic, industry, and research experience. She lectures in Data Analysis and Decision Making subjects at UWA and, as a researcher, her area of interest expanded from transport modeling, operations research, and discrete choice modeling, to incorporate artificial intelligence and simulation applications in business.

Edy Portmann is a PhD student and researcher at Information Systems Research Group at the University of Fribourg (Switzerland). After a BSc in Information Systems at the Lucerne University of Applied Sciences and Arts, he worked in different IT-related departments of Swiss companies, such as Swisscom, PricewaterhouseCoopers, and Ernst & Young. Accordingly he completed a MSc in Business and Economics at the University of Basel (Switzerland). His research interests include human–computer information retrieval, mediamatics, and soft computing. During 2010 he was an academic visitor at Keio-NUS CUTE Centre in Singapore, where he worked on human-computer interaction and data visualization.

Sharon Purchase works within the marketing discipline at the UWA Business School. Her research interests include business networks and relationships within various contexts.

Jose Sepulveda is a research fellow at the Mixed Reality Lab at the National University of Singapore. His training background includes a BSc in Physics and Doctoral work in Medical Data Analysis at the University of Valencia (Spain). His postdoctoral research focused on bioinformatics at the Center for Genomics and Bioinformatics at Karolinska Institutet (Sweden) and at the Biochemistry Department at Baylor College of Medicine (USA). His research interests focus on the use of technology to empower creativity and innovation. He is also interested on understanding the effects of Information Technology on society, and in the way that technology can be used to support knowledge management and communities of practice.

Khurram Shahzad is a PhD candidate at the Department of Software and Computer Systems (SCS), Royal Institute of Technology (KTH), Stockholm, Sweden. Shahzad received a Master's in Engineering and Management of Information Systems from KTH, and a Master's in Computer Science from the University of the Punjab, Lahore, Pakistan. He is currently on study leave from COMSATS Institute of Information Technology (CIIT), Lahore, Pakistan, where he works as an Assistant Professor in the Department of Computer Science. Shahzad has written a number of publications, several of which have been presented at international forums.

Henrik Stormer is working with the Edorex Informatik AG located in Ostermundigen, Switzerland. He studied Computer Science in Saarbrücken (Germany) and received his PhD in Zurich (Switzerland) with a focus on Business Systems and Workflow Management. Afterwards, he was Assistant Professor at the University of Fribourg where he worked in the area of Electronic and Mobile Business.

Luis Terán (1979) is currently writing a PhD in Computer Science at the University of Fribourg (Information Systems Research Group). His main research topics consist of recommender systems, e-Government, e-Democracy, e-Election, e-Voting, e-Communities, e-Passports, and fuzzy classification. He obtained a Master of Science in Communication Systems at the Swiss Federal Institute of Technology Lausanne (EPFL) in 2009. He obtained a Bachelor of Science in Engineer in Electronics and Telecommunications, Escuela Politécnica Nacional (EPN), in Quito-Ecuador in 2004. From 2004 to 2006, he headed the logistic department at TELCONET SA, a leading enterprise in provisioning telecom services in Ecuador.

Nicolas Werro is currently working for Swisscom AG as solution architect in the business intelligence department. Nicolas achieved a Diploma degree in Computer Science and Economics, a Master's degree in Computer Science, and a PhD in Information Management at the University of Fribourg (Switzerland). His research covered the themes of fuzzy logic, relational database systems, and customer relationship management.

Arch G. Woodside is Professor of Marketing, Carroll School of Management, Boston College. He is a Fellow of the American Psychological Association, Association of Psychological Science, The International Academy for the Study of Tourism, The Royal Society of Canada, and the Society for Marketing Advances. He is the Editor-in-Chief of the *Journal of Business Research*. His most recent book is Case Study Research: Theory, Methods and Practice (Emerald Publishing, 2010).

Rachel Yager is a Professor at the School of Management of Metropolitan College of New York. She specializes in developing strategies for using emerging Web technologies to attain high impact business solutions. She is an engineer with specialization in electrical engineering, industrial automation, robotics, and controls. She also has expertise in computational intelligence, knowledge engineering, and business analytics for decision support. With a doctorate scholarship from French Ministry of Education – L'Association Nationale de la Recherche et de la Technologie (ANRT) - she earned her PhD in Computer Information Systems, and a Master's Degree in Industrial Automation and Operations Management, from INSA de Lyon, Institut National des Sciences Appliquées de Lyon, France. She has a Bachelor's Degree in Electrical and Electronic Engineering from the Nanyang Technological University of Singapore. Rachel has been an advisor to Fortune 100 senior executives in emerging technologies and new product R&D, helping companies to accelerate technology transfer from leading research and academic institutions. Rachel had directed Internet strategies and delivered client services for Citigroup, Lehman Brothers, and Ernst & Young. She has extensive experience in enterprise-wide financial services IT initiatives, enterprise architecture and engineering. She has served in the World Wide Web consortium (W3C) advisory committee, and recently she was on the program committee of the IEEE conference on Computational Intelligence for Financial Engineering.

Ronald R. Yager has worked in the area of machine intelligence for over twenty-five years. He has published over 500 papers and fifteen books in areas related to fuzzy sets, decision making under uncertainty, and the fusion of information. He is among the world's top 1% most highly cited researchers with over 7000 citations. He was the recipient of the IEEE Computational Intelligence Society Pioneer award in Fuzzy Systems. Dr. Yager is a fellow of the IEEE, the New York Academy of Sciences, and the Fuzzy Systems Association. He was given a lifetime achievement award by the Polish Academy of Sciences for his contributions. He served at the National Science Foundation as program director in the Information Sciences program. He was a NASA/Stanford visiting fellow and a research associate at the University of California, Berkeley. He has been a Lecturer at NATO Advanced Study Institutes. He is a distinguished honorary Professor at the Aalborg University Denmark. He is an affiliated distinguished researcher at the European Centre for Soft Computing. He received his undergraduate degree from the City College of New York and his PhD from the Polytechnic University of New York. Currently, he is Director of the Machine Intelligence Institute and Professor of Information Systems at Iona College. He is Editor in Chief of the *International Journal of Intelligent Systems*. He serves on the editorial board of numerous technology journals.

R. Ghasemy Yaghin is a PhD student in the Department of Industrial Engineering at Amirkabir University of Technology, Tehran, Iran. His research interests include production and inventory systems, pricing theory, fuzzy optimization, and revenue management. Ghasemy Yaghin has received his BS and MS in Industrial Engineering from Buali Sina University and Amirkabir University of Technology, respectively.

Darius Zumstein (Master of Arts in Management), born the 13th of May in 1979, visited the commercial high school in Immensee (Switzerland) and studied Psychology and Management at the University of Fribourg. He is a research assistant and PhD student of the Information System Research Group in Fribourg and specialized in Web analytics, electronic business, online marketing, and customer relationship management. He is member of different associations like the Web Analytics Association (WAA), ACM, and SwissICT, and worked for many years as an assistant, Web master, and project manager in different Web (analytics) projects for several companies and non-profit organizations.

Index